*The Origins and Diversity of
Axial Age Civilizations*

SUNY Series in Near Eastern Studies
SAID AMIR ARJOMAND, *Editor*

EDITED BY
S.N. EISENSTADT

The Origins and Diversity of Axial Age Civilizations

State University of New York Press

Published by
State University of New York Press, Albany

© 1986   State University of New York

For information, address State University of New York Press,
State University Plaza, Albany, N.Y., 12246

Library of Congress Cataloging in Publication Data

The Origins and diversity of axial age civilizations.

    (SUNY series in Near Eastern studies)
    "Papers presented...in a conference on the origins
and diversity of axial age civilizations—the first of
three conferences...sponsored by the Werner-Reimer
Stiftung at Bad Homburg, the Truman Research Institute,
and the Van Leer Jerusalem Foundation...January 4-8,
1983, at the seat of the Werner-Reimer Stiftung [sic]
at Bad Homburg"—Pref.
    Bibliography: p.
    Includes index.
    1. Civilization, Ancient. 2. Comparative civilization.
I. Eisenstadt, S. N. (Shmuel Noah), 1923-
II. Werner-Reimers-Stiftung. III. Makhon le-mehkar
'al shem Heri S. Truman. IV. Mosad Van Lir
bi-Yerushalayim. V. Series.
CB311.0735   1986   930   86-14515
ISBN 0-88706-094-3
ISBN 0-88706-096-X (pbk.)

Contents

Part III
The Secondary Breakthroughs in Late Antiquity—
Second Temple Judaism and Christianity

Part IV
The Origins of the Axial Age in China and India

Part V
Islam

Contributors

G.W. BOWERSOCK, Institute of Advanced Study, Princeton.

MICHAEL COOK, School of Oriental and African Studies, University of London.

S.N. EISENSTADT, The Hebrew University of Jerusalem.

YEHUDA ELKANA, Tel-Aviv University and The Van Leer Jerusalem Foundation.

MARK ELVIN, St. Antony's College, University of Oxford.

R. FERWERDA, Manix College.

J.C. HEESTERMAN, University of Leiden.

CHO-YUN HSU, University of Pittsburgh.

S.C. HUMPHREYS, University College, University of London.

HANS G. KIPPENBERG, University of Groningen.

HERMANN KULKE, University of Heidelberg.

PETER MACHINIST, University of Arizona.

CHRISTIAN MEIER, University of München.

EDWARD SHILS, University of Chicago.

DAVID SHULMAN, The Hebrew University of Jerusalem.

MICHAEL E. STONE, The Hebrew University of Jerusalem.

GEDALIAHU G. STROUMSA, The Hebrew University of Jerusalem.

HAYIM TADMOR, The Hebrew University of Jerusalem.

STANLEY J. TAMBIAH, Harvard University.

BENJAMIN UFFENHEIMER, Harvard University.

TU WEI-MING, Tel-Aviv University.

MOSHE WEINFELD, The Hebrew University of Jerusalem.

Preface

The papers presented in this volume were presented in a conference on the Origins and Diversity of Axial Age Civilizations—the first of three conferences on the Origins and Dynamics of Axial Age Civilizations, sponsored by the Werner-Reimer Stiftung at Bad Homburg, The Truman Research Institute, and The Van Leer Jerusalem Foundation. This conference took place January 4–8, 1983, at the seat of the Werner-Reimer Stiftung at Bad Homburg.

The purpose of this conference was to explore in a systematic way the origins of Axial Age civilizations and their diversity, and especially the general conditions under which these breakthroughs developed or which have facilitated such developments, as well as the different constellations of conditions which account for the specific characteristics of each of these civilizations.

The papers and discussions dealt with five closely connected problems, which shared a common denominator. This denominator was the search for the condition of the institutionalization of the transcendental visions which characterize the Axial Age civilizations, and for the specification of the nature and direction and institutional implications of these visions.

Thus, first of all, the conference dealt with the structural-historical conditions of the emergence of these civilizations.

Second, the conference dealt with the analysis of the diversity of the major Axial Age civilizations, of how the differences in the major characteristics of these civilizations—above all the differences in the basic cultural orientations of these civilizations and in the structure of their elites—can be explained or related to the differences in the constellation of these conditions.

These problems were discussed on the basis of analysis of specific patterns of such breakthroughs and their institutionalization in Ancient Greece, Ancient Israel, China, and Brahmin India and of the later developments in Christianity, Buddhism, and Islam.

For comparative purposes, one civilization, Assyria, was analyzed in which—despite seemingly favorable conditions—such breakthrough to transcendence did not take place.

Third, attention was given to the nature of the transformation of modes of thought and symbolism attendant on the development and institutionalization of the basic conceptions of tension between transcendental and mundane orders—both in primary and secondary breakthroughs—especially on the transformation of mythical thought, symbolism, and ritual and of second-order thought.

Fourth, emphasis was laid on some of the major institutional repercussions of the institutionalization of the perception of tension between transcendental and mundane orders—especially on the tension between rulers and other elites, the development of heterodoxies, and the importance of all these for the dynamics of these civilizations.

Fifth, emphasis was laid on the problem or question of what may be called the "secondary breakthroughs," which had developed already within the framework of the first Axial Age civilizations—i.e., above all of Second Temple Judaism, Christianity, Buddhism, and Islam, as well as possibly Neo-Confucianism. The major difference between these and the primary breakthroughs lies in their having evolved as part of the process of confrontation between on the one hand the ruling "orthodoxies" and coalitions—which included already the new types of cultural elites—and on the other hand various heterodoxies and sectarian movements that developed within them. Also discussed was in what ways the combination of the various structural factors mentioned above, together with the structure of the confrontation between "orthodoxy" and "heterodoxy," have shaped the emergence and institutionalization of these secondary breakthroughs, and their specific characteristics in the symbolic and institutional realms alike.

The original papers were revised by the authors in light of the discussions at the conference.

This series of conferences is closely connected with the interdisciplinary seminars on comparative civilizations which have been taking place at the Department of Sociology and the Truman Research Institute, in cooperation with other organizations, for about the last fifteen years, as well as other international conferences and workshops many of which were published in the form of books.[1]

I would like to thank the three sponsoring institutions for their support, which made possible the convening of the Conference and the publication of this volume: the Truman Institute of The Hebrew University of Jerusalem, The Van Leer Jerusalem Foundation and the Werner-Reimer Foundation whose kind hospitality at Bad Homburg, greatly contributed to the success of the conference. I also would like to thank Ms. Esther Shashar of The Van Leer Jerusalem Foundation for help in the preparation of the volume for publication, and Mr. Moshe Levi for his help in the preparation and typing of the manuscript.

Jerusalem, September 1984

S.N. Eisenstadt

The Axial Age Breakthroughs— Their Characteristics and Origins

S.N. EISENSTADT

INTRODUCTION:

The Axial Age and the Emergence of Transcendental Visions

In the first millennium before the Christian era a revolution took place in the realm of ideas and their institutional bases which had irreversible effects on several major civilizations and on human history in general. The revolution or series of revolutions, which are related to Karl Jaspers' "Axial Age," have to do with the emergence, conceptualization, and institutionalization of a basic tension between the transcendental and mundane orders. This revolutionary process took place in several major civilizations including Ancient Israel, Ancient Greece, Early Christianity, Zoroastrian Iran, early Imperial China, and the Hindu and Buddhist civilizations. Although beyond the Axial Age proper, it also took place in Islam.[1]

These conceptions were developed and articulated by a relatively new social element. A new type of intellectual elite became aware of the necessity to actively construct the world according to some transcendental vision. The successful institutionalization of such conceptions and visions gave rise to extensive re-ordering of the internal contours of societies as well as their internal relations. This changed the dynamics of history and introduced the possibility of world history or histories.

The importance of these revolutionary changes has been recognized to some degree in the sociological and historical literature. The recognition of their importance was in the background of Weber's monumental comparative study of world religions, which focused

1

on the rationalization of these world religions.[2] Jasper's original insight into the Axial Age, concisely presented in his "Vom Ursprung und Ziel der Geschichte," was taken up in a conference organized on the initiative of Benjamin Schwartz and published in 1975 as a *Daedalus* volume under the title: *Wisdom, Revelation and Doubt*.[3] A rather parallel trend of thought and analysis, focusing mainly on Ancient Israel and Greece, has been developed by Eric Voegelin in his volume *Order and History*.[4]

But all these works notwithstanding, no full, systematic analysis of the impact of this series of revolutions on the structuring of human societies and history is available. Starting from the insights of these scholars, we shall attempt such a systematic analysis of the ways in which this series of revolutions has transformed the shape of human societies and history in what seems to be an irreversible manner.

The Nature of Axial Revolutions

What then is the nature of these Axial Age revolutions? We may quote here Benjamin Schwartz: "If there is nevertheless some common underlying impulse in all these "axial" movements, it might be called the strain towards transcendence. . . . What I refer to here is something close to the etymological meaning of the word—a kind of standing back and looking beyond—a kind of critical, reflective questioning of the actual and a new vision of what lies beyond. . . . In concentrating our attention on those transcendental breakthroughs we are of course stressing the significance of changes in man's conscious life. What is more, we are stressing the consciousness of small groups of prophets, philosophers, and wise men who may have had a very small impact on their immediate environment."[5]

These conceptions of a basic tension between the transcendental and the mundane orders differed greatly from the "homologous" perceptions of the relation between these two orders which were prevalent in so-called pagan religions in those very societies and civilizations from which these post-Axial Age civilizations emerged.

Certainly, the transmundane order has, in all human societies, been perceived as somewhat different, usually higher and stronger, than the mundane one. But in the pre-Axial Age "pagan" civilizations this higher world was symbolically structured according to principles very similar to those of the mundane or lower one. Relatively similar symbolic terms were used for the definition of God(s) and man, of the mundane and transmundane orders—even if there always was a continuous stress on the difference between them. In most such societies the transmundane world was usually equated with a concrete setting, "the other world," which was the abode of the dead, the world of spirits, and not entirely unlike the mundane world in detail.[6]

These pagan societies, of course, always recognized the moral frailty of man, the failure of people to live up to prevalent social and moral ideals. However, a conception of an autonomous, distinct moral order which is qualitatively different from both this world and "the other world" developed only to a minimal degree.

Such homologous conceptions of the transmundane and mundane worlds were very often closely connected with some mythical and cyclical conception of time in which the differences between the major time dimensions—past, present, and future—were only mildly articulated.

By contrast, in the Axial Age civilizations the perception of a sharp disjunction between the mundane and transmundane worlds developed. There was a concomitant stress on the existence of a higher transcendental moral or metaphysical order which is beyond any given this- or other-worldly reality.

The development of these conceptions created a problem in the rational, abstract articulation of the givens of human and social existence and of the cosmic order. The root of the problem lay in the fact that the development of such conceptions necessarily posed the question of the ways in which the chasm between the transcendental and the mundane orders could be bridged. This gave rise to the problem of salvation—to use Weber's terminology. The roots of the quest for salvation are given in the consciousness of death and the arbitrariness of human actions and social arrangements. The search for some type of immortality and a way to overcome such arbitrariness is universal to all human societies. In the societies in which the mundane and transmundane worlds are defined in relatively homologous terms this search for immortality is on the whole envisaged in terms of some physical continuity. It is usually seen as conditional to the fulfillment of one's concrete obligation to one's group.

This no longer holds true in the civilizations in which there is an emphasis on the chasm between the transcendental and the mundane order and a conception of a higher moral or metaphysical order. While the concept of immortality in these civilizations may or may not still be tied to bodily images and to ideas of physical resurrection, the very possibility of some continuity beyond this world is usually seen in terms of the reconstruction of human behavior and personality. This reconstruction would be based on the precepts of the higher moral or metaphysical order through which the chasm between the transcendental and mundane orders is bridged,[7] and, as Gananath Obeysekere has put it, rebirth eschatology becomes ethnicized.[8] But the very attempt at such reconstruction is always torn by many internal tensions. It is these tensions—which we shall explicate in greater detail later on—and their institutional repercussions that ushered in a new type of social and civilizational dynamics in the history of mankind.

THE EMERGENCE OF INTELLECTUALS AND CLERICS AND THE RECONSTRUCTION OF THE WORLD

The Emergence of Intellectuals and the Transformation of Elites

In order to understand these dynamics we have first of all to analyze the social actors who were most active in giving these civilizations their form.

The development and institutionalization of the perception of basic tension between the transcendental and the mundane order was closely connected with the emergence of a new social element. Generally speaking it was a new type of elite which was cited as the carrier of models of cultural and social order. Examples would include the Jewish prophets and priests, the Greek philosophers and Sophists, the Chinese Literati, the Hindu Brahmins, the Buddhist Sangha, and the Islamic Ulema.

It was the initial small nuclei of such groups of intellectuals that developed the new "transcendental" conceptions. In all the Axial Age civilizations these conceptions ultimately became institutionalized. That is, they became the predominant orientations of the ruling elites as well as of many secondary elites, fully embodied in their respective centers or subcenters.

Once such a conception of a tension between the transcendental and the mundane order became institutionalized, it was associated with the transformation of political elites, and it turned the new scholar class into relatively autonomous partners in the major ruling coalitions and protest movements. The new type of elites which resulted from this process of institutionalization were entirely different in nature from the elites which had been ritual, magical, and sacral specialists in the pre-Axial Age civilizations. The new elites, intellectuals and clerics, were recruited and legitimized according to distinct, autonomous criteria, and were organized in autonomous settings, distinct from those of the basic ascriptive units. They acquired a potential country-wide status consciousness of their own. They also tended to become potentially independent of other categories of elites and social groups. But at the same time they competed strongly with them, especially over the production and control of symbols and media of communication.

Such competition now became very intensive because, with the institutionalization of such transcendental conceptions, a parallel transformation had taken place in the structure of other elites. All these elites tended to develop claims for an autonomous place in the construction of the cultural and social order. They saw themselves not only as performing specific technical, functional activities, but also as potentially autonomous carriers of a distinct cultural and social order related to the transcendental vision prevalent in their respective societies.

The non-political cultural elites and the political elites each saw themselves as the autonomous articulators of the new order, with the other type potentially inferior and accountable to themselves.

Moreover, each of these groups of elites was not, in these societies, homogeneous. There developed a multiplicity of secondary cultural, political, or educational elites, each very often carrying a different conception of the cultural and social order.

With these new types of elites, above all the political and cultural ones, the intellectuals became the major partners in the formulative ruling coalitions as well as in the movements of protest. It is these elites that were the most active in the reconstruing of the world and the institutional creativity that developed in these societies.

Institutionalization of the Transcendental Vision and the Re-ordering of the World

The attempts at re-ordering of the world developed in most spheres of human existence and activity. Such reorganization of the world had far-reaching implications for the formation of the human personality and of personal identity in terms of the model of the ideal man. In the societies in which the perception of the tension between the transcendental and the mundane orders was institutionalized, this personal identity and the definition of man was taken beyond the primordial givens of human existence, and beyond the various technical needs of daily activities. Purely personal virtues, such as courage, or interpersonal ones, such as solidarity, were taken out of their primordial framework and were combined, in different dialectical modes, with the attributes of resolution of the tension between the transcendental and the mundane orders. In this way a new level of internal tensions in the formation of personality was generated.[9]

Similarly the institutionalization of the perceived tension between the transcendental and the mundane orders tended to create the corresponding definition of different worlds of knowledge—be they philosophy, religions, metaphysics, "science", or the like. Such definitions transformed different types of ad-hoc moral reflexion and classificatory schematization into second-order worlds of knowledge. This step constituted the starting point for what has usually been called the intellectual history of mankind.[10]

The Structuring of Legitimation of Social Centers, Traditions and Political Authority

If the legitimation of the social order in most of the great pre-Axial Age civilizations[11] was based on some fusion of sacred and primordial criteria and traditional charismatic modes of legitimation, the picture became more complicated with the institutionalization of the perception of tension between the transcendental and mundane order.[12]

In the post-Axial Age civilizations, there developed first a strong tendency to a continuous oscillation between primordial criteria on the one hand and sacred or ideological ones—defined in terms of the attributes of salvation—on the other; and a concomitant tendency to ideologize or "sacralize" the primordial attributes or to vest the sacred with primordial attributes. Second, there tended to develop a tension between "traditional" modes of legitimation and more "open" (rational, legal, or charismatic) ones. Both these tensions were given in the very stress on the basic quest to bridge the chasm between the transcendental and the mundane orders. These tensions were not purely "academic"; they constituted a continuous focus of actual political struggle.

There are far-reaching concrete institutional implications of those tensions. The most general and common has been the high degree of symbolic orientation and ideologization of the major aspects of the institutional structure. This applies in particular to the structure of collectivities, social centers, social hierarchies, and processes of political struggle.

Some collectivities and institutional spheres were singled out as the most appropriate carriers of the attributes of the required resolution. As a result new types of collectivities were created, or seemingly natural and "primordial" groups were endowed with special meaning couched in terms of the perception of this tension and its resolution.

The most important innovation in this context was the development of "cultural" or "religious" collectivities as distinct from ethnic or political ones. Some embryonic elements of this development existed in some of those societies in which no conception of tension between the transcendental and the mundane order was institutionalized. However, it was only with the development and institutionalization of this conception that those elements became transformed into new, potentially full-fledged collectivities with autonomous criteria of membership and loci of authority. The membership in these collectivities and frameworks tended to become imbued with a strong ideological dimension and to become a focus of ideological struggle.

An aspect of this ideological struggle was the insistence on the exclusiveness and closure of such collectivities and on the distinction between inner and outer social and cultural space defined by them. This aspect became connected with attempts to structure the different cultural, political, and ethnic collectivities in some hierarchical order, and the very construction of such an order usually became a focus of ideological and political conflict.

The Autonomy and Distinctiveness of the Great and Little Traditions

Related to the ordering of the major collectivities was the developing tendency towards the autonomous organization of the social centers,[13] and to a relatively strong emphasis on the symbolic distinctiveness of the centers from the periphery. Such centers have been conceived as the major loci of the charismatic attributes of the resolution of the transcendental tension, and hence also of the construction of cultural and societal orders. These attributes of centrality became "naturally" related to those institutional spheres which showed the closest affinity to the focus of resolution of the transcendental tension, and it was the centers most closely related to these spheres that became autonomous and distinct from the periphery.

At the same time the development of such distinctiveness and symbolic differentiation of the center gave rise to the tendency of the center to permeate the periphery and to reorganize it according to the autonomous criteria of the center.

These processes of center-formation and of reconstruction of collectivities were related to the transformation and construction of Great Traditions[14] as autonomous, distinct, symbolical frameworks. Such construction of centers and of Great Traditions may be evident in "external" artifacts such as great works of architecture, or in the writing and sanctification of scholarly books and codices. The structure of the Great Traditions in those societies in which the perception of tension between the transcendental and the mundane order was institutionalized went, however, beyond such external manifestations. It was above all characterized by symbolic and organizational distinctiveness from the Little Traditions of the periphery. Such distinctiveness and autonomy can be clearly identified even in those cases, as among the ancient Israeli tribes, in which the carriers of such centers and Traditions were not organized in distinct, specific frameworks. It becomes organizationally more fully visible in Imperial societies such as China and the Byzantine Empire, or in Theravada Buddhist societies.[15]

The relations between the Great and Little Traditions were transformed by processes of ideological differentiation. They gave rise both to attempts by the carriers of the Great Traditions to permeate the periphery—to pull the Little Traditions into the orbit of the Great ones—as well as to attempts by the carriers of the Little Traditions to dissociate themselves from the Great Traditions, to profane them, and, paradoxically enough, also to generate a distinct ideology of the Little Traditions and of the periphery.

The Ordering of Political Order

In all these civilizations there also took place a far-reaching reordering rooted in the conception of the relation between the political and the higher transcendental order. The political order as the central locus of the mundane order has usually been conceived as lower than the transcendental one and accordingly had to be restructured according to the precepts of the latter and above all according to the perception of the proper mode of overcoming the tension between the transcendental and the mundane order, of "salvation." It was the rulers who were usually held to be responsible for organizing the political order.

At the same time the nature of the rulers became greatly transformed. The King-God, the embodiment of the cosmic and earthly order alike, disappeared, and a secular ruler, in principle accountable to some higher order, appeared. Thus there emerged the conception of the accountability of the rulers and of the community to a higher authority, God, Divine Law, and the like. Accordingly, the possibility of calling a ruler to judgement emerged. The first most dramatic appearance of this conception appeared in Ancient Israel, in priestly and prophetic pronunciations. A different conception of such accountability, an accountability to the community and its laws, appeared in the northern shores of the Eastern Mediterranean, in Ancient Greece. In different forms this conception appeared in all these civilizations.[16]

Concomitant to the emergence of conceptions of accountability there began to develop autonomous spheres of law and conceptions of rights. These tended to be somewhat distinct from ascriptively bound custom and from purely customary law. The scope of these spheres of law and rights varied greatly from society to society but they were all established according to some distinct and autonomous criteria.

The Ordering of Social Hierarchies

Social hierarchies are another aspect of the Axial Age civilizations which were reorganized as a result of the institutionalization of the transcendental vision.[17] This is evident first of all in the organization of the group basis of stratification and in the tendency to stress groups which can be defined in wide, potentially universalistic terms.

Second, there was a marked shift in the construction of the basic criteria of stratification. The social positions which were closest to the resolution of tension became endowed with a special autonomous symbolic aura. Thus, these positions acquired a relatively high status as the criteria of evaluation became broader and dissociated from the narrow-primordial or ascriptive criteria.

Third, the holders of these positions tended to develop relatively autonomous, distinct, and broad society (or sector) wide status consciousness as opposed to more local, primordial, or sectoral ones.

Fourth, there developed a tendency to dissociate ownership and local use of resources, which might remain with the local groups, and control over the macro-social use and conversion of such resources, which tended to become vested in the holders of these "upper" positions in the social hierarchy.

New Levels of Social Conflict

These modes of organizing the major institutional spheres in the civilizations in which a conception of tension between transcendental and mundane civilizations has become institutionalized, affected the scope, intensity, and definition of social conflict in general. Insofar as the political sphere was perceived as relevant to "salvation," political conflict in particular was affected as well. New dimensions were added to the processes of conflict that developed in these societies beyond those which can be identified in the pre-Axial Age societies. The most important was the possible development of new levels of conflict beyond those of specific "narrow" interests of different groups and elites, and the definition of such conflicts in broader symbolical or ideological terms. The issues of struggle tended to become highly ideologized, generalized, and sometimes even universalized. The struggle itself tended to become organized in relatively autonomous settings. Similarly, there developed linkages between different levels of issues ranging potentially up to the very principle of legitimation of the social and political order. These new levels of conflict generated new processes of change and continuous reconstruction of the social order.

The Pattern of New Civilizational Dynamics

The Multiplicity of Visions and the Growth of Reflexivity

These new modes of continuous re-ordering of societies and entire civilizations and of social and cultural change can only be understood in connection with the tension inherent in the symbolic and ideological premises of these civilizations.

The root of such tensions lies in the very institutionalization of the perception of the tension between the transcendental and the mundane order and of the quest to overcome it. This generated an awareness of a great range of possibilities or visions of the very definition of such tensions and of the proper mode of their resolution as well as an awareness of the partiality or incompleteness of any given institutionalization of such vision.

Historically the growth of this awareness was never a simple peaceful process. It was usually connected with a continuous struggle and competition between many groups and between their respective visions.

Once the conception of a basic tension between the transcendental and the mundane order was fully recognized and institutionalized in a society, or at least within its center, any definition and resolution of this tension became in itself very problematic. It usually contained strong heterogeneous and even contradictory elements, and its elaboration in fully articulated terms generated the possibility of different emphases, directions and interpretations, all of which were reinforced by the historical existence of multiple visions carried by different groups. Because of this multiplicity of visions, no single one could be taken as given or complete.

The content of such alternative visions tended to develop in several directions, and these could also be combined in different ways. One such direction was the reformulation of the nature of the tension between the transcendental and the mundane orders. Examples of this are the cases of the Buddhist reformulation of the premises of Hinduism and the Christian reformulation of the premises of Judaism.

Second was the ideological denial of the very stress on the tension between transcendental and mundane orders and a "return" to a conception which upheld the parallelism between the transcendental and the mundane orders as if to go back to a pretranscendental stage.

The third direction of such alternative visions was the denial of the locally predominant conception of the resolution of such tension and of its institutional derivatives. This took the form of stress on other-worldly orientations in this-worldly orientations, or vice-versa, stress on learning as against military or political virtue.

Fourth was the elaboration of a great variety of religious and intellectual orientations, especially mystical and esoteric ones which went beyond the established, routinized, orthodox version of the resolution of the transcendental tension.

Fifth was the upholding of the prevalent conceptions and ideals in their pure, pristine form, as against their necessarily compromised concretization in any institutional setting.

All these alternative visions usually became combined with the perennial themes of social protest, such as the emphasis on equality and solidarity, or the suspension of social division of labor.[18]

It is this very multiplicity of alternative visions that gave rise in all these civilizations to an awareness of the uncertainty of different roads to salvation, of alternative conceptions of social and cultural order, and of the seeming arbitrariness of any single solution. Such awareness became a constituent element of the consciousness of these civilizations, especially among the carriers of their Great Traditions. This was closely related to the development of a high degree of "second-order" thinking, which is a reflexivity turning on the basic premises of the social and cultural order.[19]

This reflexivity was also closely related to the new perception of the time dimensions providing the background for the tension between the transcendental and mundane orders. Such a revision is evident in the greater stress on the possible discontinuities between the major time dimensions of time, past, present, and future, and the consequent necessity to find ways to bridge between them. While the nature of this bridge, whether it is cyclical, historical, or apocalyptic, varies greatly between different civilizations, the stress on some discontinuity is common to all of them.

Utopian visions were another common element which emerged in these civilizations. These were visions of an alternative cultural and social order beyond any given place or time. Such visions contained many of the millennarian and revivalist elements which can be found also in pagan religions, but they went beyond them by combining these elements with a stress on the necessity to construct the mundane order according to the precepts of the higher one.[20]

The Emergence of Organic Solidarity

All these visions became closely interwoven with different social groups and constituted a basic component of these civilizations, generating their specific dynamics.

One of the characteristics of these dynamics was social integration. Our preceding analysis has shown that the social recognition of the basic tension between the transcendental order, and the associated attempts to re-order the world, influence the entire pattern of social interaction and give rise to new modes of institutional creativity. They influence these patterns particularly in two directions: first towards growing symbolic articulation and ideologization of the meaning of social activities, collectivities, and institutions; and second towards the growing diversification of the ranges of social activities and frameworks.

These tendencies generate problems of social integration related to Durkheim's idea of mechanical and organic solidarity. This called for the establishment of much more flexible and differentiated frameworks of integration than the ones prevalent in the pre-Axial Age societies or civilizations.[21]

The construction of a new level of integration was necessarily difficult, fragile, and fraught with contradictions. For example, in these civilizations there emerged—if in varying degrees of intensity—proselytizing zeal, evident in the attempt to impose any given elite vision of the construction of the world on many societies. There was also the closely connected tendency to rather principled intolerance concerning the basic doctrinal and/or ritual premises and institutional results of any given definition of the tension between the transcendental and the mundane order and its resolution. This intolerance was rooted in the uncertainties generated by the construction of this tension. It stemmed from the awareness that any resolution of the tension could not be taken as given and natural, but rather that it was constructed out of different possibilities rooted in the very problems of human existence and in the consciousness of alternatives. This intolerance contrasts strongly with the relative tolerance of those societies or cultures in which the perception of tension between the transcendental and the mundane order does not exist.

The very intolerance gave rise to the establishment of official orthodoxies, upheld by the ruling coalitions of political and religious authorities, but it also contained strong elements of ambivalence. Paradoxically, it generated potential challenges to itself although such challengers could be as intolerant as those whom they challenged.

The problem of resolving the tension between mundane and transcendental orders is inherently irresolvable. But the persistent quest for a resolution results in reorganized institutions, new levels of conflict, new processes of social change, as well as a transformation of the relations between societies and civilizations.

Intellectuals and Clerics as Members of Ruling Coalitions and of Movements of Protest; and as Carriers of Conflicts and Change

A central feature of the new dynamics of civilizations was that the intellectual and clerical elites were active in both the ruling coalitions and the protest movements that developed in these societies.

As members of the ruling coalitions, these elites attempted to regulate institutional attempts to reconstruct the world according to some transcendental vision. They attempted this regulation through control over three increasingly differentiated aspects of the flow of resources in the society. First they attempted to control access to the major institutional markets, i.e., the economic, political, cultural, and religious ones. Second, and most important, they controlled the scope of these markets and the conversion of resources between them. This applied particularly to the conversion of economic resources into political and status resources. Third, they attempted to control the definition of the more complex, problematic social groups and cultural worlds.

At the same time, such elites also constituted the most active elements in the movements of protest and processes of change that developed in these societies. The participation of these elites greatly influenced the post-Axial Age character of such movements at both the symbolic and organizational levels.

First, there was a growing symbolic articulation and ideologization of the perennial themes of protest which are found in any human society, such as rebellion against the constraints of division of labor, authority, and hierarchy, and of the structuring of time dimension, the quest for solidarity and equality and for overcoming human mortality.

Second, utopian orientations were incorporated into the rituals of rebellion and the double image of society. It was this incorporation that generated alternative conceptions of social order and new ways of bridging the distance between the existing and the "true" resolution of the transcendental tension.

Third, new types of protest movements appeared. The most important were intellectual heterodoxies, sects, or movements which upheld the different conceptions of the resolution of the tension between the transcendental and the mundane order, and of the proper way to institutionalize such concepts.

The transformation of such alternative conceptions into heterodoxies resulted, of course, from their confrontation with some institutionalized orthodoxy. Since then, continuous confrontation between orthodoxy on the one hand, and schism and heterodoxy on the other, and the accompanying development of strong antinomian tendencies, has been a crucial component in the history of mankind.

Fourth, and closely related to the former, was the possibility of the development of autonomous political movements and ideologies usually oriented against an existing political center with its elaborated symbolism and ideology.

Among these new elites, it was the intellectuals in particular who were most active in the ideological development of the different types of protest. They were also especially responsible for articulating the antithesis between "rational" and "anti-rational" protest orientations. In these movements they tended to foster the antinomian tendency by focusing on the aesthetic, ritual, and mystical dimensions of human existence.[22] Out of this orientation came the most extreme expression of subjectivism and privatization.

Closely related to these changes in the symbolic dimension of protest movements were important organizational changes. The most general change was the growing possibility of structural and ideological links between different protest movements and foci of conflict. These links could be effected by different coalitions of different secondary elites, above all by coalition between "secondary" articulators of models of cultural order and political elites.

Thus, first, any single protest movement, either in the center or in the periphery, was exposed to possible links with other movements and to more central religious and political struggles.

Second, such movements could become connected with the opening up of a relatively wide range of institutional choices which resulted from the institutionalization of the transcendental tension and the quest for its resolution. Hence, they could focus not only on the specific applications of social premises, but also on the very premises themselves, and on the very bases of legitimation of the social and political order. In this way new levels of conflict were generated.

Third, a strong ideological articulation of the tension between center and periphery, between the Great and the Little Traditions, became available to these movements. Hence, the possibility of these movements impinging on the center or centers of the society increased.

New Ideological Attitudes to Change

New ways of generating, organizing, and perceiving change came out of these social conflicts, protest movements, and the awareness of a variety of choices.

While the concrete attitude toward change, negative or positive, adaptive or transformative, varied according to the society and period, all of these post-Axial Age civilizations had a common tendency toward a highly articulated symbolical and ideological attitude toward change. They shared a certain totalistic view of change which attempted to mold the changes according to the prevalent transcendental vision. Specific changes were associated with broader concepts, and in this way the possibility of the society simply absorbing piecemeal change was diminished. Instead, there developed a continuous tension between an extreme generation of change and a very principled intolerance towards the absorption of change into the symbolic and institutional framework.

These new developments ushered into the arena of human history the possibility of consciously ordering society, and also the continuous tension that this possibility caused. The new dynamics of civilization transformed group conflicts into potential class and ideological conflicts, cult conflicts into struggles between the orthodox and the heterodox. Conflicts between tribes and societies became missionary crusades for the transformation of civilizations. The zeal for reorganization informed by each society's concept of salvation made the whole world at least potentially subject to cultural-political reconstruction.

INDICATIONS FOR COMPARATIVE ANALYSIS

The Multiplicity of World Histories

The general tendency to reconstruct the world with all its symbolic-ideological and institutional repercussions was common to all the post-Axial Age civilizations. But their concrete implementation, of course, varied greatly. No one homogeneous world history emerged nor were the different types of civilizations similar or convergent. Rather, there emerged a multiplicity of different, divergent, yet continuously mutually impinging world civilizations, each attempting to reconstruct the world in its own mode, according to its basic premises, and attempting either to absorb the others or consciously to segregate itself from them.

It would be beyond the scope of this paper to analyze either these differences or to attempt to explain them—all this has to be left to further publications. It might, however, be worthwhile to point out that some of the most important sets of conditions which provide the clues to the understanding of these different modes of institutional creativity are given in the way the premises of these civilizations are crystallized and institutionalized in concrete social settings. Two such sets of conditions can be distinguished. One refers to variations in the basic cultural orientations, in the basic "ideas" or visions concerning civilization with their institutional implications. The other set of conditions refers to different concrete social arenas in which these institutional tendencies can be played out.

First of all, among the different cultural orientations there are crucial differences in the very definition of the tension between the transcendental and mundane orders and the modes of resolving this tension. There is the distinction between those cases in which the tension was couched in relatively secular terms (as in Confucianism and classical Chinese belief systems and, in a somewhat different way, in the Greek and Roman worlds) and those cases in which the tension was conceived in terms of a religious hiatus (as in the great monotheistic religions and Hinduism and Buddhism).

A second distinction, within the latter cases, is that between the monotheistic religions in which there was a concept of God standing outside the Universe and potentially guiding it, and those systems, like Hinduism and Buddhism, in which the transcendental, cosmic system was conceived in impersonal, almost metaphysical terms, and in a state of continuous existential tension with the mundane system.

Another major distinction refers to the focus of the resolution of the transcendental tensions—which, in Weberian terms, is salvation. Here the distinction is between purely this-worldly, purely other-worldly and mixed this- and other-worldly conceptions of salvation. It is probably no accident that the "secular" conception of this tension was connected, as in China and to some degree in the ancient world, with an almost wholly this-worldly conception of salvation that the metaphysical non-deistic conception of this tension, as in Hinduism and Buddhism, tended towards an other-worldly conception of salvation, while the great monotheistic religions tended to stress combinations of this- and other-worldly conceptions of salvation.

Another set of cultural orientations which are of special importance to the ordering of the broader ranges of solidarity and connecting them with the broader meanings generated by the transcendental visions can be distinguished.

First, of central importance here is the degree to which access to the central attributes of cosmic and/or social order is given directly to the members of any social category or subcategory, enabling them to act as mediators between these attributes and the broader groups.

Second is the nature of relations between the attributes of cosmic and social order and salvation and the basic attributes of the major primordial ascriptive collectivities. Here three possibilities can be distinguished. One is when the access to these broader attitudes is entirely vested within some such ascriptive collectivity. The second one occurs when there is a total disjunction between the two. The third possibility arises when these respective attributes are mutually relevant and each serves as a referent of the other or a condition of being a member of the other without being totally embedded in the other. Such a partial connection usually means that the attributes of the ascriptive collectivities are seen as one component of the attributes of salvation, and/or conversely, that the attributes of salvation constitute one of the attributes of such collectivities.

It is the different combinations of these two sets of cultural orientations that have been most important in shaping the broad institutional contours and dynamics of the different post-Axial Age civilizations.

Above all, these cultural orientations have formed the degree of the symbolic autonomy and the degree of unitary homogeneous organization experienced by the new types of elites and ruling coalitions which characterized the post-Axial Age civilizations. That is, they shaped the relations between them; their place in the ruling coalitions; the modes of control of the major institutional spheres effected by them; and the degree to which there developed different types of links between the different ruling and secondary elites and processes of change, links which could give rise to different modes of societal transformation.[23]

But the concrete working out of all such tendencies depends on the second set of conditions—the arena for the concretization of these broad institutional tendencies. These conditions included first, the economic structure of these civilizations (although they all belonged to economically relatively developed agrarian or combined agrarian and commercial societies).

Second, they varied greatly according to their respective political-ecological settings, whether they were small or great societies, whether they were societies with continuous compact boundaries, or with cross-cutting and flexible boundaries.

Third was their specific historical experience, especially in terms of encounters with other societies, especially in terms of mutual penetration, conquest, or colonization. It is the interplay between the different constellations of the cultural orientations analyzed above, their carriers, and their respective visions of restructuring of the world and the concrete arenas and historical conditions in which such visions could be concretized, that has shaped the institutional contours and dynamics of the different Axial Age civilizations. The subsequent courses of world history, and their systematic exploration, should be the objects of further systematic analysis.

The Conditions of Emergence and
Institutionalization of Axial Age Civilizations

Introduction

The emergence and institutionalization of the Axial Age civilizations have been connected with several social processes, some of
which are common to the construction of any social or institutional
order, and others are specific to these civilizations. Like all institutional, societal, or civilizational complexes the Axial Age civilizations were constructed by the combination of several major components: first, the level and distribution of resources among different
groups in a society—i.e., the type of division of labor that is predominant in a given society; second, the institutional entrepreneurs
or elites which are available—or competing—for the mobilization
and structuring of such resources and for the organization and
articulation of the interests of major groups generated by the social
division of labor; third, the nature of the conceptions of "visions"
which inform the activities of these elites and which are derived,
above all, from the major cultural orientations or codes prevalent
in a society.

Such major elites are the political leaders who deal most directly
with the exercise, regulation, and control of power in society, the
articulators of the models of the cultural order whose activities are
oriented to the construction of meaning in social life, and the
articulators of the solidarity of the major groups who address themselves to the construction of trust.

The structure of such elites is closely related on the one hand to
the basic cultural orientations or codes prevalent in a society; or, in
other words, different types of elites are carriers of different types
of orientations. On the other hand, and in connection with types of
cultural orientations, these elites tend to exercise different modes of
control over the allocation of basic resources in the society. Through
these controls they combine the structuring of trust, the establishment
of meaning, and regulation of power with the division of labor in
society—thus institutionalizing the charismatic dimension of the
social orders.

Such control is exercised by these elites (or rather by coalitions
of elites) primarily through their control over access to the major
institutional markets (economic, political, cultural, etc.); over the
conversion of the major resources between these markets; and over
the production and distribution of that information which is central
in the structuring of cognitive maps of the members of their society

(that is, the perception of the nature of their society in general and of their reference orientations and groups in particular).

Such control is effected by a combination of organizational and coercive measures, together with the structuring of the cognitive maps of the social order and of the major reference orientations of social groups.

The concretization of these tendencies takes place in different political-ecological settings. Of special importance are two aspects of such settings: one, heavily stressed in recent research, is the importance of international, political, and economic systems in general and of the place of societies within them, and of different types of relations of hegemony and dependency in particular; the second is the more general recognition of a great variety of political-ecological settings of societies, such as differences between small and large societies, their respective dependence on internal or external markets, and the like. Both of these aspects greatly affect the ways in which institutional contours and dynamics tend to develop.

Tribal Disintegration and Modes of Institutional Reconstruction

Beyond these general processes the institutionalization of the Axial Age civilizations was connected with some more specific processes of social change, and above all first, with the disintegration of relatively narrow tribal or territorial units and, second, with the concomitant crystallization of new broad collectivities and of growing internal structural differentiation within these collectivities.

These processes of disintegration and reconstruction were in all the cases connected with certain advancement in agricultural and transport technology, with growing mutual impingement of heterogeneous economic (nomad, sedentary, etc.) and ethnic populations, with some degree of international political-ecological volatility in general, and with processes of immigration and/or conquest in particular.

But even these relatively more specific processes of social change were not specific to the crystallization of the Axial Age civilizations. These processes were more intensive than those which were connected with the development of so-called "early states"[24]—mostly in pre-literate societies—but they were not entirely dissimilar from those connected with the development of Great Archaic Empires—Ancient Egypt, Assyrian ones, or the Meso-American ones.

Already in the processes of emergence of the early states it is possible to identify different modes of such breakdowns of relative narrow and of the concomitant recrystallization of broader collectivities and more complex institutional structures. The importance of such different modes becomes even more salient in comparing the processes connected with the emergence of the Archaic Empires with those which gave rise to the Axial Age civilizations.

While the details of such differences are, of course, very numerous, yet it is possible to distinguish between two broad types which can be identified already in the transition from tribal to so-called early states.[25]

These types of breakdown of tribal communities and the reconstruction of broader and more differentiated units can be distinguished according to the relations between the growing differentiation of the social division of labor on the one hand and the structure of the basic elite functions and activities and of the positions of control connected with them on the other—and especially according to the degree to which there develops a congruence—or lack of congruence—between social differentiation in terms of social division of labor on the one hand, and the performance of elite structures on the other.

Each of these modes of reconstruction denotes different ways of reconstruction of the relations between division of labor, solidarity, and power, and their interrelation with the provision of meaning, and gives rise to different types of institutional structures—of collectivities, of centers, of center-periphery relations, of social hierarchies, and of structures of collectivities.

Within congruent societies (good illustrations of which among tribal early states are, for instance, the Ashante in Africa), new cultural-political frameworks were based on the reformulation of the pre-existing—kin and territorial—criteria. Such reformulation took place above all through extension of kin units into a combination of kin-territorial entities, based on more diversified and even more encompassing sub-units still designated, nevertheless, almost entirely in such newly reconstructed kin terms.

In these cases the newly crystallized and more articulated centers tended to become embedded in the restructured, broader primordial groups defined in terms of common kin or territorial bases, without the development of distinct, autonomous and/or a differential location of different elite functions.

A broadly similar pattern of reconstruction of collectivities and of institutional complexes developed above all in many of the Archaic Empires, of which ancient Egypt is probably the best illustration, as well as in city-states such as those of ancient Phoenicia, or in various more decentralized tribal federations—all of which exhibited many so-called "patrimonial" features.[26]

In such more "developed" congruent societies the crystallization of more complex institutional structures, of what may be called the transition from one stage of differentiation to another (e.g. from early state to archaic kingdom) was usually connected with the reconstruction and widening of the kinship and/or territorial elements and ascriptive categories and symbols, with the growing importance of territorial units as opposed to purely kinship ones, and with what may be called the qualitative extension and diversification of basic cosmological conceptions. It was also characterized by the increasing specialization of elites, who were however on the whole embedded in various, even very complex and wide-ranging, ascriptive units, by a close correspondence between structural differentiation and differentiation of elite functions, and by the prevalence of cultural models and conceptions containing relatively low levels of tension between the transcendental and mundane orders.

The centers that tend to develop in such "patrimonial" societies were ecologically and organizationally but not symbolically, distinct from the periphery, and these centers crystallized around elites which were embedded in various types of ascriptive units, even if often broad and restructured ones.

In contrast a second line of development can be identified. This line of development was characterized by growing discrepancies between structural differentiation and differentiation of elite functions, and the concomitant tendency to the development of autonomous elites, articulating more radical developments or breakthroughs in cultural orientations, especially in the direction of the radical conception of the tension between the mundane and transcendental orders.

Such development can be identified in the case of early preliterate states among, for instance, some of the Yoruba states, in Ife and Oyo or the Manding in Africa, and above all it was characteristic of the development of the Axial Age civilizations discussed here.

Coalition of Elites and Institutionalization of Transcendental Visions

These different modes of social change, of reconstruction of collectivities, and of institutional changes were effected through the activities of different coalitions of elites. Of special importance in this context were the articulators of models of cultural order and solidarity and the types of coalitions they formed with political elites. The central importance of these articulators in the processes of transition from one stage to another makes their specific characteristics and the nature of their place in the social system vital to an understanding of the characteristics of the new collectivities, institutional and civilizational complexes, and of their further dynamics of the types of change and transformation which tended to become generated in it.

The crucial importance of such articulators in the emergence and crystallization of different institutional and civilizational complexes can indeed, as we have seen above, be most clearly seen in the crystallization of the Axial Age civilizations. It was these elites, originally small groups of "intellectuals" who became disembedded from tribal or territorial settings and from older traditional ruling groups that were the carriers of models of cultural and social order in particular, of the new visions of transcendental and social visions. Ultimately these conceptions or visions became institutionalized in different Axial Age civilizations. The institutionalization of these visions was effected by the carriers of the original vision and those groups—both political as well as socio-economical ones—which became, as it were, the first converts to these visions. It was these last groups that, as Weber has shown through his analysis, were of great importance in the transformation of the original vision into the premises of institutionalized order, and making the articulation of such models relatively autonomous partners in the central coalitions.

With the institutionalization of these visions, parts at least of these groups became members of the ruling coalitions of their respective societies. Thus, as we have seen, various diverse groups of intellectuals were transformed into more fully crystallized and institutionalized groups of clerics, as exemplified by the Jewish prophets and Priests, the Great Greek Philosophers, the Chinese Literati, the Hindu Brahmins, the Buddhist Sangha, or the Islamic Ulemas. At the same time they became accepted by broader strata of the population whom they are able to mobilize, thus also becoming potentially partners and competitors to the ruler.

Hence of crucial importance in our analysis is to identify the reasons that made the visions developed by these groups acceptable to other elites as well as to broader strata.

These different coalitions of elites effected different modes of reconstruction, of trust, solidarity, power, and vision of labor, generating different types of institutional structures, restructuring many crucial institutional aspects of their respective societies, including, as we have seen, the creation of special, distinct civilizations or religious collectivities and centers, as well as different types of autonomous centers, distinct from their peripheries.

These symbolic and institutional structures entailed different types of answers to some basic problems which are inherent in the very institutionalization of Axial Age civilizations. The most important of these problems are first the relations between the civilizational collectivity and various primordial ones; second, the relative evaluation of different institutional spheres as the major arenas of the crystallization of their respective transcendental visions; and third, the nature of the symbolism of the center, of the mode of center-periphery relations, and the mode of accountability of rulers.

Each of these symbolic and institutional patterns entailed also different possibilities of further dynamics, of so-called secondary breakthroughs, i.e. of the development from within these civilizations not only of sects of various secondary interpretations, but also of new overall civilizational patterns—such the development of Christianity out of Judaism, or Buddhism out of Hinduism.

Modes of Disintegration and Change

The preceding discussion does necessarily bring us to the problem of the conditions—i.e., the specific constellations of the different processes of change analyzed above—such as different advances in agricultural and transport technology, the breaking down of tribal or archaic forms of social organizations, of processes of growing mutual impingement of heterogeneous economic (nomad, sedentary, etc.) and ethnic populations, certain international politico-ecological volatility—that can explain, even if only in a preliminary way, the emergence of such different modes of breakdown of tribal and territorial communities, and of the reconstruction of new collectivities and institutional complexes.

It is, of course, obvious that such processes of change, especially those related to crystallization of new types or "stages" of social differentiation, are connected with the development of new internal or external resources, social forces and activities, and with the impingements of the structure of a given society or societies. Contrary however to assumptions of some recent researches, no single, simple combination of various demographic-ecological, economic, or symbolic resources can account for such transitions from stage to stage in general, or differences in the crystallization of the congruent modes of reconstruction of collectivities and institutional structures.

These differences certainly cannot be accounted for in terms of varying amounts or even of kinds of impinging resources and groups (e.g. nomads vs. merchants). Rather, it seems that the most important aspect of these patterns of development and impact of such resources is the degree of concentration as opposed to dispersion, of the impact of new forces—be they demographic (movements of population), economic (primarily international trade), and political (especially conquest and/or tributary relations), and the relative exposure of different institutional sectors of a given society to their influence.

While systematic research on these problems is still yet in its very beginnings, yet some preliminary indications, which can serve perhaps as starting points of such research, can be proposed.[27]

We may distinguish here again, even if in a very preliminary way, two ideal types of such processes, of modes of impingement of such social forces and resources—although, in reality, of course, the situation is much more complicated.

One such ideal pattern is characterized by the development of new types of social—material and symbolic—forces, which tend to impinge on compact political-ecological settings through the activities of their carriers in a relatively uniform manner. Another, more complicated, pattern is one in which development is connected to the development and impingement of greater variety of internal and external forces and material and symbolic resources which are located in different social and ecological settings and which impinge differentially on the various institutional spheres of a given society or sectors thereof. This pattern has usually emerged in less compact ecological settings as well as among less cohesive elites.

Each of these constellations of processes of development and of impingement can be identified in tribal societies and in the development of early as well as archaic states, as well as beyond them. Such different configurations of processes generate different patterns of relations between the extension of the scope of collectivities, the internal differentiation of the structure of the basic collectivities, the differentiation of elite functions and activities, and primarily the positions of control connected with them, and the concomitant development of different types of centers and cultural conceptions.

The more compact impingement of new forces and resources tends to give rise, as in the case of the ancient Egyptian Kingdom, to relatively centralized, uniform political entities with compact boundaries and to a close parallelism between structural differentiation and the differentiation of elite functions. Ultimately, this tends to facilitate the establishment of chiefdoms or centralized early or patrimonial kingdoms.

The more dispersed the impact of forces of change, the more they tended to give rise to discrepancies between structural differentiation and the differentiation of functions of elites and articulators, to the possible disembedment of elites from ascriptive frameworks, and concomitantly to more "radical" developments or breakthroughs in cultural orientations, both of which tend to generate special dynamics of their own. These developments were often connected with the growing openness and diversity of boundaries and with the impact of varied ecological-demographic and economic forces.

Already in various preliterate societies such constellations of forces of change facilitated the development of "non-congruent" societies with rather distinct types of centers, and the importance of such constellations becomes even more evident, as we shall see throughout, in the analysis of the conditions connected with the emergence and institutionalization of Axial Age civilizations.

But while these broad conditions or processes were common to all the Axial Age civilizations, yet there developed great differences in their concrete constellation in the different Axial Age civilizations, and these differences greatly influenced the basic contours of these civilizations.

These civilizations comprised, as we have seen, full-fledged empires (e.g. the Chinese, Byzantine, or Ottoman), rather fragile kingdoms or tribal federations (e.g. ancient Israel), combinations of tribal settings of city-states (e.g. ancient Greece), the complex decentralized pattern of the Hindu civilization, or the complex imperial and imperial-feudal ones of Europe.

The concrete institutional contours of these civilizations, centers, and collectivities and their dynamics varied greatly according to the structure of the predominant elites and their coalitions, the cultural orientations they carried, and the modes of control they exercised, as well as, of course, according to different organizational, economic, technological, and geo-political conditions in which they acted. They all denoted different modes of reconstruction of trust, solidarity, power, and division of labor, generating different institutional types of "answers" to the basic problems of these civilizations, giving rise also to different possibilities of secondary breakthroughs.

Research on the relations between the different historical, political, and ecological settings of these civilizations and the specific type of institutional and symbolic characteristics, as well as the possibility of secondary breakthroughs that developed within them, is yet in its very beginning—the papers in this volume provide some very interesting indications about these problems, and in the introductions to the various sections we shall attempt to point out some of these indications.

PART I

The Origins of the Axial Age in Ancient Greece

The Axial Age Breakthrough in Ancient Greece

S.N. EISENSTADT

I

The characteristics of the Axial Age, as they developed in Ancient Greece, evince some special features. The major breakthroughs from pre-Axial conceptions that developed in Ancient Greece did indeed entail the recognition of a far-reaching chasm between the transcendental and cosmic order and the mundane one. The homology between these two orders was no longer accepted, and the exploration of the relations between the two became one of the major intellectual concerns, especially of the new intellectual groups but also of broader strata. At the same time attempts to grope with the consequences of the recognition of this chasm on possible implementation of the new transcendental vision developed here in a rather unique way. They developed in two closely related, yet not fully interwoven or integrated, directions or spheres; first, that of philosophical speculation and analysis with strong tendencies to development of "proto-science," and second that of specialization and reconstruction of the political and to a smaller degree the broader social order.

The common denominator of both these lines of developments was a very strongly this-worldly orientation of the transcendental vision. This orientation was manifest in a strong emphasis on the exploration of the cosmos or of "nature," and of the social and political order—and to some degree also of human nature—as the major arenas of the implementation of this transcendental vision.

As indicated above, these two lines of development did not fully converge here—either symbolically or institutionally. The attitudes to the cosmic order were mostly those of exploration and much less of its creation or reconstruction in terms of the transcendental vision or of its being oriented by some transcendental power.

In this exploration in the intellectual sphere, as the papers by Y. Elkana and M. Ferwerda point out quite clearly, the major directions of such breakthroughs were very forcefully articulated containing a very strong reflexive component and a strong, although limited, tendency to second-order thinking—but without a concept of the construction of the cosmos through some transcendental power or vision.

The political order constituted the major arena or object of reconstruction in terms of some components of the transcendental vision—especially those of justice. But the vision and practice of such reconstruction were, as compared with other Axial Age civilizations, rather tenuously connected—especially in the institutional orders—with the full-fledged philosophical exploration.

Truly enough these two lines of development were closely connected in the purely intellectual sphere and were often carried by the same persons. Yet they did not converge into a relatively coherent and unified semantic map with full-fledged institutional implications as they did for instance in China or, in an entirely different mode, in early modern Europe. They did not become fully integrated—whether symbolically, conceptually, or structurally, i.e., in terms of their respective institutional implications, and to some degree also in terms of the definition of the roles of their different carriers—into a common ideological and institutional framework.

This specific pattern of Axial Age developments in Ancient Greece was closely connected with the fact that, both in the speculative philosophical and in the political arena, these breakthroughs did not obliterate the "old" religious beliefs and symbols. Truly enough these beliefs—above all those in the deities—were seemingly devaluated from their predominance in the previous age—the so-called Homeric period. Yet at the same time they were maintained as important symbols of the respective collectivities—whether of the different city-states or of the more vague Hellenistic cultural community—and to some degree even served as symbols of legitimation of the political and social order of the different city-states.

This persistence of the older religious conceptions and symbols and their embedment in the civic order were due to the fact that the transcendental vision which developed in Greece in general, and the attempts to reconstruct the political order in particular, were almost entirely disconnected from any other-worldly orientations. Such orientations were almost entirely absent not only from the mode of implementation of the transcendental vision but to a large extent also from its very definition.

At the same time the quest to integrate these two lines of development—i.e. that of philosophical exploration and that of reconstruction of the sociopolitical order; to overcome through such integration the "pagan" elements; and to find some way of coping with other-worldly orientations—constituted a perennial theme— probably even a very strong driving force—in Greek cultural creativity.

II

The emergence of this specific type of Axial Age breakthrough was connected with the special mode of disintegration of the tribal communities and of construction of new collectivities and institutional complexes.

The most important characteristics were first the concentration of population in the city-states; second, growing, yet limited internal differentiation; and third, the dispersion of the population among many single units, with many—peaceful and bellicose—contacts between them, yet without creation of a new overall community.

Thus almost all these city states were characterized by a very strong biological concentration of population. Truly enough such concentration was both relative and limited, but in terms of the realities of that time it was quite real and distinct. Moreover, this concentration encompassed, in most city-states, all the major segments of the community, even though in varying degrees and even though the lower groups participated to a lesser extent in such concentration. Only those who "did not belong"—the slaves or serfs or some of the alien groups—could be excluded from participating in the new concentrated community. But even they, on the whole, had a part in some of its ecological and institutional arrangements.

The processes of internal differentiation in the city-states were probably among the most intensive as compared with similar urban concentrations of population in archaic societies. In the economic field, we find a growing occupational differentiation between the economic ties to the land and the urban vocations, be they in trade, craft, industry, or the ritual and educational fields. This phenomenon was also very closely connected with the development of the availability of many free economic resources—partially even land and manpower resources—not bound to ascriptive social units, the concomitant development of widespread internal and external, relatively free, market activities, and the accumulation of relatively mobile capital.

Similarly, in the social field, we witness the growth of some universalistic and achievement criteria in the composition of strata which emerged from within the older community and which, in their turn, gave rise to new social divisions. The major criteria of such

division are a combination of family and kinship traditions, ownership of land, and economic, occupational, and ritual status.

In political spheres, a growing differentiation of special central
political roles and activities also took place.

In the cultural sphere the most important aspects of this development and differentiation were the breakdown of the primordial and
kinship symbols as the focuses of social, political, and cultural identity
of the community, the development of a conception of the differentiation and distinctiveness of the socio-political and the cultural
cosmic orders, and the concomitant decline of the sanctity of traditionality.

At the same time the process of differentiation that developed
with them, because of the ecological limits of the city-states and of
their strong outward orientation, was relatively limited. The high
level of differentiation and specialization that tended to develop in
most city-states was of a rather peculiar nature in that most of its
products were oriented toward external and not internal markets.
The economic production that developed outstripped by far the
internal demands. Similarly, the cultural, and sometimes also the
political, orientations that developed in at least some of these city-
states extended far beyond the boundaries of any given local community. Hence, by their very nature these communities were geared
to some international system and were naturally very sensitive to
various changes in it.

There did not develop many distinct occupational or professional
roles or a very clear distinction between the sphere of the family
and other institutional spheres.

III

As a result of all these processes there developed here a pattern
unique in the archaic world, in which the impetus to the formation
of centers originated from the same sources that created the forces
of internal differentiation of the community.

This pattern of development was carried by a very special type
of carriers, analyzed in the papers of S.C. Humphreys and Ch. Meier.
These carriers—the intellectual and the political activities—were
characterized by relatively personal autonomy in terms both of their
intellectual endeavors, as well as in terms of their political activities,
but these two types of activities—even when carried by the same
people—did not come together, despite strong intellectual yearnings
in this direction, into common institutional and intellectual frameworks.

This type of crystallization of the community, as well as of elites, was connected with a rather special type of ecological, international geo-political conditions. The most important of these conditions was the development of these communities in the interstices of Great Empires which, for some time at least, enabled the development of relatively self-enclosed enclaves, while at the same time providing these enclaves with many international markets and outlets for their activities.

IV

These patterns of breakthrough from the pre-Axial Age had far-reaching repercussions on the institutional structure of Greek polities, on the special mode of restructuring of the new collectivities, and above all on center-periphery relations that developed in Ancient Greece.

It was indeed this high level of concentration of population in a relatively limited ecological space and the tendency to differentiation together with the development of specific center-periphery relations that were most characteristic of the institutional development in Ancient Greece. Although the center which developed in the Greek city-states was almost entirely identical with the periphery (that is, with the whole collectivity in terms of membership) yet both structurally and symbolically it was almost entirely distinct from it. Structurally and organizationally the center was distinguished from the periphery in the central symbols, temples, and offices. The holders of the various central offices dealt with the internal, external, and international problems specified above.

Ecologically the center was largely identical with the more concentrated parts of the resettled tribal community and was localized usually in central places around special places of public meetings, of temples, central treasures, and courts.

Most members (citizens) of the community could also participate in the center, even though many groups could do so to a much more limited degree, as was the case especially in the more oligarchic types of city-state. But in most cases the limitations of participation in the center were not dissimilar from the social distinction made in the periphery. Most of the more active members of the community participated both in older or peripheral structures (kinship, land and family cults) and in the center. In a sense, one could talk about a continuous phase-movement of the population between these two poles. These movements created, as we shall see, a very high degree of potential social and political tension in the new political systems.

The reason for the development of this type of center-periphery relation was largely the fact that in one sense the "real" periphery or "hinterland" of many city-states lay beyond their own frontiers, in the broader economic and political international system in which they were able to perform their specialized functions.

The relatively small degree of development of a special ruling class, as distinct from the leaders of different social groups and divisions, was perhaps the most important structural outcome or derivative of the combination of a relatively high level of structural differentiation, of a structurally and symbolically distinct center, and of the overlapping of membership between the center and the periphery.

Of special importance from this point of view, of course, was the system of rotation and temporary incumbence of most public offices which was characteristic of many city-states. This system was closely related to the organizational structure of these centers, which was characterized by the development—in response to rising needs and problems—of various specialized tasks performed by relatively fluid nucleuses of elites or by representatives of various social groups and not by a high degree of structural speculation of roles and organizations.

At the same time in these city-states there developed many embryonic nucleuses of elite groups with a very high degree of potential for social, cultural, and political creativity.

The lack of distinction between membership in the community and in the center and the fact that participation in the center was very often perceived as the performance of the political roles or task of the major social divisions of the community also account for some of the major dimensions of political symbolism that tended to develop in the city-states.

The background of the development of this symbolism was the potential universalization of the pattern of participation in the political and cultural orders that were concomitant with the transpositions of the older arrangements of the tribal or semipatrimonial communities and their arrangements into the new setting. Indeed, many such arrangements were often transposed into the new settings.

Indeed one of the major characteristics of the Greek city was that the new structurally and symbolically differentiated centers were often seemingly built up on the model of the older semiequalitarian and semicommunal arrangements of the tribal communities.

There developed in the city-states attempts to transpose, on a much more differentiated and culturally sophisticated symbolic and institutional level, the basic identity between the social and the political order and the lack of distinction between center and periphery that had probably been characteristic of the older tribal communities. Paradoxically, this tendency was especially discernible in socially more differentiated or developed Greek city-states.

The most important common denominator of the political symbolism of city-states was citizenship. Particular importance was attached first to the potentially full and equal participation of individuals as individuals, freed of particularistic-primordial ties, in the body politic and second to their individual political or legal responsibility and the concomitant responsibility of the (almost always temporary) rulers before the ruled.

In its close relationship between social and political crises and in its "secular" definition of politics and of participation in the political order, the political process in the city-states resembled that of modern societies. However, in contrast to modern societies, the city-state did not allow distinction and separateness between the social and the political spheres, and it had few institutional arrangements for maintaining the differentiation between them.

V

It was probably because of the weak connection between the two lines of breakthrough from pre-Axial Age conceptions, as well as the nature of center-periphery relations and of political symbolism of the city-states, that the development of fully autonomous moral conceptions, transcending the existing social and institutional orders, was here, as compared with other Axial Age civilizations, relatively limited.

Truly enough the political symbolism and practice in Greek city-states was based on the recognition of the autonomy of the moral order as distinct from the tribal or social orders. This perception was however coupled with a quest for a reintegration of these orders through the autonomy of the individual. At the same time, the quest for reintegration was based on the conception of complete identity of the social and political order and on the assumption of "totalistic" participation of citizens in the body politic. This was extended to include the capacity of all citizens to represent the essence and center of the community. Thus there developed also the recognition of the possibility of tensions and conflicts between them, as in the "moral protest" of the autonomous individual that was depicted in some of the Greek tragedies.

Thus the possibility of full institutional working out of moral autonomy as against the state was, as Antigone or even more clearly the fate of Socrates attests, relatively very limited. Of crucial importance here was, of course, the fact that the ultimate legitimation

of the order of the polis, in terms of the existing symbols, derived
in many ways from the pre-Axial Age, even if this order itself was
already couched in terms of some of the components of the Axial
Age transcendental vision.

At the same time the recognition of this tension between the moral
and the civic order and of the limitations of the former, was probably
a very important factor in the development of some of the great
cultural achievements—above all of tragedy and of political philosophy.

VI

One of the outcomes of these specific symbolic and institutional
characteristics of the Greek Axial Age breakthrough was the very
weak possibility of internal-institutional transformability and of secondary breakthroughs.

Indeed one of the major characteristics of the Greek civilization
was the almost complete absence of the kinds of secondary breakthrough which developed, as we shall yet see in greater detail later,
in all Axial Age civilizations.

Truly enough in the purely philosophical realm far-reaching developments took place in the Hellenistic age. Many of these developments, including that of "proto" science, or of mathematical
speculation, did indeed go beyond many of the achievements in
classical Greece. Here it should, of course, also be remembered that
the great syntheses of Plato and Aristotle took place in periods of
political decline of the city-states.

Similarly the Hellenistic and later the Roman Empires constituted
of course far-reaching transformations of the original vision and
institutional arrangements of the city-states.

But these developments did not constitute, as was the case with
respect to the secondary breakthroughs of most Axial Age civilizations, further developments or restructuring of those premises which
were rooted in their Axial Age breakthroughs.

This fact was very closely connected with one of the major characteristics of the city-states—namely with the development within
them of a very strong contradiction that developed, especially in the
more dynamic of such city-states, between a very high predisposition
to internal change with relatively small capacity to absorb such
changes through the reconstruction of their institutional order.

Almost all city-states faced the problem of their ability to respond
to social demands and to absorb the various social revolutions that
could be engendered in them. At the same time, they faced the
problem how to maintain and even increase their political, executive,

and administrative abilities to deal with both such internal problems and their international involvements.

The potentialities for more radical types of change were often rooted in the tendency to universalize the political or cultural community. Insofar as this tendency was strong, there necessarily developed in these communities potentially transformative orientations, that is, orientation to development from within their own premises. But these tendencies could rarely become fully realized and institutionalized from within the political confines of the city-states.

This was due mostly to the fact that most of these universalistic orientations tended to develop in the symbolic rather than in the actual political sphere. One might say that the relations of these orientations to concrete politics were rather unrealistic in the sense that they could not be easily institutionalized in the confines of the existing political communities.

The inability to institutionalize such transformative universalistic orientations was rooted first in the small scale of the actual political community and in the fact that the conception of the totality of participation necessarily imposed great limitations on the organizational development and scope of the executive. It was also rooted in the concomitant weakness and lack of cohesion of a special political elite or ruling class capable of transcending the limits of the local community and its parts vis-à-vis the populist impingements on the center.

The conceptions of universal participation in the political or cultural order and of citizenship developed in different directions from Rome and Greece. In Rome it focused around law and legal institutions and around the possibility of extension of the idea of citizenship beyond the original confines of the local city-state. Unlike the Roman, the Greek conception did not prove capable of transcending in either legal or institutional terms the confines of the local city-state community. As a result, there was continuous tension between the universalizing tendencies of political and cultural symbolism and the institutional realities of the city-community.

Given the greater dependence of these types of city-states on international settings and exigencies, these limitations could indeed become catastrophic, stemming from the inability to deal with the external pressures and intensifying the propensities for civil war.

In some cases attempts at federative arrangements between different city-states were made. But these were not very fruitful or of long duration because basically they did not transcend the structural limitation pointed out above. They usually gave rise only to very intermittent and unstable intercity coalitions. Only in Rome did there develop from within the city-states a new, broader imperial system that maintained a relatively high degree of cultural and political continuity with the city-state, while attempting to uphold many of the political symbols of the city-state.

Rome's specific type of development was due to several factors. The first was that the peculiar structure of the Roman constitution enabled the development of a more cohesive and widely oriented ruling class and facilitated some degree of its institutional isolation from populist impingements. Second it was due to the special universalistic tendencies of Roman legal institutions. Last it was due to the fact that at a crucial point in the history of the Roman republic the decision was taken—after much dispute and civil strife—to extend the Roman citizenship to other Italian cities. But all these instances were peculiar to Rome and they only tend to emphasize the limitations of other city-states.

The different constellations of internal and international conditions greatly influenced the extent of stability in different city-states and the directions of their transformation. Insofar as it was impossible to absorb all these changes within the confines of the city-state, there developed several different types of demise or, in very rare cases, of transformation of their political systems—none of which constituted a further development of the Axial Age premises of the Greek civilization.

The first such tendency was some sort of segmentation of the given polity in the form of colonization and immigration. This was a very frequent pattern in many city-states—not totally dissimilar from the pattern of segmentation in primitive tribes, tribal federations, and patrimonial kingdoms.

Another pattern or type of change, already much more radical, was that of a tendency to total civil war, of "stasis," and of the consequent possible demise of the given system of the city-state—very often connected with and facilitating foreign conquest—and submergence in various patrimonial or imperial units of which indeed the Hellenistic and Roman Empires were the most important.

In these Empires symbolism of city-states could be perpetuated by the new rulers as sort of symbolic appendages to their own centers, but which were based on entirely different premises.

In this connection it is of crucial importance to our analysis that in these later developments in the Hellenistic and Roman Empires the relation between the two lines of development of the Axial Age vision in Ancient Greece—that of philosophical speculation and that of reconstruction of the political sphere—became even more dissociated from one another than in classical Greece.

Thus, significantly enough, in the Hellenistic Empire and to some degree in the Roman Empire, the pagan political symbolism became indeed rather fully re-enacted and the King-God reappeared.

Chapter 1

The Emergence of
Second-order Thinking
in Classical Greece

Yehuda Elkana

Understanding is an unsought condition; we inexorably inhabit a world of intelligibles. But understanding as an engagement is an exertion; it is the resolve to inhabit an ever more intelligible, or an ever less mysterious world. This unconditional engagement of understanding I shall call 'theorizing'. It is an engagement to abate mystery rather than to achieve definite understanding.[1]

The conscious resolve to demystify the world is not only about the world; it is also an effort to guide one's thoughts: it is thinking about thinking. This is what we call second-order thinking. People in all cultures 'think'. Not all 'thinking', whether it is about the world, or society, or the affairs of the individual, is second-order. The body of knowledge in any area—primitive cosmology or General Relativity—as long as it consists of thoughts *about the world,* is not second-order thinking. All 'images of knowledge'[2], i.e. our thoughts about knowledge, are second-order thinking. In my theoretical work I have tried to eliminate the inviting and tempting belief in linear development, as if second-order thinking were a highly developed form of consciousness which follows only after the highest achievements in first-order thinking. This in itself is a meta-level view, since any ordering of thought according to degrees of sophistication, complexity or achievement, is already second-order thinking. All we can say is that when we reflect about our theories of the world, i.e. about the 'body of knowledge' in any area, we find, in terms of our images of knowledge, that some of them are very sophisticated, some others very primitive, and yet both can be totally unreflective—purely first-order.

Now we ask a whole series of questions—all second-order:[3]

a. Is second-order thinking a hallmark of only some cultures or of all?

b. What is the relation between the transcendental breakthrough of the Axial Age civilizations and the emergence of second-order thinking?

c. In which bodies of knowledge and in which social context do we wake up first to the need of reflective ordering in a corpus through images of knowledge?

d. What are the mutual influences between bodies of knowledge, images of knowledge, and normative ideologies?

e. Are the carriers of the body of knowledge the same elites who carry the second-order thinking in society?

a. This is a bone of contention among relativist and realist thinkers. For me it is difficult to imagine any culture that does not reflect, ever, about its own thoughts. Even saying that our 'theory' or 'belief', "that the sun is swallowed up every night by a demon and is being reborn next morning" is a beautiful myth or a frightening fact, is an image of knowledge and it approximates second-order thinking. The real issue, therefore, arises when such images of knowledge are systematically applied to a corpus of beliefs or theories about any subject, and especially in the reflective question about their truth-value. Is there a culture which does not raise the question whether its medical beliefs are true? Probably not. Therefore the emphasis will shift to the *systematic* nature of reflexive questioning. Is it the case that in every culture there is a conscious attempt to apply *systematically* a corpus of thought about thinking to a body of knowledge? Probably not.

b. Almost by definition, if we accept the validity of the still somewhat unexplained phenomenon that during the Axial Age a number of civilizations underwent critical change more or less simultaneously and with no clear mutual influence on each other, and that the breakthroughs are characterized by a "strain toward transcendentalism," by creating a gap or tension between that newly created transcendental realm and the mundane,[4] by an urgent need to bridge that tension, and by the emergence of new elites with autonomous norms which will serve as the bridge, THEN the very strain toward transcendentalism is second-order.

c. + d. The more elaborate a corpus of views or theories about the world or society or the gods or the individual becomes, the more indispensable will become the criteria of choice between competing or contradictory views, between emerging alternatives. Awareness of alternatives is an invitation to second-order thinking. The more numerous these alternatives are, the more elaborate they are, the more natural it becomes that reflexive thinking will supply the criteria and the ordering. As we shall see, the first systematic application of reflexive thinking occurred in classical Greece not in their theories of nature, but on the one hand in the ethical-political sphere and on the other in mathematics. Only much after the idea of proof in geometry became systematically established and after conscious awareness of alternatives became the hallmark of the thinking of the sophistic 'antilogikoi', did second-order thinking penetrate and revolutionize theories of the world. The idea of proof in geometry is an image of knowledge; the idea of 'antilogikoi' in sophistic philosophy is also an image of knowledge. They stem from the normative, ideological stand of mystical Pythagoreans and sophistic educationalists respectively. The reasons for this we shall have to seek.

In geometry, once it became an intellectual enterprise, almost professionalized, the growing body of knowledge created the need for the development of criteria of validity and thus the second-order idea of proof—an image of knowledge. In politics it was the other way round: normative ideologies with competing and often directly contradictory calls for action brought about the need for a contemplative reflective ordering of these, introducing a hierarchy in values and norms and formulating chains of alternative choices: images of knowledge, second-order ideas in politics.

e. It is an accepted characteristic of the transcendental breakthroughs that the creation of the sharp dichotomy between the mundane and the transcendental (transmundane) is accompanied by a severe tension and the urgent wish to overcome that tension. It is usually beyond the capability of the old elites to perform that, and it becomes the task of new elites to support the strain for transcendence and to provide the desired salvation from that unbearable tension. Such elite groups create their own institutional settings and their own rational autonomous criteria (by definition second-order) or norms of action. They formulate their corpus of second-order thoughts about thoughts and see to it that these are then presented as a means of salvation. It is often the case that the old elite is directly concerned with the body of knowledge or with the ideological norms of conduct for their group or society and, not experiencing strain or tension, never come to grips with the need to introduce proofs or to formulate alternatives, and it comes to them as a shock to have to meet that challenge. In some cases, for example in science, such a situation brings about the creation of a new discipline, like for example *philosophy of science* as against *pure science*. The dialogue of the deaf between these two has all the characteristics of the (rare) but bitter critical dialogue between scientists and philosophers of science. For instance the road to the Pythagorean heaven leads through the well-defined corpus of the geometrical proof. This is the Pythagorean soteriology. The 'monks' or 'sages' who carry that knowledge also protect it—they serve as the gatekeepers. These new elite groups often constitute themselves as heterodoxies with relation to a central tradition or with relation to their past orthodoxy, and as such they become agents of change. Such were not only the Pythagoreans, but also the Sophists, the members of the Royal Society; such are the professional scientific societies of today. Such are, according to the experts, the Chinese literati, the Hindu Brahmins, the Judaic prophets, and the later wise men of the Islamic Ulema. The source of the concept of the Axial Age is Karl Jasper's summary formulation of previously well-known attempts to put order into universal history.[5] He described the phenomenon and introduced the concept of the Axial Age and placed it between 800 and 200 B.C.E. He surveys previous generalizations and polemicizes the views of Alfred Weber.[6]

Although it is beyond my competence to question in depth these generalizations about the Axial Age civilizations or the transcendental breakthroughs that characterize them, thinking in terms of Axial Age and transcendental breakthroughs turns out to be a very fruitful historical style and thus I shall try to briefly survey the worlds of knowledge of the Greeks in terms of breakthroughs and in terms of the point of view delineated above on second-order thinking.

TRANSCENDENCE OF THE AXIAL AGE AND ITS EXPRESSIONS

Thus we start from the view that each of the great Axial Age civilizations characterized a 'transcendental breakthrough'. This is claimed to have been characteristic of Jewish, Chinese, Greek, Iranian, and Indian civilizations. We can at best try to look for these processes in specific areas of creativity such as rhetoric, mathematics, 'sciences', ethics, or the politics of the polis. It will be my claim that at least for the case of Greece we are facing a series of breakthroughs (albeit, not all transcendental) rather than one major breakthrough. Whatever is beyond mundane life can be seen as transcendental reality: it can be conceived in religious terms as Supernatural Being, or in intellectual terms as abstract entities not accessible to the senses. Jean Pierre Vernant distinguishes between civilizations where the breakthrough was towards a transcendental *power* as in Judaism and Christianity, and others where it was towards a transcendental *order* as in Greece, where the gods themselves are subject to that order. The Homeric gods are not Supernatural Being, although they have many superhuman features as well as some very human traits. Humphreys,[7] in the same line, explains the "predominance of cosmology over theology in Greek thought" as due to the fact that "polytheists need a cosmology more than monotheists," but also as due to the early Greek social structure centered around an aristocracy. The important result of these claims is that in early Greece, as in China, there was no tension between religion and state. Thus in Homeric Greece there was no ideological tension to call for systematic discussion of alternatives, that is, for second-order thinking.

The strain towards transcendence is not identical with world-negation, but all transcendental movements negate some part of the world. The very rationalization of the mundane, the application of logos to the Homeric world of Greek philosophers or, as we learn, the banning of Gods from nature in the Hebrew prophets, is actually a negation, a limiting process. The negation of mythical authority and the recourse to violence are both aspects of rationalization of the world. Conclusive truths about the world and about human and social relations are reached by reasonable dialogue, be it on the basis of epistemic or of metic reasoning. To these truths is then attributed universal value. However, an epistemic, Socratic dialogue, sophisticated as it may be, can be first-order. It is not always so. Metic-sophistic argument by definition is second-order. If we look at transcendental breakthroughs, as typified by systematic second-order thinking, whatever happened before the emergence of second-order thinking at an early stage it could not have been a transcendental breakthrough. This relation is not symmetrical: while there is no quest for transcendence without second-order thinking—as we shall see below—not all second-order thinking results in a transcendental breakthrough.

Three major changes occurred in Greece between the fifteenth and the sixteenth centuries. The encounter between Mycenae and Crete's Minoan civilization first influenced Mycenae (about 1450 B.C.E.) and brought about the development of Linear B, which helped that influence and later led to the destruction of Crete (about 1400 B.C.E.) and the beginning of a flourishing Mycenaean civilization. It is important to think of this development as a cultural breakthrough. The expansion of the Mycenaeans brought them in touch with the Hittites, and through Rhodes with Mesopotamia and even Egypt (fourteenth–twelfth centuries). This broad exchange of communication between cultures and the creation of a new script[8] brought forth another "small" breakthrough in the form of a common Cypro-Mycenaean civilization. Finally (around 1000 B.C.E.) came the Dorian invasion which destroyed Mycenaean civilization, creating a genuine crisis and a break with tradition. After that emerged a new Greek civilization, starting with the development of phonetic script (ninth century B.C.E.), then the Homeric world[9] in the eighth century, finally leading up to the *transcendental* breakthrough of the Axial Age. Are all these really breakthroughs? Did they all follow a crisis? If the break with a previous tradition is not total, or at least not very brutal, can we speak of a crisis? These questions can be answered only according to each historian's world view. What is clear beyond doubt is that for the first of these changes the creation of the Mycenaean civilization followed an encounter of cultures, that it was a partial breach with previous traditions, and that it introduced an all-important new cultural tool: the Linear B; that it brought with it new cultural products: new archival collections, palace-in-fortress architecture, a new style of vase decoration depicting warring figures, and impressive burial sites, and with these a palace bureaucracy and great political changes. This was not a transcendental breakthrough, since it was not accompanied by second-order reflection on alternatives; there was no quest for transcendental reality in an attempt to resolve the tension. Moreover, this change was isolated in one place. However, it did result from crisis caused by contact with other civilizations. As to the second change: the Mycenaeans destroyed the Cretan civilization and created a new, widespread civilization, coming in touch with many Asian cultures. This caused a seemingly lesser crisis (can it be called a breakthrough?) but the encounter between cultures was certainly fruitful.

Then came the third change: a genuine crisis and total break with tradition—the Dorian invasion. From then on, with the phonetic script taken over from the Phoenicians, a new social structure emerged. The new script was not a 'class speciality', it served the whole society and not only the creation of a royal archives. The foundations for Homeric culture and for an egalitarian democracy were laid down with its unique cultural creations: the polis with its ethical-political theory (second-order as we shall see); a new cosmology (at first *not* second-order); a new religion: Homeric-anthropomorphic. Later followed the creation of a rational transcendental order (second-order) competing with sophisticated irrational cults and sects (also second-order). Geometry flourished at the meeting point of these two and it had to come up with a resolution: the creation of proof as a second-order idea par excellence.

That cultural encounter is indispensable for a breakthrough has been convincingly shown.[10] That a crisis and break with tradition and historical continuity serves as a new opportunity is also clear.[11] Whether we can generalize and claim that these are also sufficient conditions for a transcendental breakthrough is still an open question and will probably remain so for a long time to come.

Eric Weil reminds us that

> the history we write is always at bottom our own intellectual and political autobiography, an attempt to come to a genetic understanding of our own way of living, acting and feeling. The meanings of terms such as 'breakthrough' and 'axial time' become clear only if we use them in this context, if we acknowledge that the importance of events and dates is determined by the place we assign to them in our autobiography and not by their material weight.[12]

Eric Voegelin, in his magisterial multivolume *Order and History*, formulates a different principle:[13] "The order of history emerges from the history of order." He criticizes the efforts of Jaspers and Toynbee as oversimplifications: they, like many others, suffer from a *horror pleni*—they are overwhelmed by the "richness and diversity of spirit" and thus try to reduce all breakthroughs to some common element of cause. Especially in the theoretical introduction to volume IV of *The Ecumenical Age*. Voegelin claims that not shared origins, but structures must be looked for; hierophanic events can be explained in terms of a "structure of experiencing consciousness" which generally presupposes mutual awareness of cultures. In our terms we would say that such structures are by definition results of second-order thinking. Since East and West (Greece and China) did not know of each other's existence, they had no consciousness of thinking on any axis of history. However, here Voegelin is oversimplifying: for two different civilizations to have consciousness of thinking on an axis of history, they do not have to be mutually aware of each other: it is enough if each reaches that consciousness through awareness of other neighboring civilizations. For Greece, awareness of cultures and countries visited by Herodotus (in addition to other factors) raised that consciousness. Even the little extent to which the Greeks allowed themselves to become interested in other cultures was enough to create second-order thinking in anthropology, sociology, and history. It was the Greeks' fault, as Momigliano[14] sees it, "to have kept the Iranians, the Indians and the Chinese outside their (and our) knowledge and values." Had their consciousness absorbed the Chinese attitudes towards work, technology, labor relations, bureaucracy, etc., possibly reflexion on the relation between their physical knowledge and daily actions would have introduced the connection between proof and technology—a strain towards second-order thinking. This works in both directions: China had a technology, quite well advanced, as a body of practical knowledge, not systematically raising the issue of proof or caring about the knowledge of 'truth' about the world. Without these second-order concepts no 'science' developed from technology, just as in Greece no 'proper science' developed from their speculations about the world. 'Proof' and 'experiment' are both thoughts about thoughts—and without their joint presence no science can develop.

An important feature of a 'transcendental breakthrough' is that, after the breakthrough, authority shifts from the bearers of office in society: scribes, priests, kings, etc., to transcendental external elements: a supernatural being, a transcendental order, a theoretical cosmology, or even—as Humphreys[15] reminds us—a written code of laws ('instead' of the officers of the law).

This quest for transcendence is in itself a result of the soteriological wish to eliminate the unbearable tensions created by competing alternative world-views, and this is already a result of second-order thinking. But this now becomes systematized.

The carriers of the transcendental vision are small groups of intellectuals, often marginal to society, who contemplate the alternative views of the world in its physical aspects or its religious aspects or the world of men in its social or individual aspects. The Sophists or the philosophers had no central role to play in the political life of the city. It is important to realize that the creation of a transcendental cosmology is a result of a new body of knowledge but in itself does not yet constitute second-order thinking. Already in the Homeric poems and in Hesiod there is a rudimentary theoretical cosmology, and the pre-Socratic philosophers continued to develop it, each in his own individual direction. It would be difficult to interpret any of the extant fragments of the pre-Socratics as reflexive, a systematic critical thinking about their own thinking. True, very little is extant and we should not apply here "the argument from silence." Yet, even from Heraclitus' discussions, or from Anaxagoras' wish to sell his books (as Socrates affirms in the *Apology*), no *systematic critical* thinking about thinking can be seen. If anything, closer to second-order thinking is Xenophanes' criticism of the system of religious pantheon.[16] Yet in most of these areas second-order thinking did not create a transcendental breakthrough. Second-order, metic thinking, in politics, rhetoric, sophistic methodology are all mundane practical matters. The politicians, rhetoricians, and sophistic philosophers are not the carriers of the strain for transcendence. The dogmatic, barely reflexive, pre-Socratic philosophers and especially the elitist, rationalist, epistemic Parmenidians constitute an elite group dedicated to first-order understanding of nature, mostly non-reflexive; the static, logical intellectual style gives these intellectuals a feeling, and thus a style, of moral superiority with respect to the Sophists who are anti-epistemic and rely on cunning reason. They are not yet fully aware of the tension between the sphere of the mundane and their cosmological concerns; yet they have laid down the foundations of a 'scientific' soteriology which will be based on episteme, once it becomes conscious and reflexive after the fourth century B.C.E., and then its cosmology will become of transcendental import. Their opponents, the much maligned Sophists, became aware of alternatives, developed a reflective style and the second-order metic reasoning much earlier.

THE MORAL-POLITICAL SPHERE

Typically in the human/social sphere, conscious, systematic awareness of alternatives—second-order thought—emerges much earlier than in the philosophy of nature. Already Hesiod's "Gold, Silver, Bronze and Hero races are, like the lands visited by Odysseus, mythical models of 'alternative societies' in which the poet plays with fundamental rules and distinctions of Greek culture. . . ."[17]

The early philosophers started contemplating the origin and nature of the universe in descriptive, somewhat dogmatic fashion in terms of increasingly transcendental entities: a generalized concept of water, or *opeiron* or *nous*. Even if they were aware of each others' view and each desired that his own view be accepted, there was no critical systematic juxtaposition of alternative views with immediate practical conclusions in view, which would then constitute the tension between the this-worldly and the other-worldly. The idea that the way the basic conceptions are stated and questions formulated might influence the findings and the answers—the very basic rhetorics—did not occur to them. Thus a series of quasi-transcendental cosmologies were formulated, often quoting or opposing each other without however the emergence of second-order thinking in the philosophy of nature, and postponing the transcendental breakthrough.

On the other hand, when turning to questions of the origin and nature of the political and legal institutions, there was no way of avoiding alternative views; it happened both by comparing the past with the present and by comparing different poleis; such comparisons resulted in critically important decisions. Moreover, when the Sophists appeared on the scene and started to develop their tools of conviction and argumentative skills, the science of rhetoric developed. Systematic, critical thinking about thinking, i.e. second-order thinking, emerged in practical areas of daily life long before, and independent of second-order thinking in theology or theoretical cosmology, quasi-transcendental as they may have been.

Mathematics, or rather geometry, is different from cosmology. Here, as we shall see below, the idea of geometrical proof introduced second-order thinking at an early stage. This should not surprise us if we believe, as I do, that mathematics is invented, not discovered, and is thus a typically humanistic area of creativity.

Let us look first to the political sphere. Great scholars like Ehrenberg, Voegelin, J.-P. Vernant, and Christian Meier have studied these issues: I am merely translating their conclusions into the language of second-order thinking.

Vernant[18] describes the crisis of sovereignty in Homeric times; after the Dorian invasion and after the creation of the new phonetic script (eighth century), important social changes occurred, accompanied by moral and political changes, and in the seventh century we trace political speculations about *sophia*. This *sophia* was concerned with the human world and dealt with the human order of the city. It involved a competition—*agon*—in all areas of life; this competition presupposed basic equality; ". . . a new conception of power: *arché* was delegated every year by a human decision . . .",[19] it no longer belonged to one person but to all; oratorical contests emerged as political tools; there was strife and rivalry *(eris)* between all for everything. The *sophia* dealing with all this was clearly a *rational discourse*.

With the creation of the polis,[20] one of the greatest cultural inventions of the Greeks, the new social organization put central emphasis on speech as a political power, replacing physical (or economic) brute force. Thus rational discourse now turned naturally to the problem of how to turn speech into an effective tool of persuasion. *Peitho,* the force of persuasion, and *metis,* cunning reason: with such political tools we are in the domain of systematic critical reflection, thinking about thinking—'second-order'. With this development, speech became free debate presupposing a public; it was no longer ritual words nor precise formulae in rhetoric. This will be the main trade of the Sophists;[21] in direct, though not reflective conscious opposition to this fluidity of speech and against the metic reasoning, Parmenides will set up his rigid, static, logical, epistemic universe. Since democracy in the polis and submitting all knowledge to public criticism went hand-in-hand, it was second-order thinking on matters moral and political which was genuinely egalitarian, while the dogmatic, rational, but not reflexive natural philosophy of Parmenides and later Plato become anti-egalitarian, separatist, and often secretive.

When the crisis of the cities started thinking in second-order terms the Greeks refused to accept anomia:

What was peculiar to Greece was the reaction these changes produced in society: the refusal to accept a situation that was felt and denounced as anomia (lawlessness) and the restructuring of social life in its entirety to make it accord with communal and egalitarian aspirations.[22]

As against this, to refuse to come to terms with anomia in the natural sciences, that is, to acquire the *image of knowledge* that nature must be intelligible and lawful, took Western culture several more centuries at least to late antiquity, if not to the seventeenth-century scientific revolution!

Legal thinking is also second-order. Already in the seventh century B.C.E., which is often called the Archaic Age, even before the creation of the polis as we know it, laws became codified, securing the position of the non-nobles. A clear distinction was made between intentional and unintentional action, between murder and manslaughter.[23] This is second-order psychological thinking.

"Law as it developed was itself not a logical construction."[24] The Greeks did not have an idea of absolute law, founded upon certain principles and organized into a coherent system. For them there were different degrees of law. At one pole, law rests upon the authority of accomplished facts, upon compulsion; at the other it brought into play sacred powers, such as the order of the world or the justice of 'Zeus', again combining the rational with the irrational. In Vernant's formulation: "Divine Diké . . . includes an irrational element of brute force."[25] The consideration of what kind of a law is being encountered presupposed reflexive thinking. Below we shall also consider the absence of the concept of a 'law of nature' among the Greeks.

In the democratic polis, cultivated by the Sophists and parallel with the achievements of the Parmenidian method from the fifth century onward, there occurred a blossoming of rhetoric, the irrational domain par excellence that was sharply attacked by Plato and by anybody who professed epistemic knowledge. In contrast to what is characteristic of epistemic thought and what is customarily considered characteristic of modern science, in rhetoric the manner in which the claim is formulated determines whether the speaker will succeed in convincing his listeners of the rightness of his argument. In other words, for epistemic knowledge the meaning is in the text.[26]

It is important to note that what is considered scientific or epistemic may change diametrically with time and circumstance. Thus for example basic second-order concepts in rhetoric later became part of epistemic recovering. Let us look at this development.

In rhetoric there is no truth that can stand by itself: no text contains the meaning in its entirety; no argument has absolute authority. Rhetoric satisfies the basic democratic need: the audience decides an issue by a call of votes, with no privileged status given to those with epistemic knowledge, in accordance to whether or not it was convinced by the speaker. Rhetoric, like science, is developed in independent institutional channels—by the same elite which developed legal, political, and clinical (rather than diagnostic) thinking. Rhetoric is supported by the metic claim, metis being the 'cunning reason'. The two developed simultaneously in the Golden Age of Greece and not in sequence. More than that: some of the concepts most important for modern science developed precisely in the sphere of rhetoric; for example, the 'probable' (the Greek εικοζ), which is vital for the process of persuasion. The Platonic philosophers viewed the 'probable' as the opposite and the contradiction of the 'true'. Two thousand years and more had to pass before the 'probable' became part of the epistemic, scientific body of knowledge: it became part of the social sciences with Condorcet; of modern mathematics with Laplace; and of the very heart of physics with Boltzmann.

This process can be seen for other concepts too. The development of thought in terms of alternative truths took place in the sphere of rhetoric.[27] It was Protagoras who taught that for every issue arising there are two opposing arguments. The ability to support both an opinion and its opposite became an educational aim of the orator and formed the heart of the belief in rhetoric, a belief that is supported in its entirety by the metic, the cunning reason. It was exactly this approach that developed the awareness of alternatives, which today is considered a basic characteristic of scientific thought.

It is important to remember that although thinking in terms of second-order images of knowledge always comes after the creation of first-order bodies of knowledge, yet growth of complexity is not linear: there is sophisticated first-order thinking just as there is primitive, little developed second-order thinking. Thinking in concrete as against in abstract terms will illustrate this point.

The theme of the abstract/concrete is best illustrated by the study of the 'stages' in Greek religion. The great students of Greek religion Jane Harrison and Gilbert Murray[28] teach us that before the concrete anthropomorphic Homeric gods there was an earlier, abstract religion, a "dark primeval tangle of desires and fears and dreams," from which the Olympians later drew their vitality. These primeval gods were obviously alive but were not shaped like humans: the wind, the sun, the sea. There were powers from below: Chthonioi (literally those beneath the earth), who had to be appeased by sacrifice and ritual. To these were dedicated the early great festivals of Athens:

the Diasia, the Thermophoria, and the Anthesteria, studied in depth
by Harrison. The symbols of these ancient gods were often animals:
the snake of the Diasia, the sow of the Thermophoria, and the bull's
head of the Anthesteria. Later, after the Olympic period, they became
accompanying symbols of Olympic gods. The atmosphere of religious
dread accompanying the festivals is primordial and abstract. As
against these, the Homeric pantheon is not only anthropomorphic
but rational, close-by, and anti-magical. Unlike the abstract gods in
the ancient cosmogonic myths, the Olympic gods conquer the world—
they do not create it. Olympic religion is very human; it constitutes
a cleansing exercise—it is a moral expurgation of old rites; it brings
order into a magically created chaos, and above all it answers new
social needs in its very realistic rationalism. The Olympic gods are
very human indeed and as such, being too personal, they seem
capricious and cruel. But they rid the Greeks of the frightening power
of tribal mythology, they freed them from their dependence on the
soil (being indestructible only to return with the Dionysian and
Orphic cults), and then securely placed religion within the domain
of human imagination.[29]

Later, in the sixth and fifth centuries, many philosophers came
very close to monotheism, and this went hand-in-hand with a critique
of Homeric anthropomorphism—this is true of Xenophanes, of Parmenides discerning his sphere, and of the great tragedians Aeschylus
and Euripides.

Nor is the 'progress' of religion linear on the rational/irrational
axis. While some of the pre-Socratic philosophers of nature tended
towards a rational, almost monotheistic critique of Homeric religion,
in the cities where democracy ruled and the Sophists taught a new
irrational religious trend became powerful. By a stretch of definition
the sophistic methods of persuasion can be considered rational even
though relying on cunning reason; but the emerging Dionysian religion and the accompanying cult-movements, like the Orphics, with
their emphasis on the transmigration of the soul, the punishment
in Hades, inheritance of evil, community of all animate beings, is
in the domain of the irrational. It is in these cults that a new culture
became superimposed on that part of Mycenaean culture which
survived the Dorian destruction, namely on the popular religion of
shepherds' folklore. Such an encounter helped to create in these
religious cults, 'irrational' as they were, some beginnings of religious
control or perhaps even critique in second-order mode: this is shown
by the way the frenzy was consciously brought on and then stopped
at some point. Similarly, Vernant[30] shows in suggestive passages how
the new morality and egalitarian democracy which, as mentioned
above, abandoned brute force, brought about legislation against mur-

der (a murderer now defiled the whole community), and how this rationalization of daily life went hand-in-hand with the new "irrational" religious awakening. The cults were also preoccupied with political questions and "among the Olympian and Eleusinian divinities in the sanctuary of Demeter at Pergamun, where the religious fraternity . . . [sang] Orphic hymns . . . were a number of Orphic gods who personified abstract ideas. Among them were two pairs, Arete (Virtue) and Sophrosina (Mastery of the Self), and Pistis (Trust) and Homonoia (Unanimity)."[31]

Thus there is no linear progress from the irrational to the rational, nor from cunning reason toward epistemic reason, nor from non-reflexive thinking to second-order thinking. The 'parts' develop sometimes parallel, and sometimes sequentially, in specific intellectual domains once in one direction and at other times and domains the other way round. The only generalization that holds is that a corpus of knowledge must precede second-order thinking about it. Moreover, it is clear that these political-religious metic-irrational developments, although not transcendental in themselves, became indispensable for the transcendental breakthrough. Once the strain for transcendence becomes second-order, and a transcendental natural order was established—whether in the domain of religion or in the sphere of natural philosophy—the order itself was modelled on the moral-political order which was developed in the polis and which preceded it. Later, and in the opposite direction, as a result of the seventeenth-century scientific revolution—another breakthrough of great importance—a new transcendental social-political order was created in the eighteenth century, modelled on the natural order as developed during the scientific revolution.

The Tension Between Metis and Episteme

What typifies the pre-Socratic natural philosophers are an interest in the origin and principle of things (the order of things) and in creating conceptions of order in nature. Mostly they translate conceptions of human order—moral and political ideas—into the organization of the natural world. As we have seen above, they were dogmatic, rational, and theoretical, but not second-order. Thus the Miletians are characterized by Toynbee as having an "urge for individual freedom and self-expression" which they expressed in their individual, new, general principles (water, opeiron, air) about the world. Thus Thales, Anaximander, Anaximenes. In Anaximander, the concepts of *right* and *wrong (diké* and *adikia)* became part of the cosmic process and transformed "moral forces of social and political life and its civil struggle into an eternal order."[32]

If we call the emergence of the Ionian philosophy a breakthrough, certain of the prerequisites we noted above were there: Miletus had a flourishing international trade, and it was at the crossroads of ideas from many cultures.

Ehrenberg does not think in terms of second-order thinking, yet he brings together ideas and sources showing in great clarity how this age, the seventh and early sixth centuries, was a preparation towards a transcendental breakthrough. Natural philosophy develops a rational order, not yet second-order, based on second-order thinking in politics. A radical critique of the Homeric anthropomorphic gods is taken up by Xenophanes of Colophon (circa 580 to circa 478 B.C.E.); he has not yet created a transcendental religious order, does not show second-order thinking in religion, but an individualistic, dogmatic, egalitarian opposition to the Homeric world. Some rudimentary second-order insights can be detected here, when Xenophanes explains that "black people worship black gods, that the gods of the Thracians would have blue eyes and red hair (Fr. 16 VS[33]), even that animals, if they could draw, would draw gods as horses and cattle (Fr. 15 VS[34])": At the same time, Hecataeus of Miletus (about 530 B.C.E.) explained rationally and in human terms the ancient myths. The intense interest in the individual, again influenced by the egalitarian democratic developments, typified the mystery cults. The cult of Demeter was connected with the Eleusinian mysteries, and the wild cult of Dionysus accepted, among its initiates, citizens and slaves, rich and poor. Here the old and new, the agricultural religion with the Homeric gods, the rational and irrational merge. These cults, with their egalitarian approach and emphasis on the individual, contributed to the transcendental breakthrough as much as the rational, natural philosophers and the political thinkers of the polis. Moreover, in them there is also a beginning of the transcendental order. "As Homer's gods were the models of anthropomorphic religion, thus the Chthonian cults, the mysteries, the Orphic beliefs, reflected a divine world beyond 'human standards'. "[35]

Pythagoras, with his unique blend of philosophy and natural science, mysticism and religion, all converging in his greatest creation, geometry, stands on the verge of the transcendental breakthrough initiating second-order thinking by participating in the invention of geometrical proof.

Parmenides (515–450 B.C.E.) is the main hero of the rational deductive approach. It is he who stands for the ideology of reliance upon the ratio instead of upon the evidence of the senses. With the Eleatics, the logos (the reasoned argument) became the sole legitimate argument of philosophical-scientific investigation. Indeed, Parmenides discredited the evidence of the senses as the source of knowledge and instead placed the logos at the head of the hierarchy of the accepted sources of knowledge. This is an important development in the critical dialogue that ensued between the various components of the process of the growth of knowledge—in this case between competing images of knowledge. The significance of this development lies in the shift of emphasis from the sources of knowledge which were the property of the community at large, the sensory evidence, to sources of knowledge that had an elitist advantage for an intellectual minority. The moment when the logos—which is not bestowed upon every person in the same degree (despite Descartes' later attempts to prove otherwise)—is becoming the main source of knowledge, then the source of knowledge becomes elitist and authoritarian by nature. Consequently, it is not surprising that the fields that were built upon the Parmenidian method, that is, by strict deduction— namely mathematics and theoretical physics—became strictly authoritarian, and their practitioners began to organize themselves into exclusive groups like the Academy, the Lyceum, and some monastic orders: all these are characterized by equality among the members and authoritarian separatism towards the outside world.

Sophistic cunning reason is perhaps no less rational, the way I see rationality, than Parmenidian-Platonic epistemic reason. However, cunning reason (as mentioned above),[36] being a rhetoric device for persuasion, presupposes that the way a question is formulated will influence the kind of answer given to the question. This in its very formulation is second-order thinking. Epistemic reason, on the other hand, presupposes one true state of affairs at which we are aiming, applying our deductive scientific reason. It is presupposed that the way our question (later our experiment) is formulated, as long as our logic is used, cannot possibly influence the kind of answer we receive. Also, even in case of competing hypotheses there are no genuine alternatives, since only one is accepted to be true. There is no need to seek a release of the tension between clashing alternative choices. In a somewhat different formulation we would say that in the natural domain our questioning (experiment) will not interfere with the state of affairs (as it does in the human/social domain)— until the Heisenberg uncertainty principle (1926) or at least until the development of the electro-magnetic theory of light in the work of Maxwell and Hertz. As we have seen, such a reliance on epistemic reason need not be second-order thinking. It only becomes such when, in the context of justification, critical systematic discussion of the validity of our conclusions starts: the very concept of mathematical proof or of the critical (sometimes seen as crucial) experiment.

We should not be surprised by all this. Mystical, early cosmogonies preceded what we generally call rational thought and in all probability were created not so much to satisfy inherent curiosity as to calm down deep-seated anxieties.

Many consider the real breakthrough, the first breakthrough, to be when rationality became an ideal. Rational thinking is one of the most controversial philosophical-anthropological issues; for some even the expression 'rational thinking' will seem tautological. For us it is enough to remember that, whatever a rational attitude may be, it is not yet necessarily reflexive, critical, second-order thinking. It can be critical when a theoretical speculation is seemingly contradicted by the senses, yet this in itself does not have to become conscious systematic thinking about thinking. Pre-Socratic worldviews of the great physiologoi are rational and often critical in this above sense. But they are not examples of second-order thinking. We have referred above to the very remarkable phenomenon that ideas and concepts which are today hallmarks of the *scientific spirit* actually were born not with the early 'scientists' but on the contrary originated in the rhetorical tradition as metic means of persuasion rather than epistemic considerations of truth. Too little is known about the *mechanism that operates* when a concept or an approach is transferred from the sphere of metis to the sphere of episteme.

The concept of the 'probable' was transformed through mathematization. Mathematization gave this concept its legitimization as a scientific concept. It is more complicated to trace the transfer of the awareness of alternatives from being a rhetorical technique into the body of modern science. In rhetoric, the emphasis is not on self-examination, but the systematic, critical discussion of alternatives is a rhetorical device for the sole purpose of persuasion. It is customary to think that science is characterized by self-criticism and by the awareness of alternatives. This is true nowadays for the scientific community, but even today not generally so for the individual scientist. Indeed, almost the opposite is true: the individual scientist's characteristic image is a realistic devotion to a particular world-view. Hence, self-criticism operates on a methodological level only, and it does so for the sole purpose of better protecting the world picture to which the scientist is devoted. Extremely rare are the cases known to us in which a creative scientist exchanged one world-view for another and still continued to be creative in the new conceptual framework; whereas criticism and an openness to alternatives by the scientific community was made possible only by the organization of the scientists into a community of scientists in the framework of scientific institutions—which, as mentioned, occurred in Greece in the fifth century B.C.E.

Once more let us turn from the world of ideas to the social context of the changes. We have to turn to a political-social explanation for understanding the background that led to the blossoming of rhetoric from the fifth century onwards on the one hand, and the blossoming of the exclusive elitist methodology on the other. The Eleatic, authoritative, deductive methodology was the climax of the philosophical search of the thinkers who were active under the rule of the autocratic leadership that preceded the true democracy of the city-states. After the collapse of this form of government, and then the loss of the patronage of their ruler-defender, the philosophers and scientists sought support in newly established organizations. Rhetoric blossomed because of the secure establishment of the 'popular' democracies of the city-states; indeed, rhetoric became in time a widely influential political instrument in this form of government. Later, while the Socratic-dialectic elenchus of question and response was swallowed by the authoritarian logos in the scientific sphere, metic thought with its inherent element of persuasion grew increasingly away from science and became a hallmark of political thought only. Organized into different social institutions, each using its own language, rhetoric and science continued for centuries to conduct a critical dialogue with each other.

The central revelation of the Greek Enlightenment of the fifth century was that nothing was any longer taken for granted. Experimentation in all areas resulted, and in a new outburst of confidence reason turned a "'searchlight' upon itself".[37] It was a combination, reason and experiment, that the metis developed as a new source of knowledge. The idea of experiment is by definition a reflexive second-order concept. So is metic thinking as we have seen. Metis was taught systematically as a *techné*. It was realized that often an argument could work "more effectively upon the irrational tendencies of fellow human beings" than upon their reason. "Pity, anger, indignation and similar impulses could be manipulated." A secular psychology emerged also as a result of second-order thinking—it had no need for divine causation.

This brings us to one last quick example: the emergence of the comparative approach as a corollary to second-order thinking. Hans Blumenberg makes the point that ideas originally prevalent in antiquity about the firmament—immutability and uniformity of motion—reduced empirical attention and diverted it from accuracy. Only with the breakthrough, when mankind learned "to conceive itself as an actor not only in space . . . but in time,"[38] which is the crux of progress, does comparative thinking become prevalent. This is second-order thinking: starting with Herodotus' remark on other cultures, continuing in the growing tendency of compiling astronomical data for comparative purposes, reaching its peak with Hipparchus' catalogue of stars. Clearly "he could not have discovered the procession of equinoxes, the retrograde shift of the seasonal points along the ecliptic, if some few positional data from the beginning of the third century B.C.E. had not been available to him."[39]

We shall now look in somewhat more detail into one chapter in the emergence of second-order thinking: the geometrical proof.

THE DEBATE ON THE ORIGINS OF GREEK MATHEMATICS

Beginning in the second half of the nineteenth century, a whole series of great works on the history of mathematics was written by mathematicians/historians. Tannery, Zeuthen, Cantor, and more recently O. Neugebauer and B.L. van der Waerden showed that Greek mathematics and especially geometry, *when translated* into modern mathematical symbolism, were actually algebraic in character; then in several brilliant papers van der Waerden attempted to show that translation was superfluous; that actually the Babylonians invented the beginnings of abstract algebra and claimed that the Greeks, influenced by the Babylonians, only developed it further into geometrical algebra; this geometrical algebra is indeed strikingly familiar when expressed in modern algebraic symbolism.

Not all historians shared this whiggish view of the history of mathematics. But the main debate erupted on the pages of the *Archive for the History of Exact Sciences* with a head-on attack by S. Unguru: "On the Need to Rewrite the History of Greek Mathematics."[40]

With positivistic self-assuredness, Hans Freudenthal, the eminent historian of mathematics, writes:

> Whoever starts reading Greek mathematics is struck by large parts that are overtly algebraic as well as other parts when algebra *seems to hide under geometrical cover* [my italics, Y.E.]. This riddle was solved only after nineteenth-century mathematics has faced the same problems and solved them in a different way . . . the view that says parts of Greek mathematics are algebraic has never been challenged. (See Hans Freudenthal, n. 40.)

Neither Freudenthal nor Weil mention Jacob Klein's very important *Greek Mathematical Thought and the Origins of Algebra,*[41] which is very close to Unguru's views and to my emphasis on the role of proof in geometry and its absence in algebra.

Unguru, correctly in my opinion, calls attention to a truism which in sophisticated history of science has long been accepted, namely that form and content, even in mathematics, are mutually dependent, and it is not enough to dress old ideas up in modern formalism because their conceptual content depends not only on the total context in the body of knowledge but also on images of knowledge, in terms of which knowledge was thought about. First of all, "geometrical thinking is embodied in diagrammatical representation accompanied by a rhetorical component, the proof."[42] As against that, "algebraic thinking is characterized by operational symbolism by the preoccupation with mathematic relations rather than with mathematical objects by freedom from any ontological commitments, and by supreme abstractness."

What we are interested in here is not the disagreement between the historians of mathematics, but rather in the important concepts of *proof, abstractness,* and *rhetorical component,* on which there is agreement. There is agreement that the Greeks invented *geometrical* proof. It is a rhetorical device responding to the conscious thinking about geometrical knowledge: it is second-order par excellence. It is a rhetorical device in so far as it is introduced as a way to convince the student rather than to supply the truth. Arithmetics and algebra in Babylon or in Greece do not involve the idea of proof: they do not exhibit second-order thinking. Finally, as against the typical modernistic, whiggish interpretation, and following our argument above, abstract concepts are not necessarily more advanced or closer to reflective thinking than concrete ones.

The historian of mathematics Imre Toth says: "Zum erstenmal in ihrer Geschichte wurde die Mathematik bei den Griechen zum Gegenstand philosophischer Reflexion erhoben."[43]

Jan Mueller emphasizes the second-order nature of the proof by saying that Greek geometrists "thought about proof." That van der Waerden does not contest this, is clear: ". . . indeed what is characteristic and absolutely new in Greek mathematics is the advance by means of demonstration from theorem to theorem."[44] Clearly he is referring to geometry. For the Greeks geometrical figures and bodies were not abstract but real, even when they belonged to the world of thought. It is in this sense that Parmenides attempted to deduce the nature of reality from his famous "either it is or it is not," or Plato's wish to eliminate hypotheses by reducing all to a single unhypothetical first principle. Here is a difficulty for our own thinking: on the one hand the value of truth ascribed to geometrical theorems was not legitimized by correspondence between objects of the external world and the intellectual constructs created by man. So it is all in the world of thought:[45] thinking about thinking, i.e. second-order.

But, as Jan Mueller shows, both *conventionalism* (that is, the view that no direct sense be attached to the concept of geometrical truth)

and *formalism* (i.e., that the fundamental terms of geometry, e.g.
line, point, lie on . . ., have no particular reference) "were alien to
the Greek view." Mathematics in the thought world—although its
terms did refer to sensible objects—had to be *true* or *not true.*
Geometrical objects are not *abstract*—they are real and part of what
Plato called 'intelligibles'.[46] We deal with the intelligibles in two
different modes: by *intellection* (noésis) or by *reasoning* (dianoia).
In *reasoning* we proceed from hypotheses using *diagrams* as part of
the proof; in *intellection* we ascend to the unhypothetical first principle in terms of Platonic Forms. Now this combination of non-
abstract objects of the mind being consciously thought about and
proving convincingly their truth is very strange to us. Nor is the
Greek idea of proof identical with ours. Jan Mueller draws our
attention to the fact that they 'proved' the parallel postulate—clearly
misleading, thought of having 'proved' the squaring of the circle,
and even looked for an 'angle' between an arc and the diameter of
a circle; let us also recall Zeno's 'proof' of the impossibility of
motion. Yet for us this is not what matters.[47]

That the ancient Egyptian, Babylonian, or Chinese algebraic texts
had no idea of proof is again shown by van der Waerden. In his
papers on pre-Babylonian mathematics[48] he clearly looked for proofs.
At best he finds attempts at derivation which in our terms may look
like a proof, but no evidence of any awareness of an idea or proof.
Only much later did the idea of proof emerge with philosophy of
nature, and these created mathematical physics, one of the two
indispensable second-order ingredients of modern science. The other
is the second-order concept of experiment. Systematic reflection on
experiment as a means of deciding between alternative theories or
interpretations remained for late antiquity to develop. Second-order
reflection in mechanical Gedanken-Experimenten or with mechanical
toys became the main source of originality of scholars after Ar-
chimedes and up to Hero of Alexandria, and in this all-important
contribution their originality not only was not merely derivative of
Plato and Aristotle but exceeded them by leaps and bounds.

SUMMARY

Thus we have seen two important stages in the development of
science; what we saw seemed at first counterintuitive because too
long have we been under the influence of a whiggish (positivistic)
linear history of science. We saw that first there was Babylonian
abstract algebra; it was followed by Greek realistic geometrical thinking. While this visual realism remains, in the fifth and fourth centuries
geometrical thinking involves the idea of proof. It is thus thinking

about thinking. In addition, the idea of proof is introduced as a rhetorical device, which only strengthens its second-order character. It is part of the metic thinking of the Sophists much before it converges with the epistemic thinking of Parmenides and Plato, in later mathematical physics.

This 'progress'—realistic geometric thinking, following abstract algebraic thinking and preceding abstract mathematical physics—parallels, although somewhat later, the anthropomorphic realistic Homeric pantheon which replaced the earlier mystical abstract gods, only to give way to abstract monotheistic tendencies. Only after the creation of the homology between the realistic world of the Homeric gods and that of human beings, coming after the abstract, remote, shapeless forces which ruled the pre-Homeric world, could there occur the transcendental breakthrough in Greek religion after Homer. Contrary to what is often claimed, the abstract-mythical gives way to the concrete-realistic, which yields to a new type of transcendental abstract. In the early abstract there was no differentiation between the world and its ruling forces. Then the Homeric world, through individualization, classified the distinct but homologous worlds of the gods and of man, and only after that there occurred the transcendental breakthrough which implies a "search for authority outside the institutionalized offices and structures of the seeker's society."[49]

The same can be learned from the various stages in the development of vase painting. The Mycenaeans produced vases magnificently illustrated with warrior-figures, not very realistic but certainly not abstract. The first artistic products after the Dorian invasion excelled in their geometric style, far from primitive and fully *abstract,* only to give way, from the Homeric period onward, to the realistic figures of the black-figure and then the red-figure period. The artists of these last in all probability had read Homer and were actually 'illustrating' the *Odyssey* and *Iliad.*[50]

Thinking about the world in realistic terms was not accompanied by a conscious effort to think about thoughts. The second-order thinking in Greek 'natural science' came much later than in Greek mathematics. For Plato it was quite different from natural 'science'. It was genuine 'theoria' (literally a 'spectacle'). Mathematics became a science deeply involved with physical science (and then its humanistic origins forgotten) only after speculation about nature became a conscious second-order activity and introduced mathematical proof into its own body of knowledge as an integral part. What was missing in Greek philosophy, even long after Aristotle when the second-order concept of proof became part of 'physics', was the other indispensable second-order concept: the experiment. It is critically important that research show when this actually occurred. In my opinion it is the great contribution of the science of late antiquity.

It has often been asked: why were the Greeks no better at science? They certainly excelled in rational explanation of natural phenomena from the fifth century onward. Yet they had no notion of systematic controlled experiment. Rational explanation is about the world, not about thoughts. It is not second-order thinking, or at least it does not have to be. Controlled experiment is a thought about thought. This is why technology did not get connected with rational explanations, and technology developed only in so far as it could without reflexion on thinking. This was not much, and thus it was backward technology that held back social change, and not vice versa.[51]

The first area of natural science which involved second-order thinking was the semi-mathematical field of astronomy, where the Greeks introduced the second-order concept of the model. It occurred in the work of Plato's students, mainly Eudoxos, and was taken up by Aristotle.

The conscious attempt to 'save appearances' in astronomy and later in geometrical optics[52] was another second-order engagement: to fit the mathematics into the transcendental conceptual scheme as developed by astronomical and later optical speculations.

In Greek physics and biology, views were stated dogmatically without any critical discussion with alternative views (which would have been second-order) and although there is some metatheoretical ordering or fitting of thought processes to objects of thought, there is no systematic, critical thinking about thinking.[53]

The Greeks had no concept of law of nature either; whenever they mention laws, they refer to the moral sphere,[54] and this is not accidental. The Sophists created such a centrally important antithesis between *nomos* and *physis* that the concept of 'law of nature' became a self-conscious paradox. In other words: it was reflected upon what kind of laws existed, and after the proper consideration laws of human conduct were accepted, while the idea of laws of nature, not being a mere convention, was eliminated as 'impossible'. Even Aristotle was influenced enough to discuss the topic of *nomos* and *physis* "as a means of confusing the opponent in debate."[55] Only much later, when Aristotelian substantial forms and real qualities were rejected in the early fourteenth century and the idea of Platonic mathematical proof was reintroduced into thinking about the world, did actual second-order thinking in law-like terms make the discovery of the laws of nature possible.

In conclusion, let me reformulate what was claimed here in another way: Greek Sophists, mystics, and some philosophers discovered more or less simultaneously that man does not have a complete theory of the physical world nor of human society, not even of man himself, and that all 'rational' knowledge had to be complemented by 'irrational', i.e. mystical and religious, elements. The resulting tensions between these complementary parts and the ensuing critical dialogue between them—second-order thinking—brought about the important breakthroughs. This can be claimed for classical Athens, for St. Augustine in the fourth century C.E., for the program of the Florentine Academy, for the Newtonian revolution, for the German Naturphilosophie with its insistence on conservation ideas and the concept of energy, for Einstein's General Theory of Relativity, and possibly even for today's Grand Unification Theories.

Critical dialogue responding to an intellectual tension is mostly between competing groups of institutionalized elites like the Sophists and the Platonic Academy, or between the School Aristotelians at the Universities and Fincino's Academy. But often a breakthrough can be precipitated by an individual, if the tension between the rational and the irrational is taking place in one and the same individual. In Augustine a literal interpretation of Scripture as his main (rational) source of knowledge clashed with his neo-Platonic (irrational) mysticism. To some extent the same can be said about Newton in reverse: here the sectarian, anti-establishment, religious (irrational) fanaticism clashed with his solid, rational, epistemic knowledge of the world and of mathematics, and he used his physics and his mathematics to bridge the gap by creating a transcendental world-order centered around his conception of God and a transcendental concept of gravity.

Momigliano, in *Alien Wisdom,* accepts the Jaspersian insight and finds that all Axial Age civilizations "display literacy, a complex political organization combining a central government and local authorities, elaborate town-planning, advanced metal technology, and the practice of international diplomacy. In all these civilizations there is a profound tension between political powers and intellectual movements." So far this is what we were used to thinking. Now, however, comes an extremely interesting addition:

> New models of reality, either mystically or prophetically or
> rationally apprehended, are propounded as criticisms and
> alternative to the prevailing models. We are in the age of
> criticism—and social criticism transpires even from involuted
> imagery of Zoroaster's Gathas.[57]

Clearly for Momigliano only second-order thinking can cause a breakthrough of the Axial Age civilizations: self-criticism[58] is the central issue for him, but it is a reflexive criticism as it must be aware of alternatives, and it is, in terms of models, all second-order concepts. As we have seen above, and as Momigliano emphasizes also, such a critique was first of all *social* and such a search for alternatives is an exercise in philosophical instrumentalism. The pre-Socratic philosophers in their dogmatic realism did not create yet a transcendental order, *alternative* to other models. They were not second-order.[59]

Transcendental breakthrough occurred when in the wake of second-order weighing of clashing alternatives there followed an almost unbearable tension threatening to break up the fabric of society, and the resolution of the tension was found by creating a transcendental realm and then finding a soteriological bridge between the mundane world and the transcendental. Science could claim to constitute the salvation for its practitioners only after a theory was developed linking terrestrial motions forces and action to a transcendental world order. This was developed during many centuries, culminating in the seventeenth century. But this development could start only after late antiquity developed the second-order concept of experiment, the second cornerstone of an intellectual structure—the first cornerstone of which was the second-order concept of proof developed in classical Greece.

CHAPTER 2

The Emergence of an Autonomous Intelligence among the Greeks

CHRISTIAN MEIER

THE PROBLEM

In seeking the preconditions for the emergence of an autonomous Greek intelligence, the first factor that comes to mind is political circumstance. There must have been a connection between the development of the Greek democracy or its earlier form, the isonomy (for democracy presumably became possible only as a consequence of the Persian wars)—a phenomenon of highest significance in the history of the world, unique also within the Axial Age—and the emergence of a Greek intelligence.[1] At any rate, historical correlations between politics and intelligence in archaic times are discernible with a measure of probability. For the formation of an autonomous intelligence we find:

—a singular configuration of power within and between the archaic *poleis* as a prerequisite of the possibility;

—singular problems of coexistence in the *poleis* of the time as a challenge;

—the gradually stabilizing form and autochthonous position of political thinking, of "wisdom," and finally of philosophical thought transcending by far the problems of the *poleis* and yet in part determined by them, as a response.

An argument in favor of the connection between the formation of the autonomous intelligence and the emergence of democracy lies in the fact that, in a way which we shall define more precisely below, both amount to a particular kind of personal autonomy.

As a matter of fact, it is very difficult to attempt a reconstruction of the historical connections. Our sources are extremely sparse. They do not provide any direct information on the process of the emergence of Greek intelligence. Nevertheless they contain various indications from which one can draw conclusions about this process. And additionally, something can be deduced by inference. Theodor Mommsen calls this "the recognition of what has been from what it became through the insight into the laws of becoming."[2] Although I am reluctant to speak here of "laws," it should be conceded that from historical phenomena one may cautiously draw conclusions regarding some of their precedents. This procedure, though, must be transparent.

Above all there is a practical problem that one encounters also in epochs for which there is ample source material: namely, the question how far we are really justified in connecting intellectual processes with other factors within the society to which they belong. Whenever certain types of thinking occur once, and never again, simultaneously with a certain social structure and in addition show certain homologies, one may presume a connection. Of course, it would be better if one could observe such homologies or analogies also in different circumstances, though in a different manner. The presumable relations between thinking and social structure would become increasingly significant through such findings—despite all the questions that still remain open. At any rate, one ought to have a general knowledge about the possibilities and probabilities of such connections, acquired through observation of different societies— which we do not have. And we probably could attain this only if we made comparisons in a wider context—and above all not in juxtaposition but in direct relation to one another, viz. in a dialogue.

There would be a very strong presumption in favor of the connection between democracy and philosophy—or autonomous intelligence—if both had appeared only together, i.e. only in the Greeks. But the various cultures of the Axial Age are especially distinguished by the fact that an autonomous intelligence is formed in all of them, and particularly in China we find, independent of Greece, a philosophy that in many respects resembles the Greek and is not easily contrasted with it. Still more interesting would be a comparison between one intelligence and the other and their philosophies, as well as between the relations of intelligence and philosophy with the social structure in either culture. Such a comparison cannot be undertaken and can hardly be made exhaustively by a single human being.[3] Thus I am forced to restrict myself to the Greeks.

Within the framework of this essay it may suffice to make three fairly accurate statements: whatever thought existed in China, the thought of the responsibility of the citizens for the political order is lacking; there is no idea of an order without a monarch, i.e. without a permanently personified superior secular authority as the starting point and center of political activity and of the overall social order; and finally they seem to want also the combination of far-reaching pre- or early "civic"[4] autonomy and solidarity as a prerequisite of common political action of wide circles and strata. Precisely thereby the philosophy that subsequently emerged among the Greeks is to be clearly distinguished from that of the Chinese. Of special interest would be the question whether the Chinese also lack the idea of an order or system of laws governing the world, which is greater than each single power, encompasses everything, is not governed by any divine subject nor represented by any secular power. For on this it depends whether a homology between political order and philosophy,[5] which seems to be central for the Greeks, is or is not possible exclusively with them (and only on the road to democracy). But at this moment I do not have the means to decide this.

The question about the development of an autonomous intelligence among the Greeks has not yet, it seems to me, been dealt with satisfactorily. Nor can we do so here. However, I believe that it is possible to make some brief statements showing the direction in which the solution may possibly be found. Incidentally, the same applies to the development of democracy. The latter, too, has been given little attention by the research.[6] Numerous possibilities of its cognition have so far been neglected as well.

The research into the prehistory of Greek democracy and autonomous intelligence was largely hampered by the fact that *a priori* these Greeks are traditionally considered to be so extraordinary that their actual evolution does not seem to give much cause for thought. Often—though by no means always—it looks as if nothing else could have happened to the Greeks but to create democracy and philosophy.

This conception is typical of classicism, yet it is also familiar to the opponents of classicism. For it seems that also the latter's cognition is hampered as a result of the history of classical studies. In this context I shall confine myself to three recent works on the subject of this essay.

Under the heading " 'Transcendence' and Intellectual Roles: The Ancient Greek Case"[7] Sally Humphreys deals with the development of single intellectual roles, changes in the status of the intellectuals, in their relations to the public and to each other. Her observations are most interesting, but the connection between these roles and the thinking evolved at the time remains rather vague. Essentially, Humphreys is only following the series of our sources from various standpoints. She fails to place them in their wider contexts and draw more general conclusions from the diversity of known facts. Neither does she elaborate on the particularity of the Greeks. For elsewhere, too, there exist intellectual specialists who can also be relatively independent of separate masters (or houses) and yet remain attached to the social order as a whole. Yet in the case of the Greeks it was a matter of an entire stratum of intellectuals becoming increasingly independent of the societal context and—no matter how far intentionally—also worked toward overcoming it, while this took place directly and indirectly in different spheres (at the same time leaving open the possibility of withdrawal from politics). Clearly, the Greek intellectuals achieved this independence within the framework of an intellectual movement that was greater than the sum of their individual parts and rendered them virulent. The categories of modern sociology are hardly sufficient to apprehend this phenomenon, in any case not those applied by Humphreys.

Jean-Pierre Vernant deals far more comprehensively with the matter.[8] But oddly enough he replaces the solution by the riddle. More precisely: he extracts some questionable results of the process and places them at its beginning: thus the discussion on the market, the public opinion, rhetorics, the consciousness of a certain similarity, though not equality, of the citizens, belong for Vernant to the *polis* as such, and he describes them before starting with the crisis of archaic times. However, to this crisis these matters owe their preservation and consolidation, in any case their role in the social context, though perhaps not their existence. Vernant moreover prefers to characterize certain early phenomena in the light of later concepts. But if all this had existed in the beginning, the development of intelligence and democracy would no longer be so astonishing. Consequently Vernant contributes little to an explanation of this phenomenon. To him, democracy grows directly out of that society and then produces the particular mode of Greek thinking. In a daring operation even Anaximander's philosophy is finally deduced from the "order based on equality" of Cleisthenes' time, although it should be dated about one generation earlier, according to the dating which Vernant does not contest.[9]

Thus the proposition of Louis Gernet (to whom Vernant feels obliged), namely to regard the Greek "sans miracle"[10] does not hold. Classicism is simply turned around here: seeking the origins of philosophy in politics appears a more realistic approach. But the old assumption—that the Greeks were *a priori* different from other peoples and therefore the creation of democracy and philosophy by them was inevitable—is still maintained, the miracle becomes rather greater. G.E.R. Lloyd,[11] like Vernant, deduces the emergence of Greek philosophy and science from the political circumstances, the democratic and pre-democratic constitution.

However, it is a mistake to take for granted, unquestioningly, the democracy and singularity of the Greeks just as if they would not need explanation themselves, and then to deduce everything else therefrom. Vernant's and Lloyd's approach to the question is like a new version of the problem of hen and egg. Yet, just as it has long been clear from the theory of evolution that in the beginning there was neither hen nor egg, but a third element from which both hen and egg evolved, thus one should acknowledge that Greek thought is not simply the product of circumstances which led to democracy, but that it had itself a strong influence upon these circumstances. This evolution of Greek intelligence is in all probability equally determined by its function in the formative process of the *polis,* as this process was a matter of intelligence. Isonomy was essentially an offspring of philosophy, or more precisely, of political thinking. Political and intellectual processes were closely interwoven. To understand how the Greeks' autonomous intelligence emerged, one must first of all inquire into history. It even seems to me that one understands very little in this context, unless one reads Greek history back to front; if one does not take for granted at all what it produced, but if one regards it as very much in need of explanation.

How did democracy evolve? How did a people come to arrogate to itself the decisive power in the polity for the first time in the history of mankind? A usurper knows the position he covets. It is already there. He has only to seek the means to attain it. By contrast, the people does not know it; it cannot simply decide that it wants to replace the nobility as the ruling class. Its "rule" is fundamentally different from that of the aristocracy. When democracy comes into being there is not only a change of personalities from a relatively homogeneous class in political positions; a stratum whose members initially are hardly able to assume official functions, soon gains decisive influence on the government and assumes supreme power. This it can only do by creating or significantly consolidating the positions through which it is at all able to "rule."[12]

But whence did the broader public in Greece acquire knowledge, aspirations, and institutions? How did they know at all that anything like democracy was possible? The Greeks had no example to inspire them. How did the members of broad strata of the society prepare themselves for the overwhelming commitment without which the antique democracies could not have emerged? The first democracies of history evidently had to develop as direct democracies.[13] They even presupposed the emergence of a strong, unrivaled civic identity. This was effected mainly in the Athenian democracy but in minor degree also in its widespread precursor, the isonomy. Did not such a constitution require various intellectual anticipations, even if the precise idea of democracy need not have existed before its coming into being? Did it not necessitate distinct abstractions from the prevailing reality, a way of thinking that ultimately led to the relinquishment of the concrete attachment of the idea of rule to those who did the ruling? At any rate it is evident that the intellectuals had to bear in mind the interests of the people, even identifying with them to a certain extent, if strong activity and participation in public affairs were to develop. As a consequence, certain premises and ways of thinking were undoubtedly part of democracy's prehistory. There must have existed prior to democracy a prolonged phase of political thinking, during which the trend toward democracy grew up out of whatever knowledge and whatever intention. But such political thinking could not have persisted without leaving its imprint on other spheres of thought and philosophy. Presumably it even needed, for its own fortification and the assurance of its continued effectiveness, confirmation by analogies and cognitions in other spheres.

H.D.F. Kitto once spoke of the "passion for asking useless questions"[14] that was peculiar to the Greeks. Yet what appears to us academic in this is probably anything but academic. A people that—in whatever manner—succeeds in making its way toward culture without a monarchy suffers a twofold lack of institutions as soon as it becomes involved in the process of change and differentiation: then it not only lacks institutions which all people took for granted but also an authority which could have created new institutions. What was missing here could not be provided and/or expected either of the past or of a monarchy (with all its religious authorities). Arnold Gehlen has found that man needs institutions because his instincts are insufficient.[15] Accordingly it may be presumed that the archaic Greeks, not having sufficient institutions, needed thought. More precisely: they were to a particularly high degree in need of a manner of thinking directed to the whole, because they could not rely on any authority but only on each other, that is, on a whole community which they formed together and which presumably required particular intellectual mediation.

Out of this thinking there finally had to emerge again institutions—a whole framework of them (such as is perhaps formed by a constitution or by a legal system). But since these had to be created from within their society and not from above, a concerted, particularly intellectual preparatory effort was required in both narrow and wider circles. And just this groundwork presupposed comprehensive intellectual conceptions that went far beyond the political sphere. "Academic questions" were thus of vital importance to the Greeks.

THE PRELIMINARY POSITION

The dawn of Greek history, after the destruction of the Mycenaean culture, is shrouded in darkness. The oldest literary sources that were preserved for us are surprisingly also two of the greatest works of world literature, the *Iliad* and the *Odyssey*. Even by late dating (the end of the eighth century) they originate from a period in which the great movement from which Greek culture finally emerged had been going on for only one or two generations. Much of them is based upon ancient tradition. It is difficult to ascertain how much of them is to be ascribed to the last editor(s).

Here also ensues a scientific situation resembling that of philosophy: everybody can see that the Homeric epic poems are unique, both in their subject matter, above all its treatment, and in the kind of thinking, the rationality, expressed in them. No thorough comparison, however, has yet been made, that would elucidate what exactly should be regarded as special or not in Homer—and thus with the Greeks of his time. For the uniqueness of a phenomenon does not yet emerge from its consideration, be it ever so subtle. Do the authors of the *Iliad* or the *Odyssey* display the same "enterprising spirit" of perspicacity as is expressed in the pioneering establishment of Greek colonies which was undertaken at the same time? Did they share the same experience of the sudden opening of extraordinary possibilities, or widening of narrow horizons, of a liberation inspiring acts and works that long outlive their creators?[16] The art of writing, just recently invented by the Phoenicians, was taken over by the Greeks and adapted to their language, immediately being put to use to perpetuate the great epic poems. The subsequent history of literature is marked by a relatively quick succession of innovations, presumably faster than in other cultures—from which one may conclude that the first decades of colonization also saw dramatic change in the epos.

Beyond these and many other questions which arise in connection with Homer's poetry lies the enigma surrounding the Greeks at the end of their "dark age," at the moment when they started the process of forming their culture. Here we are facing above all the problem to what extent they were particularly moulded at that time and how far they were, on the contrary, very little moulded and therefore open. Notwithstanding all the distinctions of which various features of Homer and eventually of Greek art might provide evidence— were they really so different from many other emerging peoples

before they came under the discipline of higher civilization? Can
the specific character of their history perhaps be attributed to the
fact that numerous original, initial characteristics that others had to
give up during the process of their sociogenesis were preserved by
them and incorporated into their culture?

If, for example, one considers the people's assembly, which ultimately becomes the central constitutional organ of Greek democracy,
one sees that also in Mesopotamia, India, and elsewhere there is
evidence or indication of early people's assemblies. There, however,
they gradually lost their significance. Was, then, the people's assembly
(or the power or the will of those whose foremost organ it was)
especially developed *a priori* among the Greeks? Or was its preservation or strengthening rather a consequence of their history? Is
its early existence (and its eventual power) and not rather the
preservation of its power during their sociogenesis characteristic of
them? Or should one not even consider such alternatives for the
Greeks? Similar questions arise with regard to the peculiar license,
to the remarkable independence of the Greek aristocracy,[17] as it
appears in Homer, recurs repeatedly in later history, and finally
becomes embodied in a philosophic ideal. Could it simply be characteristic of a primitive, not highly civilized people? Did it perhaps
occur also in similar early periods of other peoples? Or does it
simultaneously presuppose a certain mobility, causally connected
with the numerous migrations of the Greeks toward the end of the
second millenium B.C.E.? Is it possible that what is astonishing, unique
in the Greeks, is only due to the fact that they were able to conserve
(and utilize) this early characteristic in the process of the formation
of their culture?

At any rate, the formation of culture in its initial phases consisted
everywhere else in the establishment of monarchies and the monop-
olization of power. Elsewhere, monarchs, officials, and priests continued to form the center of all activity, breaking the personal
independence of the members of their empires. Life, thought, and
faith were so strongly dominated by them that the society came to
view them as indispensable. The monarch, clergy, and bureaucracy
represented the keystone of a vault without which the whole would
collapse. The same applies to China, where the philosophers could
expect to influence politics only through the emperor or the high
officials. I know of only one certain exception to this rule: Israel (in
1 Samuel 8: 10ff. we have a highly graphic, critical description of
the significance of the establishment of a monarchy).

The Greeks, however, became in no way "mediatized" into parts
of a whole, which was not composed of themselves relatively concretely in form of a face-to-face society. There was no taxation—

except under the tyrants—but the members of the society bore personal responsibility for the administrative and military burdens of the community. In time the farmers also contributed to an increasing extent. Thus the people themselves constituted the commonwealth. They evidently wanted to be free and unfettered, evincing some consideration for their neighbors but completely independent of any higher authority, whether this was a monarch to whom they would have to subordinate themselves, or the restraining power of a reigning oligarchy of the Roman type to which they would have to adopt themselves, forfeiting many liberties and strictly complying with the political and military obligations of their status. This quest for maximal independence was ultimately successful. To some degree it also applied to the farmers.

The tyrants, however, always had some cohorts, and where no tyrant was at the helm the people congregated in the leading institutions of the city. But "giving oneself up" to larger political contexts still seems to have been rather limited.

Here a singular connection is revealed: the independence of the cities corresponds to the independence of the Greek aristocrats. The one could not exist without the other. Had the individuals been ready to submerge themselves in larger contexts, they would hardly have been able to withstand the development of larger complexes of power. And had greater complexes of power developed, the individuals could hardly have preserved so much of their independence.

But then, when they merely "relate to one another" (to quote Karl Marx[18]), making common cause instead of obeying a higher authority, this means that their independence had to be complemented by an ability to act in concert. This trend was weak for some time, resulting in the division into parties and even civil wars. Presumably, solidarity gained intensity only when it spread among the citizenry in its wider sense. But that it did exist is a remarkable thing in itself, since it is much more difficult to rely on one another than on a higher authority.

Still, if the aristocrats wanted to govern their cities by themselves, with as little interference as possible, and without paying taxes, special incentives for voluntary contributions to the common weal had to be offered. We find these above all in the liturgies and in the competitions for endowing and embellishing buildings, feasts, and sacraments. This may have been the particular Greek variant of conspicuous consumption. Then perhaps a connection between personal independence and a special mode of this extravagance would have developed.

Moreover, life in the small, constricted Greek cities was complemented by the formation of a comprehensive, overall Greek public, before whom the aristocrats played their roles, excelled, and became prominent, getting the feedback in their own cities. This was largely governed by social ideals, such as wealth, ostentatious celebrations, and outstanding achievements in sports. Their validity presumably was again dependent on the autarchy of the aristocrats in that it gave them wider latitude, and enabled them to evade the demands of their own cities. They did not have to adapt themselves quite so strictly to the limits of their city.

To this should be added the loosening of various bonds, including patriarchal ones, which seems to have had its simultaneous expression in religion. All these findings are corroborated by the exception to the rule: though originally they also seem to have applied to Sparta, they no longer did so after its great disciplinary reform.[19] The example of Sparta shows at the same time how little they really were necessary constants. It is by no means certain that they could have resisted any attitude, for instance the influence of strong monarchies. Herein, by the way, lie also important differences between the Greek and the Roman aristocracy. But all this—and other factors[20]—need by no means be the result of a particular early individuality of the Greeks. And in any case there are strong indications that it could only be retained and developed and strengthened because the Greeks were spared the daunting of a monarchy.

This however was due in large measure to the fact that the possibilities for evolving monarchies were relatively small. At the beginning of the eighth century the traditional monarchies were weak. And it is remarkable that the vigorous activity since around 750 B.C.E. could have emanated from a relatively broad sector of Greek society. It was concentrated upon navigation, piracy, trade and colonization. It was significant that in archaic times the Aegean was a political vacuum in which none of the larger powers had any interest. Thus fell away any incentive to consolidate a large-scale and long-lasting power, whether under the influence of an external force (like that of Minoan Crete in the middle of the second millenium) or in defence against external enemies. The geographical character of the Aegean area would not have ruled this out, for it is quite probable that in Mycenaean times larger realms existed in the same area. On the other hand, the Greeks overseas could establish close contact with the highly developed Near Eastern cultures, so that a singular combination of touch and untouchability resulted: inspirations, knowledge, patterns of life as well as numerous goods were within reach of the Greeks, without their coming under the influence of the eastern empires. This seems to have activated them and stimulated a certain process of differentiation.

Furthermore, the coastal areas of other parts of the Mediterranean as well as the Black Sea offered ample opportunities for colonization. This made it feasible to export a great number of problems that in different circumstances might or should have led to greater concentrations of power and to conquests. Greece was able to transplant on a large scale its population surplus, which was rapidly increasing at that time.[21] It was also significant that geographic or climatic reasons did not necessitate large common organizational enterprises. We do not know whether this movement necessarily started at a time when the monarchies were weak and why they were unfit to share in the increased power, wealth and prestige of this movement. It is possible that here a series of coincidences produced results in one direction. Once this had happened, the colonization and all the changes connected with it contributed considerably to strengthening the position of the numerous aristocrats who as "entrepreneurs" were the proper initiators of the establishment of colonies, deriving various benefits from the new situation.

The contingencies of this situation must have somehow combined with the attributes that, unknown to us, characterized the Greeks at the start of this epoch, in order to determine the initial conditions of their history.

The epic poems of Homer preserved important features of that time, and it may have been important that they were written down at that stage, when the kings had little institutional power,[22] when the society within which they were acting was not yet consolidated but, on the contrary, was largely dependent upon personal configurations, in which kings squabbled like farmers. Had the alphabet not yet been in existence and had there been no inducement to write the poems down at this particular time, they may have been adapted to different circumstances. In this fixed form, however, they could serve as paradigms of the relatively free, independent, unfettered character of the aristocracy.

Still, all these questions relate to details only. The decisive problem remains whether the peculiar character of the Greeks was not essentially determined by the fact that they succeeded in forming their culture from within their society and not under monarchies. And if this was not a function of their early peculiarity, it may have emerged largely from the circumstances in which their culture was shaped. The ensuing history we can in a way reconstruct.

THE CRISIS OF THE ARCHAIC PERIOD

The striking changes that took place in eighth-century Greece caused a serious crisis in due course. Different aspects of the process that brought it about are discernible in their outlines. At first a lasting differentiation grew within the aristocracy, having decisive consequences for those concerned. For with the steep rise in opportunities for various profits, the risks also increased. Where the advantages predominated, various families greatly increased their power, wealth, and ambitions. Conversely it could easily happen that other families suffered heavy losses and consequently a diminution in status, which in turn might have caused some desperate reactions. With the sharply increased demands (for which the living standard of high-ranking families in the eastern countries may have served as an example) a gap opened between aspirations and their possible realization. This in turn spurred greater activity and in the long run exploitation of public assets and, above all, of the lower classes. As certain demands became widespread also among the latter, who probably employed new methods of exploiting agricultural land through heavy investments,[23] they often sunk into debt and were sometimes obliged to mortgage their farmsteads, which could result in the debtors and their families being sold into slavery.

The relations between the higher and lower classes became considerably disturbed. We do not know whether there existed in ancient Greece patron-client relations comparable to those in Rome. But certain ties of patriarchal dependency must have existed which were irreversibly disturbed at that time. A contributing factor to this disturbance was that in view of the massive migration of population and increased opportunities that arose on the wide shores of the Mediterranean and the Black Sea, the immediate reality gave way to a wide horizon of possibilities. This, too, must have weakened existing relationships.

We are unable to reconstruct the process that led to the crisis. If the impression gained from the sources is correct (and is not merely based upon the coincidences of our tradition), during the first stage of the archaic age, i.e. approximately between 750 and 650, it was easier to resolve the conflicts, especially as a large portion of the problems was exported from the Greek mainland. But thereafter we see a distinct increase in revolts of the lower classes, in conflicts, battles between different factions, and usurpations of tyranny. Confrontations were often bloody, and expulsions of whole groups were the order of the day. It appears that the crisis spread rapidly from economic distress and social oppression to political coexistence and ultimately to its ethical foundations.

It is peculiar that relatively few, or only very limited, wars were fought on the mainland, as evidenced by the minimal (internal) expansionism. The only noteworthy exception is the conquest of Messina by Sparta. Apart from this the majority of Greek polities preserved and partly consolidated their independence. Not even the new rulers, the tyrants,[24] could on the whole effect any change in this. When a family of tyrants, such as in Corinth, took firm possession of at least some external positions, this was an exceptional case. Thus evidently even rapacious, mighty usurpers were unable to extend their sway beyond the territory of their own *polis.*

Over and above this, the tyranny shows, at least in its outcome, clear weaknesses also with regard to the task of justifying and legitimizing its own rule within the polity. Although it could at times successfully overcome economic difficulties, as a solution of the political crisis, it could not impose itself on the polity in the long run. The relative non-attachment of the Greek aristocrats, their autarchy, their limited capacity for falling into the line of larger contexts, seem to have been contributing factors.

It was these circumstances that frequently led to deadlock in the serious controversies caused by the crisis. In the course of time the contestants increasingly turned to the sages instead of to the mighty for solutions. Greater expectations were focused on political thinking. Thus evolved a dramatic reevaluation of Greek intelligence.

The Emergence of Political Thinking and of an Autonomous Intelligence

It is one of the peculiarities of the ancient Greeks that they were particularly dependent on political thinking. This was already a consequence of the necessity of the inhabitants of Greek cities to coexist without strong rulers in volatile situations. This is not to deny that monarchs also required intelligence for the establishment and administration of their rule. But it is one thing to regard a political order and its functioning from one center of power, as personified by the ruler, as the source of all public activity. And it is a different matter if one must invent regulations and institutions that have to function by themselves, to a certain measure themselves generating political activity. While in the first case the whole is ultimately oriented toward one person, in the second case many individuals must be responsible for a whole that is in their very midst. While there the interest in good order coincides with that of the monarch, here a strong divergence between general and individual interests must be balanced out. Such divergences can remain limited as long as all activity is regulated by a strong ethic that is in keeping with the situation.[25] But if this is not the case—as during the crisis of archaic times—political thinking must answer special demands. Then one must invent regulations and institutions that work independently of the particular conflicting forces. This presupposes a special degree of abstraction from the concrete reality and a particular kind of objectivity.

Another challenge for political thinking was the colonization activity. For, in addition to numerous technical requirements, the establishment of cities created a series of political problems. Whereas in the home towns the elders could be relied upon to tell (reconstruct and perhaps also invent) time-honored solutions to problematic situations, the colonizers had to do without this tried and trusted method, for they could not very well take the elders with them. Therefore one had to try to derive rules from the knowledge reproduced for each case according to its merits. Furthermore, rules had to be established by which people from different cities could live together in the new colonies.

These problems became more acute during the grave conflicts of the late seventh and the sixth centuries. In the sources of those times we also find a number of "specialists" in political thinking. These are the "legislators" (who were entrusted with the codification and mostly modification of the law that had hitherto only "been known," e.g. Zaleukos and Charondas), the "reconcilers" who were to solve the crises of the city sometimes through laws, at other times also by direct intervention (e.g. Solon), finally in general the circle of those who appear in the sources as "the seven sages."

The intelligence of these men could not be monopolized by any monarch or any clergy.[26] No authority was sufficiently powerful and extensive for this. Whatever some individuals may have said, being biased by certain interests, generally these men were moving in a void between the authorities. Their wisdom was consulted far beyond the borders of their own *poleis*. Their aims—as far as they are known to us—transcended the interests of any single power. And it seems that they created the spiritual conditions for the political advancement of the wider strata, for this ascent cannot have automatically developed from Greek society.[27] Neither could it have been the result of the peasants' participation in the conduct of wars, since the phalanx of the hoplites came into being six or seven generations before the people at large had a say in general politics. Thus the farmers remained confined for a long time in a political order that corresponded to the social structure and could expect at best to receive more respect, which found its expression in various achievements, e.g. the appointment of "legislators." But they were still a long way from isonomy.

At first the peasants' interests were directed to more concrete immediate goals: remission of debts, return of their properties, redistribution of land, economic relief, security before the law. Politically they often strove for these aims as followers of ambitious aristocrats who with their help rose to become tyrants. But for being able to demand a say in politics, in the form of a firm, regular political engagement, they evidently had to go through a lengthier process: sensibilization, raising demands, strengthening of more abstract and more distant interests, converting discontent into political claims, becoming aware of solidarity, and not least, a process of enlightenment, and securing and legitimizing the new aims. Finally the institutions had to be invented that would give permanence to the influence of wider strata. After all, wide strata, as their name implies, are always numerically superior. But only rarely, and as far as we can see never before the Greeks, did they really govern. Therefore it cannot have been easy to bring them that far. This success, as already intimated, was doubtless essentially due to a political thought process that had its center in Greek intellectual circles—and through which the latter gained its autonomy.

Still, how do intellectuals develop a concern for the needy, the weak? After all, in those times there did not yet exist a philosophy of history, nor even the urge to combine one's own luxury with a good conscience by speciously defending the underprivileged. This question should likewise be addressed to the Israelite prophets and to the particular conditions prevailing in the two societies of those centuries in the eastern Mediterranean.

In the Greek case the answer can only be vague. Yet after all we do have evidence of how a religious center in Greece was based upon providing insight and not upon power. It is not possible to make a clean separation between the two, for also Delphi, with which we are concerned here, aimed at expanding its own influence and material interests. But in the given circumstances of the Greek world it could feather its own nest only in its capacity as an advisory authority and that in the interest of those seeking counsel. Delphi hardly pursued any policy of its own, and sought no dominance or participation in government but the advancement of that "raison" on which, in Gernet's words,[28] the Greeks subsequently founded their order. It did not become a focus of political power but rather an intellectual center of religious authority. We know that it played an important role in colonization—perhaps not from its very beginning but certainly later. In this context Jacob Burckhardt speaks of "the men of Delphi."[29] This does not refer especially to the oracles of the Pythia, who on the contrary, tended to be rather cryptic for fear of undermining their authority. The actual role of Delphi in Greek history was to mediate and reinforce. And from Delphi were to spread the roots of a new order.

Curiously, the Delphic oracle is not duly appreciated by Vernant, Humphreys, or even Lloyd, possibly because they regarded Delphi's activity as primarily "theological" rather than rational, or perhaps only because certain theses on the political influence of the oracle were rejected by Louis Gernet—theses with which we are not concerned here.[30] Be that as it may, an antithesis of theology and rationality cannot apply here—if at all—since it is evident that at Delphi a high degree of rationality prevailed side-by-side with a close relation to reality.[31] Greek political thought was linked with religious realism. Theirs was above all a special brand of political theology. And rationality found its expression at Delphi particularly also where the "guilt culture"[32] was fostered, sanctioned, and recommended, but above all in the special way by which divine justice and lawfulness were sought in reality.

The importance of Delphi is a special consequence of the fact that a society extending over so many cities and (considering the means of communications) such great distances was in need of fixed centers. Then, when a single point, for whatever reason, attained a certain informational advantage, an ever increasing number of petitioners were drawn there. And a special reason for this was that the Greeks, in establishing colonies, grew to depend increasingly on consultations with oracles. When seekers for counsel arrived, the leading circles of the city became familiar with further problems, resulting in a more and more intensifying interchange of information.

In this manner a spiritual exchange center must have developed here whose attraction went far beyond the Greek world.[33] This can be concluded indirectly from the archaeological remains of innumerable delegations. For it is unlikely that the Greek cities sent deaf-and-dumb delegates to Delphi to deliver votive offerings. And it is just as unlikely that the men of Delphi were solely interested in the material treasures of the diverse delegations. Besides, we know from various reports that Delphi conducted a close correspondence with the wide circle of sages who were traditionally designated as the "seven sages." Delphi itself must have had a strong and abiding interest in giving advice in the religious as well as the political-social spheres, and perhaps only to a minor degree in the form of oracles (which of course were necessary and became remarkably authoritative). For Delphi's reputation and its material prosperity depended on these. Thus this important center represented a practically indispensable opportunity for communication in the world of many *poleis*. When, like Humphreys, one asks about the communication between the Greek intellectuals, this was without doubt much more important than, for example, the sectarian meeting under the Pythagoreans.

The centralized information provided by Delphi, though not exclusively dependent on it, was the precondition for the acceleration and dissemination of the knowledge attained among the Greeks, at the same time for spiritual discourse and mutual confirmation, and ultimately for the authority of Greek thinking. Through Delphi the Greek intelligence gained its status, its independence, and its uniqueness.

The fact that Greece consisted of innumerable, diverse, independent cities, and that there was relatively little opportunity for greater concentrations of power, certainly was a condition for the development of intelligence in the interstices between power centers and cities. And the instability of the power structures was the reason why information and advice were required repeatedly and from quite different parties. But the formation of a specific intellectual style, a specific standard of discussion presupposed especially the multiplication of communication. There was a need for an intellectual current throughout (and beyond) the Aegean world, in which primarily commonsense, knowledge, ingenuity and then also a deeper insight into the complex conditions of political and social life were appreciated—and consequently further developed. In this current there had to be built up something like a new place; a third position had to be institutionalized in order to secure the autonomy of thinking. Therein an attitude emerged which was primarily oriented toward giving good advice to the *polis* concerned. This was not a matter of course. Many interested parties must have demanded hasty, biased answers, even being ready to pay premiums for them. To counter this a mentality had to be fostered that rejected immediate benefits in favor of long-term, balanced solutions that served the general interest. And it had to become clear that such independent advice was the best—and in the end the most profitable—in the world of many *poleis*. Only in this way could the authority arise without which the autonomy of this intelligence would have been indifferent—nay impossible.

In this the reliance on Delphi was of the utmost importance. Subsequently, a second large center of Greek thought developed in Miletus, later on also in Elea and other places, before Athens became the center of Greek philosophy. The tendency is to regard Miletus as more enlightened than Delphi; this is a moot point. One would have to ask whether the relation between religion and enlightenment among the Greeks was not fundamentally different from that in modern Christian Europe. One would also have to ask whether Delphi, if indeed it was less enlightened than Miletus, was not more astute in its political thinking. And finally one would have to answer the question whether Milesian philosophy was not made possible only after Greek thinking had already passed through essential stages.

In any case, some chronological differentiations must be made. At first, the tyrants and the intellectuals thought along largely similar paths, that is, paths which the "wisdom" in ancient Egypt, in Israel, and perhaps also elsewhere tried to follow:[34] one sought means for improving economic conditions, overcoming unemployment, fostering trade, and the like. One of the "seven sages" was even himself a tyrant.

But this was not all. Political thinking—if one may use this generic term—developed different yardsticks by which tyranny did not seem to be legitimate. That the latter as a rule did not last long was certainly a contributing factor. In the long run this trend toward a non-monarchic order proved most salient and full of consequences. Presumably it was also derived from the realization that the tyrants were generally weak and in most cases unable to govern satisfactorily for any length of time. Further insights resulted from the fact that the sages were faced with the problem of giving advice applicable in the midst of precarious power structures. Then they had little choice but to work for moderation and to oppose every form of dangerous extremism, every expression of excessive power or impotence, wealth or poverty. Since even the poor could sometimes become dangerous, the sages had to side also especially with them. Thus in these precarious circumstances they had to bear in mind the overall interest of the cities, which otherwise could hardly come into play vis-à-vis the particular objectives.

When a group of people has to produce solutions to a great variety of problems, it must have certain standards. This requirement was fulfilled by the concept of Eunomia as we find it in Solon. One can reconstruct its history, at least in outline. In Hesiod we find a strong, though hardly practicable, belief in justice. It goes hand-in-hand with skepticism about the activities of the secular authorities. Solutions are sought in Zeus as the superior source of justice.[35] But the god and his daughter Dike, the personification of justice, could operate for Hesiod only if they imposed earthly punishment for earthly injustice. Therefore he could not understand the connection between injustice and punishment except by assuming direct divine intervention.

Two or three generations thereafter we find in a poem by Solon[36] the awareness that there exists a connection between injustice and ruin, which is verifiable on earth. By then it was proved that the exploitation of the peasants was deleterious not only to the victims but potentially to the whole community, since the peasants could revolt and cause civil war and slavery. Precisely therein Solon saw the temporal concatenation of things, for which the old assumption of a connection between injustice and punishment constituted only something like the background of nomologic knowledge. It was evident how divine justice works. But if this is so, the gods must also have provided a just order.

The procedure by which Solon sought to ascertain this order was conservative. He sensed the outlines of a right order behind the status quo. With this he presumed that everything that could lead to the great difficulties and conflicts in the *polis* was not provided for in the right order. Thus, for instance, the mortgage stones were contrary to it because they marked a state of affairs that ultimately caused civil unrest. In this manner there emerged the picture of eunomia in which everything had its proper place, and that on the basis of divine dispensation.

Yet this order, as Solon also found, could be reinstituted. In his poem on eunomia he asserts both the inevitability of the process toward ruin and the citizens' ability to stop it. For on the one hand he diagnosed the deplorable state of affairs and declared that it would bring inescapable doom to the city,[37] while on the other hand he appealed to the responsibility of the citizens in such a way that he could not only mean that they would have to bear the consequences of their guilt but also that they could alter the situation. After all, at the very beginning Solon emphasized strongly that Zeus and Athene were well disposed toward the city.

The contradictoriness of these three statements can only be resolved in the following manner: although there is an inescapable regularity with which civil war and tyranny follow abuses, the point of no return evidently had not yet been reached at the time of the poem. The regularity will only take effect when things get worse.[38] The result of this is the responsibility of the citizens. This responsibility, however, could not yet find its expression in their regular participation in politics, but only in their entrusting a man with extraordinary power to put things in order again. In those days this was the only possible way to initiate reform. But the citizens had to be induced to intervene in the course of things. And the best way to do this seemed to be teaching them that it tends to become fatally inescapable. Therefore just the impending inescapability of events enabled them to realize what their situation was and to take action. This must have strengthened Solon's faith in the benevolence of the gods.[39] Perhaps his praise of the gods in his poem is the expression of high-minded cognition.

Besides, the idea of the citizens' responsibility also constitutes a bridge to a deeper understanding of why the innocent have to share the suffering of the city, a fact which is evident from the empirical facts of rebellions and civil wars. And already Homer and Hesiod had stated that the city as a whole suffered through the injustice of

its leaders (as it also suffered, on the basis of the "guilt culture,"
by the presence of unexpiated murderers).[40] Here it became clear
that a share in the guilt corresponds to the suffering in case the
citizens did not intervene in good time, for—and this was a new
idea—they could do something. In this respect justice is directed
against them as well.

We do not know to what extent the ideas of eunomia are particular
to Solon and how widely held they were at the time. At any rate,
from the early years of the sixth century there existed a conception
of a recognizable good order of the *polis,* provided by the gods, in
which all forces had their place, their tasks and their rights. Solon
took it for granted that the aristocrats were entitled to the leadership,
provided that they had to act lawfully, for the people itself also had
its rights. Thus the aristocracy was especially responsible for the
good order, but in this it was not alone. The judgement over the
order and ultimately the responsibility for it was in the hands of all
citizens. This was in accordance with the idea of this order which
ultimately transcended the competence of every force, and which
could only be comprehended as an all-embracing context. There
existed, though, a distinction between the status quo and the good
order also in the largely similar conceptions of order in other cultures,
e.g. the Egyptian Ma'at, the Indian Dharma, and equivalents in
China. But there it was always the king who in the end had to bear
the responsibility for the order, whom one could at best admonish
or put under pressure. Here, however, the final responsibility for
order was borne by all—and if need be they had to resort to somebody
who would set things back into order.

The "neutrality," the "standing apart," the capacity of the sages
to see the whole and, if necessary, to set it right, reflects the third
position of this political thinking. So does the fact that the order
was conceived as a context, as a lawful relationship between the
various parts of the city, as something that must carry itself—and
in case of need must again be made to do so. This was no simple
matter: interests in the government and in the restriction of its
arbitrariness, interests of the aristocracy and of the governed had to
be taken into account. They had to be balanced in a multi-dimen-
sional perspective of the common weal as a part of which all forces
were to be understood. Laws had to be given and suggested so that
they—in conjunction with ethical maxims—formed a framework
within which the citizens could themselves cope with each other and
with their tasks. This required a measure of abstraction enabling the
recognition—beyond individual interests and the need for an equilibrium between them—of the whole that was at stake. It also required
a certain disregard for one's own involvement. It seems that these

sages as a rule did not even think of taking possession of the *polis* by way of identification with it or through some institution that could have represented them.

Yet one who has to set things on their proper course has to know their foundations and connections much better than one who in the end can and must direct them himself. The latter has to know about them only what he needs for making them dependent of and useful to him. As against this, the other has to study their nature, their particularities, the laws governing them—and their possible inter-action. Thus in time among the Greeks the problems of political life are posed much more intensely and radically, being far more directed toward principles and causes than elsewhere. Therefore it became almost inevitable that in a similar sense the Greeks also began to enquire into nature.

Where the political order in such a manner came out of joint, also the universe could no longer be taken for granted as well-ordered. Causes and laws had to be sought also in the universe. All sorts of questions, old and new, had to be answered, without regard to the activities of individual gods, as this intelligence generally no longer had any room for divine arbitrariness. Polytheism could not help. Yet one could ask for a divine principle, for a singular divine being whose regular working would be empirically recognizable.

Vernant has pointed out very aptly how especially Anaximander's philosophy is strongly determined by political categories and questions.[41] I cannot agree with him when he says it is determined by the spirit of isonomia. This not only causes great chronological difficulties, but it also relies on the interpretation of single terms which we cannot be sure Anaximander used nor whether their meaning corresponds to the political linguistic usage of the time approximately since Cleisthenes. But it is obvious that the model of a world that is ruled not by a single transcendental authority but by a law is closely related to Solon's conception. Nature is conceived as "an autarkical realm of immanent lawfulness."[42] At the same time it is clear that Anaximander, beyond Solon, saw the cohesion of the world, even the resting position of the earth within the cosmos, as founded upon geometric principles. Perhaps one ought to assume that this abstract, artificial, geometric thinking was one of the prem-ises rather than the consequences of isonomia which itself was a relatively abstract, artificial creation.[43] Anyhow something quite un-heard of and unique belonged to this constitution: namely that the political order was no longer constructed (as in Solon) in analogy to the social order, but in a fundamentally different way. For the middle classes could now effectively defy the ruling classes thanks to the institutionalization of their political participation.

This state of affairs encompassed within the *polis* a lawfulness which, according to Anaximander, clearly prevailed throughout the world. He thought that all things are in a state of ascent and descent and in this way are "doing penance" for each other. Evidently every ascent is due to an injustice which is then atoned for by descent and by the ascent of another force. As a final result the lawfulness of an order ensues here too insofar as no power can rule forever, and as all must obey the same law. But there are always some forces which keep regularly but unlawfully the upper hand while others stay below. This may be derived from nature where day changes into night, summer into winter.[44] It can also be derived from the continuous vicissitudes of the tyrants, dynasties, and empires that could be observed in the East of the Greek world—and by the way also at Miletus. In contrast to Solon's eunomia, and certainly to the expectations connected with isonomia, this world did not know the state of lawful constant restfulness that broke the vicious circle of injustice and doom, but its constancy was characterized by lawful unrest consisting in the concatenation of injustice and punishment. The equilibrium did not exist synchronously but was attained only diachronously. Later on one could turn these thoughts into the positive side of democracy, by instituting the rotation, the same alternation on earth between governing and being governed, that seemed to prevail also in the heavens. Yet there is no evidence that Anaximander thought of this. As far as we can see, he only formulated a general lawfulness within a comprehensive order that on the whole remained undisturbed. And he did this with respect to all nature. With this he went much farther than Solon, as may befit a philosopher. Only in assuming that no reign of extremes, actually no reign at all, could endure but that a law was supreme, they agreed with one another.

If laws operate in politics as in nature, their observation could mutually reinforce them. Later Heraclitus says explicitly that the laws of the city are derived from the laws governing the universe.[45] Still, one ought not to view the parallels between political and philosophical concepts too narrowly. Or should one assume that in Anaximander's Miletus things appeared differently from the Athens of Solon?

I doubt whether we are justified in regarding Anaximander's world view as transcendental (and not mundane). At any rate, the conception of eunomia in politics was intended to be realized on earth. Whatever abstractions from the given reality, from the status quo, had been achieved, eunomia was meant to be ultimately realized. And this was actually done, though differently than originally intended.

For in time it became evident that the good order was not realizable unless one granted the middle classes the right to intervene regularly. "The poor man had to be able to vote for his protection against injustice, to be judge and magistrate" (J. Burckhardt).[46] In time the political thinkers must have worked toward this. This was the consequence of their mission of creating eunomia. Herein was the source of those anticipations without which decisive participation of the broader masses of the people was almost unthinkable. From this must have unleashed the force that was responsible for the thorough overturning of interests and value judgements, from which a change in the whole social identity followed in the end. If aristocrats such as Cleisthenes, since the second half of the sixth century, sought to gain the support of wider strata by granting them political rights instead of economic concessions, surely they did so in response to expectations presented to them from the people.

It would be interesting to reconstruct in greater detail the course of thinking in those days. Many arguments support the presumption that then the conception of an equilibrium played an important role in politics. When one increased the opportunities of wider strata by creating for them "councils of opposition" or peoples' courts in competition with aristocrats' courts, this was the same expression of the idea of equilibrium, as soon thereafter, in medical thinking, the *Alkmaion* that saw health in the isonomy of the forces, differentiating between humidity and dryness, cold and heat, bitterness and sweetness. There one strove for a balance between weight and counterweight, in other words, between large groups or powers. Aeschylus in his *Oresteia* later reveals the necessity of a certain counterbalance by the aristocracy as against the people. And we find similar conceptions in some passages of Aristotle as well.[47] If they do not play an important role in our tradition, this may have been due to the fact that relatively soon another idea of equality came to the fore: because if, in order to achieve an equilibrium, one granted the people more rights, this implied a tendency toward the equality of the many with the few, or, further, to the equality of all individual citizens. For in the course of this process these had to become aware of their entitlement to equal political rights. It was just this idea which, if not *a priori,* at least very soon, determined the isonomia. And in the middle of the fifth century, when the differences between the higher and the lower classes came to a head, so that oligarchy and democracy became the most outstanding political contrast, one could think of an equilibrium at best theoretically.

The equality of the citizens was the basis of the solidarity that alone enabled the members of the community to carry the *polis.*[48] For they needed a strong cohesion. Thus they had to emphasize their citizenship most strongly—much more so than any other possible differences. Herein they had to find their primary interest. Equal rights and equal interests had to grow together.

If, according to Max Weber, men are directly governed by their interests, then "the 'world-views' created by 'ideas' . . . very often functioned as guidelines for determining the dynamics of the interests promoted by the actions."[49] When the Greek peasants had to disregard the binding force of an existing social order—and this not only in occasional rebellions but regularly—then it must seem probable that the demand for so thorough a reform had to be secured also philosophically, theologically and not lastly cosmologically—just as Aeschylus later on correspondingly secured in myth the new position of Athens after the fall of the Aeropag. The virulence that contributed to the emergence of isonomy and which itself constituted the first conclusion of the building process of the *polis*, probably resulted only from a combination of a widely held belief in justice and a confidence in man's own capacity to act.

Here it must have been a matter of formation of a new worldview. The change in social identity consolidated in civic consciousness, equality, and solidarity, corresponded to it. Through it in numerous Greek cities, in their own ways, the thoughts about the whole and the thoughts about what each individual can and should do, were combined and mutually reinforced. After all any thinking only becomes really practical when the actions of the individuals can correspond to it also in everyday life (and not, as so often at other times, when thinking and doing are so divorced from each other that the one always contradicts the other in effect). If this happens, the one reinforces the other.

Taken all in all one can say that the political thinking of archaic times was closely intertwined with the formation of the *polis*. If this reconstruction is correct, it has various consequences.

CONCLUSION: POLITICS AND THINKING

If the preceding assumptions are correct, one can observe in the development of Greek thinking a close correspondence between the position of the sages and the lawfulness they were looking for. As a consequence, the search for the reasons and correlations in nature and politics became especially intensive in those times. This was in correspondence to a vigorous realism that sought divine justice empirically in nature and in the world of men. With this the questioning of what existed probably became particularly radical—because there were special challenges and possibilities to answer.

The striving for the realization of a lawful order had the further consequence that one had to endeavor to create in the citizens the whole that was at stake. For a totality, for which no single authority could be held responsible, could only be carried by the whole community. Thus, at least in some of the more troubled cities, there evolved an identity change of the citizenry through which the common interest was turned into reality within the framework of a particular institutional order as a responsibility, conviction and object of activity.

The great number of Greek cities contributed much to the fact that the intellectuals both formed part of this whole and at the same time maintained a certain distance from it.

Certainly intellectual autonomy cannot be assured by its being to a certain extent separated from the rest of the society, but for this to be possible there must exist at the same time a certain differentiation within the rest of the society. At any rate certain terms of reference, which may be identifications, are important for an intelligence. While a particular power constellation at first left some openings within which Greek intelligence could unfold and operate, it subsequently seems to have been the cause of certain divisions within the society. In contrast to other cultures the Greeks were distinguished by the separation of lawfulness from arbitrariness, of the common interest from the singularity of all individual forces, and not by the separateness of a monarchy from a society. As a consequence, their thinking could not identify with stronger powers, not with monarchy and state, not with progress, history, the "Weltgeist," and therefore not even with the people or a class that could claim to represent in the present the mankind of the future. Rather they were relatively weak. Only through this weakness could they conceive an order within which also the weak—though only from among the citizenry—should have their part and their power. Their influence was based on the fact that they knew this weakness—and were aware that this knowledge could grant them authority.[50] The orientation toward this order provided them with the possibilities to act and secured their autonomy.

At first this may have been not so much an autonomy of the individuals but of the group of sages as a whole, precisely since, *mutatis mutandis,* the middle class citizens would develop their autonomy only through their solidarity. It seems to me that this undergoes a fundamental change only in the course of the fifth century. What was important was that the endeavors for a stronger political engagement of the citizenry could be linked with their independence, and besides that there was a fluid transition between peasants and aristocrats. Otherwise it may have been impossible to evoke the readiness of the broad strata for such a strong active involvement.

The lawfulness and the common interest that were the concern of Greek intelligence found their sociological place in strong demands and expectations emanating above all from the middle classes, from the separation of home and *polis* and from many other factors. Corresponding to this was the awareness that discussion was required, that one had to learn, that all this took place in public—and the demand that political life as a whole had to be public, and with this the debate was concerned not only with the individual interest but also the general, the *polis* and the world as a whole. In this respect the citizenry of Greece corresponded to the Greek intelligence, as this citizenry only emerged from the Greek intelligence.

It is not clear how strongly the circle of the sages stood out from the rest. Presumably it was relatively wide. It was part of the authority of at least several prominent sages that they claimed to have special access to wisdom. There was a mixture of secret and public matters not only in Delphi.[51] This circle of sages must have presented a rather colorful picture. Everything that had hitherto formed the center of my reflections was in any case only a strand of the thinking of the time, though the most consequential one. There stood others beside it. We find visionaries, miracle healers, fortune tellers. Outside public discussions, where Solon, for example, presented his arguments, they were in their element in sects and mystic communities. They answered a variety of needs. There was not only the meditation on politics but also the turning away from it into the private sphere, into ecstasy. The precarious positioning of powers and the dissolution of the institutions must have opened a multitude of intellectual possibilities. In a certain sense poetry and elaboration of myths should also be seen as media of Greek wisdom.

The success attained by Greek thought, especially in political matters, was an essential condition for its authority also in the future. Its unique intellectual engagement in the whole of the *polis,* its impartial position, continued to exert their influence as well. Both became especially palpable in the Attic tragedy.

The evolvement of early thinking, isonomy, and above all the democracy that emerged from these after the Persian wars, and that granted the citizenry free rein also over the center of the political order provided the decisive impetus to both Sophism and to Socratic philosophy. From that time onward though, Greek thought became rather a matter for specialists. Within the relationship between thinking and politics the influence of politics on thinking predominated over that of the now primary philosophical thinking on politics. But the close relationship continued up to the fourth century. And this may serve as a valid confirmation of the thesis that the emergence of an autonomous intelligence among the Greeks has a decisive connection with the origins of politics.

CHAPTER 3

Dynamics of the Greek Breakthrough: The Dialogue between Philosophy and Religion

S.C. HUMPHREYS

INTRODUCTION: FROM 'DOXA' TO OPINION

One aspect of the problem we have been asked to examine can be formulated in the question: how does it come about, in the Axial Age, that men start to ask whether human social organization and political decisions should be dominated by religious imperatives, and start to compare the claims of differing religious and/or secular accounts of the cosmos. I propose in this paper to look at the dynamics of this process by analyzing the impact on Greek (and especially Athenian) religious thought and practice, and on poetry, of the pressures towards secularization and rationalization which we can discern in Greek culture in the period between c. 550 and 300 B.C.E.

The move towards secularization begins, in archaic Greece, with a tendency towards the elimination of the supernatural from political decision-making, and with the development of increasingly sophisticated and formally rational procedural rules, voting techniques, and arrangements for sharing power. Spartan 'eunomia' even included a redistribution of land in equal lots. References to the sacred were not entirely eliminated, but the influence of seers and diviners (perhaps never very strong) was whittled down; the political elite kept the consultation of the gods largely in their own hands, through the use of oracles from extraterritorial shrines which could be manipulated and, when ambiguous, thrown open to competitive debate over alternative interpretations.

The experience of a rational and regular social order[1] must have contributed to the development in the sixth century B.C.E. of a new view of the cosmos which stressed symmetry and regularity in natural processes, and also sharply criticized the prevailing anthropomorphic conception of the gods. The radical and polemical character of this critique was favoured by the fact that religious authority was only weakly developed and it was left to poets to give competing accounts of the gods and the cosmos. This absence of religious authority also meant, however, that the defensive counter-reaction against the new secular view of the cosmos was diffuse rather than centered on any one identifiable status-group. This first version of the debate between religion and science was to a large extent internalized by Greek thinkers rather than leading to the crystallization of competing power-groups. The area of those cultural presuppositions unquestioningly accepted in all accounts of the cosmos and of man's relations with the gods shrank; by the age of the Sophists, variable opinion had taken over from unreflective 'doxa', in Bourdieu's terminology (1977), over a very wide front. But this increasing consciousness of the existence of different world-views was not accompanied by any very determined attempts by schools or sects to define their own world-views as orthodoxy. The characteristic expressions of religious thought in the classical age are on the one hand the tragedies produced by Athenian poets in a situation of open public competition, and on the other hand the doctrines of the mystery cults, protected from overt confrontation by rules of secrecy but nevertheless unable to claim the exclusive adherence of their initiates. Competition was also rife among philosophers, doctors, and historians, developing in some cases into the institutionalization of rival schools.

On the whole, therefore, the intellectual elite operated in an individualistic manner, with little formal organization. The Pythagoreans, who organized themselves into communities with shared beliefs and a distinctive way of life (Burkert, 1972a) were exceptional. The general situation of competition between world-views produced by identifiable individuals (whose views could sometimes be seen to change and develop over time) favoured a relativistic attitude, interest in 'second-order thinking' (Elkana) and criteria for judging one view superior to another, and a tendency to regard the problems of the meaning of life as something to be solved by each individual for himself, either through creative thought or by an eclectic synthesis of the competing world-views available. Clear demarcations of genre and context also prevented opposed conceptions of society and the cosmos from confronting each other too openly; to criticize the Athenian democracy in a tragedy, comedy, historical work, or philo-

sophical utopia was different from proposing a change of constitution
in the assembly.

It is against this background of intellectual pluralism, which persisted throughout classical antiquity, that Judaism, Islam, and Christianity must be seen. It was their intolerant monotheism, combined
with their origin in ethnic groups or social classes sufficiently homogeneous and remote from institutional centres of power to be
able to develop their own organization and leadership, which made
them a force to be reckoned with.[2]

But if we want to understand the endemic tension between Church
and State and within the Church between this-worldly and other-
worldly orientations which has characterized Christianity, it is worth
looking more closely at the situation in ancient Greece. The rationalist
critique of traditional beliefs set off contradictory reactions: on the
one hand attempts were made to rationalize myth, theology, and
cult, while on the other hand value was more consciously attached
to types of experience more explicitly classed as irrational or as
stretching beyond the limits of rational thought. This undercurrent
of attraction to irrationality is, I would argue, historically conditioned;
whereas Dodds (1951) tended to see it in Freudian terms as an
example of a universal psychic process, a predictable reaction generated by anxieties repressed in the increasing domination of rational
thought over Greek culture, I prefer to focus on the historical
construction by the Greeks of a concept of the irrational. A new
boundary was drawn between rational and irrational mental processes
and world-views, and this demarcation set up its own tensions; the
concept of the irrational became charged with both positive and
negative values. As with the Greek delineation of boundaries between
public and private life (see Humphreys, 1983a), a study of the
historical contexts in which an opposition which still plays a fundamental role in Western culture was first formulated can help to
uncover some of the tensions and ambiguities which it still holds
for us.

One of the striking features of this context is the intimate scale
of the debate. Though the spokesmen of the Greek intellectual
revolution were highly polemical, they were not sharply differentiated
structurally from those they criticised. Philosophers and doctors
mingled with poets and politicians; Pericles was a friend of Anaxagoras, Sophocles read Herodotus, Euripides and Aristophanes were
familiar with the ideas of the Sophists and Socrates, Lycurgus was
a pupil of Plato. The philosophers, doctors, and historians were
surrounded by people who went on writing poetry, playing prominent
parts in religious rituals, going to temples for healing, watching
tragedies, introducing new cults. And yet they knew what the ra-

tionalists were saying. The criticism was not directed just against popular superstition; and references in drama show that mass audiences were expected to have heard of the new ideas. Aeschylus, Sophocles, and Euripides all mentioned the new idea that Apollo was a personification of the sun, and a slave in Aristophanes' *Peace* (832–3) remarks, "They say we become stars when we die". New theories percolated down to all levels.

The attack directed against traditional beliefs by the prose-writers— philosophers, historians and doctors—in the late sixth and fifth centuries B.C.E. was a radical one. What the poets have told us about the gods, they claimed, is ridiculous. Who can believe that gods get wounded in battle, catch each other in adultery, or fall in love with humans? Why should the gods be supposed to have human forms and human passions? Presumably if horses had gods, they would imagine them to be like horses. Poets' statements about the past are exaggerated and full of phenomena never experienced within living memory: talking horses, fighting rivers, men coming full-grown out of the earth (Detienne, 1981, ch. 4). Popular oral tradition is no better. Hecataeus of Miletus began his work on *Genealogies* with the blunt statement, "The stories told by the Greeks are many and ridiculous". Thucydides criticised the Athenians for not knowing how the tyranny of Pisistratus and his sons had come to its end. Doctors derided the ignorance of priests who gave advice on medical questions, of magical healers, and of the ordinary patient.[3]

The new secular model of the cosmos, human society and the mind put forward by these critics was empiricist—knowledge had to be derived from direct observation or from theories based on analogies with observable processes (Heraclitus B55 D.-K.; Lloyd, 1966, 1979). The new model was also political: public life was becoming more sharply distinguished from private life, and the superiority of the public sphere was emphasised. Public life was more orderly, more rational and more important than private life (Humphreys, 1983). And finally, the new model was logical: clear reasoning and the ability to defeat opponents in argument were emphasised in philosophy and science as they were in the assembly, council, and law courts.

To each of the three aspects of this three-pronged attack—stressing empiricism, the primacy of public life, and logical argument—we can see poetry and religious thought reacting in two ways: partly modifying traditional beliefs to make them less vulnerable to attack, partly making a virtue out of what their critics claimed was a defect.

Thus, in response to empiricism, some attempts were made to rationalise and clean up myths and stories about the gods, to prune off the miraculous and undignified elements and leave a residue of credible history or allegorical statements about natural phenomena. But also more abstract conceptions of deity were developed: if gods have no bodies, their existence can not be empirically disproved.

In response to the emphasis on the importance of public life, the state cult of the gods was rationalised in various ways: the more archaic and queer-looking ceremonies got less emphasis, and the benefits to be expected from the performance of rituals were more openly stressed—the immediate benefits of distribution of sacrificial meat and the blessings expected from gods with names like Zeus Soter or Athena Hygieia. People reflected on the social functions of religious festivals: they promoted sociability and had a 'civilizing' effect (Plato, *Laws* 738, 838; Polybius iv. 20–1, cf. Borgeaud, 1979). At the same time, however, other aspects of religious life became more explicitly associated with the private sphere, with women and children, and with non-political spaces: forests and mountains, sacred shrines in remote areas.

And thirdly, in response to the demand for logical thought, we find both an influence of scientific models on religious and magical doctrines—which starts with Orphism and ends with Hellenistic astrology and magic—*and* a deliberate emphasis on the role of the irrational in human experience—of poetic inspiration, trance, possession, ecstasy.

It is these three reactions—in each case ambiguous, involving both acceptance and rejection of the rationalist criticism—that I want now to explore in more depth.

THE MATERIAL AND THE IMMATERIAL

In the case of the reaction against empiricism, it is particularly clear that we cannot always make a clear-cut distinction between those who were attacking traditional beliefs and those who were defending them (cf. Lloyd, 1979, 39–46). Philosophers and historians themselves put forward rationalizing interpretations of myth and abstract conceptions of the gods, while Orphic poets and tragedians incorporated 'philosophical' ideas into their works.

It was particularly the myths about heroes which were subject to the form of rationalisation which turned them into historical stories about real kings, which in the course of time had been deformed by poetic exaggeration (Veyne, 1983, 52ff., 70ff.). It was not until the early third century that Euhemerus extended this approach to the gods also, claiming that they too had been merely powerful mortals who had deified themselves (as contemporary kings by this time were doing: Meijer, 1981). The earlier reaction was to humanize the heroes but dehumanize the gods, turning them into physical or psychic forces. The basis for this already existed in Greek religion: Zeus was thunder and the ability of the mind to control and manipulate *(mētis)*, Aphrodite was the psychic force of love, Poseidon caused waves at sea and earthquakes on land. In the sixth century we can hardly distinguish between new religious movements and some of the new philosophies—or rather, we distinguish them solely on the basis of their later developments. Pythagoreanism and the ideas and practices associated with the name of Orpheus had a lot in common. The main difference between them seems to have been that the Pythagoreans organized themselves into communities while Orphic teachers seem to have operated in a more independent way, more loosely linked to the congregations who came to them for initiation (West, 1983a). But both offered a new kind of knowledge about the afterlife and new theories about the nature of the universe, which had a more 'scientific' tone than the traditional cosmologies.[4] Both emphasized in their teaching, and in the dietary rules which accompanied it, the separation between the believers and the rest of the world, the uninitiated. Both rejected animal sacrifice, the major rite of traditional religion.[5] Orphic teachers warned their hearers, like Hippocratic doctors, of the danger of putting themselves in the hands of charlatans who lacked true knowledge and were only interested in making money (Burkert, 1982).

Aeschylus in his *Lycurgus* trilogy presented Orpheus worshipping the sun as Apollo; he probably derived the idea from an Orphic cosmology (West, 1983a, b) and it is mentioned again several times in tragedy. In Aristophanes' *Peace* (412) the sun, moon and stars are said to be hoping that the Greeks will give up worshipping the gods and make sacrifices to them instead; Plato in the *Cratylus* (397c–d) attributes the view that primitive man worshipped the heavenly bodies to the religious specialist Euthyphro. The Sophist Prodicus, in the fifth century, said that the traditional conceptions of the gods had arisen because "primitive man deified the fruits of the earth and practically everything that contributed to his existence" (Henrichs, 1975; *P. Herc.* 1428 fr. 19), and Euripides makes Tiresias take a similar view in the *Bacchae* (274–285). Myths about the gods were given allegorical interpretations; Metrodorus of Lampsacus, a pupil of Anaxagoras, is said to have interpreted the Homeric poems as allegories about natural processes.[6]

Other allegorical interpretations took a less aggressively materialist form. Anaxagoras himself interpreted the Homeric poems as allegories about virtue and justice, and Aeschylus arguably viewed his own tragedies in rather the same way (Humphreys, 1975). The technique of allegorical interpretation allowed poets to claim that their works contained truths not immediately visible on the surface, and such claims are quite often accompanied by a deliberate obscurity of language, in the period when prose-writing is making its first impact as an alternative to poetry. Aeschylus was assumed to have deliberately chosen a highly poetic style to emphasize the seriousness *(semnotēs)* of his message, and Pindar adopts stylistic features reminiscent of the Delphic oracle: he uses enigmatic images[7] which suggest a hidden meaning—*ariston men hudōr*, best of all is water *(Olympia* 1), "There is a time when men need winds, a time for rain" *(Ol.* 11); and he also uses gnomic phrases like the famous Delphic maxims, "Know thyself", and "Nothing too much", whose application to his own circumstances the reader had to work out for himself. By means of such phrases eminent patrons could be tactfully warned that they were only mortal, and that they should aspire to virtue as well as success, in an indirect way at which they could not take offence (cf. Bacchylides iii. 85–7).

This claim that profound truths could only be expressed indirectly, in oracular or allegorical poetic language, drew some support from the difficulties which philosophers experienced in putting into words the new abstract conceptions of deity which they were developing. Complete rejection of all belief in gods, like complete rejection of all the contents of myth, was very rare (some would say unknown) in the ancient world.[8] What was rejected was the idea of gods as larger-than-life human beings. Thales said "Everything is full of gods"; Xenophanes, "There is one god, unlike men: all of him sees, all thinks, all hears". For Anaxagoras, in the fifth century, god was *Nous,* mind, the creator of the logical relationships which philosophers were discovering in the universe. Socrates' *daimonion* is a deliberately non-characterizing term. For Plato God, the supreme cause of the cosmos, existed on an entirely immaterial plane, in a world of pure forms analogous to that of pure mathematics.

For Plato education was a gradual process of initiation by which the philosopher arrived at a more direct experience of this immaterial plane of existence, which could not be described in terms which the uninitiated could understand; only a myth, an allegorical tale, could give some shadowy indication of its nature. The interplay between religious and philosophical thought led to an increasing convergence between conceptions of the psychological transformations generated by the experiences of the philosopher and the promises of revelation of a new meaning in existence offered by the mystery religions. This convergence only reaches full fruition in the gnostic and neo-Platonist texts of the Roman Empire. But there was from the beginning a potential affinity between the philosophers' struggle to express a new, more abstract, 'ineffable' conception of deity and the silence which initiates were bound to observe concerning the secret knowledge imparted to them in the 'showing' of the mysteries. The doctrine imparted in the Eleusinian mysteries was, as far as we can tell, materialist rather than abstract; but the rule of secrecy protected the rites from rationalist criticism, it created a protected space in which the idea of mystical experience could grow. In the prevailing critical atmosphere, this protective silence was important (cf. Lloyd, 1979, 228–9 for medical parallels).

The development of tragedy in the fifth century shows the increasing gap between mortals and gods which the new dematerialized conception of the gods introduced (Veyne, 1983, 52, 70ff.), and which is eventually filled, in Plato, by the idea that man himself is divided into a divine part—the soul—and a mortal, animal part—the body. The helpful divine patrons of Homer disappear; only Apollo and Athena in Aeschylus' *Eumenides* still show some resemblance to the Homeric model, and even they show the influence on Aeschylus of the rationalization of political institutions and of the philosophical ideas of the regular, unchangeable processes at work in the natural world: Athena creates the institution by which order is maintained in the city, the law-court, and Apollo represents a principle of social organization explicitly based on biology (patriliny). Gods directly enter the action in Sophocles' plays only in the *Ajax,* where Odysseus is presented as horrified by the actions of his divine patroness Athena. Comments by the chorus present a philosophical view of the gods only remotely related to the action—particularly of course in the well-known ode in the *Antigone* on the power of love.[9] Euripides' gods are dangerous, incomprehensible, alien beings: to live in close association with a god implies separation from natural political life, whether this is the radical reversal of normal life practised by the Bacchae, the exaggerated prolongation of adolescence of Hippolytus, with his devotion to Artemis, or the peaceful seclusion of the boy Ion in Apollo's temple at Delphi. Euripides, even more noticeably than Sophocles, separates action and chorus; often the sordid political manoeuvres of human actors are interrupted by interludes of lyric in which the chorus seems to portray life on another plane, an idyllic existence in which the beauty of the natural world mingles with the lost glories of the world of myth and of the heroes. By ending his plays with a reference to the religious rites by which the action they have portrayed is still commemorated, Euripides gives this dreamtime world an anchorage in real time and space (see Foley, 1985); at the same time, given the unflattering realism with which the actions of the heroes are often delineated, this reference to ritual does little to conceal the problematic nature of the relation between ritual and secular life.

PUBLIC AND PRIVATE SALVATION

We shall return to Euripides, whose plays provide an extraordinarily rich source for the often contradictory ideas and reactions of
religious thinkers in the classical period. First, however, I want to
look at the reaction to philosophical criticism as it affected the actual
practice of religion.

In Athens, Solon's codification of the laws, the end of the tyranny
of Pisistratus, and the Persian Wars mark three major steps in the
city's developing consciousness of itself: consciousness of taking part
in historical action, consciousness of taking decisions about its own
institutions. New rituals were introduced to commemorate historical
events; after the battle of Marathon, the city introduced a tribal
torch-race and a shrine on the slopes of the Acropolis to honour
the Arcadian god Pan, who had appeared to the runner Philippides
as he was returning from his unsuccessful embassy to seek Spartan
help, and had promised his own aid in the battle (Herodotus vi.
105; Pausanias 1.i.4). Conon built a sanctuary for Aphrodite of Cnidus
in the Piraeus after his victory at Cnidus in 394. The introduction
of the Panathenaic games, in 566, had marked the beginning of a
whole series of new competitive festivals; competitions in tragedy
at the City Dionysia had been introduced by the tyrants, competitions
in comedy followed in the 480s. Hephaestus and Prometheus also
had tribal torch-races in their honour; we do not know their date
of origin, but there must have been some reorganisation in the late
sixth century when Cleisthenes created new tribes. A race in honour
of the Thracian goddess Bendis was introduced about 429 (*I.G.* i³
136; cf. Pecirka, 1966, 122–130).

Beside such large-scale, spectacular festivals, funded and presided
over by the state and elected magistrates, regulated by written laws
and presenting no problems of meaning to participants or spectators—dominated by the thrill of competition and the joy of victory—
some of the older religious rituals of the city began to appear
problematic, particularly those which were organized and funded by
aristocratic clans and employed a symbolism which was not clearly
understood. The most obvious case is the ritual of the Dipolieia or
Bouphonia, ox-slaying, singled out by Aristophanes (*Clouds* 984–5)
to stand for those aspects of Athenian culture which the youngest
generation found old-fashioned and fuddy-duddy. The Bouphonia
supposedly reenacted the killing of the first sacrificial ox; the victim
had to bring its own death on itself by taking grain from the altar,
the officiants all disclaimed blame for the slaughter, the knife with
which the animal was butchered was solemnly condemned for the
killing and cast into the sea, and the skin of the ox was stuffed and

set on its feet again. Several minor aristocratic clans were involved, each with the right to appoint one of the officiants in the sacrifice. It is understandable that the urban pupils of the Sophists, more familiar with the ox in its sacrificial than in its agricultural role, could see little sense in all this.[10]

Aristophanes' comedies are often modelled on religious rituals, and his treatment gives a hint of the way different rituals were regarded. The Rural Dionysia of the *Acharnians* and the Apatouria of the *Peace* represent the traditional peacetime rural life from which the Athenians had been cut off by war. The procession to Eleusis had also been interrupted by the war (after the capture of Deceleia), except in 407 when Alcibiades had protected it with his troops; two years later, Aristophanes' use of the procession to Eleusis as basis for the *Frogs* added emotional force to his recommendation that Alcibiades should be brought back to the city.

On the other hand the Thesmophoria, which forms the basis of the *Thesmophoriazousai,* and the Skira, on which the *Ecclesiazousai* is (in a sense) based, seem to be exploited merely for their comic potential. These were rites in which only women took part: Aristophanes and the dominant male sector of his audience therefore had no official knowledge of the ritual.[11] The sacrifice which we know women carried out at the Thesmophoria (Detienne, 1979) is parodied in the sacrifice by an intruding male of the 'baby' which turns out to be a wineskin; references to Demeter and Persephone, the goddesses celebrated in the festival, are unspecific and mixed with a Bacchic song and dance and invocations of Artemis, Hera, Hermes, Pan and the Nymphs, and Athena. The salient characteristic of these rituals for Aristophanes was not the association with fertility, but the reversal of roles which put women on top, and the play with parody and transvestism for which this role-reversal provided a basis (cf. Zeitlin, 1982).

Further evidence about the aspects of ritual which educated Athenians could no longer take seriously comes from the parodies indulged in by upper-class adolescents and from Theophrastus' description of the Superstitious Man (*Characters* 16). In the late fifth century Alcibiades and his friends parodied the Eleusinian mysteries and another group of young men went round the city at night mutilating the ithyphallic Hermes figures which stood by doorways; in both cases it seems to be the use of sexual symbolism in cult which gives rise to mockery. Another group of daredevils called themselves the Triballoi—the Bongo-Bongo—and used to collect up the offerings of pigs' testicles left for Hecate at crossroads and use them for banquets (D.54 *Konon* 14, 39).[12] A further, similar group called themselves the *Kakodaimonistai,* the worshippers of bad luck;

they deliberately chose days of ill-omen for their meetings (Lys. Fr. V.2 Gernet). Theophrastus' neurotically religious type (being *deisidaimon* is being cowardly about the gods) turns everything into an omen. He spends his time performing apotropaic rituals and consulting diviners about the meaning of his dreams. He goes to the Orphic priests for purification every month with his children and his wife or, if she is busy, the nanny.[13] On the fourth and seventh of every month he spends the day tending Hermaphrodite cult-figures; these are probably singled out for special mention partly because this kind of superstitious behaviour is considered effeminate, but also because the idea of divinities with two sets of sexual characteristics seems particularly absurd. Purification was mocked because of the magical means employed: how can washing in blood make people clean? (Heraclitus B 5 D.-K.)

How did those in charge of the public cults of the city respond to such criticism? With a double process of giving increasing prominence to what appeared more rational and providing excuses for what appeared irrational.[14] There is a gradual shift of emphasis in cult, impossible to date precisely, but clearly perceptible in the long run, from archaic aspects of the gods which had come to seem incomprehensible to personifications of the blessings which men hoped for. A cult of Democracy was inaugurated in 403 after the expulsion of the junta of the Thirty, and a cult of Peace in 374. An inscription of the late fourth century listing the revenues received from selling the skins of sacrificial animals (*I.G.* ii² 1496) gives an idea of the major sacrifices of the period, as measured by the number of victims consumed. Zeus the Saviour heads the list: the temple was in Piraeus and was shared by Athena the Saviour; the cult can scarcely be earlier than the Persian Wars. This sacrifice was in the same month as the old sacrifice of the Dipolieia in honour of Zeus Polieus, god of the Polis,[15] and represented a more modern reformulation of the cult of Zeus in the city. Next came the Theseia, instituted in 475 when Cimon brought back the bones of Theseus from Scyros. Theseus symbolised Attic unity and seapower: no criticism could be made of this. Then the sacrifices to Asclepius. His cult had been introduced in 420/19 and, as seems characteristic for such late additions, the sacrifices were added on to existing festivals, the Eleusinia in honour of Demeter and Persephone and the City Dionysia. The City Dionysia rank about equal in importance with the sacrifice to Peace. Then we have the festival of Olympian Zeus, probably founded by the Pisistratids in the sixth century, the feast of Bendis (introduced c. 429), the sacrifice to Democracy and a sacrifice made by the generals to Hermes the leader which may also be associated with the restoration of democracy in 403,[16] the festival of Dionysus in Piraeus which was enlarged by the politician Lycurgus in the 330s, sacrifices to Good Fortune, and a sacrifice to Ammon (which can hardly be an early cult).

The Panathenaic cult only figures in a small way in this list because the years covered by the inscription did not include celebration of the Greater Panathenaia and the figures for the Lesser Panathenaia are incomplete. We know however from another inscription of the same period (*I.G.* ii² 334) that the lesser, annual Panathenaia by this time included sacrifices to Athena Nike, goddess of victory, and Athena Hygieia, goddess of Health; both cults were associated with the Periclean age (cf. Boersma, 1970, nos. xiv–xv).

Thus by the addition of new festivals, and new cult-titles for the old gods, the city's religious calendar was given a more rational look, the ritual activities of the state channelled into commemoration of great events of the past and petition for future blessings. Where less 'rational' elements survived they were excused as imported cults— as the feast of Bendis was and the cult of Dionysus was believed to be—or protected from criticism by secrecy, as was the central ritual of the mysteries and the rites performed by women at the Thesmophoria and Skira.

Women and children formed the links between the public aspect of ritual and the increasing pull to locate it in the private sphere. Children and the young, in particular, seem to be given a more prominent role in public ritual from the fourth century onwards. Lycurgus' reorganisation of the ritual and finances of the Panathenaia included provision of jewelry to be worn by 100 *Kanephoroi*, girl 'basket-carriers' from upper-class familes; families start to set up inscriptions commemorating their daughters' performance of this role. There are also dedications from the fourth century commemorating boys' initiation to the Eleusinian mysteries as "child from the city hearth", *pais aph' hestias,* representing the whole citizen body.[17]

It seems likely also that it was in the Lycurgan period that attendance at rituals and participation in religious processions became one of the duties of the *epheboi* when they were doing their military training from the age of 18 to 20 (see Humphreys, 1985). They became a sort of ideal representation of the citizen body which accompanied processions, manhandled sacrificial bulls, and gave military and athletic displays at festivals; watching them, their parents could feel pride and satisfaction that they were being trained in civic virtues and imbued with a sense of the city's history. There is a parallel between this use of the young in ritual and the young heroines and heroes (Menoeceus) who sacrifice themselves for the community in Euripides' tragedies; it is those who are not yet fully involved in public life who can most easily represent its ideals.[18]

An alternative, however, was to use older men in prominent religious roles. The commission which was sent on solemn embassy to Delphi, probably in 326/5 (Lewis, 1955), was led by two men in their 60s, Lycurgus and Niceratus, great-grandson of the fifth-century general Nicias; the orator Demades and the historian Phanodemus, also members, were not all that much younger. Much the same group took charge of the festival and games at the sanctuary of the healing hero Amphiaraus at Oropus, which Philip of Macedon had handed over to Athens after Chaeronea. Lycurgus and Demades were active politicians, but Niceratus and Phanodemus both, in different ways, acted as living links between present and past.

Although Lycurgus appears to have seen himself as a second Pericles, and made no attempt to change the basic institutions of the democratic state, there are some links between his programme and that of Plato in the *Laws*. Plato's *nomophylakes* are to be over 50 when they take office and continue in office until 70 (755a4–b2); priests and priestesses are to be over 60 (759d), holding office for one year (cf. Aristotle, *Politics* 1329a27–34). The function of religious rituals is to mix social classes (759b) and promote socialization generally, particularly with a view to enabling young men and women to get to know each other before choosing marriage partners (771d–772a). Here again it is the young and the old who are consciously singled out to represent the community in religious contexts.

Links can also be seen between Lycurgus' programme and the representation of religion in Euripides. I have already mentioned the altruistic devotion to the community shown by young girls and the young Menoeceus when they sacrifice themselves to ensure victory (Aélion, 1983 II, 113–124). This element in Euripides' plays has puzzled those who see him as a sceptic, satirist, and rationalist; but Euripides very often uses a contrast between the sordid scheming of men concerned with politics and public matters and a purer and more peaceful world associated with women and the young, with the wild countryside, and with sacred places remote from the bustle of the city.[19] Often it is the choral odes which, in the midst of the horrors of tragic action, lift the audience briefly on to another plane. In the *Heracles,* just before madness comes on Heracles and makes him slay his wife and children, the chorus sings an ode in praise of youth (637ff.): if the gods were wise according to human standards of wisdom, they would give a second youth to good men, and two lives, so that the good would stand out from the rest of mankind like stars shining among the clouds. But as it is, the only way of celebrating men's achievements is to wed victory, gift of the Graces, to music and song and the triumphal dances of young girls by temple doors. In the *Trojan Women* the departure of Astyanax to his death is followed by an ode in which the chorus still lament the woes of Troy, but bring into their lament the peaceful images of the island of Salamis where Telamon ruled, Ganymede's happy youth in Troy and the shining goddess Aurora, dawn, who fell in love with Tithonus. Sometimes it is the appearance of a *deus ex machina* at the end of the play—for example Castor and Pollux, the stars which guide sailors, in the *Electra*—which closes the action with an affirmation of the values of the religious plane. Their function is not to provide a retrospective justification of the mythical actions represented, nor to allow a maladroit dramatist to escape from an insoluble situation, but to point forward to the links with the mythical past which still exist in the Attica familiar to the audience; to link tragedy to ritual in a new way.

Euripides' plays help us to understand the increasing role given to the young in public ritual and the way in which great events of the historical or mythical past serve as symbols of the unity of the city and its glorious reputation. But they also illustrate the way in which religious experience was coming to be associated with private life and non-political contexts rather than with the rituals of the state. Eisenstadt's "tension between the transcendental and the mundane" (1982) is very clear here; and if sometimes the personalities and actions which make the tragic connection between the two bring salvation, as in the plays of self-sacrifice, at other times they bring only destruction *(Hippolytus, Bacchae)*. Places wholly devoted to worship, with no normal city life, have special religious power; as Lycurgus concerned himself with Delphi and the remote sanctuary of Amphiaraus, Euripides sets the *Ion* in Delphi and makes Andromache take refuge in a sanctuary outside the city. Sophocles' Oedipus dies in a sacred grove at Colonus, having in his lifetime been rejected from the *polis*. Images of the natural and mythical worlds are intertwined; for the ancient Greek (as for many modern Greek poets) the natural landscape was peopled with divine and semi-divine powers and punctuated with mythical landmarks (cf. Borgeaud, 1979; Veyne, 1983). Dionysiac imagery which associates women with religious possession and with wild mountain and forest landscapes appears in many plays, not only in the *Bacchae*. But women also represent peace as against war, continuity rather than conflict. In the *Hecuba* the story of the sack of Troy is told by the chorus as seen by a young wife whose husband had just finished celebrating the departure of the Greeks; she was just getting ready for bed, doing her hair in front of the mirror, when she heard the attack begin. Alcestis sacrifices herself to preserve her husband's 'house', his *oikos;*

as in Sophocles' *Antigone,* it is a woman who acts heroically in defence of the values of private life (Humphreys, 1983a, ch. 4). It is women who lament the dead and who remember that in the enemy's homeland there are other women weeping for *their* dead too (*Hecuba* 650–6); it is often women who tend the graves on fifth-century lekythoi. The rule against putting sculptured monuments on graves, which had been introduced about the end of the sixth century, broke down in the Peloponnesian War; families put up private monuments even to those who had died in war and had been buried in the state's graves in the Kerameikos (*I.G.* ii^2 6217); stelae showed families united, men and women, in an eternal private world (Humphreys, 1983a, ch. 5). The religious practices of Theophrastus' Superstitious Man are centred on the household and on his personal anxieties, and it is behaviour like his that Plato has in mind when he bans all private cults from his Cretan city in the *Laws* (909d–910e), particularly stressing the danger of exploitation by fraudulent 'experts'.

LOGIC AND INSPIRATION

The superstitious were reassured by the learned and quasi-scientific tone of the religious experts of the classical age: begging-priests and diviners, Plato says scornfully in the *Republic* (364b–365a), go to the houses of the rich, promising purification from misdeeds, ways of harming enemies by magic, and happiness in this life and the next, quoting a babble of books by Musaeus and Orpheus, children of the Moon and the Muses. The real development of the sciences of the irrational—magic, astrology, and other theories of the occult—belongs to the Hellenistic period; 'alien wisdom' imported from Persia, Egypt, and Babylonia contributed to their prestige (Momigliano, 1975; Dodds, 1951, 245–7; on the Greek contribution see Long, 1982, 165–70). But once the criticism of divination and magical practices as irrational had been formulated, it was inevitable that such forms of rationalization would follow. We need to distinguish more sharply than Dodds does between the process of rationalization, the aims of those involved in it, and the verification procedures they employed. On the one hand we have a dialectic between rationality and irrationality, in which each effort to fix the limits of rational thought produces fresh attempts to rationalize the irrational; on the other hand the struggle between critical enquiry and the attractions of an authority which fails to question its own assumptions.[20]

Rationalization was not, however, the only means by which the value of ideas which the philosophers derided as irrational could be defended. There was also a defence of the irrational as such: of the value of heightened 'poetic' language and of various forms of 'divine madness': Plato, in the *Phaedrus* (265b, cf. 244a–245a), refers to prophetic trances, poetic inspiration, Dionysiac possession, and love (cf. Brisson, 1974; Democritus B 17–18 D.-K.).

As I have already said, the idea of deities as psychological forces was present already in Homer (cf. Vernant, 1966). The introduction of the cult of Pan, the Arcadian god of 'panic' fear, to Athens after Marathon, whence it spread to the rest of Greece, does not represent a completely new way of thinking about the gods. However, in the success of this cult, which fused together the idea of a divine power as a psychological force, the association of divinity with remote, empty upland spaces, and the special authority of cult practices supposed to have ancient and primitive roots, we can perceive several of the main strands in classical religious thought (cf. Borgeaud, 1979).

A more conscious conception of surrender to paranormal psychological states as a form of religious worship seems to develop. The cave of Pan at Vari in Attica has a series of dedicatory inscriptions of the fifth century by Archedemos of Thera (*I.G.* i² 784–8), one of which calls him 'Archedemos ho nympholēptos'—'Archedemos the moonstruck', one might say in English. The clearest case of religious possession being associated with remote and wild areas occurs of course in the cult of Dionysus. Plato, in the *Laws* (815b–d), avoids laying down regulations for Bacchic rites and dances in which the dancers imitate nymphs and Pans and Sileni and Satyrs by defining them as "not belonging to the city", *ou politikon;* and it is significant that the chief participants in these orgiastic rites are supposedly women. Euripides' portrayal of maenads in the *Bacchae,* and other statements in our sources, probably owe more to fantasy than to experience; but from our point of view it does not matter what actually happened. What is significant is that male Athenians—vase-painters as well as playwrights and theatregoers—were deeply and ambiguously attracted to this idea of becoming totally possessed by a god during participation in his rites, of escaping completely from the framework of the *polis* and their everyday identities. Like Pentheus in the play, they both longed for the experience and feared it; they made it more acceptable to Greek ideas of decorum, and more plausible, by believing that such rites were only carried out by women, where no man could see them; but this belief in turn made their fantasies more exciting and the idea of Dionysiac madness more frightening, involving a more total loss of personality in which even gender identity would disappear.[21]

Not only were the maenads women; they were also believed to derive their rites from Thrace. What seemed strange and indecorous

in religious ritual was excused by giving it an origin either in a
barbarian region or in a particularly backward and 'aboriginal' part
of Greece, like Arcadia or Crete (Borgeaud, 1979). The foreign origin
of a god could excuse any peculiarities in the ritual performed in
his or her honour; gods, after all, have to be given the kind of
devotion they have come to expect. New foreign cults were also
introduced and in some cases given an official place in the city's
religious calendar: the Thracian goddess Bendis in c. 429, the Great
Mother (associated with both Crete and Asia), Adonis (Detienne,
1972), Isis, Aphrodite (Astarte) of Citium in Cyprus, Ammon. It was
Lycurgus himself who proposed that the traders of Citium should
be allowed to buy land to set up a temple to their native Aphrodite,
citing the similar permission given to Egyptian worshippers of Isis
as precedent (*I.G.* ii^2 337). While such proposals reflect the growing
size of the immigrant population in Athens, they also indicate a
growing taste for the exotic in religious ritual, a feeling that only
what was wild, strange, and altogether different from ordinary life
was truly religious. This is another indication of an increased feeling
of separation between religious and profane activity, an increased
tendency to regard religious activities as a matter of choice rather
than part of a taken-for-granted division of time into secular and
sacred periods; from this could develop also the idea of an existence
devoted wholly to religion, as portrayed in Euripides' *Ion* and—in
a sense—in the *Hippolytus.*

A similar attraction towards the deliberate valuation of the irrational can at times be seen in poetry. From its beginnings, Greek
poetry had encompassed a wide range of styles, from the formalized
literary dialect of epic to the use of direct everyday speech which
we find in many passages of Solon, Archilochus, or Alcaeus. Before
the late sixth-century poetry was, apart from a few brief phrases and
a small number of inscribed laws and treaties, the only form of
speech preserved in writing. The development of written prose as a
medium for the expression of individual world-views (as opposed
to collective decisions) raised questions about the relation between
prose and poetry which had not existed before. Their importance,
certainly, must not be overstressed: it is a delicate matter to distinguish the growth of a self-consciousness specific to poets from the
increasing tendency of all intellectuals at this time to dignify their
status and mission by claiming a special wisdom, *sophia* (cf. Humphreys, 1975, with bibliography cited there, plus Svenbro, 1976). An
oracular style appears in both Pindar and Heraclitus. Nevertheless
the Athenians themselves noted, in the fifth century, the appearance
of a 'dithyrambic' style confined to poetry and characterized by long
exotic-sounding words, onomatopoeia, far-fetched imagery and com-

pressed, enigmatic turns of sentence.[22] By the time of Aristophanes and Euripides this 'bardic' style had come to sound old-fashioned (*Clouds* 984–5) and pretentious. But for the generation of Pindar and Aeschylus it evidently made a significant contribution to poets' conceptions of their role. And although the dithyrambic style was mainly, as its name indicates, associated with choral poetry, other aspects of the deliberate exploration of the irrational in poetry became more deeply embedded in tragic action and lasted longer. Exotic effects were produced—and legitimized—by putting strange sounds into the mouths of foreigners (as in the *Persae*) or characters who are possessed, mad, or demonic (Cassandra, Orestes, the Furies). The more irrational, the more poetic. Many such passages of course were sung, not spoken, and the music would have heightened their effect. Euripides' tastes in coining new words were different, but he liked exotic musical effects as much as Aeschylus and was even more interested in the portrayal of different kinds of madness, and in experimenting with new kinds of music.[23]

CONCLUSION: FROM BREAKTHROUGH TO DIALOGUE

The internalization of the dialogue between the rational and the irrational in classical Greek culture becomes particularly transparent in Plato: the philosopher who considered mathematics almost the highest form of human thought yet could not express his philosophical ideas except by inventing his own myths (cf. Segal, 1978); the writer of genius who wanted to ban poetry from education; the founder of the Academy who became the patron saint of the Neo-Platonist mystics. No one was more profoundly conscious of the tensions which had been set up between the questions and methods of the new disciplines of rational thought and the other questions and ways of exploring the cosmos in thought which they brushed aside and left unanswered.

One of the main contributions of the Greek case to our general theme is, in my view, to bring into sharp focus the continuing debate which is implicit, but not perhaps sufficiently stressed, in the idea of a tension between mundane and transcendental levels of reality. Even when division of labour between different elite intellectual groups seems to succeed in averting conflict between them, some level of interaction in discourse can still be found; but in Greece what starts as polemic by those who consciously feel themselves to be voicing new ideas against the traditional beliefs of the rest of society turns rapidly into an internalised debate with which no serious thinker can avoid grappling. The 'breakthrough' of the new world-view was no easy victory, but the beginning of a long dialogue in which 'religion', as much as 'science' or 'philosophy', began to take on some of its modern contours.

CHAPTER 4

The Meaning of the Word σῶμα (Body) in the Axial Age: An Interpretation of Plato's CRATYLUS 400C

R. FERWERDA

Es ist der eigentliche Mensch, der, im Leibe gebunden und verschleiert, durch Triebe gefesselt, seiner selbst nur dunkel bewusst, nach Befreiung und Erlösung sich sehnt, und sie in der Welt schon erreichen kann.[1]

INTRODUCTION

The statement quoted above was made by Jaspers in his description of the characteristics of the "Achsenzeit," the Axial Age. According to his theory this age encompasses the years 800–200 B.C.E. and the actual or rather imaginary axis should be placed at about 500. Jaspers holds that, during that age, a fundamental change takes place in the manner in which man views not only his position in this world but also his own real being. The sentiment conveyed in our statement is, in his opinion, not to be found before the Axial Age. And in fact, when we turn our attention to Homer for instance, we discover that the Homeric man does not consider the soul to be bound by the body. During his lifetime man *was* his visible body δέμας *(demas)* and only when he *himself* was dead, his ψυχή ("soul"), a fluttering, unsubstantial shade or image, was sent to Hades *(Iliad* I, 3) and his σῶμα (corpse) was buried *(Iliad* VII, 19). The life of the soul in that netherworld was miserable. Achilles would rather be a slave on earth than a king of the dead *(Odyssey,* 11, 490). Just as the word σῶμα *(soma)* is not used in Homer for what we now call the *body,* but only for the *corpse,* the word ψυχή is not used for what we now call the *soul* but, besides *shade,* only for *life* in a broad sense as in *Odyssey* 3, 47: to hazard one's *soul* (= one's life). The same idea, however, can be expressed as well by: to hazard one's *heads* (*Odyssey* 2, 237). The faculties which we now call psychic, like wrath, desire, etc., are linked to parts of the body and, in a certain sense, *are* those parts (e.g. lungs or bile).[2] Man in the heroic age is essentially one, just as the universe he lives in is a monolithic whole to which even the immortal gods belong. The gods do not shrink back from taking part in man's activities, when the circumstances demand. There are no large states. People live usually in small communities which protect their well-being and which, occasionally, send them to war in order to secure their rights.

It is only after the Homeric age that man begins to question the existence and the power of the ancient gods and also the reliability of the traditional view of the world. Philosophers make inquiries into the metaphysical background of physical phenomena and begin to discover that there is a difference between the corporeal and the spiritual aspects of life. All kinds of sects create their own gods and strive for the salvation of that part of themselves which they now call *soul* (ψυχή). In the political field man starts to build larger states and to organize education, *inter alia* in order to create the management necessary to rule the states.

This development is by no means confined to Greece. We see it at the same time in China, in India, and in the Middle East, but it would be unwise to think that the Greeks had borrowed their new ideas from the other peoples. It is much more instructive to view it as a simultaneous process of growth of mankind in several areas of the world.[3]

So much for the general ideas of the Axial Age. It is not my bailiwick to elaborate these grand conceptions on a theoretical level. My contribution to this meeting will be a down-to-earth piece of philology. Its main entry is a discussion of Plato's *Cratylus* 400c, the translation of which runs as follows: "Some people maintain that the body (σῶμα) is the tomb (σῆμα) of the soul because the soul is buried there for this moment. And because, on the other hand, it indicates (συμαίνει) by that body whatever the soul indicates, it is also for that reason rightly called sign (σῆμα). However, it seems to me that Orpheus and his followers in the first place are the givers of that name (σῶμα) because, in their opinion, the soul is punished for which it is punished; the soul has the body as its enclosure in order to be saved (ἵνα σώζηται), just as a prison. As long as the soul pays its due, the σῶμα has that function for the soul, as its name indicates (viz. to save it). In the Orphic interpretation not even a letter needs to be changed".[4]

This passage has been taken from that part of the *Cratylus* in which Plato sums up more than a hundred more or less fantastic etymologies of Greek words. Most modern scholars[5] agree that Plato presents them tongue in cheek and that we are not to take them too seriously. So, what we will come up with after our discussion may be nothing more than the elusive and undependable result of a playful pastime.

THE TEXT

In order to understand fully what our *Cratylus* text has to say, I shall discuss it in four separate sections based on the four interpretations of the word σῶμα which Plato puts forward.

- A. According to some people the body is the *tomb* of the soul.
- B. According to the same people the body is the *sign* of the soul.
- C. According to Orpheus and his followers the body is the enclosure where the soul is *saved*.
- D. According to the same people the body is a kind of *prison* where the soul is punished.

A. *The body is the tomb of the soul*

Plato's *Cratylus* is possibly not the first occurrence in Greek literature of the association σῶμα–σῆμα. According to Clement of Alexandria (*Stromateis* III, 17) the Pythagorean Philolaus maintained that the ancient theologians and soothsayers believed that, in order to pay penalties, the soul was yoked to the body and was buried therein as in a grave.[6] He relates this statement in order to demonstrate the pessimistic attitude of the Greeks towards life on earth: the soul is bound in the body to pay some penalties for its sins. We find it also in another dialogue of Plato's (*Gorgias* 492e–493a) in the following discussion between Callicles and Socrates. Callicles wants the strong man not to repress his passions but to gratify them. That is living! For living without any desires cannot be an ideal life; on the contrary, it would make man a stone or a dead body. Socrates disagrees and says: "But life, as described by you, would be terrible as well. And then Euripides would be right in saying: 'Who knows whether living is not being dead, while being dead is living?' Perhaps we too are dead. I at least heard this from the wise men that now we are dead and that for us the body is a tomb."[7]

The third and last text of Plato where we might find an allusion to the idea that the soul is buried in the body is *Phaedrus* 250c. Plato says there that when we are in the company of Zeus, we are pure and (as most interpreters say) not buried (ἀσήμαντοι) in that which we carry around with us and call the body.[8]

So much for Plato. In later ages the formula was used and alluded to much more frequently.[9] And when we look closely at these texts, we discover that they have a very pessimistic ring, advocating a complete separation and even hostility between body and soul. For the users of the formula the soul is the "eigentlicher Mensch" of which Jaspers spoke, and its stay on earth, buried in the tomb of its body, is considered to be a dismal affair. If that was also true for the Platonic passages, our formula would be a splendid illustration of the fact that long before Plato's age the monolithic universe of Homer had completely fallen apart and the makers of this expression lived in a totally new atmosphere. However, there are a few stumbling blocks in our path which should prevent us from drawing that conclusion too rashly.

First, the playful and even ironic contexts of the *Cratylus* and the *Gorgias* passages invite us to ask whether the formula in its pessimistic sense expresses Plato's own view on the body-soul problem. Rather recently Professor De Vogel[10] argued that Socrates' and Plato's attitude towards life was not at all pessimistic. Time and again Plato has Socrates express his hope in life (*Apology* 41c8). Untimely departure from life is not only unlawful and impious (*Phaedo* 61cff.) but also painful (*Timaeus* 81c). However, I am not so certain as she is that this hope is based on a fundamental belief on Socrates' part in an afterlife of the soul, let alone in a former life. In his last speech to the judges Socrates proposes two possibilities: death is either a sort of sleep in which one has no sensations, or else it is, as people say, a change and migration of the soul from this to another place, where all the dead are. That would be a great blessing for one could meet there Orpheus and Musaeus and Hesiod and Homer and many others. However, to the description of this happy life he adds: "If that story is true" (*Apology* 40aff.). In my view, this addition expresses a certain diffidence about the religious beliefs of which he makes use,[11] and therefore I think that Socrates' optimism was (also) based on the glory that is life itself and our formula, of course, cannot be considered an adequate expression of that optimism. This seems to be confirmed by Plato himself. In the two cases where he mentions the whole formula he states explicitly that "some people" or "wise men" say that the body is a tomb. This qualification might imply that he dissociates himself from their view.

Second, the "some people" or "wise men" are generally believed to be the Pythagoreans. The line I quoted above from Clement of Alexandria apparently supports this assumption, because he says he found it in a book written by the Pythagorean Philolaus. However, we are not sure that the "theologians" of Philolaus are the Pythagoreans and, in addition to that, there are grave doubts whether this line is a literal quotation from Philolaus' book.[12] These doubts are inspired among other things by the fact that the pessimistic ring of the formula does not fit into what we know about the Pythagorean view of the world, which is built on the notion of kinship of life.[13] A spark of the divine lives in every being and our goal in life should be the assimilation to God. In this view the body is not necessarily hostile to the soul. In fact, there are Pythagorean sayings that the soul is the attunement of the body and that it is set in the body by means of number and an immortal and incorporeal harmony.[14] The soul even loves the body, because, without it, it can make no use of the senses (Claudianus Mamertus, *De Statu Animae* II, 3 [p. 120]). Besides, it is a well-known tenet of Pythagorean doctrine that man should take good care of his body so as to make sure that his soul stays in a healthy place.[15] This theory could hardly have been propounded by philosophers who contended that the body is the tomb of the soul.

Third, the history of the word σῶμα shows us that the meaning "tomb" is not the original meaning. When we first encounter the word in Homer (*Iliad* II, 814; VI, 419; *Odyssey* 2, 222 and 11, 175) it does not (negatively) indicate the grave in which the body is buried but (positively) the memorial sign (*Denkmal* in German) which is erected to keep the memory of the dead person alive.[16] Hesiod in his *Shield of Hercules* 477 even makes a distinction between σῆμα and τάφος (grave) and so does Plato in his *Phaedo* 81d. In later Greek this distinction disappears and the two words are used interchangeably. But it is wrong to suppose that in Pythagoras' time the word already conveyed the eerie meaning "grave" in which the body (or in our case the soul) was buried and lay dead.[17]

Fourth, if we accept for a moment that the word σῆμα means "grave," we cannot help raising the question what the meaning of the formula we are discussing could be. In the time between Homer and Pythagoras the ancients believed that the soul had the nature of air and that it was breathed in with air; it was, in that way, the force and source of life. In my view, it does not make sense to suppose that Pythagoras, who was well acquainted with these ideas about the soul, would have come to the conclusion that the soul was dead during our lifetime. If we go back further we see that for Homer the "soul" (ψυχή) is not active while man is alive. But that does not mean that it is dead. Modern anthropologists inform us that the Homeric soul should be called "free soul." In "primitive" tribes this "free soul" is thought to be inactive while we are awake and active while we are asleep.[18] We find the "free soul" also in post-Homeric times in Greece. Ancient authors transmit reports about supernatural powers of certain persons like Abaris, Zalmoxis, etc.[19] The learned world is in the habit of calling them "shamans" after the Siberian medicine men of that name. The part of the "shamans" that bestows the supernatural powers on them is called the "free soul." Pythagoras himself is, according to some scholars, also a kind of "shaman" and he owes much of his reputation to the activities of his "free soul." I think that it is impossible to assume that for a person with his characteristics the expression "the body is the *tomb* of the soul" would have meant anything.

In view of the foregoing stumbling blocks we may conclude that the interpretation of the σῶμα–σῆμα formula in the sense that the body is the tomb of the soul rests on very shaky grounds. I should, therefore, like to return now to our *Cratylus* passage and to the line I quoted from the *Phaedrus* in order to start the discussion of section B.

B. The body is the sign of the soul

The second explanation of the σῶμα–σῆμα formula Plato offers is that this σῶμα (body) is the means by which the soul indicates (σημαίνει) whatever it indicates. It is remarkable that Plato puts this one in the second place, because the idea expressed in it perfectly ties in with what he says about the function of language in general in other parts of the *Cratylus:* "By way of words we try to teach each other" (388b); "When you understand something, when I speak, something is made clear to you" (435a1). In other passages, for instance 393d, 394c, 436a–437a, Plato uses the verb σημαίνειν (to indicate) in the same sense as in our passage in connection with words. This is not a new development in the history of this word and the one from which it is derived (σῆμα). In Homer the word σῆμα is already used as the "sign" of a word (*Odyssey* 20, 111)[20] and we encounter it in other pre-Platonic authors as well in the same sense. So if Plato had put this interpretation first, it would have been in harmony with a long and solemn tradition and with his own way of reasoning in this dialogue. Moreover, if we now pose the question whether the Pythagoreans, to whom Socrates also attributes this interpretation, were familiar with ideas of "signification" in general, we may refer to the fact that the word μίμησισ (representation) played a very important role in their cosmology. According to Burkert[21] this representation between number and kosmos simply means that "das eine das andere deutet und erhellt." The Pythagoreans, as we have already seen, believed in the essential kinship of everything with everything and so everything could easily be called a representation or sign of everything else. For instance, the *daimones* can send signs of future disease and health to men.²² Therefore, if the Pythagoreans are the inventors of the formula, the interpretation "the body is the sign" is in perfect concordance with the rest of their philosophy.

Let us take a look now at the *Phaedrus* passage. Usually the word ἀσήμαντος which Plato uses there is translated as "not buried." But there are no other places in Greek literature where it has that meaning except Damascius, *De Principiis* 161, which is an allusion to our text. The real meaning of the word is "unmarked," "unintelligible," "without significance." That translation makes a very good sense in the *Phaedrus* passage: "In the company of Zeus we are pure and not marked by what we call the body." There is no indication whatsoever that Plato had something else in mind, and the real meaning of the text is also reflected in an interesting passage in Plotinus' *Enneads* IV, 3, 30, 43–45: "Since we have seen the body and know that it is ensouled we say that it has a soul." Here also the body is the "sign," the "proof" that the soul exists. So, we may conclude, even late Platonic writers harked back to the ancient custom of interpreting the body as a sign of the soul.

In view of all this I think that "sign" is the only genuine meaning of σῆμα here and that, for a reason I shall explain below, Plato deliberately wished to force the other one ("tomb") upon the Pythagoreans by placing it first.

C. The body is the enclosure where the soul is saved.

The third part of the *Cratylus* text refers to Orpheus and his followers as the inventors of the name σῶμα. "The soul has the body as an enclosure in order to be saved (ινα σώζηται)." Our immediate question is of course: "To be saved from what?" I do not intend to look afresh into the much debated problem of the Orphic doctrine of the "Seelenwanderung" and of what befalls the soul in that process. Ever since Wilamowitz²³ said "Eine orphische Seelenlehre soll erst einer nachweisen" the scholarly world has been rather sceptical about the Orphics having ever had clear-cut ideas about the soul. However, rather recently there was found a tiny piece of evidence of a "Seelenlehre" of the Orphics. In Olbia (South Russia) small plates of bone have been excavated in the central "temenos" of the old city. One of them has the inscription "Orphikoi," another "psyche." I agree with Burkert²⁴ that these plates do not contain an Orphic doctrine of the soul, but they seem to indicate, to say the least, that Orphics did think about the soul. From other sources we know that those who had established rites of initiation believed that the uninitiated soul would lie in the mud when it came to Hades, and most scholars think that these rites are connected with Orpheus.[25] If this assumption is correct, we have to conclude that according to the Orphic doctrine there was suffering in Hades but that the soul had a chance, during its stay in the body, to safeguard itself from it. The "punishment" our text speaks about would then point to the ascetic life which the initiated had to live on earth. But this ascetic life was not designed for the purpose of punishment for past sins (whatever that means). There is strong evidence that in the first place it prepared the believers for the liberating joys of the religious festivals.[26] These festivals took place on earth (and not in the afterlife) and were very joyful, alacritous events. That means that the stay of the soul in the body was not so unpleasant after all and consequently that the body could be called the (protecting) enclosure (περίβολος) of the soul which would save it.

It is true that the word περίβολος is often translated here as the enclosing structure which prevents the soul from leaving the body, and this sense of the word is not uncommon in Greek. In Plato's *Theaetetus* 197c for instance it definitely has the meaning "cage." But in other texts we also find the connotation of "protecting structure" which safeguards a city for example from being invaded and destroyed by enemies (Plato, *Laws* 759a).[27] The ambiguity of this word is something which Plato seems to like and to play with, especially in texts where the reader craves clarity.[28] The only thing we can do then is to look for other passages which can shed light upon the general idea of our text. Fortunately, Plato offers some help for the right interpretation in his *Timaeus* 73d: "The Demiurge built the body around the soul for a shelter." A little further on (74a) he even uses the word περίβολο ς itself: "For preserving (διασώζων!) the seed (one of the places where the soul is built into) the Demiurge closes it in with a ring-fence (περίβολο ς) of stony substance." In the same dialogue (81a) he argues that an untimely departure from this shelter is painful for the soul. I think that these texts give sufficient support to the idea that, in Plato's view, the body is meant to protect the soul rather than to punish it. That means that he understood the word περίβολο ς of our text in the sense of "protecting structure" that would keep the soul safe. This is in complete concordance with the view of the Orphics—and not only of them. We find a similar idea in an early Christian author. When Origen (*On Principles* 2,10,3) wants to describe the relationship between reason and body, he says: "Ratio quae semper in substantia corporis salva est" (The reason is safe in the body). Obviously the expression "salva est" is the translation of the Greek σώζεται.

At the end of our passage Plato has Socrates say that he likes the Orphic interpretation of σῶμα even better than the Pythagorean one, because not even a letter of the word need to be changed. He is, methinks, also happy with it because it harmonizes perfectly with his own view which, later on, he propounded in his *Timaeus.*

D. The body is a kind of prison where the soul is punished.

In the preceding section we discovered that the word περίβολοις not only had the meaning of "enclosing structure or cage" but also of "protecting structure" and we came to the conclusion that, in the *Cratylus,* Plato had the second meaning in mind. But in our discussion of the phrase we left out two Greek words: "The soul has the body as an enclosure in order to be saved, *just as a prison* (δεσμωτηρίου εἰκόνα). Does that addition not topple our hypothesis that the body is a protecting structure? In order to answer this question I would like to draw attention to a passage of Plato's *Phaedo* (62b) where he also uses a word which is mostly translated as "prison." Socrates says there that the secret doctrine that we, men, are in a kind of prison (φρουρᾷ), and must not free ourselves or run away, seems to be weighty and not easy to understand. However the word φρουρά which I translated as "prison" (following Fowler) does not necessarily have that meaning. First, it is a look-out or a watch (Aeschylus, *Agamemnon* 2; Herodotus 2, 30; Euripides, *Andromache* 1099). Second, it is a garrison (Aeschylus, *Agamemnon* 301; Herodotus, 6,26). Third, L.S.J. quotes our text and Plato, *Gorgias* 525a, as passages where it has the meaning "prison." It is evident that in the *Gorgias* φρουρά is a prison or guarded place where the souls are sent in order to be punished for sins committed in their previous life. However, that prison is not on this earth but an abode in Hades and, for that reason, strikingly different from the *Phaedo* "prison." Nevertheless, it appears that most scholars of our time believe that also in the *Phaedo* the φρουρά is a prison, especially because Socrates says that we must not set ourselves free or run away.[29] I do not intend to reexamine every facet of the complicated problem here but I want to point out two things which are important for our discussion.

First, Socrates does not say that the soul is in the prison of the body, but that the secret doctrine tells us that *we* are, on this earth, in a kind of guarded place. In this respect there is a slight difference with the *Cratylus* text. Second, he states that it would be unwise for a wise man to kill himself because he knows that there the gods are watching over him, the best overseers in the world, and that by setting himself free he would not be able to take care of himself in a better way than they do now. When I look at Socrates' elaborations I cannot convince myself that he understood the word φρουρά as "prison." For him it must be a "guarded place" where we are protected from the onslaught of evil things. It sounds rather optimistic and it lacks all the dark connotations writers of later times have put in it.[30] Since the *Phaedo* text, in contrast to the *Gorgias* passage,[31] is generally held to be based on Orphic doctrines,[32] it lends some support to what we found in the foregoing section, *viz.* that the Orphics considered our life on earth to be not as hopeless as most people maintain.

Let us return to the *Cratylus* text. The transition from περίβολο s to δεσμωτήριον (prison) is a very easy one but not accounted for by what we know about the Orphics. Moreover, it appears that Plato himself did not support either the idea that our soul is kept here as in a prison. Just as in the case of the "tomb," that is what authors of later ages thought he said and they used those images freely to illustrate their own pessimistic view on life. But that does not prove of course that Plato harboured that same view. However, the question remains to be answered why Plato endeavoured then to force this idea on the Orphics just as he forced the idea of "body-tomb" on the Pythagoreans. It is not easy to find the reasons for this behaviour since he does not mention them unequivocally. But there are some hints in his dialogues, in relation to both sects, which, I hope, will give us a clearer view on the question. I would like to examine them now in a more detailed fashion.

Plato's attitude towards Pythagoras and Orpheus

Usually Plato speaks highly of Pythagoras and his followers. As a matter of fact their philosophy is difficult to separate from Plato's own. His passion for mathematics as a glimpse of eternal truth, his talk of the kinship of all nature, his choice of musical terminology to describe the state of the soul and especially the mathematico-musical account of the composition of the world-soul, his astronomical theories—all these are evidence of a close affinity between him and Pythagoras.[33] In addition to that he openly shows his admiration for the way of life Pythagoras preached (*Rep.* 600b).

The same applies to Orpheus. Plato admires him as a singer and a poet, just as he holds Homer as a poet in high esteem (*Ion* 536b and *Laws* 829d–c), and Socrates would fain meet with Orpheus after his death in Hades (*Apology* 41a). In all his dialogues he also shows an interest in the speculations of the Orphic theologians which was near akin to reverence. They not only served to illustrate his points but they also affected the form which his way of reasoning took.[34]

However, there are also other and less favourable aspects in his dealing with Pythagoras and Orpheus. Let us look again at the only text where he mentions Pythagoras' name (*Rep.* 600ab). In discussing Homer he asks there: "But if Homer never did any public service, was he privately a guide or teacher of any? Had he in his lifetime friends who loved to associate with him and who handed down to posterity an Homeric way of life, such as was established by Pythagoras who was especially beloved for this reason and whose followers are to this day conspicuous among others by what they term the Pythagorean way of life?" Burkert[35] argues that this text is quite important because it links Pythagoras' fate with Plato's own. Plato, in fact, would have loved to be the leader in his city, but when this proved to be impossible he decided to become a teacher of private citizens and therefore he founded the Academy. I am not sure that Burkert is right in this respect. I think that the text contains a hidden reproach in that Plato implicitly blames Pythagoras for not having done any public service. At first sight this may sound strange, since we know from many sources that Pythagoras did partake in public life in Croton and that the Pythagoreans were often politically the most influential groups in their cities.[36] Therefore I need to make a few remarks on Pythagorean politics here. In the first place, as professor De Vogel[37] has pointed out, the situation of the Pythagorean Society with respect to political activities was not the same at all times.

In the middle of the fourth century B.C.E. the so-called group of Three Hundred could scarcely avoid having some of the functions in their cities. They may even have wielded political power as a group. In Pythagoras' own time there was no such organized group, but it is unimaginable that Pythagoras himself or some of his followers would not have had political influence in the cities they lived in. This political influence was, however, not the first goal of Pythagoras' teaching but only a secondary consequence.[38] Plato, on the other hand, contended that the government of a city should be entrusted to a philosopher because he possessed the best abilities to handle it (*Rep.* VI, 484b, 487b and *passim*). Therefore he must have looked askance at Pythagoras' attitude and must have considered his point of view as a lack of responsibility and as a serious shortcoming which also diminished the value of the rest of his philosophy. Ultimately it proved to be too esoteric in Plato's opinion, and in order to emphasize that aspect he thought fit to attribute to them the idea that the body was the tomb of the soul.

There may have been also another reason for Plato's reluctance to acknowledge Pythagoras' political interest. Since Aristotle it has been argued that Plato had taken (part of) his political theories from

Pythagoras.[39] This may be true, for both philosophers considered aristocracy as the highest form of government (Plato, *Rep.* VI, 497aff., and Diogenes Laertius, *Vita Pythagorae* VIII, 3). But Plato's general unwillingness to admit his indebtedness towards his predecessors is a well-known fact. For instance, he never mentioned Democritus' name in his dialogues and gossip has it that he even wished to burn his books, because he disliked his theories and did not want anybody to discover how much he had borrowed from Democritus.[40] Therefore I presume that Plato deliberately played down the political aspects of Pythagoras' doctrine and enhanced the esoteric side of it in order to disguise the close relationship between their theories.

Plato also had second thoughts about Orpheus and again this is revealed by comparing his case with Homer's. Plato admired Homer as a poet but he did not admit him in his ideal state (*Rep.* 595b), because Homer practised an imitative art which was liable to infect whole societies (*Rep.* 424c). For the same reason he must have been loath to admit there the effeminate harp-player Orpheus, who, moreover, had shown no spirit in his attempts to recover Eurydice from Hades (*Symposium* 179d). Elsewhere, Plato speaks in even less favourable terms about (Orphic) charlatans and diviners who brag about influence on the gods which, in fact, they do not possess.[41] In addition to that their political activities and interests were nil[42] and their main concern was the esoteric and the initiation into secret mysteries. They felt that initiation itself was the highest goal a man could strive for, whereas Plato believed that the truly initiated, the philosopher, should be willing to take the role of a leader in his city.

This lack (or supposed lack) of interest in political affairs is, in my view, the main reason why Plato does not always speak highly of the two sects. That is why he deliberately exaggerates the esoteric aspect of their doctrines by implying that the Pythagoreans consider the body as the tomb (and not the sign) of the soul and that the Orphics say that the soul is in the body *as in a prison*. The transitions he makes (sign → tomb and protective structure → enclosing structure → prison) are small and hardly perceptible as far as the expressions themselves are concerned. But what they caused in the minds of Plato's audience was disastrous. The slight but suggestive changes virtually inverted the meaning of the expressions and threw an unfavourable light on the whole doctrine of the people in question. But that was not the only result. Most readers of his dialogues came to believe not only that the expressions "tomb" and "prison" were a part of the esoteric doctrines of Pythagoras and Orpheus, but also that Plato himself used them to reveal his own innermost feelings of what life really was. We have already seen that there is no reason to draw that conclusion. Plato is eager to stress everywhere the fact that man is a συναμφότερον of body and soul and that we should take care of both.[43] But his ambiguous handling of our expressions in the *Cratylus* and elsewhere backfired in later ages in a way he could never have anticipated: in late antiquity Plato was considered a staunch defender of the worthlessness of life on earth.[44] Only Plotinus in his *Enneads* went out of his way to smooth down the harsh meaning of expressions like "prison of the soul," and "fall of the soul."[45] But the harm had been done, and even in our time people eagerly borrow Plato's "pessimistic" images and do not shrink back from enhancing their crudity by adding impalatable details which we look for in vain in the extant Greek literature.[46]

CONCLUSION

We may now pose the question what the examination of the ambiguous and elusive *Cratylus* text and its background has taught us about the Axial Age. My answer is that in several aspects it reflects admirably the seething and brewing of the arrival of a new era.

I. Pythagoreans and Orphics alike advocated a certain separation between body and soul, but they surely did not consider the body a worthless and abject entity in which the soul is fettered, craving for liberation. From other sources we also know that they organized a new way of life for private citizens in which new gods played a more important role than the Homeric Zeus family. Though they (at least the Pythagoreans) did sometimes partake in public life, politics were not the most important issue of their view of the world.

II. Plato knew their ideas and he agreed (more or less) with their views on the body-soul problem. But his interest was much more focused on political consequences of philosophical and religious theories. He shared this interest with most philosophers (and historians) who came after him and their theoretical elaborations laid the basis for the constitution of the empires of later ages.

III. Since Plato himself took an active part in the gradual development of new ideas, he may not always have been able to take a sufficiently distant view of what really happened in circles with which he was not intimately acquainted. But this was not the main reason why he offered a rather distorted image of the view of the Orphics and Pythagoreans on the body-soul problem. Just as, for mainly political reasons, he did not mention Democritus' name in dialogues and even wanted to burn his books, his misgivings about the (supposed) lack of political interest of the Orphics and Pythagoreans prompted him to disparage their other theories.

IV. This disparagement had an unexpected consequence. For authors of the beginning of our era the separation between body and soul had become final and the body played the role of absolute evil. The body *was* the prison, the cage, the tomb in which the soul was bound and buried, and the main striving of the soul should be its liberation from the earthly fetters which prevented it from flourishing in higher regions. These authors freely borrowed the expressions Plato had coined, and they never asked whether Plato had really believed in their appropriateness. Jaspers' description of "der eigentliche Mensch" in the Axial Age which is used as a motto of this article is much more applicable in late antiquity, and the use people made at that time of the expressions of the *Cratylus* text illustrates his ideas in a sublime fashion.

I hope that my microscopic investigation of our text has provided sufficient evidence of the gradual development of new ideas in the awakening Axial Age and also of the way people evaluated it who lived closer to it than we do.

PART II

The Origins of the Axial Age in Ancient Israel—with a Comparative Look at Assyria

INTRODUCTION:

The Axial Age Breakthrough in Ancient Israel

S.N. EISENSTADT

I

The specific cultural orientations and structure of elites of Ancient Israel—the first monotheistic civilization, as well as the conditions under which they have crystallized—were in many ways opposite from those of Ancient Greece.

The development of the Ancient Israelite Axial Age was connected with a rather different mode of breaking down of the tribal community and of reconstruction of collectivities and of new forms of trust and solidarity with new institutional patterns, and these were also connected with different sets of geopolitical conditions than those that developed in Ancient Greece.

The breaking-up of the relatively closed ascriptive tribal, and to some degree territorial, groups was characterized in Ancient Israel by several features. One such feature was the development of a relatively high level of technology, the great structural heterogeneity of the different tribal, local communities and the groups of peasants, nomads and urban dwellers, the continuous encounters among them in the same or in ecologically similar settings and the continuous process, within such settings, of social differentiation and tensions. A second feature was the fact that these groups were bound in some common bonds not entirely embedded within any one of them. These common bonds were evident in the crucial importance of the all-Israelite, as opposed to all-tribal, orientations. A third factor was the fact that these common bonds were not organized within any clear-cut, fully organized political or religious frameworks, with a consequent initial lack of any continuous, single organizational or even symbolic focus or location for such common orientations.

127

Finally, there was the absence of compact political boundaries and the continuously volatile micro- and macro-political ecological (international) settings. The micro setting was, of course, within Palestine itself, that of repeated encounters with other settled and migratory peoples; the macro setting was that of Palestine, perennially the crossroads of great empires of antiquity. The net result of this volatility was the continuous fluidity and openness of political boundaries; the constant flow and mobility of people; difficulties in the maintenance of a stable, compact political entity and even of distinct cultural identity.

II

It was in the context of these processes that there developed the specific cultural orientations, types of elites, and institutional features which were characteristic of the early Israelite society.

The major characteristic of the cultural orientations that developed in Ancient Israel was first of all the emergence of the monotheistic conception of God, of a transcendental God who created the Universe and imposed His will and law on it, who calls many nations to account to His precepts, and who recognizes the people of Israel as having entered into a specific contractual relation with Him, not because He is a tribal deity, but because He is a universal God who has chosen the people of Israel with whom to enter into a covenant. This transcendental concept resulted in a *partial* de-ritualization and demagicization of the cult, to a legitimation of the cult in terms of higher transcendental orientation—a process which has some interesting parallels to what happened in India—and led to the development of universalization and rationalization of the religious orientations and a strong emphasis on the ethical dimension of the religious experience.

In close relation to this orientation there developed a special type of multiplicity of cultural and religious orientations—cultic, with many ritual prescriptions; and a strong emphasis on legal rules and ethical injunctions. Each of these cultural and religious orientations could probably be found among many of the neighboring peoples, but the combination of all of these was very probably unique to Israel. This uniqueness was connected to the conception of one God—in the beginning probably a tribal or national God—of a type which mutually can be also probably found in many other civilizations, but which became here transformed, as indicated above, into a more dynamic conception of a transnational God. This conception was also closely related to the conception of the relationship between God and the Israeli tribes not as captive but "contractual," and which focused around the covenant with God as being the central focus of the tribal confederation.

III

Closely connected to these orientations were the characteristics of the special type of the carriers of models of cultural order, of the transcendental vision of religious orientations such as the Priests, the Levites, and above all the Prophets, as well as of different political leaders, such as various tribal leaders, the Judges, later the Kings, all of which were most active in the construction of the trans-tribal centers.

Three aspects of such carriers were of special importance: first, their multiplicity; second, the fact that they were not embedded in the various ascriptive tribal or territorial units, but were symbolically and organizationally autonomous, being recruited and defined by themselves and accepted by other parts of the population in autonomous terms as representing visions and values which were not part of the primordial symbols of the local or tribal groups, but which were yet accepted among these groups; third, the fact that these elites, who were the major carriers of common political, national and religious bonds, seemed to cut across all the tribes and be at least potentially common to all or at least to several of them.

The special characteristics of these elites shaped the unique character of the Israelite centers which distinguished them from those of Ancient Greece. Some of the characteristics of these centers can also be found in other tribal federations in the Near East or Africa, but some are specific to the Israelite situation, and it is these that are most important for our analysis. Although they are most clearly evident in the pre-monarchic period, many such characteristics persisted even into the period of the Monarchy.

The first such characteristic of the centers was that almost all of them constituted, within their broader setting, structural enclaves which were often, especially before the era of the Monarchy, but to some degree even during that era (especially in the Kingdom of Israel), short-lived and did not develop into permanent, distinct, ecological settings with continuous populations and identities of their own.

Second, even when these centers became more unified under the Monarchy—especially the Davidic one—they were always composed of several structural elements which rarely coexisted peacefully or merged into relatively homogeneous groups and elites. Between these different elites within these centers, there developed continuous tensions and conflicts—often focused around different conceptions of the nature and function of the centers in relation to the other groups in the society. In fact, no cohesive ruling class developed; rather there emerged embryonic components of such an elite which, probably only in the periods of consolidation of the Monarchy, crystallized into a relatively full-fledged cohesive group.

It was the continuous combination of and confrontation among the major structural-institutional characteristics; structural homogeneity, continuous differentiation and conflict among various social groups within a framework of common, but not fully fixed and crystallized bonds; the volatility and heterogeneity of centers; the emergence of multiple carriers of cultural models; the concomitant restructuring of common bonds between the leaders and the people often leading to diverse social movements; and finally the emerging religious orientations—that provided the setting for the breakthrough to a conception of transcendental God and within which this conception, with its specific institutional derivatives, became institutionalized.

IV

It was in connection with these developments that there crystallized some of the specific Ancient Israeli and later Jewish institutional symbolic responses to the basic problems of the Axial Age civilizations, i.e., of the definition of the relations between universalistic and primordial orientations; the concomitant definition of the civilizational collectivity, the specification of the major institutional arenas in which the predominant transcendental visions had to be implemented.

Thus, first of all, it was the socio-political arena that was designated as the major arena of implementation of the transcendental vision. This did not lead, however, as occurred partially in Greece and above all in China, to a semi-sanctification of this arena—although needless to say it generated some potentialities in this direction. Rather it connoted a very strong drive to mould this arena according to the ethical, religious, and legal components of this vision.

Interestingly enough this orientation became connected in Jewish history, because of the specific historical and geopolitical conditions in which this history developed, with a very marked fragility of its political center or centers.

This combination of the view of the sociopolitical sphere as the major arena of implementation of the transcendental vision, with the fragility of political center, gave rise later to some of the most important aspects of Jewish history and dynamics.

V

Similarly there developed here a rather special type of solution of the relations between the primordial and the universalistic orientations inherent in any Axial Age vision and the concomitant relations between Israel and other nations.

The specific Jewish solution was, apparently from the very beginning of what became Jewish history, of what indeed characterized the history of different Israeli tribes as Jewish history, in marked contrast to what later evolved in Islam and other civilizations. The primordial, i.e., "ethnic," "national," and political, symbols were evaluated positively in terms of universal religious orientations. The former were continuously incorporated into the latter, giving rise to continuous interweaving of these different symbols; each of these types of symbols was defined in terms of each other while not losing their own autonomy, thus giving rise to continuous tension between them with respect to the concrete manifestations of each and their relative importance.

Thus, from the very beginning of the specific Jewish historical experience, there developed a continuous tension between first, "ethnic" identity based upon a strong historical consciousness; second, a very strong primordial kinship identity expressed in the symbolism of descent from Abraham, Isaac, and Jacob; third, a political identity, often, but not always, coextensive with the first two; and last, a religious-cultural identity couched in potentially universalistic terms.

These varied components of collective identity combined in several ways with the cultic, legal, or prophetical-ethical elements of the specifically religious orientations. Such different combinations, which contain various religious "contents" and emphasize different elements of the collective identity, were continuously articulated by the religious and political elites and by the different carriers of models of cultural and political order mentioned above, giving rise to continuous tension between these different carriers and patterns of symbols which they represented. Whatever the differences between them, these tensions were worked out in the context of attempts to define the symbolic institutional boundaries of the Jewish nation in relation to other nations and to demarcate the parameters of collective identity in terms of its various components and of the basic religious orientations.

Thus Jewish history has been characterized by continuous attempts and internal struggle to combine the establishment of the boundaries of a unique cultural identity with efforts to establish a strong connection to other peoples and cultures—all these related to efforts to

which no single solution was ever achieved during any single period
of ancient Jewish history.

This tendency toward collective distinctiveness was accompanied
by a strong ambivalent attitude toward other nations and cultures
and tendencies to segregation from them. Such an attitude was rooted
in Judaism's claim to universalism in that it was the first monotheistic
religion, in its constant and unfriendly contact with other cultures,
and in its attempts to separate itself from them in universal terms
by claiming to transcend their particularistic religious symbols. Due
to these factors, a continuous tension between the universalism of
the religious orientation and the particularism of a primordial national community which defined itself by differentiating itself ideologically and symbolically from its neighbors through the combination of religious and primordial symbols was built into the
construction of Jewish identity from the beginning of Jewish history.

This segregation entailed the continuous combination of the symbols of primordial, ethnic, national, political, and religious identity.
But because of the growing tendencies toward universalism and the
strong competition of other religions, this solution was not purely
particularistic but contained a certain strong universalistic orientation, in contrast to the solution developed for instance by the
Samaritans. It exhibited strong tendencies to proselytization which
often were in tension with the more particularistic primordial emphases and which the sages and sects tried to resolve through their
own mode of rationalization of religious contact.

Thus even later on, in the medieval period, the Jewish people
were not just, as Weber put it, a religious pariah community or
people. Indeed many of the characteristics of a pariah people, as
depicted by Weber, were not peculiar in this period to the Jews;
they were applicable during that historical period to many nations
and religions. In a sense they were the rule within most of the
empires of antiquity as was also the experience of dispersion.

But above all it would be wrong to see in this type of situation
the most important aspect of their relationship to the international
environment.

Unlike many other minority peoples, the Jews attempted not only
to maintain some place for themselves in the tumultuous political
reality of that period, but also developed and continued claims of
the universal validity of their religion and tradition.

In other words, what was characteristic of the Jewish situation
during this period—and later on—was the combination of a precarious political and economic situation with attempts at intensive
participation in the political and cultural life of the period. They
attempted to forge out for themselves an identity and institutional

frameworks which would at the same time sustain some of their claims to universal validity.

It was also these factors that made it possible for cultural and religious innovation and change in the basic institutional mould to become combined with the maintenance of older symbols of collective identity; this was so even when the content of the symbols changed, usually through incorporation of the older symbols within the new ones.

VI

The early as well as the later Israeli cases have been compared here with another closely related society—that of Ancient Mesopotamia—represented in this volume in the two papers of Professors Machinist and Tadmor.

Their papers indicate first that there developed in Ancient Mesopotamia cultural orientations relatively close to those that developed in Ancient Israel, namely of a strong, almost transcendental God, and of an incipient responsibility of rulers to serve the mighty God.

Second they indicate that despite all these incipient developments there did not develop in Ancient Mesopotamia those breakthroughs which were characteristic of full-fledged ancient civilizations—i.e., not only of a strong God but of a truly transcendental one, the creator of the Universe which stands beyond it, as well as of full subservience of the rulers to a God who is not only a stronger being but as bearer or epitome of a higher vision, different from the more mundane role of the rulers.

Third they point out the crucial structural element which is closely connected with the lack of full development of such orientations— namely the lack of autonomous intellectual elites (prophets or autonomous priests).

Specialists in many of the more concrete or technical activities— ritual, divination, or even in giving advice to rulers—abounded in Ancient Mesopotamia and developed into relatively distinct groups, above all different groups of scribes and specialists in divination.

They all were however fully embedded either within the older primordial tribal units or within the "patrimonial" royal domains, and it was such embedment that constituted the major difference and the crucial difference from the situation in Ancient Israel.

VII

The problem of the exact conditions which generated this specific mode of development in Ancient Mesopotamia, as compared with

Ancient Israel, is rather difficult, but some indications may be not out of place.

In common with the early Israeli experience, the geopolitical situation of Ancient Mesopotamia was characterized by movements of population and by continuous waves of conquest and settlement. Yet some very important differences from the Israeli historical and geopolitical experience can be indicated. First was the fact that all these movements in Ancient Mesopotamia took place in a relatively less central international geographical location, not so much at an international crossroad of empires and in close relation with internal heterogeneity as in Ancient Israel. Second these movements of conquest and settlement here took place much more within the framework of relatively more homogeneous, less differentiated even if quite broad units, evincing many congruent characteristics. Third the pattern of settlement was based here, in comparison with Ancient Israel, on more compact, tribal, and supertribal units, with relative territorial closure.

Although these indications are rather preliminary, they do provide an approach to understanding the different modes of development in Ancient Israel and Ancient Mesopotamia.

CHAPTER 5

Myth and Reality
in Ancient Israel

BENJAMIN UFFENHEIMER

It is the central contention of this study that the essential factor
molding the spiritual world of the Bible, the Apocrypha, Rabbinic
literature, and emergent Christianity was mythical thought and
expression. In order to avoid any misunderstanding, let me emphasize
from the outset that my own approach to the problem of myth is
diametrically opposed to that of the school known as "myth and
cult," which claims that the Bible contains a Hebrew variation of
the "cult pattern" common to the ancient Near East.[1] In this view,
the absence of pagan mythology, which is one of the outstanding
features of biblical literature, or the paucity of hints at such material,
is "filled in" by pagan myths stemming from Mesopotamia, Egypt,
or Canaan. According to S. Mowinckel, the most eloquent representative of this school, one of Israel's central cultic institutions is
the so-called "Enthronement Feast of Yahweh."[2] This hypothetical
feast is a bold combination of Mesopotamian, Canaanite, and biblical
material. Moreover, the historical authenticity of the biblical material
is, according to these scholars, corroborated by its reinterpretation
in the spirit of paganism. The present writer rejects this method
because of its utter disregard of the philological discipline, essential
for an adequate appraisal of the sources.

In the following study, we intend to summarize the nature of
biblical monotheistic myth and the main differences between it and
pagan myth, which is part and parcel of ancient Near Eastern culture.
In the second part of the study, we shall sketch the political and
social impact of this myth on the culture of ancient Israel. This
analysis will also demonstrate the common basis shared by the Bible
and the literature of the Second Temple period, excluding nascent
Christianity which, by incorporating the incarnation myth from an-

cient Near Eastern religions and by accepting the dogma of the trinity, made far-reaching concessions to paganism.

This writer's approach to the problem of myth has been influenced by Martin Buber, who, at the beginning of the century, ushered in a new anti-rationalistic trend in the study of Judaism in his famous lecture, "Vom Mythus der Juden" [The Myth of the Jews] (1913). The target of the young Buber's polemics in this speech was Hermann Cohen,[3] who symbolized the rationalistic and spiritualizing tendencies within the nineteenth-century "Wissenschaft vom Judentums" (modern "Science of Judaism") which had defined Judaism as an a-mythical spiritual entity, shaped over the period of two thousand years since the destruction of the Temple in the timeless spheres of eternity, unhampered by the vicissitudes of external history.

Buber's new approach to this problem was closely connected with the rise of Zionism, the movement of Jewish national revival, at the beginning of this century. The representatives of this movement, which sought its way back into history, cherished the concrete, living elements of Jewish folk tradition, which had nothing in common with the abstract, *a priori* depictions of Judaism which were common in nineteenth-century Western European Judaic scholarship. Indeed, Buber himself was fascinated by the living faith of Hassidism, which was deeply steeped in this folk tradition. Again, he brought to our consciousness the biblical utopian myth of the kingdom of God and what it stands for. In the wake of Buber, Leo Baeck drew our attention to Jewish mysticism; but it remained for Gershom Scholem's outstanding scholarly achievements in the history of Jewish faith to reveal the crucial importance of Kabbalah and Jewish mysticism.

Thus, these scholars opened new vistas for an adequate reassessment of biblical faith and Judaism. Indeed, the problem of myth occupied a central place in all phases of Buber's thought.[4] Nevertheless, he never made any statement defining the differences between pagan and monotheistic myth. Precisely this will be the topic of the present study, within the framework of Bible and Second Commonwealth literature.

Kaufmann's Assumptions

The point of departure for our discussion will be provided by the two central assumptions of Yehezkel Kaufmann's monumental work, *Toldoth ha-Emuna ha-Yisra'elith* (History of the Religion of Israel), a major Jewish contribution to modern Bible research.[5] Kaufmann in effect translated the inherent rationalism of nineteenth-century research on Judaism, as defined and reflected in Hermann Cohen's philosophical work, *Religion der Vernunft aus den Quellen des Ju-dentums,*[6] into the language of historical-philological exegesis. In contradiction to Cohen's spiritualist and universalist interpretation of prophetic and Jewish religion, Kaufmann strove to restore to the Bible the concrete basis it had been stripped of.

His central assumptions, to be discussed below, are:

1. That monotheism is anti-mythological by definition and that all myths are pagan because they deal with the life stories and fate of the gods. The absolute otherness of the God of Israel and His transcendent nature preclude all possibility of weaving any kind of mythology about Him.

2. That monotheism cannot be explained by the principle of evolution, as Protestant scholarship in the last century would have it. Rather, it constitutes a unique, intuitive idea which forged the spirit and nature of the nation from its very beginnings.[7] It is in itself the creation of Israel's national spirit, which was molded by the work of Moses, who elim-inated the last vestiges of pagan-mythological belief from the nation's mind. Because of its monotheistic mentality, Israel was unable to value the mythological foundation of polytheism and regarded this worship as futile fetishism. Kaufmann went even further, maintaining that monotheism was so deeply ingrained in Israel's national consciousness that it prevented the emergence of any religious syncretism. He strongly re-pudiated the assumption by modern research of an Israelite-Canaanite religious syncretism, as absolutely unwarranted by the sources.[8]

THE PROBLEM OF MYTH

Before applying ourselves to these two assumptions, we must clarify three essential questions:

1. What is the nature of myth in general?
2. What are the special features of monotheistic myth?
3. What are its political and social implications?

In recent years, many scholars have dealt with the questions of the nature and function of myth. Is it to be considered a literary category, i.e. a form of expression, or a mode of thought?[9] Are myths the product of the imagination, or of memory? What are the social tasks of myths: Are they explanatory (aetiological myths), or do they represent values (paradigmatic myths)? Is their significance limited to the sphere of human existence itself, or do they hint at something beyond it, becoming a religious category? The answers given by anthropologists, sociologists, psychologists, and philosophers vary greatly, each one replying in accordance with his own views and scholarly leanings. Nevertheless, they all agree that such a fundamental concept as myth cannot be defined solely in terms of its content, i.e., the life stories and fates of the Gods, as the rationalists, including Kaufmann, would have it, according to the meaning of the Greek word *mythos,* i.e., story; they reveal rather a mode of thought and expression characterized by their concrete-pictorial nature. Myths, moreover, are not mere stories, but are conceived as living realities which have a formative effect on the mind. Furthermore, they fulfill several social functions and cannot be restricted to one sphere. Certain myths have arisen out of someone's curiosity, so that their function is allegedly "scientific," in that they explain natural phenomena, social features, etc. (aetiological myths). Some embody values and describe the exploits of individuals who have dedicated themselves to a specific ideal (paradigmatic myths). Still others deal with the basic problems of human existence: life and death, good and evil, man and his home, family relations, friendship and enmity, relations with the gods, etc. There are even myths which reflect crucial events in the lives of individuals or groups which arouse awe and wonder because they are interpreted as being the result of divine revelation or intervention in the course of history. This category includes myths which relate or hint at an individual or collective encounter between man and god or celestial creatures. In these cases, myth is the vehicle for expressing an event which cannot be defined in terms of natural causality; it thus becomes a religious category.

As to the epistemological significance of myths, some scholars have regarded myths as providing evidence of pre-logical thinking, evincing primitive or savage thought (Lévy-Bruhl). Outstanding scholars of the previous generation have attempted to outline and to examine the consistency and structure of primitive thought. The most significant and comprehensive work concerning this is Ernst Cassirer's *Philosophie der symbolischen Formen,*[10] the second volume of which analyzes myth against the background of scientific thought. This very confrontation between both modes of expression was detrimental to an adequate assessment of myth, as myth in general responds not to the questions and problems which are of major interest to science, but to those which are beyond rationality, such as basic human relationships, the relation between man and God, the problem of death, justice, and so on. Indeed, despite his sympathetic approach to myth, Cassirer admitted that, while "there is method in it," it lacks the rigorous logical structure which is the foundation of modern science.

In our generation, Claude Lévi-Strauss took the final step in demonstrating that the various forms and types of myth stand firmly on the foundation of logic, and that in this respect there is no difference between mythical and conceptual thought.

From this viewpoint, Henri Frankfort's thesis of mythopoeic thought as the basis of all ancient Near Eastern cultures is highly questionable. True, he admits that the differences between modern, that is, scientific thought, and mythopoeic thought are due to emotional attitudes and intentions rather than to the so-called pre-logical mentality.[11] However, he simultaneously argues that it is the absence of any distinctions between the subjective and objective realms which produces mythopoeic thought. This implies, however, that he is dealing with a different thought structure and not only with an emotional attitude.

This distinction between the subjective and objective is common to all ancient Near Eastern cultures, as may be seen by studying the various law codes which have come down to us. Nonetheless, scientific thought is based upon three additional elements, which are to be accounted for the increasingly wide gulf between our perception of the phenomenal world and the mythical-aetiological explanations of it.

1) Systematic, critical thinking about thought itself, i.e., the desire to understand the meaning and confines of knowledge. This unrestricted critical quest of man for self-understanding is at the very core of modern thought.

2) The second and third elements are the ideas of experiment and of logical proof as the proper ways of understanding the structure of the universe as well as the sources and goals of history. These elements, which have been revealed by Greek philosophy, are lacking in ancient Near Eastern culture. The critical search into the nature of the cosmos and of history is still hampered there by a tradition in which cultic ritual, magic, and divination predominate. These are *psychological* differences, brought about by different historical circumstances. They should, however, never be misinterpreted, either in terms of thought structure and epistemology or as the result of different emotional attitudes.

In my view, there are three psychological qualities which cause the differences between aetiological-mythical and speculative-scientific thought:

1. Myth aims at understanding phenomena by what makes them peculiar, while speculative thought is mainly interested in that which makes them manifestations of general laws.

2. Myth is the intuitive form of human expression in imagery, concrete anthropomorphic pictures and tales, as against conceptual language which is based upon analytical abstraction.

3. The very presupposition of the anthropomorphic character of the world also means that the universe is an organic unity in which every spiritual quality has its material expression. In short, spirit and matter are only different aspects of cosmic unity, in contrast to the dualistic approach of Greek philosophy which distinguishes between two ontological sources of being, the spiritual and the material.

As for the subject matter of myths, it ranges over a wide and variegated spectrum; myths deal with life and death, with relations between parents and children, between man and God, between man and his native land, etc. In brief, they include all that pertains to the meaning of human existence and to the understanding of man and society. Many of these topics are determined by historical and social components; thus, the mythic mentality as such is independent of any given historical period or social framework, being an organic function of the human mind.

Attempts have also been made to locate the mental powers which give rise to myths. Freud perceived them as a product of the imagination. Buber, on the other hand, contended that the very core of myth, its specific nucleus, was primaeval memory. It seems to me that neither of these alternatives fit the reality, as both these mental forces combine in varying degrees to create myths. Myths, such as those dealing with the creation and the various kinds of aetiological myths, whose task it is to explain the incomprehensible aspects of nature and the environment, are the product of imagination alone. Historical myths, on the other hand, namely those woven around an ancient, primitive event, are built around the nucleus of a primaeval memory handed down from one generation to the next. Nevertheless, there is no rigid connection between their mental origin and their social and psychological impact, as both memory and imagination are necessary to nourish man's mind and to maintain society. Following this brief phenomenological analysis of myth, we shall deal with the problem of its formative influence on social structure.

Pagan Myth

What, then, characterizes the myths of ancient Near Eastern religions? What distinguishes them from monotheistic myths and what have they in common with them? There would seem to be four features which typify the pagan myths of the ancient Near East:

1. The universe as well as natural forces and phenomena are explained as having a personal character, and their functioning is accounted for in the anthropomorphic terms of human will.
2. Being is based on an ontological continuum, which means that there is a natural, organic connection between man, gods, and nature, all of which are formed from the same substance and governed by the same causal framework.
3. The formation of the world is explained in two ways: the development and functioning of the universe and mankind are depicted either in terms of primaeval sexual intercourse and birth by the gods or between the gods and human beings (theogony), or as the outcome of dramatic events, such as wars and struggles between the gods or ancient monsters (theomachy). The two kinds of explanation in certain myths are intermingled. The common basis for both approaches is the principle of the ontological continuum.[12]
4. In some cases the pagan ritual is primarily the representation of the dramatic events associated with the formation of the world. These ceremonies are imbued with magical powers which aid the good, benevolent gods in their battle against the powers of disorder and death which disturb the cosmic-social harmony.

Let us examine these features briefly. As regards the personal nature of the universe, the cause of events is not the immanent laws of matter but the wishes and aspirations of the gods and their associates. Thunder, lightning, clouds, rain, floods, drought, and the like are all connected with the deeds of the gods. The sun, moon, and stars are not merely heavenly bodies but have personal features, being revered as gods or the sons of gods, they are considered members of the celestial family. Even the winds are regarded as individuals with personal qualities of their own.

As outlined above, *the ontological continuum means that the world of men and of gods is hewn from the same matter.* To be more precise, the human world is derived from divine matter, a fact which is sometimes explained by theogony (most of the Sumerian myths)[13] and sometimes by theomachy, the final outcome of which is the slaying of a monstrous god or goddess and the creation of the earth and sky from his or her body (the Babylonian myth of creation).[14] According to one Sumerian myth, even plants are of divine substance, as they grew from divine sperm.[15] One of the Babylonian myths maintains that the human body is divine, because it was formed from the blood of a murdered god and mixed with clay. All this means that the cosmos, including the gods, was formed from the same material substance, which is divine *per se*. Consequently, there are frequent transitions between the three spheres: the divine, the human, and the natural. Gods who were degraded became mortal; outstanding human individuals (Utnapishtim) were elevated and made immortal; gods and goddesses engaged in sexual intercourse with one another and with human beings and gave birth to gods, demi-gods, giants, heroes, etc. Nevertheless, despite the divine substance of the universe and the frequent transitions from one sphere to another, the creators of pagan myths were aware of the fact that ordinary human beings could not rise above their mortality. Even the epic hero Gilgamesh, who was privileged to enter the garden of the gods where he heard about the plant which bestowed immortality, failed in his mission because a snake snatched the plant away from him when he attempted to bring it up from the depths of the sea.[16] Another myth, that of Adapa, tells how man lost his opportunity to gain immortality because, influenced by the evil counsel of his god Ea, he was suspicious of the god Anu.[17] *Thus, the various myths of creation, like the myths dealing with the efforts to attain immortality, illustrate the principle of the ontological continuum, which is explained as the universal rule of biological-organic laws.* At times the continuum functions in accordance with psychological-dramatic laws to which gods, mortals and the universe are subject both in war and in peace.

This brings us to the fourth point, namely, that certain rites and rituals connected with myths served a magic purpose. Thus, one of the myths concerning the creation of man from divine blood and clay constituted an incantation for women giving birth.[18] According to Frankfort, Pharaoh's participation in the Seth ceremonies[19] was intended to maintain cosmic harmony and to ensure that the Nile would not flood the fields or natural disasters overtake the farmers. It has been claimed that during the Mesopotamian Akitu festival the creation story was recited, accompanied by symbolic magic participation in Mardukh's struggle.[20] It can be assumed, moreover, that the weeping for Tammuz described in the Bible (*Ezek.* 8:14; *Zech.* 12:11) denoted Tammuz's descent into the underworld.[21] There is probably some connection between this myth and the Ugaritic one of Baal's murder by his brother Mot, his descent into the underworld and return to life in the spring. The hymns provide a basis for assuming that some of the songs were perhaps chanted at the festival of Baal's return to life.[22]

Is There Monotheistic Myth?
(The refutation of Kaufmann's assumptions)

The above are the outlines of the pagan myth which constituted the historical and phenomenological background of the Bible and its monotheistic outlook. Before discussing the foundations of monotheistic myth, we must refer to Kaufmann's historical and sociological arguments mentioned above. First of all, let us examine his assertion that monotheism was the intuitive creation of Israel's national spirit. In his view, this belief was so deeply ingrained in the popular consciousness that Israel did not have the slightest understanding of the mythical nature of paganism. The prophets, poets, and writers condemned it as the futile, fetishist worship of trees and stones without taking notice of its mythical qualities. Indeed, this is correct (*Judg.* 6:30–32; *Isa.* 2:8, 20; 40:17–20; 44:9–20; 46:1–2, 5–7; *Ps.* 115:4–8; etc.); yet it does not imply that neither they nor anyone else in Israel knew about the mythological qualities of paganism. On the contrary, the pagan fertility rites, which involved sexual licentiousness, as is indicated by *Hos.* 2:3; 4:11–19; *Jer.* 2:28, and others, were undoubtedly not fetishistic, as they aimed to increase fertility by a magical-sympathetic imitation of the intercourse between a god and a goddess. Not only the common people, but prominent personages as well, were involved in these rituals, as indicated by *Hos.* 4:13–14 and *Ez.* 8:10–12. Moreover, popular syncretism was sometimes a mixture of Baalism and Yahwism (*Judg.* 14:4) or of Yahwism and the Moloch cult (*Mic.* 6:7) or Assyrian astral idolatry (*Jer.* 7:18; 44:19). There can be no doubt that this syncretism was based on the belief that Baal, Moloch, or the respective Assyrian divinities are living persons and not mere idols of stone and wood as Kaufmann would have it. We may therefore assume that pagan rites within Israel were also rooted in mythological consciousness.

The above picture concerning syncretism in ancient Israel is corroborated by the recent findings from Kuntillat 'Arjud, 10 km south of Kadesh at the border between Sinai and the Negev,[23] and those from Chirbet el Qôm, 14 km west of Hebron.[24]

The material discovered in Kuntillat 'Ajrud is dated at approximately 800 B.C.E. It contained the shards of a vase on which are painted red figures which show close affinity to Egyptian mythology.[25] For us, the inscription at the top of the shards is of major interest; the beginning is unreadable, while the last words are very clear. It reads:

W . . . brkt 'tkm lYhwh šmrn wl'šrth, = ברכת אתכם לה* שמרן ולאשרתה

"I bless you by YHWH our guardian (or: Shomron) and his Asherah."
(Compare *Judg.* 17:2; *I Sam.* 15:13; 23:21; *II Sam.* 2:5; *Ps.* 115:15;
etc.)
The inscription from Chirbet el Qôm reads:

1. 'rjhw hꜥšr ktbh   אריה העשר כתבה
2. brk 'rjhw lYhwh   ברך אריהו לה*
3. wmṣrjh l'šrth hwšꜥ lh   ומצריה לאשרתה הושע לה
   * the inscription has here the full Tetragrammaton.

Translation: "Uriyahu the rich wrote it: Blessed be Uriyahu by
YHWH, and saved his Ashera from her enemies" or: "from his
enemies be he saved by his Asherah."

Asherah,[26] Athrat in Ugaritic, is the Canaanite goddess of fertility
whose cult is sharply reprimanded in the Bible (*Judg.* 3:7; *I Kings*
15:13; *II Kings* 13:6; 21:7; 23:6; etc.). Here she is conceived as
YHWH's wife, a syncretistic belief which was abhorred by the biblical
writers.

Thus, the assumption concerning the anti-mythological and anti-
pagan monotheistic mentality of the people of Israel can easily be
refuted. Indeed, the Rabbis were nearer the historical truth when
they stated that the desire to engage in idol worship was "uprooted"
or "slaughtered" during the Babylonian exile, in the time of Mordecai
and Esther, or at the beginning of the Second Temple period.[27] In
other words, *Israel became a monotheistic nation in the course of a
long historical process, which reached its climax only after the psychological shock of the Destruction of the Temple.* Only after the
Babylonian Exile did paganism cease to be a national problem.
Nevertheless, we fully agree with Kaufmann that the monotheistic
idea is an ancient one and was the formative factor in the development of Israelite culture during the First Temple period.

The most serious doubts arise, however, in connection with Kaufmann's definition of monotheism as an anti-mythological belief, and
with his identification of paganism with mythology. It is unlikely
that a faith in the absolute supremacy and uniqueness of the God
of Israel would be the achievement of the people who left Egypt, as
Kaufmann implies. An abstract faith of this kind could not attract
a nation of slaves, whose bondage extended back for several generations. What would have fired the imagination of a nation in those
circumstances was the message of deliverance, namely, the concept
of a god who would liberate them and lead them to freedom. This
is indeed the way God defines Himself at the beginning of the Ten
Commandments: "I am the Lord your God, who brought you out
of the Land of Egypt, out of the house of bondage" (*Exod.* 20:2).
This motif recurs innumerable times in the Torah and the historical

books. There is no hint of Him being the one and only God. On the contrary, the Song of the Sea, one of the most ancient poems of the Bible, contains the phrase, "Who is like unto thee, O Lord, among the gods?"[28] indicating that, although other gods exist, the Lord is stronger than they are. Furthermore, during the Exodus the Lord punished not only the Egyptians themselves (*Exod.* 6:6; 7:4) but also their gods (*Exod.* 18:12; *Num.* 33:4). In the second commandment, which forbids the worship of other gods, we read: "Thou shalt have no other gods before me," (v. 3) meaning that other gods exist, but their worship has no place alongside Him. Thus, these early texts refer to the *exclusive worship* of the Lord, but not to the uniqueness of His *existence.*[29] In other words, they bear testimony to a monolatrous conception of god. The ban on making graven images or pictures of "anything that is in heaven above, or that is on the earth beneath, or that is in the water under the earth" (v. 4, 5) must also be explained in this context.

This prohibition appears to be directed against the "other gods" mentioned previously. Other passages provide evidence of their existence. Thus, *Deuteronomy* 4:19: "And lest thou lift up thine eyes unto heaven, and when thou seest the sun, and the moon, and the stars, all the host of heaven, shouldest be driven to bow down to them, and serve them, *which the Lord thy God hath divided unto all nations under the whole heaven.*" The hosts of heaven, then, are the gods which the Lord has given to all the nations on earth. In *Deuteronomy* 32:8 we find: "When the Most High divided to the nations their inheritance, when he separated the sons of men, he fixed the bounds of the peoples according to the number of the sons of God."[30] The number of nations accords with the number of their gods, each nation having its own gods, as the prophet Micah reinterpreted Isaiah's vision of the latter days, when he added: "For all people will walk *every one in the name of his god,* and we will walk in the name of the Lord our God for ever and ever" (*Mic.* 4:5). Psalm 82 indicates that these gods were members of the divine council and their task was to impose justice on mankind. One day, however, the Lord deposed them and made them ordinary mortals. The sources cited here indicate that the other gods existed and fulfilled a function in the lives of the nations, but according to Psalm 82 were ousted at some point because of their wickedness and the injustice and oppression they caused; then the Lord took it upon himself to judge the nations.

Thus, in its initial stages, monotheism emerged as a faith which centered on the exclusive *worship* of the Lord, the principal justification for which was a primaeval historical event handed down by tradition: that he released and saved Israel from the slavery of Egypt, led them through the sea, destroyed their enemies (*Exod.* 14:24–31; 15), and revealed His laws to them. At the outset, however, this focus on the sole worship of the Lord did not necessarily involve repudiation of the existence of other gods. This awareness was the outcome of an intellectual process which reached its acme in the speeches of Deutero-Isaiah (*Isa.* 40:12ff.), but can already be found in the ancient traditions of the Pentateuch (*Deut.* 6:4, etc.).

But contrary to paganism, which stands for the ontological continuum and the personalization of the universe, monotheism is based on the complete ontological detachment of God and His celestial host from the world and the reduced personalization of the universe, to the point where only two characters exist: God and man. Nevertheless, personalization recurs from time to time in poetry, particularly when the writer addresses the denizens of the upper and lower regions, calling upon them to join with him in praising God (*Ps.* 93; 96:1, 98–7–8; 114; 148). Likewise, many hymns mention nature's trembling before the Lord.[31] Personalization recurs in prose for the purpose of generating intimacy and making the land Israel's associate in shaping its life. Thus, the land vomited out the inhabitants of Canaan because of their abominations (*Lev.* 18:25, 28). Israel is warned not to behave like the nations, lest the land vomit them forth too (*Lev.* 18:28; 20:22). The land shall lie fallow ("keep a sabbath") in the seventh and fiftieth years, together with man and beast; the term "keep a sabbath" applies to everyone, without exception (*Lev.* 25:2, 4, 5, 6). If Israel does not keep the seventh and fiftieth years God will scatter them among the nations: "Then shall *the land enjoy* her sabbaths. . . . As long as it is desolate it shall rest; because it did not rest in your sabbaths, when ye dwelt upon it" (*Lev.* 26:34–35, 43). But this is only an anthropomorphic mode of speech, as neither of these objects has a will of its own. We may therefore contend that the general trend in the Bible is towards the depersonification of the universe, particularly in comparison with the pagan approach.

The foregoing leads us to two conclusions:

1. Man is distinguished from his environment by his personal nature; the universe loses all its divine and personal characteristics, becoming dead matter.
2. There is no ontological connection between God and His world, including man. On the contrary, an unbridgeable gulf separates them. God is transcendent, being totally different from this world and its very nature. He and His entourage are devoid of any material or biological substance whatsoever. There are no female members in the celestial court; angels

or the sons of god never engage in sexual intercourse with one another or with members of the human race (we will deal in the last section with the vestiges of Canaanite myth relating to this point); they neither quarrel nor envy each other, nor is there any competition among them.

3. Both these premises include another feature of major importance: God is a living personality depicted in anthropomorphic imagery, in full analogy to the human personality in its various manifestations.

We shall dwell on these features in detail:

As to the ontological detachment of God, He is conceived as the transcendent Creator, alone facing His handiwork. He uses thunder, lightning, winds, and natural phenomena for His purposes, these being objects totally devoid of all personal qualities. The celestial host surrounding God's throne and likewise the heavenly messengers sent to man on God's errands have no will of their own, no individuality or name. The meaning of their titles: Ophanim, seraphim, sons of God, assembly of saints, etc. is obscure. In any event, these are not personal but collective names.[32] Angels appear on earth as emissaries of God, to disappear once their errand has been completed. They appear in "human" form, and sometimes their supernatural nature is revealed only after they have vanished or accomplished miracles (*Gen.* 18–19; *Judg.* 13; etc.), but in all sources they remain anonymous. It is not until the Babylonian Exile and the beginnings of the Second Commonwealth that angels are individualized and given personal names. In some instances, the Bible does not draw a clear distinction between God and His minions and the angel of the Lord (*Exod.* 3:2, 4: etc.), so that it is very difficult to discern the separate existence of the angel. On another occasion, the Bible deliberately intermingles two parallel narratives, one concerning the personal appearance of the Lord and the other the arrival of three male angels, in order to obscure the anthropomorphic nature of God and the distinction between the Lord and His angels (*Gen.* 18–19).[33]

Nevertheless, despite the prohibition against making idols or graven images, i.e. attempting to reproduce God's form in any way, whether as a statue or carving, the Bible abounds in graphic and anthropomorphic descriptions of God. These recur several times in *Exodus.* According to *Exodus* 23:20–21, 23, the Lord promises to send an angel: "Behold, I send an Angel before thee, to guard thee on the way, and to bring thee into the place which I have prepared. Beware of him, and obey his voice, provoke him not; for he will not pardon your transgressions; *for my name is in him.*" This assurance is based on the assumption that the angel symbolizes the presence of God;

thus, this passage reflects a certain lack of distinction between God
and His angels. In contrast, in *Exodus* 33:2-3, we find: "And I will
send an angel before thee . . . but I will not go up in the midst of
thee since thou art a stiff-necked people; lest I consume thee in the
way." In this case it is obvious that a clear distinction is assumed
between the Lord and the angel. Moses responds by charging: "Unless
thy presence (=פניך) go, carry us not up hence" (33:15). And he
requests: "I pray thee, let the Lord go in our midst; for it is a stiff-
necked people; and pardon our iniquity and our sin. . . ." (34:9).
These verses also deal with the direct presence of the Lord, though
this time the motif of the angel is absent. This indicates that the
angel motif is omitted and direct reference is made to the "face,"
(panim) or "glory" *(kavod)*[34] of the Lord when the objective is to
eliminate all doubts regarding His direct presence. It would seem
that ancient folk legends tended to confuse these two spheres, while
theological reflection gradually drew a distinction between the Lord
and His angels. God walks in the garden in the cool of the day
(Gen. 3.8); He descends from heaven in order to see the men of
Sodom and the builders of the tower *(Gen.* 11:5; 18:21); He appears
to Abraham as he sits at the entrance to his tent in the heat of the
day *(Gen.* 18:1), walks about with him, and answers his penetrating
questions. The passage concludes with the words: "And the Lord
went, when he had finished speaking to Abraham" (18:33).

At the ford of Jabbok Jacob remains alone, "and there wrestled
a man with him until the breaking of the dawn" (32:25). When he
is unable to defeat Jacob, the mysterious man blesses him, changing
his name of Israel," for you have striven with God *(elohim)* and
with men and have prevailed" (v. 29); he leaves without disclosing
his name: "And Jacob named the site Peniel 'for I have seen God
face to face, yet my life has been preserved' " (v. 31). It follows that
Jacob thought that *God* had fought with him and that he had seen
Him face to face. According to the tradition reflected in the book
of Hosea, the 'man' was only an angel *(Hosea* 12:5), while the
narrator of *Genesis* maintains a certain lack of clarity. Be that as it
may, angels appear as men, and have no special distinguishing marks
other than the fact that, according to certain legends, they are capable
of performing miracles.

In referring to Moses, the direct presence of the Lord is stressed
in very concrete terms. We read that the Lord speaks to him "mouth
to mouth" *(Num.* 12:8), and that the Lord "knew him face to face"
(Deut. 34:10). On the other hand, God says to Moses, "Thou canst
not see my face, for man shall not see me and live . . . and thou
shalt see my back; but my face shall not be seen" *(Exod.* 33:20, 23).
The elders of Israel saw God in Sinai, "and there was under His

feet as it were a paved work of sapphire, and as it were the very sky for purity" (*Exod.* 24:10).

The dispute between these traditions relates to the question whether it is *permitted* to see Him, though all are agreed that it is *possible* to see Him. At Mount Sinai He reveals Himself before the people as a king.[35] Elsewhere Israel is depicted as His 'children' (*Deuteronomy* 14:1), His 'vassal', (not: 'peculiar treasure' *Exod.* 19:5) and His 'inheritance',[36] and He dwells among them (*Exod.* 29:45, etc.).

Micaiah the son of Imlah saw Him sitting on His throne, and all the host of heaven standing by Him (*I Kings* 22:19), in similar terms to those we find in *Job,* ch. 1–2. Isaiah saw Him sitting "upon a throne, high and lifted up, and his train filled the temple" (*Isa.* 6:1). Ezekial saw Him in his celestial "chariot" *(merkavah)* and His appearance was "of a man above upon it . . . as the appearance of fire round about within it, from the appearance of *his loins even upward,* and from the appearance of his loins even downward" (*Ezek.* 1:26, 27). Daniel beheld the "Ancient of days" sitting on his throne, "whose garment was white as snow, and the hair of his head like the pure wool" (*Dan.* 7:9). Deutero-Isaiah saw him as a man of war (compare also *Exod.* 15:3) coming "with dyed garments from Bozrah . . . glorious in his apparel, travelling in the greatness of his strength" (*Isa.* 63:1). He answers the prophet's question himself: "I have trodden the winepress alone; and of the people there was none with me; for I will tread them in mine anger, and trample them in my fury; and their blood shall be sprinkled upon my garments, and I will stain all my raiment" (*ibid.,* v. 3).

Thus, the natural tie based on common material ground between God, man, and the world is replaced by a voluntary relationship deriving from God's concern for His world and His explicit demands on man in general and Israel in particular. In the following section we shall sketch the historical setting and the social repercussions of this faith, which was paramount in forging the social structure of ancient Israel.

THE IDEA OF COVENANT AND ITS THEOPOLITICAL IMPACT

One of the most impressive assumptions of classical Bible criticism, which was generally identified with Julius Wellhausen and his school, was its exposition of the idea of monotheism in terms of evolution. In his view, the idea of monotheism was the outcome of a slow process of about two hundred years, which was initiated by the great prophets who flourished from the eighth to the sixth century B.C.E. These prophets simultaneously defied and repudiated Israel's folk religion, which was permeated with the excessive cult customs borrowed from Canaan. The first was Amos (eighth century) who emphasized the centrality of social justice in the religion of Israel, while Hosea, his younger contemporary, propagated the stern principles of sexual morality as against the licentiousness of the Canaanite cult. Again, it was Deutero-Isaiah (sixth century) who made the final breakthrough in proclaiming Yahweh's uniqueness, exclusiveness, and universality as creator of the universe, who forged world history according to His own will. Furthermore, Deutero-Isaiah ridiculed the nothingness of the pagan gods and idols by describing them as dead wood and stone. The debate over the historical validity of Wellhausen's thesis, which fascinated the positivist mentality of the nineteenth century, continues to this day.

I shall restrict myself to a short critical remark on the basic error underlying Wellhausen's ingenious historical conception: His method was based on the assumption that monotheism is basically an intellectual theory, arrived at by contemplation and speculation on the part of a small elitist group, the prophets, who fervently opposed the commonly accepted crude and primitive folk religion, pagan by nature. This basic picture of the history of monotheism is accepted to this day. We contend that this is diametrically opposed to the historical reality reflected in the biblical sources, especially in those pertaining to the Sinai covenant. These sources disclose that monotheism, far from being the speculative, contemplative faith of a small, elitist group, was the result of an overwhelming historical event involving an entire nation. While this powerful historical experience is imbedded in legend and myth, there is nevertheless no reason to doubt its essential historical reality, nor is it likely that the legend was the free invention of late writers. This experience was Israel's redemption from the house of bondage in Egypt, followed by the covenant made by the people with their divine redeemer, the so-called Sinai covenant. In other words, the nucleus of monotheism is a primaeval collective historical event, which was perceived as an encounter of the entire nation with Yahweh, their redeemer. This was an existential experience totally different from an intellectual acquisition of a small elitist group, like the ontological monism of pre-classical Greek philosophers. The Greek thinkers are characterized by speculation, by the relentless quest for universal abstract truth and the gradual development of a reflective, analytical method. Such a process can indeed be explained only in terms of evolution. Therefore, a sharp dividing line must be drawn between the two phenomena, which are completely different in character. It was not until the Hellenistic period, when Judaism encountered Hellenistic culture in Alexandria, that Jewish scholars with Greek education began to explain their biblical and Jewish heritage to themselves in terms of Greek philosophy.[37] This ushered in a new period of reshaping and molding Judaism in the spirit of Western philosophy— a process which continues to this day.

The basic historical authenticity and political or theopolitical character of the Sinai covenant have been conclusively demonstrated recently by the scholarly revelation of the close literary affinity of its biblical account to the political treaties of the Hittite kings from 1400 to 1250 B.C.E. with their vassals.[38] The full theopolitical significance of the Sinai covenant should be reassessed in this cultural setting. *Israel accepted the exclusive suzerainty of its divine king.* The prohibition against worshipping any god besides Him found its classical expression in the first commandment.[39] Indeed, this is consonant with the prohibitions found in Hittite vassal treaties, where the vassal is warned against recognizing anybody besides his suzerain, "the Sun." This is a striking parallel to the Sinai covenant in which Israel, the vassal nation, pledges absolute and exclusive obedience to Him by an act of free commitment. Thus, the Sinai covenant was tantamount to the establishment of the kingdom of God. We may therefore assume that it was the radical response of Israel to the traumatic experience in Egypt, "the house of bondage," the symbol of human enslavement and tyranny. By contrast, the kingdom of God was meant to be free of any kind of human domination and oppression. Buber, in his book *Königtum Gottes* (1936),[40] already persuasively demonstrated that this theopolitical utopia may be traced within the most ancient poetical and narrative sources of the Bible (*Num.* 10:35–36; 23:21–23; *Judg.* 5, etc.). There, the idea of human kingship is repudiated as an offence and a sin against God, the true king of Israel (*Judg.* 8:22–23; *I Sam.* 8:7ff.). In other words, the covenant between God and His people, which is the very core of biblical monotheism, is in a certain sense the transmission and reshaping of these ancient vassal treaties, in which Israel is conceived as the vassal of God.

God as Father, Lover, and Bridegroom

Before going on to analyze the socio-economic repercussions of the myth of divine kingship, let us dwell briefly on the process of its interiorization, which went far beyond the legal framework noted above. I refer to the images of personal, paternal relationship, which are found already in the ancient Near Eastern treaty formulae and recur in the Bible. According to *Exod.* 4:22, Israel is God's "first-born son"; in *Deuteronomy* 14:1 Israel is addressed with the words, "You are the sons of the Lord your God." The intimate atmosphere fostered by this mode of expression is enhanced by images and symbols of an erotic character, such as that of the faithful bridegroom and his bride (*Jer.* 2:11f.) or of God the husband and Israel the unfaithful wife (*Hos.* 1–3). This simile reaches poetic heights in Ezekiel, in which Israel is compared to a girl who has been cast out in the open field (16:5). God passed by her and saw her polluted in her own blood. "I said unto thee where thou wast in thy blood, 'Live' " (v. 6). He took care of her, and when she grew up and came to "the time of love" he covered her nakedness. "Yea, I sware unto thee, and entered into a covenant with thee, saith the Lord God, and thou becamest mine" (v. 8). He washed her, cleaned the blood from her, anointed her with oil, etc., etc. The political covenant between the divine king and his vassal nation is transmuted into the covenant of love between the divine bridegroom and his bride. A late Midrash transfers this image into the sphere of mythic realism, by reinterpreting this passage about Israel collectively to apply to each individual child, thus creating a personal, concrete relationship of love between each child and his divine savior, who appeared to him as a young man with black curls, consonant with the allegorical explanation of the *Song of Songs* 5:11: "his locks are wavy, black as a raven."[41]

Indeed, the anthropomorphic description of God, so scathingly attacked by the mediaeval philosophers, is in fact the core of the biblical concept of God, as only by being a paradigmatic personality can He command people to follow Him. He is not only a loving and merciful person, but also a jealous one, who on no account will tolerate their worshipping anyone but Himself. Each individual must be devoted to Him alone, "with all your heart and with all your soul and with all your might" (*Deut.* 6:5). Moreover, the anthropomorphic presentation of God is at the very core of *imitatio Dei,* which is the basis of biblical ethics. Only because He is a "man" can it be said that man was created "in His image and likeness." It is only for this reason that He can command the individual and the community, "Ye shall be holy, for I the Lord your God am holy" (*Lev.* 19:2). It is in this vein that Abba Saul says in *Sifra* (*Parashat Kedoshim,* par. 2): "What should the entourage of the king do but imitate the king." In other words, *imitatio Dei,* which is the basis of both individual and collective morality in the Bible and Midrash, is preconditioned by the mythical and anthropomorphic presentation of God.

THE SOCIO-ECONOMIC ASPECT

Besides the political impact, this utopia also had a socio-economic aspect. A short analysis of the main stipulations pertaining to the

Sabbath and to the Sabbatical and Jubilee years will demonstrate the decisive influence of this mythic utopia in shaping social reality. We contend that the legal amendments (*Lev.* 25:14–54) which were added to the body of the law of Sabbatical and Jubilee years (*Lev.* 25:1–13) indicate that these were implemented during the period of the First Commonwealth. It may be assumed that the amendments were meant to meet the new conditions created by the process of urbanization, which reached its pinnacle during the reign of King Solomon and later on during the reign of the Omri dynasty in northern Israel. The lawmaker then exempted the inhabited areas of the walled cities as well as the immovable property, which had been sold by the Temple administration, from the Jubilee year provisions that required the return of all lands to their original owners.[42] This central provision was designed to restore the original parcelling of the country between the tribes according to their size at the time of the Israelite conquest. The same may be said of the ancient laws of inheritance (*Num.* 27:9–11; 36:1–9) which expressly mention the preservation of "the ancestral plot" as their aim. The uniqueness of the Sabbatical and Jubilee provisions becomes evident in comparison to old Mesopotamian "misharum" provisions,[43] which contain stipulations relating to the cancellation of debts and the release of slaves. There are two outstanding differences between biblical land provisions and these royal decrees from the ancient Near East:

1. These regulations were decreed sporadically by certain Mesopotamian kings, according to their political considerations and interests. On the other hand the Sabbatical and Jubilee years, which were conceived as a divine commandment, recurred in a fixed cyclical order.

2. The "misharum" provisions were intended to improve social and economic conditions, as may be gleaned from the preamble stating: "Because the king establishes justice in the country . . ."; but as a matter of fact only a small social layer in whose welfare the king was interested took advantage of these provisions. On the other hand, the provisions of the Sabbatical and Jubilee years were relevant to Israelite society as a whole, creating a life rhythm which shaped the character of the entire nation.

The special nature of this rhythm may be seen in the literary affinity of these provisions (*Lev.* 25) to the clause relating to the Sabbath. It should be emphasized that the ancient Sabbath laws were directed against the Mesopotamian concept of the *shapattu*. Modern Near Eastern research[44] has taught us that in Babylonia *shapattu* was the fifteenth day of the month; another institution which also seems to be related to the Hebrew Sabbath were "the ill-fated days of the Assyrians" which followed one another at intervals of seven days. The *shapattu* seems to have been a day of prayer and sacrifices, called "the day of the rest of the heart" *(um nuʰ libbi),* when men calmed their gods by cultic performances. On the other hand, the ill-fated days were, according to Assyrian sources, days of bad luck when people were advised to refrain from engaging in their regular daily business. The dates of these days, as well as that of *shapattu,* were fixed according to astronomical calculations starting with the new moon, thus symbolizing the dependency on the rotations of the celestial bodies which were revered as divine beings. As against this, the Sabbath passage at the conclusion of the story of Creation emphasizes three times that it was on "the seventh day" that God finished His work, rested, and blessed the seventh day. The Sabbath commandment (*Exod.* 20:11) is likewise based on the argument that He "rested the seventh day," thus isolating the Sabbath from any affinity with the heavenly bodies. The process of regeneration inherent in the Sabbath rest embraces slaves, sojourners, and even domesticated animals: "You and your son, and your daughter, your manservant and your maidservant, and your cattle, and your sojourner who is within your gates" (*Exod.* 20:10). According to *Lev.* 25:1–13, the Jubilee is called the Sabbatical year of the country.

The rhythm of the Sabbatical and Jubilee years is based on the number seven, like the Sabbath, as may be demonstrated by the following section: "Six years you shall sow your field and six years you shall prune your vineyard and gather in its fruits; but in the seventh year there shall be a Sabbath of solemn rest for the land, a Sabbath to the Lord" (*Lev.* 25:3–4). Like the Sabbath, the Jubilee year is sacred to God and aims to demonstrate His exclusive ownership of the country: ". . . *for the land is mine, for you are strangers and sojourners with me*" (*Lev.* 25:23). The stipulations regarding the Sabbatical year require that the land be left fallow, thus including the natural environment within the process of regeneration which is essential to the ecological stability of human society. This is the first human legislation to take care not only of the inner social structure but also of environmental conditions—an aspect which has been completely neglected by modern socialist thought. In addition, it should be emphasized that the availability to all of the produce of the fields during that year creates conditions of economic equality embracing the entire social structure.

The Jubilee rhythm, which is seven times seven plus one, completes the egalitarian tendency by annulling all property transactions which have been executed during the past fifty years and restoring the land to those families to whom it was originally allotted after being captured from the Canaanites. This is intimately intertwined with the release of all slaves and their return to their families and their property. The major goal inherent in this legislation is the guarantee of human freedom in the kingdom of God, where God is conceived as the exclusive ruler: "For to me the children of Israel are servants, they are My servants whom I brought forth out of the land of Egypt" (*Lev.* 25:55).

The legislation of the Sabbatical and Jubilee years refers to the land in anthropomorphic language, demanding that it be allowed to rest. Likewise, the sanctions invoked against certain sexual relations are formulated along similar lines. Israel is warned to observe these prohibitions, saying: "That the land where I am bringing you to dwell may not vomit you out" (*Lev.* 20:22). Again, in the following admonition to the people against foresaking the Jubilee regulation Israel is threatened with destruction and exile: "Then the land will enjoy its Sabbath as long as it lies desolate" (*Lev.* 26:34); "As long as it lies desolate it shall have rest . . . and enjoy its Sabbaths" (*Lev.* 26:35, 43). Thus, the land is conceived as the full partner of man in the process of regeneration. These three concentric life cycles aim at severing the life of Israel from the natural life cycle with its inherent death and destruction. The inner cycle, the seven-day week including the Sabbath, is conceived of as the imitation of the Creator's rest; it bestows on the entire society the principle of rest. The cycle of Sabbatical year widens its orbit by including the land, thus creating the ecological equilibrium vital for the stability of every society. The Jubilee cycle completes the egalitarian tendencies by restoring all immovable property to its original owners and by commanding the release of all slaves, thus establishing the principle of freedom based upon the utopian social concept of divine kingship.

But the Hebrew lawmaker is aware that equality and freedom can never be obtained completely in this world: "For the poor will never cease from the midst of the land" (*Deut.* 15:11). While the life rhythm to be created by the legislation will draw Israel towards the ideal goal, the goal as such is out of human reach. In other words, the transcendent character of Utopia will be an eternal challenge to Israel.

I wish to conclude with some allusions to the revolutionary changes undergone by the idea of divine kingship under the impact of the tragic events which occurred in the latter part of the eleventh century, when the Israelite army was defeated by the Philistines in the disastrous battle of Eben-ha'ezer (*I Sam.* 4). The conquest of the hill country of Judaea and Samaria, which was the nucleus of Israelite settlement, the destruction of the tribal center at Shiloh, and the capture of the ark, the throne of Yahweh, shook the entire political and social structure and set in motion a chain of events which brought about the establishment of the Israelite monarchy. The echo of this deep crisis, which undermined the whole life fabric and the self-image of Israel, is reflected in *I Sam.* 8–13. These chapters sketch the transition from the old tribal system, which was the sociological setting of the kingdom of God, to the monarchic regime.[45] The penetrating discussion between Samuel, the prophetic representative of the ancient utopia, and the elders, who demanded the establishment of a kingdom, is the main topic of *I Sam.* 8. The outcome was the reluctant acceptance by Samuel of the principle of human kingship. But contrary to the absolute and divine character of ancient Near Eastern monarchy, the person of the Israelite king remained within the human sphere. His accountability before God was expressed by the motif of adoption and sonship and guaranteed by the watchfulness of the prophet, the divine messenger (*II Sam.* 7:14). This was the lasting impact of the ancient utopian idea of Divine Kingship on the social and political structure of the kingdom of ancient Israel.

This is the first breakthrough in history towards a new political order which institutionalized human freedom and the accountability of the ruler.[46] The precondition of this revolutionary change is the ontological detachment of the divine sphere from the mundane one and the appearance of the prophetic elite who pronounced the liability of king and nation to Divine law and order. This new kind of monarchy emerged after the collapse of the early utopian kingdom of God, which was originally based on the negation of all human rulership as such.

Cult, Religion, and Language

Another social sphere which was shaped under the impact of this myth was that of cult and religion. The most ancient cultic symbol of the kingdom of God was the ark of the covenant, which was conceived as the throne of the unseen king. The ark was of major importance, especially during the first stages of Israel's history, during the wanderings in the desert of Sinai. The priestly source which described the Tent of Meeting emphasizes that it contained the ark, and as such was conceived as the symbol of His indwelling in Israel (*Exod.* 25:8; 40:34–38; etc.). This tent turned out to be the tribal center during the period of the Judges (*Judg.* 21:1–4; *I Sam.* 1–4). This was of paramount importance, as the absence of a central government in peacetime during a period of two hundred fifty years impeded the political stabilization of the nation.

It is unlikely that the ramified cult prohibitions included in the Priestly Code all stem from the pre-monarchic period. Indeed, while we may assume a pre-monarchic code, this law code in its present form seems to have accumulated not earlier than the establishment of the Temple. The major tendency which may be observed in the cultic stipulations is the attempt to disenchant, i.e., to emancipate cult and ritual from magical and divinatory elements which pervade ancient Near Eastern religions.[47] The very nature of magic is the attempt of man to impose his own will on gods and demons by charms, spells, and other techniques, which may partly have been revealed to him by a god. Moreover, the magician calls on self-operating forces, which are independent of the gods and which the gods need and utilize for their own benefit. In other words, the basic idea inherent in pagan magic is that the deity is subject to a realm beside and beyond him.

As for divination, it is the science of *revealing* the hidden will or intuition of the gods as well as impending events. Like magic, it assumes the existence of a system of signs and portents which function autonomously as a part of nature, transcending the will and knowledge of the gods.

According to Bouché-Leclerq one may distinguish between two kinds of divination:

1. Inductive Divination: i.e., the observation of external signs, such as liver inspections, reading the entrails of the sacrifice, hepatocopic oracles, astrology, etc.
2. Intuitive Divination: the working of a special faculty of the soul, a charisma of the diviner who is able to get into touch with divine powers.

To summarize, magic and divination are complex and highly ramified "sciences"; knowledge of them is the privilege of a small group of magicians, priests, prophets, and sorcerers, whose secret knowledge and/or personal charisma was the source of their high social rank.

As to the Bible, it does not contain the slightest allusion to the belief that man is able to coerce God to his own will or to guess the will of God by a system of portents belonging to a realm transcending God's will or knowledge. The vast literature of magic and divination from ancient Near Eastern cultures had become meaningless in Israel. Moreover, heathen magic is banned under penalty of death (*Exod.* 22:17; *Deut.* 18:10). Nevertheless, as Kaufmann[48] has persuasively demonstrated, heathen magic was not derided as folly or nonsense, but was considered a form of human wisdom, which however had no connection whatsoever with the divine realm. In order to satisfy the general human desire to know the future, the Bible legalizes three kinds of divination, the questioning of the Urim and the Tummim, the interpretation of dreams, and the questioning of a prophet. These are the only ways in which God reveals His plans to man. There are also certain other magical practices which became legalized, such as the "Trial by Ordeal" of the woman accused of adultery (*Num.* 5:11–31)[49]; the removal of plague by incense (*Num.* 17:11f.); the use of the bronze serpent for healing (*Num.* 21:9; *II Kings* 18:4); the apotropaic nature of the atonement money of the census (*Exod.* 30:11–16); the incense brought into the Holy of Holies (*Lev.* 16:2, 13); and so forth. The efficacy of all these ancient folk customs is the result of their being conceived as the express command of God.

The major ontological assumption underlying all these vestiges of divination and magic is common to the entire fabric of the Israelite cult: namely, the belief in the unity of the universe, i.e., its organic wholeness. Spirit and matter are not two different elements which compose the universe, but two aspects thereof. There are no abstract spiritual conceptions devoid of material expressions. Therefore, the innermost feelings of man are dressed in ritual activities, on the one hand; while sins and transgressions, on the other hand, have their material repercussions: they pollute and defile man. Cultic ceremonies such as the sprinkling of blood upon the altar at the offering of certain sacrifices, or breaking a heifer's neck (*Deut.* 21:1–9), etc., aim to restore purity. The effectiveness of these ceremonies is based on the above-mentioned belief about the organic unity of the universe. On the other hand, there are no ceremonies, spells, charms, or magical techniques intended to manipulate divine decisions or to influence the divine will in any way. This is due to the underlying assumption that the pagan ontological continuum has been replaced by a dialogical, voluntary relationship between God and His world. Indeed, the few mantic customs which have survived, such as the priestly questioning of the Urim and Tummim (*Num.* 27:21; *Deut.* 33:8; *I Sam.* 28:30) or the belief that the prophet is able to foresee the future and to disclose hidden facts (*Deut.* 18:9–22; *I Sam.* 9:6, 9, 15) are conceived as a special Divine gift, as the expression of Divine grace to man, remote from any belief in the Promethean faculty of penetrating the divine sphere.

SEMANTICS

I would like to demonstrate this mode of "wholist" thought with a few examples taken from the field of biblical semantics. The Hebrew noun *nefesh,* which means life, "soul," is not an abstract concept pertaining exclusively to the realm of spirit, for blood is the material configuration or expression of *nefesh,* "for the life of the flesh is in the blood" (*Lev.* 17:11). The cultic consequence of this belief is that blood covers or wipes out *(kapper)* the sins which are polluting the soul and menacing life. The verb *kapper,* meaning "to cover" or "to wipe out," is very frequent in this context. The noun *kapparah* derived from it does not mean "atonement" in the Western, Christian sense, but covering or wiping out, i.e., expiation. The material sense of this religious category is predominant, like that of the previously mentioned noun, *nefesh* (see *Lev.* 6:19; 7:7; 8:15; 16:16–18; 17:11; *Ezek.* 43:22, 26; 45:18; etc.). The most important ritual conclusion derived from the assumption of an organic connection between life and blood is the prohibition against eating blood, "for the blood is the life and you shall not eat the life with the flesh" (Deut. 12:23). Likewise, human feelings and human intelligence are bound to the concrete physiological structure of the human body: the heart is the seat of human feelings and intelligence, while the kidneys are the seat of human conscience. Again, the semantic field of the word *ruah*[50] bears witness to the organic unity of the world, for it means both "spirit" and "wind" simultaneously. As to *mishpat, sedek, sedakah,* etc., they are no mere pneumatic-spiritual immaterial concepts. On the contrary, they are functional derivatives of concrete ways of behavior: thus *mishpat* and *sedakah* do not mean "justice" and "righteousness" as such, but "just deeds" or "righteous deeds." True, by a process of generalization these nouns slowly developed already in the Bible into abstract concepts, but the most important point is their originally concrete functional meaning. Last but not least, *davar* means "word," but the compound *devar YHVH* is not only the "word of God"; it is a concrete force of creative and destructive power: By the word God created the world (*Gen.* 1:3, etc.; *Ps.* 33:6). There is also something material in it, for God transmitted it to Jeremiah by physically touching his mouth (*Jer.* 1:9); on another occasion he coerced Ezekiel to eat the scroll which contained His words (*Ezek.* 3:1–4 ff.); it aroused a physiological reaction, for Ezekiel relates its sweetness. Its destructive faculty comes to the fore in Jeremiah, where it is supposed to uproot, destroy, and overthrow kingdoms and nations (*Jer.* 1:10).

PRIESTS AND PROPHETS

The nature and function of the priests and prophets within this social network are of deep interest. The Aaronides and the Levites were chosen by God to be the hereditary priesthood in Israel (*Exod.* 28:1ff.; 32:26ff.; *Num.* 8:5ff.; 16:5ff.; etc.).[51] The ark and the tent in the desert, the temple cult in the Land of Israel, the symbols of holiness and purity, and finally the centralization of worship—these are the major fields of activity of the priesthood, as described in the Priestly Source and in *Deuteronomy*. The priests are in charge of the temple worship (*II Kings* 23ff.) which also includes purificatory rites, such as the sprinkling of blood, which is intended to remove impurity. Other rites such as the trial by ordeal of the woman suspected of adultery (*Num.* 5) or the ceremony of the scapegoat (*Lev.* 16:21–26), which have something of a magical character, do not involve the demonic realm, as appears from the absence of exorcistic elements in them. The distinctive feature of biblical magic rites in comparison with those of paganism is that they are not performed for the purpose of banishing harm or sickness. The pagan seeks to avert harm and sickness; his purgatives in effect do battle with the baleful forces that menace men and gods. Biblical purificatory acts lack this aspect entirely. Lustrations play no part in healing the sick. The woman who bears a child, the leper, the gonnorheac, the leprous house, are all purified *after the crisis or the disease has passed*. The priest visits the leper during his sickness to examine the diseased area, to quarantine the man, and later to pronounce him free of infection, but he never performs any *therapeutic* or *exorcistic act*. His only task is to examine the sick, to watch him, and to wait until he is healed. The priestly instructions pertaining to these problems (*Lev.* 13–14) are based on mere observation; these chapters include a rational description of the various ailments and sicknesses which cause impurity. Any magic or divinatory element is lacking.

To summarize: the new monotheistic outlook reshaped the Israelite concept of cult, ritual and priesthood in terms of emancipation from magical and divinatory elements. That magical residue which has survived in the Bible, such as the above-mentioned trial by ordeal of the woman suspected of adultery or the ceremony of the scapegoat of the Day of Atonement are interpreted as an expression of the divine will. The same is true of additional examples: i.e., the removal of plague by incense (*Num.* 17:11ff.) or by sacrifice (*II Sam.* 24:18ff.); the atonement money of the census (*Exod.* 30:11–16), which has an apotropaic nature, as do the bells of the ephod-coat (*Exod.* 28:33ff.); and the incense brought into the Holy of Holies (*Lev.* 16:2, 13). If calamity is caused by the sin of an individual, the sinner or his offspring are destroyed in a specific rite, the aim of which is to propitiate and to purify (*Num.* 25:3 f.; *Josh.* 7; *I Sam.* 14:24ff.; *II Sam.* 21:1ff.). These are possibly vestiges of a popular belief in the existence of a demonic realm. But even these traces of ancient paganism have been transmuted into acts which are performed by divine command. *As for cult and ritual in general, these are conceived by the Bible as the fulfillment of God's commands and as man's free subjection to divine will.*

In this general social setting, we must assess the tasks of the Israelite priesthood: the Levites are the literati, the scholars who were engaged in teaching the divine law (*Deut.* 33:8–12; *Ezek* 44:23–24; *Mal.* 2:6ff.); moreover, in the temple service the Aaronides practice this law and, according to some sources, sit in the high court as judges. It is today widely accepted that the Priestly Source in the Pentateuch reflects the ancient priestly traditions, which developed during the period of the First Temple. It does not contain fantastic inventions of late exilic writers living in Babylonia after the Destruction of the Temple.[52] This source is the creative contribution of the priesthood to ancient Hebrew monotheistic culture.

The position and contribution of the prophets was completely different. Unlike the priests, their position was not hereditary. They were personally selected by God for their mission in Israel; personal charisma and spontaneity were the outstanding features of their election. In ancient pre-classical prophecy, magical and proto-divinatory elements still weigh heavily. They are approached both by common people and kings in order to foretell future events, to heal ailments, and to help the sick. But these activities are never conceived in terms of superhuman faculties or as the result of a special science or esoteric tradition which was at their disposal, as it was for the wizards, sorcerers, soothsayers, and priests of the neighboring pagan cultures. They are neither magicians nor diviners, but commoners who performed miracles thanks to a special divine grace, mercy, or revelation. The miracle testifies to God's omnipotence, which transcends all natural laws and human faculties or "scientific" acquisitions. This is the monotheistic transmutation of ancient Near Eastern magic and divination.

But the major significance of ancient prophecy was its political involvement in events: from Moses to Samuel, this was of an active nature, for the natural leaders of that period were prophets and charismatic judges, who were designated by divine revelation; from Samuel to Elisha, they acted as royal advisers (Nathan) or as a militant opposition (Elijah). Their militancy reached its pinnacle in the bloodstained revolution of Yehu, which was initiated by Elisha and his disciples (*II Kings* 9–10). This conspiracy, which brought about the destruction of the Omride dynasty, was directed against the cult of the Phoenician Baal introduced by the foreign queen, Jezebel. These shocking events, which crystallized in the establishment of the cruel and murderous tyranny of Yehu, brought about major changes in the attitude of Elisha's followers, the classical prophets, who refrained from any active interference in the affairs of state. As messengers of God they stuck to their primary task of reproving kings and the people only through preaching and writing. From these activities developed the bulk of prophetic literature which has come down to us through their followers, disciples, and advisers. This vast literature bears witness to their relentless struggle for justice, righteousness, and social equality, on the one hand, and to their quest for the goal and meaning of the history of Israel and its relations to the nations, on the other. Their theopolitical approach to the events of the day resulted in different historical and political approaches, and the development of eschatological systems which moulded the very core of Jewish and Christian civilization.[53]

The Idea of Creation

It is generally accepted by scholars that the biblical idea of Creation is merely a secondary development, as the fundamental basis of monotheism lies in historical experience. More precisely, the covenant between the nation and its God is the kernel of this belief and its formative basis. Only by accepting this assumption can the uniqueness of the idea of Creation be duly assessed. In the earliest sources, the principal reason given by God for His demands on Israel is His having "brought you out of the land of Egypt, out of the house of bondage," and not His having created the world. The latter is the intellectual deduction of poets and prophets who observed the universe and its marvels. This subject is also raised in Wisdom Literature, among other places in *Prov.* 8 and *Job* 28, where the descriptions are taken from early traditions, bearing substantial witness to poetic intuition and theological reflection. The features of monotheistic myth which have been sketched above are also evident in the world picture which emerges here. The formation of the world is not a matter for intercourse and birth, as depicted in the theogonies of the other nations; nor can one find here the theomachic motif which is another element in creation stories. The ontological detachment of the God of Israel from the universe obviates the presence of theogonic motifs *a priori,* and the absolute supremacy of His will inevitably rules out any dramatic explanation of the formation of the world through battles between gods. The references to wars against the sea monsters, which originated in Canaanite literature and apparently won a place in the minds of ordinary people,[54] were modified so that the great sea monsters were depicted as God's creatures who undertook a hopeless rebellion. There is no dramatic tension in these passages, because their outcome is a foregone conclusion.

The prophets and writers use various devices to neutralize and devitalize this myth. The author of the creation narrative adopts the most extreme course by stressing the fact that "the great whales" (*Gen.* 1:21) are not monstrous, unnatural creatures but were created on the fifth day together with the other denizens of the water. In *Isaiah* 27:1 "Leviathan, the piercing serpent, even Leviathan the crooked serpent" and "the Dragon that is in the sea" no longer signify real creatures but symbolize the forces of evil which the Lord will one day destroy. Deutero-Isaiah and the author of the Psalms base their request that God should demonstrate His strength and might again (*Isa.* 51:9–11; *Ps.* 74: 12–23) on these traditions concerning God's primaeval battle with these forces.

The completely new approach which emerges in contrast to the legends of the ancient Near East is the idea of *creation*. This is not the outcome of a biological or physiological process, i.e. intercourse or birth, nor is it connected with the drama of war. It is an *event* initiated by God. In other words, the act of creation is evidence of God's free, unrestricted will, an expression of His loving-kindness and concern for His world. The motif of creation *ex nihilo* which was to occupy Jewish and Christian thought is still far removed from the world picture of the Bible. The main point is that *ontological detachment* is accompanied by the *voluntary relationship* between God and His world, a fact witnessed by Israel through its own fate. This is the common ground of all creation traditions in the Bible. Israel's primaeval experience during the Exodus from Egypt, the wanderings through the desert, and the revelation of God on Mount Sinai are concrete expressions of this voluntary relationship. This is the infrastructure of the entire Bible, ranging from the narratives of the Exodus to the historiography of the Chronicler. Moreover, this is also the pattern of the patriarchal traditions; according to those, God first revealed Himself to Abraham and made a covenant with him assuring him of descendants and land. The Midrashic legends which relate that Adam and Abraham *discovered* God through observing nature date from a later period and arose from the encounter between the culture of Israel and the observing, reflective culture of Greece. The origins of monotheism lie in revelation and historical experience rather than in observation and discovery. The new cosmological truth inherent in this experience slowly unfolded in ancient Israel's culture of the First Commonwealth. The basic feature of this faith therefore lies in the obligations imposed on the individual and society rather than in the resultant intellectual cognition. Not the belief in the uniqueness of God but the exclusiveness of His service is the core of this new world view.

This God was intuitively experienced as being ontologically detached from creation. This constituted the infrastructure for the legislative, social, and cultic institutions reflecting Israel's relation to its country and other nations. It was against this background that biblical historiography and eschatology developed, forming the framework within which differences between individuals and generations were revealed; some tended towards excessive anthropomorphisms while others, regarding this as a defect, attempted to avoid mythic expression by striving for conceptualization. The mishnaic and apocryphal literature developed within this framework.

The first break in this closed network is connected with the rise of early Christianity, as acceptance of the idea of incarnation—taken from the royal tradition of the ancient East and widespread in various guises in the Hellenistic world—was the price Christianity had to pay for its considerable success in conquering the Roman Empire. By doing so, it placed itself beyond biblical, talmudic, and midrashic monotheism as well as that of most Jewish apocryphal literature, opening itself to a process of paganization from within. The attempt to come to terms theologically with the idea and meaning of incarnation occupies Christian theology and serves as a focus for its internal disputes to this day.

The Creative Dynamics of Monotheistic Myth

To sum up: The very heart of biblical monotheism is the idea of the primaeval covenant between Israel and its Divine King who revealed himself as lawgiver, warrior, loving father, bridegroom, and husband as well. The anthropomorphic language of the Bible as to the Divine King bears evidence of the sweeping, living power of this myth. Its political implication is the establishment of the kingship of God based on the repudiation of any human domination over men. Indeed, this political system was crushed by the onslaught of the Philistines during the eleventh century B.C.E. when they defeated Israel in the battle of Eben-ha'ezer (*I Sam.* 4). The Kingdom of Israel which emerged in the wake of these tragic events was the historical transmutation of the ancient idea of the kingdom of God, the very nucleus of this transmutation being the accountability of the human king before God and his emissaries, the prophets (*II Sam.* 7:14). The historical importance of this revolutionary change of the concept of monarchy lies in the fact that the person of the king remained within the human sphere, as against the absolutist and deificatory features of ancient Near Eastern kingship.

In the social sphere, monotheistic myth created the laws pertaining to the Sabbath, the Sabbatical, and Jubilee years, which are permeated by the tendency to establish social equality and to preserve the basic conditions prevailing during the period of the conquest and the settlement. The stipulations of the Jubilee year again had to be readjusted under the conditions of the Hebrew kingdom, as we have already explained. The establishment of monotheistic society and institutions is a creative dynamic process enhanced by the changing conditions of life and by a constant confrontation with the remains of pagan myth which penetrated Israel from the Canaanite environment. The end of this confrontation was to uproot pagan myth or to integrate it within the framework of the biblical world. The biblical writers adopted a variety of approaches to achieve this end.

1. *Reduction:* Some prophets and authors continued to accept the Sea myth, through reducing the sea-monster and its host from the divine level to that of titanic monsters defeated and slain by God in primaeval battles (*Isa.* 51:9–11; *Ps.* 74:13–16; etc.) or repressed and imprisoned by God (*Ps.* 89:10–11; *Job* 38:8–11; etc.).

2. *Depersonification:* Another way was to alter myth in such a way as to remove the personal nature of its protagonists. The sea and other depths became geographical concepts (*Gen.* 1:2; *Ps.* 104:25, etc.) and the great whales changed from ancient monsters into ordinary creatures, created by God (*Gen.* 1:21).

3. *Ironization:* Some writers did not have recourse to these transformations, and simply ridiculed myth to deprive it of its seriousness, as in the words of the psalmist: There is Leviathan, whom You have created to play with (*Ps.* 104:26), etc.

4. *Allegorization:* Another way of devitalizing pagan myth is through allegorical interpretation, either regarding the ancient monsters as symbols of the forces of evil whom God is to destroy in the end of the days (*Isa.* 27:1), or through historicization, the exodus from Egypt and the passage through the Red Sea being depicted in terms of God's struggle with the mythical forces of the sea (*Isa.* 51:9–11). Another example of historicization pertains to the mythical Hellel ben Shahar, who aimed to displace Elyon and establish his own throne above the stars. In the ironic dirge on the fall of the king of Babylonia Isaiah (14:4–23) describes the hybris of that king in terms of this myth. (For details advise commentaries *ad locum.*)

5. *Antiquarization:* In some cases myth is eliminated by antiquarization, as in the case in *Genesis* 6:1–4 and *Psalms* 82. *Genesis* 6:1–4 indicates that the sons of God did indeed mate with the daughters of man in ancient times, but the results of these unions have long since vanished from the earth, since the giants who were "mighty men which were of old, men of renown" (*Gen.* 6:4) no longer exist and human life has been restricted to one hundred twenty years, unlike former generations. According to Psalm 82, God

removed the sons of God from their position of authority over the
nations because of the injustice they perpetrated, and made them
ordinary mortals. "But you shall die like men, and fall like one of
the princes" (*Ps.* 82:7). Antiquarization deprives these myths of their
actuality.

These are some of the ways in which the Bible contends with
pagan myth, while at the same time creating and expanding the
monotheistic myth based on the ontological detachment of God from
His creation. This myth eventually became the formative element,
molding and shaping ancient Israel's society and culture, as we have
attempted to show.

AKH-EN-ATON AND MONOTHEISM

What is the connection between biblical myth and the long hymn
to Aton, which has been preserved from Akh-en-Aton's time (approximately 1380–1362 B.C.E.) and has been considered by many
scholars to constitute the earliest evidence of monotheism?[55] Aton
is described in it as "the sole god, with whom there is no other."
He is the creator and provider of the lands of Canaan, Nubia, and
Egypt, the creator of everything, lord of the universe, who gives life
to all creatures. The great innovation in this hymn is the liberation
from ancient Egyptian mythology. Aton created himself and his
world. Nevertheless, the term monotheism as defined above does
not apply here. Although his name is like that of one of the early
gods, he is not simply called the sun but "the wheel of the sun"
(eten-aton). This name, which had previously been used for religious
purposes,[56] is firm proof that there was pantheistic-pagan identification of the god with the sun itself.

Recent research tends to emphasize the abstract, transcendent
character of Aton. According to Assmann,[57] Aton is not simply a
sun god but the sunlight itself, symbolized by the shining sun. His
official image proclaimed by the king corresponds with the Egyptian
hieroglyph for light. He has no human or animal apparition whatsoever. Moreover, this god does not speak; communication with him
is possible only through the king, who is his prophet.

But it seems that this trend does not take into account the fact
that the very identification of this god with the sun is a variation
of ancient astral cults rather than monotheism. Moreover, the king
was considered the embodiment of the sun-god on earth, rather than
his prophet. The son of the king was "the eternal son who emerged
from the sun . . . who is reborn each morning like the sun (god),
his father." The Egyptian theologians developed a hierarchical trinity
consisting of Aton himself: "Aton who dwells in the temple of Aton

at Akhetaton," namely, his hypostasis in the temple built by the king at his new capital, and the king himself.[58] These are indications of pagan pantheism. Moreover, the new religion contained no social or ethical message and should, therefore, be defined as proto-monotheism. It led to the most crucial turning point in human history, being borne along on the waves of the syncretist culture of the late Bronze Age.

If its basic features are compared with those of biblical monotheism, two crucial differences immediately become apparent: like other pagan religions, this one is based on the ontological continuum. It emerged through observation of nature and the world, like the conceptions of the pre-Socratic Greek philosophers, though naturally in very different historical circumstances. Both were the result of contemplation by exceptional individuals and contained no new moral or religious message for mankind. Biblical monotheism, however, emerged from the historical experience of an entire nation and focused on its national, social, and ethical content. Particular emphasis should be placed on the close connection between the absoluteness of precepts in monotheism and the transcendent nature of God.

In contrast with the religion of Akh-en-Aton, which was a step towards monotheism, Christianity constituted a conceptual retreat as it accepted the ancient view of God as being inherent in man. Christianity's greatness lies in the biblical tradition and its utopian universalist ethics, but it likewise surmounts the realistically-minded ethical demands of the Pentateuch and the classical prophets.

EPILOGUE

The preceding essay is only a short sketch of the historical breakthrough towards biblical monotheism.

While lack of space has made it necessary to disregard additional motifs pertaining to the inherent religious and social creativeness of monotheistic myth, I hope to have duly demonstrated the innermost structure of this new world-view and way of life, which revolutionized human culture for the past three millennia. The attentive reader will have observed that in contending that the history of monotheism begins with the history of Israel, this presentation of the historical process deviates in a crucial respect from the customary descriptions of the history of biblical faith. It is far from being the creation of the classical prophets, as is commonly assumed. The activities, the literary and the religious achievements of the prophets, i.e. their social criticism, their personal commitment to the cause of righteousness and justice, their new approach to cult, their historiography and religious assessment of their times, as well as their eschatology, can be duly expounded only as the unfolding and deepening of their old monotheistic heritage handed down to them by their forebears. Again, biblical monotheism is conceived here as the formative element of Israel's folk culture. Its beginnings are the result of an existential experience of the whole nation rather than an intellectual achievement of a small elitist prophetic opposition. These are the historical conditions of its evolution from Moses to Deutero-Isaiah, whose speeches contain a clear-cut theological repudiation of paganism.

CHAPTER 6

The Protest against Imperialism in Ancient Israelite Prophecy

MOSHE WEINFELD

In recent years it has been established that people, especially peasants who were striving to get rid of the yoke of imperial tyranny, used to express their hope for a better future by means of oracles and prophecies. Since they learned from experience that an empire does not last forever and were convinced that the prevailing oppressing imperial regime must be overthrown, they were eager to obtain prophecies about a new rulership which would release them from their yoke and suffering. Thus for example in the Sibylline Oracles, which reflect popular Hellenistic ideology, we read:

> For all the wealth that Rome received from . . . Asia,
> threefold as much shall Asia receive back again from Rome
> and shall repay to her her . . . violence. And for all those
> children from Asia who served Italian homes, Italians to
> twenty fold shall live in bondage . . . in Asia, and shall pay
> back their debt ten-thousand times (III, 350–355).[1]

Similarly in the Persian oracle of Hystaspes:

> The name of Rome which rules now the world will be
> destroyed and the rule will be returned to Asia; then the
> Orient will rule again and the Occident will serve.
> (Lactanius, *Divinae Institutiones* VII, 15, 11)[2]

and in the Potter's oracle from Egypt:

> The Greeks will be destroyed and then a new king, who will
> be appointed by Isis, will rule the land again.[3]

Prophecies against Greek and Roman imperialism were of course most prevalent in Judea, as may be learned not only from Josephus (*Bell. Jud.* VI, 312–314) but also from Tacitus (*Historiae* V, 13, 2) and Suetonius (*Vespasianus* IV, 5). Tacitus and Suetonius tell us that a divine oracle was widespread saying that men would come out of Judea and seize world dominion. According to Tacitus and Suetonius this actually predicted the dominion of Titus and Vespasianus, coming back to Rome from Judea, but the Judeans interpreted the prophecy as applying to themselves.

It is our contention here that a similar kind of ideological resistance to imperial tyranny developed in the wake of Assyrian imperialism and is clearly reflected in Israelite prophetic literature of the eighth century B.C.E. Isaiah the prophet, who saw the apogee of Assyrian imperialistic policy, starting with Tiglath-Pileser III and ending with Sennacherib, was the first to raise his voice against Assyrian imperialism and to predict the coming of a new divine rule which would replace Assyrian tyrannic dominion. Like his followers in the Persian and Hellenistic period he decried bitterly the heavy tribute and corvée imposed on the nations by Assyria (9:3, 10:27, 14:25) and foresaw its collapse. The most outspoken anti-imperialistic document of Isaiah is found in *Isa.* 10:5–11:10, a kind of trilogy[4] which contains

    a. The protest against Assyrian dominion and its crimes (10:5–15)
    b. The destruction of Assyria (10:16–34)
    c. The rise of the divine ruler and world salvation (11:1–10)

The divine ruler actually bears the image of an emperor, though ruling not with power but with spirit (*Isa.* 11:4). The typology of measure for measure attested in the Persian and Hellenistic oracles, quoted above, is indeed characteristic of the Israelite anti-imperialistic prophetic genre:

> Woe, you plunderer. . . . when you have finished plundering you shall be plundered (*Isa.* 33:1).
> O, you who pile up what is not yours . . . because you plundered many nations all surviving peoples shall plunder you (*Hab.* 2:6–8).

This anti-imperialistic prophetic genre has not been recognized and therefore has raised misunderstandings amongst scholars. Prophecies of the sort we are discussing here were classified as prophecies against nations, a well-known type of prophetic literature, but this is hardly the case. The conventional genre of the prophecies against nations mainly contains accusations against the enemies of Israel—as for example: Aram is condemned because it threshed the people of Gilead with boards of iron (*Amos* 1:3); Ammon ripped the pregnant women of Gilead (*ibid.* 1:13), or annexed the territory of Israel (*Jer.* 49:1); Edom committed revenge on Judah (*Ezek.* 25:12); and the

Philistines exiled Israelites in order to deliver them to Edom (*Amos* 1:5).[5] Prophecies against Assyria and Babylonia, whenever concerned with inflicting Israel, belong to the same category (cf. e.g. *Micah* 5:4–5; *Isa.* 37:4,6,17,23; *Jerem.* 50–51).

However, following the rise of the Assyrian empire in the eighth century B.C.E., a new trend developed within the framework of these prophecies: nations, and indeed empires, were condemned *not* because of their hostile acts towards Israel but because of their ruthless imperialistic policy. Scholars who did not realize the existence of this type of anti-imperialistic tendency in Israelite prophecy found difficulties in the assessment and definition of prophecies of this kind. Nahum and Habakkuk, who are concerned with Assyria and Babylonia *per se,* and not with the implications of their rule for Israel, were considered not genuine; they are seen rather as cultic prophets or even false prophets.[6] This verdict was also based on the fact that these prophets did not admonish Israel as other prophets did.

Their prophecies were therefore seen as hymns or liturgies and not "prophecy."[7] The truth is that the prophecies of Nahum and Habakkuk—as will be shown—have parallels in Isaiah's prophecy and therefore cannot be considered different from classical prophecy. In fact a great part of Isaiah's prophecies, as well as the prophecies of Nahum and Habakkuk, constitute—in our view—a specific prophetic genre which it would be appropriate to name "prophecies concerning empires." It is true, every one of these prophets formed his message in accordance with the circumstances of his time: Isaiah's prophecies against the Assyrians reflect the climax of the Assyrian empire; Nahum's mockery song about the Assyrian empire was sung against the background of its collapse; while Habakkuk proclaimed his protest following the rise of the Babylonian empire. However all of the prophecies have a common denominator, the condemnation of the imperial policy as such no matter who is the ruling king or against whom he acts. Indeed because of this uniform approach to the empire it is very difficult to identify the Assyrian king whom Isaiah refers to. Is it Tiglath Pileser III, Shalmanessar V, Sargon, or Sennacherib? For the prophet who protests against the very system of imperial rule, they are all the same; they all subdue nations, exploit them, and plunder them.

This is altogether different from Aeschylus' attitude as expressed in *The Persians.* He also protests against the ruthless conduct of the Persian empire (by putting the protest into the mouth of Darius) but distinguishes between different kings. Cyrus, although subduing Ionia by force, was not hated by the gods, since he was rightminded, whereas Xerxes, who invaded the land of Hellas and ruined their altars and temples, is to be damned (759ff.). Here the attitude towards the emperor is determined by national local interests, and there is no unified approach towards the empire like the one expressed by the prophets of ancient Israel.[8] We might state then that Israel was the first nation in world history to raise its voice against imperialism. Let us survey briefly the main features of this anti-imperialistic trend in Israelite prophecy.

PROTESTS AGAINST IMPERIALISTIC BEHAVIOR

This contains roughly the following accusations:

1) annihilation of nations (*Isa.* 10:7; *Hab.* 1:17).
2) destruction of cities and devastating lands (*Isa.* 14:17; 33:8; 37:13).
3) removal of national boundaries (*Isa.* 10:13).
4) plundering and exploiting peoples (*Isa.* 10:14; 33:1,4; *Hab.* 1:9; 2:8–9; *Nahum* 2:12–14; 3:4,16–17).
5) degradation of national leaders (*Isa.* 10:8; *Hab.* 1:10).
6) exile of populations (*Isa.* 10:14; 33:3).

These accusations come boldly to expression in the prophecies of Isaiah, who witnessed the rise of the Assyrian empire to its climax: from Tiglath Pileser III (745 B.C.E.) to Sennacherib's onslaught of Jerusalem in 701. We shall adduce some salient passages of his prophecy against the Assyrian empire. In chapter 10 Isaiah quotes, as it were, the Assyrian king who says:

I have done it with my might, I removed borders of nations, I have plundered their treasures and exiled their vast populations [following the translation of H.L. Ginsberg[9]]. I was able to seize . . . the wealth of peoples . . . (10:13–14).

In the same pericope we read about the Assyrian emperor:

he has evil plans, his mind harbors evil designs, for he intends to destroy, to wipe out nations. . . . he says: 'I have kings as my captains' (10:7–8).

Similarly in the dirge about the Assyrian ruler we read:

Is this the man who shook the earth . . . who made the world like a waste and wrecked its towns, who never released his prisoners to their homes (14:17–18)?

All the six accusations enumerated above are represented here: *removing boundaries, plundering,* and *exile* in 10:13–14, *wiping out nations* and *degradation of leaders* in 10:7–8, *destruction and dev-*

astation of land in 14:17–18. These are—in the prophet's opinion—the crimes of the empire, but besides these, nations bore regularly the yoke—legitimate as it were—of taxes and corvée, and this too is mentioned several times in the prophecies of *Isaiah:* 9:3, 10:27, 14:4–5, 25 ('his yoke shall be removed from them and his burden shall drop from their backs'). Taxes and corvée for a foreign empire were rightly seen as exploitation. In contrast to taxes paid to the local government which were given in exchange for services to the local population, the taxes and corvée work for the empire were given for no exchange, and thus were rightly considered by the prophets robbery.

Nahum's mocking song on Assyria revolves around plunder and exploitation; Assyria is described there as a lion's den filled with prey (2:12–14), and most instructive in this respect is the prophecy in chapter 3:

> Woe, city of crime, utterly treacherous. Full of violence, never devoid of prey . . . who ensnared nations with her harlotries . . . (1–4).
> you had more traders than sky has stars, your agents are like locusts, your clerks like hoppers (vv. 16–17).

Habakkuk, who reacts to the rise of the Babylonian empire, proclaims:

> That fierce, impetuous nation who crosses the earth's wide spaces to seize homes not their own . . . they all come for plunder . . . and they amass captives like sand. Kings they hold in derision, rulers they despise. . . . (1:6–10) he has fished them all up with a line . . . slaughtering nations without pity (1:15–17) who has harvested all the nations and gathered all the peoples (2:5).
> Because you plundered many nations all surviving peoples shall plunder you—for crimes against men and wrongs against lands against cities and all their inhabitants (2:8).
> Ah, you who have built a town with crime and established a city with infamy . . . so that peoples have had to toil for pittance and nations to weary themselves for naught (2:12–13)[10].
> For the violence done to Lebanon shall cover you . . . for crimes against men and wrongs against lands against cities and all their inhabitants.

We do not find here *removing boundaries* and *devastation of land;* on the other hand the motif of plunder and exploitation is much elaborated here. This indeed suits the Babylonian empire, which was less involved in war and conquest and more in building activities;

the neo-Babylonian inscriptions often refer to recruitment of nations for building Babylon, which seems to be reflected in *Habak.* 2:13: peoples toil for naught in connection with the city built with crime. That this refers to the city of Babylon may be learned from the fact that the same phrase 'people toil for naught and nations weary themselves for pittance' occurs in *Jerem.* 51:58 in the prophecy against Babylon there.

Another phrase, concerning the northern power, which is common to Jeremiah and Habakkuk is:

> his chariots are like a whirlwind
> his horses are swifter than eagles (*Jer.* 4:13).
> their horses are swifter than leopards
> their steeds come from afar (*Hab.* 1:8).

We similarly find in Habakkuk an anti-imperialistic cliché identical with one in Isaiah. Habakkuk says:

> because you plundered many nations
> . . . people shall plunder you (2:8).

and Isaiah:

> When you have ceased ravaging
> you shall be ravaged
> when you have finished betraying
> you shall be betrayed (33:1).

We do not have to assume influence of one prophet on the other, for these are stock phrases characteristic of the anti-imperialistic literary genre prevalent in those days. This may be exemplified by two prophetic passages which might also be qualified as anti-imperialistic, viz. *Zeph.* 2:13–15 and *Isa.* 47:8–15. The former refers to Assyria and the latter to Babylon. Both are said in connection with the *hubris* of these empires and here we find identical phraseology:

> that says to herself: I am, and there is none but me
> (*Zephaniah* 2:15; *Isaiah* 47:8).

It is possible that the cliché was originally used in respect to Assyria and was later applied to Babylon. If this is correct this reflects an inner literary development in the genre discussed here.

Another cliché referring to the oppressing regime of the empire is *yoke (wl), burden (sbl)* and *yoke bands (mwsrwt)* which denote heavy taxes and corvée work.[11] These expressions appear in the Assyro-Babylonian inscriptions describing the imposition of the emperor's subjection upon his vassals[12] and therefore play an important role in the anti-imperialistic prophetic genre.

Thus Isaiah uses three times the phrase: *removing the burden and the yoke* (of the Assyrians) (9:3, 10:27, 14:25) while Jeremiah speaks about *breaking the yoke* and *tearing the yoke bands* so that the foreigners shall no longer subjugate them (30:8). The same cliché is found in Nahum 1:12–13:

> I will not subjugate you anymore. I will break the yoke from you and tear your yoke bands.

Two other clichés referring to the cruelty and devastating force of the empire are the figures of the lion and the flood. Both are used in the Assyrian annals describing the strength of the empire (the lion) and the sweeping attack of its army (the flood). In the prophetic writings these receive a negative connotation: the lion denotes cruelty and not strength; the flood renders devastation and not sweeping victory.[13] Isaiah speaks about Assyria as the waters which will overflow and sweep over reaching the neck (8:7–8) or the 'raging flood sweeping by' (28:15) while Nahum, close to his above-mentioned prophecy about breaking the yoke, mentions the end which God will make to the sweeping flood (1:8).

Assyria is described in *Nahum 2:12–13* as the *lion that fears victims . . . and fills his lairs with prey,* which is to be compared with *Isa.* 5:29:

> they roar like young lions, when they growl and seize a prey they carry it off and none can recover it.

Most instructive is the simile common to Nahum and Isaiah of the Assyrian tax collectors as locusts:

> you had more traders than the sky has stars a swarm which spreads out and flies away your agents are like locusts, your clerks like hoppers (*Nahum 3:16–17*).

This is to be compared with Isaiah 33:1–4:

> Ha, you ravager who are not ravaged . . . at (your) roaring[14] people have fled at your rumbling nations have scattered, spoil is swept up as if locusts swept it like a swarm of locusts (men) swarm upon it.[15]

It seems that during the Assyrian rule of Israel and Judah there developed a whole lore of popular sayings and imagery about the oppressor which is reflected in the prophetic writings concerning the empires.

THE RULING EMPIRE—A PROBLEM OF THEODICY

Not only the emperors themselves but even their subjects were aware that rule was given to the empire by a divine call or mission. The Assyrian annals open usually with the notion that the king has been called by the god Ashur and designated to rule the four corners of the world. The prophet Isaiah recognized that Assyria had been ordained by the God of Israel to rule nations and chastise them (10:5). Furthermore the Isaianic conception that Assyria is the *rod of anger* in the hands of God in order to punish sinful nations seems to be a dominant motif in the Assyrian sources. In one of the inscriptions of Esarhaddon, the King of Assyria (680–669 B.C.E.), we read:

> The great god Ashur . . . put in my hand a rod of anger *(šibirru ezzu)* to destroy the enemies, he authorized me to plunder and spoil *(ana habāti šlāli)* the land which sins . . . against Ashur.[16]

This is almost congruent with Isaiah's prophecy in *Isa.* 10:5ff.:

> Ha! Assyria, *rod of my anger.* . . . I sent him against an ungodly nation, I commanded him over a people that provokes me *to spoil and plunder* and to make it trampled like the mire of the streets.

The same applies to the Babylonian empire.

Nebuchadnezzar proclaims that he was entrusted by his god to rule all mankind and that he was given the sceptre for directing the whole inhabited world.[17] Jeremiah, his contemporary, proclaims on behalf of the God of Israel: 'I made the earth, the man and beasts who are on the earth . . . and I give it to *whomever I deem proper.* I herewith deliver all these lands to my servant, King Nebuchadnezzar of Babylon. . . . all nations shall serve him' (27:5–7). Similar to the passage of Jeremiah we hear Nebuchadnezzar proclaiming in his inscriptions that his god has chosen him as the one who is fit for him *(ša elika tābu).*[18]

The Persian emperor is also seen destined by his god to rule the world by the Persians as well as by the Israelites, Babylonians, and Greeks. The Persians considered Ahura-Mazda as the god who called the Persian kings to rule: Ahura-Mazda, who created *heaven, earth,* and *man,* appointed him (the Persian king) as king to rule over many and over many territories. . . .[19] Deutero-Isaiah formulates Cyrus' mission in an identical phraseology:

> I who made the *earth* and created *man* upon it . . . stretched
> out the *heavens* . . . roused him (Cyrus) for victory and will
> straighten his path for him (*Isa.* 45:12–13).

Is it mere coincidence that in both the Persian as well as the Israelite
passages heaven, earth, and man are mentioned? Not less instructive
is the prophecy at the beginning of *Isa.* chap. 45:

> Thus said the Lord to Cyrus . . . whose right hand he has
> grasped treading down nations before him. . . . I will march
> before you and straighten the hills . . . (45:1–2).

The phrase 'to straighten his path' (*Isa.* 45:13) is found in connection
with Nebuchadnezzar in the Babylonian inscriptions (*harrānu išartu
tapaqisu,* Langdon, *ibid.,* p. 122:60) which we quoted above. As has
been recently established, the Persian imperial style is actually derived
from Assyro-Babylonian prototypes.[20]

The idea that Cyrus was ordained as ruler of the world prevails
in the historiography of the post-exilic period. Thus we read in *Ezra*
1:2 = *2 Chronicles* 36:23:

> Thus said king Cyrus of Persia: the Lord God of Heaven has
> given me all the kingdoms of the earth. . . .

The Babylonians described the mission of Cyrus in a similar
manner (ascribing his call, of course, to the Babylonian deity):

> Marduk looked for a righteous ruler. . . . he pronounced the
> name of Cyrus to be ruler of all the world. . . . he made him
> set out on the road to Babylon going at his side like a friend
> and companion.[21]

There is an identical imagery in the Israelite, Babylonian, and Persian
descriptions of Cyrus, which may point to a common origin of the
motifs involved. Most interesting is the motif of the king as "friend"
of the god which is attested in the Persian inscriptions: 'Ahura-
Mazda is my friend' (DS; 4) as well as in Deutero-Isaiah's prophecy:

> Thus says the Lord . . . who says of Cyrus: he is my friend
> [!] he shall fulfill all my purposes (*Isa.* 44:28).

Compare:

> He whom the Lord loves [= Cyrus] will execute his purpose
> in Babylon (*Isa.* 48:14).

The Greeks conceived the role of the Persian emperor in a similar
manner:

> Our Lord Zeus first ordained . . . that one ruler should bear
> sway over all Asia with its flocks and wield the sceptre of its
> government . . . (Aeschylus, *The Persians,* 762f.).

It is clear then that the idea that the emperor—be he Assyrian,
Babylonian, or Persian—rules by grace of God was common in the
ancient world. The great difference however between the Assyrian
understanding of the mission and the Israelite one is that according
to Assyrian understanding whatever the emperor does reflects the
will of his god, while Isaiah makes a clear distinction between the
divine mission and the human fulfillment of it. There is this important distinction between the free will of man and divine predestination. God sent Ashur to punish nations because of their sins,
but the Assyrian king performs the mission not on behalf of God
but simply because he wants to wipe out nations, humiliate their
leaders, and plunder their treasures (*Isa.* 10:5–14). Furthermore, the
Assyrian king consideres his victories are stemming from his own
might and wisdom; his power is actually the prime mover of his
actions and thus is defied (see below).

Here we find a similarity with Aeschylus' presentation of Xerxes
the Persian emperor. As indicated above, the Persian emperor is
seen there too as ordained by god (Zeus) to rule the world. However
when describing the sins of Xerxes, by putting words in the mouth
of his father Darius, he says that Zeus chastises for overwhelming
pride and that Xerxes should withdraw from ravaging Hellas and
desecrating its sancta; otherwise he will suffer disaster for his pre-
sumptuous pride *(hubris)* and impious thoughts (*The Persians,* 807ff.).
However, as noted above, the sin there is against Hellas and not
against mankind as we find in Isaiah.

THE QUEST FOR UNIVERSAL REDEMPTION

As religious thinkers Israeli prophets asked themselves about the
meaning of this new phenomenon in world history: world empires
taking place of small independent nations. The question became
burning when, after the fall of the Assyrian empire, which brought
universal joy (compare *Isa.* 14:3–27, *Nahum* 3), there arose another
empire again. The question was posed in the most outspoken manner
by the prophet Habakkuk:

> You (the Lord) whose eyes are too pure to look upon evil
> . . . why do you look upon treachery and stand by idle while
> the wrong devours the right? You have made mankind like
> the fish of the sea like creeping things to rule over them[22]

. . . that is why he sacrifices to his trawl and makes offerings
to his net.
For through them his portion is rich and his nourishment fat.
Shall he keep them unsheathing his sword[23] and slaying
nations without pity (1:12–17)?

In other words, how long will tyranny prevail in the world? The
prophet plays here with the idea of "man as ruler." As we know
from *Gen.* 1:28 and *Psalm* 8:7–9 man was designated by the creator
to be master of nature and especially "to rule the fish of the sea,
the birds of the sky and all that creeps on earth." Now in the empire
system man, "the ruler," becomes himself ruled and is treated like
fish which is put in the net and like the creeping things which are
trampled upon. The prophet asks then the creator why he inverted
the order and turned man, the master, into a creeping thing. On the
other hand, he refers to the ruler's deification of his net and thus
makes clear that it is not God who makes him rule but his idol
which is his own power. The net becomes, as it were, his deity
through which he is enabled to get his venison and gather wealth.
Therefore he worships it and sacrifices to it. The same idea is
expressed in 1:11: 'and ascribes[24] to his might divine power' but it
is most elaborated at the end of his anti-imperial prophecy:

What has carved image availed . . . that he who fashioned
his product has trusted in it making dumb idols? . . . Can
that give an oracle? It is encased in gold and silver but there
is no breath inside it (2:18–19).

The empire is the embodiment of idolatry which is doomed to
failure. End of idolatry is end of empire. Bowing down to idols
made out of gold and silver means worshipping the work of one's
own hand and is tantamount to prostration and submission to the
imperial power.

This is indeed one of the profound ideas of prophecy, already
found in Hosea:

Assyria shall not save us, nor shall we ride on horse, no more
again will we call our handiwork our god (14:4). (Compare
Isa. 2:8; *Micah* 5:12.)

This outlook lies indeed at the roots of the resistance to the Roman
empire; it was especially the so-called 'fourth philosophy' described
by Josephus (*Antiq.* XVIII 23–25, comp. BJ II, 118), which fostered
the idea that submittance to human power is like idol-worshipping
punished by death.

Habakkuk then posed the question to God and waits for an answer:

> I will stand on my watch . . . and wait to see what he will
> say to me (2:1)

The Lord answered:

> Write the prophecy down, inscribe it clearly on tablets . . .
> for the prophecy is witness . . . for the appointed time that
> will come. Even if it tarries wait for it still, for it will surely
> come, without delay. . . . The righteous man will survive by
> his trust . . . (2:2–4).
> How much longer?
> Right suddenly will your creditors arise . . . and you will be
> despoiled by them. Because you plundered many nations . . .
> peoples will plunder you, for crimes against men and wrongs
> against lands against cities and all their inhabitants (2:6–8).

The answer is clear. Wait patiently until the appointed time (*mw'd,
qṣ*) comes when the oppressor will get measure for measure: the
Babylonians will be plundered as they plundered others. An identical
concept is attested in *Isa.* 33:1 in connection with Assyria: 'when
you have finished ravaging you shall be ravaged, when you have
finished betraying you shall be betrayed'. The foundation is thus laid
for the concept of change of empires which became so dominant in
Daniel.

Jeremiah a contemporary of Habakkuk, although pro-Babylonian,
anticipates a succession of empires:

> All nations shall serve him (Nebuchadnezzar) . . . until the
> turn of his own land comes, when many nations and great
> kings shall subjugate him (27:7).

In chapter 25:11 the time of the Babylonian turn is fixed as seventy
years, a sacred interval quite dominant in the soteriology of Daniel
(compare *Dan.* 9:24–27). The idea of "appointed time" for universal
redemption is most developed in Daniel, where we find very often
the concepts of 'time of the end' (*st qṣ*) and 'the appointed time'
(*mw'd*) (8:19; 11:27, 35; 12:4, 9, 13). As in Habakkuk so in Daniel
the vision (*ḥzwn*) is for a future date, it has to be concealed for
'many days' (*Dan.* 8:17, 26; 12:9). The divine kingdom set up by
God, on the other hand (*Dan.* 2:44; 7:13–14), is influenced by the
vision of Isaiah in chap. 2:1–4 (= *Micah* 4:1–4) and 11:1–9 (see
below).

THE ATTITUDE TOWARDS THE PERSIAN EMPIRE

In contrast to Assyria and Babylonia, which were severely condemned by the prophets, Persia was highly praised.[25] Deutero-Isaiah,

who denounced Babylon for its *hubris* (*Isa.* 47, cf. especially verse 8: 'that says to herself: I am and there is none but me') saw in Cyrus, the King of Persia, the ideal ruler who will be guided by the Lord in his conquests (*Isa.* 41:2–3, 45:1–2) and will restore Jerusalem and Judah (*ibid.* 44:26, 45:13); and, what is more, following his victories, peoples will abandon their idols and turn to the true God of Israel (45:6, 14–15, 20–25). The fact that he was the one who destroyed the Babylonian empire (43:14, 45:3, 48:14) added of course to his glory:

> Assemble, all of you, and listen. . . .
> He whom the Lord loves
> shall realize his plan against Babylon
> and with his might against Chaldea . . .
> I have brought him and he shall succeed in his mission
> (48:14–15)

In this respect our prophet stands on common ground with the Babylonians and Greeks (as indicated above) who glorified Cyrus. Most surprising is the title given to Cyrus: 'The God's Messiah' (45:1), a title reserved to Israelite kings of divine stature.

Metamorphosis of the Empire—The Spiritual Universal Kingdom

The same prophet who opened the campaign against imperialism formed the ideology of the spiritual world centre in Jerusalem (*Isaiah* 2:2–4; 11:1–10). This ideology of a branch of Jesse ruling with the breath of his lips, establishing external peace in the world and serving "a standard" to people who will seek his counsel (*Isa.* 11:1–9) on the one hand, and of the temple in Jerusalem serving a universal centre to which peoples from the world will ascend in order to accept the verdict of peace (*Isa.* 2:2–4) on the other, actually constitutes a transformation of a physical empire into a spiritual one.[26]

In the imperial reality nations stream to the capital of the empire to bring tribute and express submission to the emperor. In the picture of the ideal future, as depicted by Isaiah, nations come to Zion in order to express their submission to the God of Israel (*Isa.* 2:2–4).

The real emperor rules by force and dictates peace following his victory. In the Isaianic picture justice and eternal peace are established by the ideal king through the breath of his lips. Following his rule the whole earth is filled with knowledge of the Lord (*Isa.* 11:1–9). Royal-imperial characteristics come boldly to expression in the opening of this prophecy. The description of the dynastic origin of the ideal king, 'a rod from the stem of Jesse and a branch from

his roots,' is characteristic of the description of the dynastic line of
the Assyrian emperors, e.g.: "eternal offspring of Belbani son of
Adasi, King of Assyria, precious branch of Baltil, seed of Kingship,
everlasting shoot."[27] By the same token the attributes of the ideal
king that appear in *Isa.* 11:2, "wisdom, insight, counsel and valor,
knowledge and fear of god," are also characteristic of Mesopotamian
royal titles. The king is called possessor of wisdom and knowledge,
a warrior and counsellor, and one who knows and fears his god.[28]
But the godly nature of the kingdom as found in Isa. 11 is not
attested there.

This picture of a divine empire actually stands behind the image
of the kingdom of heaven which will be revealed at the 'end of the
days' following the crush of the human empires (*Daniel* 2:28, 44;
7:17).

The kingdom of heaven which is destined to replace the earthly
empire in *Daniel* 2:44 has affinities with the vision of the holy mount
of *Isa.* 2:2–4. The mountain, out of which the stone was hewn out
and the statue struck, is a divine mount which will fill the whole
earth (*Dan.* 4:34; comp. *Isa.* 11:9) and equals the mount of the Lord
in *Isa.* 2:2–4 to which at the end of the days all the nations will
stream in order to learn the ways of God. On the other hand the
image of 'the son of man' to whom kingdom will be given forever
and all the nations will serve him (7:14, compare v. 27) corresponds
to the figure of the branch of Jesse in *Isa.* 11:1, who will rule with
the spirit of the Lord and all the nations will obey him.

The concept which dominates later eschatology about a new ideal
kingdom built on the ruins of a former ruthless empire was actually
conceived for the first time in Judah in the eighth century B.C.E. It
was motivated by national feelings of oppression and subjugation
to the Assyrian empire. Similar eschatological hopes were given
expression whenever a new empire rose and oppressed nations. The
Israelite prophets who acted at the rise of the first world empire
were thus the first in world history to raise their voice against imperial
tyranny and to depict instead a glorious picture of mankind living
in harmony under divine guidance.

CHAPTER 7

On Self-Consciousness
in Mesopotamia

PETER MACHINIST

INTRODUCTION

As proposed by Karl Jaspers, S.N. Eisenstadt, and others,[1] the civilizations of the Axial Age are distinguished by two related features: one intellectual, the other social. Intellectually, they are the source and origin of new kinds of ideologies—indeed, one may say, the first real ideologies—which strive to present a comprehensive view of the world, not merely of any particular group, and argue that the main task is to remake present reality, corrupt and imperfect as it is, in accordance with the dictates of a higher moral order. Socially, Axial civilizations come to be pervaded by new kinds of groups, labelled by Eisenstadt "autonomous elites," because their existence, recruitment, and legitimacy do not depend finally on the political establishment, nor on traditional kinship ties, but on individual qualifications, especially intellectual ability. It is the *raison d'être* of these groups, in turn, to create, promulgate, and refine the new ideologies.

The two-part characterization just outlined must be judged as an "ideal type," as a model which, starting from the assumption that human society has been evolving, seeks to identify a crucial stage in that evolution, the emergence of Axial civilizations. The utility of this characterization, accordingly, depends as much on its power to explain the nature and history of non-Axial cultures as it does of Axial ones.

The present paper attempts a limited test of the Axial thesis. Our subject will be a civilization proposed as non-, or better pre-Axial: ancient Mesopotamia. Our concern will be with whether self-conscious or self-critical thinking had any place in Mesopotamian activity. Such thinking, Eisenstadt and others have urged,[2] is funda-

183

mental to the ideological enterprise in Axial cultures, for the very task of constructing a *Weltanschauung,* with a dualistic view of reality, entails explicit questioning, framed on a fairly abstract plane, about the nature of knowing, about the manner of conceptualizing problems, and about the identity of the individual vis-à-vis his work and other individuals and groups beyond him. A full examination of self-consciousness in the Mesopotamian context is impossible here. We shall look, instead, at the long and varied Mesopotamian literary record, where, if anywhere, self-consciousness might be expected to surface, and consider how or if it grapples with three related manifestations of the self-conscious mode: (1) the issue of group identity; (2) views about literature and authorship; and (3) the possibility of abstract and analytical thinking. Then, on the basis of what we find, we shall hazard some concluding conjectures about the place of self-consciousness in Mesopotamian culture, the nature of the elites concerned with its expression, and the larger implications for the relationship between pre-Axial and Axial civilizations.

GROUP IDENTITY AND THE OTHER

We may begin with a statement of the late A.L. Oppenheim, from a paper prepared for an earlier symposium on the Axial Age:

> The first shortcoming in texts from Mesopotamia is the consistent absence of any expression of that civilization's uniqueness in the face of an alien background. Thus no need is felt to contrast native ways of thinking or doing things with those of the outside world. Nor are its merits and achievements ever set forth in contradistinction to foreign views and values.[3]

Much in this statement carries conviction, for nowhere in Mesopotamian literature is there anything like a systematic ethnography of a foreign group or a treatise on Mesopotamian national character. Indeed, no word exists in the native lexicon to represent the civilization that we today label, adapting a Greek term, Mesopotamia.[4] We find only more specialized rubrics, describing the individual political, social, or cultural groups within it. Nonetheless, there are hints in the literary record—and more than that, occasional discussions—of a concern for the fabric of Mesopotamian civilization and the world beyond, which would repay our attention.

In the first place, if they yield no term for Mesopotamia, the texts reveal in other ways an awareness of the interconnections which made it up. Central to this awareness are the two regions which constituted Mesopotamia already from prehistoric times: the south or the later Babylonia, and the north or the later Assyria. In the south, the record shows a persistent ideal of political unity, even though that had to contend in practice with localistic sentiment which regularly interfered with its realization. We meet, for example, a succession of Sumerian and Akkadian terms created to denominate the region as a whole—*kalama; ki-engi ki-uri = māt Šumerī u Akkadī; māt Akkadī; māt Karduniaš*—which continued in use from the latter third millennium B.C.E. through the arrival of the Greeks in the latter first millennium B.C.E., whether actual political unity operated or not.[5] This sense of unity is also set forth in texts like the Sumerian King List, a major piece of historiography from the period 2100–1700 B.C.E., which describes the history of the south as united under a system of rule by successive cities—a system said to be the work of the gods themselves, who brought the institution of kingship from heaven for the purpose.[6]

Even more than political unity, southern texts exemplify a sense of a common cultural heritage. One crucial ingredient in this was the gods, who, though attached to particular cities, were also understood to belong to a wider Babylonian assembly. Numerous hymns, myths, and other compositions attest to the location of this assembly—in Nippur for the earlier texts, in Babylon for the later—and to its power to decide who would be the leader in heaven and the corresponding human ruler in the south.[7] A second manifestation of a common culture was the texts themselves, or more precisely, those groups of them aptly labelled by Oppenheim "the stream of tradition."[8] Assembled, transmitted, and revised over many centuries and from all parts of the south by scribes working under royal patronage, these texts spoke to the basic institutions of the culture—they included legal "codes," hymns, omens, rituals, scribal lists, inscriptions of earlier kings, etc.—and represented both the Sumerian and the Akkadian halves of the bilingual tradition, even after Sumerian had died out as a vernacular. To be sure, the collections of them which were gathered by the various southern cities were not identical; and, in turn, not every text was preserved over the entire course of southern history. But common elements and significant overlaps can be discerned among the city collections, and deliberate efforts can be observed by the ancient rulers to fill in the transmission gaps. Most assiduous in this regard were the Chaldean kings of the sixth century B.C.E., the last independent dynasty of Babylonia, whose attempts to reforge some of the broken links with the past—and so to offset the impact of their own ultimately foreign origin—included the excavation, recopying, even imitation of Agade royal inscriptions of almost two millennia earlier.[9]

The expressions of unity we have been examining from southern Mesopotamia find their counterpart in the north. Indeed there, they were much more congruent with the actual political situation, since the northern cities, particularly Ashur, formed the nucleus of the expanded Assyrian state and, unlike Babylonia, developed in close dependence upon that expansion, being created and controlled by the same ruling elite. This tighter integration of power is symbolized most concisely by the fact that one god, Ashur, remained the head of the pantheon throughout Assyrian history and that his name was identical with that of the state as a whole and the capital city at its core.[10] Integration is also emphasized in a variety of official texts, most prominently, the Assyrian King List, which organizes the entire range of Assyrian monarchs, themselves not all of the same family, into a continuous line of rule from their putative beginnings until the latter eighth century B.C.E., when the latest known edition of the list was composed.[11]

But a sense of group identity in Mesopotamia was not confined to Assyria or Babylonia separately. Although the distinctions between the two regions could never be overcome, throughout historic and even prehistoric periods a special relationship between them is discernible, in which the south assumed the role of cultural center. In historic periods, this relationship manifested itself especially in the strenuous efforts exerted by the Assyrian ruling elite—the Babylonians did not normally reciprocate—to identify with and incorporate Babylonian culture into their own. At stake was everything from the adoption or adaptation of Babylonian gods and their cults, sometimes forcibly, through the use of Babylonian literary dialects to compose Assyrian official texts, to the creation of major literary collections or libraries, absorbing "the streams of tradition" of both Babylonia and Assyria. The climax of such efforts—and of Assyrian imperial expansion, generally—came in the military-political conquest of Babylonia by the Assyrian monarchs, and their assumption of the Babylonian royal titles alongside their own. Twice, in fact, this entailed even the destruction of the leading city of Babylon and the removal of key cultural treasures to Assyria and its old capital at Ashur. The intent here, as suggested in certain Assyrian texts like the Tukulti-Ninurta I Epic, composed to celebrate the events, was literally to create a unified "Mesopotamian" polity, with Ashur replacing Babylon as the center.[12]

In sum, the literary record shows clear evidence of a regional and, though less pervasive, even a pan-Mesopotamian consciousness. Did Mesopotamians, then, go farther and seek to discover what constituted, in Oppenheim's words, "the merits and achievements" of their civilization? I believe they did, and perhaps the most significant expression of this in the texts concerns the achievement of urbanism.

Cities were a key feature of the Mesopotamian landscape, already from the prehistoric period.[13] But as we have seen, they were rather differently constituted in the Babylonian south, where they were quite numerous and often resistant to larger political structures, from the Assyrian north, where they remained just a few and were identified from the start with the Assyrian state and empire. These differences are reflected in the greater prominence and autonomy given to cities in southern texts, yet even the Assyrian tradition does not fail to affirm their importance in the political order—a stance clearly enhanced by the origin of most of the texts, whether from north or south, in urban environments. Several examples may illustrate how this political importance was articulated. From the south, there is the Sumerian King List, which, as we have seen, understands the history of the region as the divinely determined rule of successive cities. We may also recall those southern texts which show us the gods as essentially city-rooted, both in their role representing specific cities and in their participation in a wider assembly that itself was urban-based. The point here is no more dramatically illustrated than in the mythological poem Enuma elish, which narrates the defeat of chaos and the construction of an ordered universe by the god Marduk—a task not complete until he establishes as his own abode and that of his divine colleagues the city of Babylon.[14] One other marker of political importance is the city titles, like "king of Ur" and "lord of Uruk," which continued to play a conspicuous part in the repertoire of Babylonian kings, even after their sovereignty had outgrown the scope of a single settlement or two.[15] Indeed, in several cases, as with "king of Kish" or "king of Babylon," the city title was simply expanded to become one designation of the enlarged territorial state.[16] The same phenomenon might have been expected in Assyria also, whose origin and core, as we have observed, lay in the city of Ashur. But while there are Assyrian texts that emphasize the grandiose appearance and political prominence of the Assyrian cities,[17] the Assyrian kings never call themselves "king of the city Ashur" or "ruler of any other Assyrian settlement." In their titulary, rather, Ashur designates only the national god or the country,[18] bespeaking, thus, the general absorption of city into state in Assyrian ideology noted before.

We have been talking about cities as political centers in Mesopotamian literature. But there is another, perhaps more fundamental value that the texts stress: the city—or sometimes more inclusively, the city and the rural environs it is understood to dominate—as the only viable setting for the cultivation of human behavior and achievement—exactly our Latin-derived "civilization." This value is viewed polemically by the literary tradition, that is, it is normally affirmed by contrast to groups that are thought not to share in the characteristics of Mesopotamian urban life.

We must be careful here, however. There is no assertion in the literary record that cities and their environs are unique to the Mesopotamian realm. Contact had existed for too long with urban communities elsewhere in the Near East to allow such a misconception. But once one left the Tigris-Euphrates valley that constituted Mesopotamia geographically, the urban setting was not all one would find. Mesopotamian texts speak frequently of the treacherous mountain passes, rivers in flood, expansive deserts, or murky forests which lay in wait and required heroic efforts to negotiate.[19] The people who lived in such places—with no cities or at least with none in the broad plains typical of Mesopotamia—were, thus, "strange" (Sumerian *kúr*/Akkadian *ahû* or *nakru*). And of them, two types, not always clearly separated, seem to have impressed Mesopotamian writers particularly: the "nomads" and the mountaineers.

The "nomadic" Amorites, for instance, are described in The Marriage of the God Martu, a Sumerian poem from the end of the third millennium B.C.E., as:

A tent-dweller [buffeted (?)] by wind and rain . . .
  prayers. . . .
Dwelling in the mountain. . . .
The one who digs up mushrooms at the foot of the
  mountain, who does not know how to bend the knee;
Who eats uncooked meat;
Who in his lifetime does not have a house;
Who on the day of his death will not be buried.[20]

From about the same period, the mountainous Gutians appear in another Sumerian text, the Curse of Agade, as: "not classed among people, not reckoned as part of the land; Gutium, a people who know no inhibitions, with human instincts, but canine intelligence, and monkeys' features."[21] And two or three centuries later, the Old Babylonian King Hammurapi calls the Gutians and two other groups "whose mountainous regions are distant, whose languages are confused"—the later remark, a clear echo of the Greek *barbaros*.[22]

The texts just referred to belong to the third and early second millennia B.C.E. But something similar can be found in the first millennium B.C.E, especially in the inscriptions of the Neo-Assyrian kings of the eighth–seventh centuries. By this period, to be sure, a number of new nomadic and mountainous groups had emerged, like the Arabs, Aramaeans, and Mannaeans; yet not infrequently, they are described in the old, familiar ways.[23] Thus, Sargon II refers to the mountainous Mannaeans as living "in confusion," whom he has to "put into order."[24] And in another text, the same monarch talks about a route into Babylon being

> not open, [its r]oad was not passable. The country had been deserted from time immemorial. . . . (In) the inaccessible tracts, thorns, thistles, and forests predominated over them; dogs and jackals gathered inside of them, and huddled together [?] like lambs. In that desert country, Aramaean-Sutu, tent-dwellers, fugitives, treacherous ones, a race of plunderers, had pitched their dwellings, and stopped passage across it. [There were] settlements among them which had fallen into ruin for many days past. Over their cultivated ground, channel and furrow did not exist, [but] it was woven [with] spiders' webs.[25]

Significantly, in these Neo-Assyrian descriptions of nomads and mountaineers, even the older labels can reappear. Some like "Sutu" are used because they do, in fact, correspond to external reality. But others like "Gutian" clearly represent more of a literary heirloom, applied pejoratively, for by the first millennium B.C.E. the historical Gutians had long since faded from view.[26]

Taken all together, then, the descriptions of nomads and mountaineers in Mesopotamian literary texts from the third through the first millennia suggest a certain stereotyping. While there is obviously some basis in actual observed behavior, the continuity of expressions and labels in these descriptions, their tendency toward vagueness, metaphorical hyperbole, and disparagement—all argue that they cannot be considered real ethnographies. This is confirmed by the fact that where we can check on the specific groups referred to, from other sources like administrative documents and uninscribed artifacts, or from comparative study of nomads and mountaineers in other periods and regions, we find their interaction with the urban environment much more complex—indeed, overlapping and interpenetrating—than the rigid demarcation projected in our literary tradition.[27] It is also of interest that our tradition elsewhere uses some of the same images, like lawlessness and animal-like behavior, to describe primordial men at the dawn of creation, i.e. men supposed to have lived before, and without the benefit of, cities.[28]

If they cannot, thus, be trusted as sources on outsiders, what is the significance of these descriptions from the Mesopotamian literary tradition? The answer must be that they tell us about the values of the Mesopotamian urban elites themselves, the ones responsible for

their composition. In other words, the descriptions function to affirm
the centrality of the Mesopotamian city and its environment by
defining what it is not: not a "distant" or "inaccessible" place in
the order of things; not supportive of humans who are "confused"
or speak "confused" tongues, who "flout" the rules and institutions
of order, who live in "tents" or other unstable dwellings, located,
in turn, in uncultivated "wastelands," whose behavior, in brief, is
like that of "wild animals." Or, in the contrast of certain southern
texts from the late third–early second millennia B.C.E., nomads and
mountaineers are just *(nam) lū.ulu₆,* "folks," part of the undiffer-
entiated mass of humanity. They are not *un,* "people," i.e., a defin-
able, organized, sedentary community, of which Mesopotamia, it is
self-understood, furnishes the example *par excellence.*[29]

These negative descriptions, then, serve as a kind of verbal "frontier," marking what their writers consider the limits of urban civilization, much as physically the *Murīq-Tidnim* wall of Shu-Sin, or
the Great Wall of China, or the Roman *limes* functioned, in Owen
Lattimore's terms, to define the outer boundaries of Ur III Mesopotamian, Chinese, and Roman society, respectively.[30] Particularly
to be noted is that our descriptions cluster around the latter third–early
second millennia and the middle of the first millennium B.C.E., when
other sources document the full-scale emergence of the nomads and
mountaineers in Mesopotamian society, at its urban core.[31] It was,
therefore, in the urgent complexity of differentiating "outsider" from
"insider" that the descriptions seem to have been composed: an
ideological device, as it were, to co-opt at least part of the outsiders,
the "acceptable" ones, for the urban inside.[32]

This device is, of course, familiar to the self-ascriptive behavior
of most human groups in plural societies; and in the present case,
its intent is made explicit by the assertion elsewhere in the Mesopotamian literary tradition that nomads and mountaineers—and
foreigners, in general—are indeed "acceptable," providing they can
"become," or "be made to acquire," the accouterments of Mesopotamian urban life. Thus, we hear constantly in the Neo-Assyrian
royal inscriptions of the first millennium B.C.E. about "Assyrianizing"
foreign lands and peoples: "to teach them correct behavior, to fear
god and king," as a cylinder-text of Sargon II puts it.[33] "Conversion"
is also the issue at the beginning of the Epic of Gilgamesh, which
narrates the passage of Enkidu from a kind of primordial man, living
in the steppe with the animals, to a resident of the city Uruk and
companion of Gilgamesh—a passage initiated by contact in the steppe
with a woman whose profession was seen primarily as an urban one,
a courtesan.[34] And the point is addressed again in the myth about
the "nomad" god Martu, excerpted above, which tells of his marriage

to the daughter of Numushda, the god of the Babylonian city Kazallu, and his settling down as the god of another Babylonian city, Ninab.[35]

While, then, as *categories,* "nomad," "mountaineer," "foreigner" were immutable, *individuals and groups* within them were not; and regardless, the *city* always remained dominant. In this way, the Mesopotamian urban elites sought to foster ideologically their self-identity, which external reality increasingly threatened to dissolve. We should not wonder that among their own number—and among their own defenders—came to be included some of the very people, like Amorite dynasts of Old Babylonia or Aramaean bureaucrats of Neo-Assyria, who had earlier been outsiders to them.[36]

It would be remiss to conclude our discussion without mentioning one well-known text that *seems* to reverse the urban-outsider classification we have observed. It is a passage from a mythological poem, of the first millennium B.C.E., about the god Erra, in which Erra's companions come to awaken him from his slothful slumber:

> . . . Arise! To work!
> Why are you staying in town like a miserable old man?
> . . . .
> To stride into the (battle)field becomes the valiant young . . .
> Though he be a prince, he who remains in the city will not fill
> his belly with food.
> . . . .
> Though the strength of him who remains in town may be
> vigorous,
> How will he be able to prevail over the one who goes into the
> field?
> City bread, though plentiful, is not comparable to the loaves
> [baked] in the embers.
> Sweet *nashpu*-beer is not comparable to water from the waterskin.
> A palace [standing] on a foundation terrace is not comparable
> to the [shepherd's(?)] shelter.[37]

Clearly the passage at hand offers a sharp contrast between the open (battle)field and the city; but here it is the field, with its manly virtues, that appears to stand superior to the city, with its life of much shallower fulfillment. Yet if this is the opinion of Erra's companions, is it also that of the author of the poem? One suspects that the author was playing with more than a little irony, since the passage concerns a god who is described later as taking the manly virtues too much to heart, and going on a rampage of destructiveness against both gods and men—from which he is reclaimed only when he can be returned to the *city* where he was normally venerated!

LITERATURE AND AUTHORSHIP

The *communis opinio* about Mesopotamian literature, belles-lettres especially, is that it lacked the self-consciousness characteristic, say, of Classical and later Western traditions—indeed, in our present context, of Axial Age literatures generally.[38] Mesopotamian authors, in this view, did not and could not identify themselves or bare their personalities in their works. The art and craft, and purpose of composition could hardly be discussed whether in separate critical studies or in the literature itself. The possibility, in short, of a *Finnegan's Wake*, with its self-conscious reflections on the literary and linguistic process while that process was underway, would have had no place in Mesopotamia, no matter how crude we imagine the product.

Once again, as with Oppenheim's views on national and cultural identification, there is much truth here. Mesopotamian literature was largely anonymous. The few exceptions do not compensate by offering us any elaborate self-descriptions. Indeed, one exception, the scribal lists of authors with or without their works, includes a number of names which we would have difficulty accepting as authors at all, since they belong to gods or to semi-divine creatures.[39] Moreover, Mesopotamian literature was normally silent on the art and practice of composition. The instances to the contrary, such as the rubrics appended to various poetic texts, are frustratingly laconic in their apparent intention to serve as aids in identifying the poetic type and instructing on the accompanying music.[40] This laconic quality is all the more discouraging, in that no manual, like Aristotle's *Poetics* or *Rhetoric*, seems to have existed which could have explained the rubrics in a wider context.

Yet, as in our first discussion, there are some hints of self-consciousness in the literary process which should not be ignored. The first has to do with authors. While few of them did make themselves known, several of those who did made a point of introducing themselves rather artfully in their own poetic compositions. Their procedure was to put their names, often with a little pious message, in the form of an acrostic. Some years ago, W.W. Hallo speculated[41] in the case of one such acrostic that its author used it deliberately to hide his name because he knew that the views of his whole composition were too radical. But this cannot have been all of the reason; otherwise, why have run even a remote danger of discovery with the acrostic? Clearly in this instance as well as the others, there was also self-conscious play at work, in which the author was challenging his readers—who, it must be remembered, belonged with him to the tiny circle of literates in Mesopotamia—to discover the intricacies of technique the poem displayed. How elaborate the game could become is illustrated by the double acrostics in each of two prayers found on a single Babylonian tablet of the first millennium B.C.E. Here the author gave his name in one acrostic running down through the first signs of the lines of each prayer and a little piety in a second acrostic through the last signs. So that his readers would not miss his intent, he then added at the conclusion of each prayer directions for reading: "The beginning of each line and the end of each line may be read in two ways."[42]

If we move from authors to texts, we may not find much discussion about the craft of composition, but we do encounter numerous statements about the importance and even purpose of the written word. This should not be surprising in a civilization where literacy was an arduously acquired skill limited to an elite, and thus represented real societal power. For example, the inscriptions of Mesopotamian kings regularly conclude with a curse on any who would alter or deface the text and a blessing on those who would preserve it and act on its instructions.[43] A variety of kings also speak in their texts of their "heroic" journeys to distant and difficult lands, and when they do, they rarely fail to mention that they have left a written monument—normally in relief or stela form—at the limit of their travels or at the site of some feat, to tell of "my deeds of heroism, my acts of bravery"[44]—in sum, "to establish the name" (*šuma šakānu*).[45] Some of these monuments were in deliberately inaccessible places, where only the gods could know them or a future monarch might be challenged to imitate them. But in other cases, the monuments were placed for wider public view, so that they could display the king's power "for the gaze of all my foes, to the end of days."[46]

However plentiful these notices, they are all, admittedly, rather brief, without any real examination of the ways in which the power of the written word was thought to work or to mean. Some of the desired elaboration is provided by texts of a related type, the so-called *narû*'s, which read like actual stelae of historical kings, but are, in fact, fictional, composed (long) after the monarchs they purport to be quoting.[47] Perhaps because they are, then, a self-conscious meditation on the real stelae, the *narû*'s often expand explicitly on the matter of their *raison d'être*. So, in the Cuthean Legend of Naram-Sin, a Neo-Assyrian text (in this version) put in the mouth of the Agade king who lived almost two thousand years before, Naram-Sin is made to tell us at the beginning that he could not bless a predecessor, one king Enmekar, nor prosper (?), because Enmekar "did not inscribe or leave [a record] on a stela."[48] By contrast, Naram-Sin affirms at the end, he wants to make sure that his successors profit from the mistakes he was forced to make; and such wisdom can come only if they will "read this document and listen to the words thereof" and if, in turn, they will leave a record of their own, which "wise scribes will read aloud." For "you who have read my stela will prosper [?]; you who have blessed me, may a future one bless you."[49]

The sentiments involved here receive an even more searching inquiry in a text we have met with earlier, the Epic of Gilgamesh. Like the *narû*'s and the authentic royal inscriptions, this epic narrates the exploits of a royal hero in search of "making a name."[50] In the core of the epic, the phrase is taken literally, with Gilgamesh searching relentlessly after personal immortality—and ultimately failing to achieve it. The prologue and epilogue to the epic, however, which were added later,[51] supply a new meaning to the phrase. In the prologue, the reader/listener is introduced to Gilgamesh and then invited to gaze at the great wall of the city Uruk which he left behind. In the epilogue, after Gilgamesh has lost his battle to avoid death, the reader/listener is brought back to the wall, with the clear implication that this monument, not deathlessness, constitutes the hero's immortality or "making of a name." A new fragment of the prologue now complicates this picture, for it summons the reader/ listener not simply to gaze at Gilgamesh' wall, but to look for the tablet box apparently underneath, which contains "the lapis-lazuli tablet, [how] Gilgamesh went through many hardships, [sur]passing the rulers, the one of renown, possessing stature."[52] Following a convincing suggestion of Piotr Michałowski,[53] what we appear to have here is the foundation text of the wall—to which type many royal inscriptions belong—and that text is none other than the epic itself. In other words, the immortality that Gilgamesh sought in a personal sense is to be found at the wall he left behind, but only insofar as that wall points to the foundation text/epic underneath. In the final analysis, therefore, the Epic of Gilgamesh becomes a story about itself.

This last point, one might argue, as modern as it sounds, is still more implicit than explicit in the text. Let us conclude our discussion, then, by looking at one more composition, where the self-concern is more visible. The work in question is the mythological poem about the god Erra, which we have also dealt with earlier. It tells a story of how the god, awakened from an almost paralyzing sleep, goes on a rampage of universal destruction that threatens to crack the very boundaries of the cosmos. Finally, after a catharsis of bloodletting, he is calmed by his advisor, Ishum, and order is restored. The problem posed by this poem[54] is the character of Erra, in his oscillation between extremes of paralyzing sleep and boundless violence. The violence, to be sure, is checked at the end; but the question is left open as to whether it will recur. And this is where the poem steps in. To understand its role, we must first note that the story, quite strikingly, is recounted almost entirely in speeches. Even the scenes of Erra's destructiveness are presented in a long monologue by Ishum, which creates the impression that the action is taking place offstage, so to speak. And Erra's final calming is effected only when he confirms this in a *mea culpa* with a response by Ishum. The speeches, thus, lend the poem a certain introspective quality, helping to clarify the problem of Erra's character. They also point up the relevance of language itself to the problem, and the conscious emphasis on this finally becomes explicit in the conclusion. There the divine protagonists are reviewed, and even the human author of the poem—or, as he is actually called, its "compiler" (*kāṣiru*), since its true author, we are told, is the god who revealed the text to him—is introduced. But the real focus of these concluding lines is the poem itself and its crucial contribution in dealing with Erra. As the lines assert, the very remembering and reciting of the "song" with its story of Erra's rampage—not merely by men, but by the gods as well—is what will provide the needed defense against a repetition of that behavior. The poem, thus, becomes an incantation—as, in fact, we know copies of it were used—and its self-conscious concern is not any private meditation, but a forthright proclamation of the power which language, both in speech and in script, can have.

ABSTRACT AND ANALYTIC THINKING

The last area which we shall address involves the thinking process itself in Mesopotamia. As even the most cursory glance will attest, something is different when we pass from Greek philosophy and science to the equivalent fields in Mesopotamia. Indeed, the very difficulty of finding any equivalents has raised the question of whether we can really talk about rational analysis in the Mesopotamian context. Some have virtually denied the possibility, arguing that Mesopotamia, like a number of other "primitive" cultures, was hopelessly "mythopoeic" in its outlook, and so never achieved that detachment from the phenomenal world which is a prerequisite for rational inquiry.[55] Others, wishing to preserve more intellectual integrity for Mesopotamia, without at the same time dissolving the differences between it and Greece, have proposed that Mesopotamian thought does evidence a kind of rational analysis, a sort of "empirico-logical" stance, which yet lacks the power of theoretical abstraction of Greece, where the first "formal logic" appears.[56] We cannot attempt here anything like a full discussion of this complicated and, to a large extent, open-ended issue. But let us see, more simply, if there is any evidence for abstraction and analysis in Mesopotamian thought and, keeping in mind the Greek examples, of what sort it might be.

We may dispel lingering doubts straightaway. The evidence does amply attest to a Mesopotamian capacity for abstraction and analysis, including the attendant abilities of classification and generalization. It does not, thus, justify the "mythopoeic" view just noted, if that view be construed that Mesopotamia *everywhere* had an attitude of involvement in and personalization of the natural world which prevented independent, detached observation. Several examples should make this clear. The first come from mathematics, specifically from the two major types of texts known, (sample) problems and tables of numbers; and they show plainly that an ability to calculate with theorems was well established. (In the following translations, the numbers are given first in the sexagesimal form of the original, with semicolons added to distinguish between integers and fractions, and then in a decimal equivalent.)

(1) *Problem Text:*
I a[dd]ed the area and (one) side of my square, and it is 0;45(=.75). You take 1, the coefficient (?), and you break 1 into halves. You (then) multiply 0;30(=.50) by 0;30(=.50). The (result), 0;15(=.25), you add to 0;45(=.75); and the (result), 1, has 1 as a square root. The 0;30(=.50) which you multiplied you (now) subtract from 1, and 0;30(=.50) is (one) side of the square.[57]

This problem is the first, and simplest, of a whole series collected on a large tablet of the Old Babylonian period (= early second millennium B.C.E.). Underlying it clearly, as the modern editors of the tablet have pointed out,[58] is the quadratic equation $x^2 + x = 0;45(=.75)$, the solution to which, though given in narrative form, can easily be rewritten notationally as:

$$x = \sqrt{(0;30[=.50])^2 + 0;45(=.75)} - 0.30(=.50) = 0.30(=.50)$$

(2) *Table of Numbers:*

I	II	III	IV
[The *tak*]*iltu* (=number(?)) of the diagonal [which (..) the]y have subtracted, and the width . . .	The solving number (?) of the width	The solving number (?) of the diagonal	Its name
[1;59,0],15 (=1.983)	1,59 (=119)	2,49 (=169)	1

[1;56,56],58,14,50,6,15	56,7(=3367)	1,20,25	2
(=1.949)		(=4825)	
[1;55,7],41,15,33,45	1,16,41	1,50,49	3
(=1.9188)	(=4601)	(=6649)	

Only the first lines of this now famous Old Babylonian tablet, itself not fully preserved, are provided here; but they are enough to show the principles involved.[59] As recognized by the editors, O. Neugebauer and A. Sachs, columns II and III give the lengths, respectively, of the shorter leg and the hypotenuse of a series of right triangles. In column IV, these triangles are numbered for reference (there are fifteen in all preserved), while column I represents the quotient or ratio of the square of the hypotenuse of each triangle divided by the square of its longer leg. Finally, the lengths of these longer legs may have been provided, as Neugebauer and Sachs[60] conjecture, in a missing column to the left of our present column I. It is clear that the foundation of this table is the Pythagorean theorem: a^2 (longer leg) + b^2 (shorter leg) = c^2 (hypotenuse), and that what the table gives us is a list of Pythagorean prime numbers or "triples" (i.e., a, b, and c), arranged in descending size of the ratio between the square of the hypotenuse and the square of the longer leg. A. Aaboe[61] has well noted that since the numbers given are too large to have been arrived at by trial and error, they must have been calculated by a theorem, somehow related to the well known:

$$a = 2\,pq$$
$$b = p^2 - q^2$$
$$c = p^2 + q^2$$

which will produce "triples" of Pythagorean prime numbers, each triple only once, if:

$p > q > 0$;
p and q are prime numbers;
p and q are not both odd.

The sophisticated abilities evident in these mathematical examples can be found also in another area of Mesopotamian scribal activity, the tradition of lists or, as German scholarship has canonized it, the *Listenwissenschaft,* which produced compendia of such phenomena as the names of the gods, the names of human professions and occupations, legal formulae, and grammatical forms.[62] Of importance here are the principles ordering the lists; and while some of these are simple mnemonic devices, like a sequence by cuneiform sign shapes or by syllable sounds, others reflect a definite effort toward abstraction and analysis. Thus, among the lists of divine names,[63] we regularly find arrangements by rank and family, the dominant gods—at least from the viewpoint of the list—put first, with their divine relatives and retainers following. Within such arrangements, a specific development, marking the recognition of a higher level of integration of divine power, is represented by the three-column god lists, which date from the later second millennium B.C.E. on. These give the name of the main deity in the middle column, with whom a "lesser" divine name or deity in the left-hand column is equated, in terms of a particular function described in the right-hand column. For example:

^dNergal (=) | ^dMarduk | (in the function) of battle.[64]

Similarly complex are the lists of grammatical forms.[65] The first examples appear in the Old Babylonian period, and a second, Neo-Babylonian group comes from the first millennium B.C.E., both prompted by the long-standing bilingualism of Sumerian and Akkadian in Mesopotamia and, more particularly, by the need to preserve a correct knowledge of Sumerian, which by 2000 B.C.E. at the latest had passed from a vernacular to a "learned" language. Common to the two groups of texts is the comparison, in adjacent columns, of what are taken as equivalent Sumerian and Akkadian forms, the whole arranged into categories of pronouns, adverbs, prepositions and other particles, and especially verbs. But whereas the Old Babylonian texts offer mainly comparisions of full, independent forms, by the time of the Neo-Babylonian, the analytic perspective has been sharpened to a more subtle—and abstract— matching of segmented morphemes, particularly of the verb, with the morphemes now regularly identified by specific grammatical labels. Compare the following:

Old Babylonian	Neo-Babylonian
(Sumerian)[ba-an]-gar	(Akkadian)*iš-ta-ka-an*	ba	*ga!-mar!-tum* AN!.TA
"He has placed"	"ba (indicates) the perfect(?); (it is) a prefix."[66]

In sum, then, if mathematics and scribal lists are any judge, there is no question of the sophistication Mesopotamia could show in abstract analysis. What is striking about this analysis, however, is that it does not exhibit procedures common, say, to Greek and later Western tradition, especially explicit statements of principles and formal demonstrations. Thus, in the mathematical texts, while we encounter problems and tables of numbers based clearly on a knowledge of quadratic equations, the particular equations themselves are never stated nor proofs of them ever furnished. Similarly, while there are scribal lists of all kinds of phenomena, the underlying principles governing the arrangements are not articulated, nor are the phenomena as a whole ever fully discussed in the manner of a *Grundriss der vergleichenden Grammatik* or a *Summa Theologica.* (Some of the myths may well be understood as discussions of divinity, but they are not, obviously, systematic treatises.)

The question is what this lack of explicitness means. To those who say that Mesopotamian thought was "empirico-logical," it is prime evidence.[67] For they suppose that the consistent failure to state principles and proofs could not have been made by people adapted to the formal deductive and inductive procedures of the Western tradition, which operate explicitly. Such failure could only have been the work of individuals accustomed to thinking empirically: to dealing primarily with concrete experience through methods like trial and error, from which they would draw generalizations only implicitly. Indeed, the Mesopotamian texts at issue are said to demonstrate such empirical thinking directly.

But the texts do not really bear out this position. In the first place, while they list many examples of unstated principles, it is plain that the examples serve only to illustrate systematically the principles, not to generate them in some "empirical" way. The examples, in short, logically presuppose the principles, not the reverse; and the texts, it must be concluded, were not created to explain how the prnciples were arrived at. Nonetheless, there are hints in the texts of explanation; and contrary to the "empirico-logicians," some of these do suggest that the principles could be arrived at through formal, abstract methods. One such hint comes from the table of numbers discussed earlier, with its apparent knowledge of a theorem for producing Pythagorean prime "triples." Neugebauer[68] has attempted to show how Mesopotamian mathematicians might have discovered this theorem, and his proposal presumes their use of formal deductive methods. Whatever the exact details,[69] the construction of our table with this theorem and other equations indicates an ability to operate on at least some level of number theory, unconstrained by "empirical" trial and error.

This suggestion of formal theory does not mean that we should now find it everywhere in Mesopotamian thought. For in so doing, we would be making the same mistake as the "empirico-logicians," who want to see empirical methods as dominant, or as the "mythopoeists," who suppose that Mesopotamians could look at phenomena only from a perspective of empathetic personalization.[70] The point is that Mesopotamian thought had room for all three approaches, even in the same texts: thus, in a number of astronomical compilations, with their mixture of formal calculations and empir-

ically derived predictions;[71] or in the myths, which, as contemporary
structural studies should have taught us,[72] suppose much that is
formally analytical besides the personalization we have been wont
to ascribe to them.

In the light of such variety, then, how should we regard the lack
of explicit statements of principle and proof in Mesopotamian texts?
Clearly, this is no indication that formal thinking could not have
gone on. But we can be even bolder: the *mere* fact that a text lacks
such explicitness tells us nothing about what method of thinking—
formal, empirical, mythopoeic, etc.—lies behind it. For lack of explicitness in itself is not a method of thinking, but a mode of
expression.

Yet we must still ask why a mode like this was used in Mesopotamia at all. One explanation, given the apparent origin of our
mathematical tablets and lists in scribal school settings, is pedagogical.
That is, such texts would have functioned as a kind of shorthand,
providing a systematic collection of examples on the basis of which
oral class discussions would have made explicit the principles involved, and elaborated on them with demonstrations, if appropriate.
The attractiveness of this explanation is evident, all the more so as
such "shorthand" collections are well known in many places, including the educational curricula of the Western tradition. But in
the final analysis, the explanation does not go far enough, for it
cannot account for the fact that Western pedagogy uses, also, texts
that explicitly state principles and proofs, whereas the Mesopotamian
literary record seems to be characterized throughout by a lack of
this same explicitness. In other words, lack of explicitness appears
to have some kind of cultural value, but only insofar as it marks a
certain preference or style in Mesopotamia by comparison, say, with
the West, not as it prejudges the competence of Mesopotamia toward
a particular method of thinking. What that preference or style might
be will be considered in the conclusion to follow.

Conclusion

Our quest in this paper has not been without positive results. For
in the three areas we have discussed, the Mesopotamian literary
record has yielded evidence of a self-conscious, self-critical perspective. Thus, it struggled to give expression to a sense of cultural
and—what was more problematic—political unity, though such
expression was manifest more at the regional, i.e., northern or southern, than at the pan-Mesopotamian level. And being a city-based
literature, it saw the urban environment, not surprisingly, as constitutive of the Mesopotamian way of life, to emphasize which,

outside groups were brought in for comparison. Secondly, it did not lack appreciation of the literary art, occasionally allowing the personae of authors to appear and texts to play upon or talk self-consciously about their importance and purpose. Finally, the Mesopotamian literary record could evince, as its mathematical texts and scribal lists exemplify, the ability to deal abstractly and analytically with the phenomenal world around it.

And yet these achievements having been noted, it is clear that much is missing here which otherwise marks the so-called Axial civilizations. Self-conscious expressions may be found; but to judge from the areas discussed, we must work to find them, for they are infrequent, often laconic, unsystematic, and limited in their explicitness. The writing of full-scale treatises, the formal exposition of principles and their proofs, the extended probes into relations between individual and group or self and other—these were evidently not desiderata in the Mesopotamian literary materials as we know them. To be sure, we cannot dismiss the likelihood that in oral behavior, as the mathematical texts suggest, the Mesopotamian elites could be more forthcoming about themselves, their work, and their community. But the patterns in the written evidence are clear; and given the societal power and status attached to literacy and its products in Mesopotamia, these patterns must say something important about Mesopotamian civilization as a whole.

What larger importance, then, should we assign to the elusive quality of self-consciousness in Mesopotamia? The answer, it may be proposed, is bound up with the notion of traditional cultures. In such cultures, value rests not on newness and individuality, but on integration and community. Institutions and cultural forms develop in piecemeal fashion, each new development absorbed into the ongoing stream and the fact of newness quickly muted. The result is that traditional cultures have a certain elasticity and diffuseness about them, where a mixture of mutually contradictory perspectives is normative. And in that mixture, though expressions of self-consciousness do indeed appear, the important point is that they do not attain a structurally central position.

The widespread acceptance and promotion of self-conscious perspectives, on the other hand, presume a very different set of conditions. Here newness and individuality are prized; institutions and cultural forms demand sharp and often antagonistic definitions; the search for rationality and comprehensiveness in one's views becomes essential. And the underlying political and social matrix is such that no single group or class has exclusive rights to public definition and expression of cultural values. In short, we have here the conditions in which Axial ideologies can emerge and flourish.

It should be obvious that between these two cultural types Mesopotamia stood closer to the traditional. Where innovations appeared in it, the impulse in the literature and other institutions was to stress their continuity with antiquity, not their newness. And while, as we have seen, Mesopotamia was regularly beset by division into competing political units, these were dominated by small ruling elites and never really open to political and cultural participation by broad and varied elements of the society. One factor in this restrictiveness, significantly, was the very nature of literacy in Mesopotamia, for it was so complex and cumbersome a skill that it could be mastered only by an elite, and the expense involved in this was so considerable that it could be borne only by the ruling groups. The scribes, therefore, far from establishing an independent cultural and political base, simply continued to serve the ruling groups who had brought them into existence in the first place, and who remained in control of public access to them thereafter.

Mesopotamia, thus, in its integrative and conservative character, stood on the far side of the Axial threshold; and one clue to this can now be recognized in the way self-consciousness was manifest in it.

CHAPTER 8

Monarchy and the Elite in Assyria and Babylonia: The Question of Royal Accountability

HAYIM TADMOR

Ten years ago at a symposium in Venice that asked some of the questions pertaining to the Axial Age for the first time, two eminent Assyriologists—the late Professor Oppenheim, of the Oriental Institute in Chicago, and Professor Garelli of the Sorbonne—discussed the absence of a "breakthrough" in Mesopotamia. While I concur with Professors Oppenheim and Garelli as to the reasons for the "fault of the Assyrians," to paraphrase the title of Professor Momigliano's paper at that symposium, I would like to present some evidence that at least some ingredients central to the post-Axial Age societies were already present in Assyrian and Babylonian society, which in the first millennium were closely interrelated. In particular, I will single out the question of the accountability of the king to a "higher order" or to various elite groups in both the cultic and the social spheres.

Professor Eisenstadt's recent studies of the dynamics of Axial Age breakthroughs served as the impetus to apply the formulae expressed in his recent paper, "The Origins and Modes of Ideological Politics," to Mesopotamia. In Assyria and Babylonia there was no transcendental breakthrough, no attempt to restructure collectivities, and no accountability of rulers to a higher order such as that we find in ancient Israel and China. No autonomous elite of intellectuals developed to bear the ideal of "reshaping the mundane" according to transcendental norms or in light of alternative conceptions of "cultural and social order," as Professor Eisenstadt put it. Although model "law codes" existed, there was no autonomous sphere of law and its carriers. Yet, inquiries into the central role of the king and the nature of the elite do show that, in the days of Sargon and Sennacherib in Assyria and Nabonidus in Babylonia, episodic attempts to change the order did occur in the guise of religious reform. There were also political and even social realities behind the cultic-religious terminology that may justify using the term "ideological politics" even in the absence of a "transcendental breakthrough."

Despite the difficulties the historian encounters when he deals with sociological generalizations the set of questions posed by Professor Eisenstadt for this symposium has given me an opportunity to look critically at my own material from a new angle. I must stress however, that I am a historian: my tools are philological and my *modus operandi*, diachronic. Finally, a word about the chronological framework. Although our inquiry focuses on the heyday of the Assyrian Empire (eighth–seventh centuries B.C.E.) and its Neo-Babylonian successor (sixth century), the historical continuity and traditional conservatism of Mesopotamian civilization make it necessary to refer to the Old Babylonian and Old Assyrian periods of the early second millennium and the Middle Babylonian and Middle Assyrian periods of the late second millennium.

MESOPOTAMIAN KINGSHIP

In order to yield significant results, our inquiry must concentrate on the focal point of Mesopotamian civilization, the institution of kingship, which was said to have descended from heaven at the very inception of man's history.

A classical Mesopotamian composition, the Sumerian King List expresses the royal ideology of the Ur III and Isin dynasties: kingship proper could exist at only one place at any one time. The modern historian would interpret this view as essentially a historiographic justification of an actual succession of hegemonies. The harmony was somewhat undermined in the second millennium, when "kingship" existed simultaneously in a number of places. Yet rarely were there simultaneous conflicting claims to the set of titles "King of the Four Quarters," "King of the World," and "King of Sumer and Akkad." These universalistic titles were more than mere formulae or propaganda: they expressed a world-view and a political ideology, particularly in Assyria and Babylonia of the first millennium. During this period, power and authority in Mesopotamia oscillated between two centers: Babylonia in the south and Assyria to the north. The latter inherited much of the Babylonian lore, even perpetuating some aspects of Akkadian imperial patterns. Yet being on the periphery, it was also related to West Semitic civilizations. By the first millennium it was Assyria and its empire that bore the burden of the Mesopotamian continuum, transformed and reshaped to fit new political, social, and ideological-religious realities, as we shall see below.

The Sumerian and classical Old and Middle Babylonian traditions, more faithfully preserved by Babylonia, had become normative in the course of the second millennium and became the hallmarks of what is known as Mesopotamian civilization. But the region was on the decline. The traditional civilization was confined to several major temple cities, each sacred to a major divinity, such as Babylon, sacred to Marduk, chief god ever since the days of Hammurabi; Borsippa, sacred to Nabu; Sippar in the north, sacred to Shamash; and Nippur, most ancient of all, sacred to Enlil, ruler of the universe in the Sumerian pantheon. In the first millennium these traditional centers had to coexist with newcomers: Aramaean tribes east of the Tigris and Chaldaean principalities in southern Mesopotamia. The latter were powerful enough to withstand the authority of the Babylonian king, who always resided in Babylon, but they gradually became Babylonianized, replacing the older elites in the sixth century and establishing a new Chaldaean-Babylonian polity.

In contrast to the diversity of the Babylonian scene the Assyrian state of the first millennium, although not so monolithic as usually represented in its royal literature and by modern historians, did preserve the primacy of the single king. The country had grown out of a single urban nucleus—the city-state Ashur. Whereas Babylonia was called by its contemporaries *māt Akkadi* (Land of the Akkadians) or Karduniash (its older Cassite name), "Babylon" being reserved for the city, in Assyria the unity of city, god and people was never broken: one could even write the name of the city with the ideogram used for the god. Despite the identity of the people with the polity, the traditional Assyrian elite consisting of the great merchant families well attested in Old Assyrian documents from colonies in Cappadocia (nineteenth century B.C.E.) did not play a commanding role under the Empire. In the Middle Assyrian period (thirteenth to eleventh centuries) and especially under the Empire (eighth and seventh centuries), the king and his functionaries played the major role. Although originally *primus inter pares* and theoretically reappointed each year, the Assyrian king exercised sole authority, and did not share his prerogatives with any assembly of elders or traders.

The literary heritage is almost entirely "regicentric," with the king as sole protagonist. Indeed, most of our knowledge of first-century Assyria, the age of the Empire, pertains to royalty. Despite several thousand letters and economic documents relating to the functioning of the court, the royal inscriptions discovered at the outset of Assyriology (and misnamed "annals") still constitute the main body of our sources. Written in the first person singular, and sometimes apparently outlined by the king himself, these *res gestae* are in some ways the equivalent of autobiographies, though their concern is not the personal history of the royal hero but his 'έργα in the military and cultic spheres. As ever-victorious hero he conducts yearly campaigns, and as pious master-builder he restores temples. We encounter true autobiographies only when kings ascend the throne in an irregular fashion—e.g., Esarhaddon and Ashurbanipal, and retrospectively relate the history of their irregular successions.

The political correspondence of the Neo-Assyrian Empire, which has partially survived, consists largely of reports to the king or appeals directed to him. Some letters originating with the king are called "the king's words," and constitute royal orders to his functionaries. Letters, we must bear in mind, were the usual mode of communication with the king. Even the crown prince, successor to the throne, would address his father in writing prior to an oral audience. Then communications allow us to determine what the advisers told their sovereign, and to evaluate their impact on him, especially in the cases of Esarhaddon and Ashurbanipal (seventh century). The *literati*—scribes, diviners, etc.—advised the king not only on everyday cultic and divine affairs but occasionally on the conduct of war as well.

ROLE OF THE ELITE

Although the manifold officialdom consisting of royal officers, administrators, and, especially, the *literati* is often mentioned in the sources, the structure of the elite power groups and their interaction with one another are not manifest in our material. What we see, often in minute if obscure detail, are the relations between individual members of an elite grouping and the king. Even here, the record is one-sided. We lack most of the royal queries, except when one happens to be quoted in the replies in the archives of Nineveh and Calah.

We know least of all about the non-literate elite societies, including those of princes, noblemen, magnates, dignitaries, royal advisers, military commanders, provincial governors, and court eunuchs. Many of these employed scribes to whom they dictated letters, but as groups exhibiting certain partisan interests, they are outside the scope of the extant corpus of royal inscriptions, though they probably played a very real role in the social process. The omens speak of princes, noblemen and courtiers "who would kill the king," but make no mention of such threat from the *literati,* who remain technical specialists serving whichever king is in power.

Neither was there any threat from the priestly elite. The Assyrian monarch originally bore the title "priest" *(šangu)* or "vicar" *(iššiakku)* and only later that of "king" *(šarru).* He was in fact chief priest of the god Ashur in contrast to the practice in Babylonia, where the religious and civic functions were separate. He participated actively in various ceremonies, although perhaps not so frequently as the Hittite king, who would rush back in the midst of campaigning in distant lands to be on time for a festival.

The Assyrian cultic temple personnel are well documented, although not as well as those of second millennium Babylonia. Our definitions have become more accurate than in the past, when scholars applied the term "priest" also to the diviners (haruspices or augurs). We distinguish now between, on the one hand, the temple personnel, *ereb bīti* (lit. admitted to the temple), that is, priests and all technical functionaries, and on the other hand, various types of diviners, who are classed among the *literati* or "intellectuals" (A.L. Oppenheim's term), those who carried the burden of recorded traditions. Like the *literati,* the priests presumably neither endanger the king nor take part in the struggles of succession; but unlike the *literati,* they do not even give advice on state matters. Throughout Assyrian history royalty acted as the patron of the temples, which benefitted considerably from the frequent wars. Every war was by definition a sacred war ordered by the god Ashur, to whom the king reported his victories and with whom he shared the spoils.

In traditional Old Babylonian and Middle Babylonian literature the upper registers of the social order are listed in the following sequence: king, noble (dignitary or prince), royal adviser, eunuch. The old terms fall into disuse in the first millennium. They appear only as archaisms in omens such as "a nobleman *(rubû)* will kill the king," in references to foreign countries. Esarhaddon, for example, uses the terms "noblemen" and "advisers" when referring to the enemy court of the king of Shubria north of Assyria. Ashurbanipal applies them to the nobility of Elam. A more current Neo-Assyrian term for noblemen, "magnates" *(rabûti),* usually refers to the dignitaries of foreign peoples. The *res gestae* of the kings never mention this elite group within Assyria. The archaic terms appear in royal inscriptions only in the concluding sections of a text devoted to building dedications, when maledictions were invoked. But we cannot assume that the nobility plays no role in the Assyrian Empire: during Esarhaddon's reign, under the generic term "magnates," they are referred to as conspirators against royalty. A Babylonian chronicle reads: "Year eleven: Esarhaddon killed many of his magnates,"

indicating that an active elite did exist at the court capable of
opposing the king. There is some reason to believe that a power-
seeking, perhaps even ideologically-motivated group was involved
in this incident.

The Old Babylonian term for adviser, *maliku,* appears in the
traditional omen series often followed by the governor *(šakkanakku).*
But although the term is well-attested in royal inscriptions that refer
to the courts of Assyrian enemies, it is never used in the official
documents within Assyria itself. Except for the professional services
of the expert diviner (see below), the king of Assyria is generally
considered to be an omniscient decision-maker who has no need of
counsellors of any sort.

Provincial governors *(pahūte),* some of whom undoubtedly were
eunuchs *(ša rēši, šut rēši),* constituted another powerful elite in
Assyria, especially in the ninth century during a temporary decline
in royal power. Some governors ruled over vast territories, directed
courts, employed scribes, sealed tablets with their own magnificent
cylinder seals, composed inscriptions, and erected stelae. One of
them, Bel-Harran-bel-uṣur, even founded a city named after himself.
But powerful as they were, these governors, being eunuchs, could
not found a hereditary elite group to oppose the monarchy.

Under the Sargonids when irregular succession almost becomes
the norm, and the power of the queen and queen mother increases,
the chief eunuch *(rab ša rēši,* Biblical *rab saris)* is more trusted than
the *turtānu* ("viceroy" or military commander-in-chief) and replaces
him in that function. Yet even when the *turtānu* occasionally leads
the armies in place of the monarch, his victories are accredited not
to him but to the king. During the internal strife after the death of
Ashurbanipal, the chief eunuch, Sin-shum-lishir, actually usurped the
throne for several months. In an empire that thrives on the yearly
booty and spoils of defeated and annexed lands, the elite of the
army, as well as the common soldier, benefits from the king's
victories; not surprisingly we find no evidence of military uprisings
against royalty. A major defeat, however, could engender unrest; also
when the succession is atypical, as in the case of Esarhaddon, the
new ruler must have enlisted the cooperation of at least some
powerful armed units.

THE LITERATI

The elite class most deserving of our attention is that of the scribes
or *literati* (I prefer this term to Oppenheim's "intellectuals"). Fortunately, we know more about this group than about those discussed
above: After all, their creative efforts in cuneiform on clay tablets

and stone monuments are the source of most of our knowledge of Mesopotamian society. We should take note of one group of *literati,* the Aramaean scribes, often ignored by Assyriologists. Of their work little remains: a few texts written on clay or ostraca and a scroll of proverbs preserved at Elephantine in Egypt. Yet these relics point tantalizingly to a literary heritage that was recorded on parchment or papyrus, and has consequently perished.

The impact of these *literati* from west of the Euphrates should not be underestimated. In royal monuments they appear as on-the-spot recorders of military campaigns, and many of them are mentioned by name as imperial functionaries. Some masters no doubt were literate in cuneiform Akkadian and alphabetic Aramaic. Several studies during the past decade have focused attention on the effect of the Aramaeans, Israelites, Hittites, and other westerners on the language, literary genres, and social and political institutions of Assyrian and Neo-Babylonian societies, which in all probability were more diverse and open to external influence than the textbooks admit.

The delineation of the various elite groups of scribes is gradually coming into focus, thanks to an improved understanding of the Assyrian dialect of Akkadian, in which much of the royal correspondence was composed. The more prestigious, "Standard Babylonian" dialect was used for the traditional literature—epics, prayers, omens, etc.—and the royal historical inscriptions. Oppenheim delineates three categories of scribes: "bureaucrats," "poets," and "diviners"; yet the borderline between the latter two is not very sharp. A diviner who composes literary documents may also be chief royal scribe or "king's master" (the *ummānu*), and being equally versed in both disciplines was, I believe, also responsible for composing royal inscriptions.

The *ummānu* entered his name beside that of his monarch in the official canonic king-lists of Babylonia and Assyria. Was this sheer hubris, or did it reflect a comparable eminence in practice? After all, our evidence points to the fact that few Mesopotamian kings could read. The rarity of literacy among them is attested by the few who do boast of their achievement: Shulgi of the IIIrd dynasty of Ur (21st century), and Ashurbanipal, the last great monarch of Assyria (669–627), also Nabonidus, the last King of Babylonia (556–539) was apparently capable of reading cuneiform.

For our present interest the diviners (or "scholars" as they are sometimes designated) are of greater significance. Sole possessors of the rich traditional compendia of omens, they were the natural guides in divine matters for royalty, nobility, and perhaps even wealthy citizens. Most, though not all, were laymen versed in the science of divination. We find also a class of exorcists, healers, and purification priests trained to avert the evil foretold in the omens.

In the second millennium, the haruspices (*barūs*) were frequently consulted by royalty, particularly in time of war. As late as the ninth century a *barū* went at the head of the Babylonian army on its way to fight Assyria. With the refinement of astronomical observation and mathematical astronomy from the eighth century on, the celestial omen experts (often called "astrologers" in modern scholarship) became predominant among the scholars. In the documents they are usually referred to as "scribes" (*tupšarrus*) and occasionally as "scribes of *Enūma Anu Enlil*" (the major astronomical compendium). The "scholars" were consulted on matters of daily routine, such as food and health, and on the meaning of ominous occurrences. Vivid evidence comes from the brief but exceptionally well-documented reign of Esarhaddon, in the letters written to the king by his astrologers, haruspices, exorcists, and physicians. (These letters are presented now in the masterful edition of S. Parpola.) Under the shadow of the violent deaths of his father and grandfather—Sargon and Sennacherib—and suffering from a chronic illness, Esarhaddon was scrupulously guarded for his own safety and the stability of the throne.

Several extraordinary incidents bear mentioning; the most notable (studied recently and convincingly by S. Parpola) was the recurrent performance of the substitute king *(šar pūhi)* ritual. At least on five occasions during his reign the diviners advised Esarhaddon of a lunar or solar eclipse, an evil omen portending the death of the king. As prescribed in the ritual compendium a substitute king was chosen, mostly a man condemned to death. In one particular instance the *šar pūhi* was the son of the "bishop" of Esagila, a political enemy of Esarhaddon. From the moment the *šar pūhi* was enthroned until his death Esarhaddon was disguised as a peasant and letters to him bear the salutation "To our lord the peasant." In some cases the reign of the *šar pūhi* lasted 100 days, the ritually required term. The death of the *šar pūhi* during that term, or upon its completion, averted the danger in accordance with the provisions of the Ritual for the Substitute King: "The man who was given as the king's substitute shall die and . . . the bad omens will not affect that king. Things will go well with that [king] and his land will prosper" (W.G. Lambert, *Archiv für Orientforschung* XVIII, p. 110, A, 6–8).

In another extraordinary incident diviners were instrumental in helping Esarhaddon designate his royal successor. Following the example of his own selection by Sennacherib, Esarhaddon did not observe the law of primogeniture; he designated a younger son, Ashurbanipal, to be king of Assyria and thus emperor, whereas his older son, Shamash-shum-ukin, was to be the king of Babylonia. On this major state question the haruspices were consulted in addition to the astrologers. Haruspices were similarly queried about other high state appointments and about whether or not to wage war. We may well surmise that every war of Esarhaddon had the *imprimatur* of the readers of entrails; we know that they were consulted as to whether Esarhaddon should give his daughter in marriage to Bartatua, king of the Scythians, with whom a vassal treaty was being contemplated.

Haruspicy in Ashurbanipal's reign is well attested in connection with foreign affairs. On local matters a combination of haruspicy and astrology is employed, as in the rebuilding of Babylon, destroyed by Sennacherib, and in the restoration of Ashur's temple in the city of Ashur. In Babylonia, Nabonidus, the last Chaldaean king, also resorts to both disciplines on matters of state policy. Being a votary of the moon god Sin, he naturally gives preference to an omen such as a lunar eclipse.

Nabonidus seems personally to have assumed the role of diviner. A *homo literatus,* reared in the traditional lore, he claims to possess both direct access to the divine and the capacity to interpret celestial omens. In inscriptions that bear a pronounced personal imprint, he interprets his own dream-visions and even records in graphic detail the full technical "results" of several liver inspections which he himself contrived for that purpose; no other king in Babylonia or Assyria had done that.

Cultic Accountability

Such royal penetration into the secret lore must have alienated its traditional guardians, the "scholars." They express their indignation vividly at these and other unorthodox steps of this royal reformer, as we shall see in an extraordinary literary composition, a political invective in poetic form that mocks every major act of his reign. They describe the new image of the moon god fashioned by Nabonidus as an abominable fabrication, and they condemn the king's restoration of the god's temple at Harran as "an utter deceit and work of unholiness." They designate his conquest of the North Arabian oasis of Tema during his voluntary retreat to the desert as an act of senseless violence. Yet the most biting indictment is reserved for his trespass into the sphere of divination:

(It was) he (who) stood up in the assembly to praise hi[mself]
(Saying:) "I am wise, I know, I have seen (what is) hid[den]

(Even) if I do not know how to write (with the stylus), yet I
have seen se[cret things].
'The God Ilte'ri has made me see a vision, he ha[s shown to
me] everything.
[I am] aw[are] of a wisdom which greatly surpasses (even that
of the series) UD.SAR *A-num* En.líl.lá which Adapa has
composed!"
Yet he continues to mix up the rites, he confuses the
hepatoscopic oracles . . . .
To the most important ritual observances he orders an end;
As to the sacred representations in Esagila—representations
which Ea-Mummu himself had fashioned—
He looks at the representations and utters blasphemies.
                        (A.L. Oppenheim in *ANET*³, p. 314)

The composition expresses two themes important to the present
discussion: criticism of the king for his intellectual hubris, and
denunciation of his religious-cultic reforms.

Bearing in mind this potential conflict between a king-reformer
and his diviners, we turn to an earlier, generally overlooked incident
from Sargonid Assyria, described in a document dubbed in my edition
"The 'Sin of Sargon' " (subsequently Benno Landsberger suggested
calling it the "Political Testament of Sennacherib"). In this pesudo-
autobiography, Sennacherib inquires into the reasons for his father's
ignominious death in battle far from Assyria. Sargon's body has not
been recovered, a disgrace unprecedented in Mesopotamian history;
the incident also evokes the only admission of defeat in Assyrian
historical literature preserved in a contemporary chronicle. The document contains a unique assertion of cultic sins *(hiṭāti)* committed
by an Assyrian king:

I shall ask [Shamash and Adad] through an extispicy, about
the sin of Sargon my father. Let me learn (about it) so that I
[may make] taboo [to me the] sin that [Sargon my father]
had committed against God. . . .
            (H. Tadmor, *Eretz-Israel*, V, pp. 154–155 obv. 10–12)

Then Sennacherib recounts that he divided the haruspices into
several teams to work on the problem, a fine precursor to the
Septuagint story. Although the astrologers are not consulted, they
do appear later in the document, when Sennacherib is supposedly
saying: "After I had made the image of the god Anshar (=Ashur) I
wanted to make the image of [. . .]." The name of the second major
god is broken; I restore it as [Marduk]. "But the Assyrian scribes
(=astrologers) prevented me and would not let me make the image"

(*ibid.*, rev. 13–15). This is a further unprecedented admission on the part of a monarch. The diviners appear to be in a position to impose their will upon their royal master.

In order to interpret Sargon's sins and the above incident involving Sennacherib we must take into account the larger framework of religious policy. Starting with Tiglath-pileser III (745–727), whom we justly credit with the creation of the Assyrian world empire and associate with the conquest of Babylonia (729), a major religious-political shift occurs. The Assyrian emperor assumes the throne of Babylon not only with acknowledgement by the Babylonian priests but, in fact, at their invitation. From this time on, he spends part of his time in the city, fulfilling his royal obligations in the New Year ceremonies honoring the chief god Marduk. Tiglath-pileser was the first Assyrian king since Tukkulti-Ninurta I of the thirteenth century to style himself "King of Babylonia."

The policies of his successor Shalmaneser V (727–722) are not known, as his records were apparently destroyed, but Sargon II (722–705), his rival, the royal prince who replaces him, intensifies the pro-Babylonian trend. As king of Babylon he donates enormous sums to Marduk's temple: about 460 kg of gold and 4,860 kg of silver. One may assume that Babylonian *literati* gained prominence in the Assyrian court, and perhaps even replaced some of their Assyrian counterparts.

Sargon's pro-Babylonian policies and his tragic death on the battlefield so shook the empire and the throne that Sennacherib never mentioned his father's name in his inscriptions, a departure from a millennium-old practice. Sargon's newly-erected capital was abandoned and Nineveh, an ancient city, was speedily rebuilt to succeed it.

Sennacherib (705–689) declined to assume the throne of Babylonia, conferring it first on a Babylonian vassal king, and then on his son. Finally, enraged at the rebellious Babylonians, who deposed his son, delivering him to the Alamites, and brought the armies of Elam to their aid, Sennacherib destroyed the city (689), razing its walls and temples and "making its destruction more complete than that of a flood." He smashed its gods, but spared the statue of Marduk, which he removed to Assyria. These dramatic events accelerate certain developments in late eighth- and early seventh-century Assyria. The god Ashur, under the surname of Anshar, a primeval Assyro-Babylonian deity belonging to the oldest generation of gods, came to supplant Marduk as the creator of the world and sole master of the gods in official mythology.

The new theology found vivid expression in an almost henotheistic doxology:

To Anshar, king of all the gods, creator of himself, father of
the gods, whose form developed in the deep, king of heaven
and earth, lord of all of the gods, who pours out the Igigi and
the Anunnaki, fashioner of the abode of heaven and the
earth's surface, maker of all habitations, who dwells in the
"shining spheres" (constellations), Enlil (lord) of the gods, who
decrees destinies, who dwells in Esharra, which is in Ashur,
the great lord, his lord. . . .

(AR II §461)

By calling Anshar "the god who created himself," Sennacherib
introduces a new concept into official Assyrian religion, but this
gesture hardly constitutes a "new faith." In another innovation, he
rebuilds the *bit-akitu,* the New Year temple, near the city of Ashur
in 684, five years after Babylon is destroyed. Although the new
temple, appropriately endowed, is intended to supplant its Babylonian
counterpart, this innovation was presented to contemporaries as the
restoration of a highly venerated if long-forgotten ritual. The doxology
of Anshar "who created himself" is repeated verbatim in the temple's
"foundation document," and there it appears to be completely out
of context as a pious editorial gloss.

Whatever the significance of the new doxology, it can hardly be
denied that Sennacherib's attempt to elevate the city of Ashur and
her god to the place of its destroyed southern rival does constitute
a major reform that shall, I believe, be described as a case of
"ideological politics" in a pre-Axial Age society. We must consider
the counter-reform under Sennacherib's successor Esarhaddon
(680–669), who deliberately set out to restore the city, temples, divine
images and privileges of Babylon, as further evidence for the same
process. The new ruler reverted to the royal titles of Sargon, expressing the Assyrian emperor's role as viceroy or even king of
Babylonia. It was during his reign, in all likelihood, that the pseudo-
autobiographical "Sin of Sargon" was composed, to deter future
reformers. The ultimate return of Marduk's statue and priesthood
to their restored abode during the first regnal year of Shamash-shum-
ukin, Esarhaddon's son and successor on the Babylonian throne
(667), symbolizes the ephemeral nature of Sennacherib's political
and religious policies.

SOCIAL ACCOUNTABILITY

The poetic invective against Nabonidus and the "Sin of Sargon"
are evidence of some royal accountability to tradition and its guard-

ians in the cultic-religious sphere. We shall now examine the evidence for such accountability in the social-religious sphere.

Under Sargon and Sennacherib, the old Mesopotamian concept of the king as righteous ruler and just shepherd of the people gained prominence in Assyrian royal literature. Sargon (*Šarrukīn* in Akkadian) makes use of the etymological interpretation of his name as *šarru kīn,* "the king is just." Sargon, in contrast to his enemies whom he portrayed as violators of sworn treaties, styles himself:

> King of the four regions (of the world), ruler (lit. shepherd) of Assyria, guardian of the one who keeps the oath (sworn by) Enlil (and) Marduk, who carefully observes the law of Shamash, of the stock Seed of Baltil (=Ashur), the city of learning, quick of wit, who waits reverently upon the word of the great gods, never violating their ordinances, the rightful king, whose words are gracious, whose aversion (lit. abomination) is falsehood, from whose mouth (words) bringing (*lit.* doing) evil and oppression do not emanate. . . .
>
> (*AR* II, §153)

A similar motif appears in the cylinder inscription describing the foundation of Sargon's new capital Dur-Sharrukin (Khorsabad). The city was built on the lands of the town of Magganubba north of Nineveh; Sargon proclaims:

> In accordance with the name which the great gods have given me—'to maintain justice and right, to give guidance to those who are not strong, not to injure the weak'—the price [lit., silver] of the fields of that town I paid back to their owners according to the record of the purchase documents, in silver and copper, and to avoid oppression, I gave to those who did not want to [take] silver for their fields, field for field, in locations over against (facing) the old.
>
> (*AR* II, §120)

This apologetic statement can be trusted: copies of the original land deeds have been found in the archives of Nineveh.

Sennacherib takes up this *topos* of royal equity in his very first historical inscription:

> Sennacherib, the great king, the mighty king, king of Assyria, king without a rival; prayerful ruler [lit. shepherd], worshipper of the great gods; guardian of the turth, lover of justice, who lends support, who comes to the aid of the needy, who turns [his thoughts] to pious deeds; perfect hero, mighty man, first among all princes. . . .
>
> (*AR* II, §256)

Whatever the reality behind these titles, they were not mere stereotypes, as they had never appeared among the titles of Sargon's and Sennacherib's Assyrian predecessors, nor were they repeated by their successors. They express a shift in Assyrian royal ideology.

In earlier Babylonian tradition, the image of the king had been that of a just ruler, supreme judge and ultimate rectifier of wrongs. In theory, any citizen could appeal to him for judgment, and we do in fact find Babylonian letters of appeal. In Assyria as well the king was the ultimate level of appeal, but since social awareness was less developed we find fewer such letters. The monarch's self-description stresses his piety and personal valor rather than his role as guardian of justice. In contrast to Babylonia, where cases were tried by professional judges, the assembly of elders and the like, there was no separate judiciary in Assyria. Cases, as K. Deller and J.N. Postgate have shown, were tried before royal administrators, local governors, or military commanders.

A brief digression into the terms "law" and "justice" as applied to Mesopotamia is in order. As has been noted, the word "law" reflects Roman concepts and does not precisely render the sense of its Akkadian semantic counterpart *dīnum* or the Biblical Hebrew *mishpaṭ*. The Mesopotamian judge, DI.KUD. in Sumerian (lit. "decider of decision") and *dayānum* in Akkadian, pronounced his verdict *(dīnu, purrussū)* on the basis of generally accepted norms of righteousness *(kittum, ṣedek* in Biblical Hebrew). The term *kittum* could be used in non-legal contexts as well; in fact, it carried a wider semantic range than its English counterpart. In the sphere of religious thought it denoted, as E.A. Speiser put it, "the sum of cosmic and immutable truths" which were deified precisely as was its Phoenician counterpart Sydyk, known from Philo Biblius.

The king too was supposed to implement *kittum*. Such implementation was designated *mīšarum* (lit. a "straight thing," akin to the Biblical *mesharīm* and very close to the English word "justice" in its practical sense or as an act of equity). In the Old Babylonian period the king would dispense *mīšarum* in an official act, upon his accession and at periodic intervals throughout his reign. Although the practice, resembling the Greek σεισάχθεια fell into disuse by the first millennium, the terminology survived in the Babylonian royal title *šar mīšarim*, "king of equity".

As in other civilizations, the patron of justice was the sun of god, here called Shamash. He was Lord of Justice *(bēl dīni),* divine judge and guardian of the truths *(kināti)* that were embedded in the cosmic order, as J.J. Finkelstein stressed, and were not his creations. His earthly counterpart, the king, upholder of justice, was no doubt accountable to Shamash as any judge would have been. A perverse judge could be punished by the king, but what happened to a perverse king? Here lies a basic difference between Mesopotamian and Israelite societies. There is no evidence testifying to the existence of an autonomous elite that could criticize the king's equity or question his righteousness.

A pronounced freedom of expression toward former kings or current rivals did exist both in historiographic narration, mostly chronicles, and in political propaganda. Their wrongs, such as cultic sins, and especially their attitude toward the city of Babylon and its god, were criticized at times severely. Alternatively, criticism could be projected into the future in the form of prophetic (in W.W. Hallo's term "apocalyptic") schemes. Just kings were contrasted in these schemes with evildoers, who would be punished by forfeiture of their throne and dynasty. The gods were clearly the guardians of proper order, but they lacked messengers comparable to the Biblical prophets to apply transcendental criteria to the "mundane" and to demand immediate repentance from evildoing rulers.

The lack of ethical control appears more striking when we realize that Shamash (in conjunction with Adad) was also the patron of divination. The findings of extispicy, *bīru,* were called "verdicts," *dīnu* and *purussu,* the very terms used for judicial rulings. From our point of view we might expect that a society in which a vitally important institution of divination is under the patronage of the god of justice is only a short step from establishing a system of autonomous ethical control. But in contrast to Biblical *torah,* which comprised both cultic and ethical maxims, Babylonian science (largely comprising divinatory lore) never carries statements on equity. If an omen includes a negative apodosis, e.,g., the fall of a ruler, the defeat of an army or the destruction of a dynasty, the *protasis* would simply describe some morally-neutral celestial or terrestrial phenomenon, never any specific act by the ruler in violation of an ethical code. We are not saying that such a code was unknown. Ethical norms were indeed seen as part of the cosmic code and occasionally were even phrased as omens or as legal clauses; yet, unlike the omens, they were not subject to supervision by any of the groups of professional elite.

In one sphere, however, that of royal obligations toward the sacred cities of Babylonia and their privileged citizens, we do, I believe, encounter that elusive embryo of "Axial-Age" notions of the accountability of rulers that Professor Eisenstadt is looking for. It is manifested in two documents: a ritual text describing the New Year ceremonies *(akitu)* in Babylon, and a "political pamphlet" (so I.M.

Diakonoff) dubbed by B. Landsberger in F.M.Th. de Liagre Böhl's edition "Der babylonische Fürstenspiegel" ("Advice to a Prince" in W.G. Lambert's edition).

Our extant copy of the document describing the New Year rites is from the Seleucid Era, but scholars agree that it reflects a custom prevalent in Babylon at least in the Neo-Babylonian period and possibly somewhat earlier. The crucial section for our purpose recounts that on the fourth day the king enters the temple. The high priest then comes out of the holy of holies, takes away the king's staff, crown, and godly-scepter and deposits them before the god Bel. He strikes the king on his cheek, brings him to the image of Bel, slaps him on the ears and forces him to his knees. The king then is to say:

> I did [not] sin, lord of the countries, I was not neglectful (of the requirements) of your godship. [I did not] destroy Babylon; I did not command its overthrow. [I did not harm] the temple of E-sagila, I did not forget its rites . . . I did [not] hit (lit. hit the cheek) of holders of the *kidinnu*—rights . . . I did [not] humiliate them.
>
> (A. Sachs in *ANET³*, p. 334)

The term *kidinnu* (or its archaic synonym *šubarū*) relates to the traditional sacred privileges of Babylonian temple cities—their exemption from taxation, the corvée, and military service, the prohibition of imprisonment without trial, etc. Thus the king who once might have reaffirmed temple city privileges by his own free will had by now become their enforced guardian. The negative confession he had to make in the holy of holies lying stripped of his royal trappings, symbolized the victory of the temple cities in the historic struggle with the crown after the sacrilege of Sennacherib in 689.

Until recently we knew of the *Fürstenspiegel* only through a manuscript from Nineveh. A second copy has recently been unearthed at Nippur, and was edited by Erica Reiner and M. Civil. In W.G. Lambert's translation, the crucial sections read:

> If a king does not heed justice, his people will be thrown into chaos, and his land will be devastated.
> If he takes the silver of the citizens of Babylon and adds it to his own coffers, or if he hears a lawsuit involving men of Babylon but treats it frivolously, Marduk, lord of heaven and earth, will set his foes upon him, and will give his property and wealth to his enemy.
> If he imposes a fine on the citizens of Nippur, Sippar, or Babylon, or if he puts them in prison, the city where the fine

was imposed will be completely overturned, and a foreign
enemy will make his way into the prison in which they were
put.
If he mobilizes the whole of Sippar, Nippur, and Babylon,
and imposes forced labor on the people by exacting from
them a corvée at the herald's proclamation, Marduk, the sage
of the gods, the prince, the counsellor, will turn his land over
to his enemy so that the troops of his land will do forced
labor for his enemy, for Anu, Enlil, and Ea, the great gods,
who dwell in heaven and earth, in their assembly affirmed the
freedom *(šubarū)* of those people from such obligations.

(*BWL,* pp. 113–114)

In a study of this text I.M. Diakonoff has suggested that it was
composed as part of the propaganda campaign between Merodach
Baladan II of Babylonia and Sargon of Assyria, who were contesting
the right to the throne of Babylon. We know that the issue of the
privileged cities figures in that campaign. Sargon reaffirmed those
privileges after his victory and after the conquest of Babylon (710),
as did his grandson Esarhaddon when he restored the Babylonian
temple cities ruined in the interim by Sennacherib.

A recently published Neo-Babylonian letter to Esarhaddon, edited
in part by Erica Reiner, adds a new dimension to the discussion,
and may point to an earlier, perhaps much earlier, date for the
original composition of the text. The letter says: "Let the lord of
kings look at the tablet 'If the king does not heed justice,' (lit. "heed
a case") which says as follows. . . ." The writer of the letter proceeded
to quote a passage from the *Fürstenspiegel* about the privileges of
Sippar, Nippur and Babylon. His point is that Nippur, where the
letter originated, was as privileged as Babylon. The writer goes on
to suggest that the tablet, which he affirms is "reliable" (authentic),
be read before the king in full.

Should not this initiative by a celestial omens diviner, who tries
to influence the king in a question of equity or power politics, be
considered close to the concept of accountability? I believe it does.
An even more convincing example, dating back a half millennium
earlier, can be found in a Middle Babylonian letter discussed by
Landsberger. There too the writer cites ancient tablets threatening
divine wrath against a king who mistreats Nippur, Sippar, and
Babylon. There thus seems to have been a long-standing tradition
of invoking divine protection for the immunities of the temple city
elite as against the authority of the crown.

We cannot fail to observe that the warnings are phrased in the
traditional omen formula (except that the conjunction *šumma,* 'if,

is implied, not stated: the *protasis* concerns the misdeeds of the king or his functionaries and the *apodosis* involves the consequent personal or communal retribution. In fact, the first warning seems to be borrowed directly from the omen compendium *šumma ālu*, where it appears in the positive form: "if a king heeds a (just) case" ["he will enjoy a long reign . . ."]. The gods who are said to punish the rulers and judges in these cases are first of all Shamash, then Enlil and Marduk. The reference to Anu and Ea, older gods, points to the primordial origins of the privileges; they belong, so to speak, to the cosmic order and cannot be revoked.

These privileged elite groups were a hallmark of Babylonian society, and their extensive immunities were one of the causes of its decline and ultimate disappearance. Exempted from military service, the temple cities depended upon external forces for their defense. At first they use Chaldaean mercenaries, who gradually settle in the area, and finally are absorbed by the community. To fight Assyria, the aid of Elamite army was enlisted, which imposed a heavy financial burden. No wonder the temple cities sided for a while with the kings of Assyria, who reaffirmed their privileged status and undertook to defend them.

Their real problem comes with their own Babylonian monarchs, in the Neo-Babylonian (Chaldaean) Empire (626–539). The temple city privileges are not even mentioned in any royal documents of that era. True, Nebuchadnezzar II (605–562) rebuilt Babylon, making it almost the size of Augustean Rome, with the help in part of deportees from the West and conscripts from throughout the empire much as Nabonidus does later when he rebuilds the temple of the moon god at Harran. But the people of the temple cities are themselves enlisted in restoring their temples.

Nabonidus goes even farther, by interfering with the administration of the rich temples and appointing royal commissioners to supervise their treasuries. This curbing of their economic independence, in conjunction with the king's cultic reforms, must have been a major factor in stirring up priestly opposition. Both policies are overturned by Cyrus of Persia, who like Sargon before him, was invited by the priesthood of the major Babylonian temple cities to become the legal king of Babylonia.

Nabonidus' best-known innovations lie in the cultic sphere. Born to a family originating in the northern city Harran, he gradually elevates the moon god Sin, patron god of both Harran and Ur of the Chaldees, to the position traditionally held by Marduk in the Babylonian pantheon. Sin comes to be called "king of the gods," Marduk's traditional title, and even "god of the gods," an entirely new designation. The chief Babylonian deities were venerated, but their temples were now considered "the abodes of Sin's great divinity."

This phenomenon, as Garelli has correctly noted, was not monotheism. If a label is required, it might be "henotheism." Other expressions of it were the theological schemes known long ago, in which each major god was identified with a facet of Marduk, e.g., "Sin (is) Marduk who lights up the night; Shamash (is) Marduk of justice; Adah (is) Marduk of rain," etc. However, such theological speculations had no apparent impact until forcefully imposed by Nabonidus for the benefit of Sin. Yet the *novellum* should by no means be underestimated. Nor should one underestimate the impact of the ruler's ten-year absence from Babylon, which resulted in the cancellation of the New Year rites. In the past, the *akitu* celebrations had been cancelled only in cases of calamity, war or anarchy. Their prolonged non-observance was an open defiance of the priesthood and populace of privileged Babylon, to which Nabonidus himself hints in his stele from Harran:

> But the citizens of Babylon, Borsippa, Nippur, Ur, Uruk [and] Larsa, the administrators [and] the inhabitants of the urban centers of Babylonia acted evilly, carelessly, and even sinned against his great divine power, having not [yet] experienced the awfulness of the wrath of the Divine Crescent, the king of all gods; they disregarded his [text: their] rites and there was much irreligious and disloyal talk. They devoured one another like dogs, caused disease and hunger to appear among them. He [Sin] decimated the inhabitants of the country, but he made me leave my city Babylon on the road to Tema, Dadanu, Padakku, Hibra, Jadihu even as far as Jatribu. For ten years I was moving around among these [cities] and did not enter my own city Babylon.
>
> (A.L. Oppenheim in *ANET³*, p. 562)

At this point, a *caveat* is called for. "Innovation" and "reform" are our own modern terms. Nabonidus himself repeatedly claims that he is only restoring the old but forgotten ways, as when he appointed his daughter chief priestess *(entu)* of the moon god at Ur, the first appointment of an *entu* after a lapse of over six centuries.

A similar claim was made by the only religious reformer who ever sat on the throne of Assyria. In an inscription composed after the destruction of Babylon in 689, Sennacherib claims that the *akītu* temple he builds near the city of Ashur for Anshar-Ashur, and the *akītu* rite performed there, merely restored the temple and rites of long ago. In fact, his claim can be corroborated by inscriptional and archeological evidence. That very temple originally built by Tukulti-

Ninurta I over five centuries before, had fallen into disuse soon after that king was deposed by his noblemen and assassinated by his son. Parenthetically, it should be noted that Babylonian historical tradition associates this regicide with the death of Sennacherib, also killed by his son. Both murders were considered punishments for the sacrilege of conquering Babylon, destroying it (in Sennacherib's case) and removing the image of Marduk to Assyria.

We do not quite know how Nabonidus justifies the fashioning of a new image of the moon god. All that we have is his statement that people have forgotten the true worship of Sin until that deity sent the new ruler to restore it. Though fully aware of his role as Sin's apostle whose ascendance to the throne was a new departure, Nabonidus could not admit to any serious break with the past. Even so, he was eventually overpowered by Mesopotamian conservatism embodied by the elite—scholars, priests, and privileged citizens. The old order, with Babylon and Marduk at the pinnacle, prevailed almost without a struggle under the patronage of a non-Mesopotamian *homo novus*.

Cyrus, king of Anshan, assumed the traditional role of the elect of Marduk and rectifier of wrongs. This empire-builder, most likely Zoroastrian (so according to Mary Boyce), "the Lord's annointed" of Deutero-Isaiah who heralded a new order in the ancient world, paradoxically helped ensure the victory of tradition over reform in Babylonia, thus speeding up its cultural decline.

Another paradox; it was Nabonidus, not his victorious adversaries, who ultimately emerged as one of the few persons of Mesopotamian history to escape oblivion. His ten-year religious retreat at Tema in Arabia became the kernel of a Jewish-Aramaic tale which found its way into the library of the Jewish sectarians at Qumran. It was also his image that shaped the legends about Nebuchadnezzar in the book of Daniel, especially the tale in *Daniel* 3:1 in which the king erects a statue of gold "sixty cubits high and sixty cubits broad . . . in the plain of Dura, in the province of Babylon." In the guise of Nebuchadnezzar, Nabonidus became the paradigmatic "mad king" of medieval European legends. One can still catch some glimpses of his character when attending Verdi's *Nabucco*.

It is virtually axiomatic to observe that of the civilizations of the Ancient Near East, Israel alone experienced the breakthrough that provided a formidable literature of social and religious protest. Yet it is demonstrably inaccurate (and certainly misleading) to suppose that the notion of royal accountability developed in Biblical Israel *ex nihilo*. Rather, one of the challenges facing the historian of the Ancient Near East is to explain why the fundamentally traditional notion of the accountability of the king in Babylonia and Assyria remained a severely limited one. A partial answer has been found in the underlying conception of the relationship between the ruler and his society—viz. the king as the very embodiment of Justice— as an expression of a "primordial," but not "transcendental" order. Such a deep-rooted conception allows but little room for the "perception of tension between the transcendental and mundane order." In the criticism of Mesopotamian ruler, independent of fixed ritual formulae, which we have observed, there is invariably an element of projection: either a retrospective judgement of a former king or a future-oriented admonition.

Most significant in this light were those nascent breakthroughs in the cultic sphere which came as the direct result of royal initiative. It has been suggested here, on the basis of evidence generally overlooked, that Sennacherib envisioned a departure from official Assyrian religion. More obvious yet is the example of Nabonidus, whose strident cultic reforms made Cyrus one of history's most welcome conquerors. The role of tradition was so powerful in Mesopotamian civilization, however, that both Sennacherib and Nabonidus felt constrained to present their innovations as the return to ancient and venerated custom.

This conservative notion in Assyrian and Babylonian religion was perpetually reinforced by that scholarly elite bearing a wide range of literary and mantic responsibilities. Their studied inability to cross the border from hieratic techniques to ethical concern and vision left no possibility of their emergence as spokesmen for social and religious reform. How different from Biblical Israel, where the monarchy, and occasionally even the priesthood, were held accountable by an autonomous elite—the prophets—who thus became the agents of the "transcendental breakthrough." In Mesopotamia, by contrast, it was the king who periodically threatened the consensus through his abortive reforms, and it was the traditional elite of *literati* that held the royal reformer in check.

ADDENDUM: ASSYRIAN PROPHECY

I have not dealt in the body of this paper with the message-type prophecy attested in Assyria for the reigns of Esarhaddon and Ashurbanipal. While the phenomenon reveals superficial similarities to Biblical prophecy, the differences are decisive for our purposes.

Female prophets, *raggintu*'s (lit., 'those who cry out'), are occasionally referred to in the royal correspondence of the period, and several collections of prophecies uttered—in the Assyrian dialect— by female (and sometimes male) "criers" have been found among the tablets of Ashurbanipal's archives at Nineveh. In these collections the message is usually a brief prophecy of hope and salvation addressed to the king. The divinity, mostly the goddess Ishtar of Arbela, speaks in the first person through the prophet:

> Fear not, Esarhaddon! . . . I watch over your inner heart as would your mother who brought you forth. Sixty great gods are standing together with me and protect you. The god Sin is at your right, the god Shamash at your left. The sixty great gods are standing around you, ranged for battle. Do not trust human beings! Lift your eyes to me, look at me! I am Ishtar of Arbela; I have turned Ashur's favor to you. When you were small, I chose you. Fear not! Praise me! . . . [This oracle is] from the woman Baia of Arbela.
> O Esarhaddon, in the city Ashur I shall grant you long days, endless years. O Esarhaddon, in Arbela I am your good shield. O Esarhaddon, legitimate heir, son of the goddess Ninlil [=Mulissu/Mylitta/in Assyrian], I am thinking of [you]. I love [you] very much . . .
> . . . Now, O king, fear not! Yours is the kingship! Yours is the might! [This oracle is] from the woman Belit-abisha of Arbela.
>
> (R.D. Biggs in *ANET³*, p. 605)

In another oracle, Ashurbanipal is promised that rebellious kings, enemies of Assyria, will be annihilated.

Oral prophecy of this type had no place in the traditional Mesopotamian, i.e. Babylonian, "science," in which divine messages were transmitted in written form through omens. It is essentially a western phenomenon, shared by Assyria. It was current in Biblical Israel and known to have existed in the eighth-century Aramaean kingdom of Hamat in Syria. From the second millennium, similar prophecies with messages, usually connected with various cultic or political affairs but without ethical content, are attested in the rich archives at Mari on the mid-Euphrates. But once again a West Semitic milieu is involved.

While the form and content of the Assyrian oracles are indeed reminiscent of the Biblical prophecies of salvation, nowhere do we find criticism of the king or the people according to any ethical or even cultic norms, and they bear no relation to the question of accountability of rulers.

PART III

The Secondary Breakthroughs in Late Antiquity—Second Temple Judaism and Christianity

The Secondary Breakthrough in Ancient Israelite Civilization— The Second Commonwealth and Christianity

S.N. EISENSTADT

INTRODUCTION

I

The specific characteristics of the breakthrough to the Axial Age in Ancient Israel and of the conditions which were connected with it generated later on the possibility of the development from within this civilization of several secondary breakthroughs—the two most important of which were, first, the crystallization of the Jewish civilization in the period of the Second Commonwealth, and second and later on, that of Christianity.

While the directions of these two breakthroughs differed greatly, yet they shared a common background and to some degree also common characteristics—as well as continuous mutual orientations and confrontations.

First of all they shared their being secondary breakthroughs in relation to the same point of origin—namely the ancient Israeli religious and institutional mold and its various later developments.

Christianity was at least in its beginning a part of the first of these secondary breakthroughs—that of the continuous reconstruction in the Second Temple, breaking away from the fold of the Jewish civilization only at a somewhat later stage.

The very possibility of such secondary breakthroughs in general and of breaking away in particular was rooted both in some of the very specific institutional and cultural characteristics of Ancient

Israel, as well as in the new international or intercivilizational relations which have developed in this period.

Thus the development of these secondary breakthroughs was connected with the intensification of some of the socio-ecological conditions which we have identified in the development of the early Israelite Axial Age. Of special importance here were the continuous existence of international conception between different empires, movements of populations, and great internal heterogeneity. In addition there developed here the fact of the Diaspora and Exile and the intensification of international and of the intercivilizational contacts and competition.

Here of special interest from the point of view of our analysis is the development of intercivilizational competition between different "Great" Axial Age civilizations—Ancient Israel and the Hellenistic and Roman civilization. This has been probably the first such different world history and such encounter that certainly facilitated the development of secondary breakthroughs.

This encounter was of crucial importance, as Prof. M. Stone's paper shows, not only for the emergence of Christianity, but also of Second Commonwealth Judaism. This encounter generated for the first time in the Jewish history sectarianism and heterodoxies— elements which existed already in the various Jewish sects but which became most fully developed in Christianity.

Concomitantly the very breaking away of Christianity from the fold of Jewish civilization did not obliterate the common reference point—Ancient Israel—a reference which was of crucial importance in their continuous intercivilizational relations.

II

The emergence of these transformations and secondary breakthroughs was very closely connected with the specific characteristics of Ancient Israeli Axial Age. In many ways these breakthroughs— and especially the first one—were a part of the continuous reconstruction and continuity of the special combination of the basic symbolic, ideological, and institutional components of the Jewish civilization, without, however, changing their basic features analyzed above. With all the continuous changes in the social structure its major great heterogeneity of socio-economic and ecological groups; continuous differentiation and mutual impingement by these groups; and, relatively weak growing social tension—continued. The same applies to the characteristics of the major elites, of the major carriers of the models of cultural and social order. They were very numerous and continuously changing. Already in the period of the First Temple they changed from the Judges to the Kings, from the more dispersed priesthood and Levites to the more centralized cult organization; there emerged the first scribal elements; there crystallized somewhat continuous but never fully organized and always variegated clusters of prophets; there existed some form of elders, whether tribal or urban, possibly related to the earlier ones from the period of the Confederacy that continuously persisted. But whatever the changes in the concrete composition of these carriers, some of their basic structural characteristics, analyzed above, continued not only through the period of the First Temple but basically throughout Jewish history.

It was the multiplicity and changeability in the composition of the carriers along with the multiplicity of centers and subcenters that explains the tendency toward continuous transformation of the basic cultural and institutional molds in general and the evolution of multi-faceted religious orientations in particular, and that gave rise to continuous attempts to integrate and reintegrate various elements of the tradition, the most important instances of which were in the reforms of Hezekiah and Josiah in the period of the First Temple.

But the combination of such transformation with that peculiar type of continuity of collective identity which was characteristic of the Jewish people can be understood only when it is remembered that all these developments were closely related to and took place within the wider context of the development of some specific characteristics of the history of the Jewish people; above all in the context of the crystallization of the Jewish collective identity and of attempts to define its symbolic-institutional boundaries in relation to other nations.

THE CRYSTALLIZATION OF JEWISH CIVILIZATION IN THE PERIOD OF THE SECOND COMMONWEALTH

III

The directions of these secondary breakthroughs and of the civilizations that emerged out of them did of course differ, and they have to be compared with both Ancient Israel as well as Ancient Greece and Hellenistic civilization.

In the Second Jewish Commonwealth there developed new orientations, new types of carriers, and new patterns of crystallization of collective identity—albeit through a continuous reference to the older ones and evincing marked continuities with some of the basic characteristics and symbols that were crystallized in the preceding period.

The first such newly emerging orientation was an apocalyptical and eschatological one, with strong, although not exclusive, other-worldly connotations. It was only in close relation to the experience of exile and return, and the growing tension between the present and the future that began to be stressed in the last period of the First Temple, that apocalyptic and even other-worldly orientations emerged and became—even if slowly and only partially—incorporated into the Jewish religious tradition.

The second relatively new orientation was a more contemplative, ethical, or philosophical one which emerged out of the encounter with Hellenism and/or developed in relation to the literature of the Wisdom. This new orientation, however, was limited to small circles, although it was probably more widespread in the Egyptian Diaspora.

Finally, the ideology of the covenant was reinforced. It emphasized direct access of all members of the community to the sacred and thus in a sense caused a return to some of the original premises of the confederacy but in a new, non-tribal setting.

The changes in the cultural orientations were closely related to those in the composition of the elites and in the geopolitical and intercivilizational situation of the Jewish people—changes which continued, even if in different ways, throughout subsequent Jewish history.

Some of the changes—such as the disappearance of the Davidic monarchy and the emergence, in its place, of new types of political leadership—composed of communal, although no longer tribal, leaders—the "elders" of the community and perhaps the members of the Great Assembly of high priests and of new monarchs—were partly imposed by or greatly dependent on external powers, which led later, in Herod's times, to the creation of a new type of secular kingship or overlordship—of which the Hasmoneans were the major exception. Concomitantly the status of the priesthood was elevated. Thus, possibilities of new types of political linkages between the political elites and the broader strata were opened.

However, these new possibilities were actualized primarily due to the emergence of a new, crucial leadership element, a new type of the political and cultural elites. Its major constituents were the scribes (sophrim) and members of the Great Assembly and of leaders of a great variety of religious-political movements, the best known of which have been the Pharisees—who in combination with some of the scribes were the possible predecessors of the sages. This development was connected with the concomitant one of numerous semi-heterodox sects.

With the return from Babylon, and probably already in Babylon itself, this new type of elites became the most active and innovative although certainly not the only ones. It was these different types of elites that emerged as the new representatives of the highest Authority to which the rulers and the community are accountable. They were not, however, as the later historical interpretation based on rabbinical literature suggests, homogeneous. They consisted probably for a very long time, of quite distinct elements continuously evolving, modifying and interacting in various tensions or coalitions with one another.

These elites were on the whole outside of any closed ascriptive structure or groups, and were being recruited according to criteria which were in principle open to all. They were intellectuals—but oriented toward the articulation of basic models of the social cultural order of the higher Law and hence intensively involved in political life whether in the judicial halls of the Sanhedrin or Sanhedrins, in their own centers of learning and judicial institutions, or, in coalition with other groups more concerned with communal prayer and popular learning. It was these different groups of elites that were leaders of the various sects and above all the carriers of the different elements which came later together in the institutional mould of the Written Law *(Torah Shebichtav),* characterized by an increased emphasis on legal-ritual prescriptions, based on exegesis, study and continuous elaboration of the holy texts and on communal prayer.

All these new elites shared some of the characteristics of those which were active in the period of the First Temple, and which we have outlined above—especially their relative symbolic and organizational autonomy and the strong interweaving of political and religious orientations, and they also acted in a situation of great flexibility of the social structure and of geopolitical volatility. But they differed from those of the older period as well as from the priestly families in their own period, by the weakening of both ascriptive and individual-charismatic ("prophetic") orientations.

Another crucial structural development in the post-exilic period was the appearance of Diaspora as a constant feature of Jewish existence giving rise to the emergence of a multiplicity of centers, or, to use Sh. Talmon's expression, to a multi-centric situation, adding a new dimension to the heterogeneity of the structural elements in Jewish life and to the volatility of the geographical or geopolitical situation of the Jewish people.

The existence of the communities of the Diaspora added a new element to the volatility of the geopolitical situation of the Jewish people which became, in this period, even more pronounced in Palestine itself. With the ultimate disappearance of political independence it gave rise to a lack of demarcated political boundaries for the Jews and hastened the crystallization of those aspects of the relations between the Jews and their neighbors which led Weber to characterize them as pariah people.

IV

Out of the continuous interplay between the activities of the new elites and groups, the new geopolitical situation, and the new cultural orientations, there began to emerge during the period of the Second Temple several basic ideological premises which were connected with the development of a new institutional mold or rather of several incipient cultural-institutional molds, carried by the various elites and their coalitions and which in many ways persisted throughout subsequent Jewish history and are of crucial importance for the understanding of its course.

One such implication was the weakening, although not the full obliteration, of the monopoly of access to attributes of sacredness held by ascriptive groups, priests, and sometimes kings, and, paradoxically enough, as well as by the more individual and charismatic elements, such as the prophets.

Second, as a result of this participation in the central sacred sphere was opened to all members of the community. There developed a growing stress on potentially free access of all members of the community to these attributes and to the central sacred sphere, and, concomitantly there was increased emphasis on a new type of communal cohesion, based on the conception of the "holy *community*" as a constituent element of the collective religious-political identity.

Third, new criteria of leadership and elite-status were articulated. These criteria consisted of a strong elitist orientation based on the learning of the law and on a broad populist base emphasizing prayer, observation of the rules, and membership in the holy community.

Fourth, the channels of mobility into the upper religious, civic positions and political leadership was opened to all members of the community, though this was probably more true during the periods when the sages were not in power than when they were the actual rulers after the destruction of the Temple.

Fifth, and in close relation to the former, there took place a fuller crystallization of the idea of the predominance of a higher authority, and of the accountability of rulers to a higher law—albeit connected with strong competition among different elites as to who was the true representative of this higher authority.

Sixth, there developed a more diversified scope of the political-religious public and leadership creating also a basis for new more intensive types of communal conflicts.

V

Within this broad context of new cultural orientations there developed several tendencies to the rationalization of religious orientations—each carrying different institutional implications. One tendency, with indirect institutional implications, was the philosophical ethical one. It was carried mostly by relatively small, probably mainly aristocratic intellectual groups who were strongly influenced by the Hellenistic environment.

Second was the systematization and elaboration of the prophetic orientation with the addition of very strong eschatological elements which gave rise to individualistic, prophetic visions and/or to far-reaching attempts at a totalistic-rational organization of community life, which were institutionalized only within some of the sects.

The third trend to rationalization, some aspects of which Weber fully recognized, developed in conjunction with the tendency to institutionalize the new cultural mould, namely, that which focused around the crystallization of the "Oral Law" *(Torah Shebéalpeh)*—which denoted a shift from the predominance of ritual cultic elements and prophetic visions to their continuous elaboration and to the interpretation and elaboration of the economic sphere, and to an emphasis on communal prayer. The interpretation itself was based on an increasing systematization of the legal-ritual precepts according to more abstract systematic principles.

VI

Within the context of all these developments the new mold of the Oral Law became very central—ultimately the predominant one.

This new mold began to emerge out of the combined activities of the various communal leaders, the sages and their precursors, and the leaders of the major sectarian religious-social movements, and it was characterized—as implied above—by increased emphasis on legal-ritual prescriptions, based on exegesis, study, and continuous elaboration of the holy texts, and/or communal prayer as the new and ultimately, but only ultimately, dominant elements within the religious content of the tradition.

This mold was derived from a combination of the predominant this-worldly orientations together with some of the other-worldly and eschatological ones analyzed above. In this case, however, the latter did not attain the same degree of distinctiveness as they did in other monotheistic or other-worldly religions. The potentially revolutionary and universalistic implications of these orientations—most visible in some of the sects and later on in Christianity—were here reinterpreted and hemmed in within the emerging tradition of Oral Law.

But, as we have already indicated earlier, the new mold of Oral Law, with its far-reaching institutional implications, was never really as fully institutionalized.

It is however important to stress that not only did the mold of Oral Law *not* become the predominant one during the period of the Second Commonwealth, but even during this period it was far from being homogeneous, and even later on, when this mold became predominant and most of the different older orientations were incorporated and transformed within it, they were never obliterated. They often reappeared as harbingers of such trends as the mystical—philosophical, contemplative—and cross-cutting them—the messianic one.

It was not only the older elements that persisted within this mold and became transformed within it. Within the new mold tensions arose among some of its own orientations: between the elitist orientations of learning and the populist communal orientations; and between the emphasis on political leadership and activity as against religious-legal-civic activity. These struggles were interconnected with more specifically religious tensions and gave rise to a great variety of interpretations of the tradition—all of them carried by different elites and groups.

Most of these interpretations attempted to recombine the major components of the basic cultural-religious orientations, i.e., the ritual, legal, eschatological ones, with the components of national identity, i.e., political, religious, and primordial elements; they also sought to combine the former with some solution of the basic dilemmas inherent in structuring this identity, especially that between the universal and the particularistic elements of their orientations.

VII

The development of the different ideological-institutional molds within them was, as in Ancient Israel, closely related to the elaboration of the components of collective identity and boundaries, of the relations of Israel to other nations, a process which began with the very return from Babylon and in which basic continuities—but also changes—with the former period can be discerned.

The crystallization of such symbols and boundaries was central to the tensions among the different elite groups and sects. Most of them addressed themselves to the dynamic tension between the universal and the particularistic orientation, and presented some resolution to it, and in their attempts to resolve this tension continuously, and tried to recombine the major components of the basic cultural-religious orientations, such as ritual, legal, eschatological ones with the religious-universal, political and primordial elements of Jewish collective identity. Most of these solutions, with the partial exception of such groups as the Samaritans, worked within this broader common national-political-religious framework with all its diverse elements and orientations. Their different answers to the problem of construction of Jewish tradition and identity were predicated on the common continuous incorporation of the primordial national and political elements into the new religious molds and on maintenance of the tension between universalistic and particularistic orientations.

Due to the growing tendencies toward universalism and the strong competition of other religions, this solution was not purely particularistic but contained certain strong universalistic orientations which have indeed continued, as we have already indicated above, throughout Jewish history in the Diaspora.

THE CRYSTALLIZATION OF CHRISTIANITY AND OF CHRISTIAN CIVILIZATION

VIII

The development of Christianity went in directions which differed, as G. Bowersock's paper in this section shows, from Hellenistic, as well as from Second Temple and later Judaism.

The ultimate lack of success of Jewish religion and people in the great competition between different religions, which has led to the ultimate victory of Christianity, and to the crystallization of medieval Christian civilization in general and its Western European (Catholic) variant in particular—and it was indeed only an ultimate lack of success because, for a very long period of time, much longer than has been usually seen by historians, the competition between Judaism and other religions, including Christianity, and later even Islam, did go on—was due not, as has been supposed by Weber, to their having become a purely religious community, but in many ways just to opposite reasons. It was indeed above all due to the fact that the Jewish collectivity continued to combine, in its self-perception, in the construction of the symbols of its collective identity, primordial-national and political components together with religious and ethical ones.

Of crucial importance in this context has been the fact that even its ascetic elements or groups—the various sects—were indeed very closely bound to such a view of the close relations between the Jewish civilization and people.

The break of Early Christianity with Judaism—whether it occurred already in early Pauline Christianity or a bit later—must have been going on for a much longer time than has been usually supposed, and focused not only on the place of law as against faith, but in addition, and perhaps above all, on two basic changes in relation to the Jewish faith and religion.

First was the transformation of the political and primordial elements from their connection with a specific people into much more general, universal, less specifically national or ethnic elements, thus dissociating the religious from "ethnic" elements—although not necessarily totally negating these elements, as was later the case in Israel.

The second such crucial transformation of religious orientation that gradually took place in Christianity was the weakening of the emphasis on contractual or covenantal relations between God and His people, which was characteristic of the Jewish religion, an emphasis that was connected with direct access to the sacred, open to all members of the community, towards a growing emphasis on the mediatory mode of access to the sacred, first vested in the charismatic vein in the figure of Christ, then more and more institutionalized in the Church.

It was indeed the combination of these two transformations of the original Jewish religious orientation—i.e., the weakening of political and collective primordial elements in the definition of the religious and later civilizational collectivity; the emphasis on mediatory, combined with a very strong transcendental orientation, together with the growing emphasis on ritual as against the law, that has been one of the important reasons for the success of Christianity in the great religious competition in late antiquity.

Another such element was the very strong and cohesive social organizations and networks that have developed among the Christian communities, many of them based indeed on social networks in the Jewish Diaspora.

Of crucial importance in this context has indeed been the transformation and development of asceticism as it took place in early Christianity, in relation both the Jewish sects as well as various types of holy men of antiquity—a transformation which generated new transcendental visions, strong other-worldly orientations as well as strong rationalizing tendencies, and seemingly indeed involving strong depolitization especially in relation to the Jewish sects.

It was the combination of all these elements, which were characteristic of early Christianity in general and the strong transcendental vision with strong other-worldly orientation in particular, that explains the great success of Christianity in the religious competition of antiquity as well as the crystallization of the medieval Christian civilizations, after its political success with the conversion of Constantine, as well as in its later encounter with tribal elements in Europe.

IX

But such transformation was possible only if the strong other-worldly orientations of early Christianity were not of a kind which excluded any this-worldly, potentially even political, ones—even if owing both to its dissociation from the Jewish people as well as the political circumstances in late Roman Empire, these latter orientations were very subdued in early Christianity.

Truly enough these two tendencies—the strong depolitization of early Christianity and its strong other-worldly orientations, as compared with Judaism and the later fuller political involvement of Christianity and the crystallization of Christian civilizations in Europe with a very strong civilizational and political orientation—may seem to be contradictory.

Contrary to some views which stress the basic totally other-worldly orientations of early Christianity, a closer look at the evidence indicates that Christianity in general, and its monastic and ascetic groups in particular, were not totally other-worldly—in contrast, for instance, with Buddhism.

The crucial differences between the effects of the Christian conversions and Church organization and those in the realm of Buddhism do lie in the basic differences in their predominant cultural orientations, in the respective conceptions of salvation that became predominant in them, and in the specific ideological and institutional dynamics which they generated; and it is also these differences that explain the different impact and transformation of the seemingly similar outworldly orientations that developed in these civilizations.

It is here that the crucial difference between the Hindu (and Buddhist) other-worldly orientations and renunciation on the one hand, and Jewish and Christian, and to some degree Greek or Hellenic ones, stand out—with the Chinese constituting a sort of "middle" case.

In the first cases pure other-worldly orientation was in a way an extension, even if a dialectical one, of the dominant mode of orientation of conception of salvation, the other-worldly concept of salvation which has yet generated a distinct civilizational pattern. The very institutionalization of such pattern has given rise to the dialectical extension of the ideal of the renouncer as the purest embodiment of this orientation.

In the second case in general, and in Christianity in particular, there have, of course from the very beginning, developed a very strong outworldly or other-worldly orientation. Yet from the very beginning these other-worldly orientations in Christianity were a part of the attempt to crystallize a new transcendental vision in which there existed from the very beginning a combination, interweaving, as well as a very strong and continuous tension between this and other-worldly orientations.

Christianity's inherent this-worldly orientation, i.e., the vision that the reconstruction of the mundane world is a part of the way of salvation, that the mundane world constitutes at least one arena for activities which are relevant to salvation—indeed in marked contrast to Buddhism—is of course rooted in its Jewish origins.

Such this-worldly orientation, in constant tension with the other-worldly one, has been manifested by Christianity both in its basic orientations and dogma as well as institutional settings. Thus such this-worldly orientation was evident already in the very central place of the Christ, who in distinction to Buddha was conceived not only as a carrier of an other-worldly vision but as the earthly embodiment or at least earthly aspect of God.

Closely related to this has been the strong emphasis on the lack of a complete separability or even opposition between body and soul in general and on resurrection in particular—a concept which in itself contains already a strong this-worldly element or emphasis and which was strongly disputed by Platonists. Similarly strong this-worldly orientation—even in constant tension with the other-worldly or other-worldly one—is manifest in the Christian conception, inherited from Judaism, of God as the Creator of Universe, of this world, and of the centrality of eschatology in general and of the historical dimension of this eschatology, i.e., in the conception of salvation as going to occur in history for the whole of humanity.

This relatively strong this-worldly orientation of Christianity was evident for instance in its polemics—even those of its extreme ascetics—with the Platonic and gnostic schools which have stressed to various degrees, as is well known, a strongly negative attitude to the holy and to the physical world. The difficulties of Christianity with neo-Platonism, despite the strong attraction of Platonic trends of thought to patristic writers, are also important indications of this tendency.

This strong orientation to activities in the mundane world can also be found within the Christian ascetic and monastic communities. Unlike the Buddhist or the Indian renouncer the early centuries (fourth on) were oriented in some way towards this world and not to total escape from it.

Indeed as G. Bowersock has indicated one of the great advantages of Christianity in the great religious competition of late antiquity was that its other-worldly orientations and ascetic activities ultimately enabled it to come back to the world carrying a transcendental vision, and in general the strong orientations to the reconstruction of the world were indeed inherent in early Christian Ascetism and Monasticism.

It was also this strong orientation to the structuring of the community and of the Church and to the relation between the ascetic orientation and the more mundane activities that have generated the great concern with the problems of authority and organization among the early Christian ascetics.

X

Thus indeed the strong predilection to a conception of salvation which contained within itself, from the very beginning, some combination of this-worldly and other-worldly orientation, was inherent in Christianity from its very beginning. They were indeed given in Christianity's roots in Judaism and its close—not only contingent—relation, to Hellenistic civilization.

Historical circumstances—the initial low political status of Christianity, its being persecuted—made these concerns in the earlier period of Christianity submerged but did not obliterate them.

More propitious historical circumstances—the conversion of Constantine—brought out these this-worldly ideological orientations in full force, and while the conversion of Constantine was indeed a turning point in the emergence of the different medieval Christian civilization, yet these developments have built on potentialities which have existed in early Christianity from the very beginning.

Since then tension between them and the pure other-worldly or outworldly ones has been a continuous part of the history of Christianity.

These potentialities have of course developed in different ways in different parts of the Christian civilizations—in the Catholic one, the Eastern, the Byzantine, and later Russian Christianity—according to the specific combination of this- and other-worldly orientations that have developed in the respective centers; with the geopolitical circumstances and the structure of political power and elites in each of them. In all of them developed also a very special mode of other-worldly ascetism and its tension with this-worldly orientations.

XI

The crucial difference of these two civilizations from those of Ancient Greece and the Hellenistic—and to some degree the Roman—ones, was that they were continuously restructured as parts of full-fledged civilizations and not purely as components of cultural traditions in other civilizational complexes.

It is not easy to explain the reasons for these differences, but they might perhaps not be unrelated to some such differences in the nature of the basic cultural orientations, in the combination of this- and other-worldly orientations, their greater distance from any particular state of polis that was characteristic of the Jewish and Christian civilization.

Here of course the comparison with China, in which there has also developed such this-worldly orientation, is of great interest, and we shall come back to it after the discussion of the Chinese Axial-Age civilization.

CHAPTER 9

Eschatology, Remythologization, and Cosmic Aporia

MICHAEL E. STONE

Professor Eisenstadt wrote me a letter commissioning me to address myself to the rather pretentious topic to which this paper is devoted (its exact title, I must admit, is my own doing). Furthermore, in his letter he urged me to consider the ways in which the topic was influenced by the "economic, social, and geopolitical conditions and ideological-religious background." This second request compounds the problematic nature of the topic manyfold. So, instead of an immediate response to it, I shall concentrate on three transformations within Second Temple period Judaism and I trust that the consideration of them will illuminate our general theme. These are: first, the shift from oral tradition to written tradition and then to sacred scripture and the impact of this shift on the social and religious life of the Jews at the time. Second, the shift from "historical" to "meta-historical" thought and to a "cosmic" view of the world and the corresponding transformation of historiosophy and eschatology. Third, the related shift in the understanding of the human quandary that flows from the change of the view of time and place and in turn led to a different concept of redemption.

FROM ORAL TRADITION TO WRITTEN AND SACRED SCRIPTURE

Following the events of the Babylonian exile (587–6), if indeed not somewhat earlier in its preparatory stages, the national tradition of ancient Israel entered into the definite stage of written record in a standard form. The repromulgation of the Torah under Ezra, or whatever it was that happened according to *Nehemiah* 9, symbolizes that. This written tradition consisted first and foremost of the Pentateuch. It was followed by the emergence of the definitive collection of the prophets and only at the end of the Second Temple period by the "Writings." It is certain that the Pentateuch had reached its present form by the time of the Babylonian exile, the prophetic corpus by about 200 B.C.E. at the latest, while the process of the assembly and collection of the "Writings" continued with variations throughout the period. That a tradition becomes written does not mean that the written form immediately displaces the oral as authoritative. However, the written biblical books apparently soon became regarded as embodying the true divine revelation, as being the very font of religious authority, and this happened close to the "publication" of the collections of biblical writings.

When religious authority came to be embodied in a given collection of books, the way that authority was understood changed.[1] Moreover, the fact that the authoritative document was written produced manifold results. At one level,[2] developments were set afoot through which Jewish law[3] and the social groups that cultivated and transmitted it took on their particular configuration. Julius Stone has aptly commented:

> The presence of written law, and the divine origin maintained for it, meant that the unwritten law came into the charge of the exegetes, rather than the speculative philosophers. For the unwritten law could not be at large, but must respect every revealed precept and word.[4]

In biblical times, it seems, the weight of teaching and administration of divine law had been largely the task of the priests.[5] They held this position because of their sacerdotal role and the status accorded to them flowing from their cultic privileges. The written crystallization of the sacred tradition and the position accorded the written documents changed this situation, even before the concept of "canon" had fully evolved. Competition developed in society for the role of true exponent of sacred documents. Every group within the Jewish religious spectrum in the Second Temple period based itself on one or another particular claim to the unique, true interpretation of the sacred writings. The actual techniques varied.

Of the Pharisees and Sadducees Josephus (end of first century C.E.) says:

> The Pharisees had passed on to the people certain regulations handed down by former generations and not recorded in the Laws of Moses, for which reason they are rejected by the Sadducean group who hold that only those regulations should be considered valid which were written down [in Scripture] (*Antiquities* 13:397).

Josephus here says that the point of difference is over customs not written down in the "Laws of Moses". Yet, elsewhere he speaks of "the Pharisees, who are considered the most accurate interpreters of the Law" (*War* 2:162). This sounds very much like a dispute over what later came to be called "Oral Law," the idea developed by the Sages, heirs of the Pharisees, that their tradition is of Sinaitic origin and draws its authority from the Mosaic revelation. Thus they could proceed to anchor much of ancestral tradition in the authority of the written documents. That authority was expressed, however, in the reasoning of the learned, not just in divine fiat.[6] Josephus' text may indicate a greater antiquity of this idea.

It is important for our argument to observe that in one text Josephus mentions the Pharisees as introducing traditional practices into the observance of the "Law", while in the other he holds them to be its greatest exegetes. And, indeed, both points are correct. The argument is over proper and true exegesis and who possesses it. If the Torah is a written document that is exegeted by expert groups of the learned and not by the traditional priestly class, then power and authority devolve from the priests to the learned.[7] And as long as the rivalry between the groups exists, the clear development of a single new elite in society which will come to replace the priests is not perceived; there are instead rival elites vying for primacy. One clear sign of the central position taken by the exegesis of the Torah is the very attempt to root all custom in it in one way or another.

It is not clear to what extent the actual administration of justice in Jewish society in the period of the Second Temple was rooted in scripture and its interpretation.[8] This certainly was the ideal aspired to.

In the First Temple period a/the primary locus of the intellectual and learned tradition, as well as of the administration of the divine law, was the priesthood. In the Qumran sect a very primary role of the priests was maintained. They had to be at every gathering, and none of the sect's central activities, including the study of the Torah, could proceed in their absence. In this respect, the Qumran sect was conservative, indeed archaizing in character, giving the priests an even larger role than they had in fact held in earlier times. Yet, even here, the authority for the exegesis of the Torah was not uniquely located in the priesthood *qua* priesthood.

Thus, the developing role of the written Torah produced a number of results. In social structures it produced new elites who were in competition over the exegesis of the Torah and therefore over authority in society. In terms of the structure of Judaism, it led to a gradual anchoring of all Jewish law, custom, and thought in the

Torah, as it developed. This changed the view of inspiration and of inspired individuals within the society and this change is reflected in changed social and literary forms.

To use "axial" terminology, we may say that this secondary working out of the primary breakthrough is related to the change of social structures in the following manner. There were considerable changes between the period of the First Temple and its monarchy and the time of the Restoration. But by the Maccabean period the changes were even more thoroughgoing. Some of them are to be explained by developments in the general culture of the Hellenistic world. Others, however, took place within the structure of Judaism. Persian policy was partly responsible for the transformation of Judah into a Temple state and enhanced the power of the high-priesthood and of the wealthy priestly aristocracy. In a parallel development, Persian policy may also have played a role in the establishment of the Torah with imperial backing.

The working out of conceptions inherent in the "primary breakthrough" according to which the Torah was the normative embodiment of the relationship between Israel and God and of the transmundane ideal towards which Israel aspired, led to its being written down and eventually to the authority of the written document rather than of the oral tradition. As a result, the power of adjudication and the implicit incidental power of legislation and consequently, therefore, one of the centres of power of the society, seem to have shifted gradually from the priesthood. This happened in spite of the enhanced role of the priesthood in society. A number of competing groups of learned exegetes arose whose rivalry, expressed in terms of differences over the correct exegesis of the revelation, was actually over the power of adjudication and its implicitly attendant power of legislation. The struggle of the learned to perform this role was only possible because the documents were written.

The writing down of the Torah also produced a retrospective view of religious authority; the Torah, the embodiment of divine norms, had been revealed in the past. The prophets who had provided an on-going channel for transmission of divine commands and of the summons to divine norms ceased. They were replaced by various groups including the "truly inspired exegetes." The Habbakuk Commentary from Qumran says that the Righteous Teacher knew the meanings that even the prophets themselves did not know when they spoke their words. Somewhat later, but apparently reflecting earlier views, the Sages claim that their exegesis, the Oral Law, was also given to Moses on Sinai.[9] By the use of pseudepigraphical modes, the authors of the apocalypses drew authority from biblical worthies and antediluvian sages. They also, e.g. in *4 Ezra* 14, talk of a parallel or complementary tradition of revelation to that of written scripture, thus resembling the Pharisees and the Sages.

All of these developments signify a change in the centre of power which was entrusted with the task of preserving, teaching, and interpreting the divine norms to which the people were to aspire. It became largely embodied in a number of rival learned elites which claimed to draw their authority from the same source as the scripture it was their concern to exegete.

FROM HISTORY TO META-HISTORY

The hope for a future restoration is found in the literature of the First Temple period, with its most prominent but certainly not its only expression in the prophetic writings.[10] It was expected to take place in the course of historical events as they developed and sometimes it was described in ideal terms. Redemption does not usually seem to have been redemption of the cosmos, although there are certainly hints in this direction.[11] This is true even of Deutero-Isaiah, who daringly employs mythical categories to describe historical events. So he uses language of creation and exodus to talk of the return from Babylon, putting that historical event into a primordial redemptive category.[12] Even then, the course of history in which redemption takes place does not seem to refer to an end of history. Cross has observed that "history" in the biblical sense is not history as the historians would have it, for God is a protagonist and there is a mythical substratum which produces what he dubs "epic."[13] It is the balance between the mythical and the historical elements that changes in the Second Temple period (see further below).

There are some schematizations in biblical chronology, particularly in sources deriving from the priestly milieu.[14] Nonetheless, there were no presentations of history as a whole, from *Urzeit* to *Endzeit*. God was conceived of in such thought as acting in the arena of the ongoing events of the historical process in their diversity.[15] The process as a whole, its beginning, middle, and end, was not itself the object of contemplation.

In the period of the Second Temple a greater intellectual sophistication emerged and people viewed the historical process at a higher level of abstraction. It was seen with the eagle's eye, in its completeness, *sub specie aeternitatis.* God was removed, to a considerable extent, from the actual flow of historical events, although he was thought to control history as a whole. The biblical conception of God's action was stubbornly retained, but the meaning of that action and of history was sought in encompassing patterns leading from *Urzeit,* through history, to *Endzeit.*[16]

This change in conceptualization of the historical process goes hand in hand with the development of a meta-historical eschatology. That development has been attributed by some to the influence of Iranian thought.[17] Others have seen it as a development of some potentialities in biblical thought, brought about by the dire political and social conditions prevailing among the Jews in the early part of the Second Temple period. These made the idea of restoration in the course of the ordinary events of history seem so implausible that it was pushed to the end of history and beyond it.[18] This is very likely true as far as it goes. However, it does not exhaust, we submit, the reasons for the shift of the expected future redemption from history to meta-history. This shift can also be seen as part of the overall development of the concept of history and the way it was described and presented. Thus this issue enfolds three interrelated developments—historical account becomes historiosophical system; eschatology becomes meta-historical; and, following from these, redemption becomes cosmic.

REDEMPTION AND APORIA: COSMIC

One way of describing redemption is to search to characterize the quandary or condition from which redemption is sought. The nature of redemption is a correlative of the nature of the quandary. The terms in which the quandary is conceived betray the view of the world and of God and man that is inherent. The concept of God developed in ancient Israel had moved him outside nature, so that he became viewed as lord of nature and history both. His role in the cosmos was described in historical terms. History, even in the special Israelite sense, only started outside Eden.

In the Second Temple period, God is further removed from the ordinary world and course of events. He becomes more transcendent and his function is not discerned in the "little happenings" of history, but in its grand, overall pattern and its crucial, pivotal events.[19]

Speaking of the development of mediaeval art in the West, Henri Focillon made a statement that is directly applicable, *mutatis mutandis,* to our present analysis.

> Deeply immersed in the historical life of its period, it [i.e. art] was subject to the differential effects of time and place. Its development was not a consistent growth with successive stages linked by transitions in which the past made way smoothly for the future. Styles do not suceed each other like dynasties, by the death or expulsion of the last male heir. On the contrary, a country may sometimes contain a number of

different artistic currents pursuing their several courses, with greater or less vitality, side by side.[20]

So, when we make statements about "developments" or "innovations" or the like, we cannot mean that with the emergence of each new stage all vestiges of the past vanish and no intimations of the still unborn future can yet be discerned. However, since our analysis is schematic in character, it must necessarily obscure historical complexities. So it is with observations about the growing transcendence of God. In prayer and devotional texts God is addressed intimately and personally, but in many other documents we find an extolling of his power and glory, his transcendent enthronement. It is not a philosophical position, concerned about how to make predicative statements about God, nor is it a gnostic stance holding the utter otherness and unknowability of Deity. Instead he is praised, extolled and glorified. This tendency combined with the view of history that prevailed to lead to a certain disengagement of God from the daily course of events.

The need to bridge the gap to the divine, the drive towards the transcendent, became particularly acute because of the emphasis laid upon the transcendent character of God. The gap became that much more difficult to span. Moreover, the Torah was now a written document and that document and its exegesis both drew their authority from the divine realm. They embodied the goals towards which the individual and the society strove and the norms by which they assessed themselves. Yet the achievement of those goals and of the vision of "the splendor of the glory of the Most High" (*4 Ezra* 7:42) by which truth will be shown forth could only finally be achieved outside this mundane existence, whether it be in the eternal life of the individual or the meta-historical vindication of the people of Israel.[21] So there grew a consciousness of an eschatological situation which will be beyond time or beyond history.[22] In the primordial, mythical world of time, *Urzeit* is *Endzeit,* the end is the beginning, and the process of history is not the arena of action. In the Second Temple period, indeed, the *Endzeit* is parallel to and sometimes talked of in terms of the *Urzeit,* but they are not one and the same. And the events of history, perceived in their discerned, underlying structures, intervene and lead from beginning to end. It follows that this is not a complete return to the mythical view. The radical historicization of the First Temple period is modified, but its basic insights are preserved. Mythical dimensions are restored or added, but the result is something new—a different balance of the elements. This we have called remythologization.

In the thought of the Second Temple period, parallel to the development of the concept of history, the spatial or local dimension of the world was also transcended. There was a remythologization of cosmology as well as of history. In the mythological view there are this-worldly and supramundane actors, human action corresponds to or reflects that of the actors of the supra-lunar sphere. With the radical differentiation between God and all other beings that is part of the initial insight of Judaism, the supramundane action is reserved for God alone. All other action is of this world. As history is the temporal arena of action, so this world is its spatial arena.[23]

In the Second Temple period, the supramundane world reasserts itself. There are heavenly actors as well as human, and human action is related to that of the heavenly ones. Thus in *Daniel,* e.g. 10:13, patron angels fight the wars of the nations; in the Dead Sea War Scroll not only men but angelic powers too will participate in the eschatological battle (1QM 12–13); demons, angels, spirits, visions of the heavenly spheres, speculation about their structure and denizens—these and a dozen other features can be named which flow from this change.[24]

Yet, as with time so also with place, the Second Temple period did not revert fully to the mythical view of the world. It exhibits a resurgence of many elements that were older, but these are modified and transmuted by the perceptions achieved in earlier Israelite religion as a result of the primary breakthrough. There is no reversion to polytheism, even of the high-god type such as existed in Canaan. Nor are the monistic views of Hellenistic-Roman paganism accepted. The denizens of the upper world affect the life of men and women and the process of history (see, e.g. 1 *Enoch* 89:59–70). They even, in some formulations, rule this world, but always do so subject to the one supreme Deity. This statement is made neither from a sense of or out of a need for apologetics; it is simply the case.[25] There is, then, a real change in attitudes to the structure of the cosmos and it is the dual transformation of the perceptions of time and of space that may be called the remythologization of Judaism.[26]

An additional factor is at work in this complex development. A number of texts reflecting certain intellectual streams in society evince the idea of a figure of Wisdom, a sort of hypostasis or personification of divine wisdom. In the background of this figure there may lie elements of a mythical female divinity, and its development is influenced by the Hellenized Isis myth. Personified Wisdom was closely associated with God in creation, said to be his breath, or speech. She is enthroned in heaven.[27] Now, in a number of texts, e.g. *Baruch* 3:36–4:4 and *ben Sira* 24, this personified Wisdom is identified with the Torah. *Genesis Rabba,* although written well after the period we are discussing, nonetheless shows the end of this process when it states that God "consulted the Torah and created the world"; to prove it the midrash cites *Proverbs* 8:22, which verse actually says that Wisdom was with God at the time of creation (1:1).[28]

Above we discussed the increasing role of the Torah as a written document in the life of Judaism. Its authority derived from its divine authorship; the authority of the competing groups of its interpreters was the same. When Torah became identified with personified Wisdom, it took on cosmic dimensions. Then that to which men aspired is not just the divine revelation at a given historical moment (as worked out, of course, by learned expositors)—it is the very constitution of the cosmos.

Thus, one aspect of the activity of Torah moved to the cosmic realm, and it was precisely this cosmic realm that had re-entered, in a changed form, the conceptual universe of men and women in the period of the Second Temple. A particular constellation of ideas was therefore at play, for the Torah was both cosmic and at one and the same time open to human, learned exegesis. The cosmic aspect of Torah was integrated into the remythologization of time and place that happened then and its identification with Wisdom served as one of the instruments of the process. Concurrently, the move to sacred scripture and the exegetical/legal process that was stimulated by it served to re-emphasize the particularity of the revelation to Israel. These two somewhat opposed directions of development produced manifold ramifications as they were held in fruitful tension.

The stresses engendered in society by the attempt to close the gap separating the human and the transmundane became more acute. The yearning to breach the gap to the transcendent God is also the desire to live in consonance with the constitution of the universe and to make the life of man and the course of the cosmos whole. This dimension makes the dilemma, the quandary, the more acute. In these terms, therefore, the state from which redemption is desired may be called cosmic aporia. The "secondary breakthrough" developments produced intolerable stresses that had to be resolved through eschatology that would surmount the this-worldly. Cosmic aporia demanded cosmic redemption.[29]

It is by no chance, therefore, that in this age eschatological yearning became so intense and that the character of the expected redemption was, to use Scholem's terminology, "catastrophic."[30] Its roots were ancient, but the great predominance of this most radical form of eschatology in the Second Temple period resulted not only from the complexion of historical events and historical oppression, but also from the cosmic measure of the gap between mankind and the divine.

Redemption in this period is still conceived of in terms of history and meta-history, of the future of Israel and of the world. However, the conceptual dynamics we have outlined bear within themselves possibilities of development of the idea of redemption in purely individual, non-temporal and non-spatial ways. Indeed, this happened later in some strains of Jewish mysticism and also in gnostic thought.

If cosmic aporia and cosmic redemption were the only aspect of Torah and Judaism, they might be expected to find little institutional expression. This was the case, indeed, with Jewish mysticism and gnosticism. It was, however, the particular genius of Judaism that it never abandoned its specific peculiarities. The Torah is cosmic, but it is also the revelation to Israel. It is incumbent on Israel to observe it; the makers and administrators of its laws came to form an elite outside the institutional elite and in tension with them (as, differently, the prophets had been before them).[31] The "history" told by the Bible begins with creation; it is essentially, however, the epic story of the gracious acts of God towards Israel. Philo's allegorization of biblical stories is the exception, not the rule, and even Philo held fast to the *speciales leges*. When the Qumran sect takes its own history as the only significant events, since the sect sees itself as the true Israel, its history is the history of Israel. The ancient, fundamental truths of the self-understanding and national being of Israel were never lost.[32]

The grounding of the Torah in the particularities of Jewish self-understanding is the anchor keeping it from winging off into the wide spaces of cosmic, eschatological speculations. It always remains the regulation of the daily lives of men and women.[33]

Here some central aspects of the change, the secondary breakthrough of Judaism in the Second Temple period may be seen. The historical and the mythical recombine in a new way in remythologization. History is perceived as a total process; the eschaton is at its end or beyond; God withdraws but does not disappear; the cosmos is constituted by the Torah which is at the same time the particular revelation to Israel.

Institutions change too: prophecy disappears and learned interpreters of the Torah arise. Alas, we know virtually nothing of the social roles of the authors of the apocalypses or of the wisdom writings.[34] There is sectarian rivalry combined with a gradual erosion of the position of the traditional elites—the priestly aristocracy and the baronial families. They are replaced by the exegetes and the learned who stand outside the traditional structures of society and are concerned to impose the divine norms of the Torah on them.

Here the change from the social structure related to the primary breakthrough is striking; the creation of the new elites is inextricably entwined with the profound changes in the intellectual and religious world-view.

The different balances constituting the various strains of ideology at this time led to a variety of social/religious groupings differing in their character and attitudes. While in the early part of the period the groups seem to have co-existed,[35] the gradual predominance of the Pharisees can be observed. They became institutionalized with the change of circumstances that followed the failure of the revolt against the Romans in 68–70 C.E. That was still ahead, however, at the time about which we are talking.

It is perhaps by chance and perhaps inherent in the complex processes of intellectual, religious, and social development that the two dominant forms of religion that survive from this age come from very different parts of the spectrum of Judaism's combinations and balances—I refer of course to Rabbinic Judaism and Christianity.

CHAPTER 10

Old Wine and New Bottles: On Patristic Soteriology and Rabbinic Judaism

GEDALIAHU G. STROUMSA

After the third century, intellectual leadership in the Roman world had clearly moved from pagans to Christians.[1] The triumph of Christianity was not only political but also intellectual. The Church Fathers played a major role in the reinterpretation of the heritage of Antiquity and in the constitution of a new field of knowledge, which shaped Western intellectual history until the modern age. Although the recognition of the early Christian breakthrough and its importance is rarely denied, it does not often seem to be granted by intellectual historians the serious analysis which it deserves. As a small contribution to a major task, I shall here offer some reflections on the Jewish component of early Christian soteriology.[2]

It is largely thanks to its Jewish heritage that Christianity succeeded in being in tune with the new religiosity which permeated the Roman Empire better than other systems of thoughts or religious ideologies. It is this heritage, in particular, which offered early Christian intellectuals the idea of a *religious thought,* an idea absent in Greece—since it originates precisely at the meeting point between Biblical revelation and Greek intellectualism. To be sure, the pagan thinkers of late antiquity were motivated, no less than the Christians, by soteriological interest. As a typical instance of this fact, one might refer to the status given to the *Chaldean Oracles* by the late neo-Platonists, a status symptomatic of the deep self-impoverishment of philosophy under the Empire.[3] The pagan philosophers lost their battle against Christian intellectuals not because they did not ask the same basic questions, but rather because they did not succeed in developing, as well as their opponents did, the means to answer them on the intellectual level. Pagan intellectuals could not for too long, like a Galen, poke fun at the Christians, "simple fools," limited by their constant reference to *pistis* and incapable of rational argumentation.[4] The Church Fathers soon learned to integrate epistemology and soteriology in their theology, thus following in the steps of Alexandrian Jewish intellectuals—and in particular Philo, a fact forcefully argued by H.A. Wolfson.[5]

More recently, the French anthropologist Louis Dumont has offered a fresh investigation of the Christian roots of modern individualism.[6] Dumont, who follows in its great lines Troeltsch's magisterial analysis of Christian ideas, sees a very close similarity between the "otherworldly ascetism" of Jesus and the Buddha and considers Constantine's conversion as having had a major impact on what he describes as a radical transformation of Christian conceptions after Nicea. On this point Dumont's picture is far from being convincing, and this may be due in part to the fact that he completely ignores the Jewish elements in Early Christianity. The following pages are, in a sense, a contribution offered to the lively debate already aroused by Dumont's views.

Christian self-definition progressively emerged, up to what can be called the "classical stage" reached by Christian theology in the fourth century, through a process of apologetics and polemics. Of the three great challenges which thus shaped Christianity—Judaism, paganism and Gnosticism—only the first remained fully alive after the fourth century, the only true "other," outsider in a world turned Christian.[7] Dualist trends of thought, which the historian of religion can legitimately consider to be a "mutation" of monotheism, soon became a very serious threat to the young religion, for structural reasons which cannot be examined here.[8] It should be stressed, in any case, that these three major conflicts which shaped Christianity, if they cannot be seen as quite independent from one another, occurred at different levels, even if this is not always quite explicit in the sources. When Gregorius of Nyssa, for instance, says in his *Great Catechetical Oration* that Christianity is a middle path between Judaism and paganism, he does not specify that the grounds on which both are opposed are essentially different.[9]

In this regard the testimony of Faustus, the Manichaean teacher, might be enlightening. According to Augustine, Faustus argued that Paul, in moving from Judaism to Christianity, changed only his rite, not his faith.[10] These words are important: Whatever Paul might have meant when he spoke of the *telos tou nomou* (and it is hard to follow recent arguments according to which he did in no way impair the soteriological value of the Torah),[11] they indicate the extent to which a radically different soteriological conception—such as dualist Manichaeism—could see Christianity and Judaism as reflecting the same spiritual options.

Similar remarks could be drawn from Origen's *Contra Celsum:* in order to answer the arguments of pagan philosophy, Origen is often brought to insist on the spiritual affinities between Judaism and Christianity.[12] When speaking to pagans, Christian writers are often subject to what one could call "the Balaam syndrome": it is out of intellectual coercion, rather than a genuine love for the Jewish people, that they recognize their closeness to Israel. On methodological grounds, thus, a structural analysis of the links between *verus* and *vetus* Israel should take apologetic literature into serious consideration, as much as—or even more than—the repetitive *adversus Judaeos* treatises, which of necessity stress only the differences between the two sister religions. (I say "sister," since the traditional filial metaphor implicitly ignores the deep transformation of Judaism after the destruction of the Temple and the failure of the Bar Kochba revolt.)

In relation both to Judaism and to pagan wisdom, i.e., philosophy, Christianity defines itself in a fundamentally ambiguous way. Neither rejecting both totally nor considering themselves to be their simple heirs, Christian writers wish to accomplish an *Aufhebung* of both. In a manner analogous to their position as *verus Israel,* they claim to represent, vis-à-vis Greek philosophy, the *vera philosophia.*[13] Yet, this last conflict focuses on the sense and value of *knowledge*—i.e., is located on the epistemological level—while it is on the means and meaning of *salvation* that the relationship—and the controversy—with Israel is topical.

"The voice heard at Sinai and at Calvary is the voice of the same God."[14] This pregnant formulation of W.D. Davies is meant to emphasize the identity of the fundamental religious intuitions of Judaism and Christianity, not to erase the very deep structural differences between the two religions or, in other terms, between Torah and Dogma.[15] The main reason which led earliest Christianity to a parting of the ways with Judaism was its decision to break with the main ambiguity in Jewish religion: the tension between a universal God and a chosen people. Paul had seen clearly that a universal God should offer to the Gentiles which He approached throughout the Empire the same salvation He offered to the Jews—and not relegate them, as proselytizing Judaism did, to secondary status (as "God-Fearers") if they did not fully join the Jewish people.[16] Hence comes, ultimately, the idea of a *tertium genus* so admirably described, in the second century, by the anonymous author of the *Letter of Diognetus.* The new people, "nation from the nations," transcends on all grounds the categories hitherto known: Christian identity is to be found neither in geography and language, nor in a peculiar way of life. It is their faith, their spiritual world-view, which binds Christians together. It is through this new conception of peoplehood that Christianity succeeded, in opposition to the Qumrān covenanters, in transcending sectarianism. It is by breaking national boundaries that Christianity became a new religion.

Parallel to this radical turn to the Gentiles, although probably at a deeper level, the Pauline transformation of Jewish soteriology has to do with what could be called—to use the term coined by Gilbert Murray to characterize the last stage of Greek paganism—a "failure of nerve." The first question to be asked by any reflection on salvation is obviously that of evil: *From what* is one to be saved? It would seem, to schematize grossly, that the two aspects of evil, moral and objective (cf. *böse* and *schlecht* in German, or the scholastic distinction between *malum culpae* and *malum poenae*) remain clearly distinct in Jewish thought. While it is the evil tendency located inside the individual (the *yeṣer ha-raᶜ*) which brings man to sin, the notion of national and cosmic salvation at the end of times (Messianism) represents above all release from objective evil: social and political injustice, epitomized in Exile.

Paul's "failure of nerve" is rooted in his intense feeling of the *omnipresence of sin*. Rather than confronting the sins of man, or reflecting the human fear of sin *(yr'ath ḥet')*, Paul was thus brought to insist that man is in a permanent state of sinfulness. The direct implication was that the atonement for sin could not be initiated by sinful man, but only by God Himself. "Christ died for our sins": the formula of *1 Cor.* 15:3 seems indeed to express the very core of the Christian message. The new figure of the savior, Christ, was thus integrating, or conflating, personal and historico-cosmical salvation, which had usually remained distinct in Judaism.[17]

It must be noted here that even the idea of Incarnation, brandished by Jews, and later by Moslems, as a major argument against seeing Christianity as monotheistic, also provoked a violent reaction on the part of pagan thinkers. Celsus, Porphyry, and Julian witness to the absurdity of the idea of a *single* incarnation in history when viewed from a philosophical viewpoint.[18] Indeed, it is only in a monotheistic climate that the idea could emerge.

Through the suppression of national boundaries and the transformation of the concept of Messiah, Christianity thus represented from its very beginnings, to use metaphorically a term borrowed from biology, a *mutation* of Judaism. As in biological evolutionary processes, this mutation had been prepared, as it were, by deep transformations of Judaism, which had acquired in the latter period of the Second Commonwealth a new sensitivity to ethical and social issues.[19]

E.R. Dodds once noted that Christianity never succeeded, at least before John Philoponus, in desacralizing the pagan heavens.[20] Dodds' remark would seem to be mistaken. The idea of a *creatio ex nihilo* implies the disappearance of the major chasm which, in Greek thought, separated the spiritual heavens from the material earth. In monotheist thought, this chasm is displaced: it defines God's transcendence from His cosmic creation—both heaven and earth (*Gen.* 1:1). There is ample evidence that Christian thinkers recognized this implication very soon: it suffices to think of Tertullian's treatise against Hermogenes, a professed Christian who believed the world to have been created out of pre-existent matter. One might also refer to such a popular work (both in destination and in posterity) as Basil the Great's *Homilies on the Hexahemeron,* in order to realize the extent of what could be called "the Copernican revolution" achieved by Christian intellectuals in the conception of the world of late antiquity. The Good God could create only a good world: despite the deep-rooted and pernicious influences—of Greek origin— which tended to devaluate the material world, the central feature of early Christian thought, in that respect, is revealed by its final rejection of dualistic tendencies.

Like its cosmology, also the anthropology of early Christianity is basically inherited from Judaism. *Homo imago dei:* the creation of man, at the center of the universe, soon brought Christian thinkers to recognize that the Platonic conception of the close relationship *(sungenneia)* between the soul and the divine was incompatible with their own insistence on the whole of man as a created entity. It is this recognition, established on Jewish roots, which eventually permitted the development of the western idea of the person and modern conceptions of humanism.

The implications of this insistence on God's transcendence and man's unity were crucial for the conception of religious life. Christian mysticism becomes mainly defined as *imitatio Christi,* an ascetical path whose ultimate goal, the total identification with God *(homoiōsis theōi),* remains asymptotic. Here again, a central Platonic conception is integrated into Christian thought only in a highly qualified way.[21]

The insistence on ethical behavior—and this is what *imitatio Christi* is about—at the core of the religious experience highlights the profound similarity between Jewish and Christian conceptions of religion. This common insistence also emphasizes the no less profound disparity between such conceptions and the centrality of the *numinous* in the various pagan cults.

Soteria and ethics are thus integrated in Christianity as they are in Judaism. The traditional opposition of Jewish *praxis* versus Christian *theoria* is only a half truth. In the fifth century, Theodoretus, the last Christian apologist, will identify *vera philosophia* to monastic life *(politeia):* in contradistinction to pagan philosophers, Christian ascetics not only seek to interpret the world, they also act to transform it. Ultimately, the messianic roots of the Marxist dream are to be looked for in this deep transformation of the Greek patterns of thought in patristic Christianity, which insisted, in true Jewish fashion, on the direct link between personal, ethical, and spiritual *reform,* on the one hand, and world redemption, *tiqqun 'olam be-malkhut shaddai,* on the other, rather than on *apocatastasis* in the Stoic sense.[22]

This predominance of the ethical component in the definition of religious life, it should be added, is related to a *neutralization* of messianism which can be clearly discerned in the two religions in the first Christian centuries. Parallel to the de-eschatologization of Christian thought, which sought to come to terms with the postponement of Christ's Second Coming *(parousia),*[23] the Rabbis seem to have succeeded to a great extent in de-activating messianic impulses after the loss of all aspects of Jewish national life in Palestine.[24]

Between the second and the fourth centuries, those central trends of Christian thought which became known as "catholic" or "orthodox" Christianity systematically rejected both Jewish-Christian and Dualist Gnostic trends. The reason for the rejection of these two opposite attitudes towards Judaism and the Hebrew Bible is the same: both failed to offer what Christianity intended to become and to remain: a fundamental re-interpretation of Judaism. The Ebionites simply considered Jesus to be the *last prophet,* and saw themselves as "Messianic Jews." In a scathing pun, Origen derived their name from the *poverty* of their thought. Marcionism, on the other hand, radically rejected the God of the Old Testament, seeing the coming of Christ as a totally new event unrelated to the history of Israel, which was thus deprived of its status in the economy of salvation.

According to the Church Fathers, the error of both movements, although of opposite consequences, was similar in nature: both represented an inability to produce an *exegesis* of Holy Writ, because they took the Scriptures *au pied de la lettre.* This conception of a double error stemming from the same root informs, for instance, the whole structure of Origen's *magnum opus,* the *Peri Archōn.*[25] The fight against both Jewish-Christianity and Gnosticism is particularly important in our present context, since it is in fact a kind of two-front "proxy war" against Judaism and paganism. In this war, the main weapon of the Church Fathers is their method of exegesis.

I would want here to exemplify this method by referring to Origen, the most profound Christian thinker in the East, who confronted Greek philosophy more seriously than other Fathers and at the same time also showed a rather deep familiarity with the exegetical methods developed by the Rabbis.

In his *Peri Archōn* (III.1), Origen devotes a lengthy discussion to the philosophical problem of free will, in the course of which he deals at length with the biblical passage on the hardening of Pharaoh's heart (*Exod.* 9:12, 35; 10:20, 27). In the course of this discussion, Origen polemicizes explicitly with the Dualists, who make much use of these verses, either in their argumentation against the demiurge, who shows his evil qualities in the way he rules over the world (the Marcionite view), or in order to claim that there is no free-will but only predestination, and that those who are evil by nature, such as Pharaoh, cannot be saved (the Valentinian view). Rabbi Yohanan, Origen's contemporary in third-century Palestine, refers to the same argument: "R. Yohanan said: 'Hence [from these verses] the heretics *(minim)* have a pretext to say that [Pharaoh] could not repent' " (*Exodus Rabba* 13.3).

This parallelism shows that when confronted with the same radical challenges, the Church Fathers and the Rabbis could give fundamentally the same answers—although they expressed themselves in very different idiom. The Rabbis, as has become clear since the major works of Saul Liebermann and others in his footsteps, were far from being ignorant of the main problems which preoccupied their contemporaries.[26] Rather, they expressed themselves in a different *language*. Aramaic and Hebrew did not fossilize Judaism, nor did they prevent it from absorbing deep Hellenistic influences. On the contrary, the linguistic "cocoon" permitted Judaism to assimilate much of Greek thought without disappearing. It is only with the Arab conquest of the Middle East that Jewish and Christian intellectuals will be speaking the same language. Arabic will then become the theological *lingua franca* of Jews and Christians. Both would pluck from the same tree of theological arguments and counter-arguments,[27] and the closeness of the "universe of discourse" of Judaism and Christianity would become manifest. It is out of this common stock that Kalam itself will emerge in the eighth century. The linguistic factor, therefore, seems to me crucial for understanding the lack of communication, the incommensurability, as it were, which seems to raise a wall between the *Weltanschauung* of the Fathers and that of the Rabbis.

I shall illustrate here by one last and striking example the very different ways in which Fathers and Rabbis expressed a rather similar religious sensitivity. Origen's *Homilies on Joshua* is the first—and the most interesting—Patristic work on the book which the Samaritans considered to be the "sixth book of Moses," and which describes the Conquest of the Promised Land by the Israelites.[28] In the eyes of a Christian writer, the immediate importance of the book is rooted in the Septuagint's rendering of Joshua's name: *Iēsous.* Moses' successor at the head of Israel is thus, first of all, a *sacramentum* of Jesus Christ, announcing that the Law of Moses has ended and that under his guidance the new Israel will enter the spiritual Land, the kingdom of God.

The warfare described in *Joshua*—including the extermination of the seven peoples who lived in Canaan before the Hebrew conquest—was branded by the Gnostics, as well as by the Manichaeans after them, as testifying to the cruelty of the Jewish God. Origen, who refers to these attacks in his *Homilies,* feels the need to answer the heretics and to show them that a proper understanding of *Joshua* shows only God's goodness. Here, too, Jews and heretics are similar in their simplistic, literal interpretation of the text.

The Christian, then, knows that Joshua represents "Jesus, my Lord." The seven peoples who were the unworthy inhabitants of the Land before the Chosen People took possession of it are identified either with "diabolical races of inimical powers" (the demonology developed by Origen is rather striking) or with the vices *(omnes gentes istae vitiorum),* of which the second circumcision, that of the heart, frees us. Thus, all things which happened to the Israelites in figure *(figuraliter)* should be translated from the letter to the spirit, a *figuris ad veritatem.* Just as the Exodus from Egypt was a mystical exodus, the conquest of the Land represents the spiritual fight against demons and vices.

The new commandments to be followed are those of the Church *(et praeceptis ecclesiasticis parere coepisti).* Outside the Church, writes Origen, as also Cyprian, no one will be saved. The house of Rahab the prostitute, in Jericho, represents the Church in a world full of evil, and which will eventually collapse. Does this mean that Israel will not be saved? By no means, answers Origen in Paulinian fashion— but it will be saved "from afar" *(Salvabitur tamen et Istrahel, sed longe positus salvabitur):* Israel follows his way not through his own virtue, but with the help and under the protection of the priests— which means that the Christians do not need priests: they are now the "Kingdom of priests and holy people" (IV.3).

The massacre of Ai receives special treatment (VIII.1–2): why did the Holy Spirit see fit to mention precisely this one massacre, when history is full of such occurrences? It is, answers Origen, to show us that both Jews and Gentiles work together in the new Israel: Jesus divided the people into two: those who simulated flight with him represent the Jews who converted to Christianity, thus seeming to abandon the Torah, while those who attacked by surprise and murdered the people of Ai and their king (the devil), are the Gentile Christian "And they smote them with the edge of the sword . . ." (*Josh.* 8:22). When the Jews read this passage, says Origen, they become cruel, and thirst for human blood . . . while our reading—according to which the passage refers to the killing of our guilty passions—is the only way of sanctifying war (*sanctificare bellum,* VII.7). Thus, he concludes, war stories are actually a teaching of peace that is offered to us, contrary to the Jewish literal reading.

Origen appeals to the Jews: "If you come to the earthly Jerusalem, and find it in ruins, reduced to ashes and dust, do not cry, as you do now, like children. Look for a city in heaven, instead of looking for it upon earth . . ." (XVII.1). An obvious question must be asked in our present context: what was, in Origen's time, the Jewish reading of *Joshua?* The answer is striking: the Rabbis do not seem to have cared much about Joshua and his conquest of the Land. There is no *Midrash* on *Joshua,* as there is on other biblical books, and only little lore can be found in Talmudic and later Hebrew literature on these chapters.[29]

One of these few legends refers to the story of the Gibeonites, who were spared during the conquest and later demanded and obtained the heads of seven young Israelite princes: they were never totally integrated into Israel, says the *Midrash,* since they lacked *pity (rahamim),* one of the three qualities expected of Jews.[30] Indeed, the self-image of Israel developed by the Rabbis was far from that described—or rather slanderously imagined—by Origen.

The Rabbis showed no interest in *Joshua,* because ideas of *reconquista* had been more or less neutralized after the disastrous failure of the Bar Kochba revolt—and perhaps also because they did not feel quite at ease with its accounts of bloodshed. Unlike Origen, of course, they were unable to read the whole story in a purely allegorical fashion, as a *sacramentum futuri.* Thus, they preferred to remain silent.

CHAPTER 11

The Role of Christianity in the Depolitization of the Roman Empire

HANS G. KIPPENBERG

The Jews were a people which followed, the Christians a sect which deserted, the religion of their fathers. (E. Gibbon)

At the beginning of the fourth century, when Constantine granted official recognition to Christianity, Eusebius proposed a historical theology which explained why the prophesied coming of Christ had taken place only in the time of Augustus. "The prophecy remained unfulfilled as long as they [the Jews] were able to live under their own Archontes of the Ethnos [popular leaders], starting with Moses himself and continuing until the reign of Augustus, when the governance of the Judeans was bestowed by the Romans on Herod, the first foreigner (ἀλλόφυλλοφ)" (*Historia ecclesiae* I 6,2).[1] Since the Messiah is the saviour of the heathen, the ethnic limitations to his appearance had to be abolished first. Put more pointedly: the abolition of Jewish autonomy is the prerequisite for the salvation of the heathen.

Looking back from this theology to the preceding centuries, one finds indications that Eusebius was not the first to assess imperial rule as positive, whereas he regarded ethnic or civic autonomy as negative. Otherwise, how can we explain why in the third and fourth centuries Christianity found hardly any followers among the urban aristocracy, while a great number was recruited among the bureaucratic officialdom?[2] And on the same lines, how to explain why the Christians prayed for the emperor, his officials and functionaries (cf. Tertullian, *Apologeticum* 39,2)? There are ample indications that many Christians conceded a certain legitimacy to the Roman overlordship, which was rigorously, even rudely, rejected as illegitimate and ungodly by some propagandists of the apocalypse (*Apoc.*13, 1–7; 16, 12 and 17). Thus the Christian communities contributed to the depolitization, or what may be called the abrogation of the order of the polis. This theme must be precisely formulated. It would be incorrect to hold Christianity responsible for the decline of the polis; the process of depolitization went on independently.

Already before the Christian Church had begun to play a role on the political stage, the 'political' consciousness of the citizens was waning. Thus, for instance, Plutarch complained that the Greeks were turning to the jurisdiction of the Roman governor instead of to their own civic authorities (*Praecepta rei publicae gerendae* 814 ∓ f.). Internal rivalries within the cities (στάσισ), which, together with ὁμονοῖα could serve the common weal of the whole city (Philostrat, *Via Apollonii* IV 8) were now brought to court, affording the Roman authorities possibilities for intervention.[3] In this context another point is worth mentioning. It has been observed that in various parts of the Roman Empire inscriptions honoring pagan gods vanished almost suddenly after the year 260.[4] With this, paganism as a 'civic religion' became extinct. P. Brown, who has recently resumed his study of this phenomenon, tried to explain this by the collapse of inner-urban rivalries due to the partisanship of the central authority. The urban families which hitherto had been currying favor with their fellow-citizens through public donations (θιλοτιμία) either ascended into the bureaucracy or descended on the social ladder.[5] While this was happening, the Christian communities were quantitatively insignificant. Thus it has been calculated on the basis of an intimation by Eusebius (*Historia ecclesiae* VI 43,11) that there were 15,000–20,000 Christians in Rome (in 251), which means about one percent of an estimated population of one and a half million.[6] The transformation of the order of the polis into a bureaucracy had a momentum of its own and was not in need of the Christians. Incidentally, this reconstruction has also been studied in respect of architecture: by the end of the third century larger architectural compositions appeared, subjecting the single object, which hitherto had an existence of its own, to a quasi-military order, its aesthetic charm lying in this order only. Nevertheless, I would like to study ancient Christianity in this context: not because it might have *caused* depolitization, but because it *became involved* in this process. The spread of it had to do with 'status inconsistency', as W.A. Meeks recently has shown.[7] When early Christianity opened itself to the desires and interests of urban social strata that turned away from the order of the polis, it also had to meet them halfway. It is my thesis that the transformation of the prophetic apocalyptic movement into an episcopal institution must be seen in this context. Intellectual problems, of course, played a role in this (inter alia, the delay in the Parusia). Yet it is impossible to isolate the development of the Church into a state-within-the-state from the process of the disintegration of urban institutions. The urban population, which in this situation sought refuge in the Church, also made socio-political demands that had to be taken into account by the Church. It did so by integrating the small groups that centered around prophets and aspired to experience the Holy Spirit, into an official organization which could offer a measure of security to the urban poor, widows, and orphans.

THE SEPARATION IN EVERYDAY LIFE FROM THE IMPIOUS

My point of departure is a paradox. The early Christians appealed with particular intensity to the urban population, but did not take seriously the idea of an urban citizenship. "Our community of citizens (πολίτευμα) is in heaven, and from there we are also expecting the Lord Jesus Christ, our savior," writes Paul to the Christian citizens of the town Philippoi in eastern Macedonia (*Phil.* 3:20). In the 1st century there are numerous parallels in Judea to the counteraction of apocalyptic expectations against civic loyalties.

There were groups such as the Sicarians who strove for a collective liberation of Israel by military means. Their thrust was directed from the rural areas to Jerusalem.[8] Those who were led into the wilderness by prophets, there to prepare the way for the Lord, followed a different direction, as reported upon John the Baptist (*Mc* 1, 2–6; *Mt* 11,7; Josephus, *Ant. Jud.* XVIII 116–119), upon Bannus (Josephus, *Vita* 11f.), upon an otherwise anonymous Egyptian prophet (Josephus, *Bell. Jud.* II 261–263; *Ant. Jud.* XX 167–170; *Acts* 21:38), and upon Zadoq (*b Git* 56a) in varying details. This expectation was so widespread that both Josephus (*Ant. Jud.* XX 167f.) and the gospel of St. Matthew (24:26) warned against following such calls. All these were cases of relatively short-lived actions which did not institutionalize their apocalyptic expectations in the forms of everyday life.[9]

The community that had retired to Qumran near the Dead Sea was something else. As the community ordinance 105 writes, its members had separated themselves from the dwellings (môšāb) of the wicked, to go into the wilderness and there to prepare the way for the Lord (*Jes.* 40:3). This was done by studying the law and conducting the lives according to it (8, 12–18; 9, 19f.). In this ancient monastic settlement the retreat into the desert became identical with an ascetic way of life, without marriage and property.[10] Thus outside the towns and villages the apocalyptic expectation became an ascetic life-style in the wilderness.

There was, however, an apocalyptic group whose members, like the Christians, remained in their original communities: I refer to the Essenes. Philo reports on them: "They live in villages and turn away from the towns by reason of the lawlessness that had spread among their citizens. They know that such association, like polluted air, causes a sickness of the soul" (*Quod omnibus probus liber sit* 76). Hippolyte reports in a similar vein: "Therefore none of them goes into a town, that he should not pass through a gate bearing graven images" (*Refutatio* IX, 26,1).

They were averse to Hellenistic culture and not to larger settlements; for we learn from other sources that the Essenes "are living in many towns, many villages, and large populous settlements" (Philo here quoted by Eusebius, *Praeparatio evangelica* VIII 11,1). Josephus confirms this: "They have no town of their own, but many live in each" (*Bell. Jud.* II 124f.). These Essenes had no objections to marriage.

These reports are confirmed in the Damascus manuscript. The members of this community may marry (CD VII 6f.; XVI 10) and dispose of slaves and tenants (CD XI 12; XII 10). In both respects they differed from the Metrokome of Qumran.[11] They accepted the household (bêt) which formed a legally constituted hierarchy. They did not however accept its local context which entailed rights and duties. Already the terminology suggests opposition; one lives in 'camps' (mah^{a}ne) as if in a state of war or in the desert (e.g. CD VII 6f.; XII, 23; XIII, 4ff.). One must not trade with the impious except in cash transactions (CD XIII, 14–16). This agglomeration of families was headed by a supervisor (m^{e}baqqēr) who had many functions: he decided on the admission of new members, was in charge of the finances, taught the works of God and judged legal matters (CD XIII 11f.; XIV 14; XIII 7f.; IX 17–22; XIV 11f.). Internal conflicts were brought before the judges who were subordinate to the supervisor (CD X 4–7).[12] In this way the Essenes made themselves independent of the local jurisdiction. It should be noted that in antiquity the members of the urban βουλή also exercized jurisdiction (Josephus, *Bell. Jud.* II 273).[13] Through the creation of their own legal system the Essenes broke up the civil community to which they belonged by birth.

The religious community which thus came into being also undertook socio-political tasks. I quote CD XIV 12–17: "And this is the command to the many, so as to determine everything that concerns them: they shall deliver the income of at least two days to the supervisors and judges. They shall give therefrom to the orphans, support the needy and the poor ('ānî w^e 'ebyôn) as well as the aged who is about to die, the man who has lost his way, the man who was led into captivity by a foreign people, the virgin who has no saviour" (*Parallel* CD VI 21).

Here the obligations toward the needy, widows, and orphans, already postulated in the Old Testament,[14] are even increased. The community of Qumran protects also the unmarried women who do not have any free male relatives (gô'ēl); it takes care of the redemption of its fellows who fell into slavery abroad; it offers the travelling Essenes protection and shelter; it assists the dying; it helps the indigent who live by manual work; and it protects the fatherless.[15] Common property in the Metrokome is replaced in the Essene 'camps' in the villages and townships of Judea by the support lent to those who are helplessly exposed to the pressure of the mighty.[16]

In particular, the Essenes expected protection from the supervisor. About him it says in CD XIII 9f.: "And he shall have compassion for them like a father for his sons and shall (bring) back the dispersed like a shepherd his flock. And he shall remove all bonds constricting them, that there should be nobody in his community who is persecuted and oppressed."

This can hardly be taken to mean "spiritual fetters, the bonds of sin" (thus A. Dupont-Sommer),[17] for the essential concepts of the text point to a societal reality. The bonds are clearly symbols of the fetters clamped on indigent debtors and their families (Philo, *De specialibus legibus* III 160; Plutarch, *Lucullus* XX 2).[18] And the symbol of the shepherd has always had a political connotation in ancient Near East, signifying the protection of the weak by the (bureaucratic) ruler.[19] Beggars and indigents are by no means the only ones who need protection. In addition, those who have to rely on manual labor (trade or agriculture) for their livelihood, since they did not have enough to live off the proceeds of their properties without working are called 'ebyôn, dal and 'ānāw in Hebrew.[20]

This community of Essenes is an interesting parallel to the early Christians: it broke away from local jurisdiction, it rejected the cult of sacrifice in Jerusalem (Philo, *Quod omnis probus liber sit* 75; CD V 6; 1QS IX 3–6), and attached no social obligation either to common place of residence or to kinship (CD IV 11; XX 13). As a complement to this withdrawal from the community of citizens it created an organization that aided Jewish citizens without family and property to protect them. The announcement of the impending end was at the same time the renunciation of territorial and ethnic loyalties. Here I would like to refer again to J.J. Collins, who uses other words to describe this difference between referent and speech act: the eschatological doctrines do not mean to portray the future (picture model), but they do want to give structure to actual relationships (disclosure model).[21]

THE PRESENTATION OF THE END OF DAYS
BY URBAN PROPHETS

The early Christian groups followed a similar pattern. They formed a community of saints, whose members stayed on in the townships but no longer took part in public life. They expected the impending coming of Christ in his glory and did intensive missionary work, directed mainly at the Jewish synagogues (*Acts* 9:20f.; 13:5; 13:14–42; 14:1; 17:1f.; 17:10; 17:17; 18:1–11; 18:19; 19:8). The spokesmen of this apocalyptic expectation were prophets. They stood at the center of communal life, from which they were later on gradually dislodged by the Episcopoi (bishops).

Documentation of the phenomenon of early Christian prophecy is found in the Gospel of St. Matthew, the Acts of the Apostles, St. Paul's letter to the Romans 12,6, and to the Corinthians 12–14, the Apocalypsis, the Didache 11–15, the Shepherd of Hermas Mandatum 11, and patristic reports on montanist prophets.[22] A fundamental distinction should be noted: whereas the prophets of Israel confronted the people as God's emissaries and were legitimized from above, the early Christian prophets operated within the community which itself was animated by the Holy Spirit (*Acts* 2). Yoel's prophecy (3:1–5) that at the end of days God would pour His spirit over sons and daughters, old and young, bond servants and slaves, and that these, as a consequence, would begin to prophesy, had been fulfilled. The prophets did not confront the community but arose from its midst. Therefore it became this community to judge the speeches of prophets, for the διάκρίσισ πνευματων itself was part of prophecy (*1 Cor* 12:10; 14:29).[23] Not only Paul but also the shepherd of Hermas (Herm mand 11, 14f.) adhered to this view, while the Didache (11.7) no longer permitted a διακρίνειν.

Prophets and teachers as esteemed charismatic personalities are historically documented in Antioch for the first time (*Acts* 13:1f.). St. Paul, himself connected with Antioch, organized the communities founded by him in the same manner (*1 Cor* 12:28–31; 14:29–33). Also the community (of Rome) described by Herm mand 11, corresponded to this picture, although from the second century onward the prophetic constitution of the communities was overtaken and replaced by the episcopal constitution: this happened to the Valentinian Gnostics (*Interpretation of the Gnosis* NHC XI, 1; Irenaeus, *Adversus haereses* III 15,2) and to the Montanists (Eusebius, *Historia ecclesiae* V, 17), both of which continued to adhere to it.[24]

What, now, was understood as the content of prophecy? When one considers that the whole community claimed for itself the prophetic charisma and that the communities were operating in different milieux, one cannot expect to find a conception of prophecy common to all. While the Corinthians regarded prophecy as an inspired glossolalia (*1 Cor* 14:2), Paul, in contrast, stressed the intelligibility of prophetic language: it must be constructive (*1 Cor* 14:3f.31). In this contrast, though, what was presumably the historically original content of early Christian prophecy, viz. the revelation of apocalyptic secrets (*1 Cor* 13:2; *Apk* 22:6) is lost.[25] *Acts* 11:27f. may serve as an example: "Now one of them (of the prophets who had travelled from Jerusalem to Antioch) named Agabus stood up and prophesied, inspired by the Holy Ghost, that a great famine would overcome the whole inhabited earth (οἰκουμένη), which subsequently came about under Claudius." The latter was added at a later date: Agabus' message did not refer to a provincial supply crisis but to the eschatological famine that was incorporated into the apocalyptic scenario (*Mc* 13,8 par).[26]

Such apocalyptic prophets also appeared outside Christendom. Thus Josephus (*Bell. Jud.* VI 300ff.) reports that four years prior to the war against Rome (viz. 62 C.E.) a peasant called Jesus son of Ananias, during the Feast of the Tabernacles, had foreseen disaster for the city in the Temple. A hundred years later, Celsus describes men who, in Phoenicia and Palestine, "visited towns and camps"[27] as beggars, proclaiming:

> I am God or the Son of God or the divine spirit. I have come. For the world has already perished, and you people are doomed because of your iniquities. I want to save you. You will see me return with celestial powers. He who venerates me now is blessed. As to all the others, I shall throw eternal fire over their towns and the surrounding countryside.
>
> (Origines, *Contra Celsum* VII, 9)[28]

In the early Christian community, however, this traditional type of apocalyptic prophecy was met with changed demands. For this community as a whole was the "body of the prophetic status τάξισ."[29] The prophets could not make do with proclamations: they had to demonstrate convincingly and visibly the dawn of the new aeon. The Corinthians saw this happen in glossolalia. Others insisted on ascetic actions. The Didache, which—as already mentioned—no longer admitted judgements on the content of prophetic utterances (11,7), developed other criteria related to the activity of the prophets, concerning their conformity with the morals which the Lord had required of his own people (11,8). 'Prosaic rules-of-thumb'[30] were established: a prophet should not demand of a community that it support him for more than two days, "if however he stays three days, then he is a pseudo-prophet" (11,5). Also, when he asks for money or eats from a table which he has demanded for destitute people, it becomes known what he is up to (11,6.9.12). He should practice what he preaches—but he does not have to teach everything he practices (11,10f.): This is a reference to the association between male asceticist and female virgin (syneisacts).[31] Here we recognize an integration of the ascetic tradition into prophecy. Early Christian asceticism also had its roots in the expectation of an impending end of days. It anticipated the present in the direction of this end. Already in separate expressions of the synopticists (*Mt* 19:10–12 and *Lc* 20:34f., to mention only two)[32] eschatology is presented as desexualized existence. The oral tradition which demanded of Jesus' successors that they renounce home (*Mt* 8:20), and family (*Lc* 14:26), property (*Mt* 6:25) and even protection (*Mt* 5:38ff.) have been interpreted by G. Theissen as the ethos of a roving radicalism, which he relegated to a place in apocalyptics.[33] As soon as the community as a whole no longer dared judge prophecy, it became inevitable to focus attention on the behavior of the prophet instead.

Apocalyptics was given its own reality in the role which the prophets played in the Christian community. These prophets, whose status was regarded as directly below the apostles (*1 Cor* 12, 28f.) took an active part in the leadership of the communities and proved their leadership qualities. In this the presentation of Christian apocalyptics diverged from the Jewish types we dealt with above: no retreat into the wilderness, no monastic settlement on the borders of civilization, but rather—like the Essenes—a separate community of family groups. The presentation of Christianity was focused on the centers of the Roman Empire and in places were citizens who were not (yet) Christians could take part (*1 Cor* 14:23). Men and women appeared who not only proclaimed the new era but also represented it by their desecularized way of life. In principle, everybody according to his abilities was destined to attain perfection (*Did* 6:2f.). Yet this position was not maintained for long. There was a change in the Christian presentation. While at first the community collectively was regarded as endowed with the gift of prophecy, in the course of time there emerged from it specialists in prophecy. Following this change, the community no longer assessed the prophetic speech according to its content, adopting instead more objective criteria, namely ascetic conduct. Thus began the development of a two-tier ethics: only those who were perfect were expected to lead an 'angelic' life, while for the simple believers a loyalty to these was enough. This development was completed by the Gnostics with anthropolatry. The Church was different: in it another authority, besides the prophetic charisma, came to the fore. While the prophetic charisma and with it the desecularized existence became the privilege of rare virtuosos, the simple believers could declare other needs and interests. In an analogy with the Essenes one can formulate the following hypothesis: Since, on the one hand, the early Christians proclaimed their expectations of the end of days in cities (and not outside them) and demanded of their members neither legally prescribed actions (like the Essenes) nor ascetic ones, and since, on the other hand, the territorial urban citizenry lost its inner cohesion, the episcopal element, represented among the Essenes by the mᵉbaqqēr only, became increasingly prominent.

THE FUNCTIONARY WHO ORGANIZES
THE PROTECTION OF THE WEAK

The development of this episcopal constitution took place from a contrary direction: from the respect naturally due to the elders in Judaism. "White hair is a glorious crown; it is found on the road of justice" (*Prov* 16:31). It is a disgrace not to honor the elders (*Lamt* 5:12). It is a recurrent topos in apocalyptic literature that at the end of time the elders will lose this respect: "And in this generation the children will scold their fathers and elders," it says in *Jub* 23:16.[34] Also in the Gospels such an estrangement is a portent of the approaching end of the world (*Mt* 10:21; *Lc* 12:52f.). Therefore, a movement that envisaged the end of days did not set great store in such distinction without reservations. It is hardly by chance that Paul omits to mention the "elders" and speaks particularly of those whom St. Luke intentionally presents as the "oldest" of those he considered archetypal Jerusalemites (*Acts* 11:30; 21:18) in the following words: "But of those who seemed somewhat (whatsoever they were it makes no matter to me)" (*Gal* 2:6).[35] This apocalyptic radicalism was certainly decisive for the propagation of Christianity in the cities of the Roman Empire. Nevertheless, from the very outset the πρεσβύτεροι were without doubt highly esteemed. This was, of course, the effect of Jewish prototypes. Thus in the synagogue the "elders" had especially elevated seats (*Tos Mᵉgilla* 4,21b).[36] But also the Essenes, who in other respects represented apocalyptic ideas, recognized the particular authority of the "elders" (zᵉgēnîm) (Philo, *Quod omnibus probus liber sit* 81; 1 QS VI 8–10). The Judeo-Christian community in Jerusalem followed this example (*Acts* 11:30; 21:18) and regarded itself—perhaps in analogy to the Jewish Synhedrion—as the High Court of Justice and as the authoritative teaching institution (*Acts* 15; 16:4). As the Christian missionaries outside Judea also turned to synagogues, where they recruited disciples, we encounter also Presbyters in these communities (*Acts* 14:23; 20:17–38). In both passages the elders are appointed by St. Paul—a rather implausible presentation, for the Presbyterian system does not receive its support in the Epistles of St. Paul, but in a series of other writings (*Acts;* 1 *Petr Tim* and *Tit 1 Clem*).

The argument in favor of the Presbyterian system relied on the oikòs as a model for the order of the community. In the First Epistle of Peter, first the elders "are exhorted to feed the flock of God" (5:1f.). Then the younger are asked to submit themselves to the "elders" (5:5). In this context G. Bornkamm aptly speaks of the "patriarchal character of the presbyterate." In the history of early Christianity the differentiation between a bureaucratic and a patriarchal meaning of the concept has remained indistinct, and only at the end of a slow development the originally patriarchal way of thinking was replaced by a more bureaucratic conception.[37] From the very beginning, legal powers of the elders over women, children and slaves determined this order.

The pastoral letters from the second century further accelerated this development by stipulating as a criterion in the selection of the bishops or the presbyteroi that they should be of good reputation as heads of an oikos. The bishop—in *Tit* 1:5 they are the presbyteroi—

> should be blameless, have only one wife, be sober, considerate, virtuous, hospitable, skilled as a teacher, not a drunkard, brawler, but friendly, not quarrelsome, not avaricious, who is a good head of his oikos and keeps his children well-behaved and respectful (for if somebody does not know how to manage his oikos how can he take care of the community?), not a recent convert, that he should not become arrogant and fall into the hands of the devil. Also among those outsiders he should be of good reputation, that he may not be exposed to defamation and to the snare of the devil.

> (*1 Tim* 3:2–7)

But this text goes beyond the stipulation that a good episkopos has to be a good oikodespotes as well. For it expresses the idea that the episkopos is required to take care of his community in the same manner as he does his oikos. Whereas the presbyters were the representatives of the single households, the episkopos, who likewise belonged to the circle of the elders, fulfilled additional functions resulting from the social obligations of the community as a whole vis-à-vis its more needy members.[38]

In antiquity it was not a matter of course that the structure of the oikos was a model for the overall political federation. Aristotle emphatically denied this. He insisted that "the rule of the lord is not the same as that of the statesman, and that in general not all sorts of reign (arche) are the same, as some people assert. For the latter is a reign over free-born men and the former is a reign over slaves, and the administration of a household is an autocracy—for every household is administered by one person only—but the governance of the statesman is a reign over the free-born and equals in rank" (*Pol.* 1255b). This clear differentiation between the economic control of the master of the house and the political governmental power, however, was not made by Plato and Xenophon. In middle-Platonic philosophy, contemporary with the writings of the New Testament, the oikos was then, as a matter of course, seen as the model for the political federation as a whole. For instance Philo, who belongs to this tradition, can occasionally state (*De Iosepho* 38) that the polis is a large oikos, and the politeia is a communal oikonomia.[39] Also in practice this conception has determined the practice. Herod, for example (King of the Judeans from 37–34 B.C.E.) administered his land like a lord of the manor (Josephus, *Ant. Jud.* XV 305–312) and accordingly demanded obedience of his subjects (*ibid.* 368–370). This conception could easily gain acceptance, especially in Asia Minor, where the king had the traditional duty to protect the poor laborer from the rapacity of the aristocrats. This concept subsequently entered the early Church. However, it must be emphasized that the New Testament did not conceive of the oikos as despotic. Also the most recent work on the *"Haustafeln"* in the New Testament has convincingly shown again that reciprocity of obligations is stressed in the three different judicial relations: between man and wife, parents and children, masters and slaves (*Eph* 5:21–6,9; *Col* 3:18–4,1; *1 Petr*). Always the legally stronger party has charitable obligations to the weaker.[40] The oikos, as it was conceived here, did not espouse relations of subjection but of mutuality.

The importance of the episkopos increased as the Christian communities granted their members support and protection. Even though later on non-Christians could also come to enjoy such help, originally this applied to the members of the community exclusively. The sources cite particular groups who needed help: widows, orphans, strangers, and prisoners. Besides this, the community was charged with the burial of its deceased.

Already the archetypal community of Jerusalem provided care for *widows* (*Acts* 6:1ff.). Later on the pastoral letters (*1 Tim* 5:3–16) established the rule that the obligation fell first to the members of her family. Only when this was not feasible, the community was charged with the responsibility. Finally, the Apologia of Justin (from the second century) presents the community as a social confederation in the following words:

> Whosoever has the means and the desire gives what he wishes at his discretion, and what is accumulated is deposited with the head; the latter uses this to assist the widows and orphans and those who, due to sickness or for any other reason are in need, as well as the prisoners and strangers living in the community; in short, he is a provider for all the inhabitants of the city.
>
> (*I Apology* 67,6)

This was no mere wishful thinking. The Roman community (according to Eusebius, *Historia ecclesiae* VI 43,11) supported more than 1500 widows and needy (in 251 C.E.). They were outstanding: Bishop Dionysius of Corinth praised the Romans for its having relieved the poverty of the needy ('η τῶυ δεομένων πενία) and supported their brothers in the mines (Eusebius, *loc. cit.* IV 23-10) in the second half of the second century.

Besides the widows and the needy, the fatherless *orphans* are repeatedly brought into prominence. I quote the *Apologeticum* of Tertullian, who presents the Factio Christiana as a "corpus" (this is a political term) and thus develops the concept of a social community:[41]

> The administrators are always elders who have proven themselves and have earned this honor not with money but by virtue of their conduct. . . . Every individual gives a modest donation on a fixed day of the month or whenever he wishes or can do so. Nobody is compelled; one pays voluntarily. Those are quasi deposits of faith. For nothing of this is spent on orgies of eating or drinking or on superfluous festivities, but only on the support and burial of the needy (egens), for youths and maidens without means and parents, for aged servants, as well as for the shipwrecked and for those who, in mines or on islands or in prisons, have become wards of their confession—provided they got there by reason of their membership in the community of Christ.
>
> (39,5f.)

Not only in respect of their sustenance are the orphans endangered; the fact that they have no parents, and thus are under no protective patriarchal power, makes their position so precarious. The *Apologia* of Aristides points to this danger with the following words: "They rescue the orphans from violence." Already in our discussion of the Essenes we encountered this situation.

The *strangers* are also mentioned particularly: not only the ship-wrecked but all travelling Christians in general. About these the apologist Aristides has written: "When they see a stranger, they take him into their homes and are glad to have him as if he were their real brother. For they call each other brothers, not in body but in the spirit and in God" (*Apology* 15).

And finally the *prisoners* on behalf of their Christian faith were entitled to support. Tertullian and Justin refer primarily to physical sustenance, while Aristides goes further and demands that they be ransomed—whenever possible (*Apology* 15), as was also practiced by the Essenes. We learn from Eusebius' history of the Church that this was no vain illusion. This contains a report by Dionysios of Alexandria, that during the Decian persecutions (251 C.E.) in Egypt, Christians had fled into the mountains where they were enslaved by Beduins and could only be freed after strenuous efforts and large ransom payments (*Historia ecclesiae* VI 42, 3f.—a similar report on Montanists V 18, 7–9). However, the redemption of male and female slaves who served in pagan households was out of the question, although there seems to have been some such expectations never-theless. Ignatius saw cause to remark: "They [the male and female slaves] must not demand that they be freed at the expense of the community, that they should not be found slaves of avarice" (*Ign. Pol.* 4,3). The Christians felt—with some justification—that the sit-uation of these people was not precarious.[42]

The assistance afforded by the community to its needy members consisted mainly in their nutrition and in their burial.[43] But support must not be limited to these spheres only. Like the Essenes, the Christians also afforded protection to the weak. Women without male relatives, children without parental guardians, and strangers were especially vulnerable to violence,[44] as in the case of prisoners is evident. The episkopos, like an Oikonomos (*Tit* 1:7) organized the protection. But in this way his office became more powerful: the needy became directly dependent on him. The accretion of citizens seeking protection caused relations of dependence and authority that undermined the charismatic order.

This conflict is already foreshadowed in the 3rd letter of St. John. Therein a charismaticus of the old school (simply called the elder, which in this case has nothing to do with the presbyterial constitution) complained that a certain Diotrephes had refused to accept letters from the author to the community, had not received his messengers and even excluded them from the community. Here Diotrephes is acting as an episkopos who decides about the protection of others. Therefore this Diotrephes "who would like to be the first among them" (verse 9) is regarded by most of the exegetes also as a representative of the emerging office of bishopric.

> The man of the spirit who is not subject to any organization or local institution collides with the leader of the particular organized community, who, it would seem, already claims for himself the rights of a monarch. Therefore we may confidently call him a bishop who, as required by Ignatius, is fighting for the exclusiveness of his community. And in this respect he even goes beyond Ignatius, in that he practically 'excludes from the church' members of the community who will not obey him.
>
> (Hans von Campenhausen)[45]

It is almost impossible to give a better description of the controversy: Does the charisma of non-resident prophets outweigh the advantages of an exclusive organization led by an episkopos? Should the community congregate around single saints and, in a decentralized manner, attach itself to the visionaries most respected at the moment (as did the Valentinians), or was the social advantage of a tight organization preferable? In the manuscripts of the Nag Hammadi library we still find arguments in defence of the superiority of the charisma. In the Apocalypse of Peter the bishops are called "dry channels" (NCH VII 79).[46] Other ideas than those of the 1st letter of Clement, however, prevailed in the Church. Clement reproaches the community of Corinth for having dismissed presbyters who had been lawfully appointed (ch. 44). Surprisingly, the Roman army, in which common soldiers obey the orders of their officers, is presented to the Corinthians as exemplary. Each according to his ability should defer to his neighbor: "The strong shall take care of the weak, but the weak shall respect the strong; the rich shall support the poor, but the poor shall thank God for having provided for the rich who relieves his want" (32,2). It is typical, therefore, that Ignatius—the defender of the monarchic episcopate—reproaches his Gnostic adversaries (IgnSmyr 2; 5,1-3) in his letter to the Smyrnians: "They do not bother about the obligation to love, not about a widow, an orphan, a destitute (θλιβόμενοσ), a prisoner or a released prisoner, a hungry or thirsty man" (IgnSmyr 6,2). We do not know if this was the case, but surely the strength of the Episcopal Church was based upon the organization of economic aid and legal protection. The power which this official attained reflected the weakness of the institution of the polis.

THE REJECTION OF CIVIC CULTS

"They do not worship the gods, they do not sit in the municipal councils." With these words the rhetorician Aelius Aristides (or. 46, ed. W. Dindorf Vol.II 404), characterized the attitude of the Christians. At the same time they reveal a conflict between Christians and Heathen. We know today that the persecutions to which the Christians were subjected from the 1st century were not based on a general law proscribing Christianity. Prior to the Decian persecutions in 250/251 the persecutions were only local. The institutions of the state intervened only when Christians were accused before them. Trajan rejected their exposure by public institutions (Pliny, *Epistula* X 97). In case of an accusation the Roman governor could institute a lawsuit (cognitio extra ordinem). If the accused persisted in his faith, the governor had a free hand. Today it is no longer thought that the Christian churches were persecuted by the state as collegia illicita.[47] These recent insights into the persecution of the Christians before 250/251 are of major consequence for our thesis, for they indicate that the persecutions were the consequence of conflicts that arose mainly within the urban precincts. There the Christians were censured for their stubborn refusal to take part in pagan sacrificial rites and generally to eat of the flesh of sacrificial animals, as an odium humani generis, flagitia, αθεότησ, αμιξία, μισανθρωπία. This refusal made itself so strongly felt because most of the meat sold in the town of antiquity came from sacrificial animals. Anyone who refused to partake of it excluded himself from the communal meals with the other citizens. Thus the separation between Christians and Heathen was established in everyday life.

The apologists of the 2nd century are of one mind about this refusal (Aristides, *Apology* 15; Tertullian, *Apologeticum* 42,4). A passage from Plinius confirms that the Christians renounced en masse the consumption of such meat, when he records a first success of the legal proceedings against Christianity in Asia Minor, noting in a letter from the year 110:

> At least it is quite evident that the temples which were nearly abandoned are visited again, the regular sacrifices which were discontinued long ago have been resumed, and in several places the meat of sacrificial animals, for which hitherto there were hardly any buyers, could be sold again.
>
> (*Epistula* X 96, 9f.)

Now it is well worth noticing that the scriptures of the New Testament were by no means unanimous in this question. Although the apostolic decree *Acts* 15:29 strictly commands abstention from the meat of pagan sacrifices, the apostle Paul, in his description of the same procedure, knows nothing about this (*Gal* 2:6). In the community of Corinth, members who had the gnosis used to lie at table during public sacrificial meals, thereby scandalizing other Christians (*1 Cor* 8: 1-13; 10: 23-32). But Paul approved private consumation of pagan meat:

> Whatsoever is sold in the shambles, that eat, asking no question for conscience's sake: For the earth is the Lord's, and the fullness thereof (*Ps* 50:12). If any of them that do not believe bid you to a feast, and ye be disposed to go; whatsoever is set before you, eat, asking no question for conscience's sake. But if any man say unto you, 'This is offered in sacrifice unto idols,' eat not for his sake that showed it and for conscience's sake.
>
> (*1 Cor* 10: 25-28)

Here Paul clearly concedes the possibility of Christians eating together with unbelievers, yet he already posits certain restrictions. Here a parting of the ways is foreshadowed, which was subsequently to grow into a real alternative. On the one side stood the Gnostics: Valentinians ate such meat (Irenaeus, *Adversus haereses* I 6,3), the Gnostic Basilides taught "that it did not matter if one tasted of the sacrificial meat and lightheartedly foreswore the faith in times of persecution" (Eusebius, *Historia ecclesiae* IV 7,7; cf. *Apc* 2: 14f. 20). The refusal of the Gnostics to take the martyrdom upon themselves— which itself is anchored in doketic Christology— [48]presupposes such practice. The exodus of the Gnostics from the community of citizens accordingly proceeded unhindered: in this community no premia were placed on political resistance. The apologists were of a contrary opinion. A deadly conflict arose between the exponents of this doctrine, that of the Episcopal Church—which after all was organized as a competing political 'corpus'—and the adherents of the polis constitution. This conflict, which was at the root of the persecutions by the government, can be most clearly recognized in the 'αληθησ λογοσ of the anti-Christian writer Celsus and in the *Oratio ad Graecos* of Tatian. Celsus, who wrote between 177 and 180, attacked the Christians' refusal to participate in the religious ceremonies, regarding this as a breech of the political constitution:

> It is impossible for one and the same person to serve 'two masters' (here Celsus refers to *Mt* 6:24; *Lc* 16:13). This is, in his (Celsus') opinion, an incitement to rebellion (στασισ) by those who seclude themselves and set themselves apart from other human beings

thus Origines quotes the critic (*Contra Celsum* VIII 2). Celsus blames the Christians for having betrayed their Jewish πάτριοσ νόμπό (II 1), of which the Jews, too, had been guilty, since they were themselves slaves who had fled from Egypt (IV 31). The Jews were Egyptians by origin, Jewish monotheism was a defection from polytheism. "The Jews left Egypt after their revolt against the Egyptian community and despised the rites customary in Egypt. What they inflicted upon the Egyptians they suffered at the hands of those who followed Jesus and believed in him as Christ. In both cases the grounds of the innovation was the rebellion against the community (τὸ στασιάζειν πρὸσ τὸ κοινόν)" (III 5). This applies to all the Christians who rejected the customs (I 1) and renounced the πάτριοσ νόμοσ (II 4).

With the aid of the concept of the patrioi nomoi Celsus develops an entire theory of culture which lies in the tradition of Greek ethnography. Each people has its own nomoi, which was laid down for the community, and must keep faith with them. For the various parts of the earth were allotted to separate overlords and are administered accordingly in different ways. "But it is an unholy deed to dissolve that which originally had been laid down as the custom in the various regions" (V 25). Celsus places religion, viz. the conception of the gods and sacrifices according to the tradition of Herodotus' ethnography, among τὰ πάτρια or τὸ κοινόν. Each people's nomos became binding by virtue of a common decision. A religion that does not recognize the differences of the gods and of the rituals is a threat to the existing order. And Celsus was not alone in this opinion.[49] Citizenship and religion were mutually conditional. It was the aim of the persecution to bring the Christians back to the patrioi nomoi. At the end of the period of persecutions Galerius' edict of toleration, issued in 311, stated that it had been the intention of the previous persecutions to lead the Christians back to the faith of their ancestors. They were to be dissuaded from their decision to renounce the religion of their forefathers (Eusebius, *Historia ecclesiae* VIII 17, 6–8). The attempt proved unavailing, but with this one of the preconditions of the cities was destroyed.

Tatian in his *Oratio ad Graecos*, written between the years 150 and 178, argued in a vein similar to Celsus, but he assessed the position in a positive light: "I despise your legislation. Everybody should have one and the same πολιτεία. Now however there exist as many legislations as there are cities: what is shameful in some of them is good in the others" (*Oratio* 28). And Tatian regarded the view that man's origin (γένεσισ) determined his life the root of the differences. "But we (says Tatian in the name of all Christians) stand above destiny (εἱμαρμένη) and have recognized, in place of the changing demons [he means the planets], the one and only Lord and, not being driven by destiny, we have escaped their legislator" (9,2). Men are quite capable to overcome their origins (11,2). Yet they do not do so, and that is what is reprehensible: "The order of the world is good, but the actions (πολίτευμα) in it are bad" (19,2).

It only appears inconsistent that one and the same corporate body advocated both the protection of the weak and the readiness for martyrdom. The development of either conception is interconnected, and their common denominator is the intentional renunciation of the citizenship in the cities of antiquity. The martyr is first and foremost proof of the superiority of the Christian faith over political loyalties.

CONCLUSION

Finally I wish to concentrate my remarks on three points:

1. In my opinion it is impossible to interpret the metamorphosis of a prophetic apocalyptic movement into an episcopal institution as an immanent process of 'Veralltäglichung' of charisma. The episkopos somehow took his position next to the charismatic leader but he did not develop from a secularization of the latter's authority. Here one ought to distinguish between two different sources of authority. The status of the prophet was based upon the presentation of the other-worldly—that of the episkopos upon the citizens' need for protection in antiquity. Gnosticism confirms this independence of the two roots of authority, because the prophetic typos was still dominant in it even when the episcopal organization became predominant in the Church. If one wants to explain the development of the Church, one has to introduce the 'need for protection' as an external factor that was recognzied as legitimate by the Church (but not by the Gnostics). The Church legitimized the needs that received no satisfaction within the institution of the polis.

2. H. Bolkestein, in his study on "Wohltätigkeit und Armenpflege im vorchristlichen Altertum," provided evidence that the moral obligations toward the destitute, the widows and orphans were recognized in the Near East (Egypt and Israel) but not in the Greek city states. Justice (sᵉdāqā), in Israel synonymous with charity, is practiced in the Greek city states by way of public donations (the philotimia mentioned earlier). Bolkestein explains this disparity by the differences in social conditions. In the Greek city states the citizens took turns governing, the voices of the indigent in the demos carried considerable weight, and there was a predominance of smallholders. In contrast, in the Near East the economic differences were more permanent, and charity was part of the vertical coalition between the mighty and the simple producers. To the extent that

the Greco-Roman political structure became more unequal, the institutions of the polis ceased to work, and the need for an oriental type of social policy gradually increased. Christianity filled this need.[50]

3. The great significance which Christian ethics was destined to have for the actions of the laity at the beginning of the modern era in Europe (I mean Max Weber's thesis on the religious-historical premise for purposeful rational action) was foreshadowed already in antiquity. S.N. Eisenstadt saw in early Christianity a secondary breakthrough to transcendental conceptions, which differed from the Axial Age proper—the primary breakthrough—by its universality: universality because society as a whole and religious community were no longer identical. Eisenstadt had already seen much earlier the connection between this process and the formation of centralized imperia.[51] According to what was said here, one can formulate this thesis even more as a principle: Christianity has embodied in its ethic the unique process of 'depolitization' in antiquity, viz. the process of abrogation of the primordial loyalties, and turned it into a principle. Social activity was deprived of its basis in tradition. This negation of tradition could be repeated in the Middle Ages with regard to economics. There were also prototypes for this already in antiquity. Thus the Didache stipulated that a roving prophet, once he settles down, loses his right to sustenance and is required to work for it (12,3; 13,1). Weber would have enjoyed this formulation: doesn't it mean that work as an end in itself becomes here equivalent to other-worldly activity? But let us not press this sentence any further. What is important is only that antagonism to tradition was incorporated into the ethic and thus became a prerequisite for the contribution of Christianity to the breakdown of the tradition-orientedness of the economy at the beginning of the modern age. Not only bureaucracy but also capitalism have an inner connection with Christian concepts. Here we cannot use a model of causality, as A. MacIntyre has shown.[52] But one can certainly speak of affinity.

CHAPTER 12

Architects of Competing Transcendental Visions In Late Antiquity

G.W. BOWERSOCK

By the early second century of the present era, intellectuals were well established in the corridors of power as the merchants of doctrines which could bring the temporal world into harmony with the ultimate order of things. In the preceding centuries of Rome's rise to power, philosophers and sages had often whispered in the ears of great generals and potentates. Pompey had his Theophanes and Augustus his Areius. The Stoics voiced their opposition to imperial rule and felt no less free than the neo-Pythagorean Apollonius of Tyana to tell an emperor what he should be doing. But it is under Trajan in the early second century that we can see an attempt to consolidate and proclaim all this wisdom within the structure of imperial government. Dio Chrysostom's four treatises on the nature of kingship and the relation of the temporal ruler to the ideal were meant to be taken seriously by the government.[1] And that the emperor attended to the words of such a man, even if he did not always altogether comprehend them, is amply apparent in the amusing anecdote which Philostratus tells of Trajan and Dio riding together in a chariot. Trajan turns to the philosopher and says, "I know not what you are saying, but I love you as myself."[2]

The impact of visions of the ideal king upon the ideology of the state can be seen in the panegyric which the younger Pliny addressed to the emperor Trajan in the year 100 C.E., when the occasion called for rhetoric: Pliny's tribute is an attempt to give worldly substance to the philosophic ideal of the *optimus princeps.* The Platonism of Plutarch entered, in the same period, into the mainstream of Roman government through Plutarch's own connections with the highest levels of Roman society.[3] With men like Dio Chrysostom and Plutarch, who can equally address the rulers and the subjects of the Roman Empire, the opportunity for imposing their visions of an ideal order upon the organization of the Empire was far greater than anything a Theophanes or an Apollonius had ever known.

In looking at the so-called "secondary breakthrough" in the role of intellectuals during the period of late antiquity, it is important to go back to the second century, in which the institutional authority of intellectuals was crystallized. It is no accident that in less than two generations after Plutarch an avowed moralist and philosopher sat upon the throne of the Caesars. This was Marcus Aurelius, the Roman emperor who composed his *Meditations* in Greek and consorted respectfully with the most eminent professors of his day. If historians have struggled largely in vain to trace a connection between the philosophical reflections of this emperor and his conduct of public affairs, that is scarcely warrant for assuming that Marcus did not believe himself guided by the visions he took such care to publish; nor should it diminish the significance of the first appearance of a philosopher-ruler at Rome.

As Peter Brown argued five years ago in his Harvard lectures, *The Making of Late Antiquity,* many of the most important characteristics of late antiquity can be seen to have their origins in the second century.[4] For the competition of transcendental visions in the institutional history of the Roman Empire, the second century is of paramount importance as a formative age. Quite apart from the more conspicuous individual figures, such as Dio Chrysostom, Plutarch, and Marcus Aurelius, the century saw an almost unlimited development of speculative thought which often brought the traditional philosophical systems (Platonism, Stoicism, Cynicism, Epicureanism) into conflict with each other and, equally often, engendered hybrid systems which we attempt to identify by such terms as Middle Platonism, neo-Pythagoreanism, and so on. An acute observer of the scene, Lucian of Samosata, found all of this good material for satire in his essay "Philosophies for Sale," and he was able to parody with precision the influence of philosophers among highly placed persons in the society of the Empire in his work "On Hired Philosophers in the Houses of the Rich." In this period transcendental visions were not merely competing with each other: they were jostling for space.

The early theorists of Christianity were also a part of this scene; and inasmuch as they were brought up on a diet of Graeco-Roman philosophy, it is scarcely surprising to find the intrusion of pagan concepts and terminology in the new theology. The more bizarre and heretical fringes of the early Christian Church at this time show an astonishing contamination of Biblical exegesis and Platonism.

The tractates of Gnosticism discovered at Nag Hammadi furnish additional evidence of the vigor of transcendental reflection in the second century and, of course, on into the third.[5] The Gnostics point to a development which becomes essential to our understanding of late antiquity, and that is the blurring of the distinction between philosophy and religion. It is worth remembering that the canonical text of the Neoplatonists of late antiquity (when Neoplatonism was, at least for many, something very close to a religion) was the work known as the *Chaldaean Oracles.*[6] The ancients themselves traditionally dated the composition of these oracles to the second half of the second century. Although modern scholars have sometimes been skeptical, it ought to be recognized—and it often is not—that the second century would have been a most fertile ground for the generation of a work of that kind.

There is another group of intellectuals in the second century who also anticipated the developments of the fourth and later. These are the physicians who were, according to Galen's prescription for good medicine, philosophers as well as doctors. Galen himself is the best illustration of a new and potent influence of doctors in the Roman Empire.[7] He was close to the court of Marcus Aurelius as well as to the leading figures of Roman society of the time, and his voluminous writings were widely read, not only for their anatomical details but also for their observations of human behavior. Galen's view of medicine was predicated upon philosophical opinions, which were as important to his diagnoses as his experimentation with the living and the dead.

Philosophers, theologians, and doctors were all working in areas that presupposed visions of ultimate reality which they undertook to impose upon the daily life of the world around them. The ascendancy of such people in the society and government of the Roman Empire gave them an increasingly lofty sense of their own mission and naturally brought them and their doctrines into collision. The upshot of this collision could as easily be fusion as conflict, and the second century shows examples of both. It becomes increasingly difficult for the exegetes and expositors of the various doctrines to determine what is authentic and what is corrupt, or—to put it in other terms—what is orthodox and what is heterodox. The early Christian Church has a well-documented history of chasing heresies, and the history of Platonism from the second century to the end of antiquity is replete with reinterpretations of the master that seem to many to leave the pristine opinions far behind. After Middle Platonism comes Neoplatonism, and Neoplatonism is itself torn by rival teachers.

The intellectuals of the second century, as well as of the centuries to follow, came to enjoy the heady sensation that what they were doing could actually influence the course of events. The relation between their visions of the supernatural world and the conduct of life in this one was a kind of vast enlargement of the long-standing relationship between the philosophical doctrines of the doctor and the physical good which he could do to the patients he treated in the light of those doctrines. Philosophers could claim to heal the state in much the same way as a doctor a man. And the Christians could argue that what they believed could bring about the resurrection of the dead here and now. The coming together of religion, philosophy, and medicine in the second century, at a time when the intellectual elite was accorded the highest respect and influence, constituted the great beginning of the "secondary breakthrough."

It is only in the light of these extraordinary transformations in the second century that one can fully appreciate the powerful impact of the major transcendental visions of the fourth and fifth centuries. The principal competing visions in that age were Christianity and Neoplatonism; and both of these were replete with conflicting doctrines of their own. But something else impinged as well, and this was a rival vision that entered the Roman world in the third century from Iran, the vision of Mani. Manichaeism itself is another example of the institutionalization of a transcendental vision, and its proselytizing movements were closely connected with the military ambitions of the Sassanid rulers.[8] The doctrine of Mani posed a spiritual threat to Neoplatonist and Christian alike; and, together with the political might of the Iranian empire which espoused it, Manichaeism posed a considerable threat to the stability of the entire Roman world. In a celebrated utterance Diocletian attacked it in precisely those terms.[9]

The reception of Manichaeism into Graeco-Roman culture depended upon the transformation of the intellectual climate in the second century and the perpetuation of that new atmosphere in the third. In fact, Manichaeism provided an interesting third alternative in a world that was largely split between Christians of various stripes and the apostles of Plato. The interaction of Christianity and Platonism was carried still further in this age, so that we find both the Christian Origen and the Neoplatonic Plotinus sitting at the feet of the same teacher, Ammonius Saccas.[10] In Ammonius, with his influence on the Platonizing Christianity of Origen as well as on the nascent doctrines of Neoplatonic Plotinianism, we see one of the major carriers of the Hellenic traditions to the late antique world.

The role of teachers in communicating the principal transcendental visions of late antiquity to the governing class can scarcely be overestimated. The proselytizing mission of both Manichaeism and Christianity speaks for itself, but the increasingly complex and varied doctrines of Neoplatonism had their own powerful expositors. Some of these are chronicled in a work that is of supreme importance for understanding the intellectual history of the fourth century. That is the compendium of biographies of philosophers and Sophists compiled by Eunapius in self-conscious imitation of a similar compendium that had been prepared over a century before to cover the great teachers of the second century.[11] Through Eunapius' biographies we can see both the doctrines and the purveyors of them in the education of the young Christian nephew of Constantine, who ultimately converted to paganism and became the emperor Julian. The competition of other-worldly visions had no more palpable impact upon late antiquity than it did in the career of this short-lived ruler. Eunapius describes the exposure of young Julian to both the austere and the flamboyant strains of Neoplatonism, and he shows how the wonder-working of the flamboyant philosophers—the practice of theurgy—impelled the young prince to embrace a wholly new kind of life and to attempt to impose this upon the entire Mediterranean world.[12]

The two most influential advisors in the retinue of Julian during his brief reign were pagans who belonged to the traditions fixed two centuries before by men like Dio Chrysostom and Galen. Julian's counselors were the Platonist Maximus of Ephesus and the doctor Oribasius. Maximus belonged to the theurgist school of Neoplatonists and accordingly separated Julian from the more austere and abstract thinkers of the Plotinian tradition, such as the fourth-century Neoplatonist Eusebius. In the pagan domain Maximus represents two of the conspicuous developments of late antique intellectual struggles, the competition between orthodox and heterodox interpretations of transmitted doctrines and the transmutation of the study of philosophy into something very close to the practice of religion. Maximus was a philosopher, but he instructed Julian in the practice of paganism. Meanwhile Oribasius became the Galen of the fourth century by writing, at the request of Julian, a vast review of the history of medicine in antiquity. This was a history which quite obviously did honor to the curative and healing skills of paganism and thereby provided a strong counterbalance to the claims of Christianity. Nor should we forget that it was Oribasius who wrote a memoir of Julian's career which provided the basis for the most authoritative ancient accounts that survive from antiquity.

Another of the intellectual leaders with whom Julian was briefly in touch was the renowned philosopher and orator Themistius, a man who exemplifies the institutionalization of philosophic doctrines within the state in late antiquity. Deeply imbued with the thought of Plato and Aristotle but standing apart from the factions of Neoplatonism, Themistius was an influential member of the senate at Constantinople and the counselor of emperors from Constantius II down to Theodosius I. Under the latter emperor Themistius was prefect of the city and tutor of the future emperor Arcadius. His vision of monarchy and his exposition of its underlying ideology brought pagan thought into the service of the Christian establishment.

Christian leaders had long been alert to the rivalry of pagan philosophy and Christianity. The fact that the greatest Fathers of the fourth-century Church were well acquainted with Platonic philosophy made their task both easier and more difficult at the same time. They could address the Platonists on their own terms, but they could not miss the presence of Platonism in the doctrines they themselves supported. A symbiosis of Christianity and paganism is perhaps ultimately a more important theme for the understanding of late antiquity than the competition between the two. Both strove to capture the souls of men and the temporal power, and both did so by imposing a supernatural vision upon the mundane order. In daily life Christians and pagans could associate easily and freely in public struggles: they knew all too well what was vulnerable in their opponents.

But the Church found a remarkable way to break free from this strictly intellectual competition by its advocacy of a new route to wisdom, namely withdrawal into the wilderness. Gregory Nazianzen and Ambrose of Milan fought the good fight in the real world, but a new breed of Christians withdrew from the fight to seek a prayerful life far from the troubled centers of population. Such self-denial and communion with the divine was not, however, the complete renunciation that it seemed in certain individual cases. Viewed institutionally the retreat into the desert provided Christianity with a new source of power. It generated within the Church a series of holy men, who, as Peter Brown has shown so well, belong to an important tradition of spiritual leaders in the eastern Empire.[13] Antony, one of the most significant of the early saints of the desert, provided a powerful image for Athanasius, who had the political skill to use it. Athanasius wrote the biography of Antony and was able himself to exploit retreats into upper Egypt in his own interest during times of crises. Another noted anchorite of the fourth century, Moses of Egypt, was able to convert the Arab queen Mavia to orthodox Christianity and thereby to bring over a large part of the nomadic population of the Near East to the Christian church.[14] In doing this, Moses clung steadfastly to his desert outpost but may nonetheless be held responsible for Mavia's war with Valens and the triumph of her orthodoxy.

It was not long before the alternative piety which retreat to the desert represented became a stage in a Christian education. While some, like the great Simeon Stylites, maintained their eccentricities as a career, others, like bishop Rabbula of Edessa, used time in the desert as a school no less than the hours spent at the feet of philosophers and theologians. In the Syriac life of Rabbula the world and the desert are contrasted quite explicitly as the two realms with which an active Christian must become acquainted. What he learns of the other world in the desert can then be transplanted to the world itself when he returns to it. And so we see Rabbula pass from the Hellenized society of Syrian Chalcis, where one of his parents was a Christian and the other a pagan, to the austere life of a desert monastery and subsequently into deeper isolation in the more remote desert regions; but from there Rabbula is swept back into the activity of the Christian East by his appointment to the bishopric at Edessa, where he became known as the mighty "fortress of the blessed city."

Neoplatonism had nothing quite like the Christian anchorites. The Neoplatonists could contemplate a transcendental vision and communicate it to the leaders of the real world, but now the Christians could actually live a kind of transcendental life and then return into the world. The experience was more authoritative and more immediate. In short, the development of Christian withdrawal served in the long run to support rather than to weaken the Christian effort to impose its vision on the late antique order.

In the fifth century, with Rabbula in Edessa, the Neoplatonists had Proclus and his disciples in Athens. They developed an ever more rarified philosophical doctrine which gradually undermined the efficacy of this philosophical system as a practicing religion. Neoplatonism served to diminish its own authority by becoming an increasingly hermetic and academic discipline. Some young Julian of the fifth century would have found it difficult to experience among the Neoplatonists of that age the excitement which the fourth-century emperor found at Ephesus with Maximus. It may be said that in both the Christian and Neoplatonic spheres, orthodoxy won out. The withering of Gnosticism and the gradual reduction of the numerous Christian heresies of the fourth and fifth centuries contributed to the stabilization of the institutionalized Church. At the same time the more orthodox Platonism of the austere school, which was in touch with Plotinus rather than the theurgists, led to the removal of philosophy as a direct competitor to the state religion. It is probably for this reason that in the fifth and sixth centuries paganism seems to be generally tolerated in the Byzantine Empire. Some temples are still open. The school of Proclus flourishes at Athens; and, although there is a well-known tradition that the philosophers were driven out of Athens in 529, it seems clear that pagan philosophers were active there later.[15] It is a curious reflection on the course of events that the Athenian philosophers who were said to have left Athens went to Persia, where they are supposed to have made a profound impression on the Persian king. There is a certain justice in seeing these late adherents of Plato carrying their transcendental visions to the heartland of Manichaeism.

The "secondary breakthrough" in late antiquity can be traced from the second century to the sixth. It depended upon the emergence of a powerful class of intellectual elites who had the capacity to transmit their visions to the authorities of government and to influence substantially the opinion of the educated population. Platonism and Christianity held center stage, although there was enough diversity in both to create a succession of heterodox schools. A dialogue between Platonists and Christians prepared the way for the blurring of the distinction between philosophy and religion, and this in turn served to prepare the way for the intellectual invasion of the Manichees from Iran. It may be that the most brilliant stroke of the Christian theorists was the elaboration of withdrawal to the wilderness as a means of achieving piety. There the Platonists could not follow, and yet what the Christian ascetics were doing had deep roots in the actual life of the Hellenized East. The holy man proved to be a new type of carrier of a transcendental vision, and at the same time he provided an example for those coreligionists who remained in active life in the cities. In Rabbula the Christians were able to produce a figure who was, at one and the same time, a holy man from the desert and a sophisticated, Hellenized philosopher from Chalcis. As he presided over the city of Edessa, he was in his own person anchorite and bishop. The career of Athanasius had prepared the way for this, and it was something with which the Neoplatonists could not compete at all.

PART IV

The Origins of the Axial Age in China and India

The Axial Age Breakthrough in China and India

S.N. EISENSTADT

INTRODUCTION

The breakthroughs to Axial Age civilizations in China and India were, in many ways, of rather different order than those that have taken place on the eastern shores of the Mediterranean—whether in Ancient Greece and in the Hellenistic civilizations, or in Ancient Israel, Ancient Judaism, and Christianity.

With respect to the latter the major difference was that neither the Chinese nor the Hindu and Buddhist civilizations were monotheistic. At the same time in China there developed a certain—but as we shall see a rather limited—similarity in the strong stress of "this-worldliness" on viewing the mundane world, the world of political and social order, not only as the arena but also as the focus and carrier of transcendental vision with Greek and Hellenistic civilizations—but the direction of Hinduism and Buddhism was, of course, entirely different.

It is with respect to the designation of the major arena of the implementation of the transcendental vision that there has developed the most far-reaching differences between the two major Asian Axial civilizations.

Thus, as is well known, and as is fully documented in the papers presented here, within the Chinese civilization there developed a strong—perhaps the strongest ever known in human history—"this-worldly" conception of "salvation," while in the Hinduist—and later Buddhist—civilizations there developed what can be called the most far-reaching "other-worldly" civilizations.

These different conceptions of the transcendental vision and of the ways to bridge the chasm between the transcendental and the mundane orders were connected, in each of these civilizations, with some basic paradoxes.

The paradox of Hinduism and Buddhism has been that an "other-worldly" religious orientation has created a world civilization or civilizations, far beyond simple sects of renouncers going away from the mundane world.

As against this, the Chinese case presents another paradox—that between the development of the strong transcendental vision and of a perception of strong chasm between the transcendental and the mundane world, and a this-worldly conception of the bridging over this chasm.

This last paradox has already developed to some degree in Ancient Greece, in the Hellenistic, and in the Roman civilizations. As however in these last cases there did not develop such a large and continuous civilization in imperial systems, this paradox was not so fully articulated as in China where such developments have indeed taken place.

CHINA—THE PARADOX OF THIS-WORLDLY AXIAL AGE CIVILIZATION

Thus indeed, contrary to the view of many scholars, including at least partially Weber, the Chinese, above all the Confucian, tradition did not deny the existence of this tension—and accordingly there did also develop within it a very high level of rationalization of the cultural (or religious) orientations connected with the very elaboration and definition of such tension.

In Benjamin Schwartz's words: ". . . in the Analects we find considerable emphasis on his (Confucius') relationship to "heaven" which is treated not simply as the immanent Tao of nature and society but as a transcendental will interested in Confucius' redeeming mission. . . . Beyond this it is already clear that the word Tao in Confucius refers not only to the objective structures of society and cosmos but also to the inner way of man of *Jen.* . . ."[1]

There did, however, develop in China a special mode of definition of this tension, as well as a special conception of its resolution. In the classical Chinese belief systems this tension between the transcendental and mundane order was couched in relatively secular terms, i.e., in terms of a metaphysical and/or ethical—and not a religious—distinction between these two orders. Concomitantly there did develop here a basically cyclical secular, and not historical or eschatological, time conception.

This secular definition of such tension and the rationalizing tendencies it involved became here connected with a tendency to an almost wholly this-worldly conception of the resolution of such tension. The thrust of the official Confucian civilizational orientations was that the resolution of this tension was attained through the cultivation of the social, political, and cultural orders, as the major way of maintaining the cosmic harmony. Thus it focused around the elaboration of what Herbert Fingarette has defined as the cultivation of the "secular as sacred" and of "The Human Community as a Holy Rite."[2]

The this-worldly orientation that developed in China differed markedly from the one in Greek and Hellenistic civilizations. In the latter case the breakthrough to the Axial Age did not entail what may be called a "total"—even if secular—sanctification of this order in terms of the basic transcendental vision.

Moreover in Ancient Greece there developed, as we have seen above, a certain disjunction between the philosophical and the political activities and the corresponding disjunction between philosophers on the one hand and political elites on the other.

The developments in China were indeed entirely different; here there developed a strong semi-sanctification of the imperial order, a very close interweaving between the realms of speculative and of political activities, as well as between the respective elites which were here indeed more or less fused in the role of the Confucian literati.

Thus the Chinese this-worldly orientation—the Confucian-legal one—did stress the proper performance of worldly duties and activities within the existing social frameworks—the family, broader kin groups, and Imperial service—as the ultimate criterion of the resolution of the tension between the transcendental and the mundane order and of individual responsibility. Seemingly such stress could be seen as simple, traditional, ritual upholding of the existing social arrangements, and in practice this might have been the case for many Confucians. Yet in principle this was not the case. The major thrust of the Confucian orientations was the conscious taking out of these social relations from their seemingly natural context and their ideologization in terms of the higher transcendental orientations, the proper attitude to which could be only acquired through a largely demysticized and demagicized ritual, learning, and contemplation. Paradoxically enough—as can be seen especially in neo-Confucianism, the roots of which exist also in the earlier, classical Confucianism—this learning and contemplation not only allowed, but emphasized very strongly a non-traditionalistic, reflexive definition of the nature of the cosmic order and of human existence. This definition contained within itself a continuous principled awareness of the tension between the cosmic ideal and any given reality of the imperfectibility of the mundane order in general and the political one in particular; its only partial legitimation in terms of the basic cosmic harmony, and the great personal tensions involved both in the attempts to maintain such harmony through proper conduct and attitude, which necessitates a very stringent and reflexive self-discipline, as well as in the development of a critical attitude to the existing mundane world in general and political order in particular—all of which did of course develop in China among the many Confucian schools.

But indeed, as has been already alluded to above and as we shall yet see in greater detail, all these orientations and attempts had, in comparison with those which developed in other post-Axial Age civilizations, and especially in the great monotheistic civilizations, relatively limited institutional effects.

The clue to the understanding of this central problem of our analysis lies in the recognition of the fact that what was characteristic of China was not the lack of such transcendental vision or tension, but rather a "secular" definition of this tension and a this-worldly mode of its resolution.

It was the predominance of this specific mode that explains—as above all some of the discussions of Metzger's book,[3] as well as those in the conferences convened by Ted De Bary, have pointed out—why the tensions connected with a transcendental vision did not have in China those institutional, as against personal and intellectual, implications that could be found in some at least of the monotheistic civilizations.

HINDUISM AND BUDDHISM—THE PARADOX OF AN OTHER-WORLDLY CIVILIZATION

As against this the paradox of the Hinduist and Buddhist civilizations was, as we have seen, the combination of an other-worldly orientation with the construction of a this-world. Thus indeed in these cases we deal not just with recluse sects or with religious virtuosi who take themselves out from the mundane world, but with a conscious attempt to shape or reconstruct the mundane world, to construct world civilizations—yet paradoxically according to otherworldly orientations or according to orientations which seem to negate the mundane world, i.e., this very world which constitutes the arena of such construction.

Indeed the more extreme form of renunciation as enunciated by the exemplary religious virtuosi who seemed to epitomize the quintessence of Hinduism and Buddhism can—as we shall see in greater detail later on—be understood, paradoxically but significantly, only within the framework of such attempts at construction of civilizations, within the civilizational frameworks constructed by the other-worldly orientations and their carriers.

The strong civilization-building impetus of these other-worldly religions has been manifest above all in the fact that the Hindu or Brahminic belief system was of crucial importance in the construction of the specific later post-Vedic Hindu civilization, as distinct from the earlier social structure of India. Here it is of crucial importance to recognize that what has been usually designated as the caste system and often seen as the epitome of traditionalism constituted a basic part of this active construction of the mundane world. Parallelly later on, Buddhism created not only monastic organizations, but also new types of political communities, organizations, and dynamics, transforming the societies in which it has become predominant.

In other words, in both Hinduism and Buddhism the predominant other-worldly or world-negating ideological orientations have entailed some very specific ways of construction of civilizations and had accordingly some very distinct institutional implications. These implications have, however, entailed rather paradoxical and even contradictory aspects inherent in the attempts to construct civilizations on other-worldly premises.

THIS AND OTHER-WORLDLY ASIAN CIVILIZATIONS—THE MAJOR COMPARATIVE INDICATIONS. THE CHINESE INSTITUTIONAL ORDER

Each of these civilizations developed, as the papers presented here fully attest, institutional formations, specific patterns of crystallization of collectivities and collective identity, which were effected by the major coalitions of elites predominant in them.

These institutional features were, of course, closely connected to the basic characteristics of the respective carriers of the transcendental visions and their relations to other elites. They entailed different modes of reconstruction of the relations between division of labor, regulation of power and provision of trust and of meaning, and different answers to the basic problems inherent in the very institutionalization of Axial Age civilizations.

In China the very strong emphasis on this-worldly mode of "salvation" entailed a far-reaching pattern of institution-reconstruction which distinguished it both from pre-Axial Age as well as from other Axial Age civilizations.

Thus first of all there developed in China a very strong emphasis on civility or a mixture of civility and sacredness as the central criterion of the legitimation of the socio-political order, while the purely sacred or primordial criteria of legitimation have been relatively secondary or tended to disappear. The tension between them tended to be—unlike in other Axial Age civilizations—relatively weak, being funnelled into secondary areas which have been also dominated by central ones or segregated from them. Such civility tended to be formulated in a mixture of traditional and legal terms with relatively weak charismatic elements focused mostly around the office of the Emperor.

This pattern of legitimation had some very crucial repercussions on some basic institutional formats of Chinese society and civilization, on the development first of all of a rather special type of first symbolic articulation and ideologization of the major institutional spheres which, as we have seen above, is characteristic of all these post-Axial Age civilizations, and second of linkage between different institutional spheres—especially between the central and the peripheral ones. The political-cultural center and sphere were seen in Confucian-legalist China as the major focus of the resolution of the tension between the transcendental and the mundane order.

This distinctive, autonomous, absolutist political-cultural center which constituted the major locus of the attempts to maintain the cosmic harmony, tended, through mobilization and communication, to mold—but only partially—the periphery, according to its own precepts and premises. This center shared, in principle, with the periphery, a common cultural framework, but the full access to the sacred charismatic attributes of the center, although in principle open to all, was largely mediated by the center.

This structure of the center was very closely related to the structuring of the major collectivities and sub-centers, first of all evident in the ideological centrality and institutional strength of the political—albeit defined in cultural terms—collectivity, as against the institutional weakness of the civilizational frameworks or collectivity, insofar as it was not institutionally interwoven with the political ones.

Thus we find in China, among the great civilizations, the closest interweaving, almost identity, of cultural and political collectivities and centers and the concomitant weakness of any distinct cultural or religious center or centers which could compete with the political one for the definition of the major central attributes and boundaries of the society.

These tendencies are also visible in the nature of the system of law as it developed in China, and above all in the very far-reaching codification coupled with the lack of definition of an autonomous sphere of law in general and of public and civil law in particular;

in the non-development of autonomous legal roles and in the concentration of all legal affairs in the hands of officials or of representatives of lineage groups; in the non-existence of concepts of rights; in the predominance of disciplinary law based on or related to ethical considerations; and in the strong emphasis on criminal as against the weakness of civil law.

All these specific characteristics of the institutional features of Chinese society and civilization were very closely related to the specific Chinese (above all the Confucian-Legal) this-worldly orientations analyzed briefly above, and they were affected by the elites predominant in it.

The most important and distinct such elites in China were of course the famous Confucian literati and bureaucracy. These literati and bureaucrats were the major carriers of the Confucian (or Confucian-Legal) world order and orientations briefly depicted above. As such they were, especially symbolically, relatively autonomous vis-à-vis both the broader strata as well as the political center even if rather closely related to them. They were recruited, legitimized, and organized according to criteria which were directly related to—or derived from—the basic precepts of Confucian-legalistic canon, and were not mediated or controlled by either the broader strata of the society or in principle (although of course not always in practice) by the Emperor himself.

These literati were not, however, just learned men performing intellectual functions. The stratum or category of literati constituted a source of recruitment to the bureaucracy and they exercised at least a partial monopoly over venues of access to the center.

They constituted, together with the Emperors and their entourage as well as sometimes the major warlords, the major partners in the ruling coalitions—to the almost total exclusion of other groups or social elements.

Their structure and organization were influenced by their predominant this-worldly orientation. Unlike the parallel European, Byzantine, or Islamic elites, the literati combined at the same time both cultural ("religious") and administrative-political functions. Among them there developed only a relatively small degree of organizational and even symbolic distinction between these two types of elite activities. Their organizational framework was almost identical with that of the state bureaucracy (which recruited ten to twenty percent of all the literati), and except for some schools and academies they had no organization of their own. Accordingly there did not develop among them separate political, administrative, and religious organizations and hierarchies.

At the same time, and in close relation with the preceding developments, more central administrative as well as cultural elites alike had but few autonomous bases of power and resources, as against the Emperors and their entourage. It was only in one institutional sphere—the educational one—that there did develop some autonomous organizations and structures, but even here the more specific roles into which such activities crystallized were usually very closely interwoven with the political-administrative setting and oriented towards it, and rather segregated from activities of secondary elites of the periphery.

THE INSTITUTIONAL ORDER OF HINDUISM AND BUDDHISM

The major institutional contours of the Hindu and later Buddhist civilizations have, of course, been quite distinctively different from those of China, rooted in the basic other-worldly orientation—yet very paradoxical one because they attempted the construction of (by definition or by fact) a world civilization based on other-worldly premises.

This other-worldly mode of construction of civilizations has been characterized by several institutional features. First has been the construction of strong distinctiveness of the civilizational "cultural", or "religious" frameworks and their relative autonomy from other collectivities or institutional frameworks. Second has been the tendency to the "concentration" of the major institutional derivatives of the perception of tension between the transcendental and the mundane order in the so-called cultural or religious spheres. Third, and closely connected with the former, there developed in these civilizations some tendency to the stress of the coalescence, hierarchization, and mutual restructuring of the major collectivities—the primordial kinships, political and religious ones—as well as of different institutional spheres in terms of some basic ideological criteria derived from the specific other-worldly mode of resolution of this tension—but this tendency has been much weaker than in other Axial Age civilizations. Fourth has been the tendency to the reshaping, in very distinct ways, of the major institutional spheres—the political, the economic, the "cultural" or religious ones—as well as of the structuring of social hierarchies and the generation within all these spheres of new, specific types of institutional dynamics. Let's elaborate these points.

The most important single institutional construction that developed in these as well as in all other Axial Age civilizations is of course that of specific civilizational frameworks and collectivities with distinct attributes of membership as well as carriers—all of which differed greatly from the various primordial, ethnic, regional and political communities. In the case of India, it was the Hindu-Brahmanic "cultural" ritual frameworks and symbols, focused around the specific relations between King, Brahmin, and Renouncer, and the different social and religious networks that developed in close relation to them, and which were construed and carried above all by the Brahmins that constituted such distinct civilizational framework. This framework, despite its seeming embedment in ascriptive kinship units, did in fact cut across local or kinship groups and generated, through the construction of the caste system new, broader—even if ascriptive—categories and frameworks.

In the (especially Theravada) Buddhist societies, it was the Buddhist "religious" collectivity or framework, the collectivities of the adherents of the faith as constructed by the Sangha, that constituted in principle such a trans-primordial, trans-local, civilizational framework. Truly enough here these frameworks were very closely related to various national communities, but they have greatly transformed these communities, giving rise to a continuous tension between their national and transnational dimensions.

Such construction of distinct civilizational frameworks and communities was very closely related to the restructuring of the religious-cultural spheres as the major arena in which the institutional repercussions of a transcendental vision became visible; to the development within these spheres of all the artifacts and symbols of a Great Tradition—such as distinct, autonomous, religious centers and networks—all of them constructed in terms of the symbolically highly articulated conceptions of tensions between the transcendental and the mundane world and the other-worldly conceptions of resolution of such tension.

Accordingly, the civilizational frameworks constructed in those civilizations, in which the other-worldly definition of salvation was predominant, were distinguished from those in most other-Axial Age civilizations in several ways. First of all these frameworks have been in symbolic terms quite strongly, although not totally, distinct from other political, regional or "national" collectivities. Second, there has not developed in the Indian and Buddhist civilizations—as was the case in such this-worldly civilizations (as the Chinese one) and especially in the monotheistic ones—a strong tendency to coalescence and clear-cut hierarchization of these different collectivities and no continuous struggle about the principles of such hierarchization; although, as we have already indicated above, there did already emerge some very important ingredients or tendencies to such hierarchization and to such struggle.

Closely connected to the construction of specific civilizational frameworks and collectivities, and to the predominance within them of the religious spheres and centers, have been, in these other-worldly civilizations, some specific characteristics of the structuring of the major institutional spheres.

The most important such dimension has been the redefinition, broadening, and more articulate symbolization of the major ascriptive collectivities. The second such dimension has been the extension of the scope of the major institutional frameworks, the continuous expansion of the major institutional markets and contacts between different basic social units and the consequent development of some new form of social organizations.

The first major specific repercussion on the institutional structure of these civilizations—namely the redefinition, broadening and fully articulated symbolization of the major ascriptive collectivities—that has probably been the most distinctive characteristic of other-worldly civilizations—stands out against the tendency to the construction of new autonomous non-primordial, universalistic ascriptive communities, such as various religious, cultural civil ones, as well as some, even if rather few, ideologically autonomous functional (e.g. economic) collectivities, which has been characteristic of both this-worldly and combined this- and other-worldly civilizations.

The repercussions of the institutionalization of other-worldly orientations have, of course, also become fully evident in the political realm—especially in the new modes of legitimation of the political sphere, in the development of specific patterns of ideological polities in general and of accountability of rulers in particular, and of new levels of political conflicts.

First of all there developed here a basically secular conception of kingship. The King has become desacralized and his role defined largely—even if perhaps not entirely—in secular terms with a strong emphasis on the acceptance of kingship in terms of the necessity of maintenance of the social order. At the same time however demands were made on him to support the cosmic order defined in transcendental other-worldly terms, and the concomitant moral order of the community to which in principle he was seen as being subordinate. Thus in principle royalty was legitimized in terms of the predominant "other-worldly" religious symbols, but at the same time its mundane role was quite widely accepted and even defined in religious terms.

Here, in the other-worldly civilizations, these two dimensions have never been fully fused but rather continuously differentiated. Unlike, however, in civilizations in which some this-worldly (whether "pure" or connected with other-worldly) orientation to salvation has been prevalent, in the other-worldly civilizations the primordial legitimation has not usually been defined in terms of the sacred. Rather the sacred became here a dimension added to the primordial one, to some degree taking the latter out of its total embedment in primordial ascriptive units, and even devaluating it. At the same time the King's Dharma (duty) was couched in some combination of transcendental and mundane concepts and tended to some degree to minimize the tension between the sacred and the primordial modes of legitimation.

Concomitantly there developed in these civilizations a very distinct pattern of institutional dynamics which differed greatly from those of other Axial Age civilizations in which (as in China) this-worldly orientations were predominant, or from those—like the monotheistic ones—in which such this-worldly orientations were closely interwoven with other-worldly ones.

Perhaps the single most important thrust of these dynamics was the continuous restructuring of ascriptive-primordial categories and collectivities and the continuous subsumption of most (usually piecemeal) institutional changes within the framework of such restructuring.

The major thrust of these dynamics was focused around the continuous restructuring of the criteria of membership in ascriptive-primordial and religious communities, the redefinition of the boundaries of these communities and of access to them—together with periodic attempts at imbuing them with strong emphasis on equality. Here indeed the most dramatic innovation within these civilizations was the rise of Buddhism itself from within the Indian civilization and beyond it.

The restructuring of the new collectivities, the civilizational, political and religious frameworks, facilitated the continuous expansion of different social organizations. Such expansion became connected with the restructuring of these collectivities, subsuming the former under the latter.

Thus all these developments often gave rise to new organizational settings, to continuous redefinition of scope political and economic units, to changes in patterns of polities, as well as to continuous changes in the religious sphere as manifest above all in the development of new movements and sects.

But these dynamics did indeed evince several crucial differences or limits—especially as compared with other civilizations; the limits of such dynamics can be seen in the fact that whatever reorganization of mundane, institutional spheres, has taken place in these civilizations, it took place mostly on the organizational plane or level, with but very weak restructuring of the levels of symbolic articulation of these spheres, without imbuing them with new autonomous symbolic evaluation of this sphere and to the construction—as in China or in monotheistic civilizations—of autonomous centers, distinct from the periphery, with strong imperial orientations.

Conditions of Axial Age Breakthroughs in China and India

We come here to the question of the "initial" conditions—the specific patterns of the processes of the combination of breakdown of tribal and territorial units and their reconstruction that were connected with the development of the Chinese and Hinduistic Axial Age civilizations.

Here indeed we find already conditions which vary greatly from those of Ancient Greece, of Ancient Israel (and, as we shall see later on, of Islam), as well as, needless to say, great differences between these two great Asian civilizations.

The major difference between the processes of change connected with the initial breakdown of tribal and territorial units in the Mediterranean area, in the ancient Middle East, and those in India and China was that in the latter case these processes took place in very broad ecological frameworks, not only in the interstices between great kingdoms or on the thruways of many nations.

Second the fact that this pattern of change was closely connected with the dramatic encounter of continuous migrations, of relatively compact nomad groups encountering not only a small group of settled people, but large groups of settled peasants engaged in different types of intensive cultivation.

The process of such encounter was probably initially connected with what we called (in the introduction) congruent patterns of reconstruction of the new collectivities, given often rise to the patrimonial-like political units.

But in China and India alike the possibility that such units would be able to maintain their self-closure was undermined by the combination of continuous waves of nomad migrations and conquests as well as by growing interconnection between different settled groups.

It was this combination that generated the breakdown of the earlier political units that developed in these civilizations, as well as the emergence of autonomous elites who became one of the major interconnecting links between such different units.

These new intellectual and political elites were very varied and between them there developed a very strong competition, but common to most of them was indeed the tendency to become autonomous, disembedded from the existing ascriptive units.

But the mode of settlement (in itself of course closely connected to agrarian conditions and modes of production) as well as the mode of interconnection between the settled people and of their encounters with the nomad groups, differed greatly between these two civilizations. These differences may perhaps, to some degree at least, explain some of the different types of cultural orientations and types of elites that have developed in each of them.

In China, as both Hsu's and Elvin's chapters indicate, there developed a very strong interrelation between many relatively well settled groups within which there existed already semi-autonomous—or at least high specialized—cultural elites which maintained many often competitive contacts.

These contacts, political and military, were intensified through the process of nomad migration and conquest and created the possibility of new more autonomous elites and the possibility of such elites becoming indispensable parts of ruling coalitions.

Second, often closely interwoven with the former, was the fact, emphasized already many years ago by Owen Lattimore, that in China there developed a continuous incursion of nomads into those settled areas in which relatively well organized political units developed.

The combination of these processes facilitated the development in China of tendencies to political centralization as well as of autonomous elites with a very strong orientation to participation in such centralized frameworks.

The picture in India was markedly different. The pattern of settlement was much less homogeneous and compact: it was more dispersed and the mode of cultivation was not intensive as in China; the whole pattern of political organization was much more fragile. The contacts between these settled groups were less developed. Such contacts were effected more by the impact of the conquest by continuous waves of tribal or semi-tribal conquests than from within the intensive contacts between settled groups and cohesive political frameworks.

This type of contacts created a triple process. First it generated the extension and reconstruction, through the process of settlement, of broader tribal ascriptive units. Second it created a wide range of pesudo-kinship and cultural contacts and networks; but third, only relatively weak political frameworks.

The Secondary Breakthroughs in
Hinduism and in China

These conditions are also connected with the different tendencies to secondary breakthroughs which developed in each of these civilizations and which were closely related, as in all Axial Age civilizations, with the development of sectarianism and heterodoxies.

In the case of Hinduism, such a secondary breakthrough was indeed most visible in the development of Buddhism and to some degree also of Jainism and of the Bhakti movements.

In the case of China such a secondary breakthrough is much more problematic. Some scholars would even claim that such breakthrough did never take place in Chinese civilizations; others—probably a greater majority—would identify such breakthrough with the rise of neo-Confucianism.

But even those who identify the development of neo-Confucianism with such a breakthrough do admit that the institutional implication of this breakthrough differed here greatly from such breakthroughs in other Axial Age civilizations. The major difference was, of course, the fact that they did not create a totally new institutional order as was the case in Second Commonwealth Judaism, in Christianity, or in Islam.

These special characteristics of the secondary breakthrough in China are, of course, closely related to the combination of the basic premises and orientations of the Chinese civilization and the distinctive characteristics of the Chinese Empire which constituted the most continuous centralized polity in any of the Axial Age civilizations.

As against this in Hinduism there developed one of the politically most decentralized Axial Age civilizations—in many ways similar to Europe, i.e., creating a broad common civilizational framework within which there developed a multiplicity of continuously changing political formations.

The special situation of secondary breakthrough in China, as compared with other Axial Age civilizations, was connected with some interesting political-ecological conditions.

In all the Axial Age civilizations the possibility of such secondary breakthrough was very closely connected, as we have seen already above, with different types of political-ecological and demographic conditions, not unlike those which were connected with the initial emergence and institutionalization of these Axial Age civilizations.

It was indeed probably only in China that there developed a rather far-reaching difference between such conditions which were connected with the initial institutionalization of Axial Age civilizations as against later developments.

CHAPTER 13

Historical Conditions of the Emergence and Crystallization of the Confucian System

CHO-YUN HSU

This paper proposes first to identify an earlier stage of the Jasperian "breakthrough" in Chinese history which, I believe, should be regarded as the antecedent of the formation of Confucianism. The conditions for developing early Confucianism follow as a second section. And finally, there are discussions on the crystallization of Confucianism during the Han Dynasty. Special attention is to be given to the characteristics of the "carriers" and their respective roles in each stage.

APPEARANCE OF A MORAL GOD

The history of the Shang Dynasty (ca. 1765–1122 B.C.E.), a period of the bronze age, is relatively well studied because of the availability of a rich treasure of archaeological finds including a large number of oracle bones on which the Shang scribes inscribed a wide range of questions and answers relating to their religious and secular lives. From such oracle bone sources there had been virtually no traces of moral concern involved in religious practices. To spirits of ancestors and deities who were in charge of various functions were offered sacrifices routinely, as well as specifically, in order to obtain necessary protections for the living. Questions were posed to various spirits for the sake of fathoming their wills and decisions regarding future events. The Shang pantheon consisted of a great mixture of cultural heroes, deceased ancestors, celestial bodies, a cluster of natural objects which might likely originate from or be affiliated with some form of totemism. By the latter half of the Shang period, the world of deities had been pretty much organized into a mirror copy of the secular government of the Shang kingdom, obviously along the evolution process of formation of a strong monarchy. At the top of this spiritual government was a god bearing the title of Ti. The etymological origin of the term Ti is yet to be determined. It is clear, however, that Ti was an august supernatural power rather than a judge to uphold certain moral standards, because there was no mention of punishment or reward in the oracle bone record (Keightly, 1978; Shima Kunio, 1958). The Ti of the Shang period thus should be similar to the Babylonians' Marduk or the Greeks' Zeus. The conquest of Shang by the Chou people then brought about a significant transformation of the characteristics of a supreme being in ancient China.

Chou's conquest of Shang took place at the junction of the twelfth and the eleventh centuries B.C.E. The precise date of the final victory won by Chou at the suburb of the Shang capital city is still subject to much dispute. There are no less than ten different suggestions proposed by modern scholars, depending on their choices of the method of calculation. The earliest date is 1122 while the latest date is 1027 (H.G. Creel, 1970, 487–492). The conquest, however, was a gradual process, taking place in the span of three generations. The date of the final victory on a battleground is relatively less important.

What should be significant in this inquiry is the appearance of a Heaven God (T'ien) in the Chou period to replace, or more precisely to merge with, the Shang god Ti. H.G. Creel investigates such a phenomenon by observing that the frequency of appearances of Heaven (T'ien) in the Chou documents had been much more than those of the Ti. He further suggests that there might be a time when T'ien was a name for the royal ancestors as a group, although he refrains from saying that by the time of Chou's conquest there was evidence of such a notion (H.G. Creel, 1970, 493–506).

A more significant development is the adaptation of a concept of Mandate of Heaven in the Chou documents. Due to the reality that the Chou was a small nation, living for a long time under the shadow of a great and mighty Shang in both military and cultural terms, the success of bringing down such a formidable former master aroused both the conqueror and the conquered to pose a profound question: How could it happen that a minor and rustic nation overcame a major civilized power? The answer provided by the Chou leader was repeated in several documents. The general tone is represented in a speech delivered by the Duke of Chou, who was the prime minister to the King of Chou, addressing the conquered Shang people.

> Your last Shang king abandoned himself to indolence,
> disdained to apply himself to government, and did not bring

pure sacrifices. Heaven thereupon sent down his ruin. . . .
Heaven waited for five years, so that his sons and grandsons
might yet become lords of people, but he could not become
wise. Heaven then sought among your numerous regions,
shaking you with its terrors to stimulate those who might
have regard for Heaven, but in all your many regions there
was none that was able to do so. But our king of Chou
treated well the multitude of the people, was able to practice
virtue, and fulfilled his duties to the spirits and to Heaven.
Heaven instructed us, favored us, selected us, and gave us the
Mandate of Yin, to rule over your numerous regions.
(B. Karlgren, trans. 1950: 62–65)

This quotation reveals a moral commitment of Heaven to select
and guide a righteous ruler who was given the mandate, as well as
the responsibility to serve well. Creel observes that the Chou did
not charge the downfallen Shang ruler with responsibilities that the
Chou leaders themselves were unwilling to assume. The Chou king
pledged to receive punishment if he failed to meet the standard of
a ruler whose concerns were the welfare of the ruled public (H.G.
Creel, 1970: 81–99).

Thus, the significance of the Chou conquest was the emergence
of the Mandate of Heaven which endowed the supreme being with
an authority as well as the responsibility of ensuring the people to
be governed by pious and righteous rulers. I think such a transformation of characteristics of supreme being in ancient China should
be regarded as an important breakthrough.

SECULARIZATION AND HUMANISM

Throughout a period of some five centuries between the conquest
and the time of Confucius (552–479 B.C.E.) there seemed to be a
continuous trend of secularizing and rationalizing the religious concerns on the will of a supreme being. The content of the Book of
Changes (I-Ching) reveals that this handbook of divination probably
was compiled at the early stage of the Chou period. Yet the auxiliary
interpretations were attached to the text in somewhat later years,
which nevertheless could not be later than the time of Confucius
since much of the interpretation had been mentioned in the chronicle
Tso-chuan, which was derived from a long continuous record stretching from the eighth century B.C.E to the time of Confucius. In the
Book of Changes, a law of dialectism is applied to explain a variety
of phenomena in nature and in the human world. It is the predictable
law that governs the changes; no place is granted to a god to exercise

his will. Eight elements—Heaven, Earth, Thunder, Wind, Water, Fire, Mountain, Lake—constitute functional forces of interaction. Therefore, the divination on the principle of the Book of Changes was not a prayer to a deity; it was a revelation of the state in a development process (J. Needham, 1956: I, 304–314; Wilhelm/Baynes, 1967: XLIX–LVI).

Parallel to the dialectism of the Book of Changes, often people observed natural phenomena as omens to predict the correspondence in human events. Principles of such divination spanned a broad range of varieties, including astronomy, geomancy, and interaction of five elements, i.e. metal, wood, water, fire, and earth. The will and authority of divine figures were not concerned with any of these principles. It is observations based on laws of proto-science or pseudo-science rather than ways to fathom the sacred order set by super-natural beings (J. Needham, 1956: I, 351–362).

Fung Yu-lan notes correctly in his early work that some enlightened individuals preceding Confucius by a few centuries had developed the humanistic antecedent of Confucianism by means of attributing the causality of human affairs to human actions. Fung furthermore suggests that even religious ceremonies were viewed by a contemporary of Confucius as means to unite people in the community, in the kinship group, and the state (Fung/Bodde, 1952: Vol. I, 31–39). Such an ancient comment indeed sounds very much similar to modern anthropological functionalism.

I cite here two cases in order to support Fung's observation. In 639 B.C.E. a severe drought in the state of Lu caused the Duke to put into practice an exorcist ritual of burning a witch alive. His advisor Tsan Wen-chung told the Duke that the cremation of an ignorant witch would not be a way to lift the famine. Instead, he suggested that thrift and mutual assistance would help people survive the natural calamity (Tso-Chuan, p. 180)

In 523 B.C.E. a great fire spread in four states. The advisors in the court of Cheng recommended to the regent Tzu-chan that sacrifice be offered to the deities. Tzu-chan refused. He commented that the way of Heaven was too remote to be comprehended, while the way of man was to be helpful (Tso-Chuan, pp. 668–671; K.C. Hsiao, 1979: 207).

A statement by Kuan Yeh-fu, a contemporary of Confucius, symbolizes the separation of the sacred and the mundane worlds. Kuan was asked by a southern lord about the legend of the separation of Heaven and Earth. This learned person replied it did not mean that people could ascend to the Heaven; rather that there were shamans who had knowledge of serving deities and spirits by means of offering sacrifices properly. He stated that in the time of desperation people took the role of shamans until a sage king ordered two offices to be established, one of which would be in charge of the sacred affairs while the other would be in charge of human affairs. Kuan reported that such a separation of functions was the truth behind the legend of separation of Heaven and Earth. Kuan even suggested that some of the shamans' descendants who held the positions of divines and priests by heredity attempted to frighten the ordinary people by deliberately misinterpreting the history of separation of these two offices (Kuo-yü, 18/1–2). The significance of Kuan Yeh-fu's statement is in his understanding that the clergy (shamans, etc.) lost much of their monopoly of sacred affairs in the first stage and then the appearance of secular authorities created the permanent separation of the sacred and the mundane. Even Kuan attributed the happenings of such separation in the remote antiquity. It actually could have happened in the relatively recent past, namely, the junction of the Shang-Chou dynasties, because the hereditary clerical descendants whom he named were the families of the Chou time. This Kuan Yeh-fu, incidentally, is the same person who rationalized the function of religious ceremony as uniting members of a community, a kinship group, or a state, which has been cited above.

In summary, I find that the emergence of a moral god might have been associated with the phenomenon of separation of the sacred and the mundane along a process of rationalization of human intelligence and the emergence of humanistic concern. The latter, however, might have taken place a little later than the completion of the former. The professional shamans, diviners, and priests who were the "carriers" of the sacred traditions therefore had to adopt some other functions in the society.

BACKGROUND OF THE EMERGENCE OF CONFUCIANISM

The transformation of the educated minority, who were shamans, priests, diviners, etc., probably had started even before the fall of the Shang dynasty. The divines and the scribes who handled the affairs of religious ceremonies and oracle divinations had gradually turned themselves into prototyped bureaucrats in the reigns of the last two kings of the Shang. There had already been a tendency to routinize the procedure of divination as well as the arrangement of sacrificial ceremonies to serve the royal ancestors (Chen Meng-chia, 1956: 139; Tung Tso-ping, 1964: I, 2–4; 1965, 103–118). It can be surmised that the diviners and the scribes had departed from the pious practice of divination to prefer a neat regulation of the sacred orders. The fall of the Shang dynasty did not necessarily bring ill fate to them. They obviously continued to serve in the court of the

Chou kings since they probably were the only educated people whose literacy was useful in any court. Their roles were gradually diversified, however, to include many different functions: scribes, secretaries, musicians, tutors, archivists, and historians (Shirakawa Shizuka, 1973: 150–160; 280–300). Therefore, the dynastic transition from Shang to Chou probably also should coincide with the transition of roles and status of these prototyped intellectuals.

The Chou royal government was supported by a feudalistic structure which consisted of a hierarchy of lords and vassals who were scattered throughout the Chou kingdom. Such an order lasted until 722 B.C.E. when the capital region was invaded and occupied by "barbarians" from the northern frontier. Collapse of the Chou royal government brought ancient China into a five-centuries continuous internal struggle in order to gradually reshape the political as well as socio-economic institutions (C.Y. Hsu, 1965: 24–105). In the original feudal pyramid, the lowest ranked aristocratic warriors were called shih, which can be compared with the knights in medieval Europe. A shih was also the basic status which any noble must hold. Even the King himself was basically a shih whose primary role was that of a warrior and an adult member of the noble class.

By the time of the Chun-Chiu period (722–464 B.C.E.) the military function of the shih had also been blurred. He became the government functionary of the various states of dukes and even the fiefs of lower ranked lords. Since a shih did receive education in the martial aspects (such as archery and the art of driving a war chariot), literary aspects (such as reading and arithmetic), and ritualistic aspects (such as music and knowledge of rites), he was qualified to fulfill the newly expanding role of civil servant. The fight for survival in a period of intensive struggles would require the ruler to extend continuously ways and means of controlling resources which were free floating in the days of relatively less eventful social structure under the Chou royal government. Thus, there should be a development of government toward diversification and specialization in job assignments. The old-fashioned warrior-courtier type government staff had to be replaced by a staff with specific kinds of expertise. Such a development indeed took place in most of the states during the Chun-Chiu period (C.Y. Hsu, 1965: 89–90).

Intensive struggles for power and territory were constantly ongoing phenomena. Those who took part in the struggle tended to decrease in number, since the losers were eliminated one after another. More than a score of states appeared in the record at the beginning of the Chun-Chiu period. By the end of this period, the fifth century B.C.E., there were only seven major and five minor powers which had survived the brutal game of elimination taking place in a period of less than three centuries. The shih who formerly could have been retained by the now extinct states and aristocratic households became masterless. Confucius himself was one such unsettled shih. Some of his students were also members of such an unsettled shih. These new kinds of social elites still possessed their skill and expertise as potentially useful human resources. They indeed often looked for new employers while the powerholders often would also recruit these helpful people to serve as their own staff. Some of them then began to train the young who might not have been members of the shih class by teaching them skills which the teacher himself learned in the tradition of a shih. Confucius was the most eminent of such teachers, from whose informal academy anyone who aspired to learn would be taught the useful knowledge to serve a state, as well as profound wisdom to be a learned man.

Intellectual excellence was not the only goal for students to develop their potential. More important, Confucius reinterpreted the content of the code of proper conduct as a good aristocrat by universalizing such a moral requirement into fundamental virtues of a good human being. It is in this particular contribution that Confucius earns his name as the founder of a great system of thinking. Of course, Confucius was not the only person who engaged in dissemination of knowledge; there were Yang Chu, Mo Ti, and others, each of whom could have started a new school of thinking, even though their immediate function was to teach students to acquire capability in government services (C.Y. Hsu, 1965: 100–102).

In summary, the intellectual background for the emergence of Confucianism and other compatible schools of thought was mainly the trend of rationalism which was adopted by some humanistic intellectuals in the Chou period. The transformation of the shih class from the warrior-courtier type toward the bureaucrat type brought into existence a new breed of social elites who eventually developed into a group of "carriers" of new ideology. Confucius was the one who achieved most in this task and defined the intellectual heritage which the new carriers were to hand down for posterity.

INTELLECTUAL BACKGROUND IN THE CH'IN-HAN PERIOD

The unification of China under Ch'in (221–206 B.C.E.) and Han (206 B.C.E.–220 C.E.) ushered China into a long tradition of regarding the Chinese as a single nation with a single culture, a notion that the Chinese today still take for granted. The idea of a politically unified China actually had been very prevalent, even several centuries before the real unification was achieved. Mencius (385–305 B.C.E.) for instance had told several rulers that China, or more precisely, the whole world (known to him) must be unified, even though he made such a statement during a period of disunion. Mencius' ideal unification was to occur only as coherence in the world was achieved. This notion was summarized by Mencius as "Stability in Unity" (K.C. Hsiao, 1979: 167–177).

The same mode of unification might have been in the mind of several masters of learning. Each of the schools of thought which flourished during the period of free competition (sixth–third centuries B.C.E.) in fact represented an effort to establish certain kinds of intellectual orders. Customarily, there were six major schools of thought in pre-Ch'in China: Confucianism, Mohism, Taoism, Legalism, Logicism, and the Yin-Yang School. Their efforts can be summarized as follows: Confucians tried to organize an ethical order; Mohists, a religious order; Legalists, an order of political power; Logicians, an order of semantics; the Yin-Yang scholars, an order of the natural forces. Even the Taoists, who protested against all efforts of organizing ideas and people into orderly systems, could not escape from presenting their own order of counter-order.

The unification of China seemed to have also stimulated the idea of intellectual syncretism. The first notable reflection of such an idea is the gigantic project sponsored by Lü Pu-wei, the Chancellor of Ch'in who governed Ch'in on the eve of unification. Scholars of various schools were invited to participate in the compilation of a voluminous synthesis of different theories in the name of Lü-shih-Chun-Chiu. The authors boasted that this encyclopedic work was written in order to completely cover the multitudes of phenomena in the universe from antiquity to the present, and "to be based on the Heavenly principles, verified by that of the Earth, and confirmed on human affairs" (Lü-shih-Chun-Chiu, 12/9). Ironically, the synthesis reached in the Lü-shih-Chun-Chiu was a coherent system of ideas that contradicted the authoritarianism of the Ch'in court. Among the six major sources, the legalist elements were completely overcome by the combined weight of arguments of the other schools, especially those of Confucianism and Taoism (K.C. Hsiao, 1979: 557–570).

The Lü-shih-Chun-Chiu was followed by another eclectic project, the compilation of the Huai-nan-tzu (ca. 130 B.C.E.). The dominant tone of this book was Taoist, because the sponsor, Prince Huai-nan of the Han imperial household, was a Taoist. In the preface, its editors declared that the goal of this collective work was to establish an intellectual system which was not only universal but also adaptive and responsive to possible changes (Huai-nan-tzu, 21/1, 8). Its content indeed is a synthesis of Taoism, Confucius, and Naturalists' theories toward an organic relationship between Nature and Man (K.C. Hsiao, 1979: 570-582).

Recently, an archaeological excavation team turned up a group of Han tombs near the present city of Changsha in the Hunan Province. Among the abundant findings are ancient texts written on silk pieces as well as on bamboo strips. Some pieces of the text are now identified as works of one now forgotten branch of the Taoist school. The content, however, reveals a broad range of selection of items and terminology taken not only from Taoism, but also from Legalism, and the Yin-Yang Naturalism, especially its notion on correspondences between Man and Nature (Wen-wu, 1974 (10), 30-38). This piece of ancient text provides the Legalist political order with a Taoist-Naturalist cosmological theory for the purpose of justifying a permanently regulated socio-political system as confirmed by a perpetual stability of natural forces. Such an attitude definitely coincided with the need for political stability in the early Han reigns.

Early Confucian masters, such as Mencius and Hsun-tzu, were not so much concerned with cosmology, religion, or man's relationship to the supernatural order. The "salvation" in their mind was internal peace which could be achieved by means of fostering an innate goodness through self-discipline in Mencius' theory, or through education in accord with an established norm (in Hsun-tzu's theory). The sagehood was believed to be the highest status of moral order a person could aspire to achieve; yet, everyone potentially could reach such a status (D. Bodde, 1981: 262-263, 264, 287).

The Han Confucians, however, began to move into areas which were untouched by their predecessors. They made this effort to incorporate themes developed by other schools. Lu Chia, a prominent Confucian official in the second century B.C.E., in his work *Hsin-yü* (New Discourses), took a Confucian moralistic attitude toward politics. Yet he also adopted the Taoist terminology of non-action, which was reinterpreted, however, as the result of education, a considerable departure from the Taoist original connotation (*Hsin-yü*, B/6). In the *Hsin-yü*, there were some discussions on correspondence between macro-cosmos and micro-cosmos which were presented by Lu Chia as constantly changing correlationships because it was the Nature that responded to the behavior of Man (*Hsin-yü*, B/7-9). Therefore, Lu Chia in his argument seemed to recover Confucian concern of a human centered secular world by conditionally organizing into the Confucian system a few notions raised by scholars of other schools.

THE HAN CONFUCIANS

A truly comprehensive Confucian system of cosmic order was to be organized by Tung Chung-shu (ca. 179–104 B.C.E.). Tung elaborated the correspondences between macro-cosmos (universe, natural world) and the micro-cosmos (human body, human behavior, human world) and interactions at several levels of mutual influences. A major contribution of Tung Chung-shu was the inclusion of a fourth dimension, Time, into a three-dimensional universe. Such a concern with Time was taken from the historical perspective of the so-named New Text Tradition in which historical lessons as well as a pronounced verdict by historians retrospectively were regarded the primary functions of history. The record of the past therefore would serve as guidance for people in the later days to find the proper pattern for behaviors. The faith that there should be an idealized and constant normative order prompted Tung Chung-shu to condemn any deviation as abnormal. Therefore, Tung took from the Kung-yang New Text tradition of presenting his verdict upon the deviation in order that the normalcy could be safeguarded.

Tung's methodology was much influenced by those developed by Logicians and Legalists in the ancient times; the ultimate moral concern, however, was definitely Confucian. He classified his way of reaching a judgment by means of following ten principles, which nevertheless could be grouped into three categories. The first category consisted of steps to evaluate individual cases, such as selection, observation, and reaching judgment. The second category included the guiding principles to decide an order by differentiating the priority, the hierarchy, and the relationships among various components. In this category, Tung in fact attempted to establish a yardstick applicable on social relationships as well. In the third category of principles, the social order was compared to the natural normative order. Any deviation was then investigated, the degrees of deviation were measured, and a verdict on the deviant pattern rendered (Chun-chiu-fan-lu: 5/4; K.C. Hsiao, 1979: 496–500).

Tung Chung-shu used his idealized yardstick to judge reality. He even canonized Confucius as a sacred judge who took into his hand the power equivalent to that of a sovereign so that he could judge, and could reward or punish, according to the Confucian idealized ethical standard. (Chun-chiu-fan-lu, 7/5).

Derived from Tung Chung-shu's scheme of thinking, the Confucian classics were to be established as the standard of moral judgment, as part of the governance of a society. Confucian scholars then took into their hands the intellectual power of judging and criticizing the real world. Thus, a moralized orthodoxy was to be welded together with political authority. Historical incidents verified that such a consequence had been indeed reached. Chang T'ang, a renowned judicial scholar and Tung's contemporary, was often dispatched by the court to consult Tung on major policy debates. Chang subsequently recommended that students of Confucian erudition in classics be appointed to positions on the judicial staff so that judicial decisions could be based upon Confucian principles (Han-shu: 59/1–2; B.E. Wallaker, 1978: 216–228). The case of a pretender claiming to be the then missing Crown Prince was settled by a judge on the basis of a Confucian ethical code derived from an historical precedent (Han-shu: 71/2–3). The Tung Chung-shu theology therefore acquired the authority at the level of a constitution.

Another Han Confucian who combined Confucianism with thought of other schools is Kung-sun Hung, a contemporary of Tung Chung-shu, with less academic significance and more political influence than Tung. Kung-sun Hung took a court examination for an advanced position in the government. The essay topic for the candidate was related to the concept that Nature and human conduct were mutually responsive, that the consequence was revealed in favorable or adverse effects. Kung-sun Hung replied with a typical effort of syncretism. He suggested that the capable ones ought to be put in positions which matched their skills and talents, that the morally worthy should be employed, that the common people should not be deprived of the opportune time for farming, and that useless objects ought not be produced for the sake of saving labor and resources. These set concepts represented essences drawn from Legalism, Confucianism, and Mohism respectively. In the same manner, Kung-sun Hung incorporated the Mohist definition of universal love, the Confucian justice and propriety, and the Legalist notion of administrative skills in a system which gave an active and positive role to man, while the natural order would duly respond to man's actions (Han-shu 58/ 2–3); Wallaker, 1978: 221–223).

Tung Chung-shu and other Han Confucians achieved the expansion and content of Confucianism to include elements taken from other schools. The Han Confucianism had been greatly diverged from the thought of Mencius and Hsun-tzu, the early Confucian masters. Enrichment in content would also sacrifice purity in quality. Emperor Wu in 139 B.C.E. decreed the establishment of Confucian classics in the Imperial Academy as the only courses, while teachings of other schools of thought were eliminated. Emperor Wu thus acknowledged that Confucianism was an orthodoxy and Confucian classics were canonized. The seeming victory of Confucianism in fact would also mean its inevitable degeneration and vulgarization.

The first sign of vulgarization is the proliferation of materials known as prognostic and apocrypha texts. Throughout the period from Tung Chung-shu's time to the first half of the first century, people who had political interests repeatedly deliberated their interpretations on classics which were regarded as sacred anyway. Yet the classics were not so ambigious that there was much space for manipulation by misreading and misinterpretation.

Superstition in the prognostication theory and the apocrypha then appeared to be supplementaries of the classics. The classics were then called *ching* (the warp, the constant, the regular) while the apocrypha were called *wei* (the woof, the added). The common form of such materials were usually pieces of ambiguous texts attributed to mysterious origins, yet somehow associated with one of the classics in the supplementary document. Since anything related to canonized classics was regarded as sacred, the message buried in the ambiguous lines was then taken as prophecy. Political events of certain significance, i.e. changes of thrones, appointment of major positions, decisions on state policies, often would be related to the proliferation of particular deciphering of the prognostic documents (K.C. Hsiao, 1979: 210–212, 433, 472, 503, 515–522; Fung/Bode, 1953: Vol. II, 88ff.).

Thus, ironically, while Confucian stress on humanism was the result of separation of the sacred and the mundane, now the end product of an expanded Confucianism and an elevation of its status as in political influence was in the form of reemergence of an abused sacredness of the intellectual concerns of this-worldliness. Even Confucius' own image went through mythification to become a prophet, an uncrowned ruler with special mandate. The trend of prognostication reached its height around the reign of Wang Mang, the usurper, who had to justify his charisma, or lack of it, by depending upon "prophecy." Even for the sake of reviving the Han regime under the Liu household, the new leaders had to develop their propaganda by using apocryphal prophecy. It is in the second century, already several generations past the restoration of Han, that serious Confucian scholars openly discredited the prognostication as fabrication, unrelated to Confucian teaching, although some of its influence continued to be felt until the very end of the Han Dynasty (K.C. Hsiao, 1979: 522, 531–532; C. Leban, 1978: 318–322).

CONFUCIANS AND BUREAUCRATS

The Confucianization of the Han bureaucracy was mainly the result of Confucian monopoly of education and adaptation of Confucian ethics as criteria for recommendation to the government service.

The Imperial Academy was the most crucial instrument to permeate and to perpetuate the Confucian ideology. There had been so-called Erudites on the Academy's faculty ever since the Ch'in Dynasty. Their main function was in an advisory capacity in the court. They gained neither number nor influence during the early reigns of the Han period, although occasionally the staff of local governments were sent to the Academy to receive higher education (Han-shu, 89/2). The first increase in the number of intellectuals in the court occurred in the reign of Emperor Wu (140–85 B.C.E.). In 135 B.C.E., after the death of the anti-Confucian Empress, large numbers of Confucian scholars were for the first time brought into government service. Among these, Kung-sun Hung subsequently became premier (Han-shu: 88/3). In 126 Kung-sun established a student body of 50 in the Academy. Meanwhile, provincial governors were encouraged to send their staff members to the Academy. The total number of regular and special students, estimating one person per prefect, or "kingdom," was probably about 100. From that time on, the enrollment grew steadily. Emperor Chao (86–74 B.C.E.) increased the quota of 50 students to 100, not including special students. At the end of the reign of Emperor Hsuen (73–49), the number of regular students was doubled once again. Emperor Yuan (48–32) granted a quota of 1000. Meanwhile, provincial academies were established under the tutelage of local teachers who were considered members of the provincial administration. At the end of Emperor Cheng's reign (31–7) over 1000 students of the Imperial Academy gathered to protest the arrest of a popular official; the total student body must have been far larger than such a number (Han-shu: 72/4). In 5 C.E., scholars of Confucian classics as well as other specialties were summoned to the capital. Several thousand arrived (Han-shu: 12/9). This figure is probably representative of the population of established scholars in the provinces. At the conclusion of the Western Han, Wang Mang had an expanded campus for the Imperial Academy with dormitory spaces of 10,000 rooms (Han-shu: 99A/8–19). There were some thirty departments, each of which had 366 students from whom twenty-four teaching assistants for each department were chosen. The total enrollment therefore was more than 10,000 students.

Academy graduates were assigned to secretarial and clerical work in central as well as local governments. Ever since Kung-sun Hung had proposed to recruit the educated for government jobs, every level of the hierarchy was filled by learned and educated people (Han-shu: 88/4–6). While, at the local level, staff were sent to the capital for higher education, provincial academies were also established by imperial decree during the reign of Emperor Wu (Han-shu: 89/3). The grassroots level of the bureaucracy was soon also dominated by the educated. Since the curriculum in all levels of schools consisted of nothing other than Confucian classics, it is apparent that the Han government, from the time of Emperor Wu on, was a bureaucracy manned by those who in one way or another had been exposed to Confucian ideology.

The Han recommendation system was an important channel toward government positions for those who aspired to enter government service. A recruitment system based on recommendations for merit was shaped during the early reigns of the Han period in order to provide the government with competent bureaucrats who were to replace the aristocrats and military men who rose to power together with the founding of a new dynasty. The reign of Emperor Wu witnessed the upsurging influence of such civil servants, who joined the government by recommendation. During the following four reigns (86–7 B.C.E.) the Han bureaucracy and the Han recommendation system were virtually inseparable. Governments at all levels were overwhelmingly dominated by recommendees who advanced along a meticuously designed path to become a layer of social elites in government as well as in local communities (C.Y. Hsu, 1965A: 367–369; Ikeda Yuichi, 1976: 319–344).

During the Later Han (or Eastern Han) period, recommendation was the sole channel for the recruitment of candidates for government appointments. The provinces annually recommended candidates known as hsiao-lien (the filial pious and the non-corrupted) according to a complicated quota system. On the average, each prefect annually recommended one person for every 200,000 of population (Han-Hou-shu: 4/12–13, 37/12–13; Hou-Han-chih: 28/4). When this quota system was decreed during the reign of Emperor Ho (89–105 C.E.), the entire population of 53,256,229 persons should have produced at least 266 recommendees a year. Since forty less populated areas enjoyed a minimum quota, they should have produced an additional 40 recommendees with a resultant annual national figure of no less than 300 persons. During a thirty-year generation, a contingent of nine to ten thousand candidates would have entered the bureaucracy and obtained political and social eminence and influence (Hou-Han-chih: 23 B/31).

The large body of officials who were enlisted into government service were almost the same people who had attended the Imperial Academy. Furthermore, the selection of recommendees, at least nominally, was based on Confucian criteria of virtues, such as filial piety, personal integrity, fraternal love, diligent farming, etc. The whole population of social and political elites, therefore, were people who were thoroughly bred in the atmosphere of Confucianism. Confucianism seemed to have triumphantly been established as an orthodoxy.

The Post-effect of Being Established

The Han Confucians, nevertheless, had to face a difficult dilemma. Here Confucianism had been embraced by political authority to serve as the state orthodoxy, because Confucianism provided the imperial order with the concept of the Mandate of Heaven, which duly legitimized the reason for its existence. Meanwhile, Confucianism's human concerns were blended with the functions of universal forces which interacted with the human will. There was no longer the simple humanism that Confucius, Mencius, and Hsun-tzu cherished. The runaway practice of prognostication had cast a mythical mist on the otherwise intellectual clarity of early Confucianism.

The problem was further complicated by the interference of political authority in the sphere of academic development per se. The studies of Confucian classics were established in the Imperial Academy as the only curriculum through which the channel to power and glory would be paved. Since even as early as the days of Confucius there had been division of specialties among his disciples, transmission of knowledge along different lines created distinctive interpretations of the same source. Therefore, by the time Confucian teachings were established as curriculum, there was more than a single learned tradition for any of the classics, each of which had been handed down along lines of tutor-disciple transmission. At the beginning, only one of the several most renowned conventions for each of the classics was established in the Imperial Academy. Some conflict was bound to occur as scholars competed to claim that they offered the true way of understanding. The most severe competition was found between two schools of historians. Both schools developed a set of "codes" or "keys" to interpret why and how Confucius had given his evaluation and judgments on historical events in the chronicle Spring and Autumn which he allegedly compiled or edited. The competition was so heated that eventually only imperial interference could settle the issue. In 51 B.C.E. a scholar of various learned conventions was brought to the court. The debate was judged by a group of ministers, and finally the Emperor Hsuan, in person, approved the establishment of several contending traditions simultaneously in the Imperial Academy (Han-shu: 8/23; 88/25–26).

A half century later, in the reign of Emperor Ping (1–5 C.E.) more special fields of classical studies were included in the academic program. This time the new curriculum involved a number of texts which were not transmitted by means of learned tradition through a line of tutelage. These texts were the ones that were found either in the Imperial Library or even rediscovered in the ruins of old buildings, written in ancient scripts, and are therefore the earlier versions of classics without being influenced by the long tradition of editing and interpretation. Ironically, the discovery of ancient texts did not please the scholars who so far had dominated the field. The reason is simple. The establishment felt their scholarly authority was being threatened by the newly rediscovered materials which somewhat differed from the versions upon which they had worked for a long time. The struggle between the establishment and a group of scholars who were interested in the ancient texts lasted for three generations. In 79 C.E. another scholarly conference was held at the Hall of the White Tiger to settle the issue. With the full support of Emperor Chang (78–87 C.E.), the learning of ancient texts gained much influence to balance the monopoly of the established academic authority (Hou-Han-shu, 3/6).

The significance of the above-mentioned struggle between the New Text and the Old Text schools can be appreciated as a reaction against the scholasticism of the academic establishment and their misuse of Confucianism to serve political ends, even in the form of prognostication. The scholars who studied the ancient texts eventually could not completely shake off the concerns of discussing interactions between Man and Heaven, such as in the works written by Yang Hsiung. Generally speaking, however, the use of the Old Text School represents an effort to restore the original Confucianism. It can be regarded as a second separation of the sacred and the mundane after the Han Confucians once again blended the Heavenly will and Human action in their attempt to synthesize the Confucian humanism and the themes of other schools, especially those of the Yin-Yang naturalists.

The second separation was by no means a complete one. First of all, the scholars on ancient texts (or the Old Texts) could not escape the scholasticism of textural comparison, exegetic compilation, and other similar trivialities. Secondly, the scholarship of both the Old and the New Texts gradually merged into a single trend of textural studies, represented by Cheng Hsuen and other great masters of second-century Han Confucianism. They made few new breakthroughs in the ultimate concern of humanism. The opening of new dimensions of Confucianism did not take place, however, until the appearance of neo-Confucianism in the tenth century.

The lack of new breakthroughs probably should be attributed, at least partly, to the status of the carriers of Confucianism in the Han society. The above-stated struggles among academicians had made little impact on the general status of the Han elites, who were by and large Confucian intellectuals. The self-regeneration of a Confucianized bureaucracy had been automatic due to the recommendation system. The Confucian ethics of reciprocity justified the widespread nepotism and favoritism along the exercise of the recommendation system. Thus, ironically, the recommendation system which had brought new blood into government service began to restrict and negate the very function during the last phase of the Later Han. The differentiation of a group of social elites not only weakened social solidarity but also undermined the vitality of their role as cultural carriers.

Indeed, there were social critics who emerged from the Han Confucians to speak, somewhat pessimistically, of their conscience on current issues and for the Confucian ideals (Etienne Balazs 25, 1964: 213; K.C. Hsiao, 1979: 534–548). The clash between the Confucians and the imperial authority was shown in the great purge of scholars and intellectuals in the last decades of the Later Han (Hou-Han-shu, 67/1–3, 19, of Chuan 68). As a whole, the Confucians of the Later Han failed to perform their mission as standard bearers of Confucian humanism.

Moreover, there was internal differentiation among the Confucian elites. The monopoly of chances to enter bureaucracy by means of the recommendation system due to nepotism and favoritism inevitably would create a few new aristocrats whose family members for generations occupied the upper echelon of the social structure (L.S. Yang, 1936: 1007–1063; Kamada, 1962: 450ff.; Hou-Han-shu 32/4, 49/2, 61/20).

There was also a phenomenon of monopoly of elites in central core areas of the Later Han. This core consisted mainly of a few prefects near the vicinity of the capital region, in the lower middle reaches of the Yellow River Plain. Recently Hsin I-t'ien, a young colleague of mine at Academia Sinica, Taipei, combed through the Han history to trace the background and careers of the Later Han "hsiao-lien" recommendees. He collected a total of 226 names whose original place, age, and career life are recorded. Among these 226 persons, 84 came from eight prefects that constituted the core area near the capital. A census of Yang-ho years (136–141 C.E.) gives a total population of the Han Empire as 53,869,588 persons. There were 105 prefects. The eight prefects made 19.43% of the total population; their share of the top elites whose lives were well registered in history was 37.16% of the total 226 persons. Five of eight prefects, the inner of the inner, had 16% of total population; yet their share of the top elites was 30.97% of the 226 persons. The two innermost prefects, Ju-nan and Nan-Yang, produced a combined 49 persons or 21.7%; and their combined population was only 8% of the national total. These figures of elites per prefect demonstrated clearly that the central core disproportionately dominated the national distribution of top elites (for Han demography, K. Lao: 1938).

Research on the victims who suffered the anti-intellectual purges shows a compatible distribution. Chin Fa-ken collected a list of 183 scholars who suffered the purge in the decade 168 to 159 C.E. These people almost exclusively were graduates or students of the Imperial Academy. 146 of them came from 30 prefects of eastern China. Six of the eight central core prefects produced 88 persons from the 226 persons, or more than 38%. The combination of Ju-nan, Chen-liu, Shan-Yang and Yin-chuean makes a total of 70 persons, which is about one-third of the whole list. The total population of these four prefects nevertheless is about 14% (F.K. Chin, 1963: 517–520). The patterns derived from Chin's paper conform closely with that found by Hsin. In other words, in the Later Han period, a relatively small area near the capital had a high concentration of political and intellectual elites.

Thus, it seems that the Han intellectuals, most of whom were Confucians, were both geographically and socially differentiated. The existence of a small minority who dominated the whole group of cultural carriers would turn themselves into a conservative establishment who had every reason to hold onto the power if they were political figures, or to perpetuate an orthodoxy if they were intellectual elites. In the latter case, a breakthrough is most unlikely to take place. What would happen is perpetuation of old thinking with meticulous efforts to organize the current knowledge, instead of offering a new angle of speculation and a new dimension of exploration. It is not surprising that scholarship in the Later Han could have developed to such a degree that exigencies on a few words in the classics consisted of several essays of ten thousand words.

REFLECTIONS

The conditions that were associated with the first breakthrough of intellectual adventure in ancient China were, first, the dramatic change of political power in the junction of the Shang and Chou dynasties, and, secondly, the survival of the former priests who turned their roles into cultural carriers in the court of new masters. Hu Shih once suggested that the first prototype of scholars who in later days were called Confucians was actually such a group of literati of the conquered Shang (S. Hu, 1934). Fung Yu-lan rejected Hu's theory of suggesting that ancient literati were originally the low-ranked aristocrats (Y.L. Fung, 1936). Both Hu and Fung revealed one side of the same coin. Hu noticed the phenomenon of the first breakthrough by which the Shang priests were transformed. Fung, on the other hand, noticed the origins of the intellectuals of the second transformation, which took place in the Chun-chiu period when the feudal structure was in middle of collapse. These old warrior-courtiers, who were transformed into unattached intellectuals selling their knowledge and service to a "free" market, also took into their hand the function of developing universal systems of values. Confucius was one of them. The carriers of the second transformation were descendants of the aristocrats who were tutored by the "carriers" emerging from the first breakthrough.

The crystallization of Confucianism was a consequence of its being established as an orthodoxy. With the same irony, the Confucian triumph in dominating the Han bureaucracy created conditions that preoccupied the minds of Confucian carriers in either a conservative effort of scholarship or in the attempt to tangle intellect with politics (such as the prognostication of classics). They faced no crisis which should drive the intellectuals to transcendentalize the routine for more profound meanings and significances. The fact that they became the establishment deprived the Confucians of the urge to constantly search for new frontiers of intellectual adventure. Thus, after the Han political order fell, the challenge of organizing a new intellectual order was taken by other groups: the neo-Taoists and the Buddhists in the medieval era of Chinese history.

CHAPTER 14

Was There a Transcendental Breakthrough in China?

MARK ELVIN

From time's first beginning
Who can tell us the story?
Skies and earth still unformed—
How can they be studied?
The dark and the light were confused in shadow,
Who can pierce their nature?
And all things to be—disembodied potential,
By what means can one know them?
That day became day and night became night-time,
How did this happen?
The Bright Force and Dark Force in interaction,
Whence was their source? What their transformations?
The spheres of Heaven, their nine-fold storeys,
Who planned and who built them?
Whose this great work?
Who first gave it being?
. . . .

Tian Wen *(The Questions of Heaven)*[1]

As I understand it, we are concerned in our present undertaking with examining the historical emergence of certain visions in terms of which men have judged their everyday experience and everyday thinking and, in some sense or another, found them to be fundamentally wanting. Ordinary experience, and the world in which it occurs, have been deemed to be either remediably or irremediably flawed in a moral sense, and/or derivative (like the shadows in Plato's cave), or meaningless, unless placed in some transcendental context or process, or else dreamlike, or illusory and unreal in their nature. Ordinary thought, for its part, has been found imprecise, or

325

radically incomplete, or full of internal contradictions and seemingly irresolvable paradoxes, or culpable of a partial, maybe even a total, mismatch with underlying reality.[2] Although the great cultures of the ancient Old World were to a greater or lesser extent in contact with each other, they developed these visions in different ways. Is it reasonable and helpful to our understanding of history to find something in common to all of them, even if that "something" is not easily defined in terms more exact than the loose phrases used in the first sentence of the present paragraph?

I do not want to prejudge this question. My object in this chapter is to sketch this process as it occurred in China, the most isolated of these cultures, over about one thousand years (approximately 1000 B.C.E. to the turn of the eras), with the focus on the last few centuries of the first millennium B.C.E. I am not offering any original research, but a reconsideration of material that is, for the most part, well known to sinologists. If there is a preliminary conclusion, it is this: while Chinese parallels of a sort can be found for most of the main beliefs and ideas held in the western half of Eurasia during this period, Chinese culture as a whole remained untorn by those un-compromising oppositions that, in their extreme form, opened up such a wound in the European soul. By these I mean a self-existent and perfect God and an imperfect transient Creation, Good and Evil as all-pervading aspects of the universe, locked in a perpetual or at least a long-lasting struggle, Spirit and Flesh (or Matter generally), the Other World and This World, Ideal and Actual, Truth and Error (the slightest element of the latter, whether in doctrine or proof, damning utterly), and even the Religious and the Political. I would suggest that the reason for this was that the Chinese were "ecological" in their religious and philosophical thinking, that is to say, they saw *everything* as forming part of a single interacting system, in which no internal cleavages of an ultimate nature could exist, and in which every part affected every other part to some degree. Readers will have to judge for themselves the significance they think appropriate to attach to the differences and the similarities they find here when making the comparison with the rest of Eurasia.

EARLY ARCHAIC CHINA

The oracle records of the last seven kings of the Shang dynasty (whose reigns were between the late fourteenth century and the late twelfth century B.C.E.) show the existence in China of what I like to term "hypatotheism." By this I mean the worship of a supreme deity, combined with the worship of subordinate deities, and thus different from monotheism, monolatry, and polytheism pure and simple. In Shang China God was called Di or Shang Di (God on High), and the other deities were mostly the nature-spirits of mountains and rivers and the like, and selected powerful ancestors thought to dwell with God.[3] Di controlled nature, especially the weather and the crops, and human affairs such as wars and the building of cities. He was closely linked to the royal house, who may have offered Him special sacrifices,[4] and may have been thought of as its ultimate ancestor. He conferred on it good and evil fortune, and communicated with it through the medium of scapulimantic and plastromantic divination (the analysis of cracks made in an animal shoulderblade or the undershell of a tortoise by the application of a hot pointed implement), when his approval was sought regarding a proposed course of action. There is no indication in the authentic sources at our disposal of a moral element in Di's ordinances, but, likewise, being of a brief and formulaic nature, they do not rule it out as impossible.

MIDDLE ARCHAIC CHINA

The Zhou conquest of the Shang towards the end of the second millennium B.C.E. brought the appearance of another supreme God. This was Tian, usually translated "Heaven", a rendering that has the defect of concealing what was originally a clearly anthropomorphic being. The graph for Tian (which is close to that used for "big") does not appear in any context that rules out the reading "big" in the oracle records of the Shang, and the first completely certain occurrence is on a bronze from the eleventh century B.C.E.[5] The historical texts assembled in the early Zhou period (some of which purport to be from the Shang or even earlier, but which were in such cases fairly certainly either created or doctored) show a conscious effort to identify Di with Tian in syncretistic fashion. In passage after passage the two are mentioned in close proximity.[6]

It is in this age that, for the first time, the Chinese begin to perceive the world as the scene, at least to some extent, of a moral drama. This drama appears most clearly in the Zhou propaganda designed to persuade the Shang population that they had been conquered because of the transference of the "mandate" of Tian to the Zhou because of the depravity of the last Shang ruler. The essential concept was that Di/Tian demanded good behaviour of both ruler and people, and punished those who acted in evil fashion.

When Tian inspects the people below, It takes as criterion
their righteousness, and sends them down a life that is either
long or not long [accordingly]. It is not that Tian kills people

before their time has come, but that the people [themselves] cut short their fate. If some of the people do not comply with virtue, and do not acknowledge their sins, Tian assigns them their span of life, correcting their [lack of?] virtue.[7]

I have heard it said that Di on High offers guidance to the self-indulgent, but the Lord of Xia did not moderate his indulgences. Then Di descended and ascended [to partake of the sacrifices], and drew near to that [king of] Xia, but he had no respect for Di. He was licentious and dissolute in the extreme, so gaining an [ill] repute. Then Tian had no regard for him nor hearkened to him any more.[8]

To some extent Di/Tian was viewed as bestowing the "constant norms" or "standards" whereby men's lives were meant to be lived. According to the *Odes:*

Tian gave birth to humankind,
Endowing them with substance and with rules.
People hold fast to moral norms
For love of that most beauteous virtue.[9]

It is hard, though, not to have the impression that the norms were thought to have an almost autonomous existence. A bad king, for instance, was one who "does not show solicitude for his Heavenly nature, and does not follow the standards."[10]

Tian communicated by oracles and by the weather. There was, however, a lurking fear of not knowing what it was that Tian really wanted. As one afflicted monarch averred:

I am not perfected and wise, that I may lead the people to tranquillity. How much less may I enter into contact with and know the commands of Tian?[11]

LATE ARCHAIC CHINA

From perhaps the eighth century B.C.E. onwards there was a definitive transition from a concern to please God and the gods[12] by sacrifices, without making morality a primary consideration, to a belief that morally correct actions were in themselves the key to survival and success in the world. It was felt that Tian operated Its dispensations almost automatically and dependably, and that Its favours and those of the lesser gods were the natural consequence of good conduct. An illustration of the transition is the following exchange between Jiliang and the ruler of the state of Sui in the year 705:

> "Tian at this moment bestows [Its favour] on the state of Chu. . . . Why, my lord, are you in such a hurry [to attack it]? Your servant has heard that a small [state] can contend with a great one if the [true] Way reigns in the small but depravity in the great. That which is called the Way is devotion to the people and good faith towards the gods. Devotion is the preoccupation of the ruler with the well-being of the people. Good faith is truthfulness in the words of the Leader of the Prayers. At the present time the people are hungry, yet you, my lord, indulge your own desires and the Leader of the Prayers speaks falsely when he exalts [you] at the sacrifices. Your servant is not certain if it is right [to attack Chu]."
>
> The duke said: "My sacrificial beasts are flawless and of a single colour. They are fat and plump. My vessels of millet are abundant and brim-full. In what way, then, am I without good faith?"
>
> Jiliang answered: "It is the people who are the hosts [offering sacrifices] to the gods. It was on this account that the Sacred Kings first brought the people to perfection, and only afterwards turned their efforts towards the gods. Thus it is that in presenting the sacrificial beast one announces that he is broad-bodied, fully grown, fat and plump. The meaning is that the resources of the people are everywhere in good condition. . . . In offering the vessels one announces that they contain pure millet in abundance. This means that the three seasons have been without disaster, that the people are at peace with each other, and that the harvest has been plentiful. In presenting the wines, both the fermented and the sweet, one announces that these are delicious vintages [offered] with admiration and awe. This means that superiors and inferiors all possess an admirable virtue and that no heart is disobedient. What one terms the fragrance and aroma [of the sacrifices] means that there is neither slander nor evil done in secret. Thus [men] are devoting themselves to [the works of] the three seasons, perfecting themselves in the five doctrinal principles [of behaviour among kinsmen], showing affection to their relatives within the nine degrees of kinship. It is by these means that one makes a pure sacrifice. It is under these circumstances that the people are at peace among themselves and the gods send down good fortune upon them. Thus it is

that when they act, they bring what they do to success. But at the present time, everyone among the people has his own particular inclinations, and the *manes* and the gods lack anyone to be their hosts [at the sacrifice]. Although, my lord, you on your own show them liberality, what good fortune will you have?"[13]

Thus the vision by which the world and men's thoughts and actions were judged, and usually but not always found wanting, was one of a human society that ran as smoothly, harmoniously, and unvaryingly as the weather and seasons of a perfect year. If that perfection was absent, that was the fault of men:

When Tian [Heaven] violates the seasons, that is a natural disaster. When Earth violates [the usual form of] her products, that is a baleful monstrosity. When the people violate virtue, that is disorder. If disorder occurs, then baleful monstrosities and natural disasters come into being.[14]

The moral culture acceptable to Tian was revealed to mankind by the sage-kings:

Those who were kings in ancient times knew that [Tian's] mandate is not given forever. For this reason they set in place both men of wisdom and men of understanding, who implanted [in the people] customs and reputations, made distinctions for them between [the various] colours and qualities [of decorations and clothing for those of different social status], put into active effect for them the standards [of musical pitches] and the measures [of length, and so forth], displayed for them targets and ultimate ends, guided them with marks of distinction and exemplars, bestowed on them laws and institutions, proclaimed to them their instructions and norm-defining texts, gave them doctrinal education concerning what was to be guarded against and what was of advantage, commissioned them with regular duties and ranks, and spread the Way among them by means of [the system of] appropriate behaviour and ordinances, [yet] in such a way that they did not lose what was appropriate to each locality. The multitude was subordinate to these men, and depended upon them; and thereafter attained to the mandate.[15]

This vision acquired an extraordinary precision in the detailed prescriptions for "appropriate behaviour" (*li*—the term usually inadequately rendered as "ritual"). Appropriate behaviour covered the minutiae of clothing, deportment, and ceremonies as well as the basic principles of conduct such as filial obedience. The leading characters in the *Zuozhuan,* the chief surviving history of this age, are constantly criticizing each other for what appear to be relatively trivial failings in appropriate behaviour, but the significance of this becomes apparent in the context of the vision. In general, in the words of Ji Wenzi when faced with a ruler who wanted to know *why* he observed appropriate behaviour:

> Appropriate behaviour is the means by which we obey Tian. It is the Way of Tian. If one goes contrary to Tian, or even wishes to punish others [who do obey], then it is with difficulty that he will escape.[16]

But the vision of a society where "inferiors serve superiors and superiors show respect for the gods"[17] was not a transcendental one. It remained indissolubly linked with mundane good fortune, and never looked beyond worldly success to some other possible justification of action. "To violate the norms brings ill fortune"[18] was a maxim repeated in almost countless different forms. Virtue, justice, and decorum were practical means by which one attained personal security and political strength. When Tian, at first sight inexplicably, sometimes appeared to be favouring an evil ruler, It was either using him as an instrument to punish another evil-doer, after which It would abandon him, or It was preparing him for a more terrible punishment later.[19]

SECOND-ORDER THINKING

Between the late sixth and the early third centuries B.C.E. the Chinese first became aware of the intellectual problems posed by morality and truth. The archaic age had been concerned to find the secret of successful action—action in harmony with the will of Tian and the wishes of the lesser gods, foreseen by devination by the tortoise-shell, or the milfoil stalks as interpreted in *The Changes of Zhou* (*vide infra,* p. 354), and by the movements of the stars, planets, and comets. Experience and reflection had bred a measure of scepticism, and men began to look deeper into the justification of their beliefs.

At the beginning of this process of self-conscious philosophical awareness stands the enigmatic figures of Kongzi (Confucius). He is conventionally dated from 551 to 479 B.C.E.[20] His own views are difficult to distinguish from those of his disciples, and from the sayings that have gathered around his name. He seems to have had a personality that was drily sceptical and mystical at the same time, sustained by a sense of continuity and communion with the revered figures of the past.

His scepticism is evident in his refusal to talk about "supernatural events, feats of strength, disorders of nature, or the gods."[21] Presumably he thought their reality often doubtful, and their significance, if any, even harder to determine. He insisted that an essential part of knowledge was that "if you do not know a thing, recognize that you do not know it."[22] When his disciple Zilu asked how one should serve the *manes* and the gods, Kongzi answered: "You do not yet know how to serve men. How are you able to serve the *manes*?" Zilu then asked about the dead. This provoked the retort: "You do not yet understand the living. How can you know about the dead?"[23] Other sayings make it clear that he did not disbelieve in the *manes* and the gods. He insisted on the practical primacy of the human world.

His mysticism is harder to demonstrate. Being a cautious man, he did not speak of it openly. His disciples were convinced that he was hiding something from them, though he denied doing so. His conviction that he was spiritually linked to the virtuous kings of the early Zhou dynasty, as the continuator of their way of government, emerges by implication from his comment when he was in danger in the small state of Kuang:

> King Wen is dead, but is not his culture still alive in me? If Tian had intended to destroy this culture, then I, living long after him, would not have been able to take part in it. But, if Tian does not intend to destroy this culture, what harm can the men of Kuang do to me?[24]

In his later years, though, he was beset by disillusionment, realizing that he was not destined to be the instrument chosen by Tian to bring back virtuous government into the world. "How am I fallen from myself!" he said. "It is a long time now since I saw the Duke of Zhou in my dreams."[25]

Socially, Kongzi came from the lowest level of the aristocracy, the knights or gentleman-warriors. He was in impoverished circumstances in his youth, and this may in part explain why his ideals, which were aristocratic ideals, stressed nobility of character rather than of birth or rank, though appropriate behaviour *(li)* was central to his concept of society. He claimed of his teaching: "I transmit and do not create. I have faith in the past and love for it."[26] Hence his insistence on the importance of "study", the mastery of texts by which the appropriate behaviour defined in the past could be known. But this need to recover a pattern of conduct that had to some extent been lost already bespeaks the beginning of a critical and self-conscious separation from the present. And there was another, more important, break. In place of the old combination of religion and government, he put forward the conception of a state and society based on virtue in its own right, without insisting on immediate validation by God or the gods in the form of success. In other words, he began to envisage the awakening of a purely moral determination in the individual.

For Kongzi, the supreme virtue was *ren,* which means a "sensitive concern for others". It was a concept relatively little used in earlier Chinese thinking, but one that can, for example, be found applied to a prince who yielded the succession to a brother, and was also defined by its opposite, namely counting the disasters of others as one's own good fortune.[27] Kongzi exemplified this virtue in his own behaviour. For example, "when seated next to someone in mourning, he did not eat his fill."[28] When asked by Zilu what his heart was set upon, Kongzi answered: "To comfort the aged, to keep faith with my friends, and to cherish the young."[29] It was in response to a questioner who asked for a definition of *ren* that he gave the negative form of a golden rule: "Do not do to others what you would not wish for yourself."[30]

This sensitive concern for others gave a value to rituals and music that they would not otherwise have had. The "superior man", whom Kongzi regarded as the highest type of humanity, did not deserve this title if he lacked *ren.* "The superior man does not abandon his sensitive concern for others even for the length of time it takes to finish a meal. Even when harassed, he will always keep to it. Even when faced with disaster, he will always keep to it."[31] The world would turn of its own accord to a ruler who had *ren.* Zilu once asked Kongzi how Guanzhong of Qi could be regarded as having had *ren,* since he had not followed his lord in death, as prescribed by the feudal code, but had instead become the prime minister under his lord's murderer. The answer was ambiguous, and a partial justification of Guanzhong. It was due to him that Duke Huan had become hegemon "without the use of weapons or war-chariots".[32] Humanity was the essence of the matter, and the ideal with which Kongzi hoped to inspire a moral elite in whose hands government could properly rest.

Second-order thinking in the proper sense probably first appeared with Mo Di. Mo lived towards the end of the fifth century, B.C.E., and like Kongzi he came from the state of Lu. The book that bears his name (but is the work of several generations of disciples) contains the first systematically argued exposition of many of the beliefs that remained central to later Chinese tradition. Somewhat ironically, the contribution of Moism was ignored by the scholars of imperial times.

In part this was because some of its doctrines, especially "loving mankind as a whole", were regarded as heretical. In part it was because the Mo-ist school's concern for definitions, logic, and the precise use of grammar was alien to the more impressionistic, aesthetic, and pragmatic styles of thought favoured under the empire.

Mo Di maintained that a proposition should "meet three criteria". It had to have "a scriptural basis". In other words, suitable precedents for it had to exist in the acts or words of the sage-kings of the past. It had to have a "derivation" from the evidence of the senses. And due regard had to be paid to its "practical effects". That is to say, when acted on, did it bring benefit or harm to humanity? Mo did not discuss how to resolve conflicts between these criteria, perhaps believing that none could arise. The pragmatic nature of the third criterion was typical of his thought. "To put into practice the views of those who believe that there is only fate [the same word as was used for the mandate of Tian]," he said in his attack on determinism, "would be to destroy moral behaviour in the world."[33]

Moism based its political philosophy on utilitarian considerations. The immutable, hierarchical pattern of appropriate behaviour towards men and gods that had been inherited from the archaic age was set aside in favour of actions validated by a practical test, rationally applied. Moral conduct was defined as acting so as to benefit others. Tian, said Mo Di, "desires men to love each other and to benefit each other, and does not wish them to hate or to harm each other."[34] Moreover, "It loves them as a whole, and benefits them as a whole."[35] The sage-kings had made Tian their model in this, and so should everyone. Administrators should practise "the even-handedness of Tian".[36]

Utilitarian considerations justified meritocracy. In the (idealized) past, "even farmers, and those who made their living in workshops and market-places, were promoted if they were capable." "Thus officials did not always enjoy their honours as a matter of course, and the common people did not always stay in their lowly position till the end of their days."[37]

Such meritocrats had to be manipulators bringing about virtuous, that is to say socially advantageous, behaviour by incentives that worked on people's self-interest. "Encourage them with rewards and praise," said Mo Di, "overawe them with punishments, and I believe that men will tend towards love for mankind as a whole, and the exchange of mutual benefits, just as a fire leaps upwards and water flows downhill."[38]

It was vital to have uniformity of values, strict hierarchy, and perfect inter-communication between superiors and inferiors. Before the creation of government there had been chaos. Each man had

had his own particular morals and his own particular values for words. The head of each family, each community, and each state had had to unify the values of those beneath him. It was the duty of the emperor to do this for the world as a whole. "If superiors and inferiors do not share the same values, rewards and fame will not be enough to encourage people to act well, nor will punishment be adequate to prevent violence."[39] Mo Di envisaged a corporatism very different from the Western ideal of democracy. He was speaking from the point of view of a ruler when he said: "If many others assist one to hear and see, then one will be able to hear and see across vast distances. If many others help one to speak, then great numbers may be touched and calmed by one's words of virtue. If many others give one their aid in thinking ahead, then one's plans and calculations will be swiftly successful."[40]

Mo Di's feeling for mankind as a whole was the force behind his two great passions—peace and frugality. He hated war not only for its cruelty but also for its wastefulness. He argued that no war could ever be shown to have benefitted mankind, considered in its totality. He opposed extravagance in funeral rituals, in musical performances, and in objects of everyday use. "Eliminate matters that do not contribute to the function," was his rule.[41] His essential objection to the rulers of his day was that "they forcibly despoil the people of the resources they need for food and clothes."[42] If harvests failed, they starved.

Almost every one of Mo's arguments was backed by an appeal to Tian (Heaven) or to Di (God). He used both terms. Tian was the ultimate source of moral behaviour, and the authority above the emperor. Its wishes were clearly expressed, if need be through portents and the appearance of spirits. Here he was broadly in accord with archaic times, which had had their *Tianshi*—messengers from Tian— and their celestial and meteorological signs, though the latter usually required interpreting. He differed from Kongzi, who refused to speak about "the Way of Tian" and suspected that It communicated only implicitly through the passing of the seasons and the life that It gave to the multitude of living creatures.[43] For Mo the rewards and punishments of Tian were also just and certain. "If I do what Tian wants me to do," he said, "then Tian in Its turn will provide me with what I want."[44] Yet side by side with this crude confidence in virtue as a paying proposition was a real nobility of vision: "There are no great states in the world, and no unimportant states. All are the city-states of Tian. Among men there are no young and no old, no noble and no base. All are the subjects of Tian."[45]

The Mo-ists practised what they preached. "If there are no weapons stored in the armoury," said their master, "even the morally just cannot subdue the morally unjust."[46] They became famous for their technical skill in defensive warfare, especially fortifications. Their puritanical intensity drew the criticism that what they demanded was "like driving a horse without ever unharnessing him, or drawing a bow without ever unstringing it—something that can surely not be attained by beings of flesh and blood."[47] Their aim was to be like Tian that "acts far and wide, and without personal partisanship."[48] The ideal that sustained them, though it may seem drab and prosaic, had great moral power amid the slaughter of the Warring States. It was of a fair world where "the strong do not have the weak in their grasp, where the numerous do not plunder the few in numbers, where the rich do not insult the poor, where those with titles do not lord it over those of lower status, and where the cunning do not cheat the simple-minded."[49]

THE CRISIS OF CERTAINTY

In the second half of the fourth century B.C.E. there was a crisis of certainty in the Chinese intellectual world. The individualist Yang Zhu posited an opposition between human nature and the demands of society. This challenged the traditional view that rulers governed the people in such a way as to "prevent them from losing their [true] nature."[50] It raised the question, was there a philosophical basis for morality? In epistemology, the enquiries of the later Moists and the logicians into the nature of arguments led them to apparently absurd paradoxes, and undermined most people's faith in the power of logic to solve or help solve the real problems of human existence. An abyss had opened in which both conventional morality and conventional truth seemed to have been annihilated.

Yang's doctrine was to act "for myself".[51] He stressed the reality of personal pleasure and the inanity of fame. The licentious tyrants of historical legend, held up by the moralists of archaic times as proof that vice did not pay, had acted with greater sense than the self-denying sage-kings. But his hedonism was sombre and Stoic:

> Once one has been born, one should endure it with
> indifference, get as much as one can of what one wants, and
> so wait for death. When death approaches, one should endure
> it with indifference, going on to the end and thus abandoning
> oneself to extinction.

Social institutions, the conventions of appropriate conduct, were a form of torture:

> Some things are forbidden us under pain of punishment,
> some things we are urged to do with the promise of rewards.

Concern for our reputation drives us on, and the laws hold us back. We struggle fretfully for an hour of empty glory. We calculate the fame that will remain to us after we are dead. With the greatest circumspection we are concerned about what we see and hear; we worry about what is right and what wrong in our conduct and thoughts. In vain we lose the true pleasure that is suited to our years, unable to follow our inclinations for a moment. How is this different from being in a prison with many walls, and shackled in iron?

Yang urged that men should act "in accordance with their hearts, and not reject that which they spontaneously love." They should enjoy themselves "in accordance with their [inner] natures, and not rebel against that which the natural world loves." Just as Mo Di had discovered the collectivity, so Yang Zhu had discovered the individual.

The later Mo-ists, for their part, set out to develop an ethics that was no longer dependent on appeals to historical authority or to Tian, but based in rational fashion on universally valid grounds. To this end they fashioned an abstract system of analysis whose power is still impressive. To take one example to represent many, consider the technical precision seen in their rules for the use of markers or demonstrative pronouns. In modern terms it amounted to saying that if, in a valid statement, you substitute x for y, then every occurrence of y must be so changed, and all the x's of the original statement changed to something else. Otherwise the validity of the transformed statement cannot be guaranteed.[52]

The Mo-ists gave analytical definitions for geometrical figures. Thus, they said, "circular" means "having the same lengths from a single centre".[53] They touched on many of the problems covered by modern set theory, such as membership, identity, and the structure of sets. An idea of the intellectual toughness of their writing is conveyed by the following passage, which grapples with what was for them the still not quite clear notion of the conditions that determined the identity of two sets (namely that any member of either is always a member of the other). The reader versed in modern logic should refrain from automatically interpreting in the modern sense of "=" any "is" that is in or that seems to be implicit in the text. The argument is heavily over-translated so as to make it as nearly intelligible as possible. Chevron brackets "<. . .>" are used to indicate elements of which the sets are composed. Square brackets "[. . .]" enclose my own commentary.

The grounds for regarding as false the statement that "the set of <oxen and horses> is not [identical to] the set of

<oxen>" are the same as those for regarding it as true. The explanation for this paradox lies in the way composite sets are aggregated.

If some of the members of the composite set [<O + H>] are not oxen, and if the statement that "it is [i.e. has some members in common with] <not oxen>" is therefore regarded as true, then,—though some members are of course not oxen—since some of them are indeed oxen, the statement that "it is [i.e. has some members in common with] the set of <oxen>" may also on the same grounds be regarded as true.

If, for this reason, we regard as not being true *either* the statement that "the set of <oxen and horses> is not [identical to] the set of <oxen>" *or* the statement that "the set of <oxen and horse> is [identical to] the set of <oxen>", then—since a proposition must either be the case or not the case—we must also say that the statement that "the statement that 'the set of <oxen and horses> is not [identical to] the set of <oxen>' is not to be regarded as true" is also itself not a permissible proposition.

Moreover, though the set of <oxen> is not a two-fold composite set, nor is the set of <horses> a two-fold composite set, the set of <oxen *and* horses> *is* a two-fold composite set. Therefore, although the set of <oxen> is [within an unbounded universe of discourse] [identical to] the set of <not the set of <not oxen>>, and the set of <horses> is [identical to] the set of <not the set of <not horses>>, there is no difficulty about accepting as true [within a universe of discourse consisting solely of oxen and horses] the statement that "the set of <oxen and horses> is [identical to] the set composed of the [sub]set of <not horses> plus the [sub]set of <not oxen>". [That is, the union of all the subsets in a universe of discourse equals the union of the complements of these subsets.][54]

Although the argument is faulty in several respects, as the commentary makes clear, the drive towards formal rigour, and the fearless drawing of consequences, however paradoxical, are impressive.

The Mo-ists used their logical techniques to dispose of objections to their ethical doctrines. Thus, when it was argued against the obligation to "love mankind as a whole" that it could not be known a priori whether or not the earth's surface were finite, and the numbers of men on it finite or infinite, the Mo-ist rebuttal was as follows:

If men do not fill the limitless, then there is a limit to men. There is no difficulty, then, about exhausting the limited. If, *per contra*, they do fill the limitless, then the limitless *has* been exhausted. There is, then, no difficulty about exhausting the limitless.[55]

It is not surprising that in the age of the Warring States most intelligent men found this sort of discourse arid, confusing, and impractical. It takes a modern perspective to appreciate the heroic intellectual effort involved.

The paradoxes of the logicians, who did not share the stern Moist moral concern, probably appeared less justifiable still, frivolous or even mischievous. Legend has it that the Sophist Gongsun Lun got his white horse past a customs barrier by proving that "a white horse is not a horse", that is, by deliberately confusing membership of a set and the identity of sets. Perhaps this famous story symbolized the disorder that it was feared that the Sophists could introduce into society, particularly in the law-courts.

The justifications for their paradoxes have perished, but the following selection of some well-known items may give an idea of the shock effect they had. Tentative explanations are given afterwards, in square brackets.

1. Eyes do not see. [The mind does.]
2. An orphan colt has never had a mother. [When it had a mother it was not an orphan colt.]
3. If a rod one foot in length is cut short every day by one-half of its length, it will still have something left even after ten thousand generations have passed. [By definition. There will always be a half left to cut in half again.]
4. The egg has feathers. [In potentiality.]
5. Things die as they are born. [Through their transformation from one state to another. Thus the caterpillar perishes to become the chrysalis, and the chrysalis to become the butterfly.]
6. The shadow of a flying bird has never moved. [Each succeeding shadow is a different one, appearing in sequence.]
7. That which has no thickness has no bulk yet covers a thousand square miles. [The plane, presumably.]
8. Killing robbers is not killing people. ["Executing" is not "murdering" and "felons" are not "people".][56]

The language itself must have seemed to be crumbling.

Intuition and Immanence

The first to offer a resolution of the crisis in ethics created by
Yang Zhu was Mengzi, who probably lived from 371 to 288 B.C.E.
He was too early to be much affected by the undermining of the
certainty of knowledge, though he was passably adept at arguing in
the manner of the Sophists when the occasion required it. He was,
by his own description, a follower of Kongzi, and found his inspiration in the ideal of a hierarchical society that was based on man's
natural instincts of kinship, was inspired by the sense of a shared
humanity, and was well-fed, well-taught, and governed by rulers
whose own personalities had vanished in their all-absorbing sense
of social responsibility.

Where Mengzi broke new ground was in his theory of moral
sentiments. He was, in a sense, the first Chinese psychologist. Thus
he counselled fathers and sons never to reprove each other, even
with the best of intentions, lest alienation result. It is in his works
that we become aware, for the first time in Chinese philosophy, of
an inner life. "All things in the world," he said, "are already complete
in us."[57] For Mengzi, the centre of man's being was his "heart" or
"mind", the Chinese word covering both of these meanings. Man's
innate heart-mind, which he also described as "the heart-mind of a
child", was good. It took pleasure in its sensitive concern for others
and in morality, just as the mouth took pleasure in the flavours of
food, and the eyes in sexually attractive bodies. "There is no greater
pleasure," he said, "than to reflect upon oneself and to be conscious
of one's perfect sincerity."[58] Just as all men had the same essential
physical constitution, so they all had the same essential moral constitution. Innate compassion produced sensitivity to others, innate
shame created morality, innate deference was the basis of appropriate
ritual behaviour, and the innate sense of truth and falsehood led to
wisdom. "All things that are the same in kind are like to one another.
Why should man alone be different?"[59]

This innate heart-mind could be corrupted in the way that the
wooded slopes of a hill could be deforested by the hacking of axes.
Except in the case of the superior man, this was what usually
happened. But such a degraded state was not "what is essential to
man."[60] As against those who argued that man's nature was morally
neutral, and any morality he possessed therefore the result of artifice
(as cups and bowls are made by a turner from willow-wood), Mengzi
maintained that it was naturally inclined to be good. One did not
have to do violence to a man (as the turner did violence to his
wood) to make him feel a sensitive concern for others. "All men,"
he said, "have a heart-mind that cannot bear to see others suffer."[61]

He proved this by the famous example of a baby crawling towards an open well. Who could be so inhuman as not to rush forward to save it?

Evil actions, when they occurred, were due to the pressure of adverse circumstances, to what might be called "contingent corruption", rather than to any fundamental defect in the constitution of man. He did not discuss the origin of these adverse circumstances, unlike the archaic moralists, who ascribed them to Tian or the lesser gods.

Mengzi also formulated a conception of psychological self-conditioning. It was essential not "to do violence to oneself" morally, or "to throw oneself away". One had to study in order "to seek for the heart-mind that one has abandoned," and use thought, the gift of Tian, to understand what lay behind the evidence of the senses lest one became "deceived by phenomena".[62] Above all, one had to nurture one's moral vitality *(qi)*. "It is produced," he said, "by the accumulation of moral behaviour. It is not to be obtained by incidental moral acts. If some of one's actions do not make one's heart-mind contented, then one becomes starved."[63] Through self-conditioning one's heart-mind can become "immovable" in its resistance to outward pressures, but capable of transforming others.

> One who brings his heart-mind to its complete realization knows his own [intrinsic] nature. To know one's own [instrinsic] nature is to know Tian. To preserve one's heart-mind [uncorrupted] and to develop one's heart-mind [to full realization] are the means whereby one serves Tian.[64]

Mengzi gave explicit expression to the subversive idea hinted at by Kongzi, namely that the actual status order should be contrasted with an ideal status order:

> There is a nobility created by Tian and a nobility created by man. Those who have a sensitive concern for others, just principles, loyal devotion and good faith, and who take an unwearying delight in goodness, are the nobility of Tian. Dukes, ministers, and the great officers of state are the nobility of men.[65]

He also sketched what was possibly the first distinction in China between the natural and the normative, though he did not follow up its implications:

> The relation of the mouth to tastes, of the eyes to appearances, of the ears to sounds, of the nose to smells, and of the four limbs to tranquil relaxation is a matter of our

[intrinsic] nature. If there were any [element of]
commandment in these relations, the superior man would not
describe them as [intrinsic] nature. The part played by
sensitive concern in the relationship between father and son,
by just principles in that between ruler and minister, by
appropriate ritual behaviour between guest and host, by wise
perception in [recognizing] the worthy, and by the sage with
respect to the Way of Tian are matters of commandment. If
there were any [element of] [intrinsic] nature in them, the
superior man would not describe them as commandment(s).[66]

In spite of these contrasts between the actual and the ideal, the
element of real transcendence in Mengzi's thought is minimal. "Tian",
though It is the source of moral awareness, and capable of having
wishes and directing events, "does not speak" and reveals Itself
exclusively through these events, often coming close to meaning little
more than "fate", "providence", or "nature". In most contexts the
term cannot any longer be appropriately translated as "God" or
"Heaven" because It is so clearly a power immanent in the world
and not external to it. Yet, as the quotations should make clear, an
aura of Godhood lingers around it.

THE DAO

We find both the crisis of epistemological certainty and the crisis
of moral authority fully developed in Zhuang Zhou, a slightly younger
contemporary of Mengzi. It seems probable that much of the later
part of the book that bears his name, the *Zhuangzi,* was not written
by him; and although the account given here is based primarily on
the chapters accepted as authentic by all scholars, it uses material
from the others where it seems to offer a clearer expression of ideas
implicit in the first part.

Of all the great Chinese philosophers, Zhuang is the most complex
and elusive, being logical, fantastical, practical, humorous, and mystical in swift-moving succession. All his arguments, however, are in
the end a ruthless attack on the adequacy of existing human standards
of judgement, whether of fact or of logic, or of ethical desirability.
They are designed to lead the hearer to what still lies beyond when
we have come to the limit of what may be rationally spoken of:

Contingent truths come to an end. When they are at an end,
it is that of which we do not know of It what is so that we
call the Dao.[67]

Describing Its main outlines through the mouth of one of the fictitious
characters that adorn his pages, he spoke of It as follows:

My Master, oh, my Master! You chop all things to pieces and are not to be accounted moral. You fertilize generation after generation but are not to be thought of as showing a sensitive concern for others. You come from before the remotest past but are not to be reckoned old. You overarch the heavens and carry the earth on your back, you sculpt the multitude of forms, yet you are not to be regarded as ingenious.—It is here that I roam.[68]

The Dao, which literally means "the Way", was the sum-total of the patterns of potential action that made nature be the way it was.

Zhuang regarded all that was as being made of a single substance, namely *qi*, which we may overtranslate as "matter-energy-vitality", though its original sense is close to "pneuma". Specific entities were transient conglomerations of this matter-energy-vitality, each with its own particular pattern *(li)*, and were constantly being reshaped by the Transformer *(zaohua)* or Fashioner of Things *(zaowuzhe)*, a force that should be thought of as having no more than a trace element of anthropomorphic character.* Thus "the ten thousand entities are one", and "stinking putrefaction is retransformed into the spiritually extraordinary, and the spiritually extraordinary is retransformed into stinking putrefaction. Hence I say that throughout the universe there is but a single [field of] matter-energy-vitality."[69] And the *Zhuangzi* says of Zhuang Zhou: "Above he roamed with the Fashioner of Things, and below he was the friend of all who had gone beyond death and birth, and for whom there were no endings or beginnings."[70]

These transformations are given their invisible articulation by the Dao. But is the Dao transcendent, or immanent, or in some sense both? Zhuang Zhou defines it thus:

The Dao has a [certain] character and keeps faith [reliably], but It is without [specific] activities and without a [specific] shape. [An understanding of] It may be transmitted but cannot be [tangibly] received. It may be grasped but may not be seen. It is self-rooted and self-originated. Before the Heaven and the Earth were, from of old It has assuredly existed. It makes numinous the *manes* and gives godhood to God. It gave birth to Heaven and to Earth. It is prior to the Supreme Ultimate [the primal conjunction of the Dark Force and Bright Force] yet It is not elevated. It underlies the Six

---

* In archaic times the word *li* was pronounced approximately *lieg*, and the *li* meaning "appropriate ritual behaviour" was *lier*, but in recent times they have come to sound alike, though written with quite different graphs.

Extremes [the cardinal points and up and down] but It is not profound. It has been in being since before Heaven and Earth yet It is not long-lasting. It is older than the highest antiquity and yet not ancient.[71]

And the Dao is omnipresent, being even in insects, weeds, smashed tiles, and excrement and urine (and hence not to be confused with a True Controller *(Zhen Zai),* or God external to nature for whose existence Zhuang says elsewhere we obtain no sign or omen).[72] Zhuang Zhou, with his awareness and acceptance of a universe that is mostly not of man or for man, and his intuition that spiritual freedom is only possible by abandoning the self and becoming one with this universe as a whole, has no obvious ancient Western counterpart except maybe the author of the Book of Job in the speech he gives to God, answering out of the whirlwind.

Zhuang's metaphysics make it easier to understand his attack on logic. It begins with the assertion that the division of experience by words into distinct categories is already a radical falsification:

The Dao has never had boundaries. Speech has never had norms. It is through "truth by definition" that frontiers are created.[73]

The terminology itself prevents one from seeing that "things have neither development nor decay, but return into each other and interpenetrate to form a single whole."[74] And he asks, rhetorically, "Is there any argument that will prove that [speech] is different from the chatter of fledglings?"[75]

He mocked the use of such logical devices as the negation of negatives, and asked what relation they bore to reality. "Let us try nonetheless," he suggested of logicians' reasoning and ironically offered the following example:

Given "begins", we have "not yet beginning to begin", and hence "not yet beginning 'not yet beginning to begin' ".   (1)

Given "exists", we have "does not exist".   (2)

[Putting (1) and (2) together,] we have "not yet beginning not to exist", and hence "not yet beginning 'not yet beginning not to exist' ".

Existence and non-existence abruptly alternate, but we don't know what actually does or does not have existence. Now I have made some references, but I don't know if they have actually referred to anything or not.[76]

Furthermore, he said, there is no pre-existing external standard of truth outside the individual himself; and individuals differ. In what might be seen as an implicit reply to Mengzi, he argued:

> Suppose that one follows one's own heart-mind—and a heart-mind is something that comes into being [and not a permanent and universal standard]—and makes it the authority. Who is there, then, that does not have such an authority? How can it be that only the [wise] man who knows the alternatives, and whose heart-mind judges for itself between them, can have such an authority? A fool has one just as much as he has. Yet were one to say that there could be a true and a false before they came into being in one's own heart-mind, that would be as self-contradictory as to say "Going to Yue today and arriving yesterday." It would be regarding the non-existent as existing.[77]

There is also a famous passage in which Zhuang asks: "If you and I have a disputation, and you defeat me . . . are you then really in the right? Or, if I win . . . am I really right and you really wrong?" He goes on to show that appealing to a third party to arbitrate solves nothing. How can we tell if his arbitration is correct?[78]

This scepticism about logic extended into an insistence that human knowledge was inevitably incomplete and inadequate. "Our life is bounded, but knowledge is unbounded."[79] Failure to understand could be the result of personal incapacity:

> The blind have no way of joining us in the seeing of patterns. The deaf have no way of joining us in hearing the sounds of drums and bells. Why should there be only bodily deafness and blindness? It is likewise the case with knowledge.[80]

The failure could also be the consequence of limited experience. Zhuang has the God of the Northern Ocean say to the Spirit of the Yellow River:

> You cannot talk about the sea to a frog who lives in a well. He is circumscribed with respect to space. You cannot talk to the summer insects about ice. Their life is concentrated with respect to time. You cannot talk to a small-minded gentleman-warrior about the Dao. He has been bound fast by his indoctrination.[81]

Zhuang Zhou hoped to shock those who listened to him into an awareness of a universe that was immensely greater and more varied than they had imagined they lived in, but not of *another* universe, of a radically different quality. *Stricto sensu,* therefore, one cannot speak of "transcendence", but in terms of emotional impact the distinction is at most a fine one.

Finally, Zhuang argued that there was no way that everyday experience could be distinguished from a dream. "Suppose," he said, "that you dream you are a bird reaching high into the heavens, or a fish submerged in the abyss. You do not know whether what we call 'the present' is a waking or a dream."[82] For him, dreams were evidence that things constantly turned into other things, a process he compared to molten bronze taking on different shapes in the hands of a master smith. But there was no transmigration of souls. For Zhuang it was a grief that "when one's body is transformed in death, one's heart-mind goes with it in the same way." The wise man, "unable to know what went before, unable to know what will come after, submits to the transformations that make him the thing that he is, and so waits for the next unknowable transformation."[83] If life is a dream, death may be an awakening.

Zhuang condemned ordinary knowledge as a "curse" and a "weapon of contention". But he thought there was a higher kind, which he called "great" or "true" knowledge. At its simplest it was instinctive, like that of an animal:

> Fish are suited to the water. Men are suited to the Dao. . . .
> Fish forget themselves in the lakes and rivers. Men forget
> themselves in the Dao.[84]

Zhuang appreciated ecological delicacy. Like a wild animal, one should live lightly off the world, with a sense of the limited nature of one's true needs. He has one of his fictitious sages reject the offer of the empire with this observation:

> The *jiaoliao* bird nests deep in the forest, but takes only a
> single branch. The tapir drinks from the Yellow River, but
> has no more than a belly-full.[85]

What use would the empire be to him?

At a more complex level, true understanding was like the ultimately incommunicable skill of the great craftsman. This is the theme of the famous story about Master Butcher Ding cutting up an ox. Asked by his lord how he had achieved such perfection that he seemed to be performing an imperial dance, Ding answered:

> What your servant loves is the Dao, which goes beyond mere
> technique. . . . I sense [oxen] with daemonic intuition. I do
> not see them with my eyes. . . . I adapt myself to the natural
> pattern. . . . There are gaps at the joints, and the blade is
> without thickness. By inserting that which is without thickness

into these gaps, there is ample room for the edge to travel at will. . . . For nineteen years the blade of my knife has remained as fresh as though from the whetstone.[86]

The highest understanding is an all-encompassing indifference. In the words of the God of the Northern Ocean:

There are no limits to the sizes of things, no endpoints to their possible durations, no constancies in the divisions between them. Their ends and beginnings are not to be forcibly determined. So great knowledge keeps in view both the distant and the close at hand. The small does not seem inadequate, nor the great excessive, since it knows the limitlessness of sizes. It draws its proofs from both present and past. The long-enduring causes it no dull stupor, nor does the transitory make it flustered, since it knows there are no endpoints to possible duration. It scrutinizes the full and the empty. Gain brings no pleasure and loss no grief, for it understands the inconstancies of divisions. The path of tranquillity is clear to it. Life seems no happiness and death no disaster.[87]

To conclude, the vision that forms the basis for Zhuang Zhou's dissatisfaction with the human world and human understanding is of a natural wholeness of life, sentiment, and thought that has somehow been fragmented by civilization, morality, and language. Institutions, beliefs, and rigorously formulated arguments are not so much wrong as grotesque deformations that embody in lopsided form small parts of what is good or true. The sage-king, he says, is one who would "brand your face like a criminal's with a sensitive concern for others and moral obligation, and cut off your nose with caring about right and wrong."[88] But whence came this flaw, as it would seem, in the Dao, this weakening through time, he does not say.*

THE REALIST REACTION

Mengzi's optimism about human nature, the paradoxes of the logic-chopping Sophists, and Zhuang Zhou's transcendence of merely human concerns invited a realist reaction. This reaction found its clearest expression in the man-centred, secular political sociology of

---

* He does discuss the cause of the "weakening" or "impairment" of the Dao, namely, "standards of right and wrong, true and false." But this relates only to the understanding of the Dao and not to why such imperfection should have arisen in the first place.[89]

Xun Qing. Xun was born about 312 B.C.E. and died some time after 238 B.C.E. He is generally regarded as a Confucian, and professed a great respect for Kongzi. It might be better, though, to see him as a traditionalist, superbly versed in the new ideas and methods, who re-established the central tradition on a new, pragmatic basis.

He did not spare his precedessors. "Their provision of reasons for what they maintain, and the well-organized character of their arguments, are sufficient to delude the ignorant multitude." The result had been disorder. Most of the great thinkers had been one-sided:

> Mo Di's mind was darkened by his concern for utility, and he did not understand expressive forms [like appropriate ritual behaviour and music]. . . . [The logician] Hui Shi's mind was darkened by propositions, and he did not understand substantive reality. Zhuang Zhou's mind was darkened by his obsession with Tian, and he took no cognizance of man.⁹⁰

His harshest censure was for the Sophists:

> To split up propositions, and to invent names without the authorization to do so, thereby throwing the correct terminology into confusion, causing the people to have doubts and delusions, and numerous persons to engage in disputations and lawsuits, must be regarded as a major crime. Its guilt should be treated as equivalent to counterfeiting the tallies used for orders and contracts, or measures of length and capacity.⁹¹

Defining terminology should be a prerogative of the government, so as to ensure social communication and social stability. Although Xun conceded that logic could sometimes make valid points, "the superior man does not take part in disputations. They are outside the limits he has set for himself."⁹²

He swept aside the paradoxes with the assertion that words had no intrinsic reality, being merely conventionally agreed means of grouping similar objects into categories. Paradoxes arose from tampering with these conventions. To support such a view, he was obliged to create the rudiments of a new theory of knowledge:

> On what basis does one determine similarity and difference? I answer, by following one's senses. In general, those things which are of the same category and the same nature give us the same sense-impressions. By collating them, we can determine the similarity and make a generalization. It is by this means that we can all agree on a convention for the term to use, so that there are congruent expectations.⁹³

He also, in a limited way, anticipated Kant by positing an innate interpretative capacity in the mind:

> The heart-mind has the faculty of verification. It is this faculty of verification that permits it to know sounds by relying on the ear, and to know shapes by relying on the eye. But the faculty of verification has always to wait for the senses to register impressions in its categories before it can function. If the senses merely register impressions, but these are not interpreted, or if the heart-mind does verify them but cannot articulate its conclusions in words, everyone will consider this the same as ignorance.[94]

In spite of his ability to be so carefully objective, Xun Qing's insistence on the primacy of human kind made his teaching hostile to scientific investigation. Our efforts, he said, were best confined to understanding moral principles.

His most radical step was to desacralize Tian, making It merely synonymous with "Nature":

> The stars in their positions turn around, following one after another. The sun and moon shine in alternation. The four seasons preside in succession. The Dark Force and Bright Force go through their great transformations. The wind and the rains spread far and wide. Each of the ten thousand things obtains the blend that gives it birth, and the nourishment that lets it grow old. One does not see these actions, only their outcome. It is merely this that we mean by "divine". We all know the means by which they grew to completion, but none of us understands the disembodied nature [of these means, i.e. their abstract, 'scientific' character]. This is all that we mean by "Tian". The sage alone does not seek to understand Tian.[95]

Since "Tian's ways are constant", one cannot have a grievance against it for misfortune. Man's destiny is in his own hands. "If you strengthen agriculture and economize on expenditures, then Tian cannot make you poor. . . . If agriculture is left neglected and expenditures are extravagant, then Tian cannot make you rich."[96]

Man's place in this desacralized nature is seen in sociobiological terms:

> Fire and water have energy but not life. Grasses and trees have life but no intelligence. Bird and beasts have intelligence but no sense of morality. Men have energy, life, intelligence, and also a sense of morality. Therefore they are the noblest

beings on earth. Their strength is less than that of oxen; they
run more slowly than horses; yet oxen and horses serve them.
How is this? I answer, because men are able to combine
socially, whereas these others cannot. How is it that men can
combine socially? I answer, by means of the differentiation of
roles. By what means is the differentiation of roles effected? I
answer, by morality. Therefore, when morality effects a
differentiation of roles, there is a correct proportionality. A
correct proportionality makes for unity, and unity for the
multiplication of strength. The multiplication of strength
means the power to conquer other beings. . . . So it is that
men, once born, must combine together. To combine together
without a differentiation of roles leads to quarrelling.
Quarrelling leads to disorder, hence to mutual alienation, and
hence to weakness. If men are weak they cannot conquer
other beings. . . . The ruler is one who is good at causing
men to combine together.[97]

Men became what they were through cultural conditioning, as could
be seen by observing the different development of initially similar
babies brought up in different areas and among different tribes. A
person became what he was through acquiring a stock of socially
accumulated widsom. "To attempt to do everything your own way
is to be like a blind man trying to distinguish colours." In particular
this was true of morality, which had to be learned. "When a man
is born, he is certainly an inferior man."[98] Teachers and models
were indispensable.

At the heart of Xun Qing's conception of the good society was
the complementary functioning of music and appropriate ritual behaviour. "Music", in Xun's sense, must be thought of in terms of
our own singing of hymns, or listening to military pipe-bands or to
mass pop-music festivals, namely as a means of creating emotions
of various sorts that bind people together. It was a source of solidarity.
"Appropriate ritual behaviour" had something in common with the
etiquette we require in the presence of royalty, or the use of differing
and distinctive dress for priests, soldiers, policemen, and academics,
but was much stronger and more pervasive. It was a means of
expressing and structuring the differences between people. In Xun's
own words:

Music embodies the unalterable aspect of harmonious [social]
cooperation. Appropriate ritual behaviour embodies the
unchangeable aspect of orderly [social] arrangements. Music
unites what men have in common. Appropriate ritual
behaviour differentiates what sets them apart from each other.

The conjunction of appropriate ritual behaviour and music dominates the heart-minds of men.[99]

With such powers attributed to music, it was natural that Xun should regard its control by the government as essential, lest unsuitable tunes and rhythms caused "depraved and filthy influences" to corrupt the populace.

He described appropriate ritual behaviour as a disciplining of human emotion within an expressive form of action that was given power and persuasiveness by its aesthetic beauty, and capable of "serving as a pattern for countless generations". Appropriate ritual behaviour had the function of making clear, and of crystallizing, the meaning of various aspects and moments of human life. It had nothing to do with the gods, as the common people foolishly believed. It also restrained men's desires, and this restraint paradoxically produced more happiness than did a lack of self-control. Hence Xun's slightly curious assertion that appropriate ritual behaviour was "nourishing".

To sum up, appropriate ritual behaviour, conceived of in this purely sociological and psychological way, was the most significant single aspect of the social and political order. It was the framework of conduct for the whole of life.

STATE POWER AND INDIVIDUAL MORALITY

The most direct challenge to conventional morality was made by the more extreme of the theorists of statecraft. In essence they argued that the welfare of the state, or society as a whole, required standards and values diametrically opposed to those customarily regarded as admirable in relationships between individuals, and which Confucianism saw as the natural foundation of both society and polity.

A blunt version of this argument can be found in the *Lord Shang*, a work spuriously attributed to Shang Yang, the fourth-century B.C.E. prime minister of the state of Qin, but probably dating from the early third century B.C.E.:

What the present age calls "morality" is instituting what the people like and doing away with what they hate. . . . [But] if you institute what the people delight in, they will in fact suffer from what they hate. On the other hand, if you institute what they hate, the people will be happy in what they enjoy.[100]

In other words, the direct and undisciplined gratification of men's desires rapidly became self-defeating. It led to social and military weaknesses that soon made further gratification impossible. This was the general justification for the advocacy of a polity controlled by laws backed by savage punishments, and designed to coerce people in systematic fashion to work hard at farming and to fight fiercely in battle. The resulting state would be rich and secure, which was what the people really wanted, even if along the way some of the more timorous had to be executed to inspire the others to valour.

The traditional virtues were the seeds of destruction. In a society whose members practise appropriate ritual behaviour, music, filial piety, and integrity "the ruler will be unable to get the people to fight." What is more,

> A state that uses good people to govern the wicked will always suffer from disorder until it is destroyed. A state that uses the wicked to govern the good will always enjoy order, and so become strong.[101]

It was crucial to ensure that individuals were not psychologically or actually stronger than the law. Those with a powerful autonomous morality might be resistant to legal pressures and influence others in the same direction. But "if evil men are given office, the people will love the laws."[102] Culture, commerce in everything that was not a basic necessity, and scholarly learning had all to be destroyed. The people had to be made simple. "The government of the sage has many prohibitions, so as to limit the people's abilities."[103] Any independent source of moral values had to be eliminated. "States are thrown into disorder by the people having numerous private opinions as to the nature of their duty."[104] It was the state's prerogative to decide what was right and what was wrong, and to back its decisions with force. In this way, then, "if, in correcting the people, one uses what they dislike, one will eventually bring about what they do like."[105]

Statecraft theories such as those in the *Lord Shang* were an uncompromising attack, in the name of state wealth and power, on even the possibility of a vision morally and epistemologically critical of behaviour and ideas respectively, and based on its own intrinsic attractiveness and plausibility.

THE DAO AND GOVERNMENT

The Daoist philosophy of ruling that developed at approximately the same time was in some respects the opposite of this cold-blooded statism. Yet it had certain affinities with it, affinities that are easier to feel than to formulate convincingly. Both the contrasts and the similarities may be seen by comparing the *Lord Shang* with the

Scripture of the Way and Its Power. This latter is a short compilation of enigmatic sayings attributed to a probably fictitious sage called Laozi (the "Old Master"). Its date is probably third century B.C.E., but it is conventionally regarded as much older. Both books share a certain ruthlessness. The Daoist sage, following Heaven and Earth, shows no Confucian sensitive concern for others. He treats the people like "straw dogs", yet ultimately to their benefit. Like the ruler idealized in the *Lord Shang,* he is a total manipulator and controller, though he acts through an unobstrusive influence that sustains a seemingly natural order. The realist's law, though an artificial creation designed to meet particular times and circumstances, also functions in an automatic way, untouched by human feelings.

Both despise the Confucian virtues, though for different reasons. "If the state practises goodness," says the legalist, "there will be many criminals." Severity eliminates crime more surely than compassion. The Daoist sees civilized virtues and refined skills as inferior qualities that only arose when original simplicity was lost. He wishes to return to an unselfconscious innocence:

> Remove wisdom, cast off knowledge,
> The people will benefit a hundred-fold.
> Remove concern for others, cast off morality,
> The people will return to filial devotion and paternal love.
> Remove technical skill, cast off pursuit of profit,
> Robbers and thieves will vanish.[106]

Like the statecraft theorist, the Daoist wants to keep the common people uninformed. "They are hard to govern because they have too much knowledge."[107]

Both writers had a strong sense of the paradoxical nature of the world, in which ends could often only be attained by pursuing their opposites. "How did the rivers and seas gain kingship over the streams?" asks the Daoist, and answers: "Through being able to be below them."

> Therefore, if one wishes to rule the people,
> Once must speak as though one were below them.
> If one wishes to guide them,
> One must put oneself behind them.[108]

The *Scripture of the Way and Its Power* offered a vision of a society uncontaminated by progress, without labour-saving machinery, travel, the use of weapons, or books.[109] But its main polemical thrust was against the exponents of statecraft who thought, in the words of the *Lord Shang,* they could "use the death-penalty to effect a return to virtue".[110] The apparent realism of this approach was

an illusion. The nature of the world could not be caught in legalistic
verbal categories. Policies devised on their basis turned constantly
awry. "Things are often increased by seeking to diminish them."[111]
In particular,

> The more laws are promulgated,
> The more thieves and bandits there will be.[112]

Realist statesmen had yet to understand that "one does not force
the empire by the use of weapons, for such a procedure rebounds
on oneself."[113] On the contrary, "the greatest carver does the least
cutting."[114]

The methods of the Daoist ruler should be quite different. He
should nurture life gradually, always retaining a measure of under-
development and so a potential for growth. Hence he can endure.
"Obtaining All Under Heaven is done by not interfering."[115] Such
a ruler is "without any fixed heart of his own, taking the hearts of
the common people to be his heart", yet he is "able to fulfil his
personal ends."[116] But note: the element of transcendental vision
that we found in Zhuang Zhou is missing here. He could not have
imagined a sage unsagelike enough to *want* All Under Heaven.

PATTERNS AND PHENOMENA

During the last part of the first millennium B.C.E. a syncretistic
metaphysics was developed that was to be the substratum of almost
all later Chinese philosophy. Besides drawing on the ideas discussed
in the preceding sections it also contained a variety of other, originally
separate elements. There was, for example, the theory of the Five
Phases of matter. This postulated a productive cycle in which each
element engendered its successor in the sequence Wood/Fire/Earth
(i.e. ashes)/Metal (i.e. veins of ore in rocks)/Water/Wood and a
destructive cycle whereby each element consumed its successor in
the sequence Wood/Earth/Fire/Metal/Wood. There was also a magic-
square numerology connected with the so-called *Map from the Yellow
River* and the *Document from the River Luo.* The classical expression
of this syncretism was the *Scripture of the Changes,* sometimes known
as the *Changes of Zhou.*

The *Changes* is a palimpsest, made up of material put together
over perhaps a millennium. Its core is a manual of divination, said
to have been arranged by King Wen of the Zhou dynasty. This core
has been overlaid with explanations and commentaries, mostly of a
relatively late date, where the explicit philosophy is to be found.
While the book has continued to be used as an oracle, giving guidance

in the making of difficult decisions, it has also been studied as a scripture for its wisdom.

The structure is built on 64 hexagrams. These are graphic symbols composed of all the possible permutations of six parallel horizontal lines that may be either complete or broken in the middle. Traditionally the complete and the broken lines were regarded as "hard" and "soft" respectively. They also stood for Day and Night, the Bright Force *(yang)* and the Dark Force *(yin)*. When each reached the point of fullness it turned into its opposite. Each hexagram symbolized one of the 64 complex archetypal situations that structured the ceaseless transformations of the world. The Great Commentary in the *Changes* states that, when extended by analogy, the 64 hexagrams cover "all possible situations in all that is under Heaven."[117]

The commonest way of explaining the hexagrams was in terms of two superimposed trigrams. Each of the eight possible trigrams was conceived of as a network of hidden correspondences that together made up a mysteriously linked and coherent world of experience. Thus to each trigram there was ascribed a particular type of landscape and weather, particular species and varieties of animals and plants, a season, an appropriate type of activity, a place in the family structure, a colour, a temperament, a shape, a time of day, a part of the human body, a heavenly body, and other miscellaneous attributes. The nature of the hexagram was then derived from the interaction of these top and bottom trigrams, and also from the other trigrams embedded in it.

The oracle was consulted either by sorting milfoil stalks in a prescribed manner, or by tossing coins. This determined which hexagram applied to the enquirer's situation, and which of its lines were destined to change into their opposites as the situation developed. It was supposed to work because of a resonance between the archetypes defining the situation and the behaviour of the stalks and coins, and a link between both archetypes and behaviour and the symbolic forms in the book. The Wenyan Commentary on the first of the hexagrams says: "Similar frequencies will respond in resonance to each other. Similar vital forces *(qi)* will seek each other out."[118] In practice the oracle probably seemed to be responding because its ambiguous yet suggestive symbols, and its generalized and often two-sided advice, helped to put the questioner in touch with his or her subconscious perceptions of the nature of the problem to be solved.

The oracle was said to have been compiled by the sages of antiquity. The commentary called "The Discussion of the Trigrams" says of these sages:

They were in accordance with, and submissive to, the Dao
and its inner power *(de);* and they took their ordering
principles *(li = lieg)* from just distinction *(yi).* By an
exhaustive examination of ordering principles and by
exploring to the full their own natures, they had the means to
arrive at a knowledge of the commands of destiny *(ming).*[119]

According to the Great Commentary:

> The sages had the means to perceive the hidden things of the
> world, and to appraise them through their outward shapes and
> appearances. They made images *(xiang)* of these things and of
> what pertained to them. . . . The sages had the means to
> perceive the movements of the world, and to examine their
> conjunctures and interpenetrations. It was on this basis that
> they set into operation their norms and appropriate ritual
> behaviour. They appended judgments [to the images] so as to
> distinguish between good and evil fortune.[120]

The metaphysics devised to explain this system was a multi-
dimensional dualism based on a proliferation of pairs of contrasting
opposites. The Great Commentary says: "The appearance of the
Dark Force and the Bright Force in alternation—that is what is
termed the Dao."[121] Complementary to this basic contrast were the
Receptive and the Creative (the first two hexagrams), female and
male, warm and cold, container and cutting edge, mare and dragon,
form and energy, and so on. This way of thinking was organic rather
than mechanistic; and it was cyclical, perhaps reflecting the eternal
return of vegetable life, rather than progressive in a linear sense. It
did not see a force of cosmic good at war with a force of cosmic
evil, but only the interplay of good fortune and ill fortune for
individuals. The power that determined events was immanent in
the world, not outside it, let alone infinitely superior to it, as in
much of the Western tradition. Nor did it determine events in a
wholly foreordained fashion. The oracle offered a certain scope for
the operation of human choice, being a dispenser of advice rather
than of prophecies. The overall trend of a situation was at any
moment effectively given, but within the limitations imposed by this
trend an individual might act wisely or foolishly, effectively or
impotently. The sage, it was hinted, could do even more.

Above all, the *Changes* offered the lure of knowledge and power.
The most revealing statement of this can again be found in the Great
Commentary:

> Movement and rest have constant patterns. The firm and the
> soft [lines of the hexagrams] are determined thereby.

Tendencies converge according to their kind. Things are differentiated by the categories into which they are grouped. Good and evil fortune arise therefrom. The constellations take form in the skies, and on earth so do the configurations of the land. Change and transformation become apparent therefrom. For this reason the firm and the soft interact with each other, and the Eight Trigrams set each other in motion. . . . Through the easy and simple means [of the *Changes*] the inner structures *(li = lieg)* of the world may be grasped, and one's position established in their midst. The sages instituted the hexagrams so that we might see the archetypal images. They appended judgments so that we might see where good and evil fortune lie. . . . The *Changes* constitute a model of Heaven and Earth. . . . It is for this reason that we can know the causes of what is obscure and of what is visible. We search for the origins and return once again to the end. Hence we know the stages of death and birth. Semen and pneuma form beings. The flight of the soul constitutes their transformation. So we may know of the circumstances of the outgoing and incoming spirits [*gui shen,* in earlier texts close to "*manes* and gods," but not here]. We are similar to Heaven and Earth, and thus not in conflict with them. Our knowledge embraces the ten thousand things, guiding and benefitting the world. Thus there is no error. . . . We delight in Tian (Heaven) and know its commands. So we are free from anxiety. We are at ease on the earth, firm in our concern for others, and so able to express love. The scope [of the Dao, of the *Changes,* and of those who have mastered it,] embraces the transformations of Heaven and Earth in such fashion that nothing escapes.[122]

This metaphysics was a fusion of Confucian, Daoist, and magical ideas. The description given of the Dao in the Great Commentary makes this clear:

When the man of sensitive concern for others *(ren)* sees It, he calls It sensitive concern. When the man of wisdom sees It, he calls It wisdom. The common folk make use of It every day but are unaware of It, for the way of the superior man is not common. . . . Its abundance [of special objects] is termed Its great accomplishment. Its newness day after day is termed Its fullness of inner power *(de)*. That which gives life to the giving of life is called [the archetypes of] the *Changes.* That which gives actual form to the archetypes *(xiang)* is called the Creative. That which serves as the matrix for their imitation is called the Receptive. Following the numbers to their culmination [at which point the lines change into their opposites], so as to know what is going to happen, is called divination. That which runs through the transformations, linking them together, is called effect. And that which still remains impossible to foresee in the Dark Force and the Bright Force is called the daemonic.*[123]

Under the early empire, and during the first part of the ensuing period of imperial fragmentation in the middle of the 1st millennium C.E., the search continued for the all-controlling active essence that underlay phenomena. It was termed "the science of mysterious things".

CONCLUSION

This brief survey of the main currents of Chinese religious and philosophical ideas before the arrival of Buddhism around the turn of the eras suggests a few rough-and-ready conclusions. First, archaic hypatotheism, the belief in an anthropomorphic supreme God (Di or Tian) presiding in some fashion over lesser gods, gave way among the sophisticated to a belief in an amorphic and unspeaking supreme principle (later Tian, then also Dao), some of whose affinities and differences with God I have tried to suggest by using a capitalized "It" when referring to it. Hypatotheism, in a variety of forms, remained flourishing among the less sophisticated, as in the celestial hierarchy of gods under the Jade Emperor in the China of the first millennium C.E.[125] Second, this supreme principle was to all intents and purposes immanent in the everyday world of visible and tangible experience though in some cases it was (1) logically or chronologically prior to the existing universe, (2) in itself changeless, and (3) to some extent capable of abstract formal expression, as in the 64 archetypal situations of the *Scripture of the Changes.* There was no distinct Other World, whether of gods, God, or universals. Third, the limited ethicalization of late archaic religious conceptions was not developed and systematized, except by Mo Di. Rather, ethics to some extent pursued a path of their own (notably in the cases of Kongzi, Mengzi, and the late Mo-ists). The most uncompromising religious thought disdained conventional ethical concerns in the attempt to reach a mystical unity with the supreme principle (as

---

* Elsewhere in the *Changes* it is asserted that, on the contrary, it is possible to "Know what the daemonic powers are doing."[124] See also the preceding quotation in the main text.

with Zhuang Zhou). Socio-political pragmatism secularized the cosmos (as in Xun Qing and the statecraft theorists). Metaphysical pragmatism (if such a term may be permitted) returned to the archaic search for mundane success in one way or another (the *Scripture of the Way and Its Power,* and the *Changes*). It is noteworthy that there was no Hell in pre-Buddhist China, in the sense of a specific place where the souls of the dead were punished for particular transgressions committed during their earthly lives; nor was there a Heaven with corresponding rewards for good conduct.[126] The transformations of the *Changes* did not involve karma. This complex of points significantly differentiates China in the last few centuries of the first millennium B.C.E. from the other major religious cultures of the Old World.[127] Fourth, thought became conscious of itself during the post-archaic period, but precise thinking that followed logic wherever it seemed to lead came under largely effective attack on the grounds that it either (1) by its very nature falsified the understanding of ultimate reality (Zhuang Zhou), or (2) was socially subversive (Xun Qing). Whether all this amounts to a "transcendental breakthrough" or not would seem to depend on one's definition of the term.

CHAPTER 15

The Structure and Function of the Confucian Intellectual in Ancient China

TU WEI-MING

The emergence of classical Confucian humanism in the sixth century B.C.E., as an expression of the Axial Age, significantly shaped the ethico-religious direction of Chinese culture.[1] Although the mode of thought fashioned by Confucius (551–479) and by two of his many followers, Mencius (371–289?) and Hsun Tzu (fl. 298–238), was only one of several prevalent intellectual currents prior to the unification of China by the Ch'in dynasty in 221, it was the dominant spiritual force that eventually defined the otherwise nebulous concept of "Chinese culture" *(Chung-kuo wen-hua).*

Fung Yu-lan, who was associated with the anti-Confucian movement during the Cultural Revolution in the People's Republic of China, has recently attempted to formulate his interpretive stance on Confucianism. He observed that Confucianism helped inspire the self-consciousness of the Chinese people as a distinct cultural entity.[2] Fung's observation is not particularly innovative; it simply affirms what Ch'ien Mu, T'ang Chun-i, Hsu Fu-kuan, Mou Tsung-san, and other New Confucian Humanists have taken for granted for decades.[3] However, his willingness to reopen the Confucian question as *historically* significant in the Levensonian sense is unusual because it opens the door for Marxist historians to explore the roots of Chinese culture in Confucian terms without directly confronting the issue of valuating the role of Confucianism in modern China. Whether this line of questioning will inevitably lead to a complete rethinking of Confucian China and its modern transformation is unknown, but scholars in the PRC have already undertaken major research projects on the Confucian phenomenon as a necessary step toward a more sophisticated understanding of the formation of Chinese culture.[4]

From the perspective of this renaissance of Confucian studies in the last five years, Fung Yu-lan's observation is symptomatic of a collective enterprise to probe the defining characteristics of ancient Chinese thought and society. This enterprise, led by some of the most brilliant minds on the Chinese intellectual scene, may well lead to a fundamental re-interpretation of the inner logic of Confucianism, the role of Confucian humanism in traditional China, and the relevance of Confucian ethics to contemporary China, if not to a complete rethinking of Confucian China and its modern transformation.[5]

The upsurge of interest in the relationship between Confucian ethics and the entrepreneurial spirit in industrial East Asia has raised challenging questions about the Weberian thesis, not only in terms of its specific applicability to China, but also in terms of its general validity as an explanatory model for the modernizing process. A Confucian response to the Weberian interpretation of modernity, as a way of addressing the complexity of the pluralistic world view of the twentieth century, may well lead to the development of a new conceptual framework for comparative civilizational studies.[6]

My purpose in presenting this brief analysis of the structure and function of the Confucian intellectual in ancient China is twofold: to offer a phenomenological description of an important historical event in the Axial Age, particularly the institutionalization of Confucian cultural values, and to suggest a method for assessing the far-reaching implications of this event in order to understand Chinese political culture in general. I am acutely aware that this is a formidable task and that my research so far allows me to deal with these issues only in a preliminary way. However, my exposure to the most recent literature on Confucian studies East and West has reaffirmed my belief that it is through reanimation of the old that we can attain the new.[7] By "attaining the new," I am not referring to the future of Confucianism, but to a more appropriate methodology, or as I have already alluded to, a new conceptual apparatus.

In my essay on "Way, Learning and Politics in Classical Confucian Humanism," I made the following claim:

> The priestly function and philosophical role in both the public image and the self-definition of the Confucian scholar compels us to characterize him not only as a "literatus" but also as an "intellectual." The Confucian intellectual was an activist. His practical reasoning urged him to confront the world of *Realpolitik* and to transform it from within. His faith in the perfectibility of human nature through self-effort, the intrinsic goodness of the human community, and the authentic

possibility of the unity of man and Heaven enabled him to maintain a critical posture toward those who were powerful and influential.[8]

The Confucian intellectual, so conceived, was relatively weak *vis-à-vis* the power structure of his time. His moral idealism further undermined his effectiveness as a player in the power game. Lord Shang's initial failure to gain access to the king of the Ch'in state and to persuade him to follow the path of humanity and righteousness is not an isolated incident.[9] Confucius' sense of homelessness and Mencius' inability to maintain a lasting relationship with those in power clearly show that the Confucian intellectual and, by implication, the Confucian method, was not efficacious in the political arena. Hu Shih's effort to define etymologically the term "ju" (Confucian or scholar) as "weakling" is, in this connection, most suggestive.[10]

It is quite understandable that the Confucians did not exert much political influence in the period when classical Confucian humanism emerged as a major force in ancient Chinese thought. The politics of the Eastern Chou (8th to 5th century B.C.E.) was characterized by the disintegration of the feudal system *(feng-chien)* and was not at all congenial to the Confucian project of moralizing all forms of human relationship, including that between ruler and minister. As the Middle Kingdom, for a variety of economic and social reasons, gradually but definitively moved away from the elaborate ritual order that had defined the *modus operandi* of the ruling elite, the new power structure, commonly known as the *pa* (hegemony), subscribed to different rules, those of *Realpolitik*. The shapers of the new structure, as a result, were wandering scholars who knew how to flow with the tide.[11] The aforementioned Lord Shang eventually found a sympathetic ear in the king when he unabashedly discussed the concrete ways of enriching and strengthening the state.[12] Mencius, on the other hand, refused to offer advice that would "benefit" *(li)* the state of Ch'i.[13] Since the language of power was in the ascendant, the Confucian intellectuals were, at least on the surface, weaklings.

However, the commonly observed explanation that the Confucians failed politically whereas Legalists such as Lord Shang succeeded in their power struggle to influence politics is predicated on a narrow conception of how politics actually worked in ancient China. If the political arena is defined in terms of access to the decision-making body of the ruling minority, the Confucians failed miserably; and we might add that they deliberately chose to fail. Mencius' condemnation of the powerful ministers as "weaklings" is a case in point.

Ching Ch'un said, "Were not Kung-sun Yen and Chang Yi great men? As soon as they showed their wrath the feudal lords trembled with fear, and when they were still the Empire was spared the conflagration of war." "How can they be thought great men?" said Mencius. "Have you never studied the rites? When a man comes of age his father gives him advice. When a girl marries, her mother gives her advice, and accompanies her to the door with these cautionary words, 'When you go to your new home, you must be respectful and circumspect. Do not disobey your husband.' It is the way of a wife or concubine to consider obedience and docility the norm."[14]

One way of interpreting this statement is to suggest that Mencius was unrealistic and arrogant in reference to power. After all, unlike either a priest or a philosopher, Mencius was actively interested in putting his insights into the political machinery of his time. His inability to communicate with those in power seems to have undermined the very basis on which his moral enterprise was to be built. Mencius' inability to wield enough power to establish a distinctively Confucian political institution seems to indicate that in regard to power politics, he was a loser. His characterization of the powerful ministers as docile and obedient weaklings may seem to have reflected his own sour grapes mentality.

While the Confucians never gained access to the decision-making body of the ruling minority during the Warring States (403–221 B.C.E.) Period, they did become a notable social force exerting powerful control over the cultural system. This was accomplished mainly through education. The Confucian monopoly on education may have been the single most important factor for the reemergence of Confucian intellectuals in the Han dynasty (206 B.C.E.–220 C.E.) as the meaning-givers in society and the authority-legitimizers in polity.[15] This is not to say that the Confucians alone provided the symbolic resources for China to transform from the feudal states to the imperial dynasties. Far from it; the Legalists, the Yin-Yang cosmologists, the Taoists both of the Chuang Tzu and the Huang-Lao variety, and the Moists all seem to have played significant roles in this traditional period. The Confucians, with their particular interest in rituals, represented only one of the many approaches, and a relatively colorless one at that.

Yet, the Confucians were unique in transmitting what they took to be "this culture" *(ssu-wen),* the cumulative wisdom of the ancients.[16] They made education the vehicle by which they spread their influence as messengers of the Way. Confucius himself played a pivotal role in making education, which had been confined to sons of nobility, available to the commoner. This democratization of the educational process released a great deal of energy from the lower echelons of society. The channel of upward social mobility, once opened to the literatus, significantly changed its character. No longer did brute force determine the strength of a contender for power, for no matter how strong a king was militarily, he relied heavily upon the literatus to run his bureaucracy: to help him register the people, collect taxes, settle litigation, negotiate with foreign powers, establish the proper rituals; in short, to bring law and order to his regime and to enhance his presence in "international" politics.[17] To be sure, the king consolidated his position as a center of power by military conquest, but, in order to maintain his control, he had to use the civil bureaucracy to extend his influence. It seems anachronistic that the Confucian, Lu Chia, had to advise the founding father of the Han dynasty that although the empire was conquered on horseback, it could hardly be governed in the same manner.[18] For, prior to the imperial age, the civil bureaucracy had governed China for centuries.

The Confucians were not the first bureaucrats in Chinese history. The diviners, the historians, and the astronomers of the Shang and early Chou (18th to 8th century B.C.E.) performed bureaucratic functions in ancient China. Nor did the Confucians staff the feudal bureaucracies of the Warring States. Furthermore, their commitment to a holistic education to transmit the cultural norms of Confucian humanism was not primarily oriented toward government service. Yet, the Confucians were undeniably the true inheritors of the ancient texts and thus the spirit of the scribe. Unlike the Taoists who tried to transcend the written word, or the Legalists who tried to confine it to the letters of the law, or the Moists who tried to use it as an ideological weapon, or the Yin-Yang cosmologists who tried to manipulate it as a magic code, the Confucians embraced the entire literature and took it upon themselves, as a divine mission, to breathe vitality into it through the art of interpretation. Their hermeneutic efforts created one of the most comprehensive literary traditions in human history. As a result, the symbolic resources available to the Chinese civil bureaucracy for future developments greatly expanded and the institutional continuity between the feudal states and the imperial dynasties was greatly enhanced. The Confucian contribution to the identity and adaptation of the Chinese bureaucracy cannot be exaggerated.

In a broader sense, however, the most significant impact of Confucian education on Chinese political culture lies not in civil bureaucracy but in its definition of the intellectual's role in politics. This brings us back to Mencius' contempt for the powerful minister mentioned earlier. The minister was not a "great man," in part because he did not have a "home" of his own. Unlike the true great man who "lives in the spacious dwelling, occupies the proper position, and goes along the highway of the Empire,"[19] the powerful minister leaves his own abode and serves in an alien house. His respectfulness and circumspection are clear indications that he is not his own master. The analogy of a girl marrying to a new home is apt here because the minister, by accommodating himself to the demands of the king, has lost his sense of personal dignity, autonomy, and independence. The Confucian intellectual, by contrast, never leaves home to take up residence elsewhere. In other words, he defines what politics is from the center of his moral being. Since he never reverses the order of priority (morality precedes politics), he cannot be defined by politics. Even in the exercise of "expediency" *(ch'uan)*, the Confucian counterpart of the Buddhist *upaya* (skilful means), the primacy of moral rectitude is still a precondition for any circumstantial adjustment.[20] The Confucian ideal of "inner sageliness and outer kingliness,"[21] viewed in this perspective, means that sageliness takes precedence over kingliness and that only a sage is qualified to be a king.

As I have noted in "Way, Learning and Politics in Classical Confucian Humanism," since Mencius defines humanity as man's peaceful abode and righteousness as his proper path, "the spacious dwelling," "the proper position," and "the highway of the Empire" all refer to "the symbolic resources that the Confucian intellectual could tap in formulating his own distinctive form of life."[22] Concretely, the home that the Confucian intellectual constructs for himself is richly endowed with poetic, political, social, historical, and metaphysical visions. He has ready access to sagely texts, ancestral instructions, exemplary teachers, worthy friends, and the rites and music of the ancients. Moreover, since he has established an internal resonance with the basic feelings of the people, he is also in tune with the rhythm of his own community. Indeed, he is a spokesman for his fellow human beings. As such, he bears witness to the Mandate of Heaven because, as the ancient proverb states, "Heaven sees as the people see and Heaven hears as the people hear!"[23]

The transcendent reference has enabled the Confucian intellectual to extend his horizons beyond the social system so that his participation in the political arena is not confined to the social context. The common impression that the Confucian bureaucrat could only voice his discontent from within, and that he was incapable of radical protest outside his social role, fails to account for the Confucian ability to mobilize massive psychic energy through direct appeal to the transcendental principle, be it the Mandate of Heaven or the dictates of one's moral will. The convergence of the most generalizable social relevance (the sentiments of the people) and the most universalizable, ethico-religious sanction (the decrees of Heaven) has allowed the Confucian to perceive politics in terms of the ultimate meaning of life and as a basic fact of ordinary human existence.

Thus, through education, the Confucians contributed not only to the development of civil bureaucracy but also to the definition of politics in ancient China. In contrast to the powerful Legalist ministers, however, they did not play an active role in the ruling minority in the transition from feudal states to imperial dynasties. From the viewpoint of *Realpolitik,* they can be considered relatively weak, but they consciously resisted the temptation to play the game of power politics. Dictated by their core values, they initiated their project through education, from the periphery of the cultural system. Their great efforts to democratize education eventually led to a major transformation of ancient Chinese polity. Paradoxically, the weaklings who repeatedly failed to gain access to the center of power succeeded in providing the conceptual framework in which politics assumed its significance.

To characterize this transformation of ancient Chinese polity as the Confucianization of bureaucracy, however, would be one-sided. For one thing, as Confucian intellectuals became actively involved in Han bureaucracy, the values they cherished were also visibly politicized. The politicization of Confucian values as a way of enhancing the ideological control of the Han state and the moralization of politics by the Confucian intellectuals who entered the government service for idealist reasons represent two conflicting currents of thought in Han political culture. The aforementioned Lu Chia, the outspoken scholar-official Yuan Ku-sheng, the famous synthesizer Tung Chung-shu, and the literary philosopher Yang Hsiung are outstanding examples of Confucian intellectuals who wanted to bring their Way to bear upon the political process. They were concerned with the well-being of the sagely learning in the actual functioning of the Han government. Their intention to moralize politics often met with frustration, but their persistence in delivering the Confucian message through persuasion greatly contributed to a climate conducive to the eventual establishment of Confucianism as the official ideology of the Han dynasty. More important, in a broad cultural perspective, was their great contribution to the development of a political language, or more precisely, a grammar of action for all players in the political arena, including the members of the ruling minority. Remarkably, they managed to accomplish this without gaining direct access to the center of power.[24]

Needless to say, the process by which highly sophisticated philosophical ideas were translated into operational principles for governing political behavior was long and complex. The decision of the founding fathers of the Han dynasty to depart from the Legalist model of Ch'in bureaucracy, the legal and political background of those who actually designed the Han system, the necessity of a large governing machinery to run the daily routines of the empire, and other prerequisites of law and order all contributed to the emergence of Confucianism as an official ideology. The Confucian intellectuals, especially those brilliant minds who were innovative and persuasive enough to make Confucian ideas the shared assumptions of the newly emerging political order, were conscientiously involved in bringing this about. It was neither the unintended consequence of scholarly speculation nor the demand of the objective conditions that helped Confucianism become the predominant intellectual current in Han China. To be sure, the Confucians could not have been fully aware of the political implications of their scholarly work, and the circumstantial forces—the predilection of the emperor, the interests of the chief ministers, or the concerns of the bureaucrats—must have contributed to the so-called triumph of Confucianism over other trends of thought, such as Legalism and Taoism. But, the concerted effort of the Confucian intellectuals to present their teaching systematically and pragmatically as the best possible ideological line for the Han empire was the key factor in making this a political reality.

It is commonly assumed that the influential politician Kung-sun Hung (died 121 B.C.E.) and the eminent scholar Tung Chung-shu were the principal figures in making Confucianism the predominant philosophy during the reign of Wu Ti (141–87 B.C.E.). Their extraordinary feat is said to have been accomplished by converting Wu Ti, who was as blatantly ambitious and as thoroughly Legalistic as the First Emperor of the Ch'in dynasty, into a Confucian monarch. Especially noteworthy, as some historians further claim, was the manner in which this monumental phenomenon occurred: no bloodshed, no military *coup d'état*, no visible power struggle, but a peaceful transition. Although there is a measure of truth in this widely accepted account, the "triumph" of Confucianism was actually the result of a long and strenuous process, stretching over the entire period of the Han dynasty. In the perspective of intellectual history, the Confucianism that eventually emerged as the predominant court philosophy was no longer the teachings of Confucius and Mencius. Rather, it was an amalgamation of Hsun Tzu's ritualism with Legalist concepts, Yin-Yang cosmological categories, Taoist ideas, and a host of other contemporary beliefs.

The matter is further complicated by the fact that Kung-sun Hung's promotion of Confucian ideology and Tung Chung-shu's construction of Confucian cosmology belong to two significantly different modes of Confucian persuasion. Wu Ti's adoption of Confucianism as the court philosophy signified the triumph of those Confucians who rose to prominence in his reign. These Confucians were the true heirs of the spirit of Shu-sun T'ung, who, in order to find a niche in the Han bureaucracy for himself and his followers, demeaned his role as a Confucian intellectual by designing a court ritual to enhance the prestige of the emperorship.[25] Shu-sun T'ung's success in making a profession out of his expertise in ritual practices suggested a way of accommodating Confucian values to political needs.

The Confucian intellectuals, such as Lu Chia, Yuan Ku-sheng, Tung Chung-shu, and Yang Hsiung, subscribed to a radically different perception of the Confucian Way. To them, the only niche worth occupying in the government was one from which they could exert moral influence to transform politics into a human order, a world immersed in rites and music. They might serve as ministers or teachers; their primary concern was not the stability of the ruling minority, but the well-being of the people. They took part in the governing process not as servants of the emperor but as messengers of their moral ideals. Since their moral ideals were thought to have been commissioned by the Mandate of Heaven, they appealed to the transcendent as well as to the people for support. Although their relationship to the power-holders was not adversarial, they could maintain an independent posture toward the king as teacher, advisor, critic, or friend, but never as an obedient servant.

Contrary to the widely held interpretive position, Tung Chung-shu's cosmology was not an ideological justification for the divinity of the emperor. His famous thesis, "the mutual responsiveness of Heaven and man," was not intended to assign transcendent importance to the throne. Rather, he wanted to make the emperor accountable for his actions to Heaven above as well as to the people below. Thus, in establishing the supremacy of Heaven as the final arbiter of human worth, Tung perceived the power of the emperor as a relativized authority. Without the legitimizing functions of the cosmic process, the emperor's leadership remained questionable. In his interpretation of omens and portents, which features prominently in his philosophical treatise, the *Luxuriant Gems of the Spring and Autumn Annals,* Tung was engaged in the subtle art of political criticism. The whole practice was predicated on the assumption that if the empire was well governed, not only would the human world be in order, but the cosmos would also be in harmony. If the cosmic process did not proceed smoothly, the emperor was personally responsible for its failing. To correct this anomaly, the emperor had to become more cautious in his leadership.[26] The very fact that Tung and other Han Confucians were totally committed to this view as self-evidently true rendered it particularly efficacious as a principle of governance. Understandably, the Grand Historian, Ssu-ma Ch'ien (died c. 85 B.C.E.), while condemning Kung-sun Hung as subverting Confucian learning in order to please the world, praised Master Tung as a true follower of Confucius.[27]

With the establishment of the Five Erudites of the Five Classics at court in 136 B.C.E., the politicization of Confucian learning entered a new phase. The assignment of fifty official students to these Erudites in 124 B.C.E. spurred the development of an imperial university. The number of students at the university is said to have grown to a few thousand in half a century. Toward the end of the dynasty, the students constituted a major force in the political arena.[28] The implementation of examination systems and recommendations based on Confucian ethical and literary criteria further enhanced the power of the Confucian persuasion. By 1 C.E. a hundred successful candidates joined government service annually after passing through examinations administered by Confucian scholars and the number increased substantially in subsequent years. A civil bureaucracy staffed by literati trained in Confucian classics merged as a natural outcome. From Wu Ti's time on, Confucian learning was a major vehicle for training Chinese bureaucrats.[29] More significant was the establishment of government schools as centers of education throughout the empire. Since the Confucian classics were adopted as the core curriculum and Confucius was honored as the "patron saint" of the schools, Confucian ethics became the social norm for recruiting the political elite.[30] Pan Ku (died 92 C.E.), the author of *Han-shu,* suggestively commented that the path of profit and emolument contributed to the ascendancy of Confucian studies.[31]

The Confucian subversion of the Legalist bureaucracy, or, more appropriately perhaps, the incorporation of Confucian ideas into Legalist practices, resulted in a highly integrated organic system. Beyond doubt, the politicized Confucians greatly influenced the character of the government. For example, the Confucianization of law, a topic that has attracted much attention in Western sinology, began in the Han and eventually became a permanent fixture in the Chinese art of government.[32] The mixing of the kingly way with that of the hegemon, as one Han emperor frankly admitted as the "family method" of the dynasty,[33] produced a pattern of power relationships that was to become an enduring feature of Chinese politics. The idea that the Prime Minister, as the executive officer of the bureaucracy, should be treated as a respected guest of the imperial clan was

partially realized in Han political history, and the right of the worthies
to remain detached from politics was acknowledged by the power
elite. Throughout Chinese history, the government strove to elicit
either the active support or the tacit acceptance of the hermits. The
re-enactment of this venerable ritual in the Han set standards for
later dynasties. While the Confucian injunction that the ruler should
be courteous toward the worthy and humble toward the scholar was
never fully observed, it continued to inspire people of all walks of
life to show respect for the educated. It may not be farfetched to
suggest that in the Han dynasty, the idea of the literatus had already
assumed particular significance in the Chinese mind.[34]

Nevertheless, while politicized Confucian ethics represented the
predominant intellectual trend in the Han after the reign of Wu Ti
and served the Confucianized Legalist state, this is only part of the
Confucian story. The rise of Confucian classicism and the spread of
Confucian morality in society could not be subsumed under the
general rubric of Confucianism as a political ideology. To be sure,
they were closely connected with the attempt of the central government to maintain law and order by ideological persuasion as well
as by legal coercion. But, they were neither epiphenomena nor
dependent variables of political factors. Their course of development
was dictated by impulses of a nonpolitical nature, which could and
often did become politically significant. The role of the Confucian
intellectuals in those areas deserves our special attention.

Confucian learning, in its inception, took the cultivation of the
self as its point of departure. The faith in the perfectibility of human
nature through self-effort as the root of Confucian ethics provided
the impetus for cultivating one's own growth as a project of learning.
One did not study the classics simply to acquire empirical knowledge,
but also to deepen self-awareness. Tung Chung-shu's self-imposed
moratorium for three years so that he could be totally devoted to
his scholarly work was a spiritual quest as well as an intellectual
pursuit.[35] His dictum, "to rectify one's rightness without scheming
for profit; to enlighten one's Way without reckoning achievement,"[36]
meant to suggest that his rigorous effort to interpret the *Spring and
Autumn Annals* was impelled by a sense of duty to know the sagely
truth, rather than dictated by a desire to be useful. To Tung, the
choice of rightness and profit was a clear one, for the true Confucian
commitment to personal dignity, autonomy, and independence was
incompatible with the adultered Confucian interest in wealth and
power under the pretext of public service. Learning for the sake of
the self demanded that self-cultivation be recognized as a precondition for regulating the family, governing the state, or bringing peace
to the world. This sense of priority was irreversible. The insistence

that self-cultivation is the root *(pen)* and regulating the family, governing the state, and bringing peace to the world are branches *(mo)* make it explicit that political service should be a natural outgrowth of personal morality.[37] By implication, those in leadership position must observe strict rules of conduct to make them worthy of their lofty status. The idea of *noblesse oblige* is relevant here except that high birth alone did not guarantee a ready access to power and influence. One needed literary competence, social approval, and moral rectitude to climb the ladder of success. The text of the *Great Learning* captures this spirit in one of its concluding remarks: "From the Son of Heaven down to the common people, all must regard cultivation of the personal life as the root or foundation."[38]

In the realm of political culture, this universalist claim that all must regard self-cultivation as the root led to the obvious conclusion that politics was inseparable from morality and that morality must take precedence over politics. Undeniably, however, the Confucian ideal of "inner sageliness and outer kingliness" was impractical and the demand that only sages are qualified to be kings was unrealistic. Actually no emperor in the Han dynasty, or for that matter throughout Chinese history, was sagely. After all, Wu Ti, who is said to have been converted into a Confucian monarch, remained blatantly ambitious, thoroughly Legalistic, and worst of all, ridiculously superstitious. In reality, Confucian ethics rarely touched the inner lives of the rulers. Often it was abused to serve as an ideological weapon for social control. The Son of Heaven may not have been personally committed to self-cultivation, but he could appreciate the political benefit of ensuring that his ministers were. While the scholar-officials in power might not put Confucian ethics into practice themselves, they could surely see that their task of maintaining stability in society would be made relatively easy if the common people did so.

What actually happened in the Han was far more complex than this cynical view might suggest. There is, however, clear evidence that the scholar-officials in the court were critically aware of the desirability of setting standards of behavior for the society at large. The Erudites' concerted effort to reach an agreement on the governing values of proper human relationships, as reflected in the formulation of the "three bonds" and "five constancies," is a case in point. The fact that well-orchestrated court discussions were organized to ensure that the authority of the ruler over the minister, the father over the son, and the husband over the wife be firmly established, as in the "three bonds," and that the supreme importance of the five basic human relationships (father/son, ruler/minister, husband/wife, older brother/younger brother, and friend/friend) be recognized as in the "five constancies," strongly indicates that the imperial court believed that it was the business of the government to implant ethical norms in the minds of the people.[39]

To use Confucianism as a mechanism for social control turned out to be a double-edged sword for the Han regime. The establishment of the authority of the ruler, the father, and the husband may have been an effective way to ensure the stability of the society under the domination of autocracy and patriarchy. Yet, the Confucian ideology, with emphasis on exemplary teaching and mutual responsibility, also required that the ruler live up to the ideal of kingship, that the father live up to the ideal of fatherhood, and that the husband live up to the ideal of householder. The Confucian intellectuals and, to a certain extent, the scholar-officials as a whole, assumed the role of watchdog, not only for the imperial household but also for the common people. They could help the ruling minority maintain law and order in society and had some coercive power at their disposal to bring the deviants in line. Normally they would exercise their influence through moral persuasion as teachers. At the same time, they could represent the people in addressing their grievances to the higher authority. They could serve as critics and censors when they believed that the sins of the dynasty were still redeemable. They could also advocate the creation of a new dynasty, if they felt that the course of degeneration of the present one could not be reversed.

The Confucians certainly did not see their emperors as sage-kings. They also noticed that, historically, sages did not necessarily become kings. Perhaps they were impelled by the sage-king ideal when they honored Confucius as the "uncrowned king" *(su-wang)*.[40] The logic of this is not difficult to see. If only sages are qualified to be kings, it is highly desirable to make sages kings. Confucius was a sage because he embodied the virtues of humanity, rightness, propriety, wisdom, and truthfulness through moral self-cultivation. The reason that he never became king had nothing to do with his personal quality. This was a serious anomaly. If the time had been right, he would have been king. The most appropriate way to honor him, then, was to respect him as though he had been king. The implication of honoring Confucius as the "uncrowned king" is obvious. Emperors who failed to demonstrate sagely qualities were, at most, probationary kings. This Han Confucian perception is a far cry from the unquestioned loyalty towards one's ruler-father in late imperial China. It is noteworthy that once the emperor began to wonder whether he ought to be sagely, a more tender-minded approach to political matters became inevitable. Understandably, the Confucians focused their attention on the selection and education of the heir-apparent.

Unfortunately, while Confucian intellectuals may have substantially reshaped the Legalist state, they never questioned the fundamental principles of the monarchical system. They may have taken an active part in ritualizing and humanizing the *modus operandi* of the Legalist bureaucracy, but they were unable to restructure it according to the political insights of Confucius and Mencius. The Confucian literati in the *Discourse on Salt and Iron* did raise challenging issues about the nature of polity and society. They opted for a fiduciary community based on mutual respect, division of labor, pluralism, natural hierarchy, and peaceful coexistence. Yet, their idealism was undermined by the Legalist impulse for wealth and power. The arguments of national defense against the threat of the steppe people and necessary government expenditures to ensure law and order were overwhelming. As a result, the Confucian literati could only cherish their thoughts in a nostalgic, historical mode.[41] As the idea of the sage-king degenerated into the practice of king-sage, the king who failed to demonstrate any sagely quality demanded moral and ideological authority in addition to his political power. The king-sage may not have been as destructive as the warrior-despot, but his all-encompassing presence was extremely detrimental to the development of the Mencian "great man."

Confucians longed for the reappearance of the "great unity" under a universal kingship ever since the disintegration of the feudal order of the Chou dynasty. The Han Empire provided a great opportunity for Confucian ideas to become institutionalized. This was, however, a mixed blessing. The institutionalized Confucian ideology may have ritualized law and moralized bureaucracy, but it never transformed the Legalist state into a fiduciary community. Far from it: the politicization of Confucian moral symbols for the primary purpose of ideological control, rather than the Confucian intellectual's intention to humanize politics, became the Han legacy to Chinese political culture. It was the practice of the king-sage, not the idea of the sage-king, that became an enduring political reality in Chinese civilization.

CHAPTER 16

The Historical Background of India's Axial Age

HERMANN KULKE

During her Axial Age in the middle of the first millennium B.C.E. India experienced a dramatic socio-political and intellectual transformation. It culminated in the "urbanization" of the Ganges valley, the simultaneous rise of the first historical regional kingdoms, and the teachings of Buddha. The historical background of this process, however, is still a matter of controversy. The crucial problem is the question as to whether this transformation was the result of an "autonomous" Indian process of the early centuries of the first millennium or whether it derived its dynamics from much earlier Indian or even contemporary external impulses. According to their historical sequence these factors were the Indus civilization of the third and early second millennium, the coming of the Vedic Aryans to the Indus valley and Panjab in the late second millennium and the protracted process of their settlement in the Ganges valley during the early centuries of the first millennium, and, finally, on the eve of India's Axial Age, the conquest of the Indus valley by the Achaemenidian empire in the late sixth century B.C.E..

Till the early twenties of our century, the Vedic culture of the Indo-Aryans was regarded as the earliest civilization of South Asia. The discovery and excavation of the Indus cities of Harappa and Mohenjo-Daro, however, immediately ranked India among the early *Hochkulturen* of mankind. These cities captivate their spectators particularly with their sophisticated town-planning and their highly developed system of drains. Initially, the excavators overemphasized the dependency of the Indus civilization on the early *Hochkulturen* of the Near East during the third millennium.[1] But recent excavations in Baluchistan make it more and more likely that the Indus civilization had its roots in an indigenous neolithic revolution in this part of the world. Archaeological sites like Mehrgarh reveal an uninterrupted series of settlement strata from the late seventh to the third millennium which depict a continuous evolution of agriculture, handicraft, interregional trade and, finally, urbanization.[2]

With regard to the Indus civilization three important problems are still unsettled: Who were the carriers of this earliest civilization in South Asia and who were its destroyers? Because for an evaluation of the historical background of India's Axial Age it certainly matters whether the Aryan population of the later Ganges civilization either has to be directly related with the early Indus civilization or, at least, indirectly with its destruction around 1700 B.C.E.—or whether their forefathers had no contact at all with this early civilization. But even in the latter case a third question still remains open: Did other ethno-linguistic groups transmit some faint knowledge about the earlier Indus civilization which was then reactivated during the second urbanization in the Ganges valley? All these questions focus on the "Aryan problem" in early Indian history and/or the problem of an alleged continuity between the early Indus and the later Ganges civilization which are, according to the conventional dating, separated by about one millennium (ca. seventeenth to sixth centuries).

The assumption of an alleged Aryan origin of, or at least their participation in, the Indus civilization nowadays is rarely discussed outside India.[3] But the question as to whether Indo-Aryans had come into contact with it before its fall or whether they at least discovered some of its ruins, is not yet finally settled. Two factors are of particular relevance in this regard. First of all, we are not yet sure whether the Vedic Aryans who seem to have entered South Asia during the second half of the second millennium were the first Indo-Aryans or whether they had some Aryan predecessors who might have come into contact with the still existing cities of the Indus around 1800 B.C.E.[4] Secondly, a large number of cities and urban settlements of the Indus civilization were discovered after the Second World War outside the Indus valley in Rajasthan (Kalibangan),[5] Himachal Pradesh and Panjab (Rupar). These areas are definitely known to have been the regions of settlement of the Vedic Aryans in the late centuries of the second millennium.

The fact that the great Vedic god Indra has often been praised in the Rigveda as the "destroyer of the forts" *(purandar)* therefore quite understandably led to many speculations about the role played by the Aryans in the rather sudden fall of the Indus cities. Archaeologists once were even sure to have discovered signs of a "last massacre" in the Indus cities for which Indra and his Aryan following "stand accused".[6] Indologists themselves interpret the Vedic material quite differently. On the one side it has been pointed out that expressions like *pur* refer to mud or stone ramparts which don't "fit the cities of the Indus civilization."[7] On the other side, it was shown in a recent study that the term *arma* which occurs several times in the Vedic literature in regard to locations in the northwest might well have referred to *Siedlungshügel* or *tell* of former Indus cities.[8]

Very recently B. and R.A. Allchin made a truly sensational discovery in Taxila right in the heartland of early Aryan settlements. Early excavations at Taxila by J. Marshall (see below) had already revealed a series of three successive cities. The first is represented by the Bhir mound dated about 500 B.C.E., and was most probably established in the historical context of the conquest of the Indus valley by the Achaemenidian Empire. It was followed by nearby Sirkap, founded by the Indo-Greeks in the second century B.C.E. and by Sirsukh, established by the Kuṣāṇas in the first or second centuries C.E. Already in the sixties another settlement was discovered in the vicinity with two much earlier periods, i.e. neolithic and Early Indus periods. In the year 1980 the Allchins were able to fill up the gap between these early settlements and the historical cities of Taxila. Between the Bhir mound and Sirkap in the middle of Taxila they discovered on a small mound the well-known Indus pottery and "higher up on the same small mound we found the red burnished pottery which belongs to the same broad complex as that of the Gandhara graves, and which here we may believe to date from c. 1000–700 B.C.E., or perhaps earlier."[9] The Allchins are not sure whether there was a continuous occupation linking the two periods of the Indus civilization and the Gandhara Grave culture which is usually associated with the Indo-Aryans. But Taxila shows that there was at least a clear topographical continuity of settlements from the neolithicum through the historical period. It is, therefore, quite evident that the final word about the cultural continuity between the Indus civilization, the early Indo-Aryans, and the historical periods has not yet been spoken.

But the Aryans of the North Indian plain were certainly not the only possible carriers or transmitters of an albeit faint knowledge of the former *Hochkultur*. During its later phases around 2000 B.C.E. the Indus civilization spread beyond the Sind to the southeast, too. On the peninsula Kathiawar and around the Bay of Cambay in Gujarat clusters of important towns (Rangpur and Lothal) and settlements of the late Indus civilization have been discovered. And, further to the east, in Rajasthan and western Madhya Pradesh several chalcolithic cultures seem to have existed independently from the Indus cities since the early second millennium B.C.E. In fact, it is exactly this large region, which was outside the settlement area of the Vedic Aryans, where we have definite proof about a cultural continuity in double respect. In Rangpur on Kathiawar for instance several traits of the Indus civilization (pottery and graffiti) can be traced till the end of the second millennium. And in the chalcolithic cultures of the Banas valley of Rajasthan (near Udaipur)[11] and particularly at Eran in Madhya Pradesh proto-urban settlements with mud-fortifications existed continuously till the early centuries of the first millennium. Eran, for instance, is known to have been fortified from about 2000 up to the seventh century B.C.E. when Malwa with Ujjain became one of the areas of earliest "historical urbanization".[12]

It is true that no final proof has yet been established about a definite influence of these post-Indus cultures and the autonomous chalcolithic cultures of central India on early chalcolithic sites in the Ganga-Yamuna plain (Noh, Atranjikhera) and the later beginnings of the historical or "second urbanization" (Hastinapura, Kausambi, Rajghat/Benares). But in view of our hitherto still rather limited archaeological knowledge of this "dark period" an influence of the Indus civilization certainly should not be ruled out completely. This is particularly true for the more "immaterial" aspects of India's civilization, e.g. religious beliefs, iconography, symbols of early punch-marked coins, weights and measures. In a very thorough study of a large hoard of 1,150 silver coins found in Taxila, D.D. Kosambi came to the conclusion that 95% of the punch-marked coins "fell into the range of some very accurately cut stone weights of Mohenjo-Daro and Harappa." (While writing these lines Kosambi might not yet have been aware about the just mentioned discovery of a "Harappan" settlement at Taxila!) And he came to the conclusion which is of greatest relevance for our delineations: "In spite of the complete silence of all written tradition on the existence of the earlier civilization the weight standard of the Indus valley survived unchanged into Mauryan times."[13] In view of the persistency of certain societal norms and their underlying value systems during the historically documented period of India's history, it is difficult to imagine that the immaterial culture of the Indus cities had died out completely within a millennium. On the contrary, it might have well played a, though hitherto undefinable, role in the transformation of the late Vedic civilization when the Aryan population expanded over the whole of northern and parts of central India.

Whatever may be the results of future research on the problem of an assumed continuity between the Indus and Ganges civilizations, there can be no doubt that the beginnings of the culture of the Vedic Aryans were rather modest. The earliest books of the Rigveda, which seem to have been composed in an area comprising present-day North Pakistan, the Indian Panjab and Haryana during the late centuries of the second millennium B.C.E., depict a semi-nomadic and mainly pastoral culture. For instance, during this early period

the word *grāma* which later became the common expression for
"village" still means "treck" and "combat group."[14] Accordingly only
temporary horticulture but no agriculture was known. Despite various
attempts to link these early Vedic Aryans with post-Indus cultures,
e.g. the "Harappa cemetery H" culture of about the fifteenth century
B.C.E., the contemporary or slightly later "Ochre Coloured Ware"[15]
and the (contemporary?) "Copper Hoard" people or the "Gandhara
Grave" culture about 1000 B.C.E.—archaeologically the early Vedic
Aryans have not yet finally been identified.

Some time around 1000 B.C.E. or slightly later a change occurred
in the Vedic society. The late books of the Rigveda contain several
elegies with a hitherto unknown lamentation over the complaints of
the daily life. Slowly the pristine worldview and its norms were
questioned. The reasons of this new restlessness are not clear but
usually it is attributed to population growth and a scarcity of food
and land which might have increased dramatically through a climatic
change during these centuries.[16] Whatever might have been the
reasons, the result was the beginning of a new period of migration
during which the Aryans pushed eastwards down the Yamuna and
Ganges. These two or three centuries of a stepwise conquest and
settlement of the Indian *"Zweistromland" (doab)* is called the late
Vedic period. It is known to us mainly from the ritual Brāhmaṇa
texts and increasingly from archaeological evidence, too. In fact, it
is from this period that Indian archaeologists for the first time are
able to trace Aryan settlements. Their excavations during the last
three decades revealed a hitherto unknown "Painted Grey Ware
culture" which is now unanimously identified with the Aryan culture
of the late Vedic period.[17] The distribution of these archaeological
sites coincide more or less exactly with the Ganga-Yamuna doab
and its adjacent areas. The lowest settlement level of these sites
depict still a pre-urban phase of expanding settlements. Fortifications,
town planning, bricks and coins were still completely unknown. But
copper implements and in a few cases iron, too, have been discovered.

The textual sources fully confirm the archaeological evidence of
a still predominantly rural society. They even make it clear that a
considerably larger part (than historians are usually willing to admit)
of the society were still pastoralists and agriculture only slowly
emerged as the dominant occupation of the people.[18] Obviously more
important were the socio-political changes during this period. The
texts clearly depict a protracted process of detribalization or "territorialization" of the tribes and the beginning of social stratification.
The major social change which took place during this period was
the emergence of the Brahmins of as highly qualified ritual specialists
and of the Kṣatriyas as a dominant warrior and landholder caste.

The caste system of the four *varṇas,* although already known from a late text of the Rigveda, still played an insignificant role. Initially, the characteristic features of the late Vedic society were the symbiotic Brahmin-Kṣatriya relations and their dominant position vis-à-vis the village population *(viś).* Like a textbook of modern anthropology the Brāhmaṇa texts of this period depict the emergence of a dominant rural elite in a hitherto ranked society. And it is a fascinating experience to interpret many of their rituals as (initially sometimes obviously futile) attempts to establish and strengthen these beginnings of stratification by ritual and magical means.

This period of social stratification and territorialization of former Aryan tribes witnessed also the emergence of strong chieftaincies and small kingdoms. Again this process can be detected from the contemporary Brāhmaṇa texts. Their rituals illustrate the stepwise expansion of political power beyond its local clan base and the establishment of small kingdoms.[19] It is perhaps the most rewarding result of Indian archaeology during the last decades that the excavations at most of the "capitals" of the early kingdoms unearthed the Painted Grey ware Culture at their lowest levels. This is particularly true of Hastinapura the renowned "city" of the Mahābhārata. Although this epic has been written down only in the early centuries C.E., it is significant that all the major places of its legendary events including Indraprashta (in present-day New Delhi) brought this Painted Grey ware as the archaeological "key fossil" of the late Vedic period to light.[20]

Archaeological and textual evidence thus clearly shows that the Ganga-Yamuna doab for several centuries remained the centre of a decisive formative process of the Indian society, characterized by the beginning of social transformation and stratification and the development of strong chieftaincies. The importance of this late Vedic period for the crystallization of Indian culture, however, is equally based on a development which took place simultaneously in the spiritual realm. The rise of the Brahmins as highly qualified ritual specialists was accompanied by the development of an increasingly sophisticated ritualism. Very different to the mythical and heroic *Weltanschauung* of the early Rigvedic period, the world was now understood and interpreted as a rational order of rituals. The large number of Brāhmaṇa texts are perhaps the most comprehensive and elaborate corpus of a highly developed ritual rationalism which mankind ever produced. According to J.C. Heesterman "the striking feature of the Vedic ritualism is its unmythical, rational and individualistic character."[21] This Vedic ritualism of the Brāhmaṇas certainly may be regarded as a first comprehensive Indian attempt to discover, and manipulate as far as possible, the all-pervading laws of the cosmos.

The late Vedic period witnessed a further step towards the beginning of Indian history in the middle of the first millennium, i.e. the stepwise penetration into the eastern Gangetic basin between Allahabad and the (modern) Bihar-Bengal frontier east of Patna. It was this eastern region which became the focus of India's future Axial Age. The Śatapathabrāhmaṇa, the "Brāhmaṇa of the Hundred Paths", contains a famous and often quoted passage about the chieftain Māthava Videgha. With the help of the Vedic fire god Agni he moved from his homeland at the Sarasvati river in the Panjab to the east and established the early kingdom of Videha to the north of Patna. "Māthava, the Videgha, was at that time on the (river) Sarasvatī. He (Agni) thence went burning along this earth towards the east; and the Videgha Māthava followed after him as he was burning along. He burnt over (dried up) all these rivers. Now that (river) which is called 'Sadānīrā' (the modern Gandak), flows from the Northern (Himālaya) mountain: that one he did not burn over. That one the Brāhmans did not cross in former times, thinking 'it has not been burnt over by Agni Vaiśvānara'. Nowadays, however, there are many Brāhmans to the east of it. At that time (the land east of the Sadānīrā) was very uncultivated, very marshy, because it had not been tasted by Agni Vaiśvānara. Nowadays, however, it is very cultivated, for the Brāhmans have caused (Agni) to taste it through sacrifices. Māthava, the Videgha, then said (to Agni), 'where am I to abide?' 'To the east of this (river) be thy abode' he said. Even now this (river) forms the boundary of the Kosalas and Videhas".[22]

This text is quite revealing in the context of our delineation about the historical background of India's Axial Age. It shows that the Aryan civilization penetrated rather late and only stepwise into the eastern Gangetic basin, the future heartland of India's historical development. And furthermore it leaves no doubt that the orthodox Brahmins of the western doab, the "Middle Land" *(Madhyadeśa)* or "Land of the Holy Sages" *(Brahmarṣideśa)* looked down upon the "Easterners" because their land has not been "burnt over" by their purifying fire-god Agni. Although, according to this tradition, Agni had ordered the Aryan chieftain Videgha to establish the new kingdom Videha amongst the "Easterners", it is evident from the text that initially he had to perform this work without the support of the Brahmin community. Contemporary texts leave no doubt that those Brahmins who nevertheless went, for instance, to Magadha in the south of Videha were deeply disdained by their orthodox brothers in the West because Magadha was still considered as a very unusual place for Brahmins.[23] In a later period when the Śatapathabrāhmaṇa was composed (the text mentions clearly *etarhi* = now), at least Videha seems to have been regarded as "very civilized" due to the sacrifices which Brahmins meanwhile had performed in this region. But people still remembered that Agni himself, the Vedic god who was most directly connected with the orthodox Brahmanical rituals, had remained back in the "Land of the Holy Sages".

The text does not provide any clue to the time which had passed since Videgha's pristine settlement in Videha and the successive arrival of Brahmins in the eastern countries. But excavations carried out by the Archaeological Survey of India during the fifties and early sixties of our century strongly support the textual evidence that the eastern countries had remained outside the fold of orthodox Brahmanism for a considerably long time. Excavations at places which became the nuclei of future urbanization in the eastern Gangetic plain reveal in their earliest settlement strata a development which was not directly linked with the contemporary cultural evolution in western *Madhyadeśa*. For instance at Rajghat,[24] the earliest archaeological site at Benares, the first settlement period between 800 and 500 B.C.E. depicts quite a highly developed proto-urban stage of societal evolution with pottery, terracotta figurines, and a few iron implements. Towards the end of this period the settlement was even surrounded by a mud-rampart. But regarding its relations with the contemporary Brahmanical Madhyadeśa it is significant that the nearly three meters' deposit of this earliest settlement at Benares did not bring to light any trace of the "Aryan" Painted Grey ware. Even further to the west near the Ganga-Yamuna confluence, Kausambi, the oldest urban site of the whole region, seems to have yielded no genuine piece of this Painted Grey ware.[25] From the absence of this typical late Vedic ware in the east we may therefore draw the conclusion that during this early period the "Easterners" were even not equipped with the various ceramic vessels which were required for the performance of the Brahmanical rituals.

This conclusion leads us yet to another important inference. At least a considerably large number of early Aryan settlers in the eastern countries therefore seems to have remained outside, or even opposed to, orthodox Brahmanism. It is quite likely that a considerably large number of these settlers belonged to those Vedic sodalities which played an increasingly important role during this period of socio-political transformation and constant eastward movement of the Aryan population. Most important amongst these sodalities were the *Vrātyas*.[26] They are known since the Atharvaveda and one of their major habitation during the late Vedic period seems to have been the eastern countries. As they are considered as one of the

earliest heterodox groups[27] which had also retained some pre-monarchic and "tribal" institutions, e.g. the *gaṇa* and *saṃgha,* it is
quite likely that they belonged to these first groups of non-Brahmanic
Aryan settlers in the east. This fact as well as the strong indigenous
elements among the population of these eastern countries and their
unorthodox social habits and rituals might well explain the disdain
of the orthodox "western" Brahmins for the "Easterners". And in
regard to the historical background of India's Axial Age it is certainly
of greatest importance that some of the later "tribal republics" of
the east which played a decisive role in early Buddhism had also
been deeply influenced by the *Vrātyas* (e.g. the *Malla*).[28] Therefore
one still has to agree with Hermann Oldenberg who, more than a
century ago, wrote in his introduction to his famous book on Buddha:
"Whoever looks at the beginnings of Buddhism has to remind himself
that the homeland of the oldest (Buddhist) congregation was situated
in the land, or at least at its borders, to which Agni did not burn
over when he moved towards the east."[29]

But it was not only Buddhism which later on originated in the
unorthodox environment of the eastern countries. Already at the
end of the late Vedic period the first and perhaps the most revolutionary step towards the transcendental breakthrough of India's
Axial Age took place in the eastern Gangetic plain. This decisive
step is represented by the texts of the Āraṇyakas or Upaniṣads which
mark the beginning of Indian philosophical thinking. In a direct
reaction against the all-pervading ritualistic worldview of the Brāhmaṇas, but at the same time initially still deeply rooted in it, this
new philosophical thinking aimed at the discovery of the principles
of life on the basis of a hitherto unknown scientific-like approach.
The "water-cycle theory," the "wind-breath theory," and the "fire
theory" depict three successive stages of a development from an
early natural philosophy, to metaphysics (by the *ātman-brahman*
speculation) and finally to ethics (by the *karman* theory). The micro-
macrocosm speculations which had dominated the worldview of
Vedic ritualism thus gradually gave way to philosophical speculations
on the relations of the immanence and the transcendence.[30]

With regard to our attempt to correlate different stages of societal
and intellectual development of early India with the successive stages
of the eastward movement of the Indo-Aryans, it is certainly of
greatest interest that it was definitely the heterogenous East which
assumed the leadership in the course of this early transcendental
breakthrough. Whereas the orthodox ritualistic texts of the Brāhmaṇas only rarely had mentioned some of the eastern peoples, they
figure most prominently in the philosophical texts of the Upaniṣads.
It is certainly no mere coincidence that Janaka, the king of Videha,

whose country had not been purified by the Vedic fire god Agni, belonged to the leading personalities in the Upaniṣads. The famous Bṛhadāraṇyaka-Upaniṣad describes a great dispute which he arranged for Brahmins from all over the country. It was won by Yājñavalkya for his defeat of the "ritualists" and his masterful exposition of the new Ātman-Brahman theory. Another people mentioned several times in the Upaniṣads are the Kāśīs. As we have seen from the excavations at Rajghat, Benares (= Kāśī), too, had remained outside the Painted Grey Ware Culture which we had associated with the late Vedic culture of Madhyadeśa. But not only the shift from the western to the less Brahmanized eastern peoples of India is significant for this period. What is particularly striking, is the influential role played by members of non-Brahmin castes and even by women in these new and—in the eyes of the orthodox Brahmins of the West—certainly heterodox philosophical discourses.

Simultaneously with (or slightly later than) this early transcendental breakthrough of the Upaniṣads a new and perhaps the most radical sociopolitical and economic transformation of India's history took place.[31] As already mentioned, the late Vedic period had witnessed the stepwise settlement and "detribalization" of the Aryan population, the beginning of a social stratification and the emergence of early chieftaincies. But the society as a whole had remained still in a state of pastoralism and horticulture. Only during the post-Vedic period, from the seventh and sixth centuries B.C.E. onwards, five factors changed the society fundamentally and initiated the beginning of Indian history: regional kingdoms, urbanization, interregional trade, agriculture and the emergence of a new type of intellectuals. Of course, none of these factors were completely new. What was new, however, was the overall material development and a sudden awareness of change which led to a new and often radical innovative thinking. Thus India's Axial Age began.

The new kingdoms had their origins in the "territorialization" of the former tribes and the expansion of the more powerful amongst them. The settlement of the tribes *(jana)* at distinct places *(pada)* led to the emergence of *janapadas* and finally to "great" or *mahā-janapadas*. Early Buddhist and Jaina sources mention 16 *mahāja-napadas*. They covered the whole area of North and partly Central India from the Kambojas and Gandharas in the far off Northwest to Aṅga in the East and Avanti and Assaka in West and Central India respectively. In the central doab the late Vedic Kurupañcālas remained most influential. More important, however, became the "Easterners", i.e. Vaṃśa, Kāśī, Kosala, Magadha, Aṅga and the "tribal republics" of the Mallas and Vṛjjis (who settled in former Videha). During Buddha's lifetime a sanguinary warfare broke out amongst the eastern Mahājanapadas, out of which Magadha emerged as the first regional kingdom of Indian history.

This protracted political process during the late and post-Vedic periods from extended patriarchal households to chieftaincies and first monarchies may be compared to some extent with the similar process of synoikismos in Greece during its contemporary Archaic period, particularly since in both cases this development was linked with a process of early urbanization. Urbanization, too, had its pristine roots in the late Vedic period. But it is particularly this sphere where change seems to have been most radical within one century (roughly the 6th century B.C.E.).[32] Most of the larger proto-urban settlements, from Hastinapura in the west to Rajghat and Rajgir (the capital of Magadha) in the east, became early urban centres of the respective areas or Mahājanapadas. Major indicators of this change were the obvious expansion of the inhabited "urban" area and the compression *(Verdichtung)* of human habitation within it, furthermore brick (though still rarely burnt brick) structures, fortifications, and in few cases the beginning of town-planning in regard to roads and public buildings. For archaeologists the most significant indicator of the new Gangetic urban culture is the new Northern Black Polished ware which appeared in ca. 500 B.C.E. or slightly earlier. It used a hitherto unidentified technique of imparting a lustrous surface of a very high quality. According to the Indian archaeologist A. Ghosh this new ware "meant much more than the emergence of yet another regional ceramics. From its homeland in the central Ganga plains, where it is found in profusion, it was exported to cities like Taxila and Ujjain as a result of commerce."[33]

This new Northern Black Polished ware, however, is not only the archaeological *Leitfossil* of the spread of the new urbanized Gangetic culture. Even more, it is an indicator for economic growth and fast expanding interregional trade. Ghosh refers, for instance, to an early Jaina text which describes the story of a wealthy potter who owned five hundred potter's workshops and a fleet of boats which distributed his products throughout the Ganges valley. It is most likely that his product belonged to the new *de luxe* Northern Black Polished ware which became "the chief mercantile ware that was carried on boats and traded."[34] Its role as a major item and even pacesetter of early interregional trade in Northern and Central India may thus be compared to some extent with the role of the more famous Greek ceramics during a slightly earlier period in the Mediterranean world and with the Chinese ceramics in Southeast Asia about a millennium later. Another significant indicator of the emergent interregional trade during the sixth century B.C.E. was the sudden appearance of the punch-marked coins all over North India. Although they seem to have had some forerunners within rather limited distribution areas (e.g. the cast coins of Kausambi) their obviously simultaneous massive appearance with new cities of the Gangetic plain and their new Northern Black Polished ware gives them a particular meaning for the far-reaching change which took place in the sixth and fifth centuries in North India.

According to some Indian historians, this change was enabled mainly through the massive introduction of iron which by itself formed a major item of interregional trade. R.S. Sharma, for instance, argues that it was the invention of iron for agricultural implements (axe and plough) which revolutionized the early mode of agrarian production in the Gangetic plain.[35] Although iron certainly had been known in several parts of India already in the early centuries of the first millennium B.C.E., it was introduced on a large scale for agricultural work not earlier than the sixth century B.C.E. But only with the help of iron axes and large ploughs the clearance of the thick jungles in the Ganges valley was possible. Only now, agriculture became the main mode of production which soon expanded to such an extent that enough food surplus was produced for the rapidly growing population of the urban centres.

Iron and agriculture certainly played an important role during this period of rapid change. But archaeological excavations have not yet revealed any significant increase of agricultural instruments among the discovered iron implements of this period. On the other side, excavations showed a rather rapid increase of war material among the iron implements (e.g. arrowheads).[36] Iron, therefore, seems to have had a more direct impact on the intensification of the fierce political struggles which are known to us from early Buddhist literature. And the search for new iron ore deposits might have also been one of the reasons of the Magadhan expansionism into its southeastern hinterland which is known till today for its mineral wealth. And it needs no further explanation that iron production and the trade with iron ore and iron implements increased local handicraft and interregional trade.

The extension of agricultural production was certainly of great importance, although apparently it was much less influenced by a change of means of production. More important seems to have been a process of increasing social stratification in the rural countryside. As has been shown, social stratification had already begun in the late Vedic period when the Vaiśyas were more and more oppressed by an emerging elite of landholding Kṣatriyas and the Brahmins. This social stratification led both to a further expansion of agriculturally used land and exploitation of its tillers. Important centres of this expansion seem to have been the proto-urban settlements of the extended patriarchical households-courts of the leading Rajas of the early *janapadas*. It is significant that in most cases these "court-towns" became the nuclei of the early urban settlements which in turn had a direct impact on the agriculture extension in their respective hinterlands. Of major importance in this regard seems to have been the emergence of a strong and obviously very rich class of town-based traders during this period.[37] Most influential among them were the chiefs of their guilds *(śreṣṭhin* or Pali: *seṭṭhi)*. These traders retained their links with, and in some cases strengthened their hold over, the countryside through an extensive trade. Early Buddhist literature, particularly the Jātakas, shows that many of these urban traders earned the livelihood from grain trade. And we know several cases of financial transactions which these urban traders and rich householders carried out with the rural hinterland. In few cases "citizens" collected from an indebted villager up to 1000 *kahāpaṇas* which were identical with the above-mentioned punch-marked coins. The influence of the early towns thus led to an increasing monetarization of their rural hinterland which certainly resulted in an intensivation and stepwise extension of agrarian production. Urban demand for agriculture products and the demand for luxury products of urban handicrafts by the rural aristocracy, therefore, seems to have been the main reason for agricultural development rather than the introduction of new means of production.

The socio-economic changes in the middle of the first millennium B.C.E. thus clearly had their focus in the new towns and culminated in the emergence of a new urban society. Although many of the new towns had originated from early courtly settlements, they were no longer solely dominated by these princely courts. Of equal importance were rich traders and bankers and particularly the chiefs of their well-organized guilds. The early Buddhist texts are full of stories about their great influence at the courts where they were required as indispensable advisors and managers of all sorts of trade and financial transactions. A Jātaka relates the story of a son of the *seṭṭhi* of Benares who was educated by the same teacher as the crown prince. Both became friends and met frequently even after they had become successors to their fathers. Members of this non-aristocratic urban upper-class were particularly eager to provide their sons with the highest possible education. Another Jātaka, for instance, mentions that the *seṭṭhi* of Rajgir, the capital of Magadha, sent two students to a teacher even in far-off Taxila in Northwest India and payed 2000 *(kahāpaṇas?)* as a honorarium to him. Of equal importance for the growth of the urban society was the increasing number and influence of craftsmen and artisans. Their professions are known to us already from the late Vedic texts. But as most of them belonged to the despised Śūdra castes, who were explicitly excluded from the orthodox rituals, they had no chance to raise their status in the Brahmin-dominated rural society. This situation changed considerably in the new towns. Although initially their social status seems to have remained much the same, their wealth increased considerably. And, furthermore, they were able to organize themselves in powerful guilds which were completely unknown in Vedic times.

Before trying to say a few concluding words about the new social and religious movements which originated from within this new urban society it is necessary to divert from our delineations about the growth of this Gangetic society and pay attention for a moment to the contemporary historical events in the West. Around 518 B.C.E. the Achaemenidian Empire had conquered large parts of the Indus valley. For the first time in Indian history, the South Asian continent thus became directly linked with a major centre of world history outside the subcontinent. New towns at Charsada (the Indian Puṣkalāvatī) and on the Bhir mound at Taxila[38] were established which are according to our present knowledge the earliest historical towns of the Northwest. Taxila seems to have become the capital of the satrapy Gandhara. By Herodotus we are even told that India was the most populous of all the nations in the world and paid the largest sum of 360 talents of gold-dust. This levy formed nearly one-third of the total amount which the Achaemenids collected from all their Asian satrapies.

The chronological nearness, if not simultaneity, of these events in the Indus valley and the development in the central and eastern Ganges valley quite understandably raised the question as to whether the Persian conquest directly influenced the "Gangetic revolution" of India's Axial Age. The excavator of Charsada, Sir Mortimer Wheeler, whom we have already met as one of the most outspoken exponents of the theory of a direct Akkadian influence on the early Indus cities, emphasizes most strongly the direct Persian impact on the emergence of India's historical cities. According to Wheeler even the large-scale introduction of iron into Northern India was a consequence of the Persian conquest of the Indus valley.[39] Against this theory A. Ghosh argues that the excavation at Charsada and Taxila, the only two cities which "could have anything to do with Persia, has revealed nothing Persian about them, with the possible exception of an insignificant number of objects that found their way from Persia."[40] Indeed town-planning and the houses of these "Achaemenidian" towns do not reveal anything exciting about possible influences from the Near East. In fact "the plans are so chaotic that it is often impossible to determine where one house ends and another begins".[41]

But architecture and town-planning are certainly not the only possible criteria for an estimation of Persian influence in India. Certain achievements or features of Near Eastern civilization certainly have been transmitted to India under the impact of Achaemenidian rule in the Indus valley. Even if it is doubtful whether the Persian coins of the sigloi type really were copied by the Northwest Indian punch-marked coins, it is certain that a massive circulation of these coins throughout North India began after the Achaemenids had conquered parts of Northwest India. Even more evident is Persian influence in the sphere of Indian scripts. The Kharoṣṭhī script of Northwest India was directly derived from the Aramaic script which was used in the Achaemenidian Empire. Although this Kharoṣṭhī script is known for the first time only in the famous inscriptions of Aśoka in the middle of the third century B.C.E., we have good reasons to assume that the adoption of the Aramaic script in India began already soon after the Persian conquest of the Northwest. And it is true that we know next to nothing about the administrative system which the Persians had introduced in their Indian satrapies. Yet it is difficult to imagine that at least some faint knowledge about the Achaemenidian Empire should not have reached the eastern Gangetic plain exactly at the time when Magadha began to establish India's first historical supra-regional kingdom.

During the last decades a lot of thinking and writing has been devoted to the explanation of the sudden rise of the new urban-based Gangetic culture at the middle of the first millennium B.C.E. which constitutes the origin and historical background of India's Axial Age. Particularly a group of historians at the two universities of Delhi came forward with several contributions to this important question of early Indian history. Most prominently among them figure Professor R.S. Sharma who stresses—as we have seen—the material basis of this development, and Professor Romila Thapar who emphasizes more the societal aspects. In an article on "Ethics, Religion, and Social Protest in the First Millennium B.C. in North India"[42] she worked out various social tensions which arose from socio-economic changes and which were a major reason of the tremendous intellectual changes which took place during this period. Many of these changes which had their origin in the late Vedic period have already been mentioned. They began with the loss of tribal identity during the process of early state formation and the foundation of the early *janapadas*. Further, the emergence of large estates owned by individual Kṣatriya families increased the social stratification. During this process of stratification the former dichotomy of Aryans versus Dāsyus gave more and more way to opposite caste and class groupings of the Brahmin-Kṣatriya castes versus

Vaiśyas and Śūdras. The Vedic society thus slowly disintegrated into "eater" *(attṛ)* and "food" *(ādya)*.

Socio-economic changes and tensions increased rapidly during the process of early urbanization. Whereas the Brahmin-Kṣatriya elite was able to maintain their hold over the rural population, the new towns soon and increasingly felt the influence of the former's "food". As has already been mentioned, the rich bankers and traders originated mainly from the Vaiśyas and most of the craftsmen and artisans belonged to Śūdra castes.

The late Vedic society thus fell apart not only into distinct groups of social classes. In addition urbanization caused a split of the society into two different spheres with their respective urban and rural domains. They certainly cooperated economically and, to a lesser extent, socially. But it is equally true that there was a clear distinction between the old and established rural Brahmin/Kṣatriya elite and the new urban elite with its strong Vaiśya and even Śūdra components. And furthermore it is also a fact that these influential and rich urban Vaiśyas had little in common with their caste "brethren" in the countryside. According to R. Thapar there co-existed therefore also two different systems of social and economic redistribution. The agrarian *janapada* states distributed their taxes, tributes, plunders and fines in awards, salaries, grants and grand ceremonies to Kṣatriyas and Brahmins. The urban society of merchants, bankers, traders and craftsmen draw its wealth mainly from profit and interest and from urban handicrafts. This wealth was partly redistributed in social activities and in ceremonies and urban building activities of the new religious movements.

The tensions which arose in the whole of Northern India from social stratification and the emergence of a new urban society seem to have been further aggravated in the eastern countries due to the heterogeneity of their population and institutions. Aryan settlers were still a minority amongst the indigenous population. Orthodox Brahmanism and monarchical institutions, which meanwhile had become the main props of the Gangetic civilization of Madhyadeśa, had only partly been able to find a firm foothold in the eastern plain and its hilly hinterland. Nowhere in the whole of Northern India the contrast and even opposition between Brahmanical and monarchical institutions on the one side and indigenous and heterodox cults and pre-monarchical institutions on the other side seem to have been more striking than in the eastern countries. And moreover it was this region where the impact of a rather sudden urbanization with all its socio-economic consequences was more deeply felt than in Madhyadeśa. The townships of the east therefore seem to have accumulated a strong potential for new intellectual and religious movements.

It is therefore not astonishing that it was this eastern region with its peculiar socio-economic, religious and ethnic tensions where the final transcendental breakthrough of India's Axial Age took place. The carriers of this breakthrough were renouncers who opted out in a radical strife for a transcendental solution of these tensions.[43] We had already met few of them during the preceding period of the Upaniṣads. But these early renouncers had either retained their new revelation to their sylvan solitude or preached it at royal courts to sympathizing Rajas and disapproving Brahmins. Against this, the "new" renouncers of the post-Vedic Buddhist period created three institutions which formed the very basis of their sweeping success. The renouncers soon gathered followers round them and organized their congregations *(sagha)* like "republic" institutions which they knew from their non-monarchical, "tribal" surroundings of Eastern India. Furthermore they canonized their revelations and carried them as their new message *(dharma)* to the courts *and* the people. And finally they permitted laymen *(upāsaka)* as active participants of a wider community of followers and sympathizers. These three institutions effected an institutionalization of the transcendental breakthrough in the mundane order which was a precondition for the transformation of the Axial breakthrough into an Axial Age. This transformation process culminated in the third century B.C.E. in the life and mission of Emperor Aśoka who had become a Buddhist *upāsaka.*[44]

We may now try to come to some tentative conclusion. As we mentioned in the beginning, the historical background of India's Axial Age (or more precisely: the historical factors which contributed to its emergence) is still a matter of controversy. Its major issues are, firstly, the question of a *continuity* between the Indus civilization and the "second urbanization" in the Ganges valley, irrespective of who might have been the "transmitters" of certain aspects of this early civilization, secondly, the question of a direct *foreign* (and that means Achaemenidian) *influence* as the major impulse of this development and, thirdly, the assumption of an *autonomous process* neither affected by an earlier Indian nor by contemporary foreign influence.

Before trying to find a solution to these issues, it may be helpful to glance for a short while at the historical background of some other Axial Age civilizations. It turns out that the development in India had several very general, though significant features in common with the development in Persia, Greece and Israel. Firstly, all these Axial Age civilizations originated from former nomadic or semi-nomadic peoples who had settled down in their new homelands only 500–1000 years before the Axial Age. Secondly, all these newcomers had chosen as their new habitation the neighbourhood or even frontier regions of early *Hochkulturen*. Thirdly, all these peoples had undergone in a relatively short period a social change from ranked tribal to emerging stratified agro-urban societies. Fourthly, out of this rapid social change in all these societies a group of influential intellectuals arose outside or even in opposition to the established priesthood. Fifthly, during the period of their Axial breakthrough all these civilizations from India in the East to Greece in the West stood in a very direct contact with one or several of the imperial states of the Near East. Israel certainly had the longest and most troublesome experience with imperial neighbours. In comparison to this the other three enjoyed for several centuries a "splendid isolation". But after Persia took the lead under the Achaemenids, Israel, Greece and India experienced, though to a different extent, the neighbourhood of this largest empire of early history.

The first and the last stages of this process, i.e. the nomadic origin of the Indo-Aryans and the broader historical circumstances of Achaemenidian hegemony under which India finally entered the Axial Age, were thus quite similar to the cases of Iran, Israel and Greece. In the interim period there were, however, important differences. In India and Iran the continuity or direct contact with the early *Hochkulturen* was certainly much less evident than in the case of Greece and Israel. Accordingly, the social change and political development during their pre-Axial Age periods came about in a much greater isolation and autonomy in India and Iran than in Greece and particularly in Israel in its exposed location between the major powers of the Near East.

But more important than these obvious differences was another common denominator during this formative period. In all these Axial Age civilizations the socio-political change did not lead to the emergence of the rather "unitary" state societies and state religions as they are known from the early *Hochkulturen*. Instead, the rapid change in these Axial Age civilizations caused tensions of a hitherto unknown extent both in the mundane order and its divine projection. And moreover, despite the far-reaching social changes India and other Axial Age civilizations seem to have preserved still a considerably large space or *Freiraum* for the individual. It is quite likely— and in the case of India even quite sure—that this *Freiraum* was at least partly the heritage of the tribal and nomadic origin of the Axial Age peoples. Obviously the few centuries which had passed since the final settlement of these tribes till the beginning of the Axial Age have been too short to erase completely the old nomadic tradition. This rather speculative explanation of a most important characteristic feature of Axial Age civilizations might be questioned. But it remains a fact that these tensions and the social *Freiraum* existed in all these societies. And it is of equal importance that both these features were utilized and religiously institutionalized by emerging groups of socially independent intellectuals who became the carriers of the transcendental Axial breakthrough.

In order to find a solution to the problems of the historical background of India's Axial Age, one has therefore to look at India in her broader Euro-Asiatic historical context.[45] In all these cases, Axial Age civilizations originated from formerly nomadic newcomers who had settled at the fringes of early *Hochkulturen* and underwent a rather similar process of socio-political and intellectual change and who entered at a certain stage of this process into direct relations with imperial powers which were more or less direct successors to the early *Hochkulturen*. All these factors existed in India, too. Yet it is true that in the case of India we know the least about the channels of cultural transmissions between the earlier *Hochkulturen* and the newcomers and, later, between the contemporary imperial power and the emerging Axial Age civilization. But the very recent discoveries at Taxila seem to depict some continuity from the early Indus civilization to post Indus cultures, the early Aryan habitation and late Vedic proto-urban settlements and finally to a "Persian" city during the Axial Age in India. And, moreover, if we take into consideration D.D. Kosambi's findings about the possible influence of Indus weights on the punch-marked coins of late sixth century's Taxila and remember the example of the two students who were sent from Benares in the east to "Achaemenidian" Taxila, we have good reasons to believe that India's Axial Age derived its dynamics from very similar sources as the Western Axial Age civilizations. The assumption that the Gangetic culture of India's Axial Age has to be seen in complete isolation from the early *Hochkulturen* as well as from contemporary foreign influences may thus be based on our still faint knowledge rather than on the actual historical development. India's Axial Age was part of a larger historical process of the history of mankind.

CHAPTER 17

Ritual, Revelation, and Axial Age

J.C. HEESTERMAN

I

It may seem at best idiosyncratic to connect ritualism with so dramatic a concept as Karl Jaspers' Axial Age. Even if this ritualism is hallowed by the antiquity and authority of the Veda, it is still a phenomenon that seems to be the very antithesis of anything revolutionary. It is supposed to have gone on for ages past and, in the case of Vedic ritual, it goes on unchanged even in our times. Though subject to internal development, it has shown itself strangely impervious to the changes in its physical, social, intellectual and religious surroundings, all of which would, moreover, seem to militate against its very survival. To make the case for Vedic ritual even worse it is credited with the power to bring about what one desires—health, progeny, wealth. It would, in other words, be thoroughly magical and clearly at odds with all that the Axial Age stands for.

Obviously, Buddhism is an incomparably more presentable candidate for the Axial breakthrough. Buddhism, moreover, becomes intimately connected with the Maurya empire that arose together with other new empires at the end of the Axial Age. Giving the empire a new ethical legitimation, Buddhism owes to the empire the realization of its universalistic claim. Even though the Maurya empire lasted only for a relatively short time, the pattern for a new type of universalistic imperial policy, based on the intimate connection of ruler and *sangha*,[1] was set.

The Veda on the other hand kept out of such involvement. True, its ritual does contain prestigious ceremonies that are ostensibly meant for the consecration of kings and emperors, but when performing such ceremonies the royal celebrant is just a *yajamāna* like any commoner.[2] Conversely, the legal authors do not even prescribe these ceremonies for sanctioning the ruler's power. Although they were often used to enhance the standing of the ruler by documenting his access to the Veda as a proper *kṣatriya,* the Vedic ceremonies by themselves did not turn the mere ruler into a king or emperor.

Yet the contention of the present paper is that Vedic ritual—no less than Buddhism or other "heterodox" sects—reflects in its own and powerful manner the Axial breakthrough. Its lack of useful applicability as well as the restriction of its access give it a marginal place that seems to deny any such contention from the start. In post-Axial Hinduism the Veda, and even more its ritual, is, for all its high prestige, controversial, if it is not just treated as an idol that only rates a bow in passing without any further ado, as Louis Renou[3] has graphically put it. The classical proposition that the whole of the dharma rests on or is already contained in the Veda is a pious axiom that vanishes into thin air as soon as one tries to put one's finger on their supposedly intimate connection. In one point at least Veda and dharma are even disturbingly at odds with each other. The very attempts to harmonize Vedic animal sacrifice with the dharma's ideal requirement of *ahiṃsā,* or at least to reserve it a place of its own, show that the relationship of Veda and dharma is a highly problematic one.

But this contradictory valuation, running from transcendent elevation through indifference to outright rejection should put us on our guard. From the beginning the Veda has not lacked in controversy. On the other hand, its extensive body of texts has been preserved in all its intricacy with unique faithfulness which is all the more remarkable when one considers India's otherwise rather cavalier fashion of managing its textual heritage. Both the controversy surrounding it and the care spent on its preservation place the Veda in a class by itself. They may be considered as typical symptoms of the documents left by the Axial Age.

II

At this point we should recall that the Veda is viewed as ultramundane, suprahuman *(apauruṣeya)* truth, in short as "revelation". The claim to being revealed truth is in no way an unusual one for Hindu scriptures which are as a rule considered to have been taught or recited by the godhead to the sage who then hands down the revealed teaching through the teacher-pupil chain. In the case of the Veda, however, the matter is subtly different. The Veda is *śruti,* "hearing", and as such sharply differentiated from *smṛti,* "remembrance", meaning especially the dharma texts. The term *śruti,* however, requires some comment. It implies oral transmission by the teacher to the pupil who learns the text by rote. In this respect the situation is not much different from that of the *smṛti.* However, this is not the way the texts tell us the *śruti* was originally received. They were not "heard" from the godhead but "found" and, especially, "seen" by the ecstatic seers, the *ṛsis*. In contradistinction to the *smṛti* which is received and transmitted through the teacher-pupil chain, there is a sharp break between the vision of the revelation and its transmission by "hearing", *śruti*. That the Veda nevertheless goes under the name of *śruti*[4] suggests that the age of the ecstatic seers is over and the revelation complete. The only thing that remained to be done was the painfully precise transmission of the revealed knowledge by hearing and learning it by rote. From then on the Veda became a fixed and bound body of texts, like the scriptures of Buddhists or Jainas.

The point to be retained is the break between the revelatory vision of the seers and the *śruti* that purports to be the content of their vision. Though one readily understands that the seers' vision is the source of the ritual formulas *(mantras)*, it is hard to accept the notion that the ecstatic visions should be equally concerned with ritualistic minutiae. For the corpus of texts which form the *śruti* is concerned with the systematic elaboration of the utterly complicated ritual. Or, as an authoritative text has it, "Veda means *mantra* and *brāhmaṇa*,"[5] that is: ritual formula and exposition of the liturgical rules. There is, then, a decisive gap between the revelatory vision and its ritualistic substance. It is in this gap—and not in the preceding age of the seers—that the Axial turning point is situated. This turning point does not lead to the exploitation of the revelation but is aimed at overcoming it. It replaces vision and revelation with something entirely different, namely the rational order of ritualism that by itself constitutes ultimate truth and leaves no room for anything so unsettling as revelatory vision.

At first sight this may suggest a retreat from the transcendent breakthrough and its creativity towards ritualistic routinization.[6] It could even be easily construed as a backsliding into a world of myth and magic. Such an appreciation would indeed be in line with the usual evaluation of Vedic ritual thought which is at best qualified, in Hermann Oldenberg's words, as "vorwissenschaftliche Wissenschaft."[7] While this qualification acknowledges a rationalistic impulse, Vedic ritualism is generally considered the hallmark of a magic-bound Hindu world.[8] Only the "heterodox" movements, such as Buddhism and Jainism, would then be the true representatives of the Axial breakthrough. There obviously is much truth in this view, but the question is whether it can be the whole truth. For it leaves us with the obstinate problem of an ancient ritualism that has been kept alive and in exceptional esteem till the present day but is and has always been at odds with the Hindu world and its values.

III

The central concept of the *śruti* is sacrifice *(yajña)*. It is the primordial act of creation and establishes the order of the universe. In the enigmatically involute words of the Rigveda that defy interpretation it is said that "the gods sacrificed the sacrifice with the sacrifice, those were the primordial ordinances."[9] In this way, the text tells us, the gods found their place in heaven and thereby set the rules for men's activity. Starting from this mythic statement one is tempted to view sacrifice as the organizing principle of the Hindu world order.[10] But it is exactly here that the problem stands out clearest. Essential to sacrifice is the immolatory act of violence and destruction. Even if the element of death is minimized, it remains a violent attempt at gaining access to the other world. At this point, as already mentioned, sacrifice collided with the Hindu value of *ahiṃsā*. The very euphemisms for expressing the act of immolation— such as *saṃjñapana,* "making (the victim) consent"—highlight the utter gravity of the sacrificial enterprise. Rather than establishing and guaranteeing order, sacrifice overthrows order by the violent irruption of the sacred. The place of sacrifice is a battleground where one must risk life and goods in the uncertain hope of winning through to the other world. Thus the gods fought their rivals, the asuras, on the place of sacrifice and so must man. Kurukṣetra, the epic battlefield of the Mahābhārata is the gods' place of sacrifice. The ritual brāhmaṇa texts abound in references to these violently agonal procedures. But, significantly, these brief, lemma-like statements are not considered to have a founding authority. Not being by themselves authoritative rules for the execution of the ritual, they are qualified as *arthavāda,* non-authoritative explanation. They are the scattered and fossilized remnants of a lost and discredited world.

This world was the world of the heroic age that the Indian epic— like Hesiod—places in the breach that divides our present world age from its predecessor as a mythic reminiscence of an authentic Axial period. Its warriors were constrained ever again to risk their all in the agonizing sacrificial contest. The invitation to sacrifice is a challenge that the warrior can not afford to refuse on pain of losing his honour.[11] On the other hand, not being invited is a grave insult that may compel one to force his way in and challenge the host of the sacrificial festival.[12] Better still than in the flat and dry allusions of the brāhmaṇa texts the tragic predicament of the warrior ethos comes out in the epic, as when Yuddhiṣṭhira who wants to renounce the insensate violence is reminded that he is bound to stake again "the material sacrifice" (*"dravyamayo yajñaḥ"*) he has won in renewed sacrificial battle. For this, he is told, is the ever-lasting, unending way of existence, the great "ten-chariot road" *(dāśarathaḥ panthā).*[13]

Therefore too the gods are said to drive about on their chariots, while their opponents, the asuras, stayed at home. And it was through their wheeled drive that they obtained the revelatory vision of the sacrificial "work" *(karma).* The statement is, as usual, short and undramatic. The "vision" in this context is, of course, nothing more exciting than ritual procedure. But, however devoid of drama, it is nonetheless highly suggestive of a previous and totally different state of affairs. The interesting point is, however, not so much the hint at the violent warrior ethos, but the fact that this was the condition for the revelatory vision. If we look for what may have been the original context and content of such visions, there is another instance, where, again in the flattest possible manner, the story of a band of warriors is told.[14] They are attacked and plundered on their place of sacrifice—which is also their camp—apparently by a similar warrior band. Their leader is among the slain, but, while the survivors sit in mourning around his remains, one of them has the clear and sudden vision of the slain leader walking along the place of sacrifice to the offering fire at the eastern end and then upwards entering heaven. Here, it would seem, we see in abridged and all but demythologized form, the full scenario: the sacrificial encampment and battleground, the risk, defeat and death, and finally the redeeming vision of the hoped for but till the last uncertain access to heaven. But at the same time this explains why the heroic age where these visions were at home had to come to its end. Or, as Hesiod explains, the heroic race was destroyed by "evil war, some of the heroes before the city of Thebes fighting over the animals of Oedipus and others brought across the sea to Troy because of fair-haired Helen".[15]

If nothing else, the self-defeating pitch of violence to which the warrior was in honour bound time and again to expose his life and goods—even if we discount the hypertrophical elaboration in the epic—could not but call forth a radical reaction. The result was the decisive turning point where the warrior's sacrifice was replaced with the brahmin's ritualism which preserves the concept of sacrifice only in name. In fact, we are told as much by a brāhmaṇa passage, where Prajāpati, the Lord of Life, after an age-long sacrificial struggle defeats and subjects his rival, Death, by the abstract means of the new ritualism. Since then, the text triumphantly declares, there is no sacrificial struggle any more.[16]

IV

The striking feature of Vedic ritualism is its unmythical, rational and individualistic character. The mythical presence of gods and ancestors has evaporated to mere names. Their deeds no longer form the authoritative foundation of the ritual that now finds its authority in itself, in the comprehensive system of rules ordering the limited set of standardized liturgical elements—acts, formulas, recitations and chants. The paradoxical formulation of visionary truth contained the *brahma,* the mysterious inner connection of the universe, in the hollow of the unresolved cosmic riddle. Now, however, "l'énigme essentiel du Veda"[17] has been replaced by the cut-and-dried identification of the disparate elements of the divine and human worlds with those of the ritual. Indeed, identification, based on qualitative and numerical equivalence *(sampad, samkhyānam),* is said to have given Prajāpati his decisive victory over Death. It is the premier intellectual tool for organizing the disjointed universe in the perfect order of the ritual. Even though the sheer weight of intricate detail requires the services of technical experts, the priestly *rtvijah,* the system of liturgical elements and identifications is clear in itself. It has no place for mystery or enigma and, above all, it can be systematically taught and learned.

But the important achievement of the ritual system and indeed its purpose was that it took away ultimate legitimation from the violent and destructive contest for the goods of life and access to heaven. When the ritual still requires the immolation of an animal victim, it is no longer decapitated at the sacrificial stake but bloodlessly suffocated in a separate shed outside the ritual area. Violence and death have been replaced with the ritual mistake to be corrected by equally ritual means. The sacrificial battleground has been turned into a serene and perfectly ordered ritual emplacement. There, freed from the ties and contingencies of the world, the *yajamāna* strikes out on his own. Alone and without rivals or partner he constructs and controls his own universe through the artifice or the ritual. But this artificial universe, for all its systematic control of even the smallest detail, is brittle and ephemeral. The price it must pay for the perfection of its order is divorce from the world. It can only be realized outside society and for the limited duration of the ritual. At the end the ritual emplacement is abandoned[18] and the *yajamāna* goes home again, to his place in society, "as the one he was before".

There is, then, a complete break between the social world and the world of the Vedic *śruti.* The bridge between this and yonder world that sacrifice was meant to be has been broken down. The ritual that took its place could only be transcendence itself—or nothing at all. Therefore it can not be obligatory. It is left to the individual's choice whether he subjects himself to the ritual's transcendent law or not. If he does, it has no direct, visible bearing on his mundane life. In so far as it has an impact it is through the intermediary of an impersonal transcendent mechanism, namely the ritual's invisible or previously non-existent effect *(adṛṣṭa, apūrva)* that in an unknown way will bring about the intended result (say wealth or progeny). This is not however a mystical or magical entity but simply inexplicable as the ritual itself, being transcendent, is inexplicable.

V

The rise of Vedic ritualism broke the coherence of the world and produced an irreparable rift which closely resembles Max Weber's postulate of the *Entzauberung* or disenchantment of the world.[19] The tragic world of the warrior's sacrifice was certainly no enchanted Arcadia, but, at least, god and man were at one in the internecine strife for the goods of life. Even though the pitch of violence was raised to the breaking point it was still one world held together by the nexus of sacrifice. Life and death were not irreconcilable but complementary, success and defeat not decisive but reversible, good and evil not absolute but ambivalent. Nothing is definitive and everything is liable to recall at the next round of sacrifice. In the epic, Bali, the defeated king of the asuras, can still tell the victorious god Indra that at the next turn there will again be a renewal of the battle between gods and asuras, "when the sun will be standing still in the middle." Indra, however, retorts that such a day will never arrive since the sun's course has been permanently fixed, the world definitively ordered.[20] The ever renewed sacrificial hour of truth has lost its power to give meaning and coherence to the world. Instead the world has been definitively split between the transcendent order of ritual and the unreformed sphere of social life.

However, this did not lead to the disenchantment of the world, postulated by Weber. The social world was in no way divested of its mythical and magical meaning and values. It did not become a world where everything just "is" or "happens" but has no "meaning" anymore.[21] Such a disenchanted world denuded of meaning and therefore desperately looking to the transcendent sphere for a new and, this time, rational order and meaning did not arise. What happened was that ultimate value and legitimation, as it was realized and activated in the warrior's sacrifice, was taken out of the mundane sphere. Henceforth ultimate legitimation could only come from the transcendent ritual that took the place of sacrifice. For that reason the whole of the dharma had to rest on or even had to be contained in the *śruti*—a necessary fiction, but a fiction all the same. For the *śruti* is patently devoid of use or meaning for the world's affairs and it is so as a matter of principle. Closed upon itself it has no meaning other than the self-contained rationality of its system. Even if it may be supposed to offer an exhaustive pattern of life regulated by the law of ritual, it is the life of the single *yajamāna*, without regard to the surrounding society, who chooses to spend his life in ritual and can afford to do so.

True, we do find statements that claim a total cosmic effect for the ritual, for instance, that the sun would not rise without the daily performance of the *agnihotra*, the milk-offering in the fire.[22] This is, of course, in line with the ritualistic technique of identification, which equalizes the elements of macro- and micro-cosmos with those of the ritual. The ritual can in this way be viewed as the central mechanism of an ideally ordered universe. Such statements are, however, obviously *arthavāda* and therefore lacking ultimate authority, even though it would be wrong to ascribe them simply to inflated priestly self-importance. They logically follow from the system of identification. The point, however, is that if the ritual should be an essential condition for the maintenance of the universe, it is contradictory that its faithful performance is left to the decision of the single individual. But, as we already saw, the cosmic import is just *arthavāda* in praise of the *agnihotra*. That is: in the final analysis Vedic ritualism rejects its rich potential for magic meaning.

It was not the world that was "disenchanted" but the ritual, when it was stripped of the numinous meaning of sacrifice. Though the word "sacrifice" *(yajña)* suggests a deceptive continuity, it seems significant that the technical term for the central offering act is *tyāga*, "abandoning" or "renouncing", suggesting the free, non-obligatory and non-binding gift without social tension or strife.[23] "This to the god N.N., not to me", as the oblation formula has it. Indeed sacrifice is, in the theory of the four world ages too much for our fallen and spineless age. Its place is taken by the gift, *dāna*.

The result was two separate and fundamentally incompatible worlds. On the one hand the break-away transcendence of rationally systematized but meaningless ritualism; on the other hand an unreformed social world of conflict and ambivalence. Here, in the social world all things are interconnected. It is a world that does not lack in numinous and magical meaning but knows itself to be cut off from ultimate value and legitimation and its arrangements contingent and open to recall.

VI

Yet these two worlds have to exist together and must work out their mutual accommodation, even though their essential incompatibility makes all accommodation precarious. There is, of course, the temptation to exploit the magic potential of Vedic ritualism for worldly uses and abuses. Its brahmin experts could easily turn into magicians and demonstrably often did so. But we saw already that this possibility is in the last resort rejected and the brahmin is forbidden to put his Vedic expertise at the service of worldly interests. The ideal brahmin, like the Veda, stands apart from the world and cultivates the Veda by himself. The world, on the other hand, could not remain unaffected. The brahmin's standing apart illustrates how the world was impaired by the withdrawal of ultimate value and legitimation. Especially the king and the web of power relations he represents stand in need of the brahmin's legitimizing services. But it is exactly the king who is singled out as the one whom the brahmin should utterly shun.[24] The situation is the more contradictory for the fact that subsistence and survival would force the brahmin to turn to the king for his support.

The point is that Vedic ritualism, by out-lawing conflict and violence, not only makes kingship questionable but also aims at dissolving the ties of exchange and interdependence that constitute the social arena. To that end it set the *yajamāna,* as we saw, apart and isolated him on his ritual emplacement. Therefore too, it not only isolated the brahmin, but equally required the whole of society to observe absolute dividing lines, namely those between the *varṇas.* The fact that the numberless castes *(jāti)* are viewed as the outcome of inter-*varṇa* marriages breaching the dividing lines vitally impairs the caste order. Caste society—like any other society—cannot do without exchange and interdependence, but at the same time it is required to honour the principle of *varṇa*-like separation. In short, the strictly ultramundane divisiveness and individualism of the *śruti* threatens the world's vital relationships with disintegration. Hence the tension and controversy surrounding the Veda. They are the more dynamic for being irresolvable.

The unresolved tension not only affected the social world. Vedic ritualism was equally prised open to give way to further but never definitive solutions. It could either follow out the line of other-worldly individualism or it could turn back to the world in an attempt to encompass it. Both roads were indeed followed. The first led to the evaporated ritualism of the "offering in the internal fires of the breaths" *(prāṇāgnihotra),* that is, en clair: eating, ritualized by means of a few simple *mantras* and mouth rinsing.[25] However pale and evaporated this may seem to be, it is more than just a reverential bow in the direction of a hollow and outlived tradition. It is a ritual purified of the last vestiges of violence and death and solely geared to the maintenance of life. But above all it marks the individualistic independence of the eater. Alone and withdrawn into himself he follows the injunction of "sacrifice" in sovereign independence from the world. And this brings us straight-away to the brahminic renouncer who is no different from the ideal brahmin. Both stand apart and have no truck with the world. That the sovereign individualism implied in this type of ritualism is a palpable fiction makes the tension all the more poignant.

On the other hand, the attempt to encompass the world is well illustrated by the re-institution, in the prestigious *agnicayana* ritual, of a wheeled vehicle for carrying the fire that eventually will be installed on the elaborately constructed fire altar. This rite of carrying the fire clearly harks back to the raiding and transhuming treks of warrior bands carrying their fire and belongings with them—the disparaged backdrop of heroic sacrifice, frequently referred to in *arthavāda* passages but eliminated from the ritual and replaced with purely liturgical elements. In this case too the setting out on the trekking expedition and the unyoking at the resting places were replaced by simply taking up the fire in its pot, making three steps and putting it down again as well as by a particular recitation, the *vātsapra* hymn. There was, then, no need anymore even for mimicking the actual trekking. Generally the texts are content to leave it at that. However, this is exactly what a comparatively late and highly systematized text, the Śatapatha Brāhmaṇa objects to. After discussing the case our text enjoins to perform both the abstract ritual and the actual driving about of the fire on a cart. The reason given for this doubling of the procedure is significant. The abstract symbolization is said to be the divine form, the actual driving about the human form. Performing both one makes the ritual "whole and entire", encompassing both the transcendent and the human world.[26] The logic is compelling and deeply sincere, but, again, it is no more than *arthavāda*. The result is an amplification of the ritual as such. But the ritualistic injunction of aimlessly "driving about" can only mimick an archaic reality but not give it new life and meaning. The intended encompassment cannot be validly achieved.

So either way we end in a stalemate. The chasm between transcendent ritualism and mundane reality remains unbridgeable. The world, once unified in the agonal violence of sacrifice, has been irreversibly broken. Society is left unhinged. Its arrangements are permanently undermined by the withdrawal of ultimate legitimation, which in the final analysis requires no less than the dissolution of society. By the same token the source of ultimate legitimation itself could not escape doubt and controversy.

VII

If the Vedic scriptures reflect the Axial breakthrough the question of the historical conditions which led to it seems to impose itself. The question is the more pressing for the unexplained parallelism and simultaneity of the phenomenon in different areas of the old world. The answer, however, must be disappointing at best. As Jaspers has already warned us, it is an historical mystery that the progress of research can only amplify but not solve.[27] If, however, we do not immediately expect to find valid causes, but only try to fill in some of the historical back-drop, we can take advantage of the frequent and telling indications scattered throughout the Vedic ritual texts. These indications seem to centre on the transhuming and cattle-raiding warriors and the violence of their sacrificial encounters where they desperately strove for a way out of *aṃhas,* the narrows of want and insecurity, even at the price of death. It seems safe to surmise— as we already did—that the self-defeating violence of giving and receiving death must have brought on a crisis. But we can only see this in the effect it had of eliminating conflict, violence and destruction from the sacrificial ritual. The actual historical circumstances of an Axial crisis escape us.

The general picture of the ancient Indo-Aryans suggested by our texts is that of a world constantly on the move in a relentless push towards the East. This eastward move is a stereotype of the ritual texts, as in the legend of the ritual fire's triumphant progress from the Sarasvatī river in the West to the river Sadānīra in the East finally to be settled even beyond that border.[28] It is symbolically expressed in the extension of the ritual emplacement to the East and the bringing over of the fire to its new hearth at the eastern end of the extended emplacement. This is even clearer in the processional rituals *(yātsattra)* in which the whole emplacement is each day moved further east. A more balanced and realistic view of the historical process, however, seems to be contained in a passage relating the activities of the ancient Kuru-Pancālas over the year. In the cool season they set out towards the East, settle there temporarily at different places, forcibly take hold of the (winter) crop, feed their men and animals and finally, at the end of the hot season, return to the West again where they stay during the rainy season and work their own fields.[29]

The pattern, then, seems to have been a yearly circuit of transhumance and raiding starting from permanent agricultural settlements and returning there again for the agricultural operation of the monsoon crop. It seems plausible that the eastward movements of the Vedic Aryans should be viewed in these terms, as a gradual extension of these centres and their circuits into the eastern "frontier areas." That this implied a growing density of agricultural settlements—as seems also suggested by the Kuru-Pancālas' seasonal movement to apparently settled areas—seems equally plausible. This may be indicated also by the shift in meaning of the word *grāma* from "trekking warrior band" to settled "village" in the later ritual texts. There, fairly densely settled tracts with contiguous villages are, if not the standard, at least the ideal of peaceful conditions.[30] But this is as far as the Vedic ritual texts will allow us to go. We may surmise that sedentarization and expansion of settled agriculture will have played a role in the rise of Vedic ritualism, but our texts have nothing to say about this, let alone about the urban world of trade, commerce and courts found in early Buddhist texts. Instead the ritual texts keep within the imagery of the trekking warrior who is forever yoking his horses to set out again and lord it over the *kṣemya,* the stay-at-home sedentary people.[31] In this archaic world the brahmin is not yet the later priestly expert but a warrior, who is proclaimed a *brāhmaṇa* at his consecration *(dīkṣā)* and sets out on a chariot, even though the ritual has no use for chariots and wide-ranging movements anymore.

Nevertheless the chariot is interesting. In the first place it recalls the emergence of the mobile "Streitwagen-Völker" and their breaking into the old world at the end of the second millennium B.C.E. Their climactic appearance is the only possible explanation that Jaspers, following Alfred Weber, cites, but finally rejects, for the otherwise inexplicable simultaneity of the Axial Age in areas as far apart as China and the Eastern Mediterranean. Our texts show indeed an enduring fascination with the war and racing chariot to the point where the whole of the ritual is identified with it.[32] But—and this is the second point—the chariot itself is clearly a thing of the past. Its use and technique are no longer clearly understood. The ritual which is now stationary and confined to the narrow limits of its emplacement has symbolized the chariot away. Having lost its reality the chariot has gained a grandiose after-life in ritualistic imagination.

The ritual texts, then, are not concerned with the real world which surrounds them. The historical realities they refer to are those of a hallowed heroic past that the ritual was meant to overcome and replace with its own perfectly ordered world. Our texts, therefore, will not tell us about the historical conditions of the Axial Age. But they do tell us what, in their perspective, triggered the Axial movement, namely the self-destructive violence of the warrior's sacrifice, whose emblem was the chariot. Though it lived on in the imagination of the epic, agonistic sacrifice was deprived of its value and legitimacy by the ritualists' achievement. This can make us understand why the ritual texts faithfully preserved the fossilized but telling remnants of the heroic world they rejected, while neglecting their own actual surroundings. The *śrauta* ritual was created out of the dismembered ruins of the warrior's sacrifice and therefore remained tied to its disembodied memory.

VIII

There is an interesting parallel as well as a contrast with the Axial breakthrough in ancient Iran. Working under the same or at least comparable conditions and with essentially the same dismembered material the outcome was an entirely different one. Both rejected the cyclical violence and destructiveness of the warrior's circuit between settlement and trekking camp. But, while Vedic ritualism started from the menacing mobility of the trekking warrior and chariot fighter, which it transformed into the stasis of the single *yajamāna*'s ritual, the Zarathustrian reform took its stand at the other end of the circuit, in the settled community on which it built its ideal ethical order.[33]

Vedic ritualism exalts the gods who "drove about on wheels", while their rivals, the asuras, stayed at home, in their lordly halls, and lost out. With Zarathustra, however, it is the supreme asura, who holds ultimate truth against the demoniacally destructive devas. Their cyclic conflict is not eliminated but elevated to the ethical height of the battle between Good and Evil. Zarathustra's ethical dualism aimed at reforming the world; Vedic ritualism, on the other hand, taking its cue from the ancient heroes turned away from the world and in the last resort aimed at its dissolution. Both, however, irreversibly broke open the old world of violence and sacrifice.

IX

In the sacrificial arena man had ever again to risk all in the contest for the ultimate truth that held the world together—a truth that could only be expressed in the paradoxical language of the seer's *bráhma*. With the removal of the sacrificial nexus of meaning the paradoxical tension of the personal *bráhma* vision collapsed into the flatly impersonal *bráhmana* or identification of disconnected elements. Connective myth gave way to the birth of doctrine. The demise of the central nexus left an unbridgeable rift, but for the same reason invited ever new attempts at bridging the unbridgeable.

In Jaspers words:[34] "Auch die Achsenzeit ist gescheitert. Es ging weiter"—relentlessly and indefinitely.

CHAPTER 18

Aśvatthāman and Bṛhannaḍā: Brahmin and Kingly Paradigms in the Sanskrit Epic

DAVID SHULMAN

The following pages explore certain elements in the construction of post-Axial Hindu civilization, in the light of the problematic Brahminical ideals which emerged during India's Axial period. The underlying argument may be stated briefly in its essentials: it is that the emergence of classical Brahminical ideology helped to create, and to legitimate, a social order which was by nature indeterminate, disharmonious, self-transforming, self-transcending, open-ended, ambiguous in its central principles, and reflexive at its core. In other words, *despite* the transcendental breakthrough—or as a result of its absorption and institutionalization—what India shows us is *not* a society integrated around a central nucleus of transcendent values and goals, but a society integrated (if that is the right word) around a process of ceaseless *disintegration, transformation,* and flux. Here the center is not stable but deliberately ambiguous or paradoxical, while features elsewhere associated with a society's center—such as political power, on the one hand, and unequivocal ideals and goals, on the other—are relegated to the margins. Not only is the social order itself consistently opened up to questioning—under the impact of the complex of radical ideals linked with renunciation *(sannyāsa)* and the Renouncer, with whom the Brahmin partly identifies—but these same ideals are themselves questioned, undermined, systematically problematized. This process is propelled through two stages, or two dynamic movements: first, the drive toward the radical vision of freedom and transcendence associated with the Renouncer effectively deprives the king, the acknowledged guardian of the mundane order in its totality, of his authority, and vests it in the Brahmin; but the subversive power of Brahminical authority then divides the

Brahmin from within, leaving him oscillating between the affirmation
of the dharmic order with all of its inherent sacrificial violence, and
the negation of that same order. The result is a social order, largely
articulated through these two symbolic carriers, which unravels the
very fabric it weaves.

King and Brahmin together delimit the heart of the classical Hindu
state. Their relations reflect the destabilizing impact of Brahminical
ideology upon the society constructed in its name. For while the
dharma texts may depict, disingenuously, an ideal state of balanced
harmony between these two ideal figures, in reality we find a shifting,
precarious, explosive relation between two unstable entities, each
struggling with his own dilemmas and always threatening to drag
the other down with him into some new crisis. In fact, Hindu
theorists were quite aware of this reality, as innumerable stories
about kingship attest. The symbolic articulation of the Hindu order
expresses their vision of an ever unfinished world fashioned out of
conflict, imbalance, and flux. To pursue this vision, we shall concentrate here on two specific examples—a royal figure and a Brahmin—drawn from the Sanskrit Epic, the *Mahābhārata.* As the "reflexive" Hindu text *par excellence,* and as an apparently early product
of the initial post-Axial period in India, the *Mahābhārata* has much
to teach us about Hindu India's perception of its cultural realities.

The two figures I have selected are, each in his own right, something
of an anomaly. Each shows us an inversion or distortion of what
might be regarded as the normative royal or Brahmin roles. Nevertheless, I wish to argue that in the Epic's own perspective, the
anomalous may also be, in a sense, paradigmatic, and may even be
said to comprise a hidden aspect of the norm. Moreover, the two
episodes I shall describe—although they by no means exhaust the
Epic's discussion of the major types—are clearly of major interest,
dealing as they do with two of the most significant moments in the
unfolding of the Epic story. Moreover, they appear to be intimately
linked to one another, and to the core of the Epic tale as well.

The two episodes are drawn from two books, the *Virāṭa* and
Sauptika parvans, which are not usually juxtaposed. And no wonder—they could hardly be more in contrast. *Virāṭa* is, as we shall
see, one of the most lively, not to say zany, parts of the Epic—a
rich, playful, seductive book with (as van Buitenen was the first to
note) typically "carnivalesque" features of inversion, self-parody, and
ludic celebration.[1] The *Sauptika,* on the other hand, is sombre, grim,
saturated with horrors described with all the stark simplicity which
makes *real* disasters seem unreal; it leads directly into the threnodies
and poignant visions of the *Strīparvan.* The *Virāṭa* is largely comic,
gay, and at least partially optimistic: the epic battle still seems far

away, there is as yet no certainty that it will ever take place; in its stead, the *Virāṭa* gives us the mock battle of the cattle-raid. The *Sauptika,* on the other hand, follows the epic holocaust as a ghastly sequel and conclusion; its tragic tone is relentless and overwhelming; it leaves the scene as cluttered with corpses as any Elizabethan tragic drama—and with no promise, as yet, of any resurrection. Moreover, its dominant emotions—to adopt the perspective of later Indian poetics—are rage, homicidal madness, and unrelieved grief, a powerful and unmistakably tragic blend.

And yet these two books share several important features, including the one which is central to our concerns—the striking transformation of one of the major cultural roles. Both are short, dramatic, action-packed, and graced by an unusual economy of expression (hardly one of the Epic's standard qualities!). Both make extensive and seemingly premeditated use of nocturnal imagery, dreamscapes, visions; major events (Aśvatthāman's raid on the Pāṇḍava camp; Bhīma's slaying of Kīcaka) take place in darkness—either the literal darkness of night, or the metaphorical and more pervasive darkness of disguise. This nocturnal aspect seems connected to the books' fascination with inversion—as if in each case they were seeking to bring out into the open an important hidden aspect of the two basic cultural roles.[2] These transformations have recently attracted considerable scholarly attention, especially in the case of the *Virāṭa*— once regarded as a late and rather meaningless interpolation into the "original" *Mahābhārata,*[3] but now said by one scholar to embody "the 'deepest' level of their (the poets') play with symbols."[4]

We begin by taking a close look at parts of these two books, following their natural order—first the "inverted" king of the *Virāṭa,* then the violent Outcaste-Brahmin of the *Sauptika.*

BṚHANNAḌĀ: THE KING AS EUNUCH AND CLOWN

Although van Buitenen's "carnivalesque" interpretation of the *Virāṭa* has been questioned,[5] one would be hard put not to notice its largely comic tone. This comic stance is surely part of the book's hold on the imagination; as the editor of the BORI edition has noted, the *Virāṭa* is perhaps the most popular part of the entire Epic, and is often used by the Epic's reciters to begin their singing of the text.[6] And yet the book is by no means all light happiness and pleasure: like other Indian comedies, it has a strong undercurrent of sadness and pain. Indeed, the comedy seems to be predicated upon this darker dimension of feeling: the *Virāṭa* opens with the Pāṇḍava heroes on the verge of their thirteenth, and supposedly final, year of exile from their kingdom. According to the terms of the dice-game which had sent them into this exile, they must get through this thirteenth year unrecognized by friend or foe; and they elect to spend the year, in disguise, at the court of *Virāṭa,* king of the Matsyas. Their disguises have elicited much recent comment:[7] Yudhiṣṭhira, the king-to-be, becomes the Brahmin dice-player Kaṅka; the brawny Bhīma becomes Ballava, cook and wrestler; the twins, Nakula and Sahadeva, assume the guises of horse-trainer and cattle-expert, respectively; Draupadī, the common wife of the Pāṇḍava heroes, presents herself as a *sairandhrī,* servant girl and hairdresser. We have omitted the figure of primary interest to us in this paper— Arjuna, the central heroic figure of the Epic and probably, as Biardeau has argued at length, its decisive exemplar of kingship. This great warrior comes to Virāṭa's court in the most improbable disguise of all—as the eunuch *(ṣaṇḍha, klība)* Bṛhannaḍā, dance-master and musician, who is sent to the harem to instruct Virāṭa's daughter, Uttarā.

There is much to be said about each of these disguises, and about the entire context in which they are played out: there are cogent connections between the heroes' year in hiding and the *dīkṣā* rituals of separation and initiatory rebirth (the standard prelude to many types of sacrifice);[8] and the prolonged "festival" at Virāṭa, however rich in playful inversions and ludicrous situations, has a somewhat Nietzschean tone. This is particularly true of the book's first extended story, the episode of Bhīma's slaying of the lascivious Kīcaka— undoubtedly one of the MBh's finest narrative passages. We must pass over this episode here, noting only as we do so how deeply imbued it, too, is with the carnival spirit of the *Virāṭaparvan:* here Bhīma, like Arjuna throughout this book, pretends to be a woman (at his "tryst" with his intended victim, Kīcaka); Draupadī, humiliated by Kīcaka in the court, excoriates her "impotent" *(klība)* husbands in a powerful harangue reminiscent of the ritual revilings of South Indian goddess festivals, or of the Billingsgate aspect of European carnivals;[9] and the final episode—Bhīma's hair-breadth's rescue of Draupadī from a forced suttee with the body of her would-be-lover—crowns the comic melodrama with another grimly humorous slaughter, a timely reminder that these comic escapades can be deadly serious after all. The *Kīcakavadha* clearly deserves a close study of its own.

But we must concentrate on the key figure of Arjuna, who dominates the stage from chapter 33 on (the entire second half of the book). Indeed, Arjuna's disguise is a focal point of interest from the very beginning: as Dumézil has noted, "C'est Arjuna, le faux eunuque, qui a le plus richement inspiré les poètes."[10] From the moment of his arrival at Virāṭa's court, Arjuna presents an incongruous, even grotesque appearance which the Epic's authors exploit to good effect:

Then another man appeared, endowed with wondrous form,
a great man[11] covered with the ornaments of women,
with earrings like buttresses or palace walls
and gilded conch shells, resplendent and long.

Shaking his long, thick hair which fell dishevelled about him,
that great-armed hero with a wild-elephant's stride
made the earth tremble under his step
as he came toward Virāṭa in the midst of his court.[12]

King Virāṭa, beholding this apparition, is understandably perplexed: Arjuna-Bṛhannaḍā's various features simply do not harmonize (he is "a handsome man . . . with a braid and wearing earrings," 10.5). He concludes, quite correctly, that what he is seeing is an archer who is "wrongly attired" (*paridhāya cānyathā*, 10.6). For "her" part, Bṛhannaḍā sticks to her transparently inappropriate disguise, with the added remark—very much in the spirit of the *Virāṭaparvan's* own brand of comedy—"And as to why I have this form—even to talk about that increases my pain!" (*idaṃ tu rūpaṃ mama yena kiṃ nu tat prakīrtayitvā bhṛśaśokavardhanam*, 10.9). And off he goes, sad and yet comical—having somehow passed a royal inspection of his identity as a eunuch—to teach the young princess how to dance.

Arjuna-Bṛhannaḍā puts in a brief, humiliating appearance during the Kīcaka episode—he, too, has to suffer Draupadī's reproaches— but he comes into his own only later, when the Kauravas stage their cattle-raid on Virāṭa's kingdom. The king is away with Arjuna's brothers, still disguised, of course, at a second front open by the Kauravas' ally Trigarta; the defense of the kingdom therefore rests with Virāṭa's son Uttara. This sets the scene for the comic vignette in which Bṛhannaḍā will cast off "her" disguise. Once again, Dumézil has noted the essential character of this passage: "Euripide, Aristophane n'eussent pas mieux fait."[13] We may review the main points of this episode before probing further into the meaning of Arjuna's masquerade.

When the alarm is raised—the Kauravas are making off with Virāṭa's cattle—our heroes are (where else?) in the harem; the vain Prince Uttara is being entertained by the women. Upon hearing the news, he boasts that he will rout the entire Kaurava army and bring back the cattle; if he had been on the spot, the disaster could never have happened in the first place—but now the Kauravas would see him in action "as if Pārtha-Arjuna himself were tormenting them"!

Draupadī hears these boasts and feels disquieted; at her prompting, Princess Uttarā pleads with Bṛhannaḍā to serve as her brother's chariot-driver *(sūta)*. Draupadī, with her keen eye, has apparently sized up Uttara correctly—but Bṛhannaḍā at first protests disingenuously. "What power do I have to drive a chariot? If you are interested in a song, a dance, a musical recital of one kind or another, then I will be happy to help you. . . ." But he allows himself to be persuaded, although his games *(narma, 33.17)* are not yet over: he dons the armor they give him upside-down, and all the girls burst out laughing. In this lighthearted spirit, he (pointedly referred to by one of his more ominous titles, Bībhatsu, "the Terrifier"—33.26) drives off with Uttara in the direction of the Kauravas, after promising to bring the girls bright garments for their dolls *(pāñcālikārtham)* from the battlefield.[14]

From this point on we have a comic diptych—on one side, our two heroes in a clowns' duet, on the other, the Kaurava anti-heroes unwittingly indulging in their own amusing antics. This doubling is, of course, a regular feature of comedy—is it the clown's fundamental loneliness which so often makes him appear with others? Bṛhannaḍā and Uttara may not correspond in their roles here to the White Clown and the Auguste of the European circus, but they are clearly played against each other in a classical pattern of comic mirroring and surrealistic distortion. This scene depicts Arjuna in the greatest depth of his self-parody as king and hero, at the moment of his transformation back to his "native" role—as if he were required to touch bottom before bouncing back to the normative vision of himself in the world. Uttara prompts this transformation by his own ludicrous transition from vainglorious heroics to abject cowardice: no sooner does he catch a glimpse of the Kaurava army—advancing, a spectacle even more frightening than Macbeth's nightmare, "like a forest creeping through the sky" (36.5)—than he panics and wishes to go home. How can he fight, he asks his driver: he is a mere child, all alone, never tried in battle; his hairs are standing on end out of terror. But Bṛhannaḍā refuses to turn back: in what must surely be a self-conscious parody of the opening chapter of the *Bhagavadgītā* (where it is *Arjuna* who suddenly balks at the battle!), he asks Uttara why he will not fight.[15] This is followed by a grim promise: Bṛhannaḍā will drive the prince into the midst of the Kauravas, hungry as vultures for flesh, even if they are hidden inside the earth. Besides, the women would laugh at him if he came home empty-handed.

Uttara is unimpressed: "Let them laugh at me!" And in a flash he leaps from the chariot, leaving behind "his pride and his bow". But Arjuna is after him, his long braid flapping over his red skirts as he flounders over the battlefield in the wake of the cowardly

Uttara. It is an utterly ridiculous sight, and the Kauravas, watching from the distance, guffaw—until it slowly dawns on them that something here is wrong. All the incongruity of Arjuna's disguise suddenly takes on meaning: the skirts and the braid hardly seem to fit those stout arms and thick neck, that heavy gait which shakes the earth. The same doubt which had assailed Virāṭa on Bṛhannaḍā's first appearance in the court now begins to work on them: this person has "something of a man and something of a woman" (*kiṃ cid asya yathā puṃsaḥ kiṃ cid asya yathā striyaḥ,* 36.30); could it be Arjuna? They are not yet sure, but they have reason to feel afraid. Meanwhile, the duet approaches its conclusion: Bṛhannaḍā catches the fleeing Uttara by his long hair.[16] Desperately, and wholly inappropriately, the prince chooses this moment to offer his bellicose driver a bribe: he will give him 100 golden *niṣkas,* eight gems, a chariot, ten rutting elephants—if only he will let him go home. Arjuna-Bṛhannaḍā laughs and drags the whining, moaning Uttarā back to the chariot.

By now the disguise is dispensable: Arjuna announces that *he* will fight and Uttarā will drive the chariot. There is a further comic moment when Arjuna takes the prince to the *śamī* tree where the Pāṇḍavas had hidden their weapons: Uttara refuses to climb up to retrieve the hero's bow, for he has heard that a corpse is tied to this tree. And he is right—the Pāṇḍavas had indeed placed a corpse there to frighten off curious passersby. Uttara fears pollution—is this a parody of the classical motif of the king who carries a corpse?—and Arjuna blandly lies to reassure him.[17] Equipped with his great bow, Arjuna can now reveal his true identity and prepare Uttarā for his role in the battle.

As the two clowns emerge from their comic roles and assume a more properly heroic stance, their enemies become more muddled, perhaps partly in compensation. Another one of the Kauravas' interminable debates breaks out: Droṇa, the Brahmin teacher, points out a number of evil omens and urges caution. This moves Duryodhana to a satirical attack upon teachers and pundits: they are good, he remarks, at showing up others' weaknesses, at telling stories at their ease in courts and palaces, at analyzing human behavior, at finding fault with the preparation of food—but never consult them in a real emergency! (4.42.26). The discussion rambles on: Karṇa glories in the approaching fight with Arjuna, and Kṛpa turns on him with an analogy—if someone ties himself up and hangs a heavy rock around his neck in order to swim across the ocean, what manliness *(pauruṣa)* would there be in that (4.44.)? In any case, it is too late: Arjuna charges into the Kaurava army and sends one after another of the major heroes fleeing.

The poets enjoy a final ironic scene: King Virāṭa, returning home, is worried when he discovers that his son has gone to war with Bṛhannaḍā. "With a eunuch as his charioteer, I doubt that he can survive!" He is disabused of his perception when all the heroes discard their disguises. The book's conclusion—from the blood-stained dicing match to Uttarā's marriage to Abhimanyu, Arjuna's son—cannot detain us now.

What can we learn from Arjuna's adventures as the eunuch Bṛhannaḍā? What does this disguise tell us about the Epic, and specifically about its perception of kingship? The comic nature of Arjuna's experience is clear enough, as are its rapports with some sort of carnival-like inversions—but why, after all, have the poets resorted to this mode? Their choice of comedy at this juncture in the story is by no means self-explanatory. No doubt, as already noted, we have here some symbolic development of a dīkṣā, a period of womb-like concealment which must precede the great sacrifice of battle.[18] But why does it have this patently comic aspect? Biardeau's reading of Bṛhannaḍā as connected to the ideal king's ideal chastity, brahmacarya, ties in well enough with the dīkṣā theme—the dīkṣita, too, must be chaste.[19] We might even go a step farther and see Arjuna's period in the seraglio as a kind of Gandhian trial of innocence and self-restraint—it is, in fact, never made wholly clear whether Arjuna is truly reduced to the state of a eunuch or is merely masquerading as one,[20] and after it is all over Arjuna seems to imply, in an interesting speech, that it has not been easy for him in the midst of so many women (above all the lovely Uttarā, his pupil).[21] The false eunuch's self-control would put Arjuna-Bṛhannaḍā in the same class as the medieval South Indian kings, whose impassivity in various seductive situations is a conventional theme in panegyrics.[22]

Hiltebeitel, in a recent study, has delineated Bṛhannaḍā's associations with Ardhanārīśvara-Śiva, the god in his androgynous form.[23] This is instructive: although, in general, the ancient Indian king's affiliation seems to lie most closely with Viṣṇu (while, as we shall see, it is the Brahmin who is linked to Rudra-Śiva), Śiva's androgyny often evokes comic responses.[24] Indeed, the androgyne is frequently, in many cultures, a prominent clown-type: we may think, for example, of the androgynous clown Semar of the Javanese shadow-theater.[25] Actually, we should probably reverse the above way of stating the matter: clowns, by virtue of their predilection for mixing opposites, for incongruous combinations, for crossing and confusing normal boundaries and categories, have a natural affinity with the androgyne.[26] The particular power of this image (and other related clownish guises) lies in the clown's evident capacity to dissolve order back into an underlying, vital chaos; his perpetual oscillation between antithetical personae or defined roles has the effect of "framing" or offsetting them, thereby loosening their grip on our perception and diminishing their imputed reality. But we are concerned here with a specific, Indian clown and his relations with the Epic's understanding of kingship. We should note in this context that Bṛhannaḍā is not the only ancient Indian androgynous or sex-reversed king: the Epic also knows, for example, the tale of Bhaṅgāśvana;[27] but above all there is the mythic precedent provided (already in Vedic texts) by Arjuna's divine father and prototype, Indra.[28]

These stories have meaning. It is not by accident that Arjuna or his mythic multiform Indra undergo a clownlike, androgynous, quasi-impotent reversal. Nor is it simply a question of a renunciatory *dīkṣā* prior to their heroic restoration. The transformation in itself—or, more precisely, the constant, usually latent transformative potential—may be seen as an integral, constituent element of ancient Indian kingship. The Hindu king, even an ideal, paradigmatic king—and this, as Biardeau has argued, is one of Arjuna's essential images—is never at rest; he is always in danger of slipping into his own antithesis, of being swallowed by his shadow. It is the paradigmatic (though not necessarily normative!) nature of Arjuna's Epic career which lends the Bṛhannaḍā episode its power: several crucial components of kingship, as perceived in the Epic, receive classic expression in this amusing figure. There is, to begin with, the diffusion of identity, his tendency to appear masked or in flux—a constant theme throughout the *Virāṭaparvan* with its delight in secret names, prolonged masquerades, sudden revelations and identity-trials.[29] The king is, at best, an unstable amalgam of powerful and often conflicting impulses. By the same token, he eludes our grasp; no sooner do we feel that we have pinned him down in his dharmic, or heroic, or erotic exemplary role—or, for that matter, in any seemingly secure or nicely balanced relation to some other major figure—than he dissolves before our eyes. (In this sense, Yudhiṣṭhira's agonies of self-doubt are but a self-conscious, conceptually oriented variant of the more general penchant for transformation—seen in a striking symbolic form in Arjuna's more dramatic change of state.) This transformative side of kingship is directly related to the major issue of the king's authority, or rather to his lack of the latter; the Brahmin, though hardly a more stable figure (as we shall see), is abetted in his claim to ultimate authority in his society by the king's hopeless indeterminacy and unceasing oscillation among his scattered personae. But this oscillation takes on a much more specific set of connotations in the case we have been examining: here the king is not simply nebulous and elusive but quite explicitly comical or clownish. The king is an exemplar of comic inversion no less than he is, at other moments, a heroic model. Extrapolating wildly, we might discern a ludic undercurrent flowing beneath the structure of Hindu society, even subsuming that same structure—at least as perceived in the Epic text. Or we might seek to limit this notion to the discovery of a latent conception of kingship as incorporating a regressive stage *(nivṛtti)*[30] with its own peculiar blend of comic features, a renunciatory drive, hierarchical inversions, and identity-diffusion. In either case Bṛhannaḍā's comic role seems to embody a royal link to a chaotic substratum of vital disorder, a potential for transformation rooted in that connection, and, perhaps, a certain reflexive distance from any given role or definition.[31]

At the same time, the Indian king's comic persona is, as we saw, imbued with a darker side. If Arjuna-Bṛhannaḍā is never Quixotic— a wholly tragic, self-deluding clown intent, as Foucault has suggested, on turning reality into a sign[32]—neither is he a luminous, light-hearted Puck (nor, for that matter, an evolving, ever more inclusive and integrated Prince Hal). Arjuna's prolonged clowning has its roots in the tragic themes of impotence, dispossession and exile. The restorative, therapeutic aspects so pronounced in Aristophanic or Shakespearean comedy seem strangely absent from the Virāṭa masquerades. Moreover, in this respect Bṛhannaḍā, disorderly hero and king, hardly stands alone. We turn now to his far more tragic Brahmin counterpart, whose chaotic impulses explode not in carnival inversions but into nightmare.

AŚVATTHĀMAN: THE BRAHMIN AS IDEALIST AND BUTCHER

The warrior-Brahmin Aśvatthāman, though never, perhaps, a particularly popular figure, is one of the most intriguing of the MBh's portraits.[33] He could, no doubt, be most easily dealt with as an aberration—a Brahmin who abandons his proper mode of conduct in favor of the *kṣatriya*'s vocation of war.[34] Unfortunately, although this view could be supported by some passages,[35] it seems on the whole far too narrow. For Aśvatthāman, grisly parody of the ideal Brahmin as he is, at the same time embodies something of the Brahmin's essential nature: his Brahminical traits are stressed repeatedly in the course of the Epic, and, still more significantly, he performs a role which is clearly necessary in the final unfolding of the Epic tale. Aśvatthāman's brutal raid on the Pāṇḍava camp brings to completion the horrific but divinely appointed and necessary sacrifice of war. Moreover, this unpalatable figure—who turns out, as we shall see, to have certain more positive, sympathy-inducing features as well—is an incarnation of Rudra-Śiva[36] and thus the instrument for the realization of that god's destructive designs.

Throughout the earlier books of the MBh, Aśvatthāman plays a relatively minor role: he is the son of the heroes' teacher, Droṇa, who also instructs Aśvatthāman in the arts of war; and he remains with his father on the side of Duryodhana and the Kaurava anti-heroes, to whom he occasionally offers rather sound (and quite properly Brahminical) advice.[37] But if he seems somewhat neglected until the battle nears its end, the *Sauptikaparvan* is almost entirely his. Let us briefly recapitulate its description of events.

The catastrophic war is virtually over; the slaughter has been immense. Duryodhana has been mortally wounded—unfairly, of course, as in all the major confrontations between the Pāṇḍava heroes and their enemies—by Bhīma and is lying paralyzed, slowly dying, beside the pool where he had hidden. Here (as recounted in the final chapters of the *Śalyaparvan,* immediately preceding the *Sauptika*) he is visited by Aśvatthāman and two other survivors of the war, Kṛpa (another Brahmin warrior) and Kṛtavarman. The meeting of Duryodhana and Aśvatthāman is marked by powerful contrasts: on the one hand, there is the dying king who seems, on the whole, at peace with life and with fate—he has accomplished his duty and achieved a death befitting a noble *kṣatriya;* on the other hand, we have the king's Brahmin friend and supporter working himself into a fury at the unfairness of it all, and above all at the unrighteous means which the Pāṇḍavas have used against Duryodhana and most of the other Kaurava stalwarts. Aśvatthāman is simply not prepared to accept the outcome staring him in the face, and he asks Duryodhana to make him, Aśvatthāman, the last Kaurava general *(senāpati)* in the interests of revenge: he swears by all his accumulated merits, gifts, *tapas,* that he will slay all the Pāṇḍava supporters that he can find. Duryodhana acquiesces and anoints him on the spot.

This is the point at which the *Sauptikaparvan* opens: Aśvatthāman and his two followers, blood-stained and exhausted, are wandering through the night in a dense, eery, demon-infested forest near the Pāṇḍavas' encampment. Aśvatthāman, consumed by grief at Duryodhana's fate, is nursing his anger and resentment; these highly charged emotions, festering in the unsettling context of the darkness pierced by the cries of the prowling animals of the night, slowly drive him to the brink of madness. A strange vision pushes him over the brink: he sees a huge and terrifying owl swoop down on a multitude of crows sleeping peacefully on the branches of a banyan tree. This slaughter of the crows serves Aśvatthāman as a model: he has no chance of surviving an open combat with the Pāṇḍavas, but he could accomplish his goal by catching them unaware, in their sleep. And he feels wholly justified in resorting to this cruel ruse:

have not the Pāṇḍavas perpetrated deceitful and blameworthy crimes
at every step of the conflict (10.1.49)?

It is important to note the care with which Aśvatthāman's emotional state is portrayed; it is this state which allows him to take
his fateful decision. If he is mad—and he is clearly regarded as such
by his two companions when he informs them of his plan—there
is still logic in his madness: the grief and rage which overwhelm
him have a profoundly realistic basis in the cruel and conspicuously
unrighteous deaths of his friends, his king, and, closest to home, his
own father Droṇa. Let us listen for a moment to Aśvatthāman's
angry lament:

> How terrible is the sorrow of that person who must always
> recall, in this world, his father's death: it burns my heart
> relentlessly, night and day. I saw my father killed by evil
> men—you saw it all, too—and that, above all, cuts into my
> inner parts. How could someone like me live on in the world
> for even a moment after hearing from the Pāñcālas that
> Droṇa was slain? I cannot bear the thought of living unless I
> kill Dhṛṣṭadyumna in battle: he killed my father, so I must
> kill him and all those Pāñcālas who follow him. Those groans
> which I heard coming from the king as he lay with his thighs
> broken—who is so cruel that his heart would not burn at that
> sound? Who is so lacking in compassion that he would not
> weep after hearing those words of the wounded king? Those
> with whom I sided have been defeated, and I am still alive—
> that heightens my sorrow, as a raging flood fills further the
> sea. How can I sleep tonight or feel at ease, with my mind
> filled, as it is, with this single concern?
>
> (10.4.23–29)

One can hardly help but sympathize with the person crazed by so
much sorrow, and there is every reason to believe that the Epic
poets wished to arouse such an understanding, even if, on another
level, they failed to condone Aśvatthāman's actions. As we shall see,
there is also a matter of principle involved. Given the intensity of
the Brahmin's reaction to the mounting series of tragic losses, we
can also understand why Kṛpa and Kṛtavarman fail to sway him
from his chosen course. The three heroes argue, in a gloomy parody
of a Brahminical council, replete with proof-texts and logical claims
and counter-claims: once again, as in the Virāṭa episode discussed
above (but from a wholly different perspective), we seem to find
deliberate echoes of the *Gītā* (in Kṛpa's praise of proper human
effort—*utthāna, puruṣakāra*—and of yoga, 10.2.22–24). Indeed, Kṛpa
gives eloquent voice in this chapter to the complex dualism of fate

(daiva) and human effort which constitutes a major theme throughout the Epic.[38] But it is all to no avail—Aśvatthāman has by now been wholly possessed by the divine fate driving onward to disaster. He refuses his friends' advice (to get a good night's sleep, come back to himself, and then fight a fair battle in the morning) and rushes off toward his enemies' camp, with Kṛpa and Kṛtavarman following rather reluctantly behind.

Before he can enter the camp, he must pass a trial which emphasizes his identity with Rudra: a huge *bhūta* emitting flames from thousands of eyes bars his way at the gate. Unable to defeat this apparition, Aśvatthāman worships Śiva—the real source of this test[39]—and offers himself in self-sacrifice *(ātmayajña)* upon a golden altar which has miraculously appeared. The sacrifice has the desired effect—a classical Śaiva epiphany, in which Śiva reveals that the Pāñcālas' time has run out, gives Aśvatthāman a glittering sword, and enters into his body, making to glow with an unearthly brilliance.

What follows—Chapter 8, the heart and climax of the *Sauptika-parvan*—can hardly be adequately summarized; no-one who has read this passage in the original is likely to forget it. Suffice it to say that Aśvatthāman, drunk on anger, grief, and the divine power within him, rampages through the camp of his enemies, most of whom he brutally slaughters in their sleep. The first death sets the pattern: Aśvatthāman wakes Dhṛṣṭadyumna (the slayer of his father, Droṇa) with a violent kick, seizes him by the hair and pommels him into the earth; when Dhṛṣṭadyumna, still half asleep and unable to resist, pleads with his tormentor to slay him quickly, with his sword, so that he may reach the heaven of heroes killed in battle, Aśvatthāman heartlessly refuses; instead, he pounds him to death with his feet (10.8.12–21). And so it goes, in a horrendous orgy of screams and gore; the five Pāṇḍava heroes, who have gone to sleep outside the camp at Kṛṣṇa's prescient instigation, survive the slaughter, but their sons, grandsons, and allies are all killed. The few who manage to flee Aśvatthāman's avenging sword are cut down by Kṛpa and Kṛta-varman at the gates. The graphic descriptions of the holocaust are suffused throughout by sacrificial metaphors and similes; Aśvatthā-man is compared to the Destroyer let loose by time *(kālasṛṣṭa ivāntakaḥ,* 8.72). The whole grisly nocturnal scene has all the compelling horror of a nightmare coming true—and indeed the heroes see before them, in the moment of their death, the smiling, red-eyed, red-faced, red-garmented lady with a noose in her hand (Kālī, Kālarātri, Śikhaṇḍinī) of whom they had dreamt each night, in terror, since the war began (8.64–67).

At last it is over: dawn finds Aśvatthāman drenched in human blood, the hilt of his sword clenched so firmly in his hand that it

has become one with his body (8.136). And he is happy—he has
carried out his promise to Duryodhana and discharged his debt to
his father. With his two companions he hastens to inform the dying
king of his revenge, and with this comforting news Duryodhana
expires. Aśvatthāman, grieving for the king but also, it would appear,
afraid that the Pāṇḍavas will pursue him, takes to his chariot.

He has one last role to play on the Epic stage. First the Pāṇḍava
heroes must discover the extent of their loss; first reports of the
carnage inspire Yudhiṣṭhira's succinct cry of mourning, more terrible
in a way than all his subsequent agonies of remorse:

> *jīyamānā jayanty anye jayamānā vayaṃ jītāḥ* (10.10.10).
> "The others, though vanquished, have won;
> we, in our victory, have been defeated."

But it is Draupadī's bitter lament at the site of the carnage which
is most telling; and it is Draupadī who, in keeping with her character
as a fierce and high-minded *kṣatriya* wife and mother, thinks first
of vengeance. As in previous emergencies and disasters (such as the
Kīcaka episode mentioned above), she turns to Bhīma, the only one
of her five husbands upon whom she can always rely; she demands
that he bring her the jewel which Aśvatthāman has carried on his
forehead since birth. Bhīma rushes off, to be followed almost at once
by Yudhiṣṭhira and Arjuna, who have been warned by Kṛṣṇa of
Aśvatthāman's dangerous power—specifically, his possession of the
dread *brahmaśiras* weapon. They find him, covered with dust, his
hair dishevelled, but otherwise in a classic Brahminical pose—seated
on the bank of the Ganges near the venerable Vyāsa, wearing a
garment of *kuśa*-grass, his body smeared with ghee. In fact, Aśvatthāman seems at this moment like a spectre from the past: we may
be reminded of the wild Vrātya with his vision of Rudra, or of the
long-haired poison-drinking sage of the Vedic hymn.[40] And it is, it
would appear, still as a representative of Rudra that Aśvatthāman
enters into his final confrontation: he casts his weapon "for the
destruction of the Pāṇḍavas" *(apāṇḍavāya),* while Arjuna, at Kṛṣṇa's
behest, shoots to neutralize this threat. The resulting stand-off nearly
destroys the world; Arjuna accedes to the request of Vyāsa and
Nārada to withdraw his weapon, but Aśvatthāman cannot do so—
he has none of Arjuna's superb control, nothing of his truthfulness
or chastity, and he is unable to recall the missile he released in
wrath. It will end only by destroying all the embryos carried in the
wombs of the Pāṇḍava wives—including the future king Parikṣit,
who will be stillborn and then revived by Kṛṣṇa.

For this, Aśvatthāman is cursed by Kṛṣṇa: for three thousand years he will wander the earth, alone, reeking of pus and blood, without friends or companions, in forests and uninhabited countries, burdened by all forms of disease. Aśvatthāman accepts this punishment—"I shall survive," he says to Vyāsa, "*together with you* among men"—and he is, no doubt, wandering among us still.

Aśvatthāman's punishment, which puts him in a class with Cain and with the wandering Ahasuerus of medieval folklore, is clearly one of the most severe in the Epic—far worse, it would seem, than a mere death in battle (though not, perhaps, that much worse than *surviving* the war to rule a decimated world, as Yudhiṣṭhira must do). On the other hand, even this punishment appears to mimic, like the rest of Aśvatthāman's life, a classical Brahminical role—that of the lonely, homeless, forest-roaming *sannyāsin*. Aśvatthāman is something of a willy-nilly Renouncer, just as earlier he is, in a sense, a driven, unnatural sacrificial butcher. In both cases authentic elements of the Brahmin identity are distorted, unbalanced, pushed to an extreme where they are almost unrecognizable. The qualifying adverb is, however, significant—"almost" changed beyond recognition into cynical travesties of their proper forms, these Brahminical elements are nevertheless part of Aśvatthāman's natural inheritance. So, it might be argued, is the very extremism he brings to them.

This is our point of departure—the text's insistence that Aśvatthāman is carrying out a supremely necessary role, however repugnant it may appear; his identification with Śiva, and that god's part in the Epic drama of cataclysmic sacrifice and renewal; and the Brahminical components of his identity, distorted as they may be. Together, these considerations help to explain the riddle this figure poses. For if Aśvatthāman's reputation seems to have suffered at the hands of his Epic contemporaries, he does not stand wholly condemned by the Epic's traditional audience. As M.V. Subramanian has remarked,

> Aswatthama himself gets only a temporary curse. And after that, in tradition, he is one of the honoured immortals. Is this because of a lurking feeling that there was an element of justice in the recoilment [sic] on the Padavas of their own unrighteous deeds in war, and Aswatthama was just an instrument in bringing that about?[41]

The moral issue is, of course, considerably more complex—indeed, it was almost certainly *intended* to be very complex—since the Epic ideal seems to be to snatch the elusive requirements of *dharma* and to make them one's own, even, or especially, at those moments when *dharma* temporarily becomes *adharma*. But on this count

Aśvatthāman does at least as well as his Pāṇḍava enemies. Certainly, this has something to do with the divine component of his personality, his association with Rudra-Śiva. By becoming this god, or by making his human will wholly subservient to the god's purpose (in the *ātmayajña* immediately prior to the slaughter), Aśvatthāman can hardly fail to flow along with his (and the world's) fate, *daiva*— even if he still deserves to be punished for this when the deed is done!

The integral nature of Aśvatthāman's role in the wider scheme of the Epic has been discussed by Dumézil[42] and, from a different standpoint, by Biardeau.[43] For the latter, Aśvatthāman embodies the violence which the other-worldly, absolutistic Brahmin idealism (untempered by *bhakti* devotionalism) wreaks upon the world. In this sense our wild Brahmin warrior is not unlike Paraśurāma, another Brahmin fighter and sometime idealist,[44] although Aśvatthāman's lineage is more pure. Aśvatthāman does have something of the uncompromising violence of modern ideologues, convinced in murderous sincerity of the ultimate correctness of their ideals. But this idealistic streak in Aśvatthāman exists, on the one hand, within a certain emotional context, while on the other hand it must *coexist* with another major aspect of the Brahmin, i.e. his sacrificial role. As we have seen, this aspect is very pronounced in the *Sauptika* story. These apparently conflicting forces somehow combine to produce the explosion which the *Sauptikaparvan* describes.

One key to their coherence within the single figure has been elucidated by Hiltebeitel, who has pointed out the parallels between Aśvatthāman's story and the Dakṣa myth. Arguably, this perspective is close to that of the Epic's authors, who concluded the *Sauptikaparvan* with an important version of that very myth (Chapter 18).[45] Without repeating Hiltebeitel's convincing arguments here, we may note the overall replication of meaning: the excluded Śiva of the Dakṣa myth proceeds from an emotional stance similar to Aśvatthāman's to destroy—and thereby complete—his opponents' sacrifice. In an important sense, the sacrifice is carried out by someone who resents its taking place in the first place. Both Aśvatthāman and Rudra-Śiva exemplify the deeply Brahminical passion of refusing to come to terms with an imperfect, tragically limited world. We have seen how this refusal takes over Aśvatthāman's heart and mind: his personal loss, his wounded sense of a triumphant injustice grinding others into the ground, the frenzied anger this arouses—all this bursts forth in the uncontrolled fury of his attack. Moreover, as we saw, Aśvatthāman's resentment is largely justified: even from the Pāṇḍavas' perspective, the war for *dharma* is heavily burdened by *adharma*. The same protest against this basically realistic perspective activates Śiva in many of his classic myths: it underlies his attack upon the incestuous Prajāpati (an ancient multiform of the Dakṣa myth),[46] and it evokes the cry of the infant Rudra at his birth.[47] Śiva, the eternal outsider, boundary figure at the gates of order, begrudges the existence of any world which is not whole.

Yet the ambivalent Śiva is also the guardian of sacrificial order (Vāstupa, Vāstoṣpati). In his myths, as in the tale of Aśvatthāman, the *effect* of his *raudra* protest is always the same—the *performance* of the sacrifice, with all its violent horrors. In this respect, Śiva's role is passed on to the Brahmins, who are neatly bifurcated along the lines of the god's paradigmatic ambivalence—sacrificial priests, on the one hand, committed to *dharma* and the world; symbols of transcendence and other-worldly purity, on the other. The second complex of ideas (transcendence, wholeness, non-violence, renunciatory purity of heart and body) sustains their prestige and underwrites their claim to preeminence; but it remains inextricably intertwined with the demands of the sacrifice, and of life. Thus neither the Śaiva myths nor the Epic role of Aśvatthāman offer a simple idealism as part of a model for the Brahmin, or for any man. Rather, they give voice to a profound and moving vision of violent engagement in a violent world—a world in which the longing for wholeness leads to disaster, and the greatest destruction is brought about by the outsider who rejects the realities of loss, evil, and pain.

Aśvatthāman goes too far along one vector in the complex Brahmin make-up. His uncompromising stance enables him to succeed where other sacrificers are *meant* to fail—in reaching the "end of the sacrifice". For "normal" sacrifices have no proper end beyond the frustrating, impure "remnant" which will be the seed of the next sacrifice. A completed sacrifice without remnant belongs to a world without limits—a world wholly unlike the one which fascinates and perplexes the Epic poets. Therefore Kṛṣṇa must miraculously produce a remnant from Aśvatthāman's overly successful sacrifice—in the stillborn Parikṣit, the future king. In moral terms, Aśvatthāman's excess cannot go unpunished, nor can he serve as any kind of model for other Brahmins in their sacrifices, their other-worldly protests, or their wars.[48] But his story is not by any means simply a cautionary tale, a wholly negative example to be shunned by the virtuous. In living out the extreme possibilities always latent in his given role, Aśvatthāman, like Paraśurāma, offers us an "anomalous paradigm"— a conceptual device which seems to be particularly prominent in the worlds of Hindu Epic and myth.

CONCLUSION; THE CENTER WHICH DOES NOT HOLD

What do these two anomalous episodes have to teach us about the ancient Indian conceptualization of order? How do they relate to one another, to the Epic world as a whole, and to the society which gave it birth and continued to find within this text its fundamental images of itself? We began by seeking to explore the relations between the Brahmin and his king—the pair whose marriage-like bond is so often declared to be the basic unit of ordered life in the Indian universe. The peculiar problems of this marriage would seem to have something to do with its unique distribution of power, whereby the allegedly weaker partner is granted ultimate authority: the Brahmin, in reality dependent on his royal patron and donor, still sees himself (as others largely see him) as the latter's "womb," the real source of the king's ability to act, and the symbolic locus of his society's values and its link with the truth.[49] This perception is largely the result of the way Brahminical thought evolved and crystallized, in its complex relations with the sacrificial cult, in the centuries preceding the composition of the MBh.

One major thrust in this evolution was, as Jan Heesterman has shown,[50] the attempt to polarize, isolate, and stabilize major roles such as those of the Brahmin and the king—to break out of earlier patterns of cyclical interchange of identities, leaving the Brahmin secure in his symbolic mastery of his culture's semantic domain. In theory, this could be achieved only by ensuring the Brahmin's detachment or disengagement, whatever the realities of dependence may have been. But this process did not come to an end with the consolidation of the classical Brahminical theories of social order or the formal definition of the Brahmin's ideal role. Even *within* the Brahmin tradition, this role remained problematic, a constant subject for reflection and struggle. The MBh is but one forum among many in which this internal debate was continued.

The two examples we have discussed, which refract basic themes of the epic in similar patterns of inversion, exaggeration, and self-scrutiny, reveal important features of this continuing evolution. They show, first of all, that the ancient alternation in roles never really ceased, although it took on a new dynamic in the light of the Brahminical self-definition. Violent Brahmins could now contrast with detached and impotent kings, but both types appear to be categorized anew: in the two cases we have studied, the Brahmin's violence is perceived in partly idealistic, perhaps "tragic" terms, while the king acquires a comic aspect imbued with its own specific connotations. The alternation of roles involves the recovery of hidden parts of one's social identity—undercurrents of experience and feeling which turn out to be integral to these roles. An *internal* oscillation thus constitutes part of the entire dynamic of relations between Brahmin and king: each of these major figures is susceptible to his own range of transformations. The classic Brahminical attempt to achieve a stable definition of cultural roles and values must come to terms with the inherently transformational perspective of this culture.

There are several immediate consequences for the construction of the social order. The Brahmin claim to ultimate authority is partly undermined by the Brahmin's chameleon-like transformations, while the theoretical harmony of Brahmin and king is critically examined and found wanting—even the Brahmin's idealism can wreak havoc on his society. But the Brahmin's authority is always at least sufficient to *deny* authority to the king. For his part, the latter is vulnerable to periodic, necessary transformation in the direction of a *dīkṣā*-like loss of self, exile, chaotic and comic dissolution—Bṛhannaḍā exists within every king. Without such periodic inversion, kingship, it seems, might lose its affective power altogether: the king, saddled with Brahminical insistence on his inferiority, his impermanence, and his accumulating burden of evil, needs ever to be born anew to his rather thankless office. Given the basic premises of his rule, the king can never achieve a once-and-for-all rise to power: his career is not an ascending line but a confused pattern of curlicues and jagged descents with no true direction or regularity to it, but often repeating itself in part. The Brahmin's graph, whatever the theory might say, would apparently look little neater.

The resultant instability, at the very center of political and social life, should be evident. It seems, moreover, to be a matter of principle. Let us note in conclusion the peculiarly Indian nature of this resolution (if such, indeed, we may call it)—although many of its features are familiar from other cultures. After all, the close association of kings and clowns is hardly unique to India: we may think of Lear, where the interweaving of identities between king and fool is at least as obvious as in the *Virāṭaparvan;* or of Falstaff and Prince Hal. And yet there are pronounced differences as well. For one thing, there is the striking fact that Indian kingship *per se* is systematically opened—by its own exponents and epic exemplars—to a persistent questioning of its legitimacy and general value, in a way which seems far more radical than anything in the Western tradition. This is perhaps the most explicit and sustained of the MBh's many theoretical concerns. Beyond that lies the question of integration and development, the course to be followed by any exemplary figure as he becomes ever more fully identified with his role. It is not without meaning that Prince Hal, on becoming Henry V, must banish Falstaff from his realm. "Polity cannot survive this demon of jest, subversive and anarchic."[51] Or can it? The Hindu conclusion seems rather different. The "demon of jest" is internalized and thus remains alive, while Henry's option is virtually precluded for the Indian king. A latter-day Arjuna, we may be sure, will still, on some level, become Bṛhannaḍā again.

CHAPTER 19

Some Observations on the Place of Intellectuals in Max Weber's Sociology, with Special Reference to Hinduism

EDWARD SHILS

The accounts of Hindu and Buddhist beliefs presented in the scholarly sources used by Max Weber, such as the works of Oldenburg, Hopkins, Deussen, Rhys David, Fick, Jolly, Max Müller's *Einleitung* and his *Sacred Books of East*, the pertinent contributions to Chantpie de la Saussay's *Lehrbuch* and the *Census of India*, etc., made no reference to "intellectuals." The authors, interpreters, and propagators of the sacred books and teachings of Hinduism and Buddhism were not portrayed as intellectuals by the eminent German, French, and British scholars who wrote about them.

I

Max Weber never constructed formal definitions of intellectuals and literati and he did not do so in the course of his work on India. He used the terms repeatedly and there are enough references to permit a few specific delineations, but much remains unclear.

Intellectuals were a stratum of upper-class persons of literary training and activity. They came mainly from an upper-class, educated stratum, a Brahminical priestly aristocracy which was the official bearer of Indian religiosity.[1] (At one point Weber said that he would deal with the fundamental social structures of the intellectual stratum but he did not resolve the question of the position of the Brahminical intellectuals within the larger category of Brahmins.) They were linked historically with the ancient upper class of priestly singers of the ancient Vedic period and subsequently with

427

the hereditary Brahminical priesthood.[2] The intellectuals were however not coterminous with Brahmins, who constituted a wider category. Not all Brahmins were intellectuals. Not all intellectuals were Brahmins. Nevertheless, most of Max Weber's analysis was devoted to Brahminical intellectuals. Buddhist intellectuals were often not of Brahminical origin although they too came from the upper class of the laity.[3] The intellectuals of the Indian saviour-religions sometimes came from lower castes.

Although Max Weber sometimes spoke of the Indian intellectuals as a *Literatenstand*, he did not deal at all with literary intellectuals as such, unless the literary works were also religious works.[4]

The Brahminical intellectuals were a "literary status group" made up partly of court chaplains to princes, advisors, respondent and preaching theologians, and jurists, priests, and pastors *(Seelenhirten)*. They were also monks, teachers, and gurus. They formed philosophical schools. Brahmins were not confined to the roles enumerated above; they were very variously occupied, sometimes even as confidential advisors of princes. They were counsellors of princes and noblemen regarding public and private matters. He contrasted these roles of Brahminical intellectuals with those of Chinese Confucian intellectuals who were officials or aspirants to office.[5] The Brahminical intellectuals had no "official career"; they were unlike their Chinese opposite numbers for whom an official career was the only worthwhile thing.

The highest position of Brahmin intellectuals in ancient times was that of court chaplains. Thereafter, until the period of British rule, they also were high ranking consultant jurists; the senior Brahmin pandit was the highest ranking person in the country. This, again, is to be contrasted with the Chinese situation in which the Emperor was the supreme pontiff.

In the period of the earlier Jatakas and again during the medieval expansion of Brahminical Hinduism, the Indian intellectuals were a stratum of possessors of literary and philosophical knowledge who devoted themselves to speculations and discussions about ritual and philosophical and scientific questions. Also to be included among the intellectuals were the *Vyasas*—who were compilers and who replaced the earlier rhapsodists; the narrators of edifyingly elaborated myths for an intellectualistic bourgeois public; they were the reciters of law books (Dharmapakas) who replaced the older declarers of the law and who delivered opinions in doubtful cases. These reciters of law-books yielded place in about the second century C.E. to the guild of pandits who were largely a stratum of men learned in written works.[6] Brahminical hermits who had become *Yatis,* i.e., full ascetics, acted as teachers and as magical aids to those in distress. They gathered pupils and lay-venerators around themselves.

In China, the intellectuals as a rule came from the "great" families of charismatic lineage, although the personal charisma acquired through education had become important enough to enable *parvenus* to be appointed to ministerial posts. The Emperor often favored those who were without connections with the great families in order to fortify himself and his patrimonial system against the feudal powers possessed by the great families.[7] In India the situation was different. There was a never wholly resolved tension between personal charisma and the charisma of lineage. It lay with the educated priest to decide who was to be admitted to the noviciate. When the Brahmins drew abreast of the Vedic priestly aristocracy, the primacy of the charisma of lineage was settled, at least as far as official doctrine was concerned. By the time of the first universal monarchy the independent priesthood as a guild based on the charisma of lineage, i.e., as a caste with a clear educational qualification as the pre-condition for the performance of the priestly role, had so firmly established its spiritual authority as a caste that it could never be dislodged.

This position of the Brahmins first appeared in the Atharva-Veda; in the Yajur-Veda it is completely promulgated. Brahmins who had studied and taught the Vedas became "human gods."

The Brahminical intellectuals were not the only intellectuals seeking to clarify and rationalize the nature, ends and means of the attainment of sanctity and release from this world. There were upper class laymen who stood alongside the Brahmins as the bearers of Indian philosophy. Max Weber did not say of which castes they were members; presumably they were *kshatriyas* or even *vaisyas* but perhaps they were Brahmins who were not priests. There were occasionally kings who discussed with and even expounded fundamental philosophical questions to Brahmins. There were highly educated knights, the classical *kshatriya* of the time of the growth of the large monarchies. Upper-class laymen's education was well developed when Indian philosophy was at its height in about the seventh century C.E. But there can be no question of the Brahmins ever playing a secondary role in these developments.[8] Even in Vedic times the priests were very important and their power increased thereafter.

The Brahminical intellectuals had to distinguish themselves from their rivals—the magicians—from whose midst they had emerged. Laymen at times endangered the predominance of the religious philosophy of the Brahminical intellectuals. There were skeptics (tarkavadians) who taught their anti-Brahminical ideas to pupils for payment; there were also itinerant ascetic teachers who derived from the Nyaya school.[9]

Thus the Brahminical intellectuals did not hold a monopoly of the personal search for sanctity and salvation.[10] The Brahmins tried to maintain a monopoly but they could not do so. There were mystical anchorites who were worshipped as saints and wonder workers. The Brahmins refused to acknowledge the legitimacy of many of these, admitting only *sannyasis* who were Brahmins. The Brahmins were especially hostile to those *sadhus* who came from the lower strata. Even in the period of the epics, there were non-Brahminical aspirants to sanctity and wonder-working. There were also experts in popular, ecstatic magic and orgies. But the Brahmins never surrendered their claim to monopoly.

With all their divisions into various philosophical schools and despite all the competition which they faced, the Brahminical intellectuals maintained their unity and therewith provided India with the unity of a common, trans-local culture.

II

Indologists have always made it evident that Brahminical Hinduism was a body of beliefs and practices which could only be cultivated by intellectuals because belief and practice both required the study of Vedic literature and subsequent works. Max Weber was the first to declare that Brahminical Hinduism was a religion of upper-class intellectuals. In a way, this was only giving a name to already existing knowledge but in a way hard to define, the utilization of that nomenclature brought Hinduism into a different light. The statement that a certain constellation of beliefs and practices is the religion of an intellectual stratum is of course a descriptive statement which on the face of it adds little or nothing to knowledge of those beliefs and practices. Yet such a statement raises questions about the beliefs and practices in general; it causes us to ask whether there are distinctive features in the doctrines which have a special affinity with the modes of thought which are distinctive of intellectuals, whether the mode of life of intellectuals is conducive to the acceptance and development of the beliefs and practices and whether their acceptance by intellectuals leaves a substantive imprint on the beliefs and practices. It also permits the raising of a question regarding the reinforcement which the enjoyment of advantages, economic, political and social, might add to the intellectual grounds, within the setting of the given intellectual tradition, for the acceptance and espousal of the beliefs and practices in general.

It is therefore reasonable to ask in what sense Brahminical Hinduism is a religion of upper-class intellectuals. It is a religion of intellectuals because being the religion of a sacred book—the Vedas—and the vast literature produced around it, it can be accrued only by prolonged and intensive study. It is the possession of knowledge acquired by such study that defines an intellectual. Brahminical Hinduism in its various schools of philosophy is in fact the creation of intellectuals; the highly rational character of these philosophies could only be the product of the labors of persons schooled in a tradition of learning and thought. Max Weber repeatedly points out that Brahminical Hinduism is one of the most rationalized of all the world religions. It is rationalized to an extraordinary degree in its theory of the techniques for the attainment of sanctity; its doctrine of ritual is highly rationalized on a foundation of magical beliefs; its theodicy, incorporating the doctrines of *Karma* and the transmigration of souls is the most rationalized which has ever been achieved. Finally, the subtlety and rigor of the rationalization of the theory of the self in Brahminical Hinduism exceeds that achieved in any other religion. Only persons trained and experienced in textual study, speculation and rational analysis could have ever accomplished those things. By definition such persons are "intellectuals."

It may also be said that Brahminical Hinduism can only be cultivated by persons who are not just intellectual in capacity and performance but who have the wealth and income and hence the leisure to be able to devote themselves to the study and speculation required by the traditions of this type of Hinduism. It is not any deeper connection than the mere fact of the possession of wealth and income sufficient to allow the time for study.

The Brahminical intellectuals obtained benefits from the application of classical Hinduism. As priests they received fees for the performances of sacrifices and rituals. They also received prebends from wealthy landowners and princes in recognition of their learning and devoutness. They enjoyed deference throughout Indian society from rulers and subjects on the basis of religious and "social"—caste—doctrines which they themselves promulgated. This is not to say that the ideas about the place of Brahmins as the first of the four *Varnas* were invented by Brahmins in order to guarantee their advantages in Indian society. Nevertheless, it must be said to be characteristic of intellectuals in many epochs and places to accord themselves the highest "real" rank in their respective societies and so it was with the Brahminical intellectuals. It could not have been otherwise once the classical Brahminical Hinduism was established as a doctrine of sanctity and salvation; it was propounded in such a way that it could be observed in its fullest form only by intellectuals.

Similarly the reward of salvation or release although in principle available to the castes of the "twice-born" could be striven for with greater concentration by Brahminical intellectuals than by any other stratum of Indian society. These are some of the senses in which Brahminical Hinduism may legitimately be said to be a religion of upper-class intellectuals.

The Brahminical intellectuals, attentive to their high status and sensitive to the intellectuality of their religion, were extraordinarily alert to the dangers of the contamination of their beliefs coming from the religious beliefs of other strata of Indian society or persisting from epochs before the Brahminical ascendancy in the religious and social life of India had been established. They bitterly resisted religious enthusiasm, orgiastic and unintellectual methods of seeking states of sanctity. They condemned infringements on norms of the ritual purity of the various castes and they declared indifference to caste to be heretical, at least in part because such infringements or indifference was a derogation of their status within the regime of castes.

III

Brahminical Hinduism is analyzed by Max Weber within the framework constructed in the "Zwischenbetrachtungen über die Stufen und Richtungen der Weltablehnung."[11] Brahminical asceticism falls under the mystical variant of asceticism. It is a flight from the world aiming to enter into a state of sanctity by meditation and contemplation regarding the ultimate powers of existence. It rejects "the world" not in order to transform, as does "innerworldly" asceticism but to gain release from it. Salvation for the Brahminical intellectual is release from the chain of rebirth into the world. The flight from the world has many forms; it may be a flight into the loneliness of "nature," uncorrupted by contact with human institutions; it may be a flight to "the people," uncorrupted by the conventions of civilization and its institutions. It may be a secularized flight into an ideal which provides the basis for criticism of existing society. In ancient and medieval India, however, it took the form of ascetic flight from everyday ordinary experience into contact with divinity. This was the path to sanctity taken by Brahminical intellectuals. Sanctity was thought to be attainable only on condition of flight from the world which was rendered unbearable by the transience of all things, the endless chain of rebirth and the unescapable responsibility of every individual for the transgressions committed in his life on earth.

These fundamental beliefs of the Brahminical intellectuals—the belief in the ceaseless transmigration of souls and the ethical theory of retribution *(karma)*—were gradual in their emergence. The former was already present in an undeveloped form in the Brahmans, the latter appeared for the first time in the Upanishads. Taken together, they formed the rational theodicy needed to account for the world as it is. It is not sinfulness which renders the life of man valueless— there is no conception of sin in Brahminical Hinduism—it is the metaphysical valuelessness of the transient world and the grief of those who know that the world of empirical experience is a meaningless commotion which devalues the life of living creatures.[12] The transiency of the world was rationalized as the main ground for its rejection; the manifoldness of the world was the main evidence of its distance from Brahma. The rationalization of the beliefs about the transience of the world, unending rebirth and the unescapability of retribution required that Brahma became the impersonal One, hidden behind the manifoldedness of phenomena and separate from the world.

The view taken by orthodoxy that the individual could escape from the wheel of rebirth rested on the assumption of the temporal infinitude of the wheel of rebirth and the infinitude of the number of souls. The idea that the world is uncreated and without an end became part of classical beliefs of Brahminical intellectuals was consistent with and hence supported by the argument that the number of souls is infinite and that however many persons find release from the wheel of rebirth, there would always be more who would not do so and as a result the number of those who could achieve the bliss of release had to be infinitesimally small. The individual, in a cosmos which allows for no grace, is, according to this view, left to his own exertions in the striving for this release; this belief accentuates the "individualism" which inheres in the mystical striving for salvation.[13] There is no grace. Max Weber thought that only the doctrine of predestination exceeds this view in its hopelessness for the majority of individuals.

The classical Brahminical notion of salvation gave primacy to the unqualified and absolute release from the world. This extreme and thoroughgoing rejection of the world was accepted in all Indian philosophies whatever the other variations among the different philosophical schools.[14]

The flight from the world had to be a flight from the increasing transience of existence in the world. The only permanence is the permanence of transience. This is true of earthly, of heavenly and of infernal things. The world was seen as an endlessly rotating wheel of rebirth and death. Only two things were regarded permanent: the order of the world in which all experiences are transient forever and ever and the souls which are cursed with rebirth. All of Hindu religious thought was concentrated on the questions: how can souls escape from their entanglement in the causal chain of *karma* and thereby escape from the wheel of rebirth inot earthly existence. Ever since the full development of the doctrine of *karma* and *samsara,* this was the only conceivable task of the techniques of "release."[15] These ideas reached a state of complete internal consistency only after many generations of intense intellectual exertion.

Although the ideas of *karma* and *samsara* became widely accepted among all Hindus, the idea of the impersonality of the highest divinity and the idea of the uncreatedness of the world were less universally accepted. The latter ideas coexisted alongside of the ideas of personal universal gods. The emergence of Brahma as an impersonal god occurred gradually; from having been originally a magical prayer-formula and then a magical cosmic power corresponding to the magical power of prayer, Brahma became an impersonal god, displacing and supplanting the earlier personal father-god and creator of the world, Prajapati. Brahma became a supreme god because being the functional god of prayers, he could not be the object of the magic coercion by prayer.

The philosophically educated Brahminical intellectuals were the first and foremost promulgators of the idea of Brahma as an impersonal god supreme over all other. Nevertheless, there later developed, within this very stratum beliefs, in a highly personal, benevolent creator-god, superior to the swarm of local functional gods, and in a savior who brought salvation in paradise.[16] This belief in a transcendental personal god allowed for the createdness of the world, not from nothing but from the emanations of individuality.

Patanjali's version of Yoga retained the possibility of a personal, supreme god—*Isvara*—although strictly speaking, this idea was not logically consistent with belief in *karma* and *samsara.* Yogic practice with its irrationalistic asceticism and the emotional character of its experience of sanctity, did not, at least in the form given it by Patanjali, exclude a supreme personal god. The notion of a personal god who was the creator of the universe raised the difficult question as to the meaning of such a creation with all its suffering, pain and transience. The answer given in the *Maitrayana Upanishad* that he did it simply as a way of spending his time, "just to see what it was like," is an explicit renunciation of any effort to find any "meaning" in the world as it is known to human experience. The Samkhya philosophy sharply rejected the idea that a powerful and benevolent god would have done such a thing.

IV

Like many modern Western secular intellectuals and like intellectuals in other parts of the world and in other epochs, the Indian intellectuals conceived of the attainment of intellectual understanding as a step in the transformation of conduct. Unlike the modern Western secular intellectuals who have thought of the knowledge in question as primarily empirical knowledge and of the transformation of conduct as the transformation of the conduct of other persons, Brahminical intellectuals thought in the first instance of the transformation and control of their own conduct and the knowledge which they wished to use in this transformation was knowledge of divinity and the self. This control of their own conduct placed contemplation and ritual in the first place. Ritual was a magical operation.

The extraordinary rationalizing powers of the Brahminical intellectuals did not entail, as similar powers among Western intellectuals have done, the eradication of magic. Magic was never eliminated from the world-view of Brahminical intellectuals and the immense intellectual energy which they expended on the rationalization and performance of ritual was a witness to their acknowledgement of the existence and importance of magical powers. The exact performance of ritual was necessary to keep the malignancy of magical powers under control. The pressure towards the rationalization and sublimation of the magical states of sanctity was characteristic of a stratum of intellectuals. Magical sacred powers were not to be used for the purposes of the professional magician but rather for the attainment of a state of personal sanctity—a state of bliss.

The state of bliss is a condition of gnosis; it is knowledge, knowledge or sanctity—dependent for its apprehension on the existence of a state of emotionless ecstasy. This was most appropriate to the style of life of highly educated upper-class intellectuals. All seeking for sanctity by rationalization with gnostic aspirations must end up in the form of mystical seeking for divinity, mystical possession of divinity and ultimately mystical communion with the divinity.[17] The highest divinity—Brahman—was a depersonalized divine being. All these occurred in Brahminical Hinduism. Communion with divinity achieved through the Brahminical type of gnosis moved in the direction of the depersonalization of the highest divine being.

This drive towards an impersonal divine being has several sources. These sources lie in the nature of contemplative mysticism to move in that direction and partly in Brahminical thought, which gave prominence to ritual and its uninfringeability, and hence to the manifestation of the divine in the eternal, unchangeable, impersonal law-like ordering of the world. The vicissitudes of individuals could not call forth the grace of such a divinity.

The rational interpretation of the world in terms of social and ritual orders, as law-like in their structures as the laws of nature, was the third feature of the process of rationalization which the Brahmin intellectual stratum performed on the religious material. This rationalization provided the rational foundations for the goals and paths of sanctity.[18] This was the distinctive achievement of the Brahminical intellectuals.[19]

Rationalized asceticism and ecstasy were the fundamental objectives of the correct Brahminical mode of life.[20] Asceticism was pervasive first in the obligations of chastity and mendicancy of the *bramacharin* and then in the ideal mode of life of the aging Brahmin in the *Vanaprasta* phase of the four *asramas* and finally in the permanent silence of the hermit in the fourth *asrama* seeking the qualifications as a *Yati*—i.e., an ascetic inwardly liberated from the world. Even in the second stage of *asrama,* in the state of the householder *(Grihastha),* ascetic regulation was always present.[21]

Vegetarianism and abstinence from alcohol were obviously motivated by the desire of the Brahminical intellectuals to keep themselves apart form the meat-eating and alcoholic orgies; the proscription of marital infringement was likewise an act of self-distinction from orgiastic sexual activities.[22] The avoidance of anger and passion was required by the belief in the demonic and diabolical origin of all emotions. The prescriptions of strict cleanliness in the taking of food likewise originated with the rules of magical cleanliness.[23]

These beliefs were closely linked with the social situation of the Indian intellectual stratum. Unlike the Mandarins who as a political bureaucracy would have nothing to do with magical techniques and who left these despised techniques to the Taoist magicians, the Brahminical intellectuals were priests by heredity and by their activities; this required them to be magicians. The Brahminical intellectuals never freed themselves from the tradition of magical asceticism out of which they themselves came. The magical chastity of the *bramacharin,* the prescription of life in the forest are both derivative of magical asceticism.

Ritual and other virtuous actions could improve the chances of rebirth but they could not lead to salvation or release. This could be achieved only by extraordinary behavior which goes beyond the cast obligations imposed by life in the world, e.g., by asceticism or contemplation which flees from the world.[24] This was to be done, as should be expected in a stratum of intellectuals, by the rationalization and sublimation of magical states of sanctification. Instead of the cultivation of secret magical powers in the profession of the magician, the individual's state of sanctity was viewed as one of gnosis—knowledge of sacred things mainly, if not exclusively, on the basis of emotionless ecstasy; such emotionless ecstasy was, Weber said, appropriate to the status of a stratum of intellectuals. It had to aim at mystical communion with the divine. Gnosis must be the highest objective and it must be a union with an impersonal divine essence, with Brahma. Brahma was originally the functional god of magical formulae but he evolved into the highest divine essence in a way corresponding to that in which the earthly masters of prayers, the Brahmins, achieved the highest earthly status.

Indian asceticism was technically the most rationally developed of any in the world.[25] Almost every ascetic method was used in India and often they were rationalized into a technological doctrine. The origin of classical asceticism was the acquisition of magical powers—the aim of this power was to exercise power over the gods and to make them compliant to one's will.

But they did not exclude the emotionless forms of ecstasy which were the seeds of contemplative or rationalized forms of asceticism. These were not allowable to a state-mandarin class as in China but they were permissible for a priesthood. Those parts of magical asceticism and ecstasy which the Brahmins retained because they were a caste of magicians, were, since they were an upper-class intellectual group, systematically rationalized, to achieve by rationalization the coherence of all existence.

Brahminical intellectuals sought release from the world through "illumination," which is generally characteristic of the intellectual search for salvation. This illumination of the mind was sought through the exercise of the intellect.[26] This brought with it a devaluation of all that is natural, physical and sensual.

An aversion against emotional orgiastic ecstasy followed from the intellectual ascetic orientation. The asceticism aimed at the achievement of a state of ecstasy or bliss devoid of emotion. These techniques of contemplation like all the methods of attainment of a state of emotionless ecstasy, rested on the principle that "only when the creature is silent does god speak in the soul." They also rested on the traditions of magicians who had developed the effects of autohypnotic psychological techniques and physiological experiments which affect, through the regulatory slowing and temporary cessation of breathing, the function of the brain.[27]

Yogic techniques placed at the very center the regulation of breathing and the related means of emotionless ecstasy, conjointly with the concentration of conscious psychic and spiritual functions on partly meaningful, partly meaningless patterns of experience or on such patterns of experience as have a vague emotional and devotional character and subjecting all of them to rigorous self-observation; these culminate in the complete evacuation from consciousness of all that is apprehensible in rational words, leading in the end to the conscious control over the phenomena of innervation in heart and lungs and ultimately to self-hypnosis.[28]

Yoga, which was the rationalized form of the techniques of the early ecstatic magician was the most prominent of the techniques of emotionless ecstasy.[29] Yogic technique was more influential in both orthodox and heterodox doctrines of sanctity than any other technique of emotionless ecstasy. It was also the most typical form of the technique of the attainment of a sanctity practiced by intellectuals. Its practice was not however confined to Brahmins. In later times, Yoga was overtaken by the classical Brahminical technique of sanctity; nowadays a not very large but widely spread body of magicians without Vedic education are the only ones still designated as Yogins; they form a caste of their own and they are not regarded by Brahmins as their equals.[30]

The Yoga technique rested on the assumption that the comprehension or experiencing of the divine is an irrational spiritual experience to be achieved by irrational methods and having nothing to do with rationally demonstrable knowledge. The classical Brahminical intellectual's outlook had, however, no place for this view. Brahminical intellectuals placed "knowledge" as such at the very heart of all the paths to sanctity through which release from the world was to be achieved. At first this knowledge was a guild-confined knowledge of ritual. For the emancipation-seeking Brahmin however the most important thing was the metaphysical-rational gnostic interpretation of the cosmological meaning of ritual. This conception gradually developed from the ritualization and sublimation of sacred action. As in other religions, the ethically right state of mind replaced the externally correct action; so in Hinduism in accordance with the specifically Brahminical appreciation of knowledge and thought, it was the "correct idea" which came forward. A Brahmin officiating at a ritual had to have certain thoughts in his mind as a condition of the magical effectiveness of the ritual. Correct thought and correct knowledge came to be regarded as the conditions of magical effectiveness. Brahmins intellectualized the attainment of the state of sanctity and they intellectualized the practice of ritual, but the knowledge they regarded as crucial was not the ordinary kind of knowledge of things external to the power.[31] The highest state of sanctity was attainable only through the higher form of gnostic knowledge which united the knower and the known.

The objective of the Yogic-method was magical states of mind and wonder-working abilities, such as the suspension of gravity, levitation, omnipotence without external action, and omniscience or the capacity to see into the thoughts of other persons (mind-reading). In contrast with this, the classical Brahminical contemplation sought the bliss of gnostic apprehension of the divine.[32] This flight from the world into gnostic union with the divine presupposed a rejection of the world of nature and the senses.

The technique of salvation developed by Indian intellectuals aimed at the methodical expulsion from consciousness of the events of this world in order to prepare for the invasion of the sacred which had to be felt because it was ineffable. Brahmin intellectuals preferred, however, concentrated mediation which was intended to induce not a state of feeling but of gnostic knowledge of the divine. Whereas Yogic method aimed to produce magical states of mind and wonder-working powers, the Brahminical intellectuals aimed at the blissful state of gnostic apprehension and union with the divine. The intellectualistic tendency of Brahminical intellectuals went occasionally as far as the Nyaya school which regarded the rational-empirical knowledge which is cultivated as a path to sanctity; classical Brahminism did not share this view. Brahminism affirmed the metaphysical character of gnosis and hence the value of mechanical techniques of mediation for the attainment of vision as a spiritual experience. Vision could never be attained through methods of empirical proof or argument.

Nevertheless, the Brahminical intellectuals never quite rejected Yogic practice because Yoga was in its own way also a specifically intellectualistic form of achieving contact with the divine. Yoga therefore stressed the need for the conscious experience of feeling reached by increasingly intensified concentration; for this reason it was necessary to produce, by planful and rational meditative exercise, feelings of friendship (with God), sympathy (with creatures), bliss and indifference (to the world). Only at the highest stage is catalepsy attained. (Classical Yoga rejected self-mortification. Self-mortification was part of the Atha-Yoga which was the asceticism of magicians.) As a rationally systematic form of emotional asceticism, Yoga was more rationalized than the classical contemplation of Brahminical intellectuals but at the same time the latter were more rational because they strove for "knowledge" rather than for "feelings."[33] Yoga was a highly rationalized form of methodical asceticism for control of feeling but it was not rational as regards the state of mind which it sought to attain.

Brahminical intellectuals of the classic sort did not utterly reject as heterodox the self-mortification of which the world-rejecting and world-fleeing anchorites were virtuosi; they retained the magical element of self-mortification in gnosis, partly because the popular prestige of "tapas" as a means of coercing the gods was unbreakable.[34] The ordinary Brahmin preferred the more moderate technique of contemplation. In both orthodox and heterodox soteriologies, the emptying of consciousness through concentration on the mechanical repetition of the prayer syllable "om"—which had magical effects— was paramount. Whatever the techniques, the main object of classical Brahminical contemplation was emancipation from the world as it is experienced by the senses, from spiritual excitation, passions, impulses and strivings, and from the calculations of means and ends in everyday life, in order to create the preconditions for the end-state of eternal peace which is release *(mukhti, moksha)* from all earthly turmoil and union with the divine. This did not entail an external reward for ethically right conduct in the next world. Even if the soul attains to paradise, the merits stored up by earthly virtues may be exhausted so that rebirth into the world will still be un-avoidable. The idea of eternal punishment in the next world also was meaningless to Hinduism. The soul can be released from the world into a state of deep, dreamless sleep. No one knows where the soul is when it is in this deep, dreamless sleep but at least it is not entangled in the turmoil of this world.

This turning away from the world of daily life, from life and from the world as such as well as from paradise and the world of the gods was the objective of all the emancipatory techniques of all Indian intellectuals, orthodox as well as heterodox.[35]

The gods are subject to the magical influence of correctly applied ritual. The knowledge-possessing person can control them. They are as mortal as men; they are passionate and desirous; they are not identical with the divine union which is the objective of the exercises of the technicians of sanctity.

Max Weber said that the Brahminical intellectuals developed greater specialization than their counterparts in Confucian China. All branches of life and knowledge were assigned to specialists in consequence of the idea of a different *dharma* for every and each special activity. In addition to their specialized knowledge of mathematics, grammar and formal logic, they developed the idea of the syllogism which was then taken up by the Vaisesika school and which approached atomist theory by building on the results of the Nyaya school. But as the Greeks, after Democritus, could not press their atomic theory further, despite their far better mathematical foundations, because of the domination of the social critical, social ethical influence of the Socratic philosophy, in India a similar beginning stagnated be-cause of the socially supported metaphysical foundations of all phi-losophy as an orientation towards the striving for individual release.[36]

Indian intellectuals developed, instead of an ethical code or doctrine, a metaphysically and cosmologically founded doctrine regarding the procedures for deploying the technical means of achieving emancipation from this world. This was the central object of all Indian philosophical and theological interest.

V

Except for the period of some centuries when Buddhism and Jainism were at their heights, the Brahminical intellectuals were ascendant within the intellectual stratum in India and they were also ascendent in Indian society in certain very important respects. Yet there was never complete consensus either within the boundaries of the Brahminical intellectuals nor between Brahminical intellectuals and non-Brahminical intellectuals regarding what was of utmost interest to Indian intellectuals, namely, the nature of the divine, the nature of the state of sanctity and the paths to the attainment of that state.

Weber points out that Hinduism is not primarily a religion of belief; it has no dogma since it has no "church" despite the fact that in principle its members are born into it.[37] Having no church and no hierarchy, Brahminical intellectuals had no compelling authority other than their own persuasive power. When they lived under Hindu rulers, they maintained good relations with them but they could not call on the power of the earthly rulers to assert the supremacy of one particular variant of Brahminical doctrine and to render its acceptance obligatory for all non-Brahminical intellectuals, or for all of Indian society. In any case, they could not do so during most of the period of Hindu rule and of numerous princely sovereignties. Nevertheless, there was something approximating orthodoxy.

Orthodoxy was constituted by orthodoxy of ritual observance. Hinduism embraces many beliefs about the nature of divinity, about the state of sanctity and about the paths to its attainment; definitions of Nirvana varied.[38] It acknowledged as one possibility rebirth into a new, temporally delimited life on earth, less happy, or happier than, or as happy as, the preceding life on earth had been. It also accepted the possibilities of rebirth in paradise, in a divine realm, or near to god but this sojourn in paradise was limited in time and was to be followed by rebirth on earth or the cessation of individual existence either in the form of absorption into the All-One *(Sayuiya)* or of the attainment of Nirvana as a state of deep dreamless sleep.

In intellectual matters such as the discussion of natural and religious philosophy, upper-class educated laymen who were, it may

be inferred from Weber's remarks, not exclusively Brahmins, and if
Brahmins then certainly not priests, played an important part when
these discussions were at their highest point around the seventh
century B.C.E.[39] There were varieties of doctrine beyond Brahminical
intellectual influence. In religious matters Brahminical intellectuals
did not possess complete control over the personal search for sanctity
any more than they had over philosophical and scientific activities
but they certainly sought to exercise such a monopoly. They acknowledged as genuine *sramana* only the *sanniyasi* who were Brahmins by caste and who had taken to the monastic life.[40] They refused,
sometimes brutally, to give their approbation to other mystical seekers
after salvation, especially if they came from the lower strata. These
wonder-workers, who, in India as elsewhere, claimed to be endowed
with charismatic qualities, enjoyed the reverence accorded to saints
and wonder-workers. These rivals of the Brahmins demanded reverence on the basis of their claim to be saints and wonder-workers
and they, from their side, sought to monopolize this position themselves.

Since the earliest times of which we have any knowledge, the
charismatic quality which was needed to achieve a state of thought
necessary to magical practice was personal; it was not dependent on
social rank or caste. Hence, these magicians were not exclusively
recruited from an official priestly caste or from a caste of magicians
such as the Brahmins were. This wide recruitment encountered
obstacles as Brahmins became established as an upper-class stratum
of specialists in ritual, whose social claims were justified by knowledge
and upper-class education.

This suppression by the Brahmins of their rivals in magical practice
meant that the range of magical practice, including magical asceticism,
available to Indian society became narrower. The Brahminical intellectuals concentrated on "knowledge," and qualified by Vedic
education, took a strong stand against irrational orgiastic ecstasy and
enthusiastic asceticism. Its pride as an educated intellectual stratum
caused it to refuse to engage in any ecstatic therapeutic practices.[41]
These were explicitly rejected as unclassical and barbarous or they
were simply not practiced by Brahminical intellectuals. They regarded
all magicians, cultic priests and seekers after sanctity who were
without Vedic education as contemptible and fit only for extermination. They took a different attitude with regard to unemotional
forms of ecstasy—from which "contemplative techniques" were later
derived—and with regard to rationalizable ascetic practices. The
Brahmins were indeed able to prevent the formation of a unified,
organized unclassical, i.e., non-Brahminical, priesthood but they were
unable to prevent the emergence of hierarchical circles which formed

around mystagogues[42] outside Brahminical circles and even among Brahmins. Nor could they prevent the emergence of sectarian soteriologies.

Since the Brahminical intellectuals grew out of a caste of magicians, those parts of magical ascetic and ecstatic practices which could be retained as they became more of an upper-class stratum of intellectuals, could be systematically rationalized. This was something which the Chinese intellectuals, as a stratum of educated civil servants could not do, since their traditions were wholly alien to asceticism.

There were non-Brahminical upper-class intellectuals who did not accept the sacrificial and prayer formulae of the Brahmins. These educated upper-class laymen were the source of the heterodox doctrines of salvationary release *(Erlösung)* especially in the early period of Buddhism. There were also literarily highly educated kshatriya noblemen who were active in philosophical discussions. The non-Brahminical intellectuals included some who became the central figures of the popular Hindu salvationary religions, the orgiastic, ecstatic and magical Hinduism of the masses which was repugnant to the Brahminical intellectuals. The orthodox texts, like the Ramayana, show that in the time of the epics even the sudra were regarded as capable to acquiring magical wonder-working powers through asceticism.

Thus, although the Brahmins were able to prevent the formation of a unitarily organized priesthood without Vedic education, they did so at the cost of the emergence of numerous mystagogic hierarchies partly from within their own midst. They had to experience the dissolution of the consensus formed about their salvationary doctrines into sectarian soteriologies in the promulgation of which Brahmins presumably played some part.

Despite these refusals of submission, the dominant culture of India was what the Brahmins made it. The non-Brahminical intellectual movements were reactions against the dominion of the Brahminical intellectuals. Beginning already in the Vedic age, their power, although fluctuating, was always very substantial.[43] There were times when the Brahmin intellectuals were pushed back into Northern India and Kashmir; they were forced to retreat before the rapid spread of Buddhist and Jain doctrines but they did not fail, even after such reversals, to regain their dominion.

The Buddhist and Jain successors were in part manifestations of hostility of aristocratic kshatrya intellectuals against the Brahminical ascendancy. The restoration of Hinduism and the re-establishment of its dominion was less a result of the sanguinary persecution of the devotees of the two heterodox religions, although such persecutions were quite numerous, than they were of circumstances favorable to the Brahmins. It was rather a result of the fact that the Brahmins offered to the ruling strata the legitimation of their domination. This incomparable religious support for earthly authority could not be provided by either Buddhism or Jainism.[44]

Whatever the special roles of the Brahminical intellectuals, whether they were priests or court-priests, chaplains and advisors, whether they were lay intellectuals, they did nevertheless provide the theological doctrine which turned their ethnically and occupationally extremely variegated societies into a more or less unitary caste-bound society. They did not do this through the power of the state but by their acknowledged monopoly of the power to promulgate correctness in ritual behavior. Brahminical Indian intellectuals created in India a society which withstood many centuries of foreign rule and of many small states. They did this by creating a culture which spread beyond the boundaries of any single India polity.

VI

Brahminical Hinduism has, through times of prosperity and times of adversity, maintained itself as a body of beliefs for at least two and a half millennia. It has done so through its acceptance and transmission first of all through lineages of learned men, each generation of which was studious to observe the rituals appropriate to its standing as a caste and to receive the philosophical interpretation of rituals. The re-enactment of ritual performed in domestic or familial places with domestic participation gave Brahminical Hinduism a clear domination in each new generation. The life of the Brahminical intellectual required not only the observance of ritual but also a knowledge of the content of sacred writings and their philosophical interpretation. The school was the second most influential institution in the transmission of the Brahminical inheritance to each succeeding generation. When they grew into adulthood, domestic rituals and temple rituals sustained the affirmation of Brahminical beliefs among the laity.

Brahminical intellectuals were, according to Max Weber, recruited from dynasties of highly educated Brahmins. The instruction received by the male children in such dynasties was more intensive than that received by the offspring of the laity. The schools were small and informal. The guru's authority over his pupils took precedence over the fathers'. Hindu ethics attributed such great importance to the bond of piety which bound pupils and devotees to *guru* or *gosain* that it determined the pattern of all religious organizations. They were also loosely organized. The inherited qualification for participation in such schools was often a condition to being a full Brahmin, i.e., a member of that stratum of Brahmins which could perform the rituals completely and who were accordingly entitled to receive gifts and endowments *(Dakshina)*.[45] Beyond the schools were monasteries, which like the schools, were supported by endowments. Schools and especially monasteries gave the Brahminical monks who included intellectuals the possibility of devoting themselves to Vedic studies without having to work for their livelihood.[46] There were also somewhat more advanced institutions called *parishads*. They had, according to the rules of later Hinduism, to be made up of the twenty-one educated Brahmins, although in earlier times they seem to have had as few as three or four. Proper teaching of correct knowledge conferred magical powers. Knowledge which attained gnostic sanctity made its possessor capable of wonder-working. Famous wonder-working gurus inherited their capacities as teachers as the charismatic power passed on within the lineage; others were chosen by their own gurus. It was self-evident, at least by the time of the Upanishads, that one could acquire correct knowledge only from one's guru.

These loose school-communities were formed of teachers and their pupils and groups of laymen who stored up merit for themselves in the next world by providing for the support of the community while not having the standing of full members. They had a formative influence on the subsequent development of a more genuine settled monasticism which took the place of the itinerant. There was no systematic organization with fixed "rules." Purely personal relationships of a patriarchal sort prevailed. There was little formal discipline. A monk could leave the monastery at will.[47] The later monasteries *(Maths)* as systematically conducted large-scale institutions with "professional" monks emerging only at the time of competition from the sects.[48] These were, according to Max Weber, not known to Hinduism before the appearance of Buddhism. In fact, it was from the latter that Brahmin intellectuals acquired this mode of organization.

Many of the famous founders of philosophical schools left behind them hierocratic dynasties which endured for centuries, thus assuring the stability of the techniques and doctrines of gnosis.[49] The links among monasteries and monastic communities were often constituted by their dynastic affinities.

The novitiate of the priesthood which was also the first step into the life of a Brahminical intellectual was rigorously demanding. The hereditary attachment to the old schools or monastic prebendal stratum was often the pre-condition of membership of the caste of sub-caste of full Brahmins, i.e., membership in that Brahminical stratum which qualified them for the performance of rites and accordingly, to the receipt of *Dakshin*. All the others were laymen and did not have the privileges of full-caste membership.

Much of the maintenance of Brahminical philosophical and theological science was the work of intellectuals who were hermits or actively officiating priests, with their personal pupils and formally organized schools.[50] There were also lay Brahminical intellectuals, living on prebends, devoting themselves to study and reflection.

The Indian intellectuals lived withdrawn from the world, pondering and forming schools; during the expansion in the Middle Ages, they wandered from one princely court and nobleman's seat to another. Despite all the differences among themselves in matters of doctrine, the vastness of the Indian territory and the absence of hierarchical authority among Brahmins, they regarded themselves as a unitary group of intellectuals.

The sense of unity of the Brahminical intellectuals of which Max Weber spoke, was not just a product of consensus on the value of ritual, asceticism and studied knowledge culminating in gnostic knowledge, nor was it a result of common participation in central institutions, which exercised power over earthly things. There were no such central institutions in India. It was rather the result of the wandering monkish intellectuals, meeting and disputing with each other. There is no information available about the circulation of manuscripts, just as there is none on their reproduction; they were undoubtedly copied as they were in the West in antiquity and the Middle Ages. Nevertheless, there is no doubt that knowledge was being diffused by word of mouth. The long experience of oral transmission of sacred and learned works in India was not lost even when the practice lost its primary significance. Brahminical intellectuals could carry their learning with them without the encumbrance of manuscripts.

The spread of Brahminical Hinduism throughout the length and breadth of Indian society was a function of other factors than those which maintained a Brahminical intellectual center without specific spatial location. Of course, without that trans-local unity of the Brahminical intellectual stratum that diffusion of Hinduism would never have occurred. Still, the diffusion was another matter. Hinduism became the religion of the subcontinent by the actions of rulers of the numerous principalities and tribal chiefs.

The propagation of Brahminical Hinduism is paradoxical. On the one side the teachings of Brahminical intellectuals were esoteric. They were written and taught in a sacred language unknown to the laity.[51] Only those qualified by caste and hence lineage could be placed in a position where they could learn Brahminical rituals, techniques and philosophy. Hinduism is moreover not a missionary religion. It is a religion of birth and individual conversion cannot be made to it. Despite these restrictions on the movement of Brahminical sacred knowledge, it did spread. It spread largely through the decisions of rulers of the small states to assure themselves of the intellectual legitimation which only Brahmins could provide and which the rulers sought, as all rulers seek to guarantee the belief in the legitimacy of the domination over their subjects.

Once the rulers decided to assimilate themselves into Brahminical Hinduism and to accept the caste system which placed them in the high status of the Kshatrya, they also imposed the system on their subjects. The Brahmins welcomed this because it provided them with fees for the performance of sacrifices and other rituals and also with prebends, which remained in the possession of their lineages.[52] These conversions were also welcomed by Brahmins because they confirmed the superior status of Brahmins and gave them new power as legal experts. According to Max Weber, the lower classes also sought admission to Hinduism because it guaranteed their occupational monopolies. Aboriginal groups attempted to gain admission to Hindu society by their adoption of the rituals required for acceptance as a Hindu. They attempted to assimilate themselves to Brahminical Hinduism, accepting the required taboos, even attempting to have their sacrifices and rituals administered by Brahmin priests. Thus did Brahminical Hinduism become the Indian "national" religion long before anything like Indian nationality existed.

VII

The Brahmins did not attempt to rule Indian society. They had no ambition to establish a theocratic regime. Although some of them were often close to rulers—Hindu rulers had to have court-chaplains who were Brahmins and sometimes counsellors on matters of policy—the Brahmins' relations with rulers did not tempt the Brahminical intellectuals into political activity. Nor did those who were not at court stand aside in a critical attitude. They acknowledged the autonomy of the rulers[53] and they did not regard it as their responsibility to render ethical judgments on regimes, as long as the ruler treated Brahmins deferentially and as long as he was faithful and meticulous in the observance of the necessary rituals. If a ruler failed in his undertakings, which were usually military, that was interpreted as evidence of his defective magical charismatic powers, just as his magical charismatic powers were demonstrated to be genuine if he was triumphant. The Brahmins had no ideas about political obligations and they neither praised nor denounced rulers.

Unlike the Chinese intellectuals who faced an Emperor who was the head of the state religion, the Indian intellectuals confronted a large number of princes or kings of small states who had no single sovereign over them. Each ruler depended for his legitimacy on his being ritually correct; he had to adhere to the sacred tradition in his dealings with the Brahmins. Otherwise he would be regarded as a "barbarian." No Indian ruler, however great his real power even in purely ritual matters, was also a priest. According to the ancient Vedic tradition, among the Aryans, the prince from the very beginning had to accept the independent priest trained in ritual.[54] (There was nothing like this in China.) In India the princes had emerged from the campaigns of charismatic warrior-chiefs, whereas in China they grew out of the higher priesthood. No Hindu prince or monarch could claim priestly powers vis-à-vis the Brahmins.[55]

The ruler, like the incumbent of any other occupational role, had his own dharma—which was part of the sacred law interpreted by the Brahmins—and thus dharma included his independence of action in accordance with his own discretion. His dharma recommended that he make war and exercise power for its own sake. The king's dharma did not require him to observe any particular ethical rules in the conduct of war or ethical rules for the government of his subjects. Brahminical Hinduism made no place for political ethics and lacking any conceptions of natural law or universalistic ethics, of "natural rights, the observance of which all human beings had to observe," it could not have done so.[56]

The attitude of the ruler towards the Brahmin was usually a deferential one. He wished to remain in their good graces. He never presumed to be the head of anything resembling a state-church; in this regard he differed profoundly from the Chinese Emperor who was the pontifex maximus. Nevertheless, the ruler was not always subservient to the Brahmins; sometimes he attempted to play them off against the nobility. In any case, whatever his conduct towards the Brahmins, about which they had strongly held ideas, the Brahminical intellectuals did not insist that the king had obligations to the rest of society. The doctrine that each caste and occupation had its own dharma was said by Max Weber to be tantamount to an "organic theory of society" but whereas in other societies such a theory entailed obligations on the part of the upper classes for the protection of the lower classes, nothing like this followed in Hinduism.

The civil indifference of the Brahminical intellectuals was entirely consistent with their conviction that the proper end of human action should be release from the chain of rebirth. Nevertheless, the Brahminical intellectuals despite their civil indifference had great influence in Indian society. For one thing, Brahmins were very important in the legal system of the Indian states, small and large. They were often counsellors at the royal courts and although the king was the ultimate authority in cases which were brought before him, the assent of his Brahminical legal expert required for any decision he proposed gave the Brahmins much influence. The *dharmashastra* was their creation, just as Talmudic law was the creation of Talmudical scholars. Although the *dharmashastra* had no official legal status and was a statement of ideal actions rather than a body of realistic rules for application, the *dharmashastra* counted in the law courts as "books of authority." They were the work of *pandits* who were private scholars. The *dharmashastras* were in the course of the Middle Ages replaced by systematic compilations and commentaries of the "schools." The Indian legal system had no place for a licensed class of responding legal honoratiores.[57] It had no "theological jurists" responding to concrete questions such as Judaism possessed in rabbinical law-making in antiquity, in the "theological jurists" of the Talmudic age and in Islamic *sunni* jurisprudence.

As a result, Hindu legal erudition was largely scholastic, theoretical, and systematizing. It was the work of philosophers and theorists who "had little contact with legal practice."[58] These treatises abound in casuistry, dealing often with obsolete institutions. They are "compendia not of law alone but also of ritual, ethics, and occasionally social conventions and etiquette."[59]

Furthermore, much of the law governing the daily life of Indian society did not come under the jurisprudence of the *dharmashastras* and the Brahminical intellectuals who interpreted it. It was instead regulated by bodies of law which were regarded as valid by the particular occupational groups of merchants and craftsmen with consideration for which they had grown up. These bodies of law were of limited jurisdiction, being confined to problems specific to the occupational groups which accepted them, to the extent that "special law prevail(ed) over general law."[60] The Brahminical intellectuals had no voice in these matters, and partly in consequence of this, this body of particular law was never rationalized or subsumed under sacred law. Sacred law according to its Brahminical exponents was absolutely binding; in fact it was not.[61]

There was no public political life in ancient and medieval India and hence the role played by lawyers in political and public life of modern societies was not available to the Brahmins who participated in the royal courts or who wrote legal treatises and commentaries. The relative remoteness from actual daily life of Brahminical jurisprudence was part of the more comprehensive remoteness of Brahminical intellectuals from the workaday world. Their primary interest was in ritual and release from the world; their powerful intelligences were so preoccupied with the rationalization of their metaphysical and religious beliefs that they had little interest in or time for secular intellectual activities.

The structure of the Indian polity was not propitious to the exercise of influence by Brahminical intellectuals over such an immense expansion of territory. For much of Indian history except for periods of alien rule, the territory was broken up into numerous small states without any overarching legal or political structures. There were, without any constitutional provision, many parts of the various Indian societies which remained outside the jurisdiction of the monarch; in a certain sense, India was a pluralistic society, at least *de facto*, because of the weakness and traditionality of the rulers. Furthermore the Brahminical intellectuals had little in the way of institutional apparatus to convey their teachings to the mass of the oncoming generation of subjects within each state. There was no national educational system which was attended by most children. Furthermore, within each state the Brahmins, with all their pretensions to superiority to the Kashtriya and despite the deference in which they were held by that caste and particularly by the rulers who were of that caste, neither aspired to nor granted much opportunity to exploit the power of the state to dominate Indian society. Indeed the very doctrines of the Brahminical intellectuals forbade the imposition of a pattern of uniformity over Indian society, even if the institutional arrangements would have permitted it. The separation of the castes in nearly every sphere of life, and particularly the separation of the lower castes which comprised the majority of the population from the superior ones, and the Brahminical conception of the distinctiveness of the *dharma* of each caste, craft, and trade, meant that no common ethical outlook and no sense of membership in a single society could emerge. All this notwithstanding, the peoples of India did constitute a society, albeit a very loosely integrated one; the unifying elements were the rites, practices, and beliefs promulgated by Brahminical intellectuals.

The caste system was not a creation *ex nihilo* of the Brahminical intellectuals. The heterogeneity and separateness of the many smaller societies resident on Indian territory at the time of the Aryan conquest fostered the acquisition and hence the diffusion of the Brahminical view of the world and society in a way appropriate to each stratum and occupational group. There is little point to speculation about the motives which impelled the Brahmins to espouse this view; as usual, it must have been a combination of desire for and anticipation of benefits in income and social status and intellectually sustained beliefs in the meaning of human existence in the world in relation to the fundamental powers at work in the cosmos.

VIII

Alongside and prior to Max Weber's comparative sociological interests in the patterns of beliefs, their intellectual development, and their incorporation into the actions of individuals and institutions, there was his continuing interest in the conditions of the emergence of the rationalized modern industrial economy. This was his most enduring interest. The only changes in the ways in which he pursued it lay in the levels of generalization and the range of the variations of alternative paths of economic and intellectual or religious developments within which he analyzed it.

Max Weber declared that rationalized industrial capitalism was an importation into India from Great Britain. The traditions of the Brahminical intellectuals and the caste system which they helped to maintain were too strong a resistive power. The tremendous accomplishments of Brahminical intellectuals in their metaphysical and theological treatment of the nature of the cosmos and the conditions and forms of release from the bonds of earthly existence and their scarcely less considerable achievements in certain fields of science were in fact the sources of the failure of Indian society to give birth to a rationalized organization of productive labor, a rationalized technology, and the rationalized exchange of its products.

At the root of Indian intellectual activities was the unextirpable belief in the efficacy of magic; this had stereotyping effects on the economic actions of Hindus. The pervasiveness and comprehensiveness of Brahminically dominated religiosity in all spheres of life resulted in a diffusion of the stereotyping effect of belief in the efficacy of magic. The conceptions of the distinctiveness of the *dharma* of each caste and occupational group had similar stereotyping effects. The more rationalized the symbolic configurations of Brahminical Hinduism, the less the purposeful rationalization of actions and institutions. The titanic accomplishments of Brahminical intellectuals in the rationalization of their beliefs and in the methodical conduct of life organized in accordance with those beliefs, the less room and energy there was for a parallel effort in the rationalization of economic activities. In principle, *Wertrationalisierung* had its fundamental postulate in the belief in the efficacy of magic and the cultivation of ritual as a means of controlling it. The traditions of mystical gnostic asceticism which was not just rejection of the world but a more thoroughgoing flight from the world were too strong to be overcome by forces impelling towards the rationalization of empirical knowledge and the purposeful rationalization of action in the world. Although in fact few could follow out the ramifications of that flight in their mode of life, the general disposition of conduct ran in that direction.

Thus by indirection, the Brahminical intellectuals formed the Indian society which survived with extraordinary pertinacity through the invasions with volcanic force and the alternative of warring small states. It was only after the coming of the British to India and only after several centuries of British rule that the mould into which the Brahminical intellectuals had formed Indian society began to undergo changes into a direction into which Indian society had not autonomously moved. Even then and since then, the mould created by the Brahminical intellectuals has not been entirely shattered. Much still remains and is resistant to change. It would require a further study to examine the role which, over five or six generations, intellectuals of Brahminical derivation have paradoxically played in modifying the patterns so lastingly engendered and maintained by their ancestors.

CHAPTER 20

The Reflexive and Institutional Achievements of Early Buddhism

STANLEY J. TAMBIAH

This essay takes as its point of departure some propositions contained in essays by Benjamin Schwartz[1] and Shmuel Eisenstadt.[2] Schwartz has referred to Karl Jaspers' use of the term "Axial Age" to characterise certain momentous developments, certain major spiritual, moral and intellectual breakthroughs, that took place in the first millennium (more accurately the first seven or eight hundred years) B.C.E. Examples are the rise in this epoch of classical Judaism, Zoroastrianism, Buddhism, Jainism, Confucianism, Taoism, and Greek pre-Socratic and classical philosophy. A salient breakthrough, perhaps the most important one, was "the strain toward transcendence", such that the millennium in question has been called "the age of transcendence." And the transcendental breakthrough is integrally linked to the rise of small groups of prophets, philosophers, teachers and wise men, who though they may seem to have had little effect on their immediate social political and economic environment, yet opened the doors for future large-scale civilizational and imperial triumphs. Eisenstadt has emphasized how these new 'elites' in due course participated in "the active construction of the world according to some transcendental vision or command." They creatively helped to institutionalize their vision so as to generate far-reaching processes of change in the internal contours of societies and in their external relations. Indeed the new "intellectual" elites became the major partners of co-existing political and cultural elites in forming ruling coalitions and/or in launching movements of protest that had such far-reaching consequences.

At first sight early Buddhism may appear as a thorn in the side of this view of the great transformation prefigured by the transcendental breakthrough of the Axial Age. It is commonly held that the distinctive and radical Buddhist vision of "the tension between the transcendental and the mundane" resulted in the solution that veered towards "world negation" and renunciation, and therefore could not have directly launched attitudes of mind and activities that could result in the active transformation of the world.

I think there is much scope for a reinterpretation of this conventional view on the basis of a reconstruction of the social, economic and political context in which Buddhism arose. Early Buddhism can be seen as a protest movement that on the one hand reacted against features of the then prevailing dominant Brahminical religious and status evaluations and ritualism, and on the other sought patronage from certain rising commercial and landed groups within the expanding monarchical polities of Magadha and Kośala. The Buddha's renunciatory salvation ethic that he taught his *virtuoso* disciples, when placed on this sounding board, can be shown to have had consequences that in due course integrally helped to transform the historical landscape in significant ways. It is not my intention in this essay to delineate the context in which Buddhism arose or isolate those elements in its philosophical and doctrinal propagation that in due course acted as a leaven upon the political future.[3] Rather, I wish to focus on the "innovations" and "breakthroughs" that we can plausibly associate with the Buddha and his disciples, and their successor monks of early Buddhism, with regard to the codification, elaboration and transmission of their knowledge and practices directly pertaining to their transcendental vision and salvation quest. I hope to demonstrate that even with respect to the "narrow" domain of the *bhikkhu*'s a sacred knowledge and disciplinary practices, early Buddhism, say from the time of the Buddha in the sixth century B.C.E. to the early centuries C.E., made remarkable achievements, some of which may have been innovative breakthroughs, others of which may have been a greater elaboration and "rationalization" of existing techniques. These feats were indispensable for Buddhism's later civilizational triumphs in South and Southeast Asia, in Inner Asia and the Far East.

THE DHAMMA (DOCTRINE) AS ORAL KNOWLEDGE

My first point is that the early Buddhist achievements concerning the creation and transmission of sacred knowledge *preceded* the commitment of texts to writing. The remarkable thing is that the early Buddhists did not commit their sacred knowledge to writing, not because they did not know how to, but because there were special reasons why it was transmitted orally. Warder remarks: "It appears that during the Buddha's lifetime and for some centuries afterwards nothing was written down: not because writing was not in use but because it was not customary to use it for study and teaching. It was used in commerce and administration, in other words for ephemeral purposes; scholars and philosophers disdained it, for to them to study a text presupposed knowing it—by heart".[4]

There are four major implications that stem from this early Buddhist attitude, each of which we shall take up in turn. Firstly, early Buddhism's sense of a remarkable breakthrough in religious thought was accompanied by a faith in the power of the spoken word. Secondly, the sacred knowledge itself was of a complex substantive nature, and therefore had to be systematised and arranged. Thirdly, appropriate pedagogical, memory, and rhetorical techniques had to be devised so as to educate the monks in doctrine and practice, and to ensure the transmission and elaboration of knowledge from generation to generation. Fourthly, the Buddhists (together with the Jains) pioneered the establishment of the monastic community as an institution, and the rules of discipline imposed on its members, as an essential environment for the pursuit of the salvation goal, and for the acquisition and preservation of the sacred knowledge and practices.

Together all these features were essential components in Early Buddhism's extraordinary diffusion with missionary vigour into most parts of India and its peripheries in the Axial Age, an expansion that combined the force of its message with institution-building.

The Power of the Spoken Word

It is commonly said of Judaism, Christianity and Islam that they are "religions of the Book." It is perhaps even more important to recognise that they are religions of the Word. The first line of Saint John's gospel has expectably merited much exegesis: "In the beginning was the Word, and the Word was with God, and the Word was God". A few lines later we are told: "And the Word was made flesh, and dwelt among us. . . ."

The early Israelite religion exhibits another facet of the religion of the Word when it declared that the worship of YHWH and the keeping of His commandments necessarily meant the turning away from rites to images of wood and stone: "Ye shall make no idols nor graven image, neither rear you up a standing image, neither shall ye set up any image of stone in your land, to bow down unto it: for I am the Lord your God" (*Leviticus,* 26:1).

And of course Islam arising much later than all the religions of the Axial Age was not only vehemently aniconic but also more reflexive and self-conscious about the creative and aesthetic powers of the spoken word. The Qur'ān derives from the root "to recite," and Islam itself is unthinkable except in terms of the spoken Arabic word. The Qur'ān was delivered by Mohammed verbally in verses that contained majestic rhythms. It resonated with poetry. The "magic of its language" cannot be severed from the beauty and power of its conceptions. As Polk[5] remarks, "On its poetry Arabic civilization has lavished all of the inventive genuis which in other cultures has been spread over the whole range of the arts. Study, memorization, and repetition of Ancient Arabic poetry tie the modern age to previous ages and on this string is hung that sense of continuity which makes those who live in the Muslim Middle Eastern Arab states think of themselves as Arab".

Buddhism too (just like Vedic religion at the stage of moving forwards to the Upanishads) can be counted among the great creations of the Axial Age, whose transcendental vision was closely linked to a reflexive realization of the discursive as well as poetic, the metaphorical as well as the performative, role of language as a vehicle for relating the mundane to the transcendental.

The Buddha's first sermon, preached in the park at Sarnath outside Vārānasī (Benares), is expressly referred to in the Buddhist texts as "setting the Wheel *(cakra)* of the Dhamma in motion".[6] The wheel in question is loaded with many meanings: aside from solar connotations, it is the wheel of truth that rolls onward and makes a conquest of the universe non-violently and righteously.[7]

And the Buddha himself has been credited at the moment of enlightenment and meditative trance under the Bodhi tree, and afterwards while preaching, with "radiance" and "fiery energy" *(tējas)*. The *Dhammapada* (387), an early canonical text, for example, reports that the Buddha "glows with fiery energy".

The Contours of the Buddhist Sacred Texts

Buddhism, both ancient and modern, constantly affirms its "triple gem": the Buddha as the great man who showed the way, the Dhamma as the doctrine which he taught, and the Sangha, the community of his disciples who are the repository of the doctrine.

Early Buddhist traditions have it that, in the first few centuries after the passing away of the Buddha, some three great "rehearsals" *(saṃgiti)* or councils were held with monks assembling from different directions and diverse locations in order to codify and regularise, the *dhamma*.[8] The first council was held at Rajagrha immediately after the Buddha's death; the doctrine was further developed at the council of Vaiśālī which was allegedly held a hundred years later to correct wrong views that were held by certain monks. The canon in its essential parts is thought to have been completed by the third council held under King Aśoka towards the end of his reign in the third century B.C.E. The Buddhist missions to various countries are also dated from this time.

All the recensions of the *Vinaya* (texts relating to the disciplinary rules of the monks), now available and associated with the different schools of Buddhism, affirm a common story about the holding of the first Rehearsal or Council in the city of Rajagṛha (the capital of Magadha kingdom) soon after the Buddha's decease. It is said that one of the Buddha's senior disciples, Kāśyapa (Kassapa), presided over an assembly of 500 *arhants* (worthy or perfected saints) that recapitulated everything that the Buddha had said and produced a canon, which is usually referred to as the *Tripiṭaka* (Sanskrit) or *Tipiṭaka* (Pāli), the three "baskets" or collections of texts. They are the *Sūtra* (Sanskrit) or *Sutta* (Pāli) *Piṭaka,* the *Vinaya Piṭaka,* and the *Abhidharma* (Sanskrit) or *Abhidhamma* (Pāli). All schools of Buddhism agree that the first two "baskets" were codified at the First Rehearsal, while there is disagreement about the composition of the third.

The *Sūtra Piṭaka,* according to tradition, was recited by Ānanda, the Buddha's favorite disciple; its subject matter is the doctrine *(dhamma)* as taught by the Buddha in the form of discourses and dialogues. There is consensus among the schools that the *Sūtra Piṭaka* was arranged in five *nikāyas* (collections) or *āgamas* (traditions)—Dirgha Nikāya (Long Tradition), Madhyama Nikāya (Intermediate Tradition), *Samyukta Nikāya* (Connected Tradition), Ekottara Nikāya ('One-up Tradition'), and lastly, the *Kṣudraka Nikāya* (The Minor Tradition).[9] The order in which these five traditions are presented represents the order of their authenticity, the last being considered the most doubtful. These various discourses take the form of prose sprinkled with verses.

The *Vinaya Piṭaka* is an enumeration of the rules of discipline the Buddhist monks must observe, together with a vast quantity of explanatory matter about these precepts. We shall comment on the contents of this critical part of the doctrine later when we deal with the basis of monastic life.

The *Abhidhamma*'s authenticity as the words of the Buddha is a matter for disagreement.[10] Nevertheless it is clear that a substantial development of the texts that fall under this rubric had taken place within two centuries of the Buddha's death, and as a collection it is of particular interest to us as showing the sophisticated and scholastic techniques of exegesis and argumentation achieved by an "intellectual elite" of the Axial Age. Although the *Abhidhamma* texts of the various Buddhist schools do not agree as closely as their versions of the *Sutta* and *Vinaya* baskets, yet there are major agreements among them. This attests to the fact that all the variant schools do relate to a central canonical tradition, and the mechanisms of transmission, which account for their variations within a common framework, are therefore worthy of special study.

The nature of the *Abhidhamma Piṭaka* in its Pāli language version is described as follows by Geiger:[11] "The *Abhidhamma* is not a systematic philosophy, but merely a supplement to the *dhamma*. The works belonging to it mostly contain . . . detailed elucidations of various topics dealing with ethics, psychology or theory of knowledge which are mentioned in the canon.[12] Its form is throughout scholastic. The themes are schematically classified; they are not properly defined but rather described by multiplying synonyms and they are brought into all possible combinations considered as they are from the most different points of view".

These words thus plausibly describe the activities and gropings of a pioneering set of intellectual systematisers belonging to the Buddhist branch of India's reflexive renouncers.[13] An *Abhidharma* text is usually set out as an elaboration of a *mātrkā* (a set of headings serving as notes on the doctrine) that is given at the beginning. In a sense then it explains the Sūtra, but naturally it tends to go beyond this in systematising the doctrine. Most schools agree that this work of systematisation began already during the lifetime of the Buddha. The Buddha's disciple called Sāriputra is usually nominated as the first analytical expert on systematics, though certain schools associate another disciple, Kātyāyana, with the same activity.

The Politics of Schism and the Arts of Memory and Rhetoric

The activities of systematisation and hermeneutics were pursued vigorously during the early centuries of Buddhism, and inevitably these activities were accompanied by the contrapuntal development of schisms and sectarianism. These sectarian fragmentations were the product of many factors, such as genuine interpretive disagreements, which were generated in groups or communities of monks geographically dispersed, and employing different dialects of Prakrit and different languages such as Sanskrit and Pāli. Once certain schools were formed, they in turn spawned more schools, which inevitably produced their own *Abhidharma* treatises that were subsequently preserved in their separate traditions. A lively sectarianism and adversarial fragmentation may be taken to be indices of vigorous intellectual and missionary activity.

I do not intend here to give an account of the various schisms and the founding of the schools. But a few references to this topic are in order as a prelude to discussing the pedagogical and semiotic techniques by which the monks elaborated and transmitted their variant versions of a common religion.

The very first schism in the *sangha* is alleged to have taken place sometime after the Vaiśālī (Vesāli) dispute, about a hundred years after the Master's death. A community of monks based in the city of Vaiśālī was accused of relaxing certain disciplinary rules, of which the most conspicuous, as judged by the accounts of all schools, concerned the receiving by monks of gold and silver from their lay devotees and disciples.[14]

Yasa, the monk, who originally accused the Vaiśālī monks of malpractice sought support for his cause from the monastic communities located in the West, at Kausāmbi and Mathura. In due course 700 monks from various parts assembled within the boundaries of Vaiśālī to constitute a deliberative "community", and a committee proposed by both parties to the dispute was given the task of adjudication. At the conclusion of the assembly, the accounts agree that the *Vinaya* (disciplinary code) was rehearsed again, as at the first council.

The first schism is supposed to have occurred sometime after the Vaiśālī affair; the Vaiśālī faction, against whom the ruling went, was not reconciled to the decision of the assembly, and held its own "great rehearsal", out of which originated the Mahāsaṁghika School. The probable date of the first schism is thus some time between the conclusion of the Vaiśālī dispute and the period of Emperor Aśoka, say around mid-fourth century B.C.E. The sectarian bifurcation at this time was between the Sthaviravāda, who were strong in the western regions of north India, and the Mahāsaṁghika who had their heaviest representation in the east, and in the far north-west, of India.[15]

Tradition has it that the eventual number of schools at the end of the early period (i.e., excluding the subsequent Mahayāna schools) was eighteen. For example, after the time of Aśoka, three important schools hived off from the Sthaviravada, namely the Mahīsāsakas, Hamavattas and Dharmaguptakas; the Sarvāstivāda had done so even earlier. In Sri Lanka which became the subsequent centre of the Sthaviravāda, two more schools split off, the Abhayagirivāsin (Dharmarucis) around 38 B.C.E., and the Jetavanīyas (Sāgalīkas) around 300 C.E. Similarly, from within the ranks of the Sarvāstivādins were formed first the Sautrāntikas, and some time later, the Mulasarvāstivadins (around third to fourth centuries C.E.).

Now, it seems eminently plausible to surmise that the fragmentation of the monastic communities into so many rival schools or sects espousing variant doctrinal interpretations was a necessary context for the development of the discursive language and the concepts and tools of dialectical argument and the rhetoric of persuasion, which are amply present in the *Abhidhamma* texts we have already named.

That the earliest Buddhist peripatetic renouncers, organized as dispersed communities, debated with other *śramanas* equally bent on teaching and propagandising, is attested by the Brahmajāla Sutta in the *Dīgha Nikāya*, which recounts how the Buddha rejected a scheme of sixty-two opinions said to be held by some brahmans and *śramanas*, ranging from "eternalists" to "annihilationists" and so on. The theories criticised related to a medley of variant positions held by them with regard to the origin and the past states of the universe on the one hand and the soul on the other. There are other canonical discourses which suggest polemical attempts to belittle the views of contemporary rival schools such as the Ajīvikas and the Jains.[16] Rhys Davids has this to say about the Buddha's discourses celebrated in the *suttas:* "When Buddhism arose . . . hypotheses as to 'souls,' internal and external, formed the basis of all the widely differing, and very lively and earnest, religious and philosophical speculations in the valley of the Ganges, where then obtained the marvellous freedom of thought on all such subjects which has been throughout its history a distinguishing characteristic of the Indian people. Now there is one work, of more importance than any other in Buddhism, the collection of the Dialogues of Gotama the Buddha, brought together in the Dīgha and the Majjhima Nikāyas. It contains the views of the Buddha set out, as they appeared to his very earliest disciples, in a series of 185 conversational discourses, which will some day come to hold a place, in the history of human thought, akin to that held by the Dialogues of Plato."[17]

It is appropriate at this point to refer in passing to that great work enjoyed by all students of Buddhism, the *Milinda Pañhā (The Questions of King Milinda)*, a non-canonical book of didactic ethics and religious disputation, cast in the form of lively dialogues between King Menander and Nagasena, the monk. The manner in which dilemmas that puzzle ordinary laymen are resolved, and the strategies, sometimes tendentious and even sophistic, by which views contrary to orthodox Buddhism are refuted, are remarkable exercises in the art of persuasion and debating.

In the light of such suggestive parallels, it is possible that the discussion of the development of discursive techniques in Early Buddhism might profit from the findings concerning early Greece.

Geoffrey Lloyd has discussed the social and institutional context which stimulated new techniques of dialectical argument (axioms, definitions, hypotheses, types of syllogisms) and rhetorical persuasion ("forensic" in the law courts, "deliberative" in the public assemblies, and "epideictic" in ceremonial oratory), techniques which were critical for the rise of early Greek science (from the fifth to the third centuries B.C.E.). Moreover, he locates in Greek oratory the first employment of the studied use of antithesis (contrast of ideas), anaphora (the repetition of the same word or phrase in successive clauses), and chiasmus (a figure by which the order of words in one clause is inverted in a second clause).

Lloyd highlights the importance of the oral polemical debates and discussions between the Sophists, natural philosophers, and medical practitioners, and the institutions, such as the Academy and Lyceum, which provided the forum for discussion. He concludes significantly, that "although by the end of the fifth century (B.C.E.) the manufacture and production of books had begun to develop, and literacy was by then established at least in a small section of the population, the chief, even if no longer the only, medium for the propagation of scientific as well as other kinds of knowledge was still, and was for long to remain, the spoken, not the written word."[18] The intellectual milieu in which both early science and philosophy advanced was essentially oral, small-scale and face-to-face. If this was true of early Greece, it was also emphatically true of India in the Axial Age.

The fact that the sayings and discourses of the Buddha were in the early centuries of Buddhism transmitted orally necessarily implied that elaborate techniques of memorization and recitation were developed by the early monastic communities. Let us therefore now scrutinise the art of memory itself.

As far as I know, there is no text in the early Buddhist writings that quite matches that ancient Roman text, the *Ad Herennium,* which drawing on Greek sources of memory teaching, teaches how to memorize and recall in terms of the mnemonic of places and images *(loci* and *imagines).*[19] It is noteworthy that "it was as a part of the art of rhetoric that the art of memory travelled down through the European tradition. . . ."

The memory feats of Indian religious *virtuosi* is a byword, and the best known example is that of the Vedic poems which were continuously transmitted in oral form with absolute fidelity even down to the smallest phonetic details. "This astonishing feat was made possible by a hereditary priesthood which regarded the verbatim recitation and preservation of the texts as its most important duty. In addition to memorization of the connected text, two other methods of fixing the text helped to secure its stability. The first was an elaborate system of analytic recitation, including the *padapāṭha,* a form of word-by-word recitation (showing the shape of each word in *pausa*) and a variety of permutations of words. . . . Secondly, there were auxiliary treatises, themselves memorized on phonetics and philology. . . ."[20] Altogether the Vedic reciters had a sophisticated understanding of the articulatory mechanisms of speech, and it is possible that their feat of forming standardised oral editions of texts, which were transmitted unchanged over the centuries, must in part be attributed to their being tight, exclusive, highly trained and disciplined small corporations of ritual specialists.

The critical importance of India for our discussion of the Axial Age is that it is a remarkable example of a high culture, with attainments in both literature and sciences, which primarily relied on the oral medium. As Winternitz has observed: "In India, from the oldest times, up until the present day, the spoken word, and not writing, has been the basis of the whole of the literary and scientific activity. Even today, when the Indians have known the art of writing since centuries . . . Not out of manuscripts or books does one learn the texts, but from the mouth of the teacher, today as thousands of years ago.[21] The written text can at most be used as an aid to learning, as a support to the memory, but no authority is attributed to it. If today all the manuscripts and prints were to be lost, that would by no means cause the disappearance of Indian literature from the face of the earth, for a great portion of it could be recalled out of the memory of the scholars and teachers. . . ."[22] In India, as in certain other classical instances, writing, which had been developed very early, was first used for the pragmatic purposes of accounting and administration, and its use for recording literature not only came about much later, but also never assumed the importance it came to have in Europe and the Far East. In so far as India shows that it is not so much the *technique* of writing (as opposed to speech) that determines the fixity of a text but the *function* that text has in the society, it puts in jeopardy any universal claims for literacy and writing as a pre-requisite for high intellectual culture.

Let us return to our early Buddhist monks and their oral texts. It is clear that the Buddhist texts could not have achieved that total freezing into a rigid shape that the Vedic hymns achieved for two important and interrelated reasons. While Sanskrit remained for the Vedic-Brahmanical tradition the only sacred language, the early Buddhist monk missionaries and propagandists adopted the vernacular and the local dialect of the regions in which they preached. And this linguistic choice was in accord with the fact that the early monastic communities multiplied as they dispersed. The combined result was variant wordings of the canonical *Tripiṭaka* texts of different 'schools' and 'fraternities'. "The recensions of the *Tripiṭaka* preserved in different countries of India therefore differed in dialect or language from the earliest times, and we cannot speak of any 'original' language of the Buddhist canon. . . ."[23]

This flexibility in the choice of language or dialect for teaching and transmitting the doctrine surely aided the spread of Buddhism, and must certainly have contributed its share to the sectarian versions of the doctrine itself and its interpretation. However, this flexibility of the language medium, and its stimulation of variant oral texts, must be placed within the larger truth that the early Buddhist monks developed and exploited effective memorization and recitation techniques in the same way as they forged sophisticated discursive techniques of argumentation and proof.

One might surmise that as in the case of the Vedic bards and priests, the early Buddhist monks learned and recited texts, which made ample use of "formulas," which Albert Lord[24] (and Parry before him) have defined as "repeated word groups" that express an essential idea. While the Vedic bards may have insisted on an invariant recitation, the early Buddhist teachers and preachers are more likely to have used their formulaic devices, not altogether differently from—though not with the same freedom as—the Slavonic singer of epic poetry, to compose their discourses while they performed ("for the oral poet the moment of composition is the performance"). We are told by Lord that the technical equipment of the Slavonic oral poet consisted of "basic patterns of meter, word boundary, melody," and that he exploited composition devices such as the linking of phrases by "parallelism", the balancing and apposition of word order, and the substitution of key words.

"Parallelism" (the pairing of couplets, such that there are recurrent returns at the semantic, syntactic, and phonemic levels of expression), which Lowth in 1778 first brought to our attention in the Bible, which Roman Jakobson later detected with relish in Finnish and Russian oral traditions, and which now anthropologists and folklorists are collecting with ardour in many non-literate societies, as such is not a conspicuous feature of the Buddhist *sutta* discourses. But what the discourses exploit almost *ad nauseam,* no doubt because it is a device that aids memorizing and production of lengthy utterances, is that "redundancy" device at present labelled as the "substitution system" of key words. This substitution system operates both horizontally at the level of the line, and vertically at the level of the stanza, and of the grouping of stanzas into discourses. As a matter of fact, this redundant substitution device of introducing key phrases at the end of repetitive stanzas or paragraphs, was the opposite of the condensed mnemonic formula, and had its recitative uses. As

Rhys Davids pointed out: "Two methods were adopted in India to aid this power of memory. One adopted chiefly by the grammarians, was to clothe the rules to be remembered in very short enigmatical phrases (called *sutras* or threads), which taxed the memory but little, while they required elaborate commentaries to render them intelligible. The other, the method adopted in the Buddhist writings (both *Sutta* and *Vinaya*), was, firstly, the use of stock phrases, of which the commencement once given, the remainder followed as a matter of course and secondly, the habit of repeating whole sentences, or even paragraphs, which in our modern books would be understood or inferred, instead of being expressed."[25]

The *Sutta* and *Vinaya* texts show that from early times different kinds of utterances were self-consciously developed, each kind suited to a different purpose: examples are biography, narrative, question and answer dialogue, exegesis, homily and sermons, poem and verse, chant and rune. Many texts portray a combined use of these forms.

I now come to my last feature in the discussion of the art of memory of the early Buddhist monks, namely their specialization in different branches or sections of the canonical literature. This is a kind of division of labour by which the accuracy of transmission was sought to be achieved by having different groups of monks *specialize* in the memorization of certain texts (while presumably undergoing as well a general education in Buddhist doctrine). This also enabled each group specializing in certain texts to contemplate them more deeply and intensively, and thus generate fruitful commentarial and interpretive activity.

We have already mentioned that the Buddhist tradition holds that in the First Council held after the Buddha's passing away, Ananda was called upon to recite the *suttas,* Upāli the *vinaya,* and Kassapa the *abhidhamma.* The canon has references to the Buddha singling out certain of his disciples and extolling them for proficiency in certain branches of the *Dhamma.*[26] Perhaps even more significant is the *Samyutta Nikāya's* enumeration of some ten chief *theras* (elders), such as Sāriputta, Mogallāna, Mahākotthita, each of whom having some ten to forty disciples under his tutelage. Just as the *sangha* as a whole was a refraction of the Buddha, these groups of disciples were considered refractions of their *gurus,*[27] and were therefore called by epithets that characterised their teachers' special skills.

Another apposite reference which attests to groups of oral specialists is found in the *Vinaya* (IV,15.4):[28] it refers to delay that might be caused in holding the Pāvarana ceremony because "the Bhikkhus were reciting the Dhamma, those versed in the Suttantas were propounding the Suttantas, those versed in the Vinaya were discussing the Vinaya, the Dhamma preachers were talking about the Dhamma."

Dutt suggests that these distinctions which though originally not based in doctrinal differences did lead to full-fledged schools seeking proficiency in different sections of the canon which they regarded as their special preserves.

In fact Sri Lanka in the first century B.C.E. and in the early centuries C.E. provides us with good information on the prevalence of Bhāṇakas or Reciters of various portions of the Canon.[29] Indeed it is their system of oral transmission that made possible the first writing down of the *Tipiṭaka* canon in Sri Lanka in the first century B.C.E. It is this same feat of oral transmission through *bhāṇakas* that later, around the fifth century C.E., also enabled the writing down of the Pāli Commentaries *(Atthakathās)* by the famous authors, Buddhaghosa and Dhammapala.

It is noteworthy that even after the Pāli canon was committed to writing,[30] the *Bhāṇaka* system continued because it had other uses than that of simply transmitting the sacred knowledge, such as recitations at rituals at which the spoken word carried elocutionary force and performative significane. Buddhaghosa provides us with the apt example in his *Sumangalavilāsini* (a commentary on the Dīgha Nikāya) that when certain *bhāṇakas* recited the *Brahmajāla Sutta* the very earth quaked. Moreover, since the system of teaching stressed the teacher's oral transmission of knowledge to pupils and the personal face-to-face relations between them, the recitative and debating traditions continued to be important.

The Sri Lanka *Bhāṇaka* system manifested various levels and degrees of specialisation, concentrations within specialisations, and a graduated ladder of recitative attainments. At the most general level there were those who were versed in one of the three "baskets" of the *Tipiṭaka:* the *Suttas,* or *Vinaya,* or *Abhidhamma.* At the next remove there were specialists in four Nikāyas of the *Sutta* texts who were accordingly called *Catunikāyaka;* and those who mastered the collection of popular Jataka stories which were the substance of sermons to the laity were called *Jatakabhāṇakas.* The progressive mastery expected of monk scholars is indicated in the *Samantapāsādikā,* which tells us that a monk who counted ten years from his higher ordination *(upasampadā),* and who was the head of a circle of monks, should know minimally certain portions of the *Vinaya* texts together with certain portions from other sections of the canon: if he specialised in the *Dīgha Nikāya* (and was therefore a *Dīghabhāṇaka*) he had also to know the *Mahāvagga,* if he had mastery of the *Saṃyutta Nikaya,* he also had to be proficient in the first three *vaggas* of the *Mahāvagga,* and so on.

The Early Buddhist Monastic Community

All that we have discussed hitherto—the teaching vocation of the Buddha and his disciples, the codification, preservation, transmission and elaboration of the Buddha's *Dhamma* as sacred knowledge, the forging of elaborate pedagogical techniques for memorization and rhetorical argumentation, the institutionalization of teacher-pupil, preceptor-novice, and fraternal relations as crucial pathways for the passing on of authoritative knowledge, the learning and practice of meditation techniques in the company of fellow-seekers of liberation, the ensuring of reliable and organized material provisioning by laity which freed the monks for the practice of the higher vocation—all these could not have been achieved if early Buddhism, together with Jainism, had not invented the monastic community and the monastic residence.

Oldenberg has observed that the Buddha's circle of disciples even in the earliest days were by "no means a free society, bound together by merely internal bonds like the band of Jesus' disciples." Indeed he asserts that "a monastic order appeared then to the religious consciousness to be the reasonable, natural form in which alone the life of those who are associated in a common struggle for release could find expression".[31]

It seems to me that the assertion made famous by Louis Dumont that the renouncer in Indian society is "an individual outside the world" (meaning that he becomes an individual by standing outside society altogether) is as far as early Buddhism and Jainism are concerned—these are historically the most important of the "heterodox", "renunciatory" movements that arose in India—only a partial truth. In fact precisely because their most productive and creative contribution was the founding of monastic communities, we can say that these religious movements posed not so much the dichotomy of householder *versus* individual ascetic as that of the lay household (and the lay householding stratum) *versus* the religious monastic community. In fact I would go so far as to argue that it is precisely the development and far-flung situating of monastic residences—in cities and towns, along the overland trade routes, in the countryside, and in border regions—combined with the "corporate" living of monks in small-scale communities which enabled them to constitute "fields of merit" for donors ranging from royal courts, merchant guilds, trading caravans, and peasant communities, that enabled early Buddhism to successfully missionize and develop into a "world religion".

Since I have elsewhere written in some detail about the structure of the early Buddhist monastic community as can be gleaned from the *Vinaya Piṭaka,*[32] I shall merely reproduce some of the main points made there.

The *Vinaya Piṭaka* of the Pāli School is divided into two main parts, the *Vibhanga* which states the ancient formulary of confession, and the *Khandakas,* whose chief divisions are the *Mahāvagga* and the *Cullavagga,* and which are an exposition of the monastic rules accompanied by a vast amount of circumstantial detail and explanation. Many scholars, Rhys Davids and Oldenberg included, hold that the Pātimokkha is one of the oldest, if not the oldest, of all Buddhist textbooks, and that it was inserted into the *vinaya* texts as their first part.

The *Pātimokkha* which serves as a liturgical formulary during the monthly confessions is in fact a statement of the rules governing the conduct of the monks. There are a number of traditionally recognised groupings of these rules but for our purposes we can usefully recognise four main groups. There are first of all the four *pārājikā* offences which are considered grave and are punished by expulsion from the order of bhikkus. Two relate to theft and the taking of life, and the remaining two to indulgence in sexual intercourse and the making of false claims to an arhant's achievements.

The next group of crimes evoke the meeting of the monks in assembly, the suspension of the offender and his reinstatement after penance. These rules are notably concerned with sexual offences short of intercourse and offences detrimental to monastic community life. Examples of the latter kind are false accusation of another monk of a major crime, attempting to cause schism of the community, resisting disciplinary admonishment by fellow-monks, failing to request the assembly of monks to select or ratify the site of residence.

The third level of offences in the hierarchy, requiring explanation with forfeiture of the possession in question, focuses on two themes which may be described as firm rejection of the life and occupations of the householder, and a careful enumeration of the improper ways of accepting and soliciting gifts from laymen. What is noteworthy about these precepts is their manifestation of the double relation that, on the one hand, the monk's way of life is a rejection of the layman's, and on the other, that indeed a monk is in an elaborate relation of gift-acceptance from the layman.

Finally, there is a large number of rules which range over many spheres of conduct and whose infringement calls for simple expiation—they concern sexual improprieties, separation from a householder's way of life, behavior towards fellow monks, the consumption of food, and non-violence.

The *Mahāvagga* and *Cullavagga,* aside from describing the teaching career of the Buddha, state in great detail the fundamental institutions which give to the Buddhist order of monks their distinctive stamp. There are first of all important community rites and observances which give Buddhist monastic communities their identity and collective existence. These are the rituals of admission to the order; the monthly confession ceremonies; the three-month retreat during the rains *(vassa)* including the defining of the community which must attend the same confession ceremony; and the rules of residence during the rainy season; and the procedures for the *kaṭhina* ceremony, especially with regard to the distribution of the cloths received from the assembled laity.

There are then all the rules and punishments devoted to the maintenance of discipline, which, as we already saw in the Pāti-mokkha, is achieved through collective deliberations in assembly. There is a listing of the sorts of assemblies that can be convened, the criteria for deciding their lawful competence; there is an explication of the difference between a difference of opinion and a split or schism of the community; and there is a statement of the rules and etiquette of disciple-teacher relationship.

Enough has been said about the rules of monastic life to support some general statements.

I do not want to minimize in any way the central message of Buddhism to its renouncer, the *bhikkhu,* and the path of liberation it charted for him. The conceptions of *dukkha* (suffering), *anicca* (impermanence) and *anatta* (nonindividuality), of 'dependent co-origination' which explains the origins of suffering and the mode of its elimination, and the meditative techniques which enable the renouncer to acquire tranquility, one-pointedness of mind, and finally total detachment: these conceptions and techniques are primarily addressed to the individual renouncer who must depend on himself and strive by himself.

But the features of early Buddhism we have surveyed also manifest the importance placed by the Buddha and his disciples on renunciation being practised within the confines of a monastic community, to which the candidates were initiated, and in which they were subject to rules of discipleship. Moreover, if the renouncer leaves the society at large, he enters a special society of fellow adepts which provides the setting in which most of his life is lived. Although there were intimations of hierarchical organisation, the early *sangha* was essentially a 'brotherhood' of monks who through collective deliberations and collective rituals not only marked themselves off from other sects of renouncers and the laity, but also lent each other support and reinforced each other's aspirations in the pursuit of a difficult and taxing ascetic goal. It is in this way that we have to understand the so-called 'republican' model *(gaṇa sangha)* of the tribal federations (in contrast to the 'monarchical' model of the Magadha and Kosala kingdoms) which the Buddha recommended to his disciples. This aspect of the monastic fellowship emerges in better relief if we compare it with the rules which early European monastic communities endorsed, such as the Rule of St. Benedict. The Benedictine monk took a vow of obedience not only to God but also to his Abbot and undertook thus to submit himself to an institutional authority in a way no Buddhist renouncer did.

There is another major difference. The Benedictine monasteries set out, in a European feudal context, to be self-sufficient 'cells', which not only prayed and studied but also worked to materially support themselves through agriculture, crafts and other activities. Labour for the Benedictine monk had a therapeutic and material value. But Buddhist monasticism denied productive agricultural work, even the cooking of their own food, to its members; work as such was not valued; and its negation meant the monk's complete material dependence on the laity for the provision of food, clothing, and shelter. Thus the Buddhist renouncer's material dependence on the laity, specified from the beginning, cuts into his existence as 'individual-outside-society' in important ways. The *vinaya* rules we have examined testify to the fact that the relationship with lay merit makers was nearly as much an area of detailed specification as the rules of brotherly living within the sangha. And doctrinal disputes in due course regarding the propriety of a monk's taking gifts from laymen without an obligation to return attests to a tension embedded in the *bhikkhu*'s vocation.

The early canonical texts state time and again how the wandering communities of disciples provided the opportunity for conspicuous acts of feasting and donation *(dāna)*. For kings (such as those of Magadha and Kosala), nobles, and merchants (such as Anāthapindika who donated the Jetavana *ārāma*) such public acts earned them merit and legitimated their position. For the collective *sangha* such occasions provided a leverage for moral and political comment, silently and non-violently, by the mere willingness to be feasted or by their chilling rebuke of inverting their begging bowls.

These tendencies and developments that have to do with the constitution of monastic orders, the structured relations between renouncers and laymen, and between the sangha and polity, hold the principal answers for understanding how the renouncer's conceptions and practices either directly or indirectly suffused Hinduism in India, and became total religions outside it.

The corporate character of the early *sangha,* or to be more correct, of the dispersed local communities who met for *Pātimokkha* recitations and for disciplinary deliberations, is also reflected in the

ownership and use of property. Whatever the later developments in
Buddhist countries with regard to the ownership of property by
individual monks and by individual monasteries, early Buddhism's
stress that the bhikkhu was an almsman who went from home into
homelessness, rejecting the householder's values and attachments,
implied that he possessed only the minimal material requisites for
following the path—such as three robes, begging bowl, umbrella,
needle and thread, packet of medicines, and so on, making up some
'eight' requisites in all, which are still today given him at his upasampadā ordination.

The *vinaya* texts relate in extraordinary detail the circumstances
which led the Buddha to accept on behalf of the *sangha* the gift of
ārāmas from laymen, and to allow the monastic residence to be
fitted with doors, locks, and windows, and to be equipped with
acceptable furniture and rugs and the like. The *Cullavagga* (sixth
khandaka) records how the Setthi of Rājagaha (whose sister was the
wife of the conspicuous merchant donor Anāthapindika) informed
the Buddha that he had erected '60 dwelling-places made for the
sake of merit, and for the sake of heaven', and that the Buddha
replied 'Then, O householder, dedicate these 60 dwelling-places to
the *sangha* of the four directions, whether now present, or hereafter
to arrive'. And in due course when the *sangha* communities became
the recipients of residences with many rooms, of large gifts of robes
and of furishings, and of stores of food (both cooked and dry), the
Cullavagga once again describes meticulously the events leading to
the Buddha personally ordering the appointment of bhikkhu-officials
to administer the collective property of the *sangha* communities,
such as distributor of lodging-places, overseer of stores, receiver of
robes, distributor of robes, distributor of food, superintendent of the
ārāma grounds and so on. Reading between the lines, one sees in
these canonical accounts not only the establishment of corporate
property which is for the use of *bhikkhus* whose personal property
rights are limited, but also the evolving of organisational arrangements and conceptions of institutional property, which would enable
the monasteries in due course to become wealthy institutions. A
corporate body composed necessarily of mendicants attracts more
munificent endowments from the wealthy and the powerful than can
a single renouncer.

Let me conclude this section by speculating on why the Buddhist
salvation quest was thought from the beginning to be best undertaken
in a monastic context, that is by a brotherhood of seekers subject
to a monastic discipline. Buddhism has been well known for its
slogan that salvation requires the unity of 'knowledge and practice';
austerities and ascetic practices were useless unless illuminated by

the dispelling of 'ignorance' concerning the causes of attachments and mental formations, and by the mastery of the principles of 'co-dependent origination', which revealed the basis of ignorance and the manner of its extinction. It is no accident that the Buddha's very first sermon delivered, after reaching enlightenment, to his first disciples in the deer park at Sarnath near Vārānasī, which set the wheel of dhamma in motion, was on this theme. Thus the Buddhist movement, which emphasised the teachings and propagation of a certain knowledge or wisdom *(paññā)* together with the attendant ethical practices, required as its basic grouping or cell a 'master', who had acquired the 'knowledge and practice', and a following of pupils whom he instructed. We know that in the earliest phase of Buddhism, the teacher was peripatetic, his movements always in the company of disciples being punctuated by temporary residences at favourite locations. These residences were longest during retreat of the rains during which both the teaching and discussion of doctrine and the practice of discipline and meditation were intensified. It is perhaps because of this central feature of the salvation quest itself that the Buddha spearheaded the founding of the monastic way of life as the marked alternative to the householder's.

PART V

Islam

Introductory Remarks: Islam

S.N. EISENSTADT

Our discussion ends with a brief analysis of the last of Axial Age—really beyond Axial Age—the last monotheistic religion—Islam.

In some way Islam can be seen as yet another secondary breakthrough from Judaism and Christianity, in the sense that both these religions constitute its original starting point and the encounter with these civilizations, but of course especially with the Christian world, constituted a continuous part of the civilizational dynamics of Islam.

Yet quite obviously this was a rather different type of breakthrough from the ones discussed above, because it did not originate within any of these civilizations, but rather through the encounter of tribal units in Arab, with inter-civilizational dynamics that have been taking place in this period in the Near and Middle East. Michael Cook's paper analyzes some aspects of these dynamics and the ensuing crystallization of Islamic civilization.

CHAPTER 21

The Emergence of Islamic Civilisation

MICHAEL COOK

A minor event that has recently taken place in Islamic studies is the publication of a seventh-century silver coin of a hitherto unknown type.[1] It is Sasanian in style, and on the evidence of the obverse would be identifiable as a coin of the emperor Khusraw II (ruled 590–628): the image is his, and he is named in the Pahlavi superscription. The image on the reverse continues the illusion: it shows a Zoroastrian fire-temple, with attendants on either side. Only the Pahlavi superscription of the reverse gives the game away: "Year one of Yazīd", presumably to be identified with the Umayyad Caliph Yazīd I (ruled 680–3); and even here, the practice of dating by regnal years is a Sasanian one. In short, there is nothing about this coin to suggest that the Arab ruler under whom it was issued was identified with the militant and literate religion we know as Islam, or that the barbarian incursion which had established his dynasty had given rise to a new civilisation, or was in the least likely to do so.

A silver coin minted less than a generation later, in 698–9 under the Caliph 'Abd al-Malik (ruled 685–705), conveys a startlingly different message.[2] No images appear, Islamic or other—a point we can relate to the adoption in Islam of Jewish reservations on this matter. The superscriptions are entirely in Arabic, and are thoroughly Islamic. The coin is dated according to the Muslim era ("year seventy-seven"). The rest of the material is more or less Koranic. It tells us that there is no god but God, alone, without a partner; that He is one, neither begets nor was begotten, and has no equal; and that Muhammad is His apostle, "whom He sent with guidance and the religion of truth, to make it supreme above all others, whether the polytheists like it or not."

The Sasanian-style coin of Yazīd is unusual in its failure to make any gesture whatever in the direction of Islam. But in other respects it is typical of the sort of coinage which was issued under Arab rule until the last decade of the seventh century. Taken at face value, it would suggest that the barbarian conquerors of the Persian Empire, whatever havoc they may have wreaked in the short run, did not in the long run pose any serious threat to the continuance of Persian culture. A similar point can be made, *mutatis mutandis,* for the previously Roman provinces of the Arab kingdom. But the very different coin of 'Abd al-Malik is also typical of its kind, and already represents what were to become the conventions of Muslim coinage down the centuries. It marks the deliberate invention of a specifically Islamic coinage, and its superscriptions proclaim in no uncertain terms that the supposed barbarians are the bearers of God's own truth.

It would be frivolous to take the dates of these two coins as termini for the emergence of Islamic civilisation. This is a story that must go back before the 680s, and undoubtedly continues beyond the 690s. Yet this numismatic transition aptly dramatises the extraordinary speed with which this civilisation was brought into existence. It also points up other significant features of the process: the central role of a new and singularly uncompromising monotheist doctrine; the part played by the existence of a centralised Caliphal authority; and the ease with which one can imagine an alternative history in which the Arab invasion left the cultural traditions of the Near East more or less intact.

Let us begin with the problem of the sheer rapidity of the process.[3] At the beginning of the seventh century, Islam did not exist. By the end of the eighth, if not before, an Islamic civilisation existed—a *fait accompli* which possessed the kind of general and detailed plausibility—the capacity to be taken for granted—that we associate with a *Weltanschauung* several centuries old. For like any civilisation, the culture which concerns us possessed both a material basis and a world view. The material basis—food production, advanced metallurgy, urban life, the use of coinage, and the like—is, however, of little interest from our point of view. Such a repertoire was, by the first millennium of our era, pretty much the common stock of Old World civilisations; and the Islamic instance did not arise from any major advance on the material capacities of its predecessors or contemporaries. What constituted the emergence of Islamic civilisation was the formation and triumph of a new world view, and it is the rapidity of *this* process which is so surprising.

The first point to note is that we do not have to do with a process endogenous to either Arabia or the settled societies of the Fertile Crescent. That is to say, there is no question of the gradual emergence of a high culture through internal development from a state of antecedent barbarism. On the one hand, the settled lands of the Near East were civilised millennia before the rise of Islam; in this perspective, Islamic civilisation is not so much secondary as tertiary. And on the other hand, Arabia was a land of such deprivation that the endogenous development of an Arabian civilisation is hard to imagine, and never in fact took place. (There is an exception to be made in favour of the civilisation of sorts which appeared in the agricultural south of the peninsula; but this culture, whatever its origins, was not ancestral to Islamic civilisation.) The processes with which we have to deal are, in short, quite unlike those which led to the emergence of civilisation in India or China.

Nor do we have to do with the kind of endogenous transformation of values within a civilisation such as we associate with the rise of Christianity in the Roman Empire, or of Buddhism in India. Here again, small beginnings naturally require the passage of time to become great things, as Islamic culture did not. Islam is of course in many ways comparable to such new religions—it too represents a particular selection and shaping of previously available religious values. But, crucially, it was not a spiritual initiative taken from within the settled society of the Fertile Crescent; and the Arabian society within which the initiative was originally taken was not a civilisation.

Islamic civilisation thus emerged from an interaction between two adjoining but contrasting zones. The interaction was, moreover, one in which the basic material fact was the conquest of one party by the other—of the civilised by the barbarians. That there might be something catalytic in such an interaction is intuitively plausible; differences are more exciting than similarities when it comes to interaction, and conquest is a well-tried way of making history in a hurry. But that the outcome should be a new civilisation is, again, surprising.

Cultural interaction between a barbarian society and a neighbouring civilisation is a commonplace of world history; sometimes it arises in a context of barbarian conquest, but often enough without it. Most societies which come to be civilised do so through such interaction, in which the barbarians borrow the civilisation of their more advanced neighbours. They may not, of course, borrow all of it, nor need they surrender unconditionally to it. The Romans, with some reservations, decided that it was worth paying handsomely for a Greek education; but they did not replace Roman law with Greek law, and they preferred to descend from the Trojans rather than the Achaeans. In general, such cultural indebtedness tends to be accompanied by at least a measure of resentment and defensiveness on the part of the debtors—much as in modern nationalism. But these responses are attempts to set limits to one's cultural indebtedness, not to repress it.

There is, as might be expected, a strong vein of such defensiveness to be detected in Islam and its civilisation. To be a zealous monotheist by virtue of descent from Ishmael, not Isaac, is a typical strategy for remaining oneself even while subscribing to alien truths. But the Islamic case goes far beyond this point, in a brilliant application of the maxim that attack is the best form of defence. What Islam has done with its borrowings is to reshape them into an integral civilisation of its own, obliterating the overt traces of their origin. This is highly unusual. Of the numerous societies exposed to Indian or Chinese influence in eastern Asia, not one took serious steps in such a direction; the alien origin of the high cultures of Japan or Tibet is written all over them, and in no need of being discovered by academic research. In Islam it is different; it is a scholarly achievement, and often a controversial one, to identify an alien origin for any central component of Islamic culture. How then did the interaction between the Arabs and the inhabitants of the Fertile Crescent issue in something so deviant from the normal pattern? What was it about the cultural state of the Fertile Crescent, and of Arabia, that made such an outcome possible?

Culturally the Fertile Crescent on the eve of the Arab invasion was rich but messy. That it was rich is no surprise in view of the depth and variety of its cultural experience. The messiness needs more attention. It appears, first, in a notable lack of homogeneity. The area was populated by a plethora of communities differentiated in religious and other terms: Jews, Samaritans, Monotheletes, Melkites, Monophysites, Nestorians, Manichaeans, Magians, and a variety of gnostic sects. The messiness appears also in the shape of these communities. Nowhere in the Fertile Crescent was there a solid nation. The Jews were a politically dispossessed and territorially dispersed minority. The Melkite Greeks of Syria, though identified religiously and ethnically with the ruling power, were likewise a minority. The major Christian communities of the Fertile Crescent— the Monophysites and Nestorians—were politically neuter. The Persians were indeed a nation, and their own rulers; but though their capital was situated in the Fertile Crescent, their heartland lay off the stage on which Islamic civilisation was made. At the same time, the major Christian communities had neither sharply defined ethnic identities nor cultures they could call their own. They were provincials who had borrowed their monotheism from the Jews and their philosophy from the Greeks; the amalgam was for the most part Syriac only in language. The Fertile Crescent was thus littered with cultural rubble, but there was nothing formidable about the heaps in which it was distributed.

Arabia, by contrast, was distinguished by its impoverished homogeneity of culture. That it was too poor to be civilised has already been noted. There was, of course, a good deal of fall-out from civilisation—the Arabs did not live in isolation. But the kind of development which in the late Roman period produced national cultures in Christian Armenia or Ethiopia did not take place in Arabia. More remarkable is the apparent homogeneity of Arab culture. The Arabs were a single people with a single language, as the inhabitants of the Sahara or the Eurasian steppes were not; and there seems to have been a common poetic idiom that transcended differences of dialect. In part at least, this situation arises from obvious geographical factors—the Arabs were able to live over a long period undisturbed in an area with sharply defined territorial limits. There was little in this culture that could provide the substance of a settled civilisation; but, backed with the prestige of conquest, it could offer such a civilisation a language and an identity, with a mass of tribal memories that lent conviction to both. That the Arabs could not offer more is arguably crucial for the complementarity out of which Islamic civilisation emerged: had they had more of their own, they might have been less willing to take from others.

These considerations help to explain why the formation of a new civilisation was possible, and why it could happen so rapidly. But they scarcely indicate such an outcome to have been at all likely—as indeed it was not. That it did happen was due to the extraordinary deflection of the course of history through the career of an Arabian visionary—the apostle of God who is named on 'Abd al-Malik's coin.

Muhammad gave to his people an *Arab* monotheism. That is to say, he brought to Arabia an ancient idea that had become prominent in the settled world of late Roman times; and he brought it in an explicitly ethnic form, one which for the first time gave to the Arabs a central place in sacred history. This Arab monotheism was historically crucial in two ways. The first concerns us indirectly: in the hands of Muhammad, it provided a way of forming a state which transcended the divided loyalties of the tribal society in which he lived; without this it is hard to see how the Arab tribes could have been mobilised to conquer the Near East. Muhammad thus excelled at tribal politics by dint of rising above them. The second role of his monotheism is immediately relevant to our concerns. In the hands of Muhammad's successors, his doctrine provided the nucleus around which the new culture was shaped, the core of a cultural identity to which the conquerors could hold fast against the insidious pull of assimilation.

Several features of Muhammad's monotheism are relevant to this role. Some are intrinsic to monotheism as such. The simplicity of the idea rendered it detachable from the sophisticated cultures of the settled world and viable in Arabia. The power of the idea—its central image of a wilful God given to ordering His followers about— makes it a doctrine that can readily be put to use in getting things done. (Consider how much Muhammad's chances of changing the world would have been reduced had he devoted his life to the propagation of Epicureanism in Arabia.) Other features relate more to the historical context. It was important that monotheism was, by the time of Muhammad, a widely accepted premise of the civilised world; his message was accordingly an immediately intelligible one. But it was also important that the form of the monotheist tradition that seems most to have influenced him was not the prevailing one; because his message owed more to Judaism, it was better able to provide his followers with a basis for keeping their distance from the largely Christian world they had conquered. Finally, it is crucial that Muhammad's monotheism was an intrinsically Arab form of the persuasion. For if his transcendental vision was above tribes, it was by no means above ethnicity; and it was this feature of his doctrine which rendered it so apt to bring about the fusion of the cultural rubble of the Fertile Crescent with the barbarian identity of the Arabs.

Crucial though Muhammad was, the actual formation of Islamic civilisation can have taken place only after his death. Our knowledge of the concrete processes involved in this formation is pretty defective—a deficiency which is in its own way a remarkable tribute to the success of Islamic civilisation in taking itself for granted. None of our non-Koranic literary remains reflect a Muslim universe which is other than fully established, autonomous, and internally plausible. It cannot, for example, be the case that Arabic was *born* with a subtle and powerful vocabulary of theological dispute; yet the earliest theological texts we possess (whatever their exact age may be) already reveal a language so endowed. In general, we have no record of the fumbling and faltering beginnings which must initially have dominated the cultural scene, and the tendency of the Islamic sources is often to project their own classical maturity back into the earliest Islamic epochs.

What concerns us here is not so much what was done in this dusky period, but rather how it was possible to do it. One obvious precondition is straightforwardly political: the Arabs, having got their act together, had to keep it together for the duration of the formative period. For our purposes it is enough to note that, against considerable centrifugal pressures, they succeeded in doing this into the ninth century. By then Islamic civilisation was proof against the dangers of political fragmentation.

A precondition closer to our interests must obviously have been the existence of a cultural elite capable of exploiting the historical opportunity. Here we come up against a significant case of retrojected maturity. Since at least the early ninth century, Islam has been dominated by the characteristic cultural elite which we know as the 'ulamā'. This group is by no means all the elite there is in an Islamic society; but the central strands of the Islamic tradition are in its hands. From our point of view, two things are striking about this elite. First, they have little structure—no ecclesiastical hierarchy, no academies, no scholarchic succession. And second, their primary cultural role is to transmit; in emphasising this role, they become less and less inclined to see themselves as autonomous intellectuals. Thus 'opinion' becomes a dirty word ("piss on my opinion," as a distinguished Kūfan traditionist is said to have said[4]). Taken together, these two features make the classical elite an apt vehicle for the perpetuation of a tradition already shaped; but by the same token, they look peculiarly implausible as a force that could have given shape to the tradition in the first place.

How then are we to envisage the cultural elite of the formative period? One possibility is that the classical elite itself evolved from one which cultivated a more opinionated intellectual style—something of which we find considerable traces among such groups as lawyers and, still more, dialectical theologians; the anti-traditionist ideas of the latter make a fascinating chapter in the history of the idea of divine transcendence. Another possibility is perhaps historically more central. 'Abd al-Malik's coin already suggested the importance, not merely of the political unity of the conquest state, but of the existence of a locus of religious authority in the Caliphate. The creation of an Islamic coinage was, after all, a religious policy necessarily pursued by the state. That the Caliphate was endowed with such religious authority in the early Islamic period is something that the classical perspective of our sources tends to disguise; but there is evidence from a variety of sources for the view that a Caliph like 'Abd al-Malik may have played an uninhibited role in the shaping of the forms of Islamic culture of his day.[5] Less dense indications of analogous authority can be found at a provincial level. Here, then, we have at least a more plausible agent of the initial shaping of the new culture than the scholars who ultimately transmitted it.

Islamic civilisation thus emerged from a peculiar interaction between an area of ancient civilisation and one of inveterate barbarism—an interaction made possible by a rather negative cultural complementarity, and brought about through the religious and political initiative taken by one man, as continued and developed by his successors. The religious initiative, moreover, was a very specific one: a simple transcendental idea, monotheism, bonded to an immanent identity, that of the Arabs. It is all highly unlikely, but it happened, and in retrospect it is possible to understand something of the way it happened.

What this leaves is the question of the extent to which this unusual origin gave to Islamic civilisation a distinctive character. The analysis set out above has two obvious implications here. The first is that the way in which the civilisation came about gave to a single overriding religious idea a cultural salience that is without parallel among the world's major civilisations; and the idea in question was at once a powerful and an exclusive one. The second implication is that the same genesis gave to Islam an overwhelmingly Arab colouring. In itself, this is not remarkable; civilisations start somewhere, and so tend to have the ethnic colouring of their place of origin. But the ethnic environment from which Islamic civilisation took its colouring was, unusually, a self-consciously barbarian one—the ethos of a tribal and largely pastoral society which saw itself in contradistinction to the prevailing civilisations. The effect of this identification is again an exclusive one. The negative result of these factors was a high level of allergy in Islamic civilisation towards overtly alien influence; the legacy of the ancient world tended either to be appropriated and reshaped, or to be held at arm's length. The positive result was that monotheism and the tribal legacy alike played a notably constitutive role in the formation of the civilisation. The basic political vocabulary of Islam, for example, reflects the centrality of both—and the downgrading of alien influences that goes with it. All in all, Islamic civilisation is marked by an intensity of focus which arises directly from its genesis.[6]

Notes

NOTE TO PREFACE

For publications stemming out of these seminars see:

S.N. Eisenstadt and Yael Azmon (eds.), *Socialism and Tradition,* The Van Leer Jerusalem Foundation, 1975 (German edition in Tübingen: J.C.B. Mohr, 1977).

The papers in the series of studies in Comparative Modernization, Sage Research Papers in the Social Sciences (Series Number 90–003) (Beverly Hills and London: Sage Publications, 1973–75).

S.N. Eisenstadt and L. Roniger, *Patrons, Clients and Friends* (Cambridge: Cambridge University Press, 1984).

S.N. Eisenstadt and A. Schachar, *Culture, Society and Urbanisation* (Sage Publications, forthcoming 1985).

S.N. Eisenstadt, M. Abitbol, and N. Chazan (eds.), *The Origins of the State Reconsidered* (Philadelphia: ISHI Press, forthcoming).

S.N. Eisenstadt and I.F. Silber, *Cultural Traditions and Worlds of Knowledge—Explorations in the Sociology of Knowledge* (Philadelphia: ISHI Press, forthcoming 1985).

The special issue (Summer 1984) on Comparative Liminality and Dynamics of Civilizations, of *Religion.*

Among the publications of international seminars, see:

S.N. Eisenstadt and S.R. Graubard (eds.), *Intellectuals and Tradition* (New York: Humanities Press, 1973).

S.N. Eisenstadt (ed.), *Post-Traditional Societies* (New York: Norton, 1972). (These two were initially published as special issues of *Daedalus*).

S.N. Eisenstadt, R. Kahane and D. Shulman (eds.), *Orthodoxy, Heterodoxy and Dissent in India* (Berlin & New York: Mouton, 1984).

Notes to Introduction

1. K. Jaspers, *Vom Ursprung und Ziel der Geschichte* (München: Piper Verlág, 1949), 15–106.

2. See Max Weber, *Gesammelte Aufsatze zur Religionsoziologie* (Tübingen: J.C.B. Mohr, 1922, 1978) and the English translation: *Ancient Judaism* (New York: The Free Press, 1952), *The Religion of India* (New York: The Free Press, 1958), *The Religion of China* (New York: The Free Press, 1951, 1964). On Weber's thematic and vision see: W. Schluchter, "The Paradox of Rationalization," in G. Roth and W. Schlucher, *Max Weber's Vision of History, Ethics, and Methods* (Berkeley, Los Angeles, London: University of California Press, 1979), 11–64; see also P. Bourdieu, "Une interprétation de la théorie de la religion selon Max Weber," *Arch. Europ. Sociol.* 12 (1971), 1–24; R. Lennert, "Die Religionstheorie Max Webers, Versuch einer Analyse seines religionsgeschichtlichen Verstands," Inaugural Dissertation, Stuttgart, 1955; F.H. Tennbruck, "The Problem of Thematic Unity in the Works of Max Weber," *The British Journal of Sociology* 31, no. 3 (1980), 316–351; Stephen Kalberg, "The Search for Thematic Orientations in a Fragmented Oeuvre; the Discussion of Max Weber in Recent German Literature," *Sociology* (1979) 13, 127–139.

3. K. Jaspers, *Vom Ursprung und Ziel der Geschichte, op. cit.,* n. 1; *Wisdom, Revelation, and Doubt: Perspectives on the First Millennium B.C., Daedalus,* Spring 1975.

4. E. Voegelin, *Order and History,* vols. 1–4 (Bâton Rouge: University of Louisiana Press, 1954–1974).

5. B.I. Schwartz, "The Age of Transcendence," in *Wisdom, Revelation, and Doubt, Daedalus,* Spring 1975, 3–4.

6. For some out of the many analyses of these premises of pagan religions see for instance: M. Fortes and G. Dieterten, eds., *African Systems of Thought* (London: Oxford University Press, 1965), esp. 7–49; the analysis in E. Voegelin, *Order and History,* vol. 1, Israel and Revelation; the papers by Oppenheimer and Garelli in *Wisdom, Revelation, and Doubt, op. cit.,* n. 3; H. Frankfort, *Kingship and the Gods* (Chicago: University of Chicago Press, 1948; for a case of individual transcendental vision which was not institutionalized see: G. Wiley, "Mesoamerican Civilization and the Idea of Transcendence," *Antiquity,* L (1976), 205–215.

7. See Max Weber, *Gesammelte Auftsatze zur Religionsoziologie, op. cit.,* n. 2; and G. Roth and W. Schluchter, *Max Weber's Vision of History, op. cit.,* n. 2.

8. G. Obeysekere, "The Rebirth Eschatology and Its Transformations: A Contribution to the Sociology of Early Buddhism," in W. Doniger O'Flaharty, ed., *Karma and Rebirth in Classical Indian Traditions* (Berkeley and Los Angeles: University of California Press, 1980), 137–165.

9. See, for instance, E.H. Erikson, ed., *Adulthood* (New York: W.W. Norton & Co., 1978).

10. The relations between the eschatological premises of civilizations and the construction of worlds of knowledge is one of the neglected—but also perhaps one of the most promising—arenas of sociology of knowledge. They

are being now worked out in an interdisciplinary seminar at the Hebrew University in Jerusalem. Some interesting indication can be found in B. Nelson, *Der Ursprung der Moderne Vergleichende Studien zum Zivilisationsprozess* (Frankfurt: Suhrkamp, 1977).

11. On Egypt see H. Kees, *Ägypten—Die Kulturgeschichte des Orients,* (Munich: 1933); and J. Wilson, *The Burden of Egypt* (Chicago: University of Chicago Press, 1951). On Japan see J.W. Hall, *Japan from History to Modern Times* (London: Weidenfeld and Nicholson, 1970).

12. These terms are derived from E. Shils, "Primordial, Personal, Sacred, and Civil Ties," in E. Shils, ed., *Center and Periphery, Essays in Macro-Sociology,* (Chicago: University of Chicago Press, 1975), pp. 111–126.

13. These terms are derived from E. Shils, "Center and Periphery; and Society and Societies—The Macrosociological View," in E. Shils, ed., *Center and Periphery, op. cit.,* n. 12, 3–11 and 34–48; and see also their elaboration and application in S.N. Eisenstadt, ed., *Political Sociology* (New York: Basic Books, 1971); and S.N. Eisenstadt, *Revolution and the Transformation of Societies* (New York: The Free Press, 1978).

14. The concept of Great Tradition is derived from R. Redfield, *Human Nature and the Study of Society* (Chicago: University of Chicago Press, 1962), passim.

15. This point is more fully elaborated in S.N. Eisenstadt, *Revolution and the Transformation of Societies, op. cit.,* n. 13, esp. chs. III and IV.

16. See S.N. Eisenstadt, "Cultural Traditions and Political Dynamics, The Origins and Modes of Ideological Politics," *The British Journal of Sociology* vol. 32, no. 2 (June 1981), 155–181.

17. See also this in greater detail in S.N. Eisenstadt, *Social Differentiation and Stratification* (Glenview: Scott Foresman & Co., 1971), ch. 6; and S.N. Eisenstadt, "Convergence and Divergence of Modern and Modernizing Societies," *International Journal of Middle East Studies* 8 (1977), 1–18.

18. S.N. Eisenstadt, *Tradition, Change, and Modernity* (New York: John Wiley & Sons, 1973), 140–151.

19. See on this the various discussions in *Wisdom, Revelation, and Doubt, op. cit.,* n. 3.

20. The literature on Utopia is, of course, immense. For a good survey see G. Kaleb, "Utopias and Utopianism," *International Encyclopedia of the Social Sciences,* vol. 16 (New York: MacMillan and Free Press, 1968), 267–270; and for a fascinating collection of essays: *Vom Sinn der Utopie, Eranos Jahrbuch, 1963* (Zurich: Rhein Verlag, 1964).

21. E. Durkheim, *De la division du travail social* (Paris: Alcan, 1983). English translation: *The Division of Labor in Society* (Glencoe: The Free Press, 1960). See also R. Aron, *Les étapes de la pensée sociologique* (Paris: Gallimard, 1967), 319–330.

22. See S.N. Eisenstadt, "Intellectuals and Tradition," in S.N. Eisenstadt and S.R. Graubard, eds., *Intellectuals and Tradition* (New York: Humanities Press, 1973), 1–21; and E. Shils, "Intellectuals, Traditions and the Tradition of Intellectuals," *ibid.,* 21–35.

23. See S.N. Eisenstadt, "Some Observations on the Dynamics of Traditions," *Comparative Studies in Society and History* 2 (1969), 451–475.

24. See S.N. Eisenstadt, M. Abitbol, and N. Chazan, "The Origins of the State Reconsidered: Theoretical Considerations and an Introduction to African States," in idem (eds.) *The Origins of the State Reconsidered* (Philadelphia: ISHI, forthcoming).

25. See S.N. Eisenstadt, M. Abitbol, and N. Chazan, "The Origins of the State Reconsidered," *op. cit.*

26. See S.N. Eisenstadt, "Traditional Patrimonialism and Modern Neo-Patrimonialism," *Sage Research Papers in the Social Sciences,* in Comparative Modernisations Series, Beverly Hills and London: Sage Publications, 1973.

27. This follows the discussion in S.N. Eisenstadt, M. Abitbol, and N. Chazan, "Conclusions," *op. cit.,* n. 24.

NOTES TO CHAPTER 1

These are the reflections of a historian of modern science who is equipped only with "little Latin and less Greek." I am grateful for the critical remarks of my colleagues Zev Bechler, Shmuel Eisenstadt, Radi Malkin, and Sabetai Unguru.

1. Michael Oakeshott, *On Human Conduct* (Oxford, 1975), p. 1.

2. See my "A Programmatic Attempt at an Anthropology of Knowledge," in E. Mendelsohn and Y. Elkana, eds., *Sciences and Cultures,* Sociology of the Sciences, Vol. 5 (Dordrecht, Boston, London: Reidel, 1981), pp. 1–77.

3. A word about the expression 'second-order': The way it is used here, namely as reflexiveness, i.e., conscious, systematic thinking about thinking, is often encountered in philosophical, anthropological, and psychological literature but has not yet been evaluated in a critical mode as a theoretical concept. In 1972 the University of Ife, under Robin Horton's guidance, established a thoughtful journal concentrating on comparative issues of Western and African culture and science. The journal is called *Second Order* and it is dedicated to cultural reflexivity. The editors did not think it necessary to explain the name of the periodical.

4. See here the Spring 1975 issue of *Daedalus: Wisdom, Revelation, and Doubt: Perspectives on the First Millennium B.C.,* and Benjamin J. Schwartz's Introduction: "The Age of Transcendence." Also S.N. Eisenstadt's recent work, and especially his "Heterodoxies, Sectarianism and Dynamics of Civilizations," *Diogenes* 120 (Oct.–Dec. 1982).

5. Karl Jaspers, *Von Ursprung und Ziel der Geschichte* (München: R. Piper, 1949).

6. Alfred Weber, *Kulturgeschichte als Kultursoziologie* (München, 1950 [1935]).

7. S.C. Humphreys in *Daedalus, op. cit.,* n. 4, p. 92.

8. J.P. Vernant, in his *The Origins of Greek Thought* (Ithaca: Cornell University Press, 1982 [1962]), p. 22, relates that this Cypro-Mycenaean civilization in which Mycenaean-Minoan and Asian elements intermingled used a new script (derived, like the Mycenaean syllabus, from Cretan Linear

A); are we not witnessing a breakthrough (albeit smaller) resulting from "alien wisdom" of some importance leading up towards the 5th century?

9. J.M. Redfield, *Nature and Culture in the Iliad* (Chicago: The University of Chicago Press, 1975).

10. Especially see A. Momigliano, *Alien Wisdom* (Cambridge: Cambridge University Press, 1975).

11. This is one of the theses of Arnold Toynbee's posthumous *The Greeks and their Heritages* (Oxford: Oxford University Press, 1981).

12. Eric Weil, "What is a Breakthrough in History?" in *Daedalus, op. cit.*, n. 4, pp. 21–36.

13. Eric Voegelin, *Order and History*, 4 vols. (Bâton Rouge: Louisiana State University Press, 1954–1974).

14. A. Momigliano, "The Faults of the Greeks," *Daedalus, op. cit.*, n. 4, pp. 9–19.

15. *Daedalus, op. cit.*, n. 4, pp. 105–107.

16. On this point I am grateful to Dr. Erad Malkin.

17. S.C. Humphreys, *Daedalus, op. cit.*, n. 4, p. 96.

18. Chapter 3 of *Origins of Greek Thought, op. cit.*, n. 8.

19. *Ibid.*, p. 42.

20. Ch. Meier, *Die Entstehung des Politischen bei den Griechen* (Suhrkamp Verlag, 1980).

21. G.B. Kerford, *The Sophistic Movement* (Cambridge: Cambridge University Press, 1981).

22. Vernant, *op. cit.*, n. 8, p. 74.

23. Victor Ehrenberg, *Society and Civilization in Greece and Rome* (Harvard: Harvard University Press, 1965), p. 28.

24. E.A. Havelock, *The Greek Concept of Justice* (Harvard: Harvard University Press, 1978).

25. J.P. Vernant and P. Vidal-Naquet, *Tragedy and Myth in Ancient Greece* (Harvester Press, 1981), p. 3.

26. On this again in my "A Programmatic Attempt at an Anthropology of Knowledge," *op. cit.*, n. 2, pp. 34–38.

27. G. Kennedy, *The Art of Persuasion in Greece* (Princeton: Princeton University Press, 1963).

28. Jane E. Harrison, *Prolegomena to the Study of Greek Religion* (London, 1976); *Themis: A Study of the Social Origins of Greek Religion* (London, 1979). Gilbert Murray, *Five Stages of Greek Religion* (Doubleday Anchor Books, 1955).

29. G. Murray, ch. II.

30. Vernant, *op. cit.*, n. 8, p. 75; on this also L. Gernet, *The Anthropology of Ancient Greece* (John Hopkins, 1981).

31. Vernant, *op. cit.*, n. 8, pp. 89–90.

32. Ehrenberg, *op. cit.*, n. 23, p. 38. Ehrenberg also claims that "the Ionian mind always tended to be rational"—a view which in details I cannot judge but tend to find unacceptable on general theoretical grounds; I do not believe that rationality is a racial characteristic and I think few historians today would endorse such a view.

33. *Ibid.*, p. 39. VS refers to that unique collection of the fragments of the pre-Socratics: *Die Fragmente der Vorsokratiker*, ed. H. Diels, 6th ed. by W. Kranz (Berlin: Weidmann, 1952).

34. Ehrenberg, *op. cit.*, n. 23; VS, *ibid.*

35. Ehrenberg, *op. cit.*, n. 23.

36. M. Detienne and J.P. Vernant, "Cunning Intelligence in Greek Culture and Society" (Harvester Press, 1978); Y. Elkana, "Of Cunning Reason" in Thomas Gieryn, ed., *A Festschrift for Robert K. Merton: Science and Social Structure* (The New York Academy of Sciences, 1980), pp. 32–42.

37. F. Solmsen, *Intellectual Experiments of the Great Enlightenment* (Princeton: Princeton University Press, 1975), p. 4.

38. Hans Blumenberg, "On a Lineage of the Idea of Progress," *Soc. Res.* 91 (1971), p. 8.

39. *Ibid.*, p. 13.

40. S. Unguru, "On the Need to Rewrite the History of Greek Mathematics," *XIV Internat. Cong. His. Sci. Proc. 2* (1975), 169.

It is fascinating to see to what emotional pitch this debate rose, or rather sank. The eminent mathematician André Weil (see below) opens his letter to the editor thus: "Some time ago your Archive printed a paper on Greek Mathematics which in tone and style as well as in content fell significantly below the usual standards of that journal": What arrogance!

See also, S. Unguru, "On the Need to Rewrite the History of Greek Mathematics," *Arch. H. Ex. Sci.* (hereafter *AHES*) 15 (1975), 67–114; B. van der Waerden, "Defence of a 'Shocking' Point of View," *AHES 15* (1976), 199–210; B. van der Waerden, "Die Postulate und Konstruktionen der frühgriechischen Geometrie," *AHES 18* (1978), 343–358; Hans Freudenthal, "What is Algebra and What has It been in History?" *AHES 16* (1976), 189–200; André Weil, "Who Betrayed Euclid?" (extract from a letter to the Editor), *AHES 19* (1978), 91–93; B. van der Waerden, "On Pre-Babylonian Mathematics (I) and (II)," *AHES 23* (1980), 1–25 and 26–46 respectively; Jan Mueller, "Coping with Mathematics (the Greek way)," Publication No. 2, 1980, of the Morris Fishbein Center for the Study of the History of Science and Medicine.

41. Jacob Klein, *Greek Mathematical Thought and the Origins of Algebra* (MIT Press, 1968).

42. See Unguru's article in the *XIV Internat. Cong. His. Sci. Proc. (op. cit.,* n. 40).

43. Imre Toth, "Die nicht-euklidische Geometrie in der Phenomenologie des Geistes," *Eidos, Beiträge zur Kultur,* Bd. 23 (Frankfurt, 1972).

44. B.L. van der Waerden, *Science Awakening*, as quoted by Mueller, *op. cit.,* n. 40, p. 2.

45. Imre Toth, *op. cit.,* n. 43, p. 11, "Mathematical objects and especially geometrical figures and bodies belong exclusively to the world of thought." (Plato, *Epist.* VII 342B, *Theat.* 150B, 191B–194B; *Menon* 86B.)

46. Plato, *Republic,* 509.

47. Bruno Snell's classic, *The Discovery of the Mind* (Harper Torchbook, 1960), is still very relevant to this discussion.

48. *Op. cit.,* n. 40.

49. S.C. Humphreys, "Transcendence and Intellectual Roles: The Ancient Greek Case," *Daedalus, op. cit.,* n. 4, p. 92.

50. Victor Ehrenberg, *op. cit.,* n. 23, p. 22.

51. See Sir Desmond Lee, "Science, Philosophy and Technology in the Graeco-Roman World." I. *Greece & Rome 20* (1973) 65–78; II. *Greece & Rome 20* (1973) 180–193.

52. A. Mark Smith, "Saving the Appearances: The Foundations of Classical Geometrical Optics," *AHES 24* (1981), 73–99. Also see: G.E.R. Lloyd, "Saving the Appearances, a critique of Duhem's book of the same title," *Classical Quarterly 28* (1978), 202–222.

53. On this see Heinrich Gomperz, "Problems and Methods of Early Greek Science," *J.H.I.* 4 (1943), 161–176.

54. See John R. Milton, "The Origin and Development of the Concept of the Laws of Nature," *Arch. Europ. Sociol.* 22 (1981), 173–195. Milton finds two weak expectations: Plato, once, talking of the human body, mentions laws (*Timaeus* 83c), and Aristotle, once talking of Pythagorean number mysticism (*De Caelo* 268a, 14).

55. Aristotle, *De Caelo* 268a, 14.

56. *Op. cit.,* n. 10.

57. Momigliano, *op. cit.,* n. 10, p. 9.

58. Further down he says: "Mesopotamia and Egypt still lived in a world which had been built in the second millennium upon the power of monarchy . . . built on conquering others rather than criticizing herself. The men of Greece, Judaea, Iran, India and China, who transformed their countries through their criticisms of traditional order, did not communicate with one another and did not create an international civilization." (*Ibid.,* 10.)

59. Two important books to which this study is greatly indebted are: G.E.R. Lloyd, *Magic, Reason and Experience* (Cambridge: Cambridge University Press, 1979); and S.C. Humphreys, *Anthropology and the Greeks* (R.K.P., 1978).

Notes to Chapter 2

1. To this and the following in general cf. Ch. Meier, *Die Entstehung des Politischen bei den Griechen,* Frankfurt: 1980 (Paperback 1983). "Die Griechen: die politische Revolution der Weltgeschichte" in: *Saeculum* 33, 1982, 133ff. The essays printed there are, in part, intended to be in preparation of a book on the origins of political thinking among the Greeks, which I am still planning to write. The situation of humanistic research in Germany, however, does not permit this before my retirement, i.e. before the end of this century, if at all.

2. *Reden und Aufsätze,* Berlin: 1905, p. 199.

3. Cf. e.g. L. Gernet/J.-P. Vernant in *Bulletin G. Budé,* 1964.

4. Citizen is understood here as citoyen, not as bourgeois.

5. As it is maintained by J.-P. Vernant, *Les Origines de la Pensée Grecque.* Paris: 1962, 119ff. (see also below).

6. Some important deliberations in this context can be found mainly in the historiographic works of Chester G. Starr and Alfred Heuss.
7. In *Anthropology and the Greeks*, London: 1978, 209ff.
8. Cf. above, n. 5.
9. *Ibid.*, 125, 100, 95ff.
10. Cf. L. Gernet, *Les Grecs sans Miracle*, Paris: 1983.
11. *Magic, Reason and Experience, Studies in the Origin and Development of Greek Science*, Cambridge: 1979, 246ff.
12. *Entstehung*, 283, to this state of affairs from the aspect of the history of concepts. Against these statements one could argue that Herodotus twice uses the phrase "placing the government *(arche)* in the midst of the people" to describe the change from Tyranny to isonomia, and that for the late 6th century (3,142,3.7,164,1. Cf. 3,80,2 where the same is said about things. M. Detienne in *Annales* 20,1965,425ff.). Only this does not say that by this reason it already belongs into the 6th century and not into the times of Herodotus. If this were so, then this phrase could not be understood otherwise than in the double meaning: that the people be consulted on all political affairs (cf. 3,80,6) and dispose of the offices (by allotting them through elections to aristocrats and later through ballots). Then one should take into account the possibility that already in the late 6th century the government, i.e. the dominance, belonged to and was common to the people. It would remain significant that this order is called isonomia (Herodotus 3, 142,3) and that evidently for another half a century the accent lies on the equality of the citizens instead of on their "governance". And there would remain a long way from the government that is placed in the midst of all to the people that governs—and to the governance that is the decisive criterion of order. Besides, in this context the people and the aristocracy do not yet constitute alternatives. In this case the statements quoted above would have to be modified at most.
13. *Entstehung*, 127ff.
14. *The Greeks*, Penguin Books, 1951, 178.
15. *Anthropologische Forschung*, Reinbeck: 1961, 23f.
16. W. Schadewaldt, *Der Aufbau der Ilias*, Frankfurt: 1975, 91ff., 7ff. A. Heuss in: *Gnomosyne, Festschrift W. Marg*, Munich: 1981.
17. Cf. A. Aymard, "Hiérarchie du Travail et Autarcie Individuelle dans la Grèce Archaique," in: *Revue d'Histoire de la Philosophie et d'Histoire Générale de la Civilisation* 2, 1943, 124ff.
18. *Grundrisse der Kritik der politischen Oekonomie*, Berlin, 1974, 379.
19. There also the equality in an early "nomistic" form is developed on the basis of the exceptional role of the hoplites (P. Spahn, *Mittelschicht und Polisbildung*, Frankfurt/Bern/Las Vegas: 1977, 98ff.).
20. E.g. the role of the agora (Vernant, 7.44ff.) or of the sacrificial communities (W. Burkert, *Griechische Religion der archaischen und klassischen Epoche*, Stuttgart: 1977, 98. "Opfertypen und antike Gesellschaftsstruktur," in G. Stephenson, *Der Religionswandel unserer Zeit im Spiegel der Religionswissenschaft*, Darmstadt: 1976, 168ff.).
21. O. Murray, *Das frühe Griechenland*, Munich: 1982, 80f. 140.150.235.277.

22. Cf. Ch. Meier, "Macht und Gewalt," in: O. Brunner, W. Conze, R. Koselleck, *Geschichtliche Grundbegriffe* 3, Stuttgart: 1982, 820ff.

23. Cf. the references in Ch. G. Starr, *The Economic and Social Growth of Early Greece*, New York/Oxford: 1977, 245 (who is sceptical himself).

24. H. Berve, *Die Tyrannis bei den Griechen*, Munich: 1967.

25. It is even thinkable that within an aristocratic community a center is institutionalized, whose—alternating—members develop a personal interest in maintaining the rules and the uniformity of politics (Ch. Meier, "Die Ersten unter den Ersten des Senats," in *Gedächtnisschrift für Wolfgang Kunkel*, Frankfurt: 1984, 85ff.). But this presupposes the preservation of social homogeneity, which got lost among the Greeks. Perhaps something similar existed in Venice.

26. J. Burckhardt, *Griechische Kulturgeschichte,* 3. 1956, 280.

27. Thus it appears e.g. in Vernant.

28. See n. 10, 23.

29. See n. 26, 2. 313.

30. See n. 10, 223ff.

31. Burckhardt (see n. 26) 2.312f.; 4.69f.

32. E.R. Dodds, *The Greeks and the Irrational,* Berkeley/Los Angeles: 1951.

33. A. Heuss in: *Propyläen Weltgeschichte* 3, Berlin: 1962, 192.

34. *Les Sagesses du Proche-Orient Ancien. Colloque de Strasbourg* 17–19 Mai 1963. G. von Rad, *Weisheit in Israel*, Neukirchen/Vluyn: 1970.

35. Humphreys (as in n. 7), 216f.

36. Elegy 3 (*Anthologia Lyrica Graeca.* Ed. E. Diehl 1. Leipzig: 1958). Cf. Ch. Meier, *Entstehung des Begriffs Demokratie,* Frankfurt: 1970, 18ff.

37. Verse 17. This passage is often mistranslated. It does not say that a doom is inescapable but that an inescapable doom is approaching.

38. This may also be indicated by the double *tacheōs*, verse 18.21.

39. We encounter a similar turn of phrase in the *Odyssey* (H. Fränkel, *Dichtung und Philosophie des Frühen Griechentums,* Munich: 1962, 253), but there the concern is with matters that men have brought upon themselves through their own wickedness and which they cannot escape above all. Solon's trust in the benevolence of the gods seems to me connected with the efforts made at the time to combat the fatalism that resulted from such attributions of guilt (cf. H. Schwabl, *Realencyclopädie der classischen Altertumswissenschaft,* Supplement 15. 1270,1275.

40. Hesiodus, *Erga,* 226ff.; *Odyssey* 19,108ff.; *Iliad* 16, 386ff.; Dodds.

41. See n. 5, 119ff.

42. U. Hölscher, "Das existentiale Motiv der frühgriechischen Philosophie," in: F. Hoermann, *Probata-Probanda,* Munich: 1974, 67.

43. It is hard to say how much meaning the analogy has in Anaximander that the world lies in the middle of all extremes and in isonomia the power lies *en mesoi*, especially as, if it is taken seriously, the citizens have to be regarded as being outside the world, like the planets.

44. It is unlikely that Anaximander has in mind single trials in court, for that would refer to individuals only. Rather, here he means big powers, whole parts of the world.

45. Fragment 114 in H. Diels, *Die Fragmente der Vorsokratiker*, 10th ed., 1961.

46. See n. 26, 1,206.

47. *Entstehung*, 82—*Alkmaion*, Fragment 4 in Diels (see n. 45). G. Vlastos, "Equality and Justice in Early Greek Cosmologies," in *Classical Philology* 42, 1947, 156ff. Aeschylus, *Eumenides*. To this: *Entstehung des Politischen*, 200f., 203ff. Thucydides 4,86,4ff. Euripides, Fragment 626 Nauck. Aristotle, *Politics* 1291 b 30ff. D. Sternberger, *Drei Wurzeln der Politik*, 1. Frankfurt: 1978, 151ff.

48. This was initiated in the phalanx of the hoplites. Vernant, 58f. Cf. Burkert, *Homo Necans*. Berlin: 1972, 32ff., on the solidarity producing role of the ritual. The sharing of certain characteristics as a premise for civic solidarity reappears in the myth of Protagoras.

49. Max Weber, *Gesammelte Aufsätze zur Religionssoziologie*. 1, Tübingen: 1921, 252.

50. This, then, is the subject of Aischylus' *Prometheus*. Cf. Ch. Meier, "Zeus nach dem Umbruch. Aischylos und die politische Theologie der Griechen" (forthcoming in *Historische Zeitschrift*).

51. On the extent of the circle of sages cf. e.g. the evidently quite accidental mention of Demonax in Herodotus 4, 161f. On the mystery men, Vernant, 52ff.; Burkert in R. Hägg, *The Greek Renaissance of the Eighth Century B.C.*, Stockholm: 1983, 115ff.

NOTES TO CHAPTER 3

1. Humphreys, 1978, chs. 9–10. I would not stress, as Christian Meier does (this volume, p. 65ff), the influence of Delphi on the development of Greek political thought and institutions, but the innovations which took place within different city-states and the effects of the interruption by the tyrants of the development towards more regular forms of power-sharing, in making the elite more conscious of the value of law and order.

2. Monotheists can, of course, be just as intimately engaged in dialogue with opposing world-views as those whose attitude is more tolerant; see Murray, 1925, ch. 5 and Liebeschuetz, 1979, 252–277 on the similarities between pagan and Christian thought in the 3rd–4th centuries C.E. The difference lies in the effort made by monotheist leaders to control their followers' beliefs.

3. See Lloyd, 1979, 15–21, 26–29. Criticism of rival doctors was equally sharp.

4. See West, 1963, on Alcman's contribution to the development of a more "physiological" cosmogony.

5. Detienne, 1972, 76–114; 1979. As Kirk, 1981, points out, animal sacrifice was already felt to be problematic by Hesiod (because of the worshippers' consumption of the meat). The Dipolieia, which in the form we know, involving the law court in the Prytaneion, is probably not earlier than the 7th century, may represent an expression of disquiet over animal sacrifice in ritual form (see the suggestive but not wholly satisfying account in Burkert,

1972b, 153–161). Surprisingly the mainstream philosophical tradition seems to have little to say on animal sacrifice until Theophrastus presents the arguments against it in his *Peri Eusebeias* (*On Piety;* see Bernays, 1866, 129–131; Pötscher, 1964; note also Plato, *Laws* 782c). The history of the growth of repugnance for animal sacrifice, which by the 4th century C.E. was clearly widespread even among pagans, still needs study.

6. Richardson, 1975; note that this allegorizing process was by the 4th century B.C.E. being applied within the Orphic tradition, as the Derveni papyrus shows (West, 1983a). Naturist allegory in Aeschylus, frags 105, 125 Mette (1959).

7. On the role of riddles and riddle-solving in archaic Greek thought see Veyne, 1983, 41–2; both divination and the use of oracles encourage this attitude. Note the parody of the riddling language of oracles in Aristophanes, *Peace* 1065ff. The gods, when they did not communicate by signs, tended to speak through oracles in verse, and this may have encouraged poets to sound an 'oracular' note; Aeschylus' fondness for 'kennings' should be noted here. On Pindar's use of the distance between contemporary mortals and the heroic world of myth both to flatter his clients and to maintain the dignity of his own position, Veyne *(ibid.),* 30–31.

8. Myth: Veyne, 1983; Dodds, 1937 (1973, 96–7). Atheism unknown, Meijer, 1981; Bremmer, 1982; on Critias' *Sisyphus,* Dihle, 1977. *Contra,* Henrichs, 1975. Certainly ancient Greeks labelled some thinkers *atheoi,* accused them of not believing in the gods and persuading others not to believe (a charge levelled at Euripides in Aristophanes' *Thesmophoriazusae,* 443–458), and at times took action against unbelievers (Momigliano, 1973; Dover, 1975).

9. Cf. the choral ode of Aeschylus, *Agamemnon* 160–183, with the comments of Smith, 1980. In the *Oedipus Tyrannus* Tiresias' complete knowledge of past, present and future makes him a representative of the divine plane of existence, but he can neither explain the facts he reveals nor change them. The breakdown of communication between him and Oedipus is in a sense paradigmatic of the general human condition. The gods act on humans, they no longer interact with them.

10. See Durand, 1977; Detienne, 1972, 105–8; n. 5 above and Gernet, 1917, 164–7. Clans: Toepffer, 1889, 149–160; Humphreys, 1983b. Historians of religion who assume that there is a constant emotional current in the response to sacrifice, through all periods and in all social milieux, as Burkert (1972b) and Girard (1972) tend to do, overlook essential differences in the way in which this emotion is felt and handled. When Aristophanes in the *Peace* (1017–1022) arranges for the sacrificial lamb to be slaughtered offstage, like a tragic victim, he draws a parallel which is implicitly valid but which nevertheless, by being made explicit, becomes absurd. Girard, 1978 (e.g. pp. 61f.) recognizes the problem but treats the Judaeo-Christian reaction against sacrifice (which has Greek parallels) as a unique discovery rather than as the basis for a historical approach to religious change.

11. It is not clear whether women watched plays or not (Pickard-Cambridge, 1968, 264–5). The Skira was a festival in which the chief religious officials of the Acropolis left the city to go in procession to the (early)

boundary of Attica, and women were left in possession of the city (Burkert, 1972b, 161–8; I am not however convinced that it was the Kerykes of Eleusis who came to the Acropolis two days later to celebrate the Dipolieia); there are parallels with the rituals and myths associated with the women of Lemnos (Burkert, 1970). When Aristophanes in the *Ecclesiazusae* makes the women of Athens decide at the Skira to dress as men and join the Assembly, the reference seems to be to this reversal of male and female roles rather than to actual ritual transvestism (Gjerstad, 1929; Jacoby, 1954, 285–305, on *F.G.H.* 328 F 14–16; but see Vidal-Naquet, 1981, 166–7). There is some evidence, not entirely conclusive, that in the late 4th century and Hellenistic period public business continued on the days of the Thesmophoria (Mikalson, 1975).

12. As the Greeks became increasingly conscious of the difficulties of reconciling theological and materialist conceptions of the cosmos, the natural sacraments of commensality, sexual intercourse, and procreation, instead of serving as metaphors and analogies used to bridge the gap between human experience and the divine, became obstacles to the acceptance of myths and rituals which incorporated them. Myths were altered and reinterpreted by poets (cf. Untersteiner, 1972), but ritual was more difficult to manipulate. Parodies, however, can be illuminating. Webs of association linking points of ambiguity and marginality in society and culture persisted but acquired new meanings: the Triballoi are a case in point. Hecate was an ambiguous figure (cf. Theophrastus, *Characters* 16.7) and the idea of a goddess who ate pigs' testicles must surely at some level have been disquieting; pigs were marginal animals, crossroads liminal space. Hecate was *Kourotrophos*, youth-nurturer, and adolescent males had a marginal place in the city; in their symposia they played with the boundaries between public and private life (Humphreys, 1983a, 16–18), between male and female and—as we see here—between the sacred and the profane. Unconsciously, the Triballoi pick up patterns of mythical association which add spice to their parody.

13. See Bolkestein, 1929. Plato, *Laws* 907d–901e (cf. Bernays, 1866, 104) anticipates Theophrastus in associating atheism and *deisidaimonia* as the two extremes between which the mean of proper behaviour towards the gods, *eusebeia,* is found (Pötscher, 1964, 127–8). (Xenophon presents Socrates as converting an *atheos* to philosophical religion in *Memorabilia* 1. iv.) The seers, diviners, and oracle-mongers of classical Athens are frequently mocked by Aristophanes, and Plato pokes fun at Euthyphro's pretensions to expert knowledge on questions of piety (leading him to charge his father with homicide) and modern theology (rationalistic etymologies of the names of the gods) in the *Euthyphro* and *Cratylus*. Cf. the presentation of Tiresias in Euripides' *Bacchae* 266ff. (Henrichs, 1968).

14. Possibly the interest taken by the Athenians in the cult of Themis and Nemesis at Rhamnous in the 5th century represents an early stage in this process of rationalization? See Nilsson, 1952; Hamdorf, 1964.

15. A. Mommsen (1898, 526–32) thought that both festivals were held on the same day; the date of the Diisoteria is still not known (see Mikalson, 1975, 170, 180).

16. Hermes Hegemonios is mentioned in Aristophanes' *Plutus* (1159), but at present we can only guess that this may be a topical reference to a new cult. A fuller account of Athenian public cults in the Lycurgan period will appear in Humphreys, 1985.

17. *Kanephoros, I.G.* ii² 3457; on their number see Brelich, 1969; on Aristophanes' *Lysistrata* 641-7, Vidal-Naquet, 1981, 197-8. *Pais aph' hestias,* Clinton, 1974, 98-114 (cf. Kourouniotis, 1923, fig. 8; Mylonas, 1961, p. 203 and fig. 80). A mention is plausibly restored in *I.G.* i³ 6 C 25, and certain in Clinton 1980, frag. d 5 (mid-4th century; the restoration of another reference to the *aph' hestias* in a 41 does not suit the context), but it is not clear whether early *paides* were children or adolescents (though I am not suggesting that the mystery cults, with their ranked initiation grades, should be confused with initiation as a *rite de passage* for adolescents). There seems to me to be a gradually increasing interest in the classical period in the conceptualization and portrayal of gods as infants or children which is, towards the end of the 4th century and in the Hellenistic period, accompanied by (though not systematically associated with) an increased use of pre-pubertal children, as well as adolescents, in ritual. But the extent and chronology of this trend are by no means clear. It is presumably connected, in part, with the increasing tendency to see myth as only suitable for the early stages of children's education.

18. The leading figures in ritual are no longer acting to maintain their status in the city and relations with the gods, but *representing* values which are felt to have affinities with ritual. Similarly, those granted dining rights in the Prytaneion are not given this privilege to increase their power, as in the archaic period, when dining at the archons' table gave a man a seat at the centre of *polis* business, but so that they may serve as living icons of the city's past glories (cf. Schmitt-Pantel, 1980), flesh-and-blood counterparts to the statues in the Agora, a civic and permanent equivalent of the representation of dead ancestors in aristocratic Roman funerary rituals (cf. the use of living stand-ins for dead kings among the Merina of Madagascar, Bloch, 1981).

19. My comments on Euripides owe much to Helene Foley's *Ritual Irony* (1985), which I had the privilege of seeing in manuscript and found extremely illuminating and stimulating—though she should not be held responsible for the directions in which her ideas have led me.

20. See Weber, 1968, 196-200, on the formal rationalization of divination and other magical practices; doctrine is systematically elaborated but this increasing sophistication is not accompanied by any critical 'second-order thinking' (cf. Elkana) about methodology and verification procedures. Cf. Gascoigne, 1983, for some remarkable contemporary examples.

21. See Just, 1975; Henrichs, 1978, 1982; Padel, 1983. Freudian influence has made it fashionable to see Euripides' portrayal of Pentheus as a case study of a man with transsexual leanings, revealed in his reaction to dressing in women's clothes. This is, I think, a reversal of Euripides' interest: to reduce religious experience to sex makes nonsense of his play. He was surely using sex—or rather, gender—as a way of talking about religious experience. For a Greek male to abandon himself to ecstasy was like becoming a

woman—unstable, emotional, open to penetration. Nevertheless the idea held a fascination (cf. Girard, 1978, 421). It is essential, for this view that Pentheus' ambiguous feelings about gender identity function as a metaphor, that he should not be presented or perceived as a psychiatric case, that the audience should be able to empathize with his feelings. It may be relevant here that he is presented as a youngish man—unmarried—so not far removed from an age at which playing the coquette and taking a female sexual role was socially accepted (*neanias, Bacchae* 274, 974).

22. Murray, 1940, 59–68; Stanford, 1942 (note pp. 38–40 on links between Aeschylus and Orphic texts, though we cannot say in which direction the influence travelled); Rosenmeyer, 1982, ch. 4, warning against the tendency to exaggerate this element in Aeschylus' style. In his work we can see some of the roots of the classicizing tradition of poetic grandeur *(semnotēs)* which we have inherited, but we must not project the whole later development back into the early 5th century B.C.E.

23. Barbarians: Aélion, 1983, II, ch. 6; madness, *ibid.*, ch. 8.

BIBLIOGRAPHY

Aélion, Rachel (1983), *Euripide héritier d'Éschyle* I–II, Les Belles Lettres, Paris.

Bernays, J. (1866), *Theophrastos' Schrift über Frömmigkeit*, Hertz, Berlin.

Bloch, M. (1981), "Tombs and States" in S.C. Humphreys and Helen King, eds., *Mortality and Immortality*, Academic Press, London, pp. 137–147.

Boersma, J.S. (1970), *Athenian Building Policy from 561/0 to 405/4 B.C.*, Wolters and Noordhoff, Groningen.

Bolkestein, H. (1929), *Theophrastus' Charakter der Deisidaimon als religionsgeschichtliche Urkunde*, Töpelmann, Giessen.

Borgeaud, Ph. (1979), *Recherches sur le dieu Pan*, Institut Suisse, Rome.

Bourdieu, P. (1977), *Outline of a Theory of Practice*, University Press, Cambridge (French ed. Droz, Geneva, 1972).

Brelich, A. (1969), *Paides e Parthenoi*, Ateneo, Rome.

Bremmer, J. (1982), "Literacy and the origins and limitations of Greek atheism" in J. den Boeft and A. Kessels, eds., *Actus: Studies in Honour of H.L.W. Nelson*, Instituut voor Klassieke Talen, Utrecht, pp. 43–55.

Brisson, L. (1974), "Du bon usage du dérèglement" in J.-P. Vernant et al., *Divination et rationalité*, Seuil, Paris, pp. 220–248.

Burkert, W. (1970), "Jason, Hypsipyle and new fire at Lemnos", *Classical Quarterly*, 20, pp. 1–16.

Burkert, W. (1972a), *Lore and Science in Early Pythagoreanism*, Harvard University Press, Cambridge, Mass. (first ed. 1962).

Burkert, W. (1972b), *Homo Necans. Interpretationen altgriechischer Opferriten und Mythen*, De Gruyter, Berlin.

Burkert, W. (1982), "Craft versus sect: the problem of Orphics and Pythagoreans as alternative groups" in Meyer and Sanders, 1982, pp. 1–22.

Clinton, K. (1974), *The Sacred Officials of the Eleusinian Mysteries, Transactions of the American Philosophical Society*, N.S. 64.3

39. D. Lührmann, "Neutestamentliche Haustafeln und Antike Ökonomie," in *NTS* 27 (1981), 83–97; on Middle-Platonism: C. Zintzen (ed.), *Der Mittelplatonismus* (Darmstadt: 1981).

40. D.L. Balch, *Let Wives be Submissive* (Scholars Press: 1961); likewise already J.E. Crouch, *The Origin and Intention of the Colossean Haustafel* (Göttingen: 1972), 102f.

41. The most important literature on this subject is: M. Hengel, *Eigentum und Reichtum in der frühen Kirche. Aspekte einer frühchristlichen Sozialgeschichte* (Stuttgart: 1973); the article by E.A. Judge and R.L. Wilken in W.A. Meeks (ed.), *Zur Soziologie des Urchristentums* (Munich: 1979), 131–193; R.M. Grant, *Christen als Bürger im Römischen Reich* (Göttingen: 1981).

42. H. Gülzow, *Christentum und Sklaverei in den ersten drei Jahrhunderten* (Bonn: 1969), 115–127.

43. Aristides, *Apologia* 15; Tertullian, *Apologeticum* 39,6.

44. R. MacMullen (see n. 16) 11; Stählin, Art. χήρα in *ThW* IX (1973), 428–454 mentions on p. 431 the legal tribulations of widows who are frequently sold into slavery to cover debts (*Lam.* 1,1 gives the parallel between 'widow' and 'become tributary'); Stählin, Art. ξένοσ in: ThW V (1954) 1–36 on p. 6: "Still in the imperial era the stranger was theoretically homeless and without rights; only if he acquired a host did he obtain the possibility of finding shelter . . ., and only if he was subordinate to a *patronus* did he receive the protection of the law"; H. Ringgren, Art. jātôm in: *Theologisches Wörterbuch zum Alten Testament* III (1982) 1075–1079.

45. See n. 37, 133. On the interpretation of the 3rd letter of St. John see the list of literature by G. Strecker in W. Bauer, *Rechtgläubigkeit und Ketzerei im ältesten Christentum* (Tübingen: 1964²) supplement 304–306.

46. K. Koschorke, *Die Polemik der Gnostiker gegen das kirchliche Christentum* (Leiden: 1978), 60ff.

47. G. de Ste. Croix, "Why were the Early Christians Persecuted?" in *Past and Present* 26 (1963), 6–38; W.H.C. Frend, *Martyrdom and Persecution in the Early Church* (Oxford: 1965); A. Wlosok, *Rom und die Christen* (Stuttgart: 1970).

48. The historical material on this: in W.H.C. Frend (n. 47) 244–247 and 353ff.; E. Pagels, *Versuchung durch Erkenntnis. Die gnostischen Evangelien* (Frankfurt: 1981) 120–156, discusses the Gnostic reasoning. The Elkesaits in particular practised the principle of the denial of the faith vis-à-vis strangers (later on described in Islam as ketmān/taqīya (Epiphanius, *Panarion* XIX, 1,8f. and Eusebius, *Historia ecclesiae* VI 38). Besides the above-mentioned reason of the Doketism, something else played a role. The fact that indeed there were martyrs among the Marcionites (Eusebius *loc. cit.*, V 16,21 and VII 12) is connected with their understanding of the revelation: to them the revelation was established with certain writings of the New Testament, whereas some Gnostics, by virtue of their visions, regarded themselves as superior also to the apostles and generally believed in a continual revelation through visions (E. Pagels, "Visions, Appearances and Apostolic Authority: Gnostic and Orthodox Traditions," in *Gnosis. Festschrift für Hans Jonas* (Göttingen: 1978) 415–430).

49. C. Andresen, *Logos und Nomos. Die Polemik des Kelsos gegen das Christentum* (Berlin: 1955), demonstrates how Celsus was influenced by Herodotus (pp. 192–197). Andresen emphasizes that Celsus' accusation should be seen in the context of his theory of history (pp. 209–224). His conclusion that "The 'community' does not mean the political body of the state but the community of people united in the Nomos" (p. 217) is however based upon an untenable distinction between religion and politics and is rejected— as incompatible with the texts—by M. Borret in his Edition (*Origène contre Celse* II (Paris; 1968) 22f. n. 1). E. Peterson has dealt with the political logic of Celsus' argumentation: "Der Monotheismus als politisches Problem," in idem, *Theologische Traktate* (Munich: 1951) 45–147.

50. Cf. n. 20.

51. *The Political System of Empires* (New York: 1963); "Religious Organizations and Political Process in Centralized Empires," in: *Journal of Asian Studies* 21 (1961/2), 271–294.

52. "A Mistake about Causality in Social Science," in: P. Laslett & W. Runciman (eds.), *Philosophy, Politics and Society* (Oxford: 1967) 48–70.

NOTES TO CHAPTER 12

1. See C.P. Jones, *The Roman World of Dio Chrysostom* (Harvard: 1978), pp. 115–123.

2. Philostratus, *Vitae Sophistarum* 1.7, p. 488 (Olearius).

3. R.M. Jones, *The Platonism of Plutarch* (Menasha, Wisconsin: 1916).

4. Peter Brown, *The Making of Late Antiquity* (Harvard: 1978), pp. 27–53 ("An Age of Ambition").

5. See J.M. Robinson (ed.), *The Nag Hammadi Library* (San Francisco: 1977).

6. H. Lewy, *Chaldaean Oracles and Theurgy: Mysticism, Magic, and Platonism in the Later Roman Empire*, ed. Tardieu (Paris: 1978).

7. G.W. Bowersock, *Greek Sophists in the Roman Empire* (Oxford: 1969), pp. 59–75 ("The Prestige of Galen"). Most recently, V. Nutton (ed.), *Galen: Problems and Prospects* (London: 1981).

8. See now the large literature spawned by the important publication by A. Henrichs and L. Koenen of the Cologne Mani codex: *Zeitschrift für Papyrologie und Epigraphik* 5 (1970), 97–216; 19 (1975), 1–85; 32 (1978), 87–199; 44 (1981), 201–318; 48 (1982), 1–59.

9. *Mos. et Rom. leg. coll.* 15.3.

10. See the new volume edited by H.J. Blumenthal and R.A. Markus, *Neoplatonism and Early Christian Thought: Essays in Honour of A.H. Armstrong* (London: 1981).

11. L. Ruggini, "Sofisti Greci nell'Impero Romano," *Athenaeum* 49 (1971), 402–425.

12. Eunapius, *Vitae Philosophorum et Sophistarum*, pp. 474–475 (Boissonade). Cf. G.W. Bowersock, *Julian the Apostate* (London: 1978), pp. 28–29.

13. Peter Brown, "The Rise and Function of the Holy Man in Late Antiquity," *Journal of Roman Studies* 61 (1971), 80–101, reprinted in *Society and the Holy in Late Antiquity* (California: 1982), pp. 103–152.

14. G.W. Bowersock, "Mavia, Queen of the Saracens," *Studien zur antiken Sozialgeschichte: Festschrift für Fr. Vittinghoff* (Cologne: 1980), pp. 477–495, especially 487–488.

15. Alan Cameron, "The Last Days of the Academy at Athens," *Proceedings of the Cambridge Philological Society* 195, new series 15 (1969), 7–29.

NOTES TO INTRODUCTION, PART IV

1. Benjamin I. Schwartz, "Transcendence in Ancient China," *Daedalus,* Spring 1975, pp. 57–69.

2. Herbert Fingarette, "Human Community as Holy Rite, An Interpretation of Confucius' Analects," in *Harvard Theological Review,* vol. 59, 1966, no.1, pp. 53–67; idem, *Confucius, The Secular as Sacred,* New York: Harper & Row, 1972.

3. Review Symposium: Thomas A. Metzger's "Escape from Predicament" in *The Journal of Asian Studies,* vol.39, no.2, 1930; Guy S. Alido, "Introduction," pp. 237–243; H.D. Harootunian, "Metzger's Predicament," pp. 245–254; E.T. Ch'ien, "The Transformation of Neo-Confucianism as Transformative Leverage," pp. 255–258; Hao Chang, "Neo-Confucian Moral Thought and its Modern Legacy," pp. 259–272; T.A. Metzger, "Author's Reply," pp. 273–290.

BIBLIOGRAPHY TO CHAPTER 13

Balazs, Etienne, (tr. by H.M. Wright), *Chinese Civilization and Bureaucracy.* New Haven: Yale University Press, 1964.

Bodde, Derek, *Essays on Chinese Civilization.* Princeton: Princeton University, 1981.

Chen, Meng-chia, *Yin-hsu-pu-tzu tsung-shu* (General Introduction of the Oracle Inscription). Peking: Science Press, 1956.

Chin, Fa-ken, "Tung han Tang-ku jen-wu-ti fen-shi," ("The Partisans during the Later Han Dynasty"). *Bulletin of the Institute of History and Philology,* XXXIV (2), 1962, 505–558.

Chun-Chiu-fan-lu, Ssu-pu-pei-yao edition.

Creel, H.G., *The Origins of Statecraft in China.* Chicago: University of Chicago Press, 1970.

Fung, Yu-lan, "Yuan Ju Mo" (On the Origin of the Confucians and Mohists). *Ching hua Journal* 10 (1936), 279.

Fung, Y.L. and D. Bodde (tr.), *History of Chinese Philosophy,* 2 vols. Princeton: Princeton University Press, 1952.

Han-shu, Han-shu-pu-chu (Han History with Complete and Supplementary Commentaries). I-Wen Reprint edition.

Hou-Han-chih, (Gazetteers and Treatises of the Later Han Dynasty.) Taipei: I-Wen Reprint edition.

Hou-Han shu, Hou-Han-shu-chi-chieh (History of the Later Han Dynasty with Collections of Annotations). Taipei: I-Wen Reprint edition.

Hsiao, Kung-Chuan (tr. by F.W. Mote), *A History of Chinese Political Thought* Vol. 1. Princeton: Princeton University Press, 1979.

Hsin-yü, Ssu-pu-pei-yao edition.

Hsu, Cho-yun, *Ancient China in Transition,* Stanford: Stanford University Press, 1965.

Hsu, Cho-yun, 1965A, "The Changing Relationship Between Local Society and the Central Political Power in Former Han," *Comparative Studies in Society and History,* 1965, Vol. 7, No. 4.

Hu, Shih, "Shuo Ju" (On Origins of the Confucians), *Bulletin of the Institute of History and Philology,* IV (3).

Huai-nan-tzu, ssu-pu-pei-yao edition.

Ideda, Yuichi, "Chugoku Kodai'ni Okeru," *Chungoku Kodaishi Kenkyu,* ("On Chinese Antiquity", Studies on Ancient China.) Vol. IV (Tokyo: Yuzan Kaku, 1976).

Kamada, Shigeo, *Shinkan seiji seido no kenkyo* (Studies on Ch'in-Han Political Institutions). Tokyo: Nihongakujutsu Shinko-Kai, 1962.

Karlgren, Bernhard (tr.), "The Book of Documents," *Far Eastern Antiquities,* XXII, 1950, 1–81.

Keightley, David N., "The Religious Commitment: Shang Theology and the Genesis of the Shang Political Culture," *History of Religion,* 17 (1978), 211–225.

Kuo-yü, (Discourses of the States), ssu-pu-pei-yao edition.

Lao, Kan, "Liang Han chun-kwo mien-chi chih Ku-chi chi K'ou-shu tseng-chien chih tui-tse," ("On Sizes of the Han Prefects and Their Demographic Fluctuation"), *Bulletin of the Institute of History and Philology,* V (1938).

Leban, Carl, "Managing Heaven's Mandate: Coded Communication in the Accession of Ts'ao P'ei A.D. 220," Roy and T.H. Ts'en (ed.) *Ancient China: Studies in Early Civilization.* Hong Kong: Chinese University of Hong Kong Press, 1978, 315–342.

Lü-shih-chun-chiu, ssu-pu-pei-yao edition.

Needham, Joseph, *Science and Civilization in China,* Vol. I. Cambridge: Cambridge University Press, 1956.

Shima, Kunio, *Inkyo Bukuji Kenkyu* (Studies on Oracle Book Inscription from the Yin Site). Tokyo: Kyuko Shonin, 1958.

Shirakawa, Shizuka, *Kokotsu Kimbungaku Ronso* (Studies on Oracle Bone and Bronze Inscriptions). Kyoto: Hoyu Shuden, 1973.

Tso-Chuan, (Tso's Chronicles), Translation by James Legge, in *The Chinese Classics,* Vol. V. *(The Chun-ts'ew with the Chuen),* Hong Kong Reprint, 1960, 1970.

Tung, Tso-ping, *Yin-li-pu* (Chronology of the Yin Calendar). Nankang: Academia Simica, 1964.

Tung, Tso-ping, *Chia-ku-ksueh liu-shih-niem* (Sixty Years of Oracle Bone Studies). Taipei: I-wen, 1965.

Wallaker, B.E., "Han Confucianism and Confucian in Han," in David Roy and T.H. Tsien (ed.), *Ancient China: Studies in Early Civilization.* Hong Kong: Chinese University of Hong Kong Press, 1978, 215–227.

Wen-wu, "Chang-sha Ma-wang-tui Han-mu chu-tu Lao-tzu ipeng-chuang-chien Ku-i-shu shih-wen," *Wen-wu,* 1974 (10) 30–40. ("Text of the Ancient Document Found on Silk Preceding the Lao-tzu Text from Han Tombs, at Ma-Wang-tui, Changsha").

Wilhelm, Richard/Cary, Baynes, (tr.), *The I Ching or Book of Changes.* Princeton: Princeton University Press, 1967.

Yang, Lien-sheng, "Tung Han-ti Hao-tsu," (Powerful Clans in the Eastern Han), *tsing-Hua Journal,* XI (4), 1936.

NOTES TO CHAPTER 14

Wherever possible references to Chinese sources are accompanied by a reference to a translation into a European language, for the convenience of non-sinological readers. It should be noted, however, that the translations offered in this chapter are the author's own.

1. Su Xuelin, *Tianwen zhengjian* ("The Questions of Heaven" Correctly Analyzed) (Taibei: 1974), p. 33. Cp. D. Hawkes, *Ch'u Tz'u. The Songs of the South* (Oxford: 1959), pp. 47–61. The date of this poem may be as early as the 4th century B.C.E. Su's book presents a detailed case, which requires a considerable re-ordering of the text, for extensive influences from Western Eurasia in this poem, whose interpretation has long baffled commentators. Even if one retains grave doubts about her central thesis (which includes the alleged incorporation of a compressed version of *Berē'shith* as far as the tower of Babhel: *op. cit.,* pp. 174–190), many of the detailed notes are extremely valuable.

2. The most uncompromising ancient Western exponent of the unreality of ordinary experience and the inadequacy of ordinary thought was probably Parmeides, whose work "proceeds, by the sole use of reason unaided by the senses, to deduce all that can be known about Being, and . . . ends by denying any truthful validity to the senses or any reality to what they appear to perceive": G. Kirk and O. Raven, *The Presocratic Philosophers* (Cambridge: 1957), p. 266. The most dramatic vision of the universe as the conflict between good and evil, and more particularly between the Truth and the Lie, the Holy Spirit and the Evil Spirit, and eventually Ohrmazd and Ahriman, was that of Zoroastrianism and the systems of belief deriving from it. See R.C. Zaehner, *The Dawn and Twilight of Zoroastrianism* (London: 1961). On the problem of explaining the flaw latent in the creator (Ahura Mazda, later Zurvan) according to this vision, see *ibid.,* pp. 51, 207–208, and 212–215. In India, the Buddhist criticism of early Hinduism offers an unusually clearcut example of dissatisfaction with the cosmos: "The world is so confused and out of joint, why does Brahmā not set it straight? . . . Why did he make the world with deception *[māyā],* lies, and excess, with injustice *[adhamma]?*" See W.D. O'Flaherty, *The Origins of Evil in Hindu Mythology* (Berkeley: 1976), p. 5.

3. Shima Kunio, *Inkyo bokuji kenkyū* (Researches on Oracle Texts from the Ruins of the Yin Capital) (Tokyo: 1958), pp. 189–190, and 192–196. Later standard hypatotheistic formulae of the early 1st millennium were "God on High, *manes,* and gods" *(Shangdi gui shen)* and "God on High and the gods possessed of intelligence" *(Shangdi mingshen).* See *Guoyu* (The Discourses of the States) (Shanghai: 1935, reprinted 1959), *Wuyu,* p. 221, and *Zhouyu shang,* p. 12, respectively. A useful introduction to Chinese myths, a subject not touched on here, is K.C. Chang, *Early Chinese Civilization: Anthropological Perspectives,* chaps. 8 and 9. For a brief description of Shang and Zhou society, see C. Blunden and M. Elvin, *A Cultural Atlas of China* (Oxford: 1983), pp. 54–75.

4. Shima, *Inkyo bokuji kenkyū,* pp. 198–200. Cf. *ibid.,* pp. 202 and 204. The question is controversial. Many scholars think Di did not receive sacrifices. E.g. Chang, *Early Chinese Civilization,* p. 156.

5. Shima, *Inkyo bokuji kenkyū,* pp. 216–217.

6. Examples may be found in B. Karlgren, *The Book of Documents* (Stockholm: 1950), p. 39, and B. Karlgren, *The Book of Odes* (Stockholm: 1950), p. 186. The composite title was "Huang Tian Shang Di", meaning approximately "August Heaven God on High": Karlgren, *Documents,* p. 48, and Karlgren, *Odes,* p. 225. See also Li Du, *Zhong-Xi zhexue sixiang-zhong-de Tian Dao yu Shangdi* (Heaven, the Way, and God in Chinese and Western Philosophical Thought) (Taibei: 1978), pp. 15–20.

7. Karlgren, *Documents,* p. 26.

8. *Ibid.,* p. 55.

9. Karlgren, *Odes,* p. 228. Compare Karlgren, *Documents,* p. 30, which describes how Tian gave "The Great Plan" to the sage-king Yu.

10. Karlgren, *Documents,* p. 27.

11. *Ibid.,* p. 36. Communication from Tian was the function of the oracle: *ibid.,* pp. 37, and 39.

12. A list of the categories of divinities may be found in S. Couvreur, *Tch'ouen Ts'iou et Tso Tchouan. La chronique de la principauté de Lou* (Ho-Kien-fou: 1914; reprinted Paris: 1951), 3 vols., Xianggong 11, II, p. 272, as the guarantors of an oath of alliance: "Superintendents of Circumspection, Superintendents of Treaties of Alliance, Famous Mountains, Famous Rivers, the multitude of gods, the multitudes of those to whom sacrifices are made, the earliest sovereigns, the earliest dukes, the [founders of the] seven [princely] surnames, the ancestors of the twelve states, may [these] gods possessed of intelligence destroy [anyone unfaithful to the treaty] in such fashion that his people desert him and the mandate of [Tian] pass from him." It is to be noted that the clear "separation of the world of gods from the world of ancestors" after the eighth century B.C.E. posited by K.C. Chang *(op. cit.,* pp. 193, and 171) is not supported by this passage. For an instance of ancestors dwelling with Tian, see Blunden and Elvin, *Cultural Atlas,* p. 75.

13. Couvreur, *Tch'ouen Ts'iou,* Huangong 6, I, pp. 87–89.

14. *Ibid.,* Xuangong 15, I, p. 655.

15. *Ibid.,* Wengong 1, I, p. 471.

16. *Ibid.,* Wengon 15, I, p. 531.

17. *Ibid.,* Zhaogong 10, III, p. 129. It was a mark of virtue in a population that its people did not try to change their occupations: *ibid.,* Xianggong, II, pp. 238–239.

18. *Ibid.,* Xianggong 19, II, p. 349. The process involved could be almost mechanical. E.g., "When a man breaks a taboo, his vital energy becomes inflamed and thereby attracts [an evil omen]. Evil omens arise from men. If a man is without such inflammation, an evil omen will not arise of its own accord. If the norms are abandoned, then there are evil omens.": *ibid.,* Xuanggong 14, I, p. 160.

19. *Ibid.,* Zhaogong 11, III, pp. 183–184. Cf. *ibid.,* Xianggong 28, II, pp. 513–514. A partial parallel is God calling Nebuchadnezzar *'abhedi,* "My servant": *Yirēmēyahu* 25.9. An aggrieved Chinese statesman said of two evildoers, "If in five years they have not been destroyed, then there is no Tian": Couvreur, *Tch'ouen Ts'iou,* Xianggong 20, II, p. 358.

20. The best short general life of Kongzi is still probably Shigeki Kaizuka, *Confucius* (London: 1956).

21. J. Legge, *The Chinese Classics,* I, *Confucian Analects, The Great Learning, and The Doctrine of the Mean* (Oxford; 1893), p. 201. See also A. Waley, *The Analects of Confucius* (London: 1938), p. 127.

22. Legge, *Confucian Analects,* p. 151; Waley, *Analects,* p. 91.

23. Legge, *Confucian Analects,* p. 240; Waley, *Analects,* p. 155.

24. Legge, *Confucian Analects,* pp. 217–218; Waley, *Analects,* p. 139.

25. Legge, *Confucian Analects,* p. 196; Waley, *Analects,* p. 123. Dreams were the commonest means whereby men spoke with the gods and with the dead. E.g. Couvreur, *Tch'ouen Ts'iou,* Xigong 28, I, p. 399 (the god of the Yellow River); Xuangong 3, I, p. 578 (an angel = "an envoy of Tian"); Zhaogong 1, III, pp. 31–32 (Di Himself); etc.

26. Legge, *Confucian Analects,* p. 195; Waley, *Analects,* p. 123.

27. Couvreur, *Tch'ouen Ts'iou,* Xigong 9, I, pp. 268–269; Xigong 14, I, p. 290. Other passages mentioning *ren* suggest that it was "a consideration for others" (*ibid.,* Wengong 3, I, pp. 455–456, a passage attributed to Kongzi himself), and the opposite of "having a disposition to harm others" (*ibid.,* Zhaogong 1, III, p. 6).

28. Legge, *Confucian Analects,* p. 197; Waley, *Analects,* p. 124.

29. Legge, *Confucian Analects,* p. 183; Waley, *Analects,* p. 114.

30. Legge, *Confucian Analects,* p. 251; Waley, *Analects,* p. 162.

31. Legge, *Confucian Analects,* p. 166; Waley, *Analects,* p. 103.

32. Legge, *Confucian Analects,* p. 282; Waley, *Analects,* pp. 184–185.

33. *Mozi jijie* (The Works of Mozi Annotated) (Shanghai: 1931. Reprinted, Taibei: 1971), ed. Zhang Chunyi, *feiming shang,* p. 319; Y.P. Mei, *The Ethical and Political Works of Motse* (London: 1929), p. 184. On the three criteria, see *Mozi jijie, feiming zhong,* p. 325; and Mei, *Motse,* p. 189.

34. *Mozi jijie, fayi,* p. 33; Mei, *Motse,* p. 14.

35. *Mozi jijie, fayi,* p. 33; Mei, *Motse,* pp. 14–15.

36. *Mozi jijie, shangtong zhong,* p. 116; Mei, *Motse,* p. 65.

37. *Mozi jijie, shangxian shang,* pp. 66 and 67; Mei, *Motse,* pp. 32 and 33.

38. *Mozi jijie, jian'ai xia,* p. 169; Mei, *Motse,* p. 97.

39. *Mozi jijie, shangtong zhong,* p. 117; Mei, *Motse,* p. 66.
40. *Mozi jijie, shangtong zhong,* pp. 119–120; Mei, *Motse,* pp. 67–68.
41. *Mozi jijie, jieyong shang,* p. 212; Mei, *Motse,* p. 119.
42. *Mozi jijie, ciguo,* p. 49; Mei, *Motse,* p. 23.
43. Legge, *Confucian Analects,* pp. 117 and 326; Waley, *Analects,* pp. 110 and 214. It should be noted that in the second passage Kongzi, implicitly comparing himself to Tian, is justifying his own preference for not speaking.
44. *Mozi jijie, Tianzhi shang,* p. 241; Mei, *Motse,* p. 136.
45. *Mozi jijie, fayi,* p. 33; Mei, *Motse,* p. 15.
46. *Mozi jijie, qihuo,* p. 44; Mei, *Motse,* p. 20.
47. *Mozi jijie, sanbian,* p. 59; Mei, *Motse,* p. 28.
48. *Mozi jijie, fayi,* p. 32; Mei, *Motse,* p. 14.
49. *Mozi jijie, jian'ai zhong,* p. 141; Mei, *Motse,* p. 82.
50. Couvreur, *Tch'ouen Ts'iou,* Xianggong 12, II, p. 309. Wrong behavior, in the late archaic view, was not so much due to the influence of an evil force or spirit as to a sort of disability, not unlike blindness or deafness. "For the heart not to take as its laws the guidelines of virtue and moral principle is to be lacking in perception [or, alternatively, "to be stubborn"]": *ibid.,* Xigong 24, I, p. 361.
51. J. Legge, *The Chinese Classics,* II, *The Works of Mencius* (London: 1861), prolegomena, pp. 95–102, gives Chinese texts and translations of the surviving fragments by Yang Zhu.
52. A.C. Graham, *Later Mohist Logic, Ethics and Science* (London: 1978), pp. 40 and 440–441. I owe a considerable debt to this remarkable book, here and elsewhere in the present chapter.
53. Graham, *Later Mohist Logic,* p. 58.
54. Graham, *Later Mohist Logic,* p. 439, retranslated.
55. Graham, *Later Mohist Logic,* pp. 448–449.
56. Graham, *Later Mohist Logic,* pp. 43 and 58; Hu Shih, *The Development of the Logical Method in Ancient China* (Shanghai: 1922. Reprinted, New York: 1963), pp. 111 and 118–119.
57. Legge, *Mencius, jinxin,* p. 326.
58. *Ibid., jinxin,* p. 327.
59. *Ibid., Gaozi,* pp. 280–281.
60. *Ibid., Gaozi,* p. 278.
61. *Ibid., Gongsun Chou,* p. 77.
62. *Ibid., Gaozi,* p. 294.
63. *Ibid., Gongsun Chou,* p. 66.
64. *Ibid., jinxin,* pp. 325–325.
65. *Ibid., Gaozi,* pp. 294–295.
66. *Ibid., jinxin,* pp. 365–366. The word translated here as "commandment" is *ming,* which is usually rendered as "mandate" (*sc.* of Tian) or "fate" (in Mozi). The basic senses are "an order", "a designation", and "life" in the sense of "allotted span".
67. *Zhuangzi jishi* (The *Zhuangzi* with Collected Explanatory Notes) (Beijing: 1961), 4 vols., ed. Guo Qingfan, *qiwulun,* I, p. 70. The concept of *yinshi,* "contingent truth", is related to the possibility of defining one and the same reality in a number of different ways. Cf. *ibid.,* I, p. 79.

68. *Ibid., dazongshi,* I, p. 281.
69. *Ibid., zhibeiyou,* III, p. 733.
70. *Ibid., Tianxia,* IV, p. 1099.
71. *Ibid., dazongshi,* I, p. 246.
72. *Ibid., qiwulun,* I, p. 55.
73. *Ibid., qiwulun,* I, p. 83.
74. *Ibid., qiwulun,* I, p. 70.
75. *Ibid., qiwulun,* I, p. 63.
76. *Ibid., qiwulun,* I, p. 79.
77. *Ibid., qiwulun,* I, p. 56.
78. *Ibid., qiwulun,* I, p. 107.
79. *Ibid., yangshengzhu,* I, p. 115.
80. *Ibid., xiaoyaoyou,* I, p. 30.
81. *Ibid., qiushui,* III, p. 563.
82. *Ibid., dazongshi,* I, p. 275.
83. *Ibid., qiwulun,* I, p. 56, and *dazongshi,* I, p. 274.
84. *Ibid., dazongshi,* I, p. 272.
85. *Ibid., xiaoyaoyou,* I. p. 24.
86. *Ibid., yangshengzhu,* I. p. 119.
87. *Ibid., qiushui,* I, p. 568.
88. *Ibid., dazongshi,* I, p. 279.
89. *Ibid., qiwulun,* I, p. 74. The creation of right and wrong, and true and false, gives rise to partiality and hence the loss of all-embracing unity in one's feelings.
90. *Xunzi jijie* (The Annotated Works of Xunzi) (Shanghai: *circa* 1891. Reprint, n.p.: n.d.), ed. Wang Xianqian, *fei shier zi,* 2, pian 6, p. 13, and *jiebi,* 4, pian 21, p. 5; H. Dubs, *The Works of Hsuntze* (London: 1927), p. 78.
91. *Xunzi jijie, zhengming,* 4, pian 22, pp. 18–19; Dubs, *Hsuntze,* p. 282.
92. *Xunzi jijie, xiushen,* 2, pian 2, p. 20; Dubs, *Hsuntze,* p. 50.
93. *Xunzi jijie, zhengming,* 4, pian 22, p. 20; Dubs, *Hsuntze,* p. 284.
94. *Xunzi jijie, zhengming,* 4, pian 22, p. 21; Dubs, *Hsuntze,* p. 285.
95. *Xunzi jijie, Tianlun,* 3, pian 17, pp. 53–54; Dubs, *Hsuntze,* p. 175.
96. *Xunzi jijie, Tianlun,* 3, pian 17, pp. 52–53; Dubs, *Hsuntze,* p. 173.
97. *Xunzi jijie, wangzhi,* 2, pian 9, pp. 60–61; Dubs, *Hsuntze,* pp. 136–137.
98. *Xunzi jijie, rongru,* 1, pian 4, p. 41; Dubs, *Hsuntze,* p. 61.
99. *Xunzi jijie, yuelun,* 3, pian 20, p. 101; Dubs, *Hsuntze,* p. 254.
100. "Shang-jun shu" Critical Annotation Committee, *Shang-jun shu pingzhu* (The *Book of Lord Shang* with critical annotations) (Beijing: 1976), *kaise,* pp. 117–118; Duyvendak, *The Book of Lord Shang* (London: 1928), p. 229.
101. *Shang-jun shu, quqiang,* p. 65; Duyvendak, *Lord Shang,* pp. 199–200.
102. *Shang-jun shu, shuomin,* p. 80; Duyvendak, *Lord Shang,* p. 207.
103. *Shang-jun shu, suandi,* p. 102; Duyvendak, *Lord Shang,* p. 222.
104. *Shang-jun shu, huace,* p. 222; Duyvendak, *Lord Shang,* p. 290.
105. *Shang-jun shu, kaise,* p. 118; Duyvendak, *Lord Shang,* p. 230.
106. D.C. Lau, *Tao Te Ching* (Hong Kong: 1982), pp. 27 and 293. Lau's book reproduces both the received and the recently excavated variant texts.

The *Daodejing* (The Scripture of the Way and Its Power) is of course more than just an anthology of items on government.

107. Lau, *Tao Te Ching*, p. 97.

108. *Ibid.*, pp. 97 and 237–239.

109. *Ibid.*, pp. 115–117 and 239–241.

110. *Shang-jun shu, kaise,* p. 120; Duyvendak, *Lord Shang,* p. 232.

111. Lau, *Tao Te Ching,* pp. 53 and 321. Lau translates: "If you would have a thing shrink, you must first stretch it."

112. *Ibid.*, p. 83.

113. *Ibid.*, pp. 45 and 313.

114. *Ibid.*, pp. 43 and 311. Or "a great carver does not sever".

115. *Ibid.*, p. 71, and cf. p. 83.

116. *Ibid.*, pp. 11, 71, 181, 207, and 275. A possibly older version read "The sage is constantly without a heart of his own, . . ."

117. *Zhouyi Yaoshi-xue* (The Changes of Zhou annotated by Yao [Pei-zhong]) (mid-19th century, Reprint, Taibei: 1965), 3 vols., *xici shang,* III, p. 60; R. Wilhelm, *The I Ching or Book of Changes* (New York: 1950), trans. C. Baynes, 2 vols. in one, I, p. 336.

118. *Zhouyi Yaoshi-xue, wenyan zhuan,* I, p. 26; Wilhelm, *Changes,* II, p. 15. This resonance theory can also be found expressed in *Zhouyi Yaoshi-xue, xici shang,* III, p. 61.

119. *Zhouyi Yaoshi-xue, shuoqua,* III, pp. 118–119; Wilhelm, *Changes,* I, p. 281.

120. *Zhouyi Yaoshi-xue, xici shang,* III, pp. 48–49; Wilhelm, *Changes,* I, p. 327.

121. *Zhouyi Yaoshi-xue, xici shang,* III, p. 43; Wilhelm, *Changes,* I, p. 319.

122. *Zhouyi Yaoshi-xue, xici shang,* III, pp. 32–33, 35–36, 39, and 40–42; Wilhelm, *Changes,* I, pp. 301–318.

123. *Zhouyi Yaoshi-xue, xici shang,* III, pp. 44–46; Wilhelm, *Changes,* I, pp. 321–323.

124. *Zhouyi Yaoshi-xue, xici shang,* III, p. 61; Wilhelm, *Changes,* I, p. 337.

125. E. Werner, *A Dictionary of Chinese Mythology* (Shanghai: 1932. Reprinted, New York: 1961), pp. 598–601. The Jade Emperor is described as the "Supreme Lord of the physical world, and the saviour of men" who "receive[s] delegations from other gods his subordinates, and intimate[s] to them his orders."

126. Sawada Mizuho, *Jigokuhen* (Changing [Ideas of] Hell) (Kyoto: 1968), pp. 9–14.

127. S. Brandon, *The Judgment of the Dead* (London: 1967), though not specifically concerned with Hell in the strict definition given here, provides a useful general survey, and notes the early appearance of Hell in Hinduism: p. 167. See also J. Pavry, *The Zoroastrian Doctrine of the Future Life* (New York: 1929) and B. Law, *Heaven and Hell in Buddhist Perspective* ([New] Delhi: 1973). A belief in Hell as a place of retributive punishment (as contrasted with an afterworld, whether gloomy or pleasant, that provided much the same conditions for all, or made distinctions according to rituals

performed rather than according to moral status) seems to have been common to most faiths in Southern and Western Eurasia in the centuries before the turn of the eras, including Judaism of the post-biblical period and classical paganism (see, for example, Lucretius' magnificent but unavailing attack on the popular belief in Acheron).

NOTES TO CHAPTER 15

1. For the idea of the "Axial Age," see K. Jaspers, *Vom Ursprung und Ziel der Geschichte,* Teil Weltgeschichte (Zurich: 1949), pp. 15–106. For a discussion of the Chinese case in the perspective of the "transcendental breakthrough," see Benjamin I. Schwartz, "Transcendence in Ancient China," *Daedalus* (Spring 1975), 57–69.

2. For an indication of his current thinking on the matter, see his Response at the Columbia University Convocation in his honor on September 10, 1982; *Proceedings of the Heyman Center.*

3. For a general discussion of the shared assumptions of the New Confucian Humanists, see Chang Hao, "New Confucianism and the Intellectual Crisis of Contemporary China," in Charlotte Furth, ed., *The Limits of Change: Essays on Conservative Alternatives in Republican China* (Cambridge, Mass.: Harvard University Press, 1976).

4. See *Chung-kuo che-hsüeh nien-chien* (*Zhongguo zhexus nianjian,* Year Book of Chinese Philosophy), ed., The Philosophy Institute, Academy of Social Sciences (Beijing: The Chinese Encyclopedia, 1982), pp. 104–114.

5. Especially noteworthy in this regard are works by Li Che-hou (Li Zehou), P'ang P'u (Pang Pu) and T'ang I-chieh (Tang Ijie). See Li's article on the reevaluation of Confucius in the second issue of the *Chinese Social Sciences* (1980).

6. For a panoramic view on this issue, see S.N. Eisenstadt, "This Worldly Transcendentalism and the Structure of the World—Weber's 'Religion of China' and the Format of Chinese History and Civilization." The German version of this essay is included in W. Schluchter, ed., *Max Webers Studie über Konfuzianismus und Taoismus* (Frankfurt: Suhrkamp, 1983), pp. 363–411.

7. Tu Wei-ming, *Humanity and Self-Cultivation: Essays in Confucian Thought* (Berkeley: Asian Humanities Press, 1979), xxii.

8. Tu Wei-ming, "Way, Learning and Politics in Classical Confucian Humanism," a paper prepared for the Conference on the Axial Age and Its Diversity, Bad Homburg (January 4–8, 1983), pp. 17–18.

9. Ssu-ma Ch'ien, *Ssu-chi* (The historical records; Beijing: Chung-hua, 1959) in 10 volumes, *chaua* 68, biography 8 (VII: 2228).

10. Hu Shih, "Shuo *Ju*" (On the character *ju*), in *Hu Shih wen-ts'un* (Collected literary works of Hu Shih; Taipei: Yuan-tung t'u-shu, 1953), in 4 volumes, vol. IV, pp. 1–103.

11. Cho-yun Hsu, *Ancient China in Transition: An Analysis of Social Mobility, 722–222 B.C.* (Stanford: Stanford University Press, 1965), pp. 140–174.

12. Ssu-ma Ch'ien, VII:2228.

13. *Mencius,* 1A:1.

14. *Ibid.,* 3B:2. For this translation, see D.C. Lau, trans., *Mencius* (Middlesex, England: Penguin Classics, 1970), p. 107.

15. Yü Ying-shih, "Ku-tai chih-shih chieh-cheng ti hsing-ch'i yü fan-chan" (The rise of the ancient intellectual class and its development), in his *Chung-kuo chih-shih chieh-cheng shih-lun—ku-tai p'ien* (A historical discussion of the Chinese intellectual class—ancient chapter, Taipei: Lien-ching, 1980), pp. 1–108.

16. *Analects,* 9:5.

17. Yü Ying-shih, "Tao-t'ung yü cheng-t'ung chih chien- Chung-kuo chih-shih fen-tzu ti yuan-shih hsing-t'ai" (Between the tradition of the Way and the tradition of politics—an original mode of the Chinese intellectual) in his *Shih-hsüeh yü ch'uan-tung* (Historical scholarship and tradition; Taipei: China Times, 1982), pp. 30–70.

18. Hsü Fu-kuan, "Han-ch'u ti ch'i-meng ssu-hsiang chia—Lu Chia" (Lu Chia—the enlightenment thinker in early Han) in his *Liang-Han ssu-hsiang shih* (History of thought of the Han) in 3 volumes (Taipei, Hsueh-sheng, 1976), vol. II, pp. 85–108.

19. *Mencius,* 3B:2: D.C. Lau, p. 107.

20. *Analects,* 9:30; *Mencius,* 4A:18, 7A:26. For an interpretive essay on the concept of *ch'uan,* see Chao Chi-pin, "Shih ch'uan" (On *ch'uan*), *Chung-kuo che-hsüeh* (Chinese Philosophy) (Beijing: San-lien, 1983), IX, 18–29.

21. This expression is found in the "T'ien-hsia" chapter of *Chuang Tzu.* See *Chuang Tzu Ying-te* (Index to Chuang Tzu, Harvard-Yenching Institute, 1947), 91/33/15.

22. Tu Wei-ming, "Way, Learning and Politics in Classical Confucian Humanism," pp. 18–19.

23. *Mencius,* 5A:5. For a historical note on this saying, see D.C. Lau, p. 144.

24. Yü Ying-shih, "Tao-t'ung yü cheng-t'ung chih chien," pp. 64–70.

25. For a general historical account of this transformation from a "materialist" viewpoint, see Hou Wai-lu et al., eds., *Chung-kuo ssu-hsiang t'ung-shih (A general history of Chinese thought),* in 5 volumes (Beijing: Jen-min, 1957-), vol. II, pp. 40–63.

26. For a suggestive study of Tung Chung-shu, see Hsü Fu-kuan, "Hsien-Ch'in ju-chia ssu-hsiang ti chuan-che chi t'ien ti che-hsüeh ti yuan-ch'eng" (The transformation of pre-Ch'in Confucian thought and the completion of the philosophy of Heaven), in his *Liang-Han ssu-hsiang shih,* vol. II, pp. 295–438.

27. Ssu-ma Ch'ien, *chüan* 121, biography 61 (X:3128).

28. Hou Wai-lu et al., eds., vol. II, pp. 331–363.

29. *Ibid.,* pp. 364–414.

30. *Ibid.,* pp. 50–55.

31. See Pan Ku's comment on Emperor Wu's establishment of the Five Erudites, cited in Hou Wai-lu et al., eds., vol. II, p. 48.

32. Ch'ü T'ung-tsu, *Law and Society in Traditional China* (Paris: Mouton, 1961), an English version of the author's earlier work in Chinese.

33. Ssu-ma Kuang, *Tzu-chih t'ung-chien* (Comprehensive mirror for aid in governance; Beijing: Chung-hua, 1971), in 4 volumes, *chüan* 27, Han-chi 19 (I:880–881).

34. Yu Ying-shih, "Han-Chin chih chi shih chih hsin shih-chüeh yü hsin ssu-ch'ao" (New currents of thought and new self awareness of the literatus during the transition from Han to Chin), in his *Chung-kuo chih-shih chieh-cheng shih-lun*, pp. 205–230.

35. Ssu-ma Ch'ien, *chüan* 121, biography 61 (X:3127).

36. See Tung Chung-shu's memorial to the King of Chiao-hsi, quoted in his biography in the *Han-shu*. See Pan Ku, *Han-shu* (Beijing: Chung-hua, 1959).

37. *Ta-hsüeh* (The great learning), see Wing-tsit Chan, trans. and comp., *A Source Book in Chinese Philosophy* (Princeton: Princeton University Press, 1969), p. 87.

38. *Ibid.*

39. See Hou Wai-lu et al., eds., pp. 232–247. For an English version of the famous discussions in the White Tiger Hall, see Tjan Tjoe Som (Tseng Chu-sen), *Po hu t'ung, The Comprehensive Discussions in the White Tiger Hall* (Leiden: Brill, 1949–52).

40. For a Han use of the term, see the "Kuei-te" chapter of Liu Hsiang's *Shuo Yuan*. For the precise reference, see *Index to Shuo Yuan, Harvard-Yenching Sinological Index Series,* no. 1 (reprint; Taipei: Chinese Materials and Research Aids Service Center, 1966), 5/2a.

41. Hsü Fu-kuan, "Yen-t'ieh lun chung to cheng-chih she-hui wen-hua wen-t'i" (The political, social and cultural issues in *Discourse on Salt and Iron*), in his *Liang-Han ssu-hsiang shih*, vol. III, pp. 117–216. For an English translation of chapters 1–19 of the *Discourse*, see Huan K'uan, *Discourse on Salt and Iron: a Debate on State Control of Commerce and Industry in Ancient China*, trans. E. Gale (Leiden: Brill, 1957).

NOTES TO CHAPTER 16

1. M. Wheeler, *The Indus Civilization,* 2nd ed., Cambridge: 1962, p. 101.

2. J.-F. Jarrige and R.H. Meadow, "Vorläufer der Stadtkultur im Industal," in *Spektrum der Wissenschaft,* Oktober 1980, pp. 61–62 (translated from *Scientific American*).

3. Of great relevance for this matter is still P. Thieme, "The 'Aryan' Gods of the Mitanni Treaties," in *Journal of the American Oriental Society,* 1960.

4. For "pre-Rigvedic" Aryans see: A. Parpola, "Interpreting the Indus Script," in *Indus Civilization. New Perspectives,* ed. by A.H. Dhani, Islamabad: 1981, 117–131 (121).

5. B.B. Lal, "Kalibangan and Indus Civilization," in *Essays in Indian Protohistory,* ed. by D.P. Agrawal and D.K. Chakrabarti, Delhi: 1979, pp. 65–97.

6. M. Wheeler, *op. cit.,* p. 99.

7. W. Rau, *The Meaning of Pur in Vedic Literature,* München: 1976, p. 52.

8. H. Falk, Vedisch *árma*, in *Zeitschrift der Deutschen Morgenländischen Gesellschaft*, 131 (1981) 160–171.

9. F.R. Allchin, "How old is the city of Taxila?" in *Antiquity*, 56 (1982) 8–14.

10. S.R. Rao, "Excavations at Rangpur and other explorations in Gujarat," in *Ancient India*, 18/19 (1963) 5–207.

11. H.D. Sankalia (et al.), *Excavations at Ahar*, Poona 1969; Z.D. Ansari and M.K. Dhavalikar, "New Light on the Prehistoric Cultures of Central India," in *World Archaeology*, 2 (1970) 337–346.

12. For Eran see: A. Ghosh, *The City in Early Historical India*, Simla: 1973, pp. 62f.

13. D.D. Kosambi, "Scientific Numismatics," in *Scientific American*, 1966, 102–111. For coin symbols see: K.K. Dasgupta, *Indian Coins and Coin Symbols*, Presidential Address, Numismatic Society of India, 71st Session, Madras: 1980.

14. W. Rau, *Staat und Gesellschaft im alten Indien*, Wiesbaden: 1957, pp. 51ff.

15. In his recent book *Zur Vedischen Altertumskunde* (Wiesbaden: 1983, pp. 48ff.) W. Rau associates the (early?) Vedic Aryans with the Ochre-Coloured Ware.

16. For pollen-analytical studies in Rajasthan see: Gurdip Singh, "The Indus Valley Culture," in *Ancient Cities of the Indus*, ed. by G.L. Possehl, New Delhi: 1979, 234–249; B.K. Thapar, "Climate during the Period of the Indus Civilization: Evidence from Kalibangan," in *Ecology and Archaeology of Western India*, ed. by D.P. Agrawal and B.M. Pande, Delhi: 1977, 67–73.

17. B.B. Lal, "Excavations at Hastinapura and other Explorations in the Upper Ganga and Sutlej Basins 1950–52," in *Ancient India*, 10/11 (1954/55) pp. 5–151; V. Tripathi, *The Painted Grey Ware. An Iron Age Culture of Northern India*, New Delhi: 1976.

18. For the socio-economic change during the late Vedic period see: W. Rau, *op. cit.* (see note 14); R.S. Sharma, *Material Culture and Social Formation in Ancient India*, New Delhi: 1983; K. Mylius, "Die gesellschaftliche Entwicklung Indiens in jungvedischer Zeit nach den Sanskritquellen," in *Ethnographisch-Archäologische Zeitschrift*, 12 (1971) 171–197; 13 (1972) 321–365.

19. R. Thapar, "State Formation in Early India," in *International Social Science Journal*, 33 (1980) 655–669 and *From Lineage to State*, Delhi: 1984.

20. B.B. Lal, "The two Indian Epics vis-à-vis Archaeology", in *Antiquity*, 55 (1981) 27–34.

21. J.C. Heesterman, "Ritual, Revelation, and Axial Age," *infra*.

22. *Śatapatha Brāhmaṇa*, I, 4,1,14–17, transl. by J. Eggeling, Oxford University Press 1882, pp. 105f. (Sacred Books of the East, vol. XII).

23. Śrautasūtra of Kātyāyana, 22,4,22 quoted by W.B. Bollée, "The Indo-European Sodalities in Ancient India," in *ZDMG*, 131 (1981) 174; see also J.P. Sharma, *Republics in Ancient India, c. 1500 B.C.E.–500 C.E.* Leiden: 1968, pp. 136ff.

24. A.K. Narain and T.N. Roy, *Excavations at Rājghāt (1957–58; 1960–65)* 5 vols., Varanasi: 1976–1978.

25. G.R. Sharma, *The Excavations at Kausambi 1957–59,* Allahabad: 1960. For a criticism of Sharma's dates etc. see Ghosh, *op. cit.,* pp. 80f.

26. For the Vrātyas see the recent studies of W.B. Bollée *(op. cit.)* and H. Falk, "Das Würfelspiel im Veda. Untersuchung zur Entwicklungsgeschichte des Śrauta-Opfers" (Habilitationsschrift Freiburg 1984 particularly ch. I "Der Männerbund in Indien", pp. 5–48).

27. W.D. O'Flaherty, "The Origins of Heresy in Hindu Mythology," in *History of Religions,* 10 (1971).

28. J.P. Sharma, *op. cit.,* p. 137.

29. H. Oldenberg, *Buddha* (1881), quoted from the new ed., München: 1961, p. 18.

30. E. Frauwallner, *Geschichte der indischen Philosophie,* Salzburg 1953, vol. I, pp. 48–96; U. Schneider, "Upaniṣad-Philosophie und früher Buddhismus," in *Saeculum,* 17 (1967) 245–263.

31. See note 18.

32. See A. Ghosh, *op. cit.,* and D. Schlingloff, *Die altindische Stadt,* Wiesbaden: 1969.

33. A. Ghosh, *op. cit.,* p. 15.

34. *Ibid.*

35. R.S. Sharma, "Iron and Urbanization in the Ganges Basin," in *India Historical Review,* 1 (1974) 98–104.

36. D.K. Chakrabarti, "Distribution of Iron Ores and the Archaeological Evidence of Early Iron in India," in *J. of the Economic and Social History of the Orient,* 20 (1977) 166–184.

37. For the Buddhist material see R. Fick, *Die sociale Gliederung im nordöstlichen Indien zu Buddhas Zeit,* Kiel: 1897 (Engl. transl. by S.K. Maitra, Calcutta: 1920).

38. J. Marshall, *Taxila,* 3 vols., Cambridge: 1951; M. Wheeler, *Chārsada,* Oxford: 1962.

39. M. Wheeler, *Early India and Pakistan,* London: 1959.

40. A. Ghosh, *op. cit.,* p. 87.

41. J. Marshall, *op. cit.,* vol. I, p. 92.

42. R. Thapar, "Ethics, Religion and Social Protest in the First Millenium B.C. in North India," in *Daedalus,* 104 (1975) 119–133 (repr. in: R. Thapar, *Ancient Indian Social History. Some Interpretations,* New Delhi, 1978, pp. 40–62); see also her *Presidential Address of Indian History Congress,* 44th Session, Burdwan: 1983.

43. S.N. Eisenstadt, "Cultural Traditions and Political Dynamics: The Origins of Modes of Ideological Politics," in *British Journal of Sociology,* 32 (1981) 155–181.

44. Max Weber, *Hinduismus und Buddhismus* (Gesammelte Aufsätze zur Religionssoziologie, Bd. II), Tübingen: 1920, pp. 251ff.

45. H. Kulke, "Gibt es ein indisches Mittelalter. Versuch einer eurasiatischen Geschichtsbetrachtung," in *Saeculum,* 33 (1982) 221–239.

NOTES TO CHAPTER 17

1. Cf. H. Bechert, "Einige Fragen der Religionssoziologie und Struktur des südasiatischen Buddhismus," *Intern. Jahrbuch für Religionssoziologie* 4 (1968), 251–95, esp. 260f. The starting point of formal relations between the temporal power and the *sangha* was the momentous purge of the internally divided *sangha* by the Maurya king Aśoka (see H. Bechert, "Aśokas Schismenedikt und der Begriff *sanghabheda*," *Wiener Zeitschrift für die Kunde Süd- und Ostasiens* 5 (1961) 18–52.

2. Cf. J.C. Heesterman, *The Ancient Indian Royal Consecration*, The Hague: 1957, 226.

3. L. Renou, "Le Destin du Veda dans l'Inde," *Etudes védiques et panindéennes* 6 (Paris, 1960), 2.

4. On the terms *śruti* and *smṛti* cf. A. Ludwig, *Der Rigveda* III, Prague: 1878, 21–24.

5. Āpastamba Śrautasūtra, 24.1.31.

6. K. Jaspers, *Vom Ursprung und Ziel der Geschichte*, Zürich: 1949, 24.

7. H. Oldenberg, *Die Weltanschauung der Brāhmaṇa-Texte*, Göttingen: 1919, 1. Cf. also S. Lévi, *La Doctrine du Sacrifice dans les Brāhmaṇas*, 2ᵉ éd., Paris: 1966, 3f., where the systematic, "scientific" nature of the texts is equally given attention.

8. Thus Max Weber stresses priestly magic as "das absolut beherrschende Element" (*Ges. Aufsätze zur Religionssoziologie* II, 136).

9. Ṛgveda 1.164.50 ab, 10.90.16 ab.

10. Thus, for instance, the interesting attempt to study "le tronc commun de l'hindouisme" "autour de la notion de sacrifice" (M. Biardeau-Ch. Malamoud, *Le Sacrifice dans l'Inde ancienne*, Paris: 1976, 13).

The notion of sacrifice has certainly undergone a wide-stretched extension, as when the peasant patron is called *jajmān*, "sacrifical patron" *(yajamāna)*. But this should not make us overlook that such usage does not so much prove continuity but rather patches over an unsettling discontinuity.

11. Aitareya Brāhmaṇa 6.34.4.

12. Ibid., 7.27.

13. Mahābhārata 12.8.34–37.

14. Jaiminīya Brāhmaṇa 2.299 (W. Caland, *Auswahl*, no. 156).

15. Works and Days, 161–165; cf. P. Walcot, "Cattle Raiding, Heroic Tradition and Ritual," *History of Religions* 18 (1979), 326–51, esp. 327.

16. Jaiminīya Brāhmaṇa 2.69–70 (W. Caland, *Auswahl* no. 128); cf. J.C. Heesterman, "Brahmin, Ritual and Renouncer," *Wiener Zeitschrift für die Kunde Süd- und Ostasiens* 8 (1964), 8–31, esp. 12f.

17. Cf. L. Renou-L. Silburn, Sur la notion de *bráhman*, *Journ. asiatique* 1949, 7–46 (repr. in L. Renou, *L'Inde fondamentale*, Etudes d'indianisme réunies et présentées par Ch. Malamoud, Paris: 1978, 83–116).

18. In a performance of the *agnicayana* ritual by Nambudiri brahmins of Kerala in 1975 (recorded on film and tape by J.F. Staal and R. Gardner) the whole of the ritual emplacement was even burned. The spectacle distinctly brought to mind the *pralaya* conflagration at the end of a world period.

19. Cf. M. Weber, *op. cit.*, I, 564; W. Schluchter, *Rationalismus der Weltbeherrschung*, Frankfort/Main: 1980, 16.

20. Mahābhārata 12.225.30–36.

21. Cf. M. Weber, *Wirtschaft und Gesellschaft* (Studienausgabe hrsg. von J. Winckelmann), Köln-Berlin: 1964, 396.

22. Śatapatha Brāhmaṇa 2.3.1.5.

23. Interestingly, where *tyāga* occurs in the Ṛgveda, it is the giving up of his life by the warrior in (sacrificial) battle (4.24.3).

24. Mānava Dharmaśāstra 3.64, 153, 4.84–85, 218.

25. Cf. J.C. Heesterman, "Vedisches Opfer und Transzendenz," in G. Oberhammer, *Transzendenzerfahrung*, Wien: 1978, 29–44, esp. 42f.

26. Śatapatha Brāhmaṇa 6.8.1.4.

27. K. Jaspers, *op. cit.*, 33.

28. Śatapatha Brāhmaṇa 1.4.1.10–17.

29. Taittirīya Brāhmaṇa 1.8.4.1–2; ŚB.5.5.2.5; Cf. W. Rau, *Staat und Gesellschaft im alten Indien*, Wiesbaden, 1957, 15. on the *vrātya* expeditions of the "sons of the Kuru-brahmans" also Baudhāyana Śrautasūtra 18.26:374.8.

30. W. Rau, *op. cit.*, 51–54.

31. On *yoga* (yoking) and *kṣemya* see H. Oertel, *The Syntax of Cases*, Heidelberg: 1926, 223–27 (Excursus on . . . yogakṣema); also J.C. Heesterman, "Householder and Wanderer," *Contrib. to Indian Sociology* N.S. 15 (1981), 251–71.

32. Aitaraya Brāhmaṇa 2.37.1; Kauṣītaki Brāhmaṇa 7.7

33. On the geographical and historical context of Zarathustra and on his reform of sacrifice cf. K. Rudolph, "Zarathustra—Priester und Prophet," *Numen* 8 (1961), 81–116 (repr. in: B. Schlerath, *Zarathustra*, Darmstadt: 1970, 270–313).

34. K. Jaspers, *op. cit.*, 43.

Note: An extended version of this paper has been published in J.C. Heesterman, *The Inner Conflict of Tradition*, Chicago, 1985, 95ff.

NOTES TO CHAPTER 18

1. J.A.B. van Buitenen, trans. and ed., *The Mahābhārata*, Book 4, *The Book of Virāṭa*, Book 5, *The Book of the Effort* (Chicago: University of Chicago Press, 1978), pp. 3–10; Madeleine Biardeau, too, has stressed the *Virāṭa*'s associations with play *(krīḍā* and *līlā)* in her Compte-rendu, *Annuaire, École Pratique des Hautes Études,* 5th sec., Sciences religieuses 82 (1973–74), p. 91.

2. In addition, the two books share intriguing themes and motifs, e.g. the role of the goddess—Kālī in the allegedly interpolated hymn at the start of the *Virāṭa;* Kālarātri in the *Sauptika* (1.24; 8.64–66); and note Draupadī's identification with Kālarātri in the Kīcaka episode (4.13.21; 4.21.19). Cf. M. Biardeau, "L'arbre *śamī* et le buffle sacrificiel," *Puruṣārtha* 5 (1981), pp. 215–43, especially pp. 216–18; A. Hiltebeitel, "Draupadī's Hair," *Puruṣārtha* 5 (1981), pp. 179–214. Similarly, the close association of Draupadī and Bhīma replicates itself in both *parvans* (the slaying of Kīcaka, the pursuit

of Aśvatthāman—both at Draupadī's insistence). The laments for the king
in distress (Draupadī for Yudhiṣṭhira, 4.17-19; Kṛpa for Duryodhana, 10.9)
seem to echo one another. These are but a few of the many striking parallels.
    3. This was the view of E.W. Hopkins, among others; see van Buitenen's
discussion, pp. 18-21.
    4. A. Hiltebeitel, "Śiva, the Goddess, and the Disguises of the Pāṇḍavas
and Draupadī," *History of Religions* 20 (1980), p. 148. Cf. G. Dumézil,
Mythe et épopée, Vol. I (Paris: Gallimard, 1968), pp. 93-94; M. Biardeau,
"Études de mythologie hindoue (V)," *Bulletin de l'École Française d'Extrême-
Orient* 65 (1978), pp. 187-200.
    5. By J.W. de Jong in a review of van Buitenen's translation, *Indo-Iranian
Journal* 22 (1980), pp. 58-62.
    6. Raghu Vira (ed.), The *Virāṭaparvan* (Poona: Bhandarkar Oriental Re-
search Institute, 1936), p. xvii.
    7. See sources cited in notes 1 and 4 above; also Heino Gehrts, *Mahāb-
hārata: Das Geschehen und seine Bedeutung* (Bonn: Bouvier Verlag Herbert
Grundmann, 1975), pp. 215-228.
    8. Biardeau, "Études V," pp. 187-88 (n. 3); Gehrts, *loc. cit.*
    9. See M.M. Bakhtin, *Rabelais and his World*, trans. Helene Iswolsky
(Cambridge, Mass.: MIT Press, 1968); also Claude Gaignebet and Marie-
Claude Florentin, *Le carnaval, essais de mythologie populaire* (Paris: Payot,
1974). For South Indian festivals to the goddess, see Richard L. Brubaker,
*The Ambivalent Mistress: A Study of South Indian Village Goddesses and
their Religious Meaning*, Ph.D. dissertation, University of Chicago, 1978.
Ritual abuse remains an important feature at festivals such as the Bharaṇi
celebration to Bhagavatī at Kŏṭunkolūr (Cranganore).
    10. Dumézil, p. 93.
    11. *bṛhatpumān;* cf. Biardeau, *op. cit.,* p. 189.
    12. 4.10.1-2.
    13. Dumézil, *loc. cit.*
    14. On this rather loaded term, see Hiltebeitel, "Disguises," pp. 166, 171;
Biardeau, "Études V," pp. 197-99. Whatever the suggestive overtones of
the word, we should note its mirroring capacity—the doll *(pāñcālikā)* calls
up the image of Pāñcālī/Draupadī, herself reduced in Virāṭa to a restricted
and impure image of her normal role.
    15. See Dumézil, *loc. cit.,* and van Buitenen, pp. 15-16, on the link with
the *Gītā's* opening scene.
    16. We might note that the *Virāṭaparvan* appears almost obsessively
fascinated by hair (Bṛhannaḍā's long locks; Draupadī's unbound hair, a
theme stressed in the context of her appeal to Bhīma, 4.15.36; Kīcaka grabs
Draupadī by the hair. 4.15.7. while Bhīma grabs Kīcaka by *his,* 4.21.47).
See Hiltebeitel, "Draupad'ami's Hair," *passim.*
    17. Biardeau, "Compte-rendu," p. 99, offers a different interpretation.
    18. The heroes spend the year in hiding "like creatures dwelling in the
womb" *(garbhavāsa iva prajāḥ,* 4.12.11), in the text's own phrase (see
comments by Hiltebeitel, "Disguises," p. 149; Gehrts, p. 217).
    19. Biardeau, "Études V," pp. 189-93.

20. As Hiltebeitel remarks, "The epic descriptions leave it amusingly imprecise and ambiguous whether Arjuna is physiologically a eunuch, a hermaphrodite, or simply a transvestite." "Disguises," p. 154.

21. 4.67.1–7.

22. E.g. the Tamil *ulā* poems, which describe the monarch's procession past hundreds of love-sick, brazenly seductive women. I do not, of course, wish to imply that the king is devoid of erotic susceptibility—witness Arjuna's own considerable experience in this area in other sections of the Epic.

23. Hiltebeitel, "Disguises," *passim.*

24. See D. Shulman, "Imperfect Paradise: Some Uses of the Androgyne," in press (in a volume to be edited by R. Brubaker).

25. See J. Scott-Kemball, *Javanese Shadow Puppets* (London: 1970), plate 19.

26. See Don Handelman, "The Ritual-Clown: Attributes and Affinities," *Anthropos* 76 (1981), pp. 321–70. For another androgynous clown, see Paul Bouissac, *Circus and Culture: A Semiotic Approach* (Bloomington and London: Indiana University Press, 1976), p. 174. I discuss Indian clown-types, especially royal clowns, in a forthcoming study of South Indian social symbolism.

27. MBh 13.12.2–49, discussed in D. Shulman, *Tamil Temple Myths* (Princeton: Princeton University Press, 1980), pp. 303–304.

28. Indra is disguised as a woman in the house of Vṛṣaṇaśva: see *RV* 1.51.13. And cf. Hans Oertel, "Contributions from the Jāiminiya Brāhmaṇa to the History of the Brāhmaṇa Literature," *Journal of the American Oriental Society* 26 (1905), p. 177; also Hiltebeitel, "Disguises," p. 158 n. 43. Indra's relation to Arjuna thus seems to extend to this feature as well. The *Pañcavaradakṣetramāhātmya,* a late work on Uttaramerūr, connects the Virāṭa stories with a local myth about Indra, who was cursed by his mother to become a leper because he dressed as a woman in her presence (chapter IV, end): F. Gros and R. Nagaswamy, *Uttaramērūr—Légendes, histoire, monuments* (Pondicherry: Institut Français d'Indologie, 1970), pp. 17–18 of the text. On androgyny and sex-reversal in Indian myth, see W.D. O'Flaherty, *Women, Androgynes, and other Mythical Beasts* (Chicago: University of Chicago Press, 1980), pp. 283–334.

29. The interest in secret nomenclature is nicely stated by M.V. Subramanian, *Vyasa and Variations* (Madras: Higginbothams, 1967), p. 143: "In buccaneering vein they also settle on a set of code names for all the five brothers. . . ."

30. See the interpretation of the Epic by G.J. Held, The *Mahabharata—an Ethnological Study* (Amsterdam: 1935), pp. 127–29, 139–47; and cf. R. Inden, "Ritual, Authority, and Cyclic Time in Hindu Kingship," in J.F. Richards (ed.), *Kingship and Authority in South Asia* (Madison: University of Wisconsin, 1978), pp. 58–59 (broadly distinguishing two phases, "transcendent" and "immanent" in the internal dynamic of Indian kingship).

31. This reflexivity is a regular feature of comedy; yet the Indian king is, even in his comic phase, on the whole *less* reflexive than the self-conscious Brahmin clowns. As A.K. Ramanujan has said (private communication, Mysore, 1980), "We laugh *at* the king, but we laugh *with* the clown." The

difference has something to do with the king's lack of awareness, his un-premeditated (hence partly tragic) comic stance.

32. M. Foucault, *The Order of Things* (New York: Pantheon Books, 1970), pp. 46–48.

33. He is, however, claimed as the mythical progenitor of medieval dynasties (e.g. the Pallavas); and he is traditionally said to be present whenever the MBh is recited or discussed (like Hanuman for the *Rāmāyaṇa*).

34. This is the basic perspective adopted by Iravati Karve in an illuminating study: *Yuganta, the End of an Epoch* (New Delhi: Sangam Books), pp. 107–21.

35. Thus in 10.3.21, Aśvatthāman says he became a follower of the *kṣatriyadharma* through ill fortune *(mandabhāgyatā)*.

36. More precisely, he is born from a mixture of Mahādeva (Śiva), Antaka (the Destroyer), Krodha (Anger) and Kāma (Desire): MBh 1.61.66. See discussion by Dumézil, *op. cit.*, p. 213.

37. As in the Virāṭa debate mentioned above: 4.45.1–26. This side of Aśvatthāman—his classical Brahminical wisdom—is even more pronounced in Villiputtūrār's Tamil MBh (e.g. 8.179–81).

38. See the statement of the question by John D. Smith, "Old Indian: The Two Sanskrit Epics," in A.T. Hatto (ed.), *Traditions of Heroic and Epic Poetry* (London: Modern Humanities Research Association, 1980), pp. 67–68. The Epic's dualism is a persistent theme in Biardeau's ongoing research and interpretation.

39. See discussion by Stella Kramrisch, *The Presence of Śiva* (Princeton: Princeton University Press, 1981), pp. 85–88.

40. RV 10.136.1–7. See Kramrisch, pp. 88–91, on the Vrātya hymns.

41. Subramanian, p. 295. The "rehabilitation" of Aśvatthāman is carried considerably further in the medieval South Indian sources such as Villiputtūrār's MBh; *Bhāgavatapurāṇa* 1.7.13–58.

42. Dumézil, pp. 213–22.

43. M. Biardeau, "Études de mythologie hindoue (IV), *Bulletin de l'École Française d'Extrême-Orient* 63 (1976), pp. 209–214.

44. I have discussed Paraśurāma at length in "The Brahmin Integration of Hindu Civilization: 'Great', 'Medium' and 'Little' Versions of the Myth of Paraśurāma," to appear in a volume of papers from the Colloquium on Max Weber's Study of Hinduism and Buddhism (Bad Homburg, 1981).

45. As Hiltebeitel notes in his study: *The Ritual of Battle* (Ithaca and London: Cornell University Press, 1976), pp. 312–35. Certain features of this version of the Dakṣa myth are discussed in *Tamil Temple Myths*, pp. 114–16.

46. *Śatapathabrāhmaṇa* 1.7.4.1–8; see discussion by Kramrisch, chapter 1.

47. *Kauṣītakibrāhmaṇa* 6.1–4.

48. We may note at this point that Brahmin warriors, generals, and rulers are prominent throughout the medieval period in South India (see the paper cited in n. 44).

49. See J.C. Heesterman, "Brahmin, Ritual and Renouncer," *Wiener Zeitschrift zur Kunde des Süd- und Ostasiens* 8 (1964), pp. 1–31.

50. *Ibid.*, also "The Conundrum of the King's Authority," in Richards (n. 30 above), pp. 1–27.

51. Ruth Nevo, *Comic Transformations in Shakespeare* (London and New York: Methuen, 1980), p. 16.

NOTES TO CHAPTER 19

1. Gesammelte Aufsätze zu Religionssoziologie II, *Hinduismus und Buddhismus*, p. 31 J.C.B. Mohr (Paul Siebeck), Tübingen: 1921 (1978). (hereafter R.S.)

2. *Ibid.*, p. 135.
3. *Ibid.*, II, p. 152.
4. *Ibid.*, p. 137.
5. *Ibid.*, p. 138.
6. *Ibid.*, II, p. 163.
7. *Ibid.*, II, p. 140.
8. *Ibid.*, p. 155.
9. *Ibid.*, p. 157.
10. *Ibid.*, p. 152.
11. *Ibid.*, I, pp. 536–573.
12. *Ibid.*, pp. 175–176.
13. *Ibid.*, p. 174.
14. *Ibid.*, II, p. 172.
15. *Ibid.*, p. 172, see also pp. 116ff.
16. *Ibid.*, pp. 173–174.
17. *Ibid.*, II, p. 154.
18. *Ibid.*, II, pp. 149–151.
19. Idem, see also *ibid.*, pp. 37ff.
20. *Ibid.*, II, p. 151.
21. *Ibid.*, p. 151.
22. *Ibid.*, p. 151.
23. *Ibid.*, pp. 151–152.
24. *Ibid.*, p. 154.
25. *Ibid.*, p. 149.
26. R.S. I, p. 436; *Wirtschaft und Gesellschaft*, 5th revised edition, ed. by J. Windelman, J.C.B. Mohr, Tübingen: 1976 vol. I, p. 307.
27. R.S. II, p. 168.
28. R.S. II, pp. 168–169.
29. *Ibid.*, p. 168.
30. *Ibid.*, pp. 149–150.
31. *Ibid.*, II, p. 169.
32. *Ibid.*, II, p. 170.
33. *Ibid.*, II, p. 170.
34. Idem.
35. *Ibid.*, II, pp. 171–172.
36. *Ibid.*, II, p. 146.
37. *Ibid.*, II, p. 22.

38. *Ibid.,* II, pp. 23–24.

39. *Ibid.,* II, p. 155.

40. *Ibid.,* II, p. 157.

41. *Ibid.,* p. 150.

42. *Ibid.,* pp. 157–158.

43. *Ibid.,* II, p. 155.

44. *Ibid.,* II, p. 19.

45. *Ibid.,* II, pp. 158–159.

46. *Ibid.,* p. 158.

47. *Ibid.,* p. 160.

48. *Ibid.,* p. 158.

49. *Ibid.,* p. 160.

50. *Ibid.,* p. 158.

51. R.S. II, p. 162. The esoteric restriction on the spread of Brahminical knowledge beyond the boundaries of the Brahmin caste was by no means consistently observed. Some of the sacred knowledge was included in the education of youths of the knightly stratum. In this way, Vedic knowledge entered into the culture of the laity in the Kshatriya caste (*Ibid.,* p. 156).

52. *Ibid.,* p. 137.

53. *Ibid.,* p. 141.

54. *Ibid.,* p. 139.

55. *Ibid.,* p. 140.

56. *Ibid.,* p. 145.

57. R.S. II, p. 54; *Wirtschaft und Gesellschaft,* Vol. II, pp. 459–460 (1967 edition).

58. *Wirtschaft und Gesellschaft,* Vol. II, p. 460.

59. Idem.

60. R.S. II, pp. 54–55; *Wirtschaft und Gesellschaft,* Vol. II, p. 473.

61. *Wirtschaft und Gesellschaft,* Vol. II, p. 473.

NOTES TO CHAPTER 20

1. Benjamin I. Schwartz, "The Age of Transcendence," in *Wisdom, Revelation and Doubt, Perspectives in the First Millennium B.C., Daedalus,* Spring 1975.

2. S.N. Eisenstadt, *The Axial Age; Rise of Transcendental Visions; The Emergence of Intellectuals and of Clerics and the Structuring of World History,* unpublished essay; also another unpublished essay: "Heterodoxies, Sectarianism and Dynamics of Civilizations."

3. I have dealt with the first issue in a separate essay entitled "A Critique of Weber's Discussion of Early Buddhism" written for a colloquium organized by Werner-Reimers-Stiftung. The second issue has been discussed in my *World Conqueror and World Renouncer,* Cambridge University Press, 1976.

4. A.K. Warder, *Indian Buddhism,* Motilal Banarsidass, Delhi: 1970, pp. 205–206.

5. William R. Polk, *The United States and the Arab World,* Third Edition, Harvard University Press, 1975.

6. This is a literal translation of the sermon's Pāli language title: *Dhammacakkapavanasutta*. Verse 25 states: "And when the royal chariot wheel of the truth had thus been set rolling onwards by the Blessed One, the gods of the earth gave forth a shout, saying . . . "that wheel . . . not by anyone in the universe, can ever be turned back."

7. It is the opposite of the discus *(cakra)* of Vishnu which is a weapon he throws and conquers through violence and bloodletting, as for example in the myth of "the churning of the ocean".

8. On the views of scholars regarding the historicity of these councils, see Charles S. Prebish, "A Review of Scholarship on the Buddhist Councils", *Journal of Asian Studies,* 33, Feb. 1974, pp. 239–254.

9. The above names are the Sanskrit titles. The Pāli names for these collections are *Dīgha Nikāya, Majjhima Nikāya, Saṁyutta Nikāya, Anguttara Nikāya,* and *Khuddaka Nikāya.* Famous discourses such as the Brahmajāla Sutta and the Mahāparinibbāna Sutta (an account of the last weeks of the Buddha's life) are found in the first collection; the most famous discourse in the third collection is the Buddha's first sermon, *Dhammacakkappavattana Sutta.* The much admired anthology of 432 memorial verses, the *Dhammapada,* and the Theragāthā and Therīgathā, strophes and poems attributed to monks and nuns, appear in the last collection.

10. The accounts of two of the oldest schools, the Sthaviravāda and the Mahasamghika do not mention the recitation of the *Abhidhamma* at the First Council; however the Mahāsaṁghika mentions it as among the texts that were handed down. However, the Sarvāstivāda and the Dharmaguptaka Schools have it (as stated in their *Vinayas*) that Ānanda recited the Abhidhamma as well as the Sutta texts.

11. Wilhelm Geiger, *Pāli Literature and Language* (translated into English by Batakrishna Ghosh), University of Calcutta, 1956, pp. 22–23.

12. The precursors of the *Abhidhamma* are already found in the *Sutta Piṭaka,* for example, in some of the schematic enumerations of the *Anguttara Nikāya,* the last two discourses of the *Dīgha Nikāya,* and similar pieces.

13. In the Pāli canon the following seven works belong to the *Abhidhamma.* 1) *Dhammasaṅgani* ("enumeration of psychical phenomena") is a psychological work. 2) *Vibhaṅga* ("differentiation") is a supplement and continuation of the preceding. 3) *Kathāvathu* is a great commentarial work attributed by the Sthaviravāda School to Mogaliputta Tissa as the author during the time of King Aśoka; this text contains the refutation of 252 different "wrong" teachings. 4) The *Puggalapaññatti* ("description of individuals") deals in the form of questions and answers with various personalities. 5) The *Dhātukathapakaraṇa* ("discussions of the elements") deals with various psychic phenomena and their relation to the categories. 6) The *Yamaka* ("book of pairs") is a work on applied logic, using the method of thesis and antithesis. 7) The *Paṭṭhānappakaraṇa* or *Mahāpaṭṭhana* is a volumnious work dealing with causality, and is said by the experts to be very difficult to understand.

An example of some major agreements in the *Abhidhamma* of various schools is the following; The *Vibhaṅga* of the Sthaviravāda, the *Dharmas-*

kandha of the Sarvāstivāda, and the *Sāriputrābhidharmaśāstra* of the Dhar-maguptakas (this last attribution is not certain) are parallel exercises.

14. The Mahāsaṁghika school (which was the first to break away) mentions only the matter of cash donations while the Sthaviravāda lists nine grounds for dispute, the receipt of money being one of them.

15. Przyluski (in his *Concile de Rājagrha*. Paris:Paul Geuthner, 1926–28) identified three main centres of Buddhism at this time: Vaiśālī, Kausambi and Mathura. Kausambi and all the south-western regions subsequently became the seat of the Theravādins, while Mathura and the regions of the north-west that of the Sarvāstivādins. Thus at the time of the first schism the Westerners were probably composed of the Sthavirās and Sarvāstivadins, while the Easterners who had their headquarters at Vaisālī were the Mahāsaṅghikas and their offshoots.

16. See Majjhima Nikāya No. 76 where Ānanda ridicules those who claimed omniscience for their leaders; in No. 79 the Jaina leader, Mahāvīra, is belittled.

17. These words are to be found in the 'Introduction' (pp. xxii–xxiii) to T.W. Rhys Davids (transl.), *The Questions of King Milinda*, Part II, Dover Publications, 1963.

18. G.E.R. Lloyd, *Magic, Reason and Experience, Studies in the Origin and Development of Greek Science*, Cambridge University Press, 1979, p. 98.

19. Frances Yates, *The Art of Memory*, The University of Chicago Press, 1974, p. 2. The idea behind this memo-technics is that of "visual memorization": the words and mental images to be recalled are assigned to a series of places in a building, so that the ancient orator moves in imagination through his memory building whilst he is making his speech, drawing from the memorized places the images he had placed on them. The five parts of rhetoric in ancient Latin conception were *inventio* (invention), *dispositio* (disposition), *elocutio* (elocution), *memoria* (memory) and *pronuntiato* (pronunciation).

20. Paul Kiparsky, "Oral poetry: some linguistic and typological considerations", in *Oral Literature and the Formula* (eds. Benjamin A. Stolz and Richard S. Shannon III) Center for the Coordination of Ancient and Modern Studies, The University of Michigan, Ann Arbor: 1976.

21. It is noteworthy that "Among Vedic priests, writing was even regarded as an unclean activity which required subsequent ritual purification". *Ibid.*, p. 101.

22. M. Winternitz, *A History of Indian Literature*, transl. by Mrs. S. Ketkar, University of Calcutta, 1927, pp. 33–34.

23. A.K. Warder *op. cit.*, pp. 206–207. The Buddha himself presumably spoke the dialect of Kośala, though he also preached in Māgadha.

According to Geiger *(op. cit.)*, Pāli, the language in which is composed the *Tipiṭaka* of the Theravādins, was an archaic Prākrit of the Middle-India region. Pāli is not a homogeneous language, and is perhaps a compromise of various dialects. Scholarly opinion varies as to the exact region whose dialect Pāli was—Magadha, the Kalinga country, and Ujjain have been mentioned. Geiger says Magadha was the most probable region.

24. Albert Lord, *The Singer of Tales,* Harvard University Press, 1958.

25. T.W. Rhys Davids, *Buddhist Suttas. The Sacred Books of the East,* ed. F. Max Muller, Vol. XI, Oxford: 1881, p. xxiii.

26. From *Vinaya* and *Saṁyutta Nikāya* texts, for example, we can extract these reputations. Sāriputta, the foremost of the wise, was credited with skill in *Abhidhamma;* Mahāmoggalana was credited with supranormal powers *(iddhi)* on account of his expertise in meditation; Mahākassapa was known for his ascetic practices *(dhutanga);* Punna Mahātāniputta was the foremost of the preachers of the *dhamma;* Revata was the foremost of forest recluses, etc.

27. See *Vinaya Texts,* transl. by T.W. Rhys Davids and Hermann Oldenberg, Part I, Motilal Banarsidass, Delhi: 1974, p. 339.

28. See Nalinaksha Dutt, *Buddhist Sects in India,* Motilal Banarsidass, Delhi: 1978, pp. 43–44. Dutt provides this information: Sāriputta enjoyed the epithet *mahāpaññanaṁ* (highly wise); his disciples were called *mahāpannāvantā;* Mahakassapa's pupils were similiarly called *dhūtavāda,* and so on. A thousand years later Yuan Chuang (Xuan Zang) reported during his travels in India that on auspicious days the Abhidhammikas worshipped Sāriputta, the Vinayists Upāli, the Samādhists Mahāmoggalana, the bhikkhunis (nuns) Ananda, and so on.

29. See E.W. Adikaram, *Early History of Buddhism in Ceylon* (or "State of Buddhism in Ceylon as Revealed by the Pāli Commentaries of the Fifth Century A.D."), Colombo: 1946.

30. This act of writing itself highlights some of the dangers inherent in the dependence on oral transmission alone. In Sri Lanka the anxieties generated by foreign invasions and degenerating internal political circumstances appear to have motivated monks to committing their knowledge to writing so that it would not disappear. According to the Tibetan historian Bu-ston, the *Tripiṭakas* of the "eighteen schools" were written down in the first century C.E. or earlier on account of the dangers of faulty memorizing.

31. Hermann Oldenberg, *Buddha, his Life, his Doctrine, his Order,* London: Williams and Norgate, 1882.

32. See my "The renouncer: his individuality and his community", in *Way of Life: King, Householder, Renouncer, Contributions to Indian Sociology,* New Series, Vol. 15, Nos. 1 and 2, 1981.
The rules of conduct regulating the conduct of monks are to be found in *Vinaya Texts,* transl. by T.W. Rhys Davids and Hermann Oldenberg, Parts 1, 2 and 3, Delhi: Motilal Banarsidass, 1968.

NOTES TO CHAPTER 21

1. M.I. Mochiri, 'A Sasanian-type coin of Yazīd b. Muʻāwiya,' *Journal of the Royal Asiatic Society,* 1982, 137–41.

2. J. Walker, *A Catalogue of the Arab-Byzantine and Post-Reform Umaiyad Coins,* London: 1956, 104.

3. In what follows I have drawn freely on the ideas put forward in Patricia Crone and Michael Cook, *Hagarism: the Making of the Islamic World,*

Cambridge: 1977, and to a lesser extent on Patricia Crone, *Slaves on Horses: the Evolution of the Islamic Polity*, Cambridge: 1980, chapter 2, and my own *Early Muslim Dogma: a Source-critical Study*, Cambridge: 1981, chapter 16. I have also been influenced by unpublished work of Fritz Zimmermann.

4. Ibn Saᶜd, *Kitāb al-tabaqāt al-kabīr*, ed. E. Sachau and others, Leiden: 1904–21, vol. 6, 174.

5. A central question here is the role of Caliphal authority in the formation of Islamic law; much relevant material has been collected by Patricia Crone in unpublished research.

6. I am grateful to Fritz Zimmermann and to several members of the conference for their comments on this paper, and to Dr. A.D.H. Bivar for advice on a numismatic point.